EIGHTH EDITION

Health Care USA

Understanding Its Organization and Delivery

Harry A. Sultz, DDS, MPH

Professor Emeritus
Social and Preventive Medicine
School of Medicine and Biomedical Sciences
Dean Emeritus
School of Health Related Professions
State University of New York at Buffalo
Buffalo, New York

Kristina M. Young, MS

School of Public Health and Health
Professions
Instructor and Co-director, Health Services
Administration Concentration
State University of New York at Buffalo
Buffalo, New York
President
Kristina M. Young & Associates Inc.
Buffalo, New York

JONES & BARTLETT
LEARNING

World Headquarters
Jones & Bartlett Learning
5 Wall Street
Burlington, MA 01803
978-443-5000
info@jblearning.com
www.jblearning.com

Jones & Bartlett Learning books and products are available through most bookstores and online booksellers. To contact Jones & Bartlett Learning directly, call 800-832-0034, fax 978-443-8000, or visit our website, www.jblearning.com.

Substantial discounts on bulk quantities of Jones & Bartlett Learning publications are available to corporations, professional associations, and other qualified organizations. For details and specific discount information, contact the special sales department at Jones & Bartlett Learning via the above contact information or send an email to specialsales@jblearning.com.

Production Credits

Executive Publisher: William Brottmiller
Publisher: Michael Brown
Editorial Assistant: Sean Fabery
Editorial Assistant: Chloe Falivene
Production Manager: Tracey McCrea
Senior Marketing Manager: Sophie Fleck Teague
Manufacturing and Inventory
  Control Supervisor: Amy Bacus

Composition: diacriTech
Cover and Title Page Design: Kristin E. Parker
Cover and Title Page Image: © KvnKrft/ShutterStock, Inc.
Printing and Binding: Edwards Brothers Malloy
Cover Printing: Edwards Brothers Malloy

To order this product, use ISBN: 978-1-284-02988-8

Library of Congress Cataloging-in-Publication Data
Sultz, Harry A.
  Health care USA: understanding its organization and delivery / Harry A. Sultz, Kristina M. Young. — 8th ed.
    p.; cm.
  Includes bibliographical references and index.
  ISBN 978-1-4496-9451-7 (pbk.)
  I. Young, Kristina M. II. Title.
  [DNLM: 1. Delivery of Health Care—United States. 2. Health Policy—United States. W 84 AA1]
  RA395.A3
  362.10973 dc23
                        2013012427

6048

Printed in the United States of America
17 16 15 14 13   10 9 8 7 6 5 4 3 2 1

This book is dedicated to our parents, William and
Marabelle Sultz and Jacob Jay and Marie Young.
Guiding these warm, loving, and dignified people
through the health care system during the last years of
their lives taught us more about the feats, functions, and
foibles of medical care than all the research conducted,
literature read, and services administered.

Contents

Foreword

Already having survived many legislative and judicial challenges, the implementation of the Patient Protection and Affordable Care Act (ACA) of 2010 is well underway. Although all of its provisions will not have full force and effect until 2019, many of its provisions are already manifest in system operational changes and demonstration projects of the Centers for Medicare and Medicaid Services and other federally directed programs and initiatives. Both those opposed to and in support of the ACA agree that this legislation will result in the most significant overhaul of the health care delivery system in the history of the U.S. health care enterprise. Respected economists and system analysts from independent organizations and major universities predict that, by aligning a focus on population health with new reimbursement incentives, this legislation will provide opportunities to improve the quality and lower the costs of health care. Much experimentation with new models of health care delivery will ensue over the next several years to identify best practices. Concurrently, physicians, other health professionals, and organizational providers will undertake adjustments and adaptations to the delivery system's new premises.

In this period of immense change, the eighth edition of *Health Care USA* has heightened significance. The text offers a clear overview of the evolution of the health care industry's components and describes the technical, economic, political, and social forces that shaped their development. In this context, the authors provide concise reviews of the major features of the ACA as it affects system components and the practitioners and organizations within them. This information is highly relevant for students of health care and related professions as well as neophyte practitioners who require a broad understanding of the reformed U.S. health care system to function effectively, and to relate intelligently, to its various sectors.

In this edition, as in previous ones, the authors have meticulously screened vast amounts of new information and included the most critical points to update this work. Because a "population" rather than an "individual" health care perspective is the predominant theme of the reformed system, the authors' public health orientation makes this text particularly valuable. Their combined experience in the public health and health care management fields allows them to objectively interpret health care developments. This is an important feature in an introductory text that strives toward analysis of evidence, not advocacy, thereby allowing the formulation of one's own position.

Michel A. Ibrahim, MD, PhD
Professor of Epidemiology
Editor-in-Chief, "Epidemiological Reviews"
Johns Hopkins Bloomberg School of Public Health
and
Dean and Professor Emeritus
School of Public Health
University of North Carolina at Chapel Hill

Acknowledgments

Because one of us has an academic base as a professor emeritus of social and preventive medicine and as a former academic dean, and the other has served in a variety of executive positions in voluntary agencies, hospitals, a managed care organization, in her own consultant business, and as executive director of a regional public health organization, we bring different experiences to our interpretations of health care developments. When we taught together, as we often did, our students were at first amused and then intrigued by the differences between academic and applied perspectives. They learned, by our willingness to debate the merits of different interpretations of the same information, to appreciate that health care is fraught with variance in understandings, dissonance in values, and contradictions in underlying assumptions.

We are grateful therefore to the students in the Schools of Medicine, Public Health and Health Professions, Management, Law and Millard Fillmore College of the University at Buffalo, who contributed to our knowledge and experience by presenting challenging viewpoints, engaging us in spirited discussions, and providing thoughtful course evaluations. Over the years, their enthusiasm for the subject stimulated us to enrich our coursework constantly in an effort to meet and exceed their expectations.

We acknowledge with our sincerest gratitude Philip J. Kroth, MD, MS, and Susan V. McLeer, MD, MS, for their respective contributions of the chapters on health information technology and mental health services. As consummate clinicians and academicians, their expertise, effort, and enthusiastic participation have provided exceptionally clear and insightful overviews of the complex issues and system responses in their fields. Dr. Kroth's and Dr. McLeer's professional summaries appear in the "About the Contributors" section. We are grateful to Michel Ibrahim, MD, PhD, professor, Johns Hopkins Bloomberg School of Public Health and Dean and professor emeritus of the School of Public Health at the University of North Carolina at Chapel Hill, who encouraged us to write the first edition of this book in 1993 and has contributed the "Foreword" to each edition.

We also appreciate those who helped turn teachers into authors by providing the necessary editing, literature searches, word processing, and other support services. This and earlier editions of this book benefited inestimably from the health care and library and information science research expertise of Karen Buchinger. Sharon Palisano word processed all manuscripts of the eight editions of this book with meticulous attention to every detail of the publisher's requirements. We remain extremely grateful for her unparalleled professional skill and patience with the complex details of these large texts. We also wish to recognize the important contributions of our publisher's staff who encourage our efforts, help shape the results, and motivate us to improve the book's utility to its users. To each of you we offer our profound thanks.

About the Authors

Harry A. Sultz, DDS, MPH, is professor emeritus of Social and Preventive Medicine at the University at Buffalo School of Medicine and Biomedical Sciences and dean emeritus of its School of Health Related Professions. He has also served as adjunct professor at the School of Law; adjunct professor, Health Systems Management, School of Management; and clinical assistant professor, Department of Family Medicine.

Dr. Sultz has written six previous books, contributed chapters to several other books for professional audiences, and published numerous articles for medical and allied health journals. An epidemiologist, health care services planner, and researcher, he established and, for 26 years, directed the Health Services Research Program of Buffalo's School of Medicine. His extensive research experience serves as background for the various editions of this book and for the courses that he taught about health care and health policy. He also has long service as an expert consultant to several governmental and voluntary agencies and institutions.

Kristina M. Young, MS, is an instructor and co-director of the health services administration concentration at the University at Buffalo, School of Public Health and Health Professions, State University of New York, where she teaches graduate courses in health care organization and health policy for students in the fields of public health, law, and management. She also is president and owner of Kristina M. Young & Associates Inc., a management consulting and training firm specializing in health and human services organizations. Previously, she served as executive director of an organization that administers government and private funds to support public health activities in western New York; as president of a corporate training and development organization; as executive vice president of a not-for-profit organization dedicated to advancing the joint interests of a major teaching hospital and a health maintenance organization; and as the vice president for Research and Development for a teaching hospital system and executive director of its health, education, and research foundation.

About the Contributors

Philip J. Kroth, MD, MS, is the director of Biomedical Informatics Research, Training, and Scholarship at the University of New Mexico (UNM) Health Sciences Library and Informatics Center and is Associate Chief Medical Information Officer for UNM Hospitals. Before joining UNM in 2004, he received a BS degree in computer engineering from the Rochester Institute of Technology in 1987 and his MD degree from the Medical College of Ohio in 1995. He completed his residency in internal medicine at the State University of New York at Buffalo in 1999 and is board certified in internal medicine. He completed a research fellowship in biomedical informatics at the Regenstrief Institute at Indiana University Medical Center where, at the same time, he earned an MS degree in clinical research in 2003.

In addition to directing a postdoctoral research fellowship in biomedical informatics, Dr. Kroth's research focus areas include adapting electronic clinical records for research, assessing the value of various design aspects of electronic health records, and the promotion of open access publication. He continues to practice internal medicine in Albuquerque, New Mexico and assists with the implementation of UNM Hospitals' electronic health record system.

Susan V. McLeer, MD, MS, is professor and chair of the Department of Psychiatry at the Drexel University College of Medicine and former professor and chair of the Department of Psychiatry at the State University of New York at Buffalo School of Medicine and Biomedical Sciences. Board certified in both Psychiatry and Child and Adolescent Psychiatry and with a master's degree in psychiatric administration, she has extensive experience in managing and integrating services at all levels of care, both within public and private behavioral health systems. She has been a fierce advocate for improvements in the public sector system of care and has taught multiple generations of medical students and residents aspiring to care for people who are in need of psychiatric and/or behavioral health services.

Dr. McLeer has 85 publications to her credit, including peer-reviewed journal articles, book chapters, and published abstracts. Combining her experience at the medical schools in Buffalo, New York and Philadelphia, Pennsylvania, she has been the Chair and Chief Clinical Officer for an academic department of psychiatry for more than 19 years and has been in academia for 36 years. She currently serves and provides expert consultation for the American Psychiatric Association's National Council on Health Care Systems and Financing, a position she has held for more than 6 years. Additionally, she is an active member and contributor to the Council's Workgroup on Public Sector Psychiatry, a group that has been actively studying the impact of the U.S. economy on public sector behavioral health systems.

Introduction

The U.S. health care system has remained a complex puzzle to many Americans and the new health reform legislation will doubtless add additional complexity to the puzzle. Medical care in the United States is an enormous $2.7 trillion industry. It includes thousands of independent medical practices and partnerships and provider organizations; public and nonprofit institutions such as hospitals, nursing homes, and other specialized care facilities; major private corporations that manufacture drugs and devices; and huge health insurance corporations. Health care is by far the largest service industry in the country. In fact, the U.S. health care system is the world's eighth largest economy, second to that of France, and is larger than the total economy of Italy.[1,2]

More intimidating than its size, however, is its complexity. Not only is health care labor intensive at all levels, but also the types and functions of its numerous personnel change periodically to adjust to new technology, knowledge, and ways of delivering health care services.

As is frequently associated with progress, medical advances often create new problems while solving old ones. The explosion of medical knowledge that produced narrowly defined medical specialties compounded a long-standing shortcoming of American medical care. The delivery of sophisticated high-tech health care requires the support of an incredibly complicated infrastructure that allows too many shortcomings which result in patients falling through the cracks between its narrowly defined services and specialists. In addition, the system has proved to be inept in securing even a modicum of universal coverage, with more than 49 million uninsured Americans in U.S. today.

The size and complexity of health care in the United States has contributed to its long-standing problems of limited consumer access, inconsistent quality, and uncontrolled costs. In addition, the U.S.

health care system has done little to address the unnecessary and wasteful duplication of certain services in some areas and the absence of essential services in others.

These problems have concerned this country's political and medical leaders for decades and motivated legislative proposals aimed at comprehensive reform by eight U.S. presidents. President Clinton's National Health Security Act of 1993 produced an unusually candid and sometimes acrimonious congressional debate. Vested interests advocating change and those defending the status quo both lobbied extensively to influence public and political opinion. Ultimately, stakeholders in the traditional system convinced Americans that the Clinton plan was too liberal, and too costly. The Clinton plan never reached Congress for a vote.

Health care reform has been occurring as a market-driven, not a policy-driven, phenomenon that began well in advance of the new health care reform legislation.[3] In a world of accelerating consolidation to achieve ever higher standards of effectiveness and economy, there has been a surge of health care facility and service organization mergers and acquisitions, and new roles for individual and organizational providers that signal the onset of fundamental changes throughout the system. Hospitals are competing for patients, independently operated clinics are springing up in unprecedented numbers with convenient locations and venues, and physician group practices are forgoing their independence to embrace hospital employment to join with integrated systems of care that leverage population-based reimbursement schemes of the reformed system.[3]

The Patient Protection and Affordable Care Act (Public Law 111-148)[4] and the Health Care and Education Reconciliation Act (Public Law 111-152),[5] signed by President Barack Obama on March 23, 2010 and March 30, 2010, respectively, enact the most sweeping transformation of the U.S. health care delivery system since the passage of Medicare and Medicaid legislation in 1965. The two laws are commonly referred to as the Patient Protection and Affordable Care Act and throughout this textbook will be referred to as the Affordable Care Act (ACA). Over a period of several years of implementation that began in 2010 and will continue through 2019, the spectrum of the ACA provisions will change how U.S. health care is delivered and financed in ways that vastly exceed the impacts of Medicare and Medicaid. Medicare and Medicaid affected specific populations of individuals qualified by program criteria; the ACA affects virtually all Americans.

The timing of the development of the ACA, and ultimately its passage, represented the Obama administration's rapidly seizing a "policy window of opportunity" to put comprehensive health reform legislation on the agenda for legislation development. As described by John Kingdon, this "policy window of opportunity" for new or amended legislation arises when problems have reached a magnitude of scope and urgency allows their survival in competition from other issues; potentially feasible solutions can be identified; and sufficient political will exists to drive the process forward.[6] In the case of the proposed ACA, problems included the widely acknowledged economic unsustainability of rising health care costs linked with the all-important issue of the rising federal deficit; the moral, social, and economic implications of more than 49 million uninsured citizens; and the system's well-documented shortcomings in quality. Proposals for potential solutions to these problems had a very lengthy and evidence-based research history. Political will to move comprehensive health reform onto the legislative agenda was established early by the three highest profile contenders for the 2008 Democratic party presidential nomination (Hillary Clinton, John Edwards, and Barack Obama), agreeing that they would support "universal coverage."[7] Also, in early 2008, the very powerful and highly respected health reform advocate Senator Edward Kennedy agreed to endorse Mr. Obama's candidacy with the pledge of Obama's commitment to make health care reform his top domestic priority, including a commitment to universal coverage.[8] Finally, with a new president elected on a platform of change and Democratic majorities in both the Senate and House of Representatives, the "policy window of opportunity" opened for moving the comprehensive health reform agenda forward. Recognizing the failure of the Clinton administration's "White House-centered" approach to its failed reform plan, and that "delay was the enemy of reform," President Obama requested that reform be enacted in the first year of his term and delegated the development of the plan to congressional leaders.[9] To ensure involvement of key stakeholders who had been neglected in the Clinton plan, he urged "administration officials to negotiate with key interest groups, emphasizing the need to compromise and build incrementally off the current system."[9]

During the months following President Obama's request to congressional leaders, complicated and convoluted events ensued among the loyalties of key supporters and key stakeholders' positions. The chronicle of rancorous partisan political debates, passionate outcries from a misinformed citizenry, negotiations with interest groups, and intervening events, such as the death of Democratic Senator Kennedy and his replacement with a Republican, and White House shifts in strategy, fills volumes in the history of the ACA. Nevertheless, the ACA was signed into law just 14 months following President Obama's taking office, representing an incredible and unparalleled time trajectory for legislation of this magnitude, scope, and complexity. On the occasion of signing the new law, President Obama commented, "Our presence here today is remarkable and improbable."[8] Now, more than 3 years since its implementation, the ACA has survived many hurdles—including a U.S. Supreme Court challenge on the constitutionality of its core provisions for the "individual mandate" and "Medicaid expansion"—and much has been accomplished on enacting the scheduled 2010–2012 provisions.[10,11]

We have worked in the academic and health system management spheres for decades while we have assiduously studied and followed developments in the health care delivery system. In the past seven editions of this textbook, we have attempted to objectively describe the status quo and delineate new efforts aimed toward system changes and improvements using a topic framework of the system's major components. As we researched to prepare this eighth edition that includes explanation of the ACA provisions and their effects, it became apparent that in terms of its organizational framework, this is a transitional edition. As the ACA achieves its intended effects, the prior health care delivery system will emerge from its old form of fragmented, piecemeal services and payments and opaque quality assessments to a form of integrated systems that rewards continuity of care and requires transparent quality assessments. It is clear that old lines of demarcation among delivery system components will blur and in some cases disappear. For example, the ACA offers experiments in which patients' illnesses are treated and paid for as a single "episode of care" by all involved providers—primary care physicians, specialists, hospitals, and other providers in a seamless continuum rather than in a series of disconnected encounters.[12] While major system components will remain largely intact, the ways in which they operate and interact with each other will change dramatically and, in that regard, so will the future organizational framework of this textbook. This eighth edition required difficult decisions about how best to assist instructors and students with navigating the most significant features of the extremely complex, 907-page ACA in the context of the current delivery system components. We hope that our treatment of the subject matter provides a foundation for comprehending major facts as well as the significance of the ACA and encourages further curiosity about continuing developments and the effects of this landmark legislation as its implementation proceeds. We also note that in just the first two years since its passage, proposed rules and regulations to implement the ACA have already undergone changes and revisions. As with any legislation of this complexity, these changes and revisions can be expected to continue in what will be an ongoing and dynamic process.

This book is intended to serve as a text for introductory courses on the organization of health care for students in schools of public health, medicine, nursing, dentistry, and pharmacy and in schools and colleges that prepare physical therapists, occupational therapists, respiratory therapists, medical technologists, health administrators, and a host of other allied health professionals. It provides an introduction to the U.S. health care system and an overview of the professional, political, social, and economic forces that have shaped it and the provisions of the ACA that will continue to do so.

To facilitate its use as a teaching text, the book's chapters both stand alone as balanced discussions of discrete subjects and, when read in sequence, provide incremental additions of information to complete the reader's understanding of the entire health care system. As in prior editions, decisions about what subjects and material were essential to the book's content were relatively easy but decisions about the topics and content to be left out were very difficult. This was especially challenging as we researched the ACA and made decisions about the breadth and depth of its subject matter to include. The encyclopedic nature of the subject and the finite length of the final manuscript were in constant conflict.

Thus, the authors acknowledge first that information presented on the ACA is limited to what we believe most pertinent to the text's major subjects' focus, and we note that the information is not exhaustive. Indeed, exhaustive treatment of the ACA continues to generate its own texts. Copious references are provided to lead interested readers to explore the ACA in more detail and depth. Second, we respectfully acknowledge that nurses, dentists, pharmacists, physical and occupational therapists, and others may be disappointed that the text contains so little of the history and the political and professional struggles that characterize the evolution of their important professions. Given the centrality of those historical developments in students' educational preparation, it was assumed that appropriate attention to those subjects, using books written specifically for that purpose, would be included in courses in those professional curricula. To be consistent with that assumption, the authors tried to include only those elements in the history of public health, medicine, and hospitals that had a significant impact on how health care was delivered.

The authors made a similar set of difficult decisions regarding the depth of information to include about other subjects. Topics such as epidemiology, the history of medicine, program planning and evaluation, quality of care, and the like each have their own libraries of in-depth texts and, in many schools, dedicated courses. Thus, it seemed appropriate in a text for an introductory course to provide only enough descriptive and interpretive detail about each topic to put it in the context of the overall subject of the book.

This book was written from a public health or population perspective and reflects the viewpoint of its authors. Both authors have public health and preventive medicine backgrounds and long histories of research into various aspects of the health care system, have planned and evaluated innovative projects for improving the quality and accessibility of care in both the public and voluntary sectors, and have served in key executive positions in the health field.

The authors have used much of the material contained in *Health Care USA: Understanding Its Organization and Delivery* to provide students, consumers, and neophyte professionals with an understanding of the unique interplay of the technology, workforce, research findings, financing, regulation, and personal and professional behaviors, values, and assumptions that determine what, how, why, where, and at what cost health care is delivered in the United States. In this eighth edition, as in each previous edition, we have included important additions and updates to provide a current perspective on the health care industry's continuously evolving trends.

The authors hope that as this book's readers plan and expand their educational horizons and, later, their professional experiences, they will have the advantage of a comprehensive understanding of the complex system in which they practice.

References

1. Trading Economics. Italy GDP. 2013. Available from http://www.trading economics.com/italy/gdp. Accessed February 13, 2013.

2. Trading Economics. France GDP. 2013. Available from http://www.trading economics.com/france/gdp. Accessed February 13, 2013.

3. Healthcare Financial Management Association. What's your organization's position in the next mergers and acquisitions wave? May 2009. Available from http://www.hfma.org/content.aspx?id=2465. Accessed January 14, 2013.

4. U.S. Government Printing Office. Patient Protection and Affordable Care Act of 2010. March, 23, 2010. Available from http://www.gpo.gov/fdsys/pkg/PLAW-111publ148/pdf/PLAW-111publ148.pdf. Accessed November 14, 2012.

5. U.S. Government Printing Office. Health Care and Education Reconciliation Act of 2010. March 30, 2010. Available from http://www.gpo.gov/fdsys/pkg/PLAW-111publ152/pdf/PLAW-111publ152.pdf. Accessed November 14, 2012.

6. Kingdon JW. *Agendas, Alternatives, and Public Policies, 2nd ed.* New York: HarperCollins College Publishers; 1995.

7. LifeHealthPro. PPACA: a history. Available from http://www.lifehealthpro.com/2012/06/12/ppaca-a-history. June 12, 2012. Accessed May 13, 2013.

8. Staff of the Washington Post. *Landmark.* New York: Perseus Books Group; 2002:7.

9. Kovner AR, Knickman JR, editors. *Health Care Delivery in the United States, 10th ed.* New York: Springer Publishing Company; 2011:36.

10. Henry J. Kaiser Family Foundation. A guide to the Supreme Court's Affordable Care Act Decision. June 29, 2012. Available from http://www.kff.org/healthreform/upload/8332.pdf. Accessed July 9, 2012.

11. Surgeon General. 2012 annual status report; national prevention, health promotion, and public health council. June 13, 2012. Available from http://www.surgeongeneral.gov/initiatives/prevention/2012-npc-status-report.pdf. Accessed February 11, 2013.

12. U.S. Department of Health and Human Services. Centers for Medicare & Medicaid. Center for Medicare & Medicaid Innovation. Bundled payments for care improvement (BPCI) initiative: general information. Available from http://innovation.cms.gov/initiatives/bundled-payments/index.html. Accessed January 19, 2013.

New to the Eighth Edition

In addition to updating all key financial, utilization, and other data with the latest available information, the eighth edition includes a new chapter on health information technology, a completely revised chapter on mental health services and, as relevant, discussions of the impacts of the American Reinvestment and Recovery Act of 2009 (ARRA) and Patient Protection and Affordable Care Act of 2010 (ACA). The eighth edition also provides "Key Terms for Review" at the conclusion of each chapter and a glossary of the key terms.

Chapter 1: Overview of Health Care: A Population Perspective

- Definition and discussion of the Patient Protection and Affordable Care Act (ACA) in a population context
- Comparisons and contrasts among the U.S. health status indicators and costs with other developed nations
- ACA proposed remedies to ongoing U.S. health care delivery system problems
- Discussion of ACA public/health population goals and alignment challenges of the current delivery system
- Role of insurers in offsetting ACA costs
- Key Terms for Review

Chapter 2: Benchmark Developments in U.S. Health Care

- Discussion of the political circumstances and prelude to the Patient Protection and Affordable Care Act (ACA) introduction for congressional action
- Discussions linking the ACA provisions with historically intransigent problems of cost, quality, and access in the health care delivery system
- Overview of judicial challenges to the ACA and final U.S. Supreme Court decisions
- Discussion of historical significance of the ACA
- Listing of ACA provisions on an implementation time line, 2010–2019
- Key Terms for Review

Chapter 3: Health Information Technology

- New chapter
- Key Terms for Review

Chapter 4: Hospitals: Origin, Organization, and Performance

- Updates on hospitals' adoption of health information technology
- Recent trends in hospital consolidations and mergers and impacts on the marketplace: competitiveness, cost, and quality
- Numerous ways the ACA impacts hospitals via the shift to a "population focus," transition from a "volume-based" to a "value-based mentality" through value-based purchasing requirements and other payment reforms, readmission penalties, and voluntary participation in bundled payment initiatives
- Emergence of hospitals as one component of integrated, community-based continuums of care
- Key Terms for Review

Chapter 5: Ambulatory Care

- Emerging trends in hospital employment of physicians
- A new section on "Integrated Ambulatory Care Models": the "patient-centered medical home" and "accountable care organizations" in the context of ACA initiatives
- Trends in urban emergency department closures
- Trends in number of retail clinics and increase in patient utilization
- Trends in federally qualified health center utilization and declining Medicaid revenue
- Key Terms for Review

Chapter 6: Medical Education and the Changing Practice of Medicine

- Update on major changes in evaluating medical residency program accreditation in future years through an outcomes-based evaluation system
- Discussion of the ACA impacts on medical residency and training, incentives to increase primary care and physician supply in under-served areas
- Updates on physician workforce trends and ACA initiatives
- Updates on physician hospital employment trends as a response to market forces
- Updates on incentives and other support for adopting and achieving "meaningful use" of electronic health records via ARRA and ACA requirements
- Future perspectives based upon the HITECH ACT, ACA, and related market forces
- Key Terms for Review

Chapter 7: The Health Care Workforce

- Trends in registered nurse education and employment
- Trends in educational qualification changes for certain occupations

- Trends in complementary and alternative medical utilization and costs
- Highlights of the ACA health workforce initiatives and goals
- Data on the highest projected demand in health care occupations
- Key Terms for Review

Chapter 8: Financing Health Care

- Most current national health care expenditure data with updated graphics
- Updated data on health insurance coverage and costs
- Brief overview of the political "prelude" to passage of the Affordable Care Act
- Reviews of major health care financing provisions of the Affordable Care Act, including the individual mandate, Medicaid expansion, health insurance exchanges, accountable care organizations, value-based hospital purchasing, bundled payments for care initiative and the Independent Payment Advisory Board
- Key Terms for Review

Chapter 9: Long-Term Care

- Discussion of a U.S. General Accountability Office report on quality of for-profit versus not-for-profit nursing homes and ACA new accountability standards for nursing home monitoring and public disclosures
- Descriptions of ACA Medicare and Medicaid provisions to decrease institutional care by expanding access to home and community-based services
- Description of Medicare payment for respite care
- Updated definitions of continuing care retirement communities and continuing life care communities
- Discussion of the ACA's CLASS Act provision to enact national voluntary long-term care insurance and the Act's failure
- Key Terms for Review

Chapter 10: Mental Health Services

- New data on prevalence, treatment, and diagnoses in the primary care sector
- New figure with data on the burden of neuropsychiatric disorders compared with other leading categories of diseases and disorders in the United States and Canada
- New figure with data on the total annual costs of serious mental illness
- Discussion of three recent paradigm shifts toward a more integrated mental health services system
- Discussion of the ACA relative to financing of mental health services
- Key Terms for Review

Chapter 11: Public Health and the Role of Government in Health Care

- Explanation of the ecological model in public health
- Definition and discussion of the three core functions of public health
- Description of the ten essential public health department responsibilities
- New figure depicting the relationships among the 3 core functions of public health and 10 essential services of public health departments
- Listing of added topics in *Healthy People 2020*
- Description of the origin and listing of the 12 Principles of Ethical Public Health Practice
- Description and discussion of the major public health-related provisions of the ACA
- Key Terms for Review

Chapter 12: Research: How Health Care Advances

- Updates on the roles of the Agency for Healthcare Research and Quality with particular note of its prominence in the quality initiatives of the ACA

- Discussion of the ACA-created Patient-Centered Outcomes Research Institute and its priorities and challenges
- Updated information on research challenges concerning antibiotic resistant microbes
- Key Terms for Review

Chapter 13: Future of Health Care

- Discussion of the future of employer-sponsored health insurance
- Discussion of the shortage of primary care physicians and other primary care practitioners
- Review of key features of Patient Protection and Affordable Care Act effects on the workforce
- Description of the impact of the Patient Protection and Affordable Care Act's public health focus on the existing delivery system
- Discussion of challenges in implementing health information technology
- Key Terms for Review

CHAPTER 1

Overview of Health Care: A Population Perspective

This chapter provides a broad overview of U.S. health care industry, its policy makers, its values and priorities, and its responses to problems and changing conditions. A template for understanding the natural histories of diseases and the levels of medical intervention is illustrated and explained. Major influences in the advances and other changes to the health services system are described with pertinent references to the Patient Protection and Affordable Care Act (ACA). Issues of conflicts of interest and ethical dilemmas resulting from medicine's technologic advances are also noted.

Health care continuously captures the interest of the public, political leaders, and all forms of media. News of medical breakthroughs, health system deficiencies, high costs and, most recently, federal health care reform through the Patient Protection and Affordable Care Act (ACA) attract high-profile attention. Consuming over 17% of the nation's gross domestic product,[1] exceeding $2.7 trillion in costs,[2] and employing a workforce of over 16 million,[3] it is understandable that health care occupies a central position in American popular and political discourse. In large measure, the development and passage of the ACA resulted from decades-long problems with rising costs, questionable quality, and lack of health care system access for large numbers of un- or underinsured Americans. If the ACA is successful in accomplishing its intended goals by 2019, it will extend health insurance coverage to 32 million presently uninsured people; the remaining uninsured will be illegal immigrants, low-income individuals who do not enroll in Medicaid, and others who choose to pay a penalty rather than purchase coverage.[4] The current projected cost of ACA implementation is just under $1.1 trillion.[5] Compared with seven other developed nations (the U.K., Germany, Sweden, Canada, France, Australia, and Japan), Americans' health status lags sorely behind on important indicators. The United States ranks eighth behind all of these nations in life expectancy at birth, highest in infant mortality rate, and highest in the probability of people dying between the ages of 15 and 60 years.[6] These are startling outcomes given that the United States continues a per capita annual health care expenditure that is triple that of Japan, which has the best health outcomes, and more than double that of several other of the aforementioned nations.[2,7] Although the ACA will provide vastly increased access to health care for 30+ million Americans, there are strong reasons for policy makers' focus on whether increased access can result in measurable improvements in Americans' health status. "Health policy researchers are increasingly aware of the dangers of overstating the link between insurance and health."[8] As some suggest, ultimately improvements in population health will require the ACA's success in merging the concepts of public health into the reformed system's approach to personal medical care.[4] With the ACA's overarching emphasis on prevention and wellness and realigned financial incentives to support these, there is even reason for optimism that "over time, prevention and wellness could become a dominant aspect of primary care."[4]

For many, the fortunes and foibles of health care take on deeply serious meanings. There was a widespread sense of urgency among employers, insurers, consumer groups, and other policy makers about the seemingly unresolvable problems of inadequate access, rising costs, and questionable quality of care. Passionate debates about the ACA in health care reform focused many Americans on the role health care plays in their lives and about the strengths and deficiencies of the complex labyrinth of health care providers, facilities, programs, and services.

Problems of Health Care

Although philosophical and political differences historically fueled the debates about health care policies and reforms, consensus finally emerged that U.S. health care system is fraught with problems and dilemmas.

Despite its decades-long series of impressive accomplishments, the health care system exhibits inexplicable contradictions in objectives; unwarranted variations in performance, effectiveness, and efficiency; and long-standing discord in its relationships with the public and with governments.

The strategies for addressing the problems of cost, access, and quality over the 75 years since the passage of the Social Security Act reflected the periodic changes in political philosophies. The government-sponsored programs of the 1960s were designed to improve access for older adults and low-income populations without considering the inflationary effects on costs. These programs were followed by regulatory attempts to address first the availability and price of health services, then the organization and distribution of health care, and then its quality. In the 1990s, the ineffective patchwork of government-sponsored health system reforms was superseded by the emergence of market-oriented changes, competition, and privately organized managed care organizations (MCOs).

The failure of government-initiated reforms created a vacuum, which was filled quickly by the private sector. There is a difference, however, between goals for health care reform of the government and those of the market. Although the proposed government programs try to maintain some balance among costs, quality, and access, the primary goal of the market is to contain costs and realize profits. As a result, there remain serious concerns that market-driven reforms may not result in a health care system that equitably meets the needs of all Americans and may even drive up costs.[9]

As the recent querulous debate over health care reform illustrated, when the dominant interest groups—government, employers, insurers, the public, and major provider groups—do not agree on how to change the system to accomplish widely desired reforms, the American people would rather continue temporizing. They are "unwilling to risk the strengths of our existing health care system in a radical effort to remedy admittedly serious deficiencies."[10]

Understanding Health Care

Health care policy usually reflects public opinion. Finding acceptable solutions to the perplexing problems of health care depends on public understanding and acceptance of both the existing circumstances and the benefits and risks of proposed remedies. Many communication problems regarding health policy stem from the public's inadequate understanding of health care and its delivery system.

Early practitioners purposely fostered the mystique surrounding medical care as a means to set themselves apart from the patients they served. Endowing health care with a certain amount of mystery encouraged patients to maintain blind faith in the capability of their physicians even when the state of the science did not justify it. When advances in the understanding of the causes, processes, and cures of specific diseases revealed that previous therapies and methods of patient management were based on erroneous premises, new information remained opaque to the American public. Although the world's most advanced and proficient health care system provides a great deal of excellent care, the lack of public knowledge has allowed much care to be delivered that was less than beneficial and some that was inherently dangerous.

Now, however, the romantic naïveté with which health care and its practitioners were viewed has eroded significantly. Rather than a confidential contract between the provider and the consumer, the health care relationship now includes a voyeuristic collection of insurers, payers, managers, and quality assurers. Providers no longer have a monopoly on health care decisions and actions. Although the increasing scrutiny and accountability may be onerous and costly to physicians and other providers, it represents the concerns of those paying for health care—governments, insurers, employers, and patients—about the value received for their expenditures. That these questions have been raised reflects the prevailing opinion that those who now chafe under the scrutiny are, at least indirectly, responsible for generating the excesses in the system while neglecting the problems of limited access to health care for many.

Cynicism about the health care system grew with more information about the problems of costs, quality, and access becoming public. People who viewed medical care as a necessity provided by physicians who adhere to scientific standards based on tested and proven therapies have been disillusioned to learn that major knowledge gaps contribute to highly variable use rates for therapeutic and diagnostic procedures that have produced no measurable differences in outcomes. Nevertheless, as the recent discussions about system-wide reforms demonstrated, enormously complex issues underlie the health industry's problems. "The quest for greater efficiency in the delivery of health care services is eternal in a country that spends far more on health care than any other, consistently has growth in spending that outstrips that of income, is unable to provide insurance coverage to at least 17% of its population, and ranks poorly among industrialized countries in system-wide measures such as life expectancy and infant mortality."[11]

Why Patients and Providers Behave the Way They Do

The evolution of U.S. hospital system makes clear the long tradition of physicians and other health care providers behaving in an authoritarian manner toward patients. In the past, hospitalized patients, removed from their usual places in society, were expected to be compliant and grateful to be in the hands of professionals far more learned than themselves. More recently, however, recognizing the benefits of more proactive roles for patients and the improved outcomes that result, both health care providers and consumers are encouraging patient participation in health care decisions under the rubric of "shared decision making."[12]

Indexes of Health and Disease

The body of statistical data about health and disease has grown enormously since the late 1960s, when the government began analyzing the information obtained from Medicare and Medicaid claims, and computerized hospital and insurance data allowed the retrieval and exploration of clinical information files. In addition, there have been continuing improvements in the collection, analysis, and reporting of vital statistics and communicable and malignant diseases by state and federal governments.

Data collected over time and international comparisons reveal common trends among developed countries. Birth rates have fallen and life expectancies have lengthened so that older people make up an increasing proportion of total populations. The percentage of individuals who are disabled or dependent has grown as health care professions have improved their capacity to rescue otherwise moribund individuals.

Infant mortality and maternal mortality, the international indicators of social and health care improvement, have continued to decline in the United States but have not reached the more commendable levels of countries with more demographically homogeneous populations. In the United States, the differences in infant mortality rates between inner-city neighborhoods and suburban communities may be greater than those between developed and undeveloped countries. The continuing inability of the health care system to address those discrepancies effectively reflects the system's ambiguous priorities.

Natural Histories of Disease and the Levels of Prevention

For many years, epidemiologists and health services planners have used a matrix for placing everything known about a particular disease or condition in the sequence of its origin and progression when untreated; this schema is called the natural history of disease. Many diseases, especially chronic diseases that may last for decades, have an irregular evolution and extend through a sequence of stages. When the causes and stages of a particular disease or condition are defined in its natural history, they can be matched against the health care interventions intended to prevent the condition's occurrence or to arrest its progress after its onset. Because these health care interventions are designed to prevent the condition from advancing to the next, and usually more serious, level in its natural history, the interventions are classified as the "levels of prevention." Figures 1-1, 1-2, and 1-3 illustrate the concept of the natural history of disease and levels of prevention.

The first level of prevention is the period during which the individual is at risk for the disease but is not yet affected. Called the "prepathogenesis period," it identifies the behavioral, genetic, environmental, and other factors that increase the individual's likelihood of contracting the condition. Some risk factors, such as smoking, may be altered, whereas others, such as genetic factors, may not.

When such risk factors combine to produce a disease, the disease usually is not manifest until certain pathologic changes occur. This stage is a period of clinically undetectable, presymptomatic disease. Medical science is working diligently to improve its ability to diagnose disease earlier in this stage. Because many conditions evolve in irregular and subtle processes, it is often difficult to determine the point at which an individual may be designated "diseased" or "not diseased." Thus, each natural history has a "clinical horizon," defined as the point at which medical science becomes able to detect the presence of a particular condition.

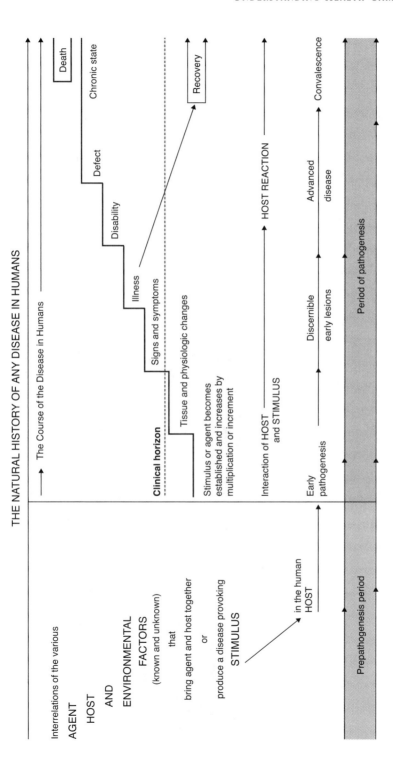

FIGURE 1-1 Natural History of Any Disease in Humans.

Source: Reprinted with permission from H. R. Leavell and E. G. Clark, *Preventative Medicine for the Doctor in His Community: An Epidemiologic Approach*, 3rd edition, p. 20, © 1965, The McGraw Hill Companies, Inc.

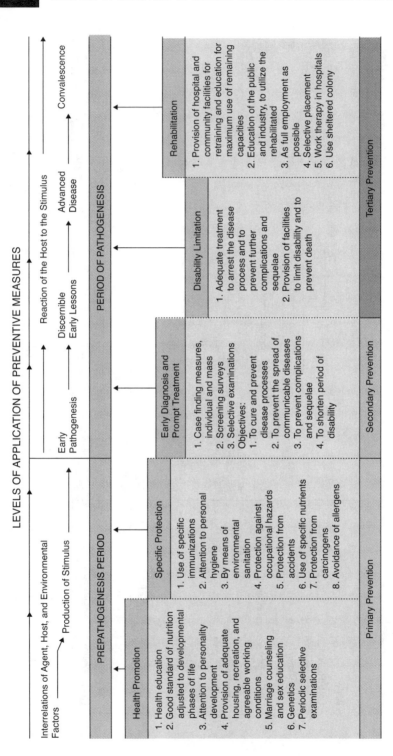

FIGURE 1-2 Levels of Application of Preventative Measures.

Source: Reprinted with permission from H. R. Leavell and E. G. Clark, *Preventative Medicine for the Doctor in His Community: An Epidemiologic Approach*, 3rd edition, p. 21, © 1965, The McGraw Hill Companies, Inc.

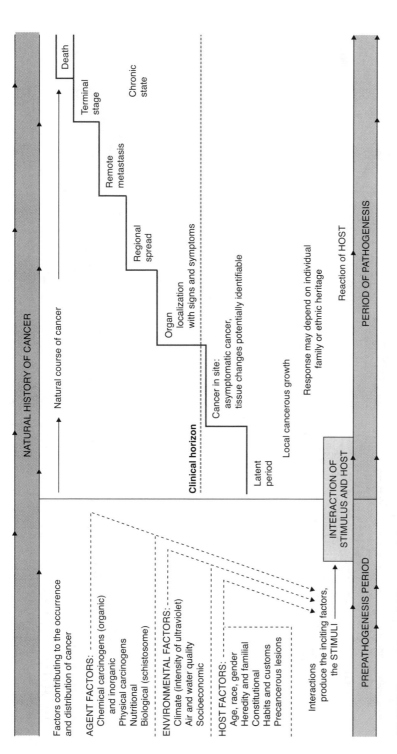

FIGURE 1-3 Natural History of Cancer.

Source: Reprinted with permission from H. R. Leavell and E. G. Clark, *Preventative Medicine for the Doctor in His Community: An Epidemiologic Approach*, 3rd edition, pp. 272–273, © 1965, The McGraw Hill Companies, Inc.

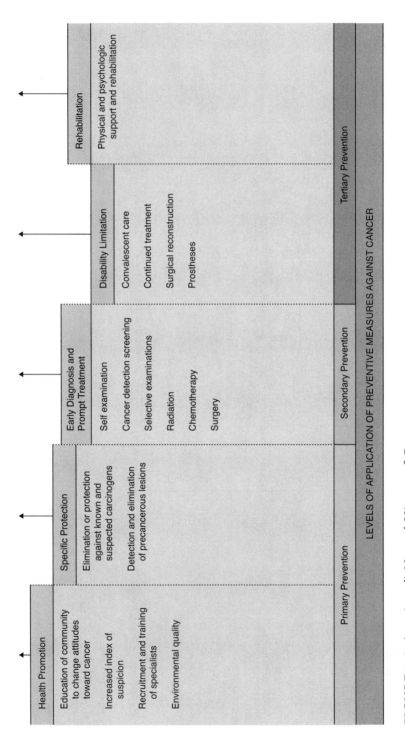

FIGURE 1-3 (continued) Natural History of Cancer.

Source: Reprinted with permission from H. R. Leavell and E. G. Clark, *Preventative Medicine for the Doctor in His Community: An Epidemiologic Approach*, 3rd edition, pp. 272–273, © 1965, The McGraw Hill Companies, Inc.

Because the pathologic changes may become fixed and irreversible at each step in disease progression, preventing each succeeding step of the disease is therapeutically important. This concept emphasizes the preventive aspect of clinical interventions.

Primary prevention, or the prevention of disease occurrence, refers to measures designed to promote health (e.g., health education to encourage good nutrition, exercise, and genetic counseling) and specific protections (e.g., immunization and the use of seat belts).

Secondary prevention involves early detection and prompt treatment to achieve an early cure, if possible, or to slow progression, prevent complications, and limit disability. Most preventive health care is currently focused on this level.

Tertiary prevention consists of rehabilitation and maximizing remaining functional capacity when disease has occurred and left residual damage. This stage represents the most costly, labor-intensive aspect of medical care and depends heavily on effective teamwork by representatives of a number of health care disciplines.

Figure 1-4 illustrates the natural history and levels of prevention for the aging process. Although aging is not a disease, it is a condition that is often accompanied by medical, mental, and functional problems that should be addressed by a range of health care services at each level of prevention.

The natural history of diseases and the levels of prevention are presented to illustrate two very important aspects of U.S. health care system. First, it quickly becomes apparent in studying the natural history and levels of prevention for almost any of the common causes of disease and disability that the focus of health care historically has been directed at the curative and rehabilitative side of the disease continuum. The serious attention paid to refocusing the system on the health promotion/ disease prevention side of those disease schemas reflected in the National Prevention Strategy of the ACA[13] came about only after the costs of diagnostic and remedial care became an unacceptable burden and the lack of adequate insurance coverage for over 49 million Americans became a public and political embarrassment.

The second important aspect of the natural history concept is its value in planning community services. The illustration on aging provides a good example by suggesting health promotion and specific protection measures that could be applied to help maintain positive health status.

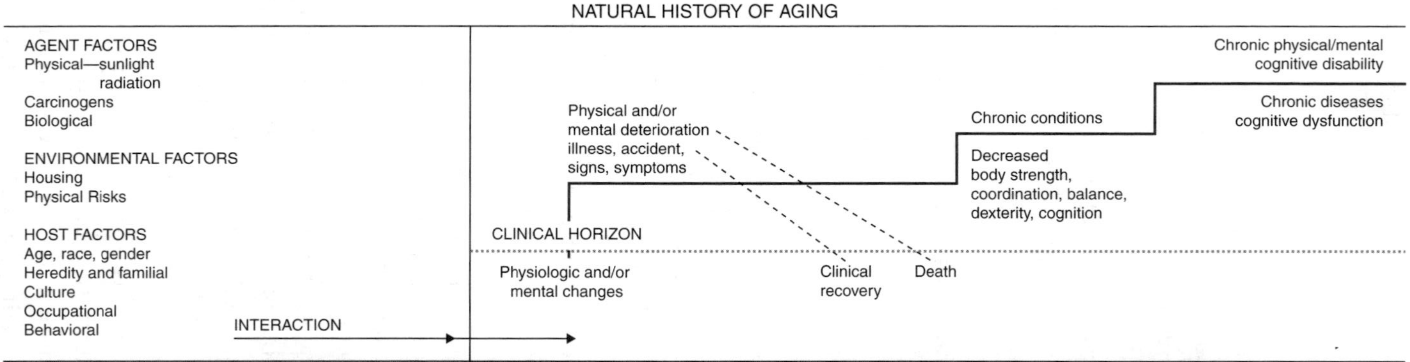

PREPATHOGENESIS PERIOD		PERIOD OF PATHOGENESIS			
Health Promotion	Specific Protection	Early Diagnosis and Treatment	Disability Limitation	Rehabilitation	Long-Term Support
Health education Wellness promotion Nutrition Exercise Adequate housing Avoidance of alcohol, drugs, and tobacco Stress reduction	Immunization Personal hygiene Driver's education Seat belts Accident protection Reduction of risk factors—cholesterol, weight, etc.	Periodic physicals Self-examination Primary care centers for older adults Mental health counseling Preventive care/screening centers Acute care	Subacute care Hearing and vision services Convalescent care Psychiatric care Home care Home-based chemotherapy Personal emergency response Housing for older adults	Physical and psychological rehabilitation Cardiac and stroke rehabilitation Inpatient and outpatient occupational and physical therapies, speech, respiratory therapies Home care	Social and medical models Adult day care Congregate dining Institutional and noninstitutional skilled nursing care Assisted living with board and care Personal services for activities of daily living Home care Home delivered meals, equipment, transportation, housekeeping, structural changes, hemodialysis, respiratory, etc.

FIGURE 1-4 Natural History of Aging.
Source: Reprinted with permission from H. R. Leavell and E. G. Clark, *Preventative Medicine for the Doctor in His Community: An Epidemiologic Approach,* 3rd edition, pp. 272–273, © 1965, The McGraw Hill Companies, Inc.

Major Stakeholders in U.S. Health Care Industry

To understand the health care industry, it is important to recognize the number and variety of its stakeholders. The sometimes shared and often conflicting concerns, interests, and influences of these constituent groups cause them to shift alliances periodically to oppose or champion specific reform proposals or other changes in the industry.

The Public

First and foremost among health care stakeholders are the individuals who consume the services. Although all are concerned with the issues of cost and quality, those who are uninsured or underinsured have an overriding uncertainty about access. It remains uncertain as to whether U.S. public will someday wish to treat health care like other inherent rights, such as education, but the passage of the ACA suggests that there is general agreement that some basic array of health care services should be available to all U.S. citizens. As the country waits to judge the success of the ACA in opening access to the previously uninsured, consumer organizations, such as the American Association of Retired Persons, and disease-specific groups, such as the American Cancer Society, the American Heart Association, and labor organizations, remain politically active on behalf of various consumer constituencies.

Employers

Employers constitute an increasingly influential group of stakeholders in health care because they not only pay for a high proportion of the costs but also take proactive roles in determining what those costs should be. Large private employers, coalitions of smaller private employers, and public employers wield significant authority in insurance plan negotiations. In addition, employer organizations representing small and large businesses wield considerable political power in the halls of Congress.

Providers

Health care professionals form the core of the industry and have the most to do with the actual process and outcomes of the service provided. Physicians, dentists, nurses, nurse practitioners, physician assistants, pharmacists, podiatrists, chiropractors, and a large array of allied health providers working as individuals or in group practices and staffing health care institutions are responsible for the quality and, to a large extent, the cost of the health care system. Recognizing the centrality of individual providers to system reform, the ACA is now offering numerous opportunities for the participation of physicians and other health care professionals in innovative experimentation with integrated systems of care.[14,15]

Hospitals and Other Health Care Facilities

Much of the provider activity, however, is shaped by the availability and nature of the health care institutions in which providers work. Hospitals of different types—general, specialty, teaching, rural, profit or not-for-profit, and independent or multifacility systems—are central to the health care system. However, they are becoming but one component of more complex integrated delivery system networks that also include nursing homes and other levels of care and various forms of medical practices.

Governments

Since the advent of Medicare and Medicaid in 1965, federal and state governments, already major stakeholders in health care, have become the dominant authorities of the system. Governments serve not only as payers but also as regulators and providers through public hospitals, state and local health departments, veterans affairs medical centers, and other facilities. In addition, of course, governments are the taxing authorities that generate the funds to support the system.

Alternative Therapies

Unconventional health therapies—those not usually taught in established medical and other health professional schools—contribute significantly to the amount, frequency, and cost of health care. In spite of the scientific logic and documented effectiveness of traditional, academically based health care, it is estimated that one in three adults uses alternative forms of health interventions each year.[16] Because of their popularity, state Medicaid programs, Medicare, and private health insurance plans provide benefits for some complementary therapies.[16]

It is estimated that over $9 billion per year is spent on such alternative forms of health care as Rolfing, yoga, spiritual healing, relaxation techniques, herbal remedies, energy healing, megavitamin therapy, the commonly recognized chiropractic arts, and a host of exotic mind–body healing techniques.[16]

The public's willingness to spend so much time and money on unconventional therapies suggests a substantial level of dissatisfaction with traditional scientific medicine. The popularity of alternative forms of therapy also indicates that its recipients confirm the effectiveness of the treatments by referring others to their practitioners. The National Institutes of Health has established a National Center for Complementary and Alternative Medicine to fund studies of the efficacy of such therapies. Thus, as a somewhat paradoxical development, some of the most ancient concepts of alternative health care are gaining broader recognition and acceptance in an era of most innovative and advanced high-technology medicine.

More for monetary than therapeutic reasons, a number of hospitals are now offering their patients some form of alternative medicine. According to an American Hospital Association survey, over 15% of U.S. hospitals opened alternative or complementary medicine centers by the year 2000. With a market estimated to be over $27 billion and patients willing to pay cash for alternative medicine treatments, hospitals are willing to rationalize the provision of several "unproven" services.[17]

Health Insurers

The insurance industry has long been a major stakeholder in the health care industry and has played a highly significant role in the development of the ACA. The industry will be a major contributor to offset the ACA's costs. In the years 2014–2018, health insurers will pay annual fees totaling $47.5 billion with future years' fees based on the previous year increased by the rate of premium growth.[18] MCO insurance plans are the predominant form of U.S. health insurance. MCOs may be owned by insurance companies, or they may be owned by hospitals, physicians, or consumer cooperatives. MCOs and the economic pressures they can apply through the negotiation of prepaid fees have produced much of the change that has occurred in the regional systems of health care during the past three decades.

Long-Term Care

The aging of U.S. population will be a formidable challenge to the country's systems of acute and long-term care. Nursing homes, home care services, other adult care facilities, and rehabilitation facilities will become increasingly important components of the nation's health care system as they grow in number, size, and complexity. The ACA's creation of seamless systems of integrated care that permit patients to move back and forth among ambulatory care offices, acute care hospitals, home care, and nursing homes within a single network of facilities and services will provide a continuum of services required for the more complex care of aging patients.

Voluntary Facilities and Agencies

Voluntary not-for-profit facilities and agencies, so called because they are governed by volunteer boards of directors, provide significant amounts of health counseling, health care, and research support and should be considered major stakeholders in the health care system. Although the voluntary sector traditionally has not received the recognition it deserves for its contribution to the nation's health care, it is often now viewed as the safety net to replace the services of government or other organizations that are eliminated by budgetary reductions.

Health Professions Education and Training Institutions

Schools of public health, medicine, nursing, dentistry, pharmacy, optometry, allied health, and other health care professions have a significant impact on the nature, quality, and costs of health care. As they prepare generation after each succeeding generation of competent health care providers, these schools also inculcate the values, attitudes, and ethics that govern the practices and behaviors of those providers as they function in the health care system.

Professional Associations

National, state, and regional organizations representing health care professionals or institutions have considerable influence over legislative proposals, regulation, quality issues, and other political matters. The lobbying effectiveness of the American Medical Association, for example, is legendary. The national influence of the American Hospital Association and the regional power of its state and local affiliates are also impressive. Other organizations of health care professionals, such as the American Public Health Association, America's Health Insurance Plans, the American Nurses Association, and the American Dental Association, play significant roles in health policy decisions. The American insurance industry lobbyists from organizations such as America's Health Insurance Plans had major influences on the provisions of the ACA.[19]

Other Health Industry Organizations

The size and complexity of the health care industry encourage the involvement of a great number of commercial entities. Several, such as the insurance and pharmaceutical enterprises, are major industries themselves and have significant organizational influence. The medical supplies and equipment business and the various consulting and information and management system suppliers also are important players.

Research Communities

It is difficult to separate much of health care research from the educational institutions that provide for its implementation. Nevertheless, the national research enterprise must be included in any enumeration of stakeholders in the health care industry. Government entities, such as the National Institutes of Health and the Agency for Healthcare Research and Quality, and not-for-profit foundations, such as the Robert Wood Johnson Foundation, the Commonwealth Fund, the Henry J. Kaiser Family Foundation, and the Pew Charitable Trusts, exert tremendous influence over health care research, policy development, and practice by conducting research and widely disseminating findings and supporting and encouraging investigations that inform policy decision making.

Rural Health Networks

Rural health systems are often incomplete, with shortages of various services and duplications of others. Federal and state programs have addressed this situation by promoting rural health networks' development.[20]

Networks may be formally organized as not-for-profit corporations or informally linked for a defined set of mutually beneficial purposes. Typically, they advocate at local and state levels on rural health care issues, cooperate in joint community outreach activities, and seek opportunities to negotiate with MCOs to provide services to enrolled populations. Most of these networks strive to provide local access to primary, acute, and emergency care and to provide efficient links to more distant regional specialists and tertiary care services. Ideally, rural health networks assemble and coordinate a comprehensive array of services that include dental, mental health, long-term care, and other health and human services.

With costs increasing and populations declining in many rural communities, it has been difficult for rural hospitals to continue their acute inpatient care services. Nevertheless, rural hospitals are often critically important to their communities. Because a hospital is usually one of the few major employers in rural communities, its closure has economic and health care consequences. Communities lacking alternative sources of health care within reasonable travel distance not only lose payroll and related business but also lose physicians, nurses, and other health personnel and suffer higher morbidity and mortality rates among those most vulnerable, such as infants and older adults.[21]

Some rural hospitals have remained viable by participating in some form of multi-institutional arrangement that permits them to benefit from the personnel, services, purchasing power, and financial stability of larger facilities. Many rural hospitals, however, have found it necessary to shift from inpatient to outpatient or ambulatory care. In many rural communities, the survival of a hospital has depended on how quickly and effectively it could replace its inpatient services with a productive constellation of ambulatory care, and sometimes long-term care, services.

Rural hospital initiatives have been supported by federal legislation since 1991. Legislation provided funding to promote the essential access community hospital and the rural primary care hospital. Both were limited-service hospital models developed as alternatives for hospitals that were too small and geographically isolated to be full-service acute care facilities. Regulations regarding staffing and other service requirements were relaxed in keeping with the rural settings[22] and included allowing physician's assistants, nurse practitioners, and clinical nurse specialists to provide primary or inpatient care without a physician in the facility if medical consultation is available by phone.

The Balanced Budget Act of 1997 included a Rural Hospital Flexibility Program that replaced the essential access community hospital/rural primary care hospital model with a critical access hospital (CAH) model. Any state with at least one CAH may qualify for the program, which exempts CAHs from strict regulation and allows them the flexibility to meet small, rural community needs by developing criteria for establishing network relationships. Although the new program maintained many of the same features and requirements as its predecessor, it added more flexibility by increasing the number of allowed occupied inpatient beds and the maximum length of stay before required discharge or transfer. The new program also allowed a swing bed program to provide flexibility in their use. The goal of the CAH program is to enable small rural hospitals to maximize reimbursement and meet community needs with responsiveness and flexibility.

The Balanced Budget Act also served rural hospitals by providing Medicare reimbursement for "telemedicine" and other video arrangements that link isolated facilities with clinical specialists at large hospitals. Telemedicine technology makes it possible for a specialist to be in direct visual and voice contact with a patient and provider at a remote location. The ACA contains significant support for the continued expansion of telemedicine programs that began with prior Medicare-supported pilot projects.[23]

Priorities of Health Care

The priorities of America's health care system—the emphasis on dramatic tertiary care, the costly and intensive efforts to fend off the death of terminal patients for a few more days or weeks, and the heroic efforts to save extremely low birth-weight infants at huge expense while thousands of women go without the prenatal care that would decrease prematurity—contribute to the obvious mismatch between the costs of health care and the failure to improve the measures of health status in the United States. It is difficult to rationalize the goals of a system that invests in the most expensive neonatal services to save high-risk infants while reducing support for relatively inexpensive and effective prenatal services with potential to prevent high-risk births in the first place.

If health care were to be governed by rational policies, the benefits to society of investing in primary prevention that is unquestionably cost-effective would be compared with both human and economic costs of salvaging individuals from preventable adverse outcomes. Unfortunately, priorities have favored heroic medicine over the more mundane and far less costly preventive care that results in measurable human and economic benefits. As noted previously in this chapter, major tenets of the ACA are designed to shift the focus from curative to preventive priorities though the implementation of the National Prevention Strategy.[13]

Tyranny of Technology

In many respects, the health care system has done and is doing a remarkable job. Important advances have been made in medical science, which have brought measurable improvements in the length and quality of life. The paradox is, however, that as technology grew in sophistication and costs, increasing numbers of people were deprived of its benefits. Health care providers can be so mesmerized by their own technologic ingenuity that things assume greater value than persons. For example, hospital administrations and medical staffs commonly dedicate their most competent practitioners and most sophisticated technology to the care of terminal patients while allocating far fewer resources to primary and preventive services for ambulatory clinic patients and other community populations in need of basic medical services.

Some hospitals recognize this disparity by conducting outreach and education programs for the medically underserved. Now with the ACA aligning reimbursement with prevention and wellness efforts, it is likely that more institutions will find it beneficial to initiate and maintain prevention initiatives and allocate staff to the potentially more productive care of discharged patients and ambulatory clinic populations.

The recurring theme among health services researchers assessing the value of technologic advances is a series of generally unanswered questions:

1. How does the new technology benefit the patient?
2. Is it worth the cost?
3. Are the new methods better than previous methods, and can they replace them?
4. Is treatment planning enhanced?
5. Is the outcome from disease better, or is the mortality rate improved?

Although many of the latest advances have gained great popularity and widespread acceptance, rigorous assessments that address these basic questions remain sorely needed.

Much of the philosophy underlying the values and priorities of the health care system today can be attributed to the unique culture of U.S. medicine. That philosophy owes much to the aggressive "can do" spirit of the frontier. Diseases are likened to enemies to be conquered. Physicians expect their patients to be aggressive too. Those who undergo drastic treatments to "beat" cancer are held in higher regard than patients who resign themselves to the disease. Some physicians and nurses feel demoralized when dying patients refuse resuscitation or limit interventions to palliative care.

The treatment-oriented rather than prevention-oriented health care philosophy has been encouraged by an insurance system that, before managed care's prevention orientation and efforts to curb unnecessary interventions, rarely paid for any disease prevention other than immunizations. It is also understandable in a system prizing high-technology medicine and rewarding volume regardless of value, that there has been much more satisfaction and remuneration from saving the lives of the injured and diseased than in preventing those occurrences from happening in the first place.

Social Choices of Health Care

The American emphasis on cure over prevention disinclined the health care professions to address those situations over which they have had little control. Behavioral issues such as acquired dependence on tobacco, alcohol, and drugs must be counted among the significant causes of impaired health in our population. If left unchanged, the future effects on health and medical care associated with these addictions probably will exceed all expectations. Similarly, the AIDS epidemic is as much a social and behavioral phenomenon as it is a biologic one. Nevertheless, outside of the public health disciplines, the considerable influence and prestige of the health care professions have been noticeably absent in steering public opinion and governmental action toward an emphasis on health. Similarly, in comparison with resources expended on treatment after illness occurs, relatively little attention had been given to changing high-risk behaviors even when the consequences are virtually certain and nearly always extreme.

Aging Population

The aging of U.S. population will have wide-ranging implications for the country. As the United States ages over the next several decades, its older population will become more racially and ethnically diverse. Projecting the size and structure in terms of age, sex, race, and Hispanic origin of the older population is important to public and private interests, both socially and economically. U.S. Census Bureau projects that nearly one in five residents will be aged 65 or older by 2030 and that by 2050 the number of Americans aged 65 and older will be 88.5 million, which is more than double its projected population in 2010.[24] Between 2010 and 2050, U.S. Census Bureau projects that the proportion of U.S. population comprising persons over 85 years old will increase from 14% to 21%[24] (see Figure 1-5).

In the same period, the minority composition of the older population is expected to more than double from 20% to 42% and the older Hispanic population is projected to more than triple[24] (see Figure 1-6). The growth of the older population will present serious challenges to policy makers and programs, such as Social Security and Medicare and will also affect families, businesses, and health care providers.

As medical advances find more ways to maintain life, the duration of chronic illness and the number of chronically ill individuals will increase with a concomitant increase in the need for personal support. The intensity of care required by frail older adults also has the potential of affecting worker productivity as it is common for family members to leave the workforce or to work part time to care for frail relatives.

The increased number of older persons with chronic physical ailments and cognitive disorders raises significant questions about the capability and capacity of U.S. health care system. Health care professionals are just beginning to respond to the need to focus health care for older adults away from medications or other quick-fix remedies. The system is slowly acknowledging that the traditional medical service model is inappropriate to the care of those with multiple chronic conditions.

The growing number of older adults faces serious gaps in financial coverage for long-term care needs. Unlike the broad Medicare program coverage for the acute health care problems of older Americans, the long-term care services needed to cope with the chronic disability and functional limitations of aging are largely unaddressed by either Medicare or

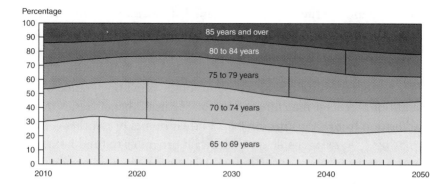

Note: Line indicates the year that each age group is the largest proportion of the older population.

FIGURE 1-5 Distribution of the Older Population by Age: 2010 to 2050. *Source:* Reproduced from U.S. Census Bureau, *The Next Four Decades: The Older Population in the United States: 2010 to 2050.*

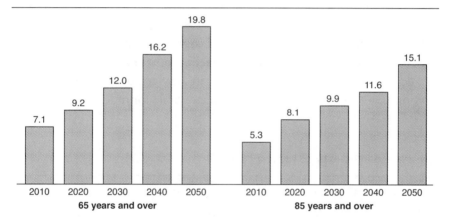

FIGURE 1-6 Percent Hispanic for the Older Population by Selected Age Groups for the United States: 2010 to 2050. *Source:* Reproduced from U.S. Census Bureau, *The Next Four Decades: The Older Population in the United States: 2010 to 2050.*

private insurance plans. With the exception of the relatively small number of individuals with personal long-term care insurance, the costs of long-term care services are borne by individual older adults and their caregivers.

As a last resort, the Medicaid program became the major public source of financing for nursing home care. Medicaid eligibility, however, requires that persons "spend down" their personal resources to meet financial eligibility criteria. For those disabled older adults who seek care in the community outside of nursing homes, Medicaid offers very limited assistance. Provisions of the ACA make some progress in addressing these issues. The reform plan, called "Medicaid Money Follows the Person" (MFP), set demonstration projects in motion by providing grants to states for additional federal matching funds for Medicaid beneficiaries making the transition from an institution back to their homes or to other community settings.[25] Grants enable state Medicaid programs to fund home- and community-based services for individuals' needs, such as personal care assistance to enable their safe residency in the community. Other long-term care provisions under the ACA include "Community First Choice Option in Medicaid," which provides states with an increased federal Medicaid matching rate to support community-based attendant services for individuals who require an institutional level of care,[26,27] and a "State Balancing Incentive Program," which enhances federal matching funds to states to increase the proportion of Medicaid long-term services and support dollars allocated toward home- and community-based services.[27] It is hoped that these demonstrations will yield results that may be expanded to address the serious gaps that exist in services between home- and community-based and institutional care available for older Americans.

Access to Health Care

Much attention has been paid to the economic problems of health care, and considerable investments of research funds have been made to address the issues of health care quality. However, the third major problem—that of limited access to health care among the estimated 49 million uninsured or underinsured Americans—has continued to confound decision makers for decades and evolved into both a moral and an economic issue.

Polar positions have been taken by those who have addressed the question of whether society in general or governments in particular have an obligation to ensure that everyone has the right to health care and whether the health care system has a corresponding obligation to make such care available. Consider these opposing viewpoints by P. H. Elias and R. M. Sade, respectively:

> Physicians who limit their office practice to insured and paying patients declare themselves openly to be merchants rather than professionals. . . .

Physicians who value their professionalism should treat office patients on the basis of need, not remuneration.[28]

The concept of medical care as the patient's right is immoral because it denies the most fundamental of all rights, that of a man to his own life and the freedom of action to support it. Medical care is neither a right nor a privilege: it is a service that is provided by doctors to others who wish to purchase it.[29]

Although health care providers debate their individual and personal obligations to provide uncompensated care, the system itself finessed the problem for many years by shifting the costs of care from the uninsured to the insured. This unofficial but practical approach to indigent care was ethically tolerable as long as the reimbursement system for paying patients was so open ended that the cost of treating the uninsured could easily be passed on to paying patients. The cost shifting that worked under old reimbursement systems that paid for virtually everything after the fact was not feasible under new payment schemes of the 1980s and beyond that pay a preestablished and fixed price in advance of treatment based on diagnosis. The ACA's insurance and reimbursement mechanisms recognize that a transparent approach to providing insurance coverage for low-income persons will address the long-standing inequities in a system previously required to cryptically manage uncompensated care. In this regard, the ACA's provisions are a pointed example of the need for government intervention on behalf of its citizenry when markets are unable or unwilling to respond.

Ideally, U.S. health policy makers would have preferred to assure the public that the health care system would provide all citizens with comparable access to health care and to assure physicians and other health care providers that they would be free of government interference in decisions about service production and delivery. However, a very long history of failed attempts at free-market approaches has resulted in the indisputable conclusion that government intervention is needed to materially improve the access problem.

Quality of Care

Another health care system problem area is variations in the quality and appropriateness of medical care. The uncertainty that pervades current clinical practice is far greater than most people realize. Problems in the quality and appropriateness of many diagnostic and therapeutic procedures impact heavily on costs.

Since the 1999 report of the Institute of Medicine that estimated that medical errors take from 44,000 to 98,000 lives per year, the Congress, the president, medical institutions, and the public have been stirred to respond to a problem that has existed for decades. The increasing complexity of the health care system, the potency of its pharmaceuticals, the dangers inherent in surgical procedures, and the potential for error in the many information transfers that occur during hospital care combine to put patients at serious risk.

Health care errors are a leading cause of preventable deaths in the United States.[30] The overall burden on society is much greater when both fatal and nonfatal events are counted and when medical mishaps in medical offices, ambulatory centers, and long-term care facilities are considered.[31]

Conflicts of Interest

One of the greatest advantages of U.S. high-technology health care systems is the ability of physicians and patients to benefit from referrals to a broad range of highly specialized clinical, laboratory, rehabilitation, and other services.

In recent years, however, increasing numbers of physicians have begun to invest in laboratories, imaging centers, medical supply companies, and other health care businesses. In many cases, these are joint ventures with other institutions that conceal the identity of the investors. When health care providers refer patients for tests or other services to health care businesses that they own or in which they have a financial stake, there is a serious potential for conflicts of interest. For the last several years both federal and state governments and the American Medical Association have conducted studies that confirm that physician-owned laboratories, for example, perform more tests per patient at higher charges than those in which physicians have no investments.[32] These conflicts of interest undermine the traditional professional role of physicians and significantly increase health care expenditures. In another dimension of conflicts of interest, the ACA includes "Sunshine" provisions that arose from activities related to enforcement of the federal kickback statute pertaining to financial relationships between health industry (pharmaceutical, biologics, and medical device companies) and health care providers.[33]

The ACA "requires reporting of all financial transactions and transfers of value between manufacturers of pharmaceutical/biologic products or medical devices and physicians, hospitals and other covered recipients that are reimbursed by U.S. federal government."[33] In addition, the ACA requires the Centers for Medicare & Medicaid Services to establish a Web site to post information pertinent to these transactions in a searchable, downloadable database.[33] Fines for manufacturer noncompliance with reporting requirements can reach up to $1 million per reporting year.[33]

Health Care's Ethical Dilemmas

Once almost an exclusive province of physicians and other health care providers, moral and ethical issues underlying provider–patient relationships and the difficult decisions resulting from the vast increase in treatment options are now in the domains of law, politics, journalism, health institution administrations, and the public. During the last few decades, the list of ethical issues has expanded as discoveries in genetic identification and engineering, organ transplantation, a mounting armamentarium of highly specialized diagnostic and therapeutic interventions, and advances in technology have allowed the lives of otherwise terminal individuals to be prolonged. In addition, an energized health care consumer movement advocating more personal control over health care decisions, economic realities, and the issues of the most appropriate use of limited resources are but a few of the topics propelling values and ethics to the top of the health care agenda. There is a social dimension to health care that never existed before and that the health professions, their educational institutions, their organizations, and their philosophical leadership are now beginning to address.

Clearly, the rapid pace of change in health care and the resulting issues have outpaced U.S. society's ability to reform the thinking, values, and expectations that were more appropriate to a bygone era. Legislative initiatives are, correctly or not, filling the voids.

The 1997 decision of the U.S. 9th Circuit Court of Appeals permitting physician-assisted suicide for competent, terminally ill adults in the state of Oregon is an unprecedented example. The New York state's 1990 passage of health care proxy legislation that allows competent adults to appoint agents to make health care decisions on their behalf if they become incapacitated is another. Living wills that provide advance directives regarding terminal care are now recognized in all 50 states.

Issue by issue, the country is trying to come to grips with the ethical dilemmas that modern medicine has created. The pluralistic nature of this society, however, and the Judeo-Christian concepts about caring for the sick and disabled that served so well for so long make sweeping reformation of the ethical precepts on which health care has been based very challenging.

Continuing Challenges

As the United States pushes forward with the implementation of the ACA and its experimentation with new models to test strategies for cost reductions, quality improvement, and increased access, these basic issues will persist for the immediate future, likely joined by other emerging concerns. How to improve Americans' health behaviors, how to involve consumers more effectively in health care decisions, and how to appropriately balance responsibilities and accountability between the government and private sectors remain among the looming challenges of this unprecedented era of health reform.

Key Terms for Review

Natural History of Disease   Secondary Prevention
Primary Prevention   Tertiary Prevention
Rural Health Networks

References

1. The Henry J. Kaiser Family Foundation. Health care costs: a primer, key information on health care costs and their impact. May 2012. Available from http://www.kff.org/insurance/upload/7670-03.pdf. Accessed January 26, 2013.
2. U.S. Department of Health and Human Services, Centers for Medicare & Medicaid Services. National health expenditures tables. 2011. Available from http://www.cms.gov/Research-Statistics-Data-and-Systems/Statistics-Trends-and-Reports/NationalHealthExpendData/downloads/tables.pdf. Accessed January 26, 2013.

3. U.S. Department of Labor, Bureau of Labor Statistics. Monthly labor review. January 2012. Industry employment and outlook projections to 2020. Available from http://www.bls.gov/opub/mlr/2012/01/art4full.pdf. Accessed July 1, 2012.

4. Gostin LO, Jacobson PD, Record KL, et al. Restoring health to health reform: integrating medicine and public health to advance the population's well-being. *Pennsylvania Law Review.* 2011. Available from http://scholarship.law.georgetown.edu/facpub/609. Accessed January 16, 2013.

5. Congressional Budget Office. Updated estimates for the insurance coverage provisions of the affordable care act. 2012. Available from http://www.cbo.gov/sites/default/files/cbofiles/attachments/03-13-Coverage%20Estimates.pdf. Accessed February 17, 2013.

6. Charting the Economy.com. Healthcare. 2009. Available from http://chartingtheeconomy.com/?cat=18. Accessed February 17, 2013.

7. The Henry J. Kaiser Family Foundation. Health expenditure per capita. Global health facts.org. 2010. Available from http://www.globalhealthfacts.org/data/topic/map.aspx?ind=66. Accessed February 15, 2013.

8. Pollack H. Health reform and public health: will good policies but bad politics combine to produce bad policy? *University of Pennsylvania Law Review.* 2011;159:2061. Available from http://www.pennumbra.com/issues/pdfs/159-6/Pollack.pdf. Accessed February 9, 2013.

9. Roy A. How hospital mergers increase health costs, and what to do about it. *Forbes.* 2012. Available from http://www.forbes.com/sites/aroy/2012/03/01/how-hospital-mergers-increase-health-costs-and-what-to-do-about-it/. Accessed February 4, 2013.

10. Ginzberg E. Health care reform: why so slow? *New England Journal of Medicine.* 1990;32:1464,1465.

11. Nichols LM, Ginsburg BA, Christianson U, et al. Are market forces strong enough to deliver efficient health care systems? Confidence is waning. *Health Affairs.* 2004;23:8–21.

12. Bernabeo E, Holmboe ES. Patients, providers and systems need to acquire a specific set of competencies to achieve truly patient-centered care. *Health Affairs.* 2013;32:251–254. Available from http://content.healthaffairs.org/content/32/2/250.full.html. Accessed February 6, 2013.

13. U.S. Department of Health and Human Services. Obama administration releases national prevention strategy. 2011. Available from http://www.hhs.gov/news/press/2011pres/06/20110616a.html. Accessed January 18, 2013.

14. Reid RJ, Coleman K, Johnson EA, et al. The group health medical home at year two: cost savings, higher patient satisfaction, and less burnout for providers. *Health Affairs.* 2010;29:835. Available from http://content.healthaffairs.org/content/29/5/835.full.html. Accessed January 15, 2013.

15. HealthCare.gov. Accountable care organizations: improving care coordination for people with Medicare. 2011. Available from http://www.healthcare.

gov/news/factsheets/2011/03/accountablecare03312011a.html. Accessed January 15, 2013.

16. Davis MA, Martin BI, Coulter ID, et al. US spending on complementary and alternative medicine during 2002–08 plateaued, suggesting role in reformed health care system. *Health Affairs*. 2013;32:45–47. Available from http://content.healthaffairs.org/content/32/1/45.full.html. Accessed February 11, 2013.

17. Abelson R, Brown PL. Alternative medicine is finding its niche in nation's hospitals. *The New York Times*. April 13, 2002:B1, B3.

18. The Henry J. Kaiser Family Foundation. Focus on health reform. 2011. Available from http://www.kff.org/healthreform/upload/8061.pdf. Accessed February 9, 2013.

19. Common Ground. Who wrote Obamacare? 2012. Available from http://commongroundamerica.net/Who_Wrote_the_PPACA.html. Accessed February 16, 2013.

20. U.S. Department of Health and Human Services. Health Resources and Services Administration. Rural health network development program. 2012. Available from http://www.hrsa.gov/ruralhealth/about/community/networkprogram.html. Accessed February 1, 2013.

21. Fickenscher K, Voorman ML. An overview of rural health care. In: Shortell SM, Reinhardt UE, Eds. *Improving Health Policy and Management: Nine Critical Research Issues for the 1990s*. Ann Arbor, MI: Health Administration Press; 1992:133–134.

22. Fickenscher K, Voorman ML. An overview of rural health care. In: Shortell SM, Reinhardt UE, Eds. *Improving Health Policy and Management: Nine Critical Research Issues for the 1990s*. Ann Arbor, MI: Health Administration Press; 1992:127.

23. Medical News. American Telemedicine Association. Telemedicine benefits from Supreme Court ruling. 2012. Available from http://www.news-medical.net/news/20120629/Upholding-PPACA-will-have-positive-impact-on-development-adoption-of-telehealth-ATA.aspx?page=2. Accessed February 17, 2013.

24. U.S. Department of Commerce. U.S. Census Bureau. The next four decades: the older population in the United States: 2010–2050. 2010. Available from http://www.census.gov/prod/2010pubs/p25-1138.pdf. Accessed February 17, 2013.

25. The Henry J. Kaiser Family Foundation. Kaiser Commission on Medicaid and the Uninsured. Money follows the person: a 2011 survey of transitions, services and costs. Executive summary. 2011. Available from http://www.kff.org/medicaid/upload/8142-02-2.pdf. Accessed January 19, 2013.

26. American Association of Retired Persons. Health care reform improves access to Medicaid home and community-based services. 2010. Available from http://assets.aarp.org/rgcenter/ppi/ltc/fs192.hcbs.pdf. Accessed January 19, 2013.

27. The Henry J. Kaiser Family Foundation. Medicaid long-term services and supports: key changes in the health reform law. 2010. Available from http://www.kff.org/healthreform/upload/8079.pdf. Accessed January 19, 2013.

28. Elias PH. Letter to editor. *New England Journal of Medicine.* 1986;314:314–391.

29. Sade RM. Medical care as a right: a refutation. *New England Journal of Medicine.* 1971;285:1281, 1289.

30. The Lancet. Medical errors in the USA: human or systemic? *The Lancet.* 2011;377:1289. Available from http://www.thelancet.com/journals/lancet/article/PIIS0140-6736(11)60520-5/fulltext?rss=yes. Accessed February 17, 2013.

31. Kizer KW. Patient safety: a call to action: a consensus statement from the national quality forum. *Medscape General Medicine.* 2001;3:1–7. Available from http://www.medscape.com/viewarticle/408114_4. Accessed February 18, 2013.

32. Kirkner RM. The enduring temptation of physician self-referral. *Managed Care Magazine Online.* October 2011. Available from http://www.managedcaremag.com/content/enduring-temptation-physician-self-referral. Accessed February 17, 2013.

33. Lauer K, Patel M, Pepitone K. Physician payment Sunshine Act: potential implications for medical publication professionals. *American Medical Writers Association Journal.* 2012;27:7–8. Available from http://www.amwa.org/default/publications/journal/vol27.1/v27n1.007.feature.pdf. Accessed February 18, 2013.

2

Benchmark Developments in U.S. Health Care

This chapter describes the important legislative, political, economic, organizational, and professional influences that transformed health care in the United States from a relatively simple professional service to a huge, complex, corporation-dominated industry. The effects of medical education, scientific advances, rising costs, changing population demographics, and American values and assumptions regarding health care are discussed. This chapter concludes with a brief discussion of judicial challenges to the Patient Protection and Affordable Care Act (ACA) and a review of the ACA provisions that address basic, cost, quality, and access issues of U.S. health care system.

From its earliest history, health care, or, more accurately, medical care, was dominated by physicians and their hospitals. In the 19th and early 20th centuries, participation in U.S. medicine was generally limited to two parties—patients and physicians. Diagnosis, treatment, and fees for services were considered confidential between patients and physicians. Medical practice was relatively simple and usually involved long-standing relationships among physicians, patients, and their families. Physicians set and often adjusted their charges to their estimates of patients' ability to pay and collected their own bills. This was the intimate physician–patient relationship that the profession held sacred.

Free from outside scrutiny or interference, individual physicians had complete control over where, when, what, and how they practiced. In 1934, the American Medical Association (AMA) published this statement: "No third party must be permitted to come between the patient and his physician in any medical matter."[1] The AMA was concerned about such issues as non-physician-controlled voluntary health insurance, compulsory health insurance, and the few prepaid contracts for medical services negotiated by remote lumber or mining companies and a few workers' guilds. For decades, organized medicine repeatedly battled against these and other outside influences that altered "the old relations of perfect freedom between physicians and patients, with separate compensation for each separate service."[1]

As early as the 19th century, some Americans carried insurance against sickness through an employer, fraternal order, guild, trade union, or commercial insurance company. Most of the plans, however, were simply designed to make up for lost income during sickness or injury by providing a fixed cash payment.[1] Sickness insurance, as it was originally called, was the beginning of social insurance programs against the risks of income interruption by accident, sickness, or disability. Initially, it was provided only to wage earners. Later, it was extended to workers' dependents and other people.[2]

Around 1915, the drive for compulsory health insurance began to build in the United States, after most European countries had initiated either compulsory programs or subsidies for voluntary programs. The underlying concern was to protect workers against a loss of income resulting from industrial accidents that were common at the time. Families with only one wage earner, often already at the edge of poverty, could be devastated by loss of income caused by sickness or injury, even without the additional costs of medical care.

At the time, life insurance companies sold "industrial" policies that provided lump-sum payments at death, which amounted to $50 or $100 to pay for final medical expenses and funerals. Both Metropolitan Life and Prudential Insurance Company rose to the top of the insurance industry by successfully marketing industrial policies that required premium payments of 10–25 cents per week.[2]

In 1917, World War I interrupted the campaign for compulsory health insurance in the United States. In 1919, the AMA House of Delegates officially condemned compulsory health insurance with the following resolution[3]:

> The American Medical Association declares its opposition to the institution of any plan embodying the system of compulsory contributory insurance against illness or any other plan of compulsory insurance which provides for medical service to be rendered contributors or their dependents, provided, controlled, or regulated by any state or the federal government.

Most of physician opposition to compulsory health insurance was attributed to an unfounded concern that insurance would decrease, rather than increase, physician incomes and to their negative experience with accident insurance that paid physicians according to arbitrary fee schedules.[1]

The Great Depression and the Birth of Blue Cross

As the Depression of 1929 shook the nation, it also threatened the financial security of both physicians and hospitals. Physician incomes and hospital admission rates dropped precipitously as individuals were unable to pay out of pocket for medical care, and hospitals began experimenting with insurance plans. The Baylor University Hospital plan was not the first, but it became the most influential of those insurance experiments. By enrolling 1,250 public school teachers at 50 cents a month for a guaranteed 21 days of hospital care, Baylor created the model for and is credited with the genesis of Blue Cross hospital insurance. Baylor started a trend that developed into multihospital plans that included all hospitals in a given area. By 1937, there were 26 plans with more than 600,000 members, and the American Hospital Association began approving the plans. Physicians were pleased with the increased availability of hospital care and the cooperative manner in which their bills were paid. The AMA, however, was characteristically hostile and called the plans "economically unsound, unethical, and inimical to the public interest."[4]

The AMA contended that urging people "to save for sickness" could solve the problem of financing health care.[2] Organized medicine's consistently antagonistic reaction to the concept of health insurance, whether compulsory or voluntary, is well illustrated by medicine's response to the 1932 report of the Committee on the Costs of Medical Care. The committee's establishment represented a shift from concern about lost wages to concern about medical expenses. Chaired by a former president of the AMA and financed by several philanthropic organizations, a group of prominent Americans from the medical, public health, and social science fields worked for 5 years to address the problem of financing medical care. After an exhaustive study, a moderate majority recommended adoption of group practice and voluntary health insurance as the best way of solving the nation's health care problems. However, even this relatively modest recommendation was rejected by some commission members who in a minority report denounced voluntary health insurance as more objectionable than compulsory insurance. Health insurance, predicted the minority, would lead to "destructive competition among professional groups, inferior medical service, loss of personal relationship of patient and physician, and demoralization of the profession."[5] In 1933, the AMA's House of Delegates again reiterated its long-standing opposition to health insurance of any kind by declaring that the minority report represented "the collective opinion of the medical profession."[6] The dissenting physicians did, however, favor government intervention to alleviate physicians' financial burden, resulting from their obligation to provide free care to low-income populations.

From the turn of the 20th century to the present, there have been many efforts to enact various forms of compulsory health insurance. It was only when the proponents of government-sponsored insurance limited their efforts to older adults and low-income populations; that they were able to succeed in passing Medicaid and Medicare legislation in 1965. Voluntary insurance against hospital care costs became the predominant health insurance in the United States during those decades. The advocates of government-sponsored health insurance had little success in improving patient access to medical care, but the Blue Cross plans effectively improved hospitals' access to patients.

Following World War II, the federal government gave a huge boost to the private health insurance industry by excluding health insurance benefits from wage and price controls and by excluding workers' contributions to health insurance from taxable income. The effect was to enable employees to take wage increases in the form of health insurance fringe benefits rather than cash. Also following World War II, the federal government began heavily subsidizing the health care industry's expansion through hospital construction and medical research, with physician resources as an overriding policy objective.

Because insurance companies simply raised their premiums rather than exerting pressure on physicians and hospitals to contain costs, the post–World War II private health insurance system pumped an ever-increasing proportion of the national income into health care. There was little regard for cost growth, and attention was focused on avoiding any infringement on physicians' or hospitals' prerogatives to set prices and control costs. Medicare and Medicaid followed the same pattern. In fact, the preamble to those original legislative proposals specifically prohibited any interpretation of the legislation that would change the way health care was practiced.

Dominant Influence of Government

Although the health insurance industry contributed significantly to the spiraling costs of health care in the decades after World War II, it was only one of several influences. The federal government's coverage of health care for special populations played a prominent role. Over the years, U.S. government developed, revised, and otherwise adjusted a host of categorical or disease-specific programs designed to address needs not otherwise met by state or local administrations or the private sector. Federally sponsored programs account for about 40% of this country's personal health care expenditures.[7] In much smaller amounts, the federal government also provides funds for research and development and public health activities.[7]

In the evolution of U.S. health care delivery system, the policy implications of certain federal initiatives cannot be overemphasized. By establishing the principle of federal aid to the states for public health and welfare assistance, maternal and child health, and children with disabilities services, the Social Security Act of 1935 was the most significant social initiative ever passed by any Congress. It was the legislative basis for a number of significant health and welfare programs, including the Medicare and Medicaid programs.

The government increased its support of biomedical research through the National Institutes of Health, which was established in 1930, and the categorical programs that addressed heart disease, cancer, stroke, mental illness, mental retardation, maternal and infant care, and many other conditions. Programs such as direct aid to schools of medicine, dentistry, pharmacy, nursing, and other professions and their students and support of health planning, health care regulation, and consumer protections, which were incorporated in the various 1962 amendments to the Food, Drug, and Cosmetic Act of 1938, were all part of the Kennedy–Johnson presidential policy era called Creative Federalism. The aggregate annual investment in those programs made U.S. government the major player and payer in field health care.

Grants-in-aid programs alone, excluding Social Security and Medicare, grew from $7 billion at the start of the Kennedy administration in 1961 to $24 billion in 1968 under President Johnson's administration. Several other programs beside Medicare and Medicaid were initiated during the Johnson administration to address mental illness and to support health care professionals' role. The Health Professions Educational Assistance Act of 1963 provided direct federal aid to medical, dental, nursing, pharmacy, and other professional schools, as well as to their students. The Nurse Training Act supported special federal efforts for training professional nursing personnel, and during the same period, the Maternal and Child Health and Mental Retardation Planning Amendments initiated comprehensive maternal and child health projects and centers to serve people with mental retardation. The Economic Opportunity Act supported the development of neighborhood health centers to serve low-income populations.[8]

In 1970, in a direction labeled New Federalism, President Nixon expressed his intent to rescind the federal government's direct administration of several health care programs and shift revenues to state and local governments through block grants. In spite of his efforts, federal grants-in-aid programs grew to almost $83 billion by 1980. Congress had resisted block grants and allowed only limited revenue sharing to take place.[8]

In the meantime, with no effective controls over expenditures, federal and state governments underwrote skyrocketing costs of Medicare and Medicaid. The planners of the Medicare legislation had made several misjudgments. They underestimated the growing number of older adults in the United States, the scope and burgeoning costs of the technologic revolution, and the public's rising expectations for use of advanced, diagnostic, and treatment modalities.

The Medicare and Medicaid programs provided access to many desperately needed health care services for older Americans, people with disabilities, and low-income populations. Because rising Medicare reimbursement rates set the standards for most insurance companies, however, their inflationary effect was momentous. In the mid-1960s, when Medicare and

Medicaid were passed, the United States was spending about $42 billion on health care, or approximately 8.4% of the gross domestic product. The costs of U.S. health care now exceed $2.7 trillion and consume over 17% of the gross domestic product.[7, 9]

Three Major Health Care Concerns

The three major health care concerns of cost, quality, and access have comprised a generations-long conundrum of U.S. health care delivery system. Virtually, all attempts to control one or two of these concerns have exacerbated the one or two remaining. The federal government's improvements in access to care by measures such as the post–World War II hospital expansion and the Medicare and Medicaid legislation, which extended government health insurance to millions of older and low-income Americans, were accompanied by skyrocketing expenditures and quality issues. These measures resulted in the health care system's excess capacity, and while virtually unchecked funding improved access to competent and appropriate medical care for many, it also resulted in untold numbers of clinical interventions of questionable necessity. Almost all the federal health legislation since the passage of Medicare and Medicaid and the Balanced Budget Act of 1997 were targeted at reducing costs but with little focus on the reciprocal effects of reducing both the access and the quality of health care.

Efforts at Planning and Quality Control

The federal government did not ignore the issues of cost and quality, but efforts to address those concerns were doomed to be ineffectual by their designs. Powerful medical and hospital lobbies exerted great influence over any legislation that might alter the existing constellation of health care services or that would scrutinize the quality of clinical practice. Any legislation had to be "provider friendly," allowing physicians, hospital administrators, and other health professionals to maintain control over how the legislation was interpreted and enforced.

Two legislative initiatives of the 1960s typify the circumstances surrounding federal legislative efforts to address the cost, quality, and access concerns of the health care delivery system. In 1965, the Public Health Service Act was amended to establish the Regional Medical Program initiative, a nationwide network of medical programs in designated geographic areas to address the leading causes of death: heart disease, cancer, and stroke. Throughout the nation, groups of physicians, nurses, and other health professionals met to deliberate innovative ways to bring the latest in clinical services to the bedside of patients. Representatives of each constituency advocated for funding in their respective disciplines. As a consequence, the regional medical programs improved the educational and clinical resources of their regions but did not materially improve prevention or cost reductions in the treatment of the target conditions.

A parallel program, the Comprehensive Health Planning Act, was passed in 1966 to promote comprehensive planning for rational systems of health care personnel and facilities in designated regions. The legislation required federal, state, and local partnerships. It also required that there be a majority of consumers on every decision-making body.[10]

Almost all the Regional Medical Programs and Comprehensive Health Planning Act programs across the country soon were dominated by medical–hospital leaders in their regions. Many productive outcomes resulted from the two programs, but conflicts of interest regarding the allocation of research and development funds were common, and there was general agreement that the programs were ineffective in achieving their goals.

The Johnson-era programs of 1966–1969, especially Medicare and Medicaid, entrenched the federal government in the business of financing health care. President Johnson's ambitious creative federalism enriched the country's health care system and improved the access of many impoverished citizens, but it also fueled the inflationary spiral of health care costs that has persisted until today.

The National Health Planning and Resources Development Act of 1974 ultimately combined the Regional Medical Health Program and Comprehensive Health Planning Act programs with political rather than objective assessments. The Congress apparently assumed that combining two ineffective programs would result in one successful program. Nevertheless, the legislation established a new organization, the Health Systems Agency (HSA), which required broad representation of health care providers and consumers on governing boards and committees to deliberate and recommend health care resource allocations to their respective federal and state governing bodies.

HSAs were largely ineffective for many of the same reasons as their predecessor organizations had failed to provide meaningful strategies to address cost, quality, and access concerns. The general ineffectiveness of HSAs in their regions was acknowledged by the federal administration, and support ultimately was withdrawn.[11,12]

Managed Care Organizations

In 1973, the Health Maintenance Organization Act supported the development of health maintenance organizations (HMOs) through grants for federal demonstration projects. An HMO is an organization responsible for the financing and delivery of comprehensive health services to an enrolled population for a prepaid, fixed fee. HMOs were expected to hold down costs by changing the profit incentive from fee for service to promoting health and preventing illness.

The concept was accepted widely, and between 1992 and 1999, HMOs and other types of managed care organizations experienced phenomenal growth, accounting for the majority of all privately insured persons.[13] Subsequently, the fortunes of managed care organizations changed as both health care costs and consumer complaints increased.

Beginning in 2001, a derivative of managed care organizations, preferred provider organizations (PPOs), gained in popularity. Although PPOs encompass important managed care characteristics, they were organized by physicians and hospitals to meet the needs of private, third-party, and self-insured firms. By 2002, PPOs had captured 52% of covered employees.[14] Although most Americans are now receiving their health care through some sort of prepaid managed care arrangement, the evidence that significant savings will be realized is fragmentary. Stiff increases in HMO premium rates suggest that the widespread application of HMO concepts will not provide the long-sought containment of runaway health care costs. In addition, both consumers and providers are suggesting that the HMO controls on costs are compromising the quality of care. Consumer concerns about restrictions on choice of providers, limits on availability of services, and quality of health care evoked a managed care backlash and generated support for government regulation of managed care organizations.[15]

The Reagan Administration

Beginning with the Reagan administration in 1981, attempts continued to shrink federally supported programs begun in the 1960s and 1970s. Unlike Nixon and Ford, Reagan succeeded in implementing New Federalism policies that were all but stymied in previous administrations. A significant reduction in government expenditures for social programs occurred. Decentralization of program responsibility to the states was achieved primarily through block grants. Although his attempts at deregulation to stimulate competition had little success, Reagan's implementation of Medicare prospective payment to hospitals based on diagnosis-related groups, rather than retrospective payment based on hospital charges, signaled the new effort to contain health care costs that were widely adopted as standard by the health insurance industry.[16]

The conversion of categorical and disease-specific programs to block grants, the withdrawal of federal support for professional education, and the creation of a Medicare resource-based relative value scale to adjust and contain physicians' fees are but a few other examples of presidential or congressional efforts to reduce the federal government's financial commitment to health care.

Biomedical Advances: Evolution of High-Technology Medicine

Health care in the United States dramatically improved during the 20th century. In the first half of the century, the greatest advances led to the prevention or cure of many infectious diseases. The development of vaccines to prevent a wide range of communicable diseases, from yellow fever to measles, and the discovery of antibiotics saved vast numbers of Americans from early death or disability.

In the second half of the 20th century, however, technologic advances that characterize today's health care were developed and the pace of technologic development accelerated rapidly. The following are a few of the seminal medical advances that took place during the 1960s:

- The Sabin and Salk vaccines ended annual epidemics of poliomyelitis.
- The tranquilizers Librium and Valium were introduced and widely prescribed, leading Americans to turn to medicine to cure their emotional as well as physical ills.

- The birth control pill was first prescribed and became the most widely used and effective contraceptive method.
- The heart-lung machine and major improvements in the efficacy and safety of general anesthesia techniques made possible the first successful heart bypass operation in 1964. Three years later, the first human heart transplant took place.

In 1972, computed tomography was invented. Computed tomography, which unlike x-rays can distinguish one soft tissue from another, is installed widely in U.S. hospitals and ambulatory centers. This valuable and profitable diagnostic imaging device started an extravagant competition among hospitals to develop lucrative patient services by making major capital investments in high-technology equipment. Later, noting the convenience and profit associated with diagnostic devices such as computed tomography and magnetic resonance imaging, medical groups purchased the devices and placed them in their own facilities. This practice represents one example of how hospitals, physicians, and other health service providers came to act as isolated economic entities rather than as members of a community of health care resources established to serve population needs. The profit-driven competition and resulting redundant capacity continued to drive up utilization and costs for hospitals, insurers, and the public.[17]

New technology, new drugs, and new and creative surgical procedures have made possible a wide variety of life-enhancing and life-extending medical accomplishments. Operations that once were complex and hazardous, requiring hospitalization and intense follow-up care, have become relatively common ambulatory surgical procedures. For example, the use of intraocular lens implants after the removal of cataracts has become one of the most popular surgical procedures. Previously requiring hospitalization, these implants are performed in outpatient settings on over 3 million Americans annually,[18] with the procedure taking less than 1 hour.

Technical Advances Bring New Problems

Almost every medical or technologic advance seems to be accompanied by new and vexing financial and ethical dilemmas. The increased ability to extend life raises questions about the quality of life and the right to die. New capabilities to use costly and limited resources to improve the quality of life for some and not others create other ethical problems.

Whatever its benefits, the increased use of new technology has contributed to higher health care costs. Some believe, however, that if the new technology were used properly and not overused for the sake of defensive medicine or to take advantage of its profit potential, it would actually lower health care costs.[19]

Both the AMA and the federal government developed programs to explore these issues and to provide needed information for decision makers. The AMA established three programs to assess the ramifications of medical advancements: the Diagnostic and Therapeutic Technology Assessment Program, the Council on Scientific Affairs, and the AMA Drug Evaluations.[20]

In the Technology Assessment Act of 1972, Congress recognized that "it is essential that, to the fullest extent possible, the consequences of technologic applications be anticipated, understood, and considered in determination of public policy on existing and emerging national problems."[21] To address this goal, the Office of Technology Assessment (OTA), a nonpartisan support agency that worked directly with and for congressional committees, was created. The OTA relied on the technical and professional resources of the private sector, including universities, research organizations, industry, and public interest groups, to produce their assessments and provide congressional committees with analyses of highly technical issues. Established by a democratically controlled Congress because of distrust of the Nixon administration, it was intended to help officials sort out increasingly complex scientific information without advocating particular policies or actions. The OTA was shut down in 1995 as a result of political controversies adverse to the then Republican-controlled Congress.[22]

The Agency for Health Care Policy and Research, created by Congress in 1989 and now called the Agency for Healthcare Policy and Quality, is intended to support research to understand better the outcomes of health care at both clinical and systems levels. It has a particularly challenging mission as technologic and scientific advances make it ever more difficult to sort out the complexities of health care and determine what works, for whom, when, and at what cost.

Roles of Medical Education and Specialization

Medical schools and teaching hospitals in the United States are the essential components of all academic health centers and are the principal architects of the medical care system. In addition to their research contributions to advancements in health care and their roles as major providers of health services, they are the principal places where physicians and other professional personnel are educated and trained.

From post–World War II to the mid-1970s, there were numerous projections of an impending shortage of physicians. The response at federal and state levels was to double the capacity of medical schools and to encourage the entry of foreign-trained physicians.[23]

The explosion of scientific knowledge in medicine and the technologic advances in diagnostic and treatment modalities encouraged specialization. In addition, the enhanced prestige and income of specialty practice attracted most medical school graduates to specialty residencies. It soon became evident that specialists were being produced in numbers that would lead to an oversupply. Also, they needed to be close to their referring doctors and to associate with major hospitals, which caused graduates to concentrate in urban areas. At the same time, the shortage of primary care physicians among rural and inner-city populations grew.

In response, medical schools and hospitals developed a more acceptable physician workforce policy to maintain or increase their training capacities. Schools erroneously assumed that producing an oversupply of physicians would force more physicians into primary care in underserved rural and inner-city areas. Unfortunately, this trickle-down workforce policy did little to change supply distribution problems and only added to the swelling ranks of specialists. Hospitals added to the problem by developing residencies that met their own service needs without regard for oversupply. Supplemental Medicare payments for teaching hospitals and indirect medical education adjustments for hospital-based residents were and still are strong incentives for hospitals to add residents.[24]

The rapid growth of managed care plans in the 1990s with their emphasis on prevention and primary care was expected to produce profound changes in the use of the physician workforce and cause a significant oversupply of specialists by the year 2000. To stave off the surplus, many medical schools and their teaching hospitals endeavored to produce equal numbers of primary care and specialist physicians instead of the one-third-to-two-third ratio that had existed for years.

As soon as the effort produced a sizable increase in the number of primary care physicians, new medical workforce projections refuted the prior predictions and forecasted a shortage, rather than a surplus, of specialists. Clearly, estimating a future physician shortage or surplus is a tenuous endeavor.

The forces of reform are exerting increasing pressures on schools of medicine and other major health professions to change their curricula in keeping with the new emphasis on population-based thinking, prevention, and cost effectiveness. The inflexibility of traditional departmental organization and the relatively narrow areas of expertise required of faculty, however, present formidable obstacles to needed educational reforms.

Influence of Interest Groups

Many problems associated with U.S. health care result from a system shared among federal and state governments and the private health care industry. The development of fully or partially tax-funded health service proposals initiated waves of lobbying efforts by interest groups for or against the initiatives. Federal and state executives and legislators receive intense pressure from supporters and opponents of health care system changes.[25] Lobbying efforts from special interest groups have become increasingly sophisticated and well financed. Since the 1970s, former congressional staffers appear on the payrolls of private interest groups, and former lobbyists assume positions on Capitol Hill. This strong connection between politicians and lobbyists is evidenced by the record number of dollars spent to defeat the Clinton Health Security Act of 1993 and both "for" and "against" President Obama's health care reform plans.

Five major groups have played key roles in debates on tax-funded health services: providers, insurers, consumers, business, and labor. Historically, physicians, the group most directly affected by reforms, developed the most powerful lobbies. Although the physician lobby is still among the best financed and most effective, it is recognized as not representing the values of large numbers of physicians detached from the AMA. In fact, several different medical lobbies exist as a result of political differences among physicians.

The American Medical Association

The AMA, founded in 1847, is the largest medical lobby, with a membership of 217,000 individuals, yet it represents only 17% of medical professionals and medical students.[26] The AMA was at the height of its power from the 1940s to the 1970s, opposing government-provided insurance plans by every president from Truman through Carter. Compromises gained in the final Medicare bill still affect today's program. In the 1980s, however, the AMA steadfastly opposed cuts in Medicare proposed by the Reagan–Bush administration.

In 1989, the AMA changed its relationship with Congress. Initially locked out of White House discussions on the Clinton plan, the AMA was later included and supported, at least publicly, by the Obama plan for expanding health care access to all Americans. Nevertheless, cost containment, malpractice reform, and physician autonomy still remain as areas of contention.[27]

Insurance Companies

Even more than physicians, nurses, or hospitals, insurers' political efforts have been viewed as completely self-serving. The efforts of insurance companies to eliminate high-risk consumers from the insurance pools and their frequent premium rate hikes contributed significantly to the focus on cost containment and the plight of the uninsured and underinsured in the debate on health care reform. Nevertheless, the Health Insurance Association of America, founded in 1956 and representing some 300 small companies, was responsible for a robust onslaught of television commercials featuring middle-class people worrying about the limited choice of physicians and other potential dangers of cost containment in the Clinton plan.

The insurance companies played an even stronger but more deceptive role in the debates about President Obama's health care reform effort by appearing to support the general idea while vigorously opposing the idea of a public option that would severely limit their profits. The amount of dollars spent in lobbying efforts by insurers and others with vested interests in the status quo and in misinforming the public to raise unwarranted fears about the proposed health care reform legislation hit a new high in deception and a new low in political machinations.[28]

Consumer Groups

Although provider groups have been most effective in influencing health care legislation, the historically weak consumer movement has gained strength. Much of the impetus for health care reform on the national scene was linked to pressure on politicians from consumers concerned about rising costs and lack of security in health care coverage. Despite widespread disagreement among groups about the extent to which government involvement was needed, all were concerned about the questions of cost, access, and quality in the current health care system.

Better educated and more assertive citizens have become more cynical about the motives of leaders in both the political and the health arenas and are much more effective in influencing legislative decisions. A prominent example is the American Association of Retired Persons (AARP). Founded in 1958, the AARP is one of the most influential consumer groups in the health care reform movement. Because of its size and research capability, it wields considerable clout among legislators who are very aware that the AARP's 40 million older citizens are among the most determined voters.

Although a single consumer group may have some influence in shaping a legislative proposal, consumer group coalitions that rally around specific issues are much more effective in generating political pressure. For example, a political battle over revamping the U.S. Food and Drug Administration (FDA) was initiated in 1995 when conservative think tanks and drug company officials urged a receptive Congress to make major changes in the agency's operations. These changes were intended to weaken the agency's investigative powers and reduce the time required for drug companies to introduce new drugs to the consumer market. The proposed changes would require the FDA to meet deadlines for investigating and approving new drugs and allow pharmaceutical companies to submit one, rather than two, well-controlled studies as proof of effectiveness.

Consumer groups entered the debate on both sides of the issue. The biggest and best organized was the Patients' Coalition, which is made up of more than 50 national nonprofit health groups. It includes such dissimilar organizations as the American Cancer Society, National Hemophilia Foundation, Arthritis Foundation, and several AIDS organizations such as the AIDS Action Council and Gay Men's Health Crisis. The coalition rushed to the FDA's defense and urged Congress to reject the proposals that could hurt consumers. Other consumer groups support the positions of the Pharmaceutical Research and Manufacturers Association, the main industry trade group that claims that FDA reforms could be accomplished without risking safety and effectiveness.[29]

The battle continues, however, between those who believe that keeping new drugs from the market while safety and effectiveness are carefully tested is denying help to those patients who might benefit from them and those who presume that drug manufacturers would take advantage of less rigorous testing to foist unproven or dangerous drugs on the market for profit. Although the two sides continue to debate, administrative changes have taken place that shortened the assessment time for cancer-treating drugs in an effort to prolong life for dying patients.[30]

Business and Labor

The National Federation of Independent Businesses, founded in 1943, has 350,000 individual members and is the largest representative of small firms.[31] The National Association of Manufacturers founded in 1895 represents the interests of large employers and has a current membership of 11,000.[32] The U.S. Chamber of Commerce was founded in 1912 and represents 3 million businesses of all sizes.[33] The Chamber and the National Association of Manufacturers have similar views on reform; they both generally welcome the equalizing effect of an employer mandate but are wary of intense government regulation and, particularly, of more government-run health care.[32,33]

Whenever business groups are involved in an issue, and especially one of the magnitudes of health reform, labor unions will have a strong presence to represent their members' interests. The American Federation of Labor and Congress of Industrial Organization (AFL-CIO), once over 14 million individuals strong,[34] has had a tremendous influence on national health policy. Although job losses during the current economic downturn have reduced membership by over a million members, the influence of organized labor is significant. Intimately connected with the AFL-CIO is the Service Employees International Union, founded in 1921. It is the largest union representing health care workers, with a membership of 2.1 million individuals, 1.1 million of whom are in the health professions.[34] During the mid-1940s, labor unions demanded and received health care benefits as an alternative to wage increases prohibited by postwar wage and price controls. The two major national unions, the AFL and the CIO, consolidated their power by merging in 1955. During the late 1960s, they were able to address the issues of occupational safety and health and achieved passage of the Occupational Safety and Health Act of 1970. Today, occupational safety and health hold prominent places on the national agenda.

Pharmaceutical Industry

In recent years, the profit-laden pharmaceutical industry increased its spending on lobbying tactics and campaign contributions to unprecedented levels. With prescription drug prices and pharmaceutical company profits at record highs, the industry correctly anticipated public and congressional pressure to legislate controls on drug prices and drug coverage for older adults on Medicare.

In 2003, as lawmakers moved to add a prescription drug benefit to Medicare that would include price controls, the pharmaceutical industry deployed more than 1,000 lobbyists.[35] The pharmaceutical industry was given a large role in crafting the 2003 Medicare Part D prescription drug benefit plan. As a result, the final plan prohibited Medicare and the federal government from using its enormous purchasing power to negotiate prices with drug companies.[35]

One of the most contentious elements in the Medicare Part D drug plan was the so-called "doughnut hole." Beginning in 2006, the legislation required ending federal payment for a person's drug purchases after an annual spending limit was reached. Federal support resumed only after the beneficiary spent $3,600 out of pocket for prescription drugs. The "doughnut hole" directly affected the middle-class and disabled retirees who do not qualify for special poverty assistance yet still lived on limited incomes.

Public Health Focus on Prevention

Although the groups discussed in the previous section are primarily concerned with the diagnostic and treatment services that constitute over 95% of U.S. health care system, there is an important public health lobby that speaks for health promotion and disease prevention. Often overlooked because of this country's historical emphasis on curative medicine, public health organizations have had to overcome several negative perceptions. Many health providers, politicians, and others associate public health with governmental bureaucracy or link the care of low-income populations with socialism. Nevertheless, the American Public Health Association, founded in 1872 and having an aggregate membership of approximately 30,000, has substantial influence on the national scene, and in 2012 in its advocacy role, reported over 150 individual meetings with congressional members.[36]

Economic Influences of Rising Costs

The single most important impetus for health care reform throughout recent history has been rising health care costs and insurance premiums. Since the introduction of Medicare and Medicaid in 1965, almost all federal health law has been aimed at cost containment but without success. Growth in health spending has been advancing much faster than the rest of U.S. economy.[7,9]

The number of Americans without adequate or any health insurance was estimated at 37 million during the health care reform debates of 1994. As noted above, census bureau estimates now put the number of uninsured at 49 million Americans or 17% of the total population.[9] Of most importance, when considering the magnitude of this problem, is that the composition of that uninsured population is constantly changing. When those on Medicaid or other unemployed persons find jobs that provide group health insurance, those individuals leave the ranks of the uninsured. They are replaced, however, by those who become unemployed or lose Medicaid coverage.

Health Insurance Portability and Accountability Act

The Health Insurance Portability and Accountability Act, or HIPAA, signed into law in 1996, was intended to address the problem of the growing number of uninsured. The legislation permits individuals to continue insurance coverage after a loss or change of employment by mandating the renewal of insurance coverage except for specific reasons, such as the nonpayment of premiums. The Act also regulates the circumstances in which an insurance plan may limit benefits because of preexisting conditions. It also mandates special enrollment periods for individuals who have experienced certain changes in family composition or employment status.

More sweeping in its effects is the part of the law called "Administrative Simplification." It required medical records to be computerized by October 2003. Although yet to be achieved, it is intended to reduce the costs and administrative burden of health care by standardizing the electronic transmission of many administrative and financial transactions. The standardization must also maintain the privacy of health information. Subsequent major support for health information technology development occurred with President Bush's executive order of 2004 establishing the Office of the National Coordinator for Health Information Technology.[37] In 2009, President Obama signed the American Recovery and Reinvestment Act that designated $20.8 billion to incentivize physicians and health care organizations to adopt electronic health records.[38] As a result, virtually, the entire health care industry is involved in a high-technology upgrade of complex medical care delivery information.

Aging of America

The elimination or control of many infectious diseases through immunization and antibiotics; the implementation of basic public health measures that contribute to the safety of food, water, and living and working conditions; a far more nutritious food supply; and constantly improving medical care have all combined to extend the life expectancy of people in the United States. Although AIDS, accidents, and violence are causing an increasing number of deaths among young people, the vast majority of Americans live to advanced ages. U.S. Census Bureau projects that nearly one in five residents will be aged 65 or older by 2030 and that by 2050 the number of Americans aged 65 and older will be 88.5 million, more than double its projected population in 2010.[39] Between 2010 and 2050, U.S. Census Bureau projects that the proportion of U.S. population comprised by persons over 85 years old will increase from 14% to 21%.[39]

Although the medical model of curing illness, maximizing function, and preventing premature death has been beneficial to many older Americans, it has offered little to the growing number of older citizens who are not acutely or morbidly ill but who have irreversible physical or mental limitations that require diligent care by others.

Of increasing importance to the future health care system are mechanisms to support caregivers as older person care becomes the responsibility of more and more Americans. Changes in U.S. social structures have increased the stress on today's adults because they are required to provide financial, functional, or emotional support to aging family members. More women working outside the home, a high divorce rate, the geographic dispersion of family members, an increase in the number of adults simultaneously caring for both children and aging relatives beg for additional respite services, adult day care, and other strategies to reduce stress and caregiver burnout.

Oregon Death with Dignity Act

November 8, 1994 was a pivotal date in U.S. social legislation. Oregon voters approved Ballot Measure 16, the Oregon Death with Dignity Act, also known as the Oregon Physician-Assisted Suicide Act. The Act legalized physician-assisted suicide by allowing "an adult resident of Oregon, who is terminally ill to voluntarily request a prescription for medication to take his or her life."[40] The person must have "an incurable and irreversible disease that will, within reasonable medical judgment, produce death within six months." The Death with Dignity Act was a response to the growing concern among medical professionals and the public about the extended, painful, and demeaning nature of terminal medical care for patients with certain conditions. An additional consideration for some voters was the worry that the extraordinary costs associated with lengthy and futile medical care would exhaust their estates and leave their families with substantial debts.

A survey of Oregon physicians showed that two-thirds of those responding believe that physician-assisted suicide is ethical in appropriate cases. Also, almost half of the responding physicians (46%) said that they might assist in a suicide if the patient met the criteria outlined in the act.[41]

The issue of euthanasia and physician-assisted suicide has been debated for years in other countries. Although among Westernized countries only Northern Australia has legalized physician-assisted suicide, the Netherlands has a long history of allowing euthanasia within the medical community.[42]

Physicians must meet multiple requirements before they can write a prescription for a lethal combination of medications. The physician must ensure that the patient is fully informed about the diagnosis, the prognosis, the risks, likely result of the medications and alternatives, including comfort care, pain control, and hospice care. A consulting physician must then confirm that the patient's judgment is not impaired and that the decision is fully informed and voluntary. The patient is then asked to notify next of kin, although family notification is not mandatory. After a 15-day waiting period, the patient must again repeat the request. If the patient does so, the physician is then permitted to write the fatal prescription. Although it varies from year to year, not all patients requesting physician prescriptions opt to use them.[43]

In November 2008, the State of Washington initiated its own Death with Dignity Act along the same lines as that of Oregon.[44] On the last day of 2009, the Supreme Court of the State of Montana ruled to maintain the state law that protects doctors from prosecution for helping terminally patients die.[45] With issues of the burgeoning aged U.S. population and this population group's increasing political strength in numbers, consumer pressure for more states to enact "right to die" legislation will be a subject of increasing interest in the years to come.

Internet and Health Care

Data collection and information transfer are critical elements of the health care system, and thus it is not surprising that the Internet has become a major influence in U.S. health care. A 2012 Pew Foundation survey report noted that "one in three U.S. adults have gone online to diagnose a condition and about half consulted a medical professional about what they found."[46] The Internet provides consumers with access to vast resources of health and wellness information, the ability to communicate with others sharing similar health problems, and the ability to gain valuable data about medical institutions and providers that permit well-informed choices about services and procedures. Internet users are becoming more educated and participatory in clinical decision making, challenging physicians and other providers to participate with a more knowledgeable and involved patient population.

Physicians and other health care providers also are entering the online world of health care communication. After a slow start, provider-sponsored websites are proliferating at a rapid pace. In addition to information for consumers about the provider's training, competencies, and experience, many providers encourage email exchanges that invite queries and provide opportunities to respond to consumer informational needs.

A wide variety of other web-based entrepreneurial ventures have also begun to take advantage of the huge and growing market of Smartphone users with "apps," that "give consumers access to health information wherever and whenever they need it."[46] Both professionally reliable and questionable entrepreneurs are offering consumers opportunities to cyber-shop for pharmaceuticals, insurance plans, medical supplies and equipment, physician services, and other health-related commodities, making the public well advised in exercising caution.

Landmark Legislation: The Patient Protection and ACA of 2010

"The first promise Obama made as a presidential candidate was to enact a universal health care plan by the end of his first term."[47] Many months prior to his inauguration, senate Democrats led by Senators Max Baucus, chair of the powerful Senate Finance Committee, and Senator Edward Kennedy were collaborating with a diverse group of stakeholders to craft a plan.[47] Only days after President Obama's 2008 election, Senator Max Baucus, released a white paper on November 12, 2008, "A Call to Action: Health Reform 2009," in which he outlined goals to improve access to quality, affordable health care, and to control costs in the U.S. Health Care system.[48] Some in the new administration opposed advancing the cause of universal coverage at a time when the President also had to advance his pledges for economic stimulus package, education reform, and bailouts for banks and the auto industry.[49] Nevertheless, believing "that rising medical costs were crippling average families, cutting into corporate profits, and consuming more and more of the federal budget,"[49] President Obama moved the health care agenda forward through a tortuous and often rancorous maze of political machinations and public reactions.[50] Decades-long analyses and assessments by the most prestigious academic research and industry experts overwhelming noted that U.S. health care system focused on providing excellent care for the individuals with acute conditions, although virtually ignoring the more basic health service needs of larger populations who could benefit enormously from primary preventive care. The system continued to reward providers for the volume of services delivered with piecemeal reimbursement rather than with financial incentives to maintain or improve health status among populations of service recipients.

Given that a succession of federal administrations beginning in 1945 with President Harry Truman had proposed and failed at enacting some form of universal health care coverage,[51] the ACA was an achievement of historic proportion. The groundbreaking nature of the ACA resides in its addressing what have been historically intractable system problems of cost, quality, and access.

Through a variety of measures, the ACA intends to reverse incentives that drive up costs, to enact requirements that increase both accountability for and transparency of quality, and by 2019, to increase access by expanding health insurance coverage to an additional 32 million Americans.[52,53] The ACA also adds important new consumer protections and enhances access to needed services for the nation's most vulnerable populations.[54]

Judicial Challenges

On the day the ACA was signed into law, the state of Florida filed a federal district court lawsuit challenging the constitutionality of the law's requirement for individual coverage and its expansion of the Medicaid program. Twenty-five additional states, the National Federation of Independent Businesses, and other plaintiffs also filed suit in Florida.[55] The Virginia state attorney general also filed a separate lawsuit challenging the federal requirement to purchase health insurance.[56]

The primary issues of contention were whether Congress had the authority to impose the individual coverage mandate with personal financial penalties for noncompliance under either its authority to regulate interstate commerce or its taxing power; and whether Congress had the authority to make all of a state's existing Medicaid funding contingent on compliance with the ACA's Medicaid expansion provisions.[55] The U.S. Supreme Court agreed to decide the two issues and heard oral arguments from proponents and detractors of the ACA provisions during the spring of 2012. On June 28, 2012, in a 5-4 decision, the court upheld the constitutionality of the individual mandate with Chief Justice Roberts writing, "The mandate is not a legal command to buy insurance. Rather it just makes going without insurance just another thing the government taxes."[57] The court determined that the Medicaid expansion as described in the ACA was unconstitutionally coercive of states but remedied this violation of states' rights by prohibiting the federal government from making states' existing Medicaid funding contingent on participation in the expansion. The court's decisions made no changes to the preexisting Medicaid law and the federal government's authority to require states' compliance with existing Medicaid program rules.[55]

The ACA Implementation Provisions

The ACA is over 900 pages in length written under 10 titles[58] and is organized under 4 broad headings that highlight its major goals:

- Providing new consumer protections
- Improving quality and lowering costs
- Increasing access to affordable care
- Holding insurance companies accountable

The following outline of the ACA provisions is provided as an overview with a suggestion to interested readers to use this chapter's references and their Internet links to obtain further information and detail.

Largely excerpted and edited from a federal government Website managed by the Department of Health and Human Services, the overview describes key features of the ACA by year of scheduled implementation. In the dynamic process of implementation, schedules are updated and amended; current information is available from the federal Websites. The "time-line" format provides a sequenced view of the ACA provisions as scheduled to take effect by 2019.

2010

New Consumer Protections

- Putting Information for Consumers Online: establishes a website on which consumers can compare health insurance coverage options and choose their preference.
- Prohibiting Denying Coverage of Children Based on Preexisting Conditions: new rules to prevent insurance companies from denying coverage to children under the age of 19 because of a preexisting condition.
- Prohibiting Insurance Companies from Rescinding Coverage: new rules that make it illegal for insurance companies to deny payments

for a subscriber's illness because of technical or other errors discovered in a subscriber's original insurance application. In the past, insurance companies could search for an error or other technical mistake on a customer's application and use this error to deny payment for services when the subscriber experienced an illness.

- Eliminating Lifetime Limits on Insurance Coverage: prohibits insurance companies from imposing lifetime dollar limits on essential benefits, such as hospital stays.
- Regulating Annual Limits on Insurance Coverage: prohibits insurance companies' use of annual dollar limits on the amount of insurance coverage a patient may receive under new plans in the individual market and all group plans. In 2014, the use of annual dollar limits on essential benefits like hospital stays will be banned for new plans in the individual market and all group plans.
- Appealing Insurance Company Decisions: provides consumers with a way to appeal coverage determinations or claims to their insurance company and establishes an external review process.
- Establishing Consumer Assistance Programs in the States: provides federal grants to states that apply to help set up or expand independent offices to help consumers navigate the private health insurance system. These programs help consumers file complaints and appeals; enroll in health coverage; and get educated about their rights and responsibilities in group health plans or individual health insurance policies.

Improving Quality and Lowering Costs

- Providing Small Business Health Insurance Tax Credits: up to 4 million small businesses are eligible for tax credits to help them provide insurance benefits to their workers. The first phase of this provision provides a credit worth up to 35% of the employer's contribution to the employees' health insurance. Small nonprofit organizations may receive up to a 25% credit.
- Offering Relief for 4 Million Seniors Who Hit the Medicare Prescription Drug Reimbursement Gap: provides a one-time, tax-free $250 rebate check for uncovered prescription drug costs.
- Providing Free Preventive Care: all new plans must cover certain preventive services such as mammograms and colonoscopies without charging a deductible, co-pay or coinsurance.

- Preventing Disease and Illness: a new $15 billion Prevention and Public Health Fund will invest in proven prevention and public health programs that can help keep Americans healthy—from smoking cessation to combating obesity.
- Reducing Health Care Fraud and Abuse: invests new resources and requires new screening procedures for health care providers to boost federal antifraud and waste initiatives in Medicare, Medicaid, and Child Health Insurance Program.

Increasing Access to Affordable Care

- Providing Access to Insurance for Uninsured Americans with Preexisting Conditions: the Preexisting Condition Insurance Plan provides new coverage options to individuals who have been uninsured for at least 6 months because of a preexisting condition. States may operate these programs or opt for the Department of Health and Human Services to do so in that state.
- Extending Coverage for Young Adults: young adults will be allowed to stay on their parents' plan until they turn 26 years old.
- Expanding Coverage for Early Retirees: creates a $5 billion program to provide needed financial help for employment-based plans to continue providing health insurance coverage to people who retire between the ages of 55 and 65, as well as their spouses and dependents.
- Rebuilding the Primary Care Workforce: provides new incentives to expand the number of primary care doctors, nurses, and physician assistants through funding for scholarships and loan repayments for primary care doctors and nurses working in underserved areas.
- Holding Insurance Companies Accountable for Unreasonable Rate Increases: provides eligibility for $250 million in new grants to states that have or will implement measures requiring insurance companies to justify premium increases; also may bar insurance companies with excessive or unjustified premium levels from participation in the new health insurance exchanges.
- Allowing States to Cover More People on Medicaid: provides federal matching funds for states covering some additional low-income individuals and families under Medicaid for whom federal funds were not previously available.

- Increasing Payments for Rural Health care Providers: provides increased payments to rural health care providers to help them attract and retain providers.
- Strengthening Community Health Centers: provides new funding to support the construction of and expand services at community health centers, allowing these centers to serve some 20 million new patients across the country.

2011
Improving Quality and Lowering Costs

- Offering Prescription Drug Discounts: provides Medicare recipients who reach the prescription drug coverage gap with a 50% discount when buying Medicare Part D covered brand-name prescription drugs; for the next 10 years, seniors will receive additional savings on brand-name and generic drugs until the coverage gap is closed in 2020.
- Providing Free Preventive Care for Seniors: provides certain free preventive services, such as annual wellness visits and personalized prevention plans for seniors on Medicare.
- Improving Health care Quality and Efficiency: establishes a new Center for Medicare & Medicaid Innovation to test new ways of delivering care to patients to improve the quality of care, and reduce the rate of growth in costs for Medicare, Medicaid, and the Children's Health Insurance Program (CHIP); DHHS will also submit a national strategy for quality improvement in health care, including these programs.
- Improving Care for Seniors after Hospitalization: establishes The Community Care Transitions Program to help high-risk Medicare beneficiaries avoid unnecessary readmissions by coordinating care and connecting patients to services in their communities.
- Introducing New Innovations to Reduce Costs: establishes a new Independent Payment Advisory Board to develop and submit proposals to Congress and the President aimed at extending the life of the Medicare Trust Fund by focusing on ways to target waste in the system, recommend ways to reduce costs, improve health outcomes for patients, and expand access to high-quality care.

Increasing Access to Affordable Care

- Increasing Access to Services at Home and in the Community: allows states to offer home and community-based services to disabled individuals through Medicaid rather than institutional care in nursing homes through the Community First Choice Option.

Holding Insurance Companies Accountable

- Reducing Health care Premiums: ensures that premium dollars are spent primarily on health care, by generally requiring that at least 85% of all premium dollars collected by insurance companies for large employer plans are spent on health care services and health care quality improvement; for plans sold to individuals and small employers, at least 80% of the premium must be spent on benefits and quality improvement. Failing to meet these goals, insurance companies must provide rebates to subscribers.
- Addressing Overpayments to Big Insurance Companies and Strengthening Medicare Advantage: eliminates additional Medicare costs from Medicare managed care plans (Medicare Advantage) and provides bonus payments to Medicare Advantage plans that provide high-quality care.

2012
Improving Quality and Lowering Costs

- Linking Payment to Quality Outcomes: establishes a hospital Value-Based Purchasing program in Traditional Medicare, offering financial incentives to hospitals to improve the quality of care; requires hospitals to publicly report performance for certain diagnoses and patients' perceptions of care.
- Encouraging Integrated Health Systems: provides incentives for physicians, hospitals to join together to form "Accountable Care Organizations" to better coordinate Medicare beneficiary patient care and improve the quality, help prevent disease and illness and reduce unnecessary hospital admissions.
- Reducing Paperwork and Administrative Costs: institutes a series of changes to standardize billing and requires health plans to begin

adopting and implementing rules for the secure, confidential, electronic exchange of health information.

- Understanding and Reducing Health Disparities: requires any ongoing or new federal health program to collect and report racial, ethnic, and language data to help identify and reduce disparities.

Increasing Access to Affordable Care

- Providing New, Voluntary Options for Long-Term Care Insurance: intended to create voluntary long-term care insurance program, "Community Living Assistance Services and Supports Act (CLASS)," to provide cash benefits to adults who become disabled. CLASS was officially abandoned by the DHHS in October, 2011 and will not be implemented.

2013

Improving Quality and Lowering Costs

- Improving Preventive Health Coverage: provides new funding to state Medicaid programs that choose to cover preventive services for patients at little or no cost to expand the number of Americans receiving preventive care.
- Expanding Authority to Bundle Payments: establishes a national pilot program, Bundled Payments for Care Improvement (BPCI), to encourage hospitals, doctors, and other providers to work together to improve the coordination and quality of patient care by paying a flat rate for a total episode of care rather than billing Medicare for individual services. The BPCI aligns the incentives of those delivering care, with any savings shared between providers and the Medicare program.

Increasing Access to Affordable Care

- Increasing Medicaid Payments for Primary Care Doctors: requires states to pay primary care physicians no less than 100% of Medicare payment rates in 2013 and 2014 for primary care services, with full federal funding of the increase; the requirement anticipates an influx of new Medicaid enrollees into the system.

- Providing Additional Funding for the CHIP: provides states with two additional years of funding to continue coverage for children not eligible for Medicaid.

2014

New Consumer Protections

- Prohibiting Discrimination Due to Preexisting Conditions or Gender: prohibits insurance companies from refusing to sell coverage or renew policies because of an individual's preexisting conditions and in the individual and small group insurance market, prohibits insurance companies from charging higher rates because of gender or health status.
- Eliminating Annual Limits on Insurance Coverage: prohibits new plans and existing group plans from imposing annual dollar limits on the amount of coverage an individual may receive.
- Ensuring Coverage for Individuals Participating in Clinical Trials: prohibits insurers from dropping or limiting coverage because an individual chooses to participate in a clinical trial; applies to all clinical trials that treat cancer or other life-threatening diseases.
- Improving Quality and Lowering Costs
- Making Care More Affordable: makes tax credits available for middle-class individuals with incomes between 100% and 400% of the federal poverty level who are not eligible for other affordable coverage to make insurance coverage more affordable.
- Establishing the Health Insurance Marketplace: enables individuals to purchase health insurance directly in the Health Insurance Marketplace if their employers do not offer health insurance; individuals and small businesses can buy affordable and qualified health benefit plans in this new transparent and competitive insurance marketplace, offering a choice of plans that meet certain benefits and cost standards.
- Increasing the Small Business Tax Credit: implements the second phase of the small business tax credit for qualified small businesses and small nonprofit organizations; in this phase, the credit is up to 50% of the employer's contribution to provide health insurance for employees; there is also up to a 35% credit for small nonprofit organizations.

Increasing Access to Affordable Care

- Increasing Access to Medicaid: enables Americans who earn less than 133% of the federal poverty level eligible to enroll in Medicaid; provides states with 100% federal funding for the first 3 years to support this expanded coverage, phasing to 90% federal funding in subsequent years.
- Promoting Individual Responsibility: requires most individuals who can afford it, to obtain basic health insurance coverage or pay a fee to help offset the costs of caring for uninsured Americans; if affordable coverage is not available to an individual, he or she will be eligible for an exemption.

2015

Improving Quality and Lowering Costs

- Paying Physicians Based on Value Not Volume: a new provision ties physician payments to the quality of care provided. Physicians will see their payments modified so that those who provide higher value care will receive higher payments than those who provide lower quality care.[59]

Increasing Access to Affordable Care

- Increasing Federal Match for CHIP: provide states with a 23% increase in their CHIP matching rate up to 100%; CHIP eligible children excluded from the program because of enrollment caps are eligible for tax credits in the state health insurance exchanges.[53]

2016

Increasing Access to Affordable Care

- Increasing Competition and Choices: creates Health Care Choice Compacts that allow selling health insurance across state lines to increase competition among plans and consumer choices; Compacts provide consumer protections to ensure that policies will be subject to the laws and regulations of the state in which the policy was issued and must offer the same benefits required by the consumer's state of residence.[60]

2018

Improving Quality and Lowering Costs

- Imposing an Excise Tax on High-cost Insurance Plans: creates incentives to limit the costs of health insurance plans to a tax-free amount with the intent to generate revenue to help pay for covering the uninsured and to make the most expensive plans less attractive.[61]

The Congressional Budget Office (CBO) 2012–2021 estimate of the net cost of the PPACA for insurance coverage provisions for 32 million newly insured individuals is just under $1.1 trillion, with deficit reductions derived from new taxes, penalties, and other revenues of $510 billion.[62]

ACA implementation is proceeding in a variety of ways that include new agency programs, grants, demonstration projects, guidance documents, and regulations. The ACA contains over 40 provisions that require or permit agencies to issue rules with some allowing agencies to "prescribe such regulations as may be necessary."[56] It is anticipated that the ACA will generate scores of rules over the years of its implementation that must be published to allow public comments before issuance of a final rule and, as such, are subject to change.[56] In making financial estimates, the CBO notes that "projections of the budgetary impact and other impacts of health care legislation are quite uncertain because assessing the effects of making broad changes in the nation's health care and health insurance systems—or of reversing scheduled change—requires assumptions about a broad array of technical, behavioral, and economic factors."[63] It is certain that financial projections will continue to evolve as the ACA is implemented over succeeding years.

It remains very early to speculate on the ACA's success in achieving its intended changes in the organization, delivery, efficiency, and effectiveness of a monstrously complex industry that encompasses over 17% of the nation's economy. As implementation rules are published and challenges are navigated in the courts, outcomes will be determined over the next several years. Regulatory and legal changes enacted by the ACA are indeed only two components of the equation. A multitude of other factors as far-ranging as the nation's economy, the political environment, and provider and consumer reactions and behaviors to name only a few, will determine the outcomes of this landmark legislation.

Key Terms for Review

Block Grants
Health Maintenance Organization Act of 1973
Health Systems Agencies
Medicaid

Medicare
Oregon Death with Dignity Act of 1994
Social Security Act of 1935
The Health Insurance Portability and Accountability Act of 1996 (HIPAA)

References

1. Numbers RL. The third party: health insurance in America. In: Vogel MJ, Rosenburg CE, Eds. *The Therapeutic Revolution: Essays in the Social History of American Medicine*. Philadelphia, PA: University of Pennsylvania Press; 1979.

2. Starr P. Transformation in defeat: the changing objectives of national health insurance, 1915–1980. In: Kindig DA, Sullivan RB, Eds. *Understanding Universal Health Programs, Issues and Options*. Ann Arbor, MI: Health Administration Press; 1992.

3. American Medical Association. Minutes of the House of Delegates. JAMA. 1920;74:1317–1328.

4. Leland RG. Prepayment plans for hospital care. *JAMA*. 1933;100:113–117.

5. American Medical Association Committee on the Costs of Medical Care. *Medical Care for the American People: The Final Report of the Committee on the Costs of Medical Care*. Chicago, IL: University of Chicago Press; 1932.

6. American Medical Association. Minutes of the Eighty-Fourth Session, 12–16 June 1933. *JAMA*. 1933;100:44–53.

7. U.S. Department of Health and Human Services, Centers for Medicare & Medicaid Services. National Health Expenditures Tables. 2011. Available from http://www.cms.gov/Research-Statistics-Data-and-Systems/Statistics-Trends-and-Reports/NationalHealthExpendData/downloads/tables.pdf. Accessed January 26, 2013.

8. Lee PR, Benjamin AE. Health policy and the politics of health care. In: Lee PR, Estes CL, Eds. *The Nation's Health, 4th ed*. Sudbury, MA: Jones and Bartlett; 1994.

9. U.S. Department of Commerce. U.S. Census. Highlights 2010. 2011. Available from http://www.census.gov/hhes/www/hlthins/data/incpovhlth/2010/highlights.html. Accessed April 23, 2013.

10. Litman TJ, Robins LS. *Health Politics and Policy, 2nd ed*. Albany, NY: Delmar Publishers; 1991.

11. Cheekoway B, O'Rourke T, Macrima DM. Representation of providers on health planning boards. *International journal of health services*. 1981; 11:573–581.

12. Mueller K, Comer J. The case of health systems agencies: some correlates of health policy in the United States. *State and Local Government Review.* 1991;23:13–15.

13. McGinley L. HMO fracas moves to who makes medical decisions. *Wall Street Journal.* February 18, 1999:A24.

14. Hurley RE, Strunk BC, White JJ. The puzzling popularity of the PPO. *Health Affairs.* 2004;23:56–68. Available from http://content.healthaffairs.org/content/23/2/56.full.html. Accessed February 19, 2013.

15. Blendon RJ, Brodie M, Benson JM, et al. Understanding the managed care backlash. *Health Affairs.* 1998;17:82–85. Available from http://content.healthaffairs.org/content/17/4/80. Accessed February 19, 2013.

16. Lee PR, Estes CL. *The Nation's Health, 4th ed.* Boston, MA: Jones and Bartlett; 1994.

17. Ropes LB. *Health Care Crisis in America.* Santa Barbara, CA: ABC-CLIO; 1991.

18. Statistic Brain. Cataract Statistics. 2012. Available from http://www.statistic-brain.com/cataract-statistics/. Accessed February 21, 2013.

19. Gallwas G. The technological explosion: its impact on laboratory and hospital costs. *Pathologist.* 1980;31:86–91.

20. McGivney WT, Hendee WR. Technology assessment in medicine: the role of the American Medical Association. *Archives of pathology & laboratory medicine.* 1988;112:1181–1185.

21. Office of Technology Assessment. *Assessing the Efficacy and Safety of Medical Technologies.* Washington, DC: Government Printing Office; 1978.

22. Sadowski J. The much-needed and sane congressional office that Gingrich killed off and we need back. *The Atlantic.* Available from http://www.theatlantic.com/technology/archive/2012/10/the-much-needed-and-sane-congressional-office-that-gingrich-killed-off-and-we-need-back/264160/#. Accessed February 20, 2013.

23. Reinhardt UE. Reinhardt on reform (interview done by Donna Vavala). *Physician Executive.* 1995;21:10–12.

24. Eisenberg JM. If trickle-down physician workforce policy failed, is the choice now between the market and government regulation? *Inquiry.* 1994; 31:241–249.

25. Oberlander J. The politics of paying for health reform: zombies, payroll taxes, and the Holy Grail. Health Affairs. 2008;27:w544–w555. Available from http://content.healthaffairs.org/content/27/6/w544.full.html. Accessed February 19, 2013.

26. Walker EP. AMA makes small gain in membership. MedPage Today. 2012. Available from http://www.medpagetoday.com/Meetingcoverage/AMA/33320. Accessed February 20, 2013.

27. Fuchs VR. Health reform: getting the essentials right. Health Affairs. 2009;28:w180–w183. Available from http://content.healthaffairs.org/content/28/2/w180.full.html. Accessed February 20, 2013.

28. National Journal. Influence Alley. Exclusive: AHIP gave more than $100 million to Chamber's efforts to derail health care reform. 2012. Available from http://www.nationaljournal.com/blogs/influencealley/2012/06/exclusive-ahip-gave-more-than-100-million-to-chamber-s-efforts-to-derail-health-care-reform-13/. Accessed February 18, 2013.

29. U.S. Department of Health and Human Services. U.S. Food and Drug Administration. FDA Sees Rebound in Approval of Innovative Drugs in 2003. FDA News Release. 2004. Available from http://test.fda.gov/NewsEvents/Newsroom/PressAnnouncements/2004/ucm108225.htm. Accessed February 18, 2013.

30. Murray A. Trade group fight against drug review is self-defeating. *Wall Street Journal.* November 30, 2004:A4.

31. Pickert K. Is the NFIB really a voice for small businesses? Time.com. Available from http://swampland.time.com/2010/05/14/is-the-nfib-really-a-voice-for-small-businesses/. Accessed February 16, 2013.

32. National Association of Manufacturers. About the NAM-manufacturing in America. 2013. Available from http://www.nam.org/about-us/about-the-nam/US-manufacturers-association.aspx. Accessed February 18, 2013.

33. U.S. Chamber of Commerce. About the U.S. chamber of commerce. 2012. Available from http://www.uschamber.com/about/. Accessed February 18, 2013.

34. AFL-CIO Now. Overall union membership notches up from 2010–2011. 2012. Available from http://www.aflcio.org/Blog/Organizing-Bargaining/Overall-Union-Membership-Notches-Up-from-2010-to-2011. Accessed February 18, 2013.

35. Singer M. Columbia Broadcasting System. Under the influence. 2009. Available from http://www.cbsnews.com/8301-18560_162-2625305.html. Accessed April 23, 2013.

36. American Public Health Association. Annual report: fiscal year 2012. 2013. Available from http://www.apha.org/NR/rdonlyres/7ACA7C23-9C65-4F8E-BC56-D15CAC87D325/0/Annual_Report2012.pdf. Accessed February 17, 2013.

37. Bush GW. Executive Order: Incentives for the Use of Health Information Technology and Establishing the Position of the National Health Information Technology Coordinator. 2004. Available from http://georgewbush-whitehouse.archives.gov/news/releases/2004/04/20040427-4.html. Accessed September 25, 2012.

38. One Hundred Eleventh Congress of the United States of America. *The American Recovery and Reinvestment Act.* Washington, DC; U.S. Government Printing office; 2009.

39. U.S. Department of Commerce. U.S. Census Bureau. The next four decades: The older population in the United States: 2010–2050. 2010. Available from http://www.census.gov/prod/2010pubs/p25-1138.pdf. Accessed February 17, 2013.

40. Emanuel EJ, Daniels E. Oregon's physician-assisted suicide law: provisions and problems. *Archives of internal medicine.* 1996;156:46, 50.

41. Lee MA, Nelson HD, Triden UP, et al. Legalizing assisted suicide: view of physicians in Oregon. *New England journal of medicine.* 1996;334:310–315.

42. De Wachter MAM. Active euthanasia in the Netherlands. *JAMA.* 1989;262:3316–3319.

43. Hedberg K, Tolle S. Putting Oregon's death with dignity act in perspective: characteristics of decedents who did not participate. *The Journal of clinical ethics.* Summer 2009;20(2):133–135.

44. Washington State Department of Health. Death with Dignity Act. 2011. Available from http://www.doh.wa.gov/dwda/. Accessed February 11, 2013.

45. Johnson K. Ruling by Montana Supreme Court bolsters physician-assisted suicide. *The New York Times.* January 1, 2010:A16.

46. Pew Research Center. Pew survey of Americans' online health habits. 2013. Available from http://www.chcf.org/publications/2013/01/pew-survey-online-health. Accessed February 18, 2013.

47. Connolly C. Senators hurry to keep health care in forefront. 2008. The Washington Post. Available from http://www.washington-post.com/wp-dyn/content/article/2008/11/11/AR2008111102511.html?sid=ST2008111200035. Accessed February 22, 2013.

48. Hayes K. Overview of policy, procedure, and legislative history of the affordable care act. *Journal of the National Academy of Elder Law Attorneys.* 2011;1:2.

49. Staff of the Washington Post. *Landmark.* New York, NY: Perseus Books Group; 2002:13.

50. Frakes VL. Partisanship and (un)compromise: a study of the patient protection and affordable care act. *Harvard Journal on Legislation.* 2012;49:135–139. Available from http://www.harvardjol.com/wp-content/uploads/2012/03/Frakes_Article.pdf. Accessed February 21, 2013.

51. The Henry J. Kaiser Family Foundation. Timeline: history of health reform in the U.S. 2010. Available from http://healthreform.kff.org/flash/health_reform-print.html. Accessed February 12, 2013.

52. Gostin LO, Jacobson PD, Record KL, et al. Restoring health to health reform: integrating medicine and public health to advance the population's well-being. Pennsylvania Law Review. 2011. Available from http://papers.ssrn.com/sol3/papers.cfm?abstract_id=1780267. Accessed January 18, 2013.

53. The Henry J. Kaiser Family Foundation. Summary of the new health reform law. 2011. Available from http://www.kff.org/healthreform/upload/8061.pdf. Accessed February 9, 2013.

54. The Henry J. Kaiser Family Foundation. Summary of coverage provisions in the Patient Protection and Affordable Care Act and the Health Care and Education Reconciliation Act of 2010. 2012. Available from http://www.kff.org/healthreform/upload/8023-R.pdf. Accessed February 16, 2013.

55. The Henry J. Kaiser Family Foundation. A Guide to the Supreme Court's Affordable Care Act Decision. 2012. Available from http://www.kff.org/healthreform/upload/8332.pdf. Accessed February 23, 2013.

56. Chaikind H, Copeland CW, Redhead SC, et al. PPACA: a brief overview of the law, implementation, and legal challenges. Congressional Research Service. 2011. Available from http://www.nationalaglawcenter.org/assets/crs/R41664.pdf. Accessed February 3, 2013.

57. Pazanowski MA. Split court upholds PPACA constitutionality, limits Medicaid. Bloomberg BNA. 2012. Available from http://www.bna.com/split-supreme-court-n12884910401. Accessed February 22, 2013.

58. U.S. Government Printing Office. Patient Protection and Affordable Care Act of 2010. 2010. Available from http://www.gpo.gov/fdsys/pkg/PLAW-111publ148/pdf/PLAW-111publ148.pdf. Accessed November 14, 2012.

59. HealthCare.gov. Key features of the affordable care act by year. 2013. Available from http://www.healthcare.gov/law/timeline/full.html. Accessed February 12, 2013.

60. U.S. Department of Health and Human Services. Statement by Steven B. Larsen: Expanding health care options: allowing Americans to purchase affordable coverage across state lines. 2011. Available from http://www.hhs.gov/asl/testify/2011/05/t20110525a.html. Accessed February 23, 2013.

61. Gold J. "Cadillac" insurance plans explained. Kaiser Health News. 2010. Available from http://www.kaiserhealthnews.org/stories/2010/march/18/cadillac-tax-explainer-update.aspx. Accessed February 23, 2013.

62. Congressional Budget Office. Updated estimates for the insurance coverage provisions of the affordable care act. 2012. Available from http://www.cbo.gov/sites/default/files/cbofiles/attachments/03-13-Coverage%20Estimates.pdf. Accessed February 17, 2013.

63. Congressional Budget Office. Statement of Douglas W. Elmendorf: CBO's analysis of the major health care legislation enacted in March 2010. 2011. Available from http://www.cbo.gov/sites/default/files/cbofiles/ftpdocs/121xx/doc12119/03-30-healthcarelegislation.pdf. Accessed February 9, 2013.

CHAPTER 3

Health Information Technology

Philip J. Kroth, MD, MS

This chapter outlines major historical developments in the evolution of health information technology and discusses government initiatives to support its implementation. It highlights both benefits and challenges of using this new technology and progress in implementation to date.

Historical Overview

Applying modern information technology (IT) to the health care system to improve its quality and reduce its costs is not new. On April 27, 2004, President Bush created the Office of the National Coordinator for Health Information Technology (ONCHIT or "the ONC") by Executive Order as the first step to create the Nationwide Health Network.[1] On February 17, 2009, President Obama signed the American Recovery and Reinvestment Act (ARRA) that designated $20.8 billion through the Medicare and Medicaid reimbursement systems to incentivize physicians and health care organizations to adopt and achieve "Meaningful Use" of electronic health records (EHRs).[2]

These programs are the latest in a long history of government health information technology (HIT) initiatives. One of the earliest government inquiries into the potential benefits of HIT occurred in the Kennedy Administration in the early 1960s. A report from the

President's Science Advisory Committee, "Some New Technologies and their Promise for the Life Sciences," was optimistic about the benefits HIT would bring to biomedical research and the health care system. Ironically, the report written a half century ago is still relevant to current HIT issues:

> The application of computer technology to the recording, storage, and analysis of data collected in the course of observing and treating large numbers of ill people promises to advance our understanding of the cause, course, and control of disease. The need for a general-purpose health information technology stems in large part from increasingly rapid changes in the pattern of illness in the United States and from equally significant changes in the way medicine is practiced. The acute infectious diseases from which the patient either recovered or died have largely given place to chronic disorders which run an extremely variable course dependent on many factors both in the environment and within the patient himself. . . . Within any sizable community there are numerous administrative organizations charged with providing health services. It is not uncommon for a single patient to be cared for by a large number of agencies in a single city, and workers in any one agency usually cannot find out about the activities of others; sometimes they even fail to learn that other agencies are active at all. . . . Modern data-processing techniques make it possible to assemble all the necessary information about all the patients in a given geographical or administrative area in one place with rapid access for all authorized health and welfare agencies. Such a system would produce an immediate and highly significant improvement in medical care with a simultaneous reduction in direct dollar costs of manual record processing and an even greater economy in professional time now wasted in duplicating tests and procedures.[3]

To date, despite a half century of government programs and technological advancement, the best and most current scientific evidence indicates that the benefits of HIT on the quality and cost of health care are at best, mixed.[4] This chapter will explore the history of how HIT has evolved, the imprint HIT has made on the current health care system, and speculate about how HIT will likely influence the future of health care and the health care system as a whole.

Using computers to improve health care in many ways parallels the development of modern IT. The late 1960s and early 1970s saw several pioneering efforts at a small number of universities to apply IT to various aspects of the health care delivery process. Early systems were not the web-based, interactive systems of today but were usually a hybrid of computer and paper integrated into a clinical work process. One early example was a system at

Indiana University where a small army of data entry clerks manually entered data into a computer on key parts of all patients' medical records.

The night before a patient's clinic appointment, a one-page, paper encounter form was printed for the appointment listing the patients' name, record number, medical problem list (i.e., the known diagnoses and medical problems), medication list, medication allergies, and suggestions based on the data in the computer system. A suggestion was printed on the list when the computer software detected any of 290 agreed-upon patient care protocols or conditions defined by rules applied to the computer's database. When a physician saw the patient in the clinic, they would handwrite encounter notes on the appropriate section of the paper encounter form and manually annotate the computer-printed problem list, medication list, and other items. The next day, a team of data entry clerks would review all encounter forms and update the computer data to reflect the physician's orders and updates to the patient's condition. The paper form would then be filed to the patient's chart. The Indiana group conducted a study demonstrating a 29% improvement in adherence to agreed-upon treatment protocols in the group of physicians who received the computer "suggestions" for recommended treatment protocols on the encounter forms versus those who did not.[5] With the introduction of the IBM PC in the late 1970s and early 1980s, paper forms were mostly eliminated and physicians began interacting with the patient's EHR in real time on the video screen. Similar experimental systems were designed and built during the same time period at a number of other U.S. universities, including The University of Pittsburgh,[6] The University of Utah,[7,8] Vanderbilt University,[9,10] Duke,[11] and Harvard University/Massachusetts General Hospital.[12] These early systems were custom designed, built, and maintained by in-house dedicated teams of computer programmers and systems engineers. Because of the custom designs, the unique work process that existed at each institution, and the advanced nature of these early systems, they were not portable and could not be transplanted to other institutions without extensive software design rework. More importantly, because each of these early systems had a unique design, they were incapable of electronically transferring any of the patients' records to any other system. Despite these limitations, the pioneering works done with these early systems laid the foundation for modern EHR design.

It was not until the 1990s that commercially produced comprehensive EHR systems were marketed and sold to health care institutions in high volume. These commercially produced systems allowed hospitals to implement EHRs without the prohibitive expenses of building custom systems. Instead, hospitals could buy an "off the shelf" system that although not completely customized to institutional work flows, could be configured to meet most of their perceived HIT institutional needs. However, as with the pioneering EHR systems at academic institutions, the "off the shelf," commercially produced EHRs of today still require extensive configuration to accommodate the unique and varying work processes at each institution. The configuration differences between institutions are often so significant that even institutions with the same commercial EHR systems cannot electronically exchange patients' records without customized software. The ONC Website reports that there are a total of 2,648 certified ambulatory EHR products and a total of 878 inpatient products currently on the Certified HIT Product List.[13] While many of these are merely different versions of the same software, there are at least 200 unique systems. None of these systems is designed to interface with each other for patient data sharing across different software platforms. Due to this lack of standardization, regional health information organizations (RHIOs) have been created to facilitate the exchange of patient data among different health care institutions to support improved patient care. RHIOs and health information exchanges (HIEs) are discussed in more detail later in this chapter.

The 2009 HITECH Act created several programs to incentivize individual physicians and health care organizations to buy, install, and adopt EHR systems in the hope that this will yield significant benefits by reducing the cost and improving the quality of care.[2] "The provisions of the HITECH Act are specifically designed to work together to provide the necessary assistance and technical support to providers, enable coordination and alignment within and among states, establish connectivity to the public health community in case of emergencies, and assure the workforce is properly trained and equipped to be meaningful users of EHRs."[14] The scope of this text does not allow detailed delineations of HITECH Act programs; however, the following brief descriptions of programs created and supported by the HITECH Act provide an overview of its comprehensive approach to HIT implementation[14]:

- Beacon Community Program to assist communities in building their HIT infrastructures and exchange capabilities

- Consumer eHealth Program to help empower Americans' access to their personal health information and use this as a tool to gain more control over their health
- State Health Information Exchange Cooperative Agreement Program to support states in establishing HIE capability among health care providers and hospitals in their jurisdictions
- HIT Exchange Program to establish regional extension centers for education and training of health providers in use of EHRs
- Strategic Health IT Advanced Research Projects to fund research advances to overcome major barriers to EHR adoption

While the HITECH Act and its funding provide a new thrust toward EHR adoption, the state of EHR technology does not allow most systems to interface with each other. Despite this large government investment and over half a century of technological development, U.S. health care system HIT still consists of a large number of disparate "siloed" systems that cannot electronically exchange patient records in an efficient and secure manner.

Historical Challenges in Implementing HIT

Figure 3-1 illustrates the three essential components required for successful HIT implementation.

The first essential component is the technology. Organizations often focus on this first component with the mistaken belief that merely selecting the "right" technology or the "right EHR" is the most important aspect of HIT implementation. The essential technologies needed to implement an EHR

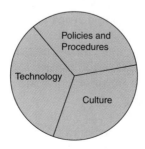

FIGURE 3-1 The Three Essential Components of a Successful HIT Implementation.

system are a relational database, a computer network, and computer workstation. All three technologies have existed for more than 40 years, begging the question of why adoption of HIT in the clinical environment has been so slow compared to the adoption of IT in other industries such as the airline industry's reservation system. The second component of successful implementation, work policies and procedures, makes implementing HIT systems in the clinical environment extremely challenging due to wide variations in work policies and procedures among different organizations and institutions.

An organization's policies and procedures describe and define the processes through which work is carried out. The process component is complex, because it requires HIT system implementers to fully understand all existing work processes. Many such processes are not written or formalized, having evolved over the years to accommodate the unique characteristics of a particular organization. Often existing work processes are significantly different from those officially documented or assumed to be in place, while many critical work processes are not documented at all. When a HIT system is implemented, it is common for many of the undocumented processes to become apparent for the first time.[15] Undocumented or unknown work processes have been the root cause for many HIT implementation failures.[16]

In addition, it is well known that the most significant component of HIT implementation is the institutional and organizational culture—what people are willing to do.[17] This is the most critical, least studied, and least understood of the HIT implementation components.[18] Ash and Bates summarized the importance of organizational culture with regard to EHR adoption[19]:

> The organizational culture must be ready to support adoption by the individuals within it. There has been a period when clinicians have not experienced a sense of collaboration and trust between them and hospital administration. Consequently, if clinicians believe the administration wants to force them to use Computerized Physician Order Entry (CPOE), for example, they may dig in their heels. They may be more resistant to arguments based on safety and patient care benefit if the level of trust is not there. On the other hand, if the impetus comes from the clinical staff, other clinicians may be more apt to adopt sooner, and readiness will be at a higher level. One gauge of readiness is the extent to which certain categories of people hold positions within the organization. In particular, administrators at the highest level must offer both moral and financial support and demonstrate that they really believe in the patient care benefits of the systems. There must be clinical leaders, including a chief medical information officer if at all possible, who understand the fine points of implementation strategies, and opinion leaders among the clinical staff

members. In addition, there need to be sufficiently skilled implementation, training, and support coordinators who understand both clinical and technical issues.*

There is a significant publication bias in the biomedical literature against publishing on HIT implementation failures. Because of the human tendency to avoid publicizing individual's mistakes, the body of literature is strongly skewed toward successful implementations and studies. Unfortunately, this has made it difficult to study and understand causes of HIT implementation failures. A significant advance for the HIT industry as a whole would be a shift in its culture toward not only reporting HIT failures, but viewing them as valuable learning opportunities rather than events to be downplayed and forgotten.

One major example of a HIT implementation failure occurred at the prestigious Cedars-Sinai Hospital in Los Angeles, California, in 2002. After implementing a new $34 million HIT system, several hundred physicians refused to use the new system 3 months after it was turned on. Cedars-Sinai attempted to implement a new electronic medical record that changed the way physicians ordered patient treatments and tests in the hospital. Prior to implementing the new system, physicians wrote their orders on paper forms in the patients' paper charts. After new patient orders were written, physicians gave the chart to nurses or ward clerks to read and implement the orders. The new system required physicians to type orders directly into a computer workstation, where the software provided the physician with immediate feedback if they attempted to enter an order that the computer either did not understand or interpreted as a mistake. An article in the *Washington Post* reported[20]:

> A veteran physician at the prestigious Cedars-Sinai Medical Center here had been mixing up a certain drug dosage for decades. Every time he wrote the prescription for 10 times the proper amount, a nurse simply corrected it, recalled Paul Hackmeyer. The computers arrived—and when the doctor typed in his medication order, the machine barked at him and he barked back. . . . "What we discovered was that for 20 years he was writing the wrong dose."

This failure illustrates the three principal HIT implementation components described above. Technology: With physicians required to enter

*Reproduced from the *Journal of the American Medical Informatics Association*, "Factors and forces affecting EHR system adoption: report of a 2004 ACMI discussion," by JS Ash and DW Bates, Issue 12.1, pages 8–12, © 2005, with permission from BMJ Publishing Group Ltd.

orders directly to the computer system, time required to enter orders became dependent on the computer's ordering input format and system response time. Process: Many undocumented processes in the old system were not carried to the new system. In this example, the nurse's automatic correction of an obvious dosage error was a critical, undocumented, process step—a check on the orders' accuracy. Although the new system caught the error, the physician user in this case could no longer rely on the nurse's checking and correcting his orders. Culture: The new system required physicians to interact with a computer, which took more time than writing orders on paper forms. The new system required physicians to change the way they practiced medicine in the hospital and as is common, people dislike change. This was a significant change in physicians' work culture in which nurses had routinely checked and corrected physician orders without communicating the corrections. Physicians also had to deal with a barrage of system alerts when they were imprecise or inaccurate in entering their orders. While possibly enhancing patient safety, responding to the system alerts increased the time required for physicians to place orders.

Another historical barrier to broad implementation of HIT is the chasm between those who bear the costs of the technology and those who receive its benefits. The purchase and operation of an EHR system represent a major investment for large health care organizations and especially for small private physician groups. Not only must physician groups bear the costs of the hardware and software, but they must also support ongoing IT maintenance, staff training, and software upgrade costs. Because small practice groups often have no experience or expertise with IT issues, they also experience anxiety about making decisions necessary to convert from paper to electronic charting. While economies of scale make the marginal costs of adopting EHR technology somewhat lower for large health care organizations, these organizations often do not realize costs savings from their investment. For example, a health care system participating in a HIE may reduce the number of duplicate laboratory and imaging tests saving the patient and the payer significant expense, but the health care system may actually lose money by not receiving revenue for the duplicate tests. As with large health care systems, small practices that invest in EHR technology may not directly benefit from the technology. Patients may receive better age appropriate screening[21,22] and preventative care[23] as well as reduced duplicate testing because of physician access to HIEs and patient records from outside of the practice group or health system.[24] However, from a practice financial perspective, these factors actually may produce a significant disincentive for adopting EHRs.

The Federal Government's Response to HIT Implementation Challenges

The federal government's financial incentive programs for large health care organizations and private practices that adopt and demonstrate "meaningful use" of EHRs are an effort to bridge the chasm between costs and benefits. On April 27, 2004, President Bush created the ONCHIT or "the ONC" by Executive Order.[1] In 2009, the ONC was also tasked in the Health Information Technology for Economic and Clinical Health Act (HITECH Act)[25] to be "the principal Federal entity charged with coordination of nationwide efforts to implement and use the most advanced HIT and the electronic exchange of health information."[26] The ONC's mission is to promote the development of a nationwide HIT infrastructure, provide leadership in the development of standards, provide the certification of HIT products, coordinate HIT policy, perform strategic planning for HIT adoption and HIE, and establish the governance for the Nationwide Health Information Network. Figure 3-2 depicts the ONC's organizational structure.[27]

The ONC employs 191 full-time staff and operates with an annual budget of $66 million in fiscal year 2013, excluding the $20.8 billion in HITECH funding in incentive payments for physicians and health care organizations administered through the Centers for Medicare and Medicaid Services for achieving meaningful use of EHRs. In addition to these resources, the HITECH Act created a HIT Policy Committee and a HIT Standards Committee under the auspices of the Federal Advisory Committee Act. Both committees have multiple workgroups with representatives from payers, academia, and the health care industry. They address a variety of HIT-related issues including certification/adoption, governance, HIE, meaningful use, privacy and security, quality measures, implementation, and a HIT vocabulary standards committee.[28]

> The Health IT Policy Committee will make recommendations to the National Coordinator for Health IT on a policy framework for the development and adoption of a nationwide health information infrastructure, including standards for the exchange of patient medical information. The American Recovery and Reinvestment Act of 2009 (ARRA) provides that the Health IT Policy Committee shall at least make recommendations on the areas in which standards, implementation specifications, and certifications criteria are needed in eight specific areas.
>
> The Health IT Standards Committee is charged with making recommendations to the National Coordinator for Health IT on standards,

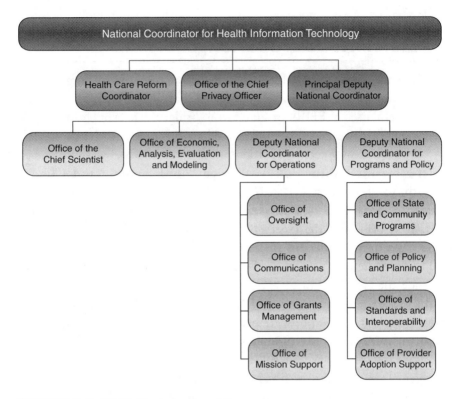

FIGURE 3-2 ONC Organizational Structure.
Source: Reproduced from Office of the National Coordinator for Health
Information Technology Newsroom, http://www.healthit.gov/newsroom/about-onc.

implementation specifications, and certification criteria for the electronic
exchange and use of health information.

As noted previously, the ONC also has funded several programs to
facilitate the adoption of EHRs. Examples include training programs to
increase the number of professionals with IT skills required in the health
care domain. Other programs fund the development of HIE standards
across multiple EHR vendor platforms. The ONC also funds annual surveys to track HIT adoption.

Meaningful Use Incentives

The $20.8 billion included in the HITECH Act created the Medicare
and Medicaid EHR incentive programs for eligible professionals (individual physicians in solo or multiphysician practice groups) and hospitals

as they adopt, implement, upgrade, or demonstrate meaningful use of certified EHR technology to improve patient care.[20]

Eligible professionals may receive up to $44,000 through the Medicare EHR Incentive Program and up to $63,750 through the Medicaid EHR Incentive Program. Eligible professionals may participate in either the Medicare or Medicaid EHR Incentive Programs but not both. Eligible hospitals can participate in both the Medicare and Medicaid incentive programs.[29] Each hospital incentive includes a base payment of $2 million plus an additional amount determined by a formula based on the number of discharges per year.[30,31] The Medicare Program is a 5-year program administered through the federal government while the Medicaid program is a 6-year program funded by the federal government but administered through individual states. Table 3-1 compares Medicare and Medicaid adoption incentive programs for eligible professionals and hospitals.[29–37] CMS also publishes a flow chart to help Eligible Professionals determine qualifications to meet program requirements.[32]

To receive EHR incentive payments, providers and hospitals must demonstrate that they are "meaningfully using" their EHRs by meeting thresholds for several specific objectives. In a partnership with the ONC, CMS has established the objectives for "meaningful use" that eligible professionals and eligible hospitals must meet in order to receive incentive payments.[38] The CMS meaningful use criteria are developed by the experts who comprise the various work groups in the ONC's Health IT Policy Committee. The level of evidence for the majority of meaningful use objectives is only at the expert opinion level. The science of HIT awaits rigorous research studies to validate the choices and designs of the meaningful use criteria.

To receive incentive payments, eligible professionals and health care organizations must meet specific meaningful use criteria in three stages. Stages 1 and 2 have been defined, but stage 3 is yet to be developed. Stage 1 includes objectives for capturing patient data and sharing data in a standardized format with patients and other health care professionals. Stage 2 includes objectives for advanced clinical processes. Stage 3 will reportedly be related to measuring and reporting clinically relevant patient outcomes.

To receive the full Medicare incentive, physicians and hospitals were required to apply for Stage 1 certification by 2012 or the maximum amount of the Medicare incentive payments decreases each year until 2015 when the Medicare incentive stops.[39] The Medicaid incentive payments for eligible professionals are higher under the Medicaid EHR

Table 3-1 Comparison of Medicare and Medicaid Adoption Incentive Programs for Eligible Professionals (Individual Physicians in Solo and Group Practices) and Hospitals (Including Critical Access Hospitals)[29-37]

	Medicare Program	Medicaid Program
Eligible Professionals	• Administered by CMS • $44,000 Maximum per physician (over 5-year period) • 90% or more of practice must be outpatient based • Cannot participate in Medicaid Program if enrolled in Medicare Program • Must apply for Stage 1 Meaningful Use by 2012 to obtain the maximum incentive • Medicare imposes payment penalty on those failing to demonstrate Meaningful Use by 2015	• Administered by State Medicaid Agency • $63,750 Maximum per physician participate (over 5 years) • Must have ≤30% Medicaid patient volume or ≤20% Medicaid patient volume and be a pediatrician or practice predominantly in a Federally Qualified Health Center or Rural Health Clinic and have ≤30% patient volume attributable to needy individuals • ≤90% of practice must be outpatient based • Cannot participate in Medicare Program if enrolled in Medicaid Program • Can begin to certify for Meaningful Use by 2016 and still receive full incentive • Non-participants exempt from Medicaid payment reductions
Hospitals (including Critical Access Hospitals)	• Administered by CMS • Can begin receiving incentive FY 2011 to FY 2015, but payments will decrease for hospitals that start receiving payments in FY 2014 and later • Medicare and Medicaid Program eligible	• Administered by State Medicaid Agency • Acute care hospitals (including critical access and cancer hospitals) with at least 10% Medicaid patient volume are eligible • Children's hospitals are eligible regardless of their Medicaid volume

- Must apply for Stage 1 Meaningful Use by FY 2013 to receive maximum incentive
- Hospitals that do not successfully demonstrate Meaningful Use will be subject to Medicare payment penalties beginning in FY 2015
- Incentive payments are based on several factors, beginning with a $2 million base payment

- Can apply for both Medicare and Medicaid Programs
- Incentive payments are based on a number of factors, beginning with a $2 million base payment

Source: Centers for Medicare and Medicaid Services. Eligible Hospital Information. 2012; http://www.cms.gov/Regulations-and-Guidance/Legislation/EHRIncentivePrograms/Eligible_Hospital_Information.html. Accessed October 30, 2012; Centers for Medicare and Medicaid Services. EHR Incentive Program for Medicare Hospitals. 2012; http://www.cms.gov/Outreach-and-Education/Medicare-Learning-Network-MLN/MLNProducts/downloads/EHR_TipSheet_Medicare_Hosp.pdf. Accessed October 30, 2012; Centers for Medicare and Medicaid Services. Medicaid Hospital Incentive Payments Calculations. 2012; http://www.cms.gov/Outreach-and-Education/Medicare-Learning-Network-MLN/MLNProducts/downloads/Medicaid_Hosp_Incentive_Payments_Tip_Sheets.pdf. Accessed October 30, 2012; Centers for Medicare and Medicaid Services. Flow Chart to Help Eligible Professionals (EP) Determine Eligibility for the Medicare and Medicaid Electronic Health Record (EHR) Incentive Programs. 2012; https://www.cms.gov/Regulations-and-Guidance/Legislation/EHRIncentivePrograms/downloads/eligibility_flow_chart.pdf. Accessed December 21, 2012; Centers for Medicare and Medicaid Services. EHR Incentive Programs. 2012; http://www.cms.gov/Regulations-and-Guidance/Legislation/EHRIncentivePrograms/index.html?redirect=/ehrincentiveprograms/. Accessed September 24, 2012; Centers for Medicare and Medicaid Services. Medicare Electronic Health Record Incentive Program for Eligible Professionals. 2012; http://www.cms.gov/Outreach-and-Education/Medicare-Learning-Network-MLN/MLNProducts/Downloads/CMS_eHR_Tip_Sheet.pdf. Accessed December 22, 2012; Centers for Medicare and Medicaid Services. An Introduction to the Medicaid EHR Incentive Program for Eligible Professionals. 2012; http://www.cms.gov/Regulations-and-Guidance/Legislation/EHRIncentivePrograms/Downloads/EHR_Medicaid_Guide_Remediated_2012.pdf. Accessed December 22, 2012; Centers for Medicare and Medicaid Services. An Introduction to the Medicare EHR Incentive Program for Eligible Professionals. 2012; http://www.cms.gov/Regulations-and-Guidance/Legislation/EHRIncentivePrograms/Downloads/Beginners_Guide.pdf. Accessed December 22, 2012; Centers for Medicare and Medicaid Services. Medicaid Electronic Health Record Incentive Payments for Eligible Professionals. 2012; http://www.cms.gov/Outreach-and-Education/Medicare-Learning-Network-MLN/MLNProducts/Downloads/EHRIP_Eligible_Professionals_Tip_Sheet.pdf. Accessed December 22, 2012.

Incentive Program. Unlike the Medicare EHR Incentive Program, the Medicaid EHR Incentive Program does not penalize those who begin to certify meaningful use after 2012. In fact, an eligible professional can begin to certify meaningful use in the Medicaid Program as late as 2016 and still receive the same total incentive payment as those who began to certify in 2011. Those eligible professionals who begin to certify under the Medicaid Program after 2016 will receive no incentive. Regardless of which of the two programs certifies an eligible professional, beginning in 2015, Medicare will impose payment penalties upon providers who fail to demonstrate meaningful use. Table 3-2 summarizes the timetable for meaningful use criteria implementation.[40]

Detailed information on the Meaningful Use requirements for Stage 1 is available for eligible professionals[41] and eligible hospitals.[42] Some examples of meaningful use requirements for Stage 1 for Eligible Professionals include:

- CPOE
- Drug–Drug Interaction and Drug–Allergy Checking
- Up-to-Date Problem List of Current and Active diagnoses
- Electronic or "e-prescribing" (of at least 40% of prescriptions)

Table 3-2 Meaningful Use Implementation Timeline[40]

Stage 1: 2011–2012	Stage 2: 2014	Stage 3: 2016
Meaningful use criteria focus on:	Meaningful use criteria focus on:	Meaningful use criteria focus on:
• Electronically capturing health information in a standardized format • Using that information to track key clinical conditions • Communicating that information for care coordination processes • Initiating the reporting of clinical quality measures and public health information • Using information to engage patients and their families in their care	• More rigorous health information exchange (HIE) • Increased requirements for e-prescribing and incorporating lab results • Electronic transmission of patient care summaries across multiple settings • More patient-controlled data	• Improving quality, safety, and efficiency, leading to improved health outcomes • Decision support for national high-priority conditions • Patient access to self-management tools • Access to comprehensive patient data through patient-centered HIE • Improving population health

Source: Office of the National Coordinator for Health Information Technology. Stages of Meaningful Use. http://www.healthit.gov/policy-researchers-implementers/meaningful-use; United States Department of Health and Human Services. Meaningful Use. 2012; http://www.healthit.gov/policy-researchers-implementers/meaningful-use. Accessed December 21, 2012.

- Maintaining an Active Medication List
- Record and Chart Changes in Vital Signs
- Recording Smoking Status for Patients 13 Years and Older
- Reporting Ambulatory Clinical Quality Measures to CMS and States
- Implementing Clinical Decision Support
- Providing Patients with an Electronic Copy of Their Health Information Upon Request
- Providing Clinical Summaries to Patients for Each Office Visit

Stage 1 also includes a "menu" of requirements from which physicians must achieve a total of 5. Examples of requirements include the capability to generate lists of patients by specific conditions, proactively sending reminders to patients for preventive/follow-up care, providing patients with electronic access to health information, reconciling patient medication lists, and producing summaries of records for transitions of care. Stage 2 requirements build those of Stage 1 and contain 17 required objectives and a menu of six items from which to choose three. The complete list of meaningful use objectives and metrics for individual physicians and health care organizations are available.[43,44] The list of meaningful use objectives to attain Stage 3 compliance is not yet published but scheduled for release in time for the first Stage 3 certifications in 2016.

HIT Opportunities: Improving Health Care Delivery Quality, Effectiveness, and Efficiency

With mediocre evidence to date for HIT goals to improve health care quality and reduce costs, the question looms: What is the driving force behind U.S. quest to implement HIT? The answer resides in understanding the limitations of the human brain and limited attention span. A healthy human's performance begins to measurably decrease in about 40 minutes while monitoring a continuous process.[45] These limitations explain regulations for work-time breaks for air traffic controllers, anesthesiologists, and work-hour limitations for airplane pilots and commercial truck drivers, and more recently work hour limitations for medical students and residents.[46] These regulations recognize that human performance is limited by innate biology and physiology and that fatigue degrades performance; no amount of training or willpower can overcome these biological and physiological limitations. These acknowledgements apply to health care delivery where a physician in a busy outpatient clinic or inpatient ward is much like an air traffic controller monitoring a continuous process. Patients are tightly scheduled with additional patients often "doubled-booked" at the last minute because of acute illness. Every patient must be seen and volumes of data accessed, processed, and synthesized to formulate a diagnosis and a plan of care. At the same time, the physician must document the encounter in detail, complete all required forms and insurance paperwork, respond to electronic pages and phone calls, speak with consultants, manage correspondence, and in many cases supervise midlevel providers, nursing and office staff. Stead and Hammond have shown that the amount of data accessed and used by clinicians per medical decision is increasing exponentially despite the fact that physicians' ability to cope with the higher information load remains constant.[47] The driving concept behind EHRs' potential to improve the quality and reduce the cost of health care is represented by Figure 3-3.[48]

The ultimate goal is to combine the intuitive strengths of humans and data retention strengths of computers to create a hybrid system that is intuitive with a tireless data processing capability. The computer reminds the physician to do what they already know how to do, and what they want to do, in a manner that makes it easy to implement. Meeting these parameters results in an efficacious computerized decision support system (CDSS). For CDSS to work, the computer system must provide the right information at the right place and at the right time. If any of these

FIGURE 3-3 Why EHRs have Potential to Improve Quality and Reduce Costs.
Source: Adapted from Friedman CP. What informatics is and isn't. *J Am Med Inform Assoc.* 2012;0:1–3.
Computer: © iStockphoto/Thinkstock.
Head: © Lightspring/Shutterstock, Inc.

three requirements are missing, the system will tend to fail. With EHRs, the right place and time are often when the physician is entering patient orders at a computer workstation, a process termed CPOE. At this place and time, the physician's mind is focused on the patient just seen or the patient they are currently thinking about. It is also this place and time at which it is easiest for the physician to take action, such as writing new orders that result in timely follow-through for a patient's care.

For example, when a physician has completed a patient interview and examination and is using an EHR to enter e-prescriptions that will be sent securely over the internet to the patient's pharmacy, the computer can present the physician with a pop-up "reminder" that the patient is allergic to the medication being prescribed. It can also indicate that the prescribed requires at least annual kidney function monitoring and that the last record of kidney function laboratory work is more than a year old. In this event, the system can present the physician with an option to order the appropriate laboratory work or to ignore the warning with one keystroke or mouse click. Most decision support is designed with these "soft stops" or interventions that allow the physician to heed or ignore the warning as he or she believes to be most appropriate. CDSS "hard stops" do not allow physician options to ignore a warning. An example of a "hard stop" could be the use of a very expensive, broad spectrum antibiotic that by hospital policy can only be ordered by an infectious disease specialist. In this case, the CDSS would not allow the physician to order the medication but would inform them that an infectious disease consult is required to order the drug and would make ordering that consult a mouse click away. A nonmedical example of a "hard stop" is the automobile design preventing the shift of an automatic transmission out of Park and into Drive unless the brake petal is depressed. This was implemented after reports of multiple accidental injuries and deaths attributed to unanticipated automobile movements. In this, like the medical example, the decision support system prevents the operator from making an error with high probability of significant adverse consequences.

Like the first example that used a computer–paper hybrid system in the 1970s, CDSS reminds the physician to do what they already know how to do—at the right place and time and in the most convenient manner possible. Because the computer never fatigues, the reminders compensate for physicians' biological limitations and the human–computer hybrid system outperforms what either could accomplish on their own.

There are hundreds of studies and randomized controlled trials published in the peer-reviewed, biomedical literature that have demonstrated how CDSS can have a dramatic impact on improving physician performance in myriad different health care venues. CDSS similarly designed to produce pop-up warnings and recommendations to physicians have been shown to improve the ordering of age appropriate screening tests,[21,22] appropriate antibiotic prescribing for inpatients,[49] appropriate advance directive discussions with patients,[50] the use of preventative care for hospitalized patients,[21] appropriate weaning of patients from mechanical ventilators,[51] appropriate reductions of inpatient resource utilization,[52] the prevalence of Methicillin-Resistant Staph Aureus (MRSA) in a community,[53] the isolation rates of patients admitted to the hospital with drug-resistant infections,[54] the screening for sexually transmitted diseases in the Emergency Department,[55] the accurate capture and recording of patient temperatures by nurses in the inpatient setting,[56] and many others. Despite these very promising studies, until recently, most of these studies were performed at major university health care centers that had custom designed and maintained EHR software systems, maintained by local IT departments with relatively large IT support budgets compared with smaller community hospitals' budgets.[18] In 2006, Chaudhry et al. published a systematic review of 257 CDSS studies published up to 2005 that concluded 25% of the studies were from four major academic institutions that all had custom designed systems and ". . . only 9 studies evaluated multifunctional, commercially developed systems."[18] Therefore, while there are hundreds of studies demonstrating the potential for CDSS to improve the quality of care and/or reduce its costs, the appropriateness of this research to typical health care settings in other than large academic institutions is mostly unknown.

The Agency for Health Research and Quality commissioned the most systematic, rigorous, and comprehensive CDSS review of prior studies to date and published the results in 2012.[57] The systematic review analyzed 311 studies in the biomedical literature and found moderately strong evidence confirming three previously reported factors associated with successful CDSS implementation:

1. Automatic provision of decision support as part of clinician workflow
2. Provision of decision support at time and location of decision making
3. Provision of a recommendation, not just an assessment

The study also identified six additional factors that were correlated with the successful implementation of CDSS:

1. Integration with charting or order entry system to support workflow integration
2. No need for additional clinician data entry
3. Promotion of action rather than inaction
4. Justification of decision support via provision of research evidence
5. Local user involvement in development process
6. Provision of decision support results to patients as well as providers

The study found a high strength of evidence for CDSS to improve the ordering and completing of preventative care and ordering and prescribing recommended treatments "across academic, VA, and community inpatient and ambulatory settings that had both locally and commercially developed CDSS systems."[57]

There was a moderate strength of evidence that CDSS improves appropriate ordering of clinical studies, reduces patient morbidity and cost of care, and increases health care provider satisfaction.

Studies demonstrated a low strength of evidence for CDSS impact on efficiency of the user, length of hospital stay, mortality, health-related quality of life, and "adverse events" or medical errors.

The study also pointed out some significant voids in the current biomedical literature. None of the studies addressed the impact of CDSS on health care delivery organization changes, on the number of patients seen per unit of time, on user knowledge, on system cost-effectiveness, or on physician workload.

In summary, the current cumulative evidence for the benefits of EHRs with CPOE and CDSS is mixed. Even in areas where there is a high strength of evidence such as improvement in the ordering and completing of preventative care, the effective magnitude of the improvement is small, even though statistically significant.[57]

Health Information Exchanges

Virtually none of the commercially available EHR systems available in today's market or the custom-designed systems at large academic institutions can easily exchange patients' health information with care providers outside of their institutions. Despite 50 years of efforts, patients' health information remains siloed and "It is not uncommon for a single patient to be cared for by a large number of agencies in a single city, and workers in any one agency usually cannot find out about the activities of others; sometimes they even fail to learn that other agencies are active at all."[3] Barriers to sharing patient information across multiple providers often become immediately apparent when a patient with a significant illness sees a number of different specialty physicians and attempts to coordinate the flow of information among them. Unlike other industries such as the airlines that have cooperated to create a standardized ticketing system, the health care system has been marginally successful in designing a common platform or standard to allow a patient's records to be compatible with multiple vendor systems. In addition, health domain data are orders of magnitude larger and more complex than data for ticketing in the airline industry. In addition, the Health Insurance Portability and Accountability Act (HIPAA) regulations have had a chilling effect on health care institutions' willingness to share data with other institutions because they are responsible for patient privacy and the security of patient data.

These and other factors led to development of HIEs with their corresponding administering organizations, Regional Health Information Organizations (RHIOs). RHIOs attempt to create systems, agreements, processes, and technology to manage these factors in order to facilitate the appropriate exchange of health care information between institutions and across different vendor platforms. While most all states and regions of the United States have RHIOs, the actual state of implementation and real data exchange varies widely. For example, some states have active RHIOs that are in the planning stages of establishing relationships with all key stakeholders, creating administration agreements, creating governance structures, securing funding, attempting to develop business models for sustained funding of the organization, etc. Other RHIOs have functioning HIEs where medical data are actually being exchanged between institutions and across disparate software EHR platforms. The ONC has funded many RHIOS to develop and test their national standards for HIE with the ultimate goal of creating the "Nationwide Health Information Network" that would be a network of regional networks. Despite the testing and demonstration projects to date, actively functioning HIEs exist only at regional levels.[58]

Each vendor's building toward one common standard would significantly reduce the technical complexity of data exchange. Unfortunately, vendors' products are still not being built toward one national standard to facilitate electronic HIE. Despite these limitations, there have been significant accomplishments in implementing the data and IT standards necessary to facilitate the exchange of health information among multiple EHR platforms. Today, most institutions participating in HIEs must build or configure "interface engines" that convert the institution's data format to the form used by the HIE. This is a major challenge as there is no single standard that provides sufficient specification of data formats and communication protocols. Rather, there are a number of standards that address various domains of data management. In addition, the voluminous scope of modern health care and continuous advancements in knowledge and technology make managing data in the health care domain extremely dynamic and complex.

As an example of this complexity, the Logical Observations Indexes Names and Codes (LOINC) standard was developed in the 1990s to solve a problem with an older health information communication protocol that specified how clinical data should be identified for transmission between computer systems. LOINC uniquely defines codes for information such as blood chemistry laboratory tests and clinical observations, such as patient blood pressure that can be recorded in many different formats. There are currently over 70,000 LOINC defined codes for uniquely reporting laboratory tests and clinical observations.[59] For example, there are 419 different codes for reporting blood pressure. With its unique codes for laboratory tests and clinical observations, LOINC enables computer systems receiving the data to generate exact interpretations. This is called semantic interoperability. Semantic interoperability is essential for patient record transmission from one EHR system to another so that the meaning of the critical data contained within the records is not at risk of erroneous interpretation.

Because new laboratory tests are constantly being developed and existing assays are being improved, LOINC creates and disseminates new codes so that semantic interoperability can be maintained. Old codes are not deleted from the system, ensuring that researchers using prior clinical data bases can retrieve prior results comparable with new codes. LOINC is supported by the National Library of Medicine (NLM), a division of the National Institutes of Health. The LOINC Committee publishes quarterly updates and holds bi-annual, national meetings to discuss proposed new clinical observations and laboratory tests for the assignment of new LOINC codes.

For a HIE to transfer information accurately, each EHR system must map its own internal code for each datum to a standard code to ensure that information passed from one EHR to another in the exchange is interpreted exactly the same by the receiver as it is in the sender's system. LOINC is one of the many HIT-related standards. The Systematic Nomenclature of Medicine (SNOMED) was originally developed by the College of American Pathologists (CAP) to exactly specify tissue pathologic diagnoses. The same group also developed a standard for clinical observations called SNOMED Clinical Terms (SNOMED-CT). LOINC and SNOMED-CT domain standards overlap but their design characteristics are valuable in different situations; for example, exchanging laboratory results versus coding patient problem lists within EHRs. Similar to LOINC, CAP also provides periodic updates to SNOMED-CT codes.

To keep track of the many coding standards and the terms within, the NLM built and maintains the Unified Medical Language System (UMLS), which houses a massive "metathesaurus" and a variety of tools for mapping between and discovery of over 200 biomedically related terminology standards.[60] Because LOINC, SNOMED-CT, and the 200 or so other standards are periodically updated, the UMLS is also regularly updated to keep the interstandard terminology mapping current and accurate.

Using HIEs, designated member groups of health care institutions exchange data in a standardized format using a combination of the previously described standards. This cooperation enables the access to a comprehensive clinical data set on individual patients across multiple institutions and multiple EHR vendor platforms.

There are two kinds of HIE architectures: "monolithic" and "federated."

The monolithic architecture is a design where all member institutions periodically send copies of their clinical data to one central repository where all the data reside together in one format. The advantage of this approach is that a patient's comprehensive data can be maintained in one place and in one format. However, this approach has several disadvantages. First, the frequency with which members contribute and update copies of institutional data can vary making the comprehensive HIE medical record potentially out of date. Second, aggregating data from multiple institutions creates administrative complexity with regard to HIPAA regulations. HIPAA requires each health care institution to maintain security of patient data. If an institution's data are "mixed" in the HIE database with data from other institutions, the responsibility of who ensures patient privacy and data security reverts to all HIE member institutions. HIPAA requirements make fulfilling health care organization obligations to insure patient privacy more difficult and complex. Third, when data are aggregated by a third party or HIE, the ability of the source institution to assert control over data contributed to the collective HIE is limited. If, for example, an institution desires to stop participating in an HIE because of concern for patient privacy and data security, it may be technically difficult and time consuming to selectively delete all data from one institution from the HIE database. The monolithic model is depicted in Figure 3-4.

The federated model is the most widely used design, allowing contributing institutions to maintain control over data for which they are responsible under HIPAA. In this model, institutional data resides only within each institution's system. The HIE database is small, containing only a master patient index (MPI) housing the identifiers for each patient in the form of each institution's unique patient record numbers along with only sufficient patient demographic data to facilitate accurate identification of individual patients with the same or similar names. This information is mapped to all of the institutional-specific patient identifiers in the exchange. Figure 3-5 depicts the federated model.

For example, a patient who has medical records at more than one institution in the HIE would have all their medical record numbers from the

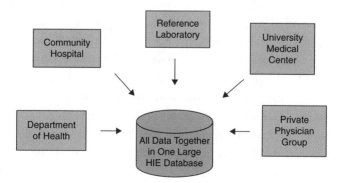

FIGURE 3-4 HIE Monolithic Model. Institutions periodically send copies of their clinical data to one central repository. Individual transinstitutional patient records are maintained in the central database where they can be accessed by authorized users.

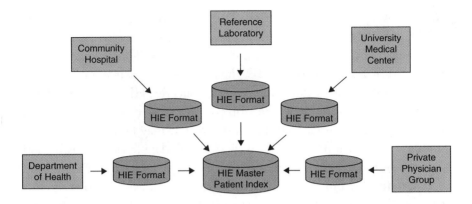

FIGURE 3-5 HIE Federated Model. Institutions maintain copies of their own data at their site in the format used by the health information exchange (HIE). Individual trans-institutional patient records are assembled in real time by searching all institutions' databases only when needed/requested by authorized users. Individual institutions can "op-out" of the HIE at any time by disabling access to their database.

various institutions where they have clinical data stored, linked together in the common MPI along with basic demographics such as address, date of birth, and social security number. This allows for fast and accurate identification of patients named "John Smith" because the MPI maintains only sufficient identifying information to ensure selection of the correct patient among all institutions in the exchange. "John Smith" would be identified from others with the same name by parameters such as date of birth, social security number. No clinical data are stored in the MPI. Clinical data are usually maintained in the proprietary format of the particular EHR system used by each institution. A copy of the same data is also maintained but is formatted in the standard used by all members of the HIE. For example, all HIE members could agree to code all laboratory test results using the LOINC standard described earlier. Each institution would create and maintain a database of all patients' laboratory results coded with LOINC. When a user requests a comprehensive record from the HIE, the system would query all of its institutional members in real time to send all the data available on a particular patient as identified using the MPI. In this way, when an HIE receives a records request on a particular patient, each institution sends data on the requested patient from the database where all clinical data are in the

HIE format. This process ensures that the data are collected securely, assembled into a comprehensive record, and made available to authorized users in real time. This comprehensive record is only accessible on a patient-by-patient basis for immediate patient care purposes; it is not copied to any institution's system. When the user logs out of the HIE, the comprehensive record assembled for that episode of patient care is deleted.

The federated model has several advantages over the monolithic model. With the federated model, each institution maintains complete control over its data, simplifying compliance with HIPAA regulations. If, for example, a data breach occurs in the database of an HIE that uses the monolithic model, responsibility for the data breach is not always clear. Data breaches in a federated system are always clearly attributable to a particular institution and not the HIE (unless there is a data breach of the MPI). Another benefit of the federated system is that trans-institutional data are up-to-the-minute accurate because each time a user requests access, the clinical data from all institutions are assembled in real time. Institutional HIT administrators typically favor the federated model. With this model, HIT administrators have the option of withdrawing from the HIE at any time in order to maintain control of their responsibilities for patient information and data security under HIPAA guidelines.

While communities with HIEs generally appreciate the benefits, the current reality is that most of the operating HIEs are heavily subsidized with federal research grant funding. The RHIOs that administer the HIEs and seek funding have not developed a business model that can be used in all communities in order to sustain their HIEs independent of federal funding. Some HIEs have developed services for payers, charging them for access to the comprehensive records available in the HIE. These services allow payers to increase their claims processing efficiency. Other HIEs have developed services to generate comprehensive quality reports to sell to payers desiring to track physician and health plan outcomes or to help them meet the meaningful use requirements for CMS financial eligibility incentives. Some communities are resistant to allowing payer access to a data resource they believe should be solely dedicated to improving patient care and quality.[61] An excellent example of this is the State of Vermont's 2006 law that prevented data miners from selling physicians' prescribing data to pharmaceutical companies who wanted the information to inform their marketing practices. In 2011, the law was struck down by the Supreme

Court on a First Amendment basis.[62] Physicians may feel uncomfortable participating in an exchange they know government, payers, or pharmaceutical companies may use for monitoring of individual practice outcomes and patterns. While the benefits of HIEs are documented and desirable, solving the cultural and business model issues will be essential to obtaining the national goal of a network of regional exchanges that will constitute the Nationwide Health Information Network.

The Veterans Administration Health Information System

No discussion of HIT, EHRs, and HIEs would be complete without noting the HIT system used by the Veterans Administration (VA). The VA is a model representing a single-payer health care system in the United States. For example, the VA HIT system supports only one payer, one pharmaceutical formulary, one provider group, and one supplier of laboratory testing. All VA physicians are employees of the same organization, so new policies and practices can be communicated, implemented, and monitored much more easily and efficiently than in U.S. multipayer, multiformulary, siloed system. Also, key is that the VA has one, universal EHR system with CPOE and CDSS. The VA EHR is able to code all data in one format that allows veterans who move from state to state to have their entire VA medical record seamlessly follow them. All these factors have allowed the VA to offer high-quality care at a relatively reasonable cost. Until the United States creates a single payer system and uses the same EHR universally, the larger system will suffer from the enormous complexity and costs of developing and maintaining multiple data standards to support the exchange of health information among institutions and across vendor platforms.

EHR Adoption Progress in the United States

One of the legislated functions of the ONC is to perform periodic surveys of EHR adoption. The ONC performs two national surveys. One surveys physician offices and the other surveys hospitals. The ONC defines two levels of adoption defined as "Basic" and "Full."[63] This distinction is important because many other surveys report EHR adoption rates but do not define in any detail what "EHR adoption" means. The ONC survey uses an exacting definition of "Basic" and "Advanced" EHR adoption that produces results that are much more valid than surveys where "adoption" is not well defined. Figure 3-6 from the January 2012 ONC report to Congress, "Update on the Adoption of Health Information Technology and Related Efforts to Facilitate the Electronic Use and Exchange of Health Information," illustrates the rate of EHR "Basic" adoption among non-hospital-based physicians. These results demonstrate a steady increase in the adoption of "Basic" EHRs[64]:

> As of 2011, 34% of non-hospital-based physicians had adopted a "basic" EHR. This is double the adoption rate among non-hospital-based physicians in 2008. Adoption among primary care physicians, a key focus area of the HITECH Act, grew to approximately 40 percent; adoption among this same group has nearly doubled since 2008. These results are initial indications of the effects that the HITECH Act and CMS and ONC programs have had to date in accelerating the adoption of health IT and EHRs.[63]

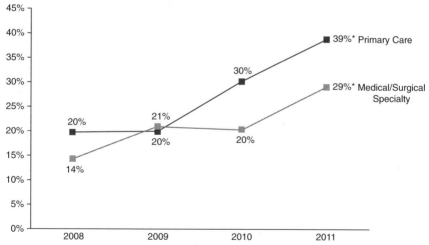

*Significantly higher than previous year estimate, or in the case of primary care all other physicians, at *p*<0.05. Adoption of "Basic" electronic health records as defined in: Hsiao CJ, et al. Electronic Medical Record/Electronic Health Record Systems of Non-hospital-based physicians: United States, 2009 and Preliminary 2010 State Estimates Health E Stats. National Center for Health Statistics, Centers for Disease Control.

FIGURE 3-6 Adoption of "Basic" Electronic Health Records Among Non-Hospital-Based Physicians.
Source: Reproduced from ONC report to Congress. Update on the Adoption of Health Information Technology and Related Efforts to Facilitate the Electronic Use and Exchange of Health Information: A Report to Congress. Jan 2012, Page 8.

Figure 3-7 from the ONC report noted above, illustrates the adoption rate of "Basic" EHRs among nonfederal acute care hospitals[64]:

The report states "Nearly 19 percent of non-federal acute care hospitals adopted a 'basic' EHR by 2010. This represents over a 50 percent increase in adoption among hospitals since 2008."[64]

The adoption rate of electronic prescribing or "e-prescribing" has been much more successful than the overall adoption of basic EHRs. The ONC report of 2012 further noted:

> Data from Surescripts, the nation's largest electronic prescribing network, shows that the percent of non-hospital based physicians active on the Surescripts network using an electronic health record has increased more than three-fold since 2008, to 44 percent. Pharmacies have reached near-universal adoption of electronic prescribing at 93 percent.[64]

The report also attributes much of the increase to the CMS financial incentive program for e-prescribing. Figures 3-8 and 3-9 from the January 2012 ONC report provide the adoption rates for e-prescribing by non-hospital-based physicians and retail community pharmacies.[64]

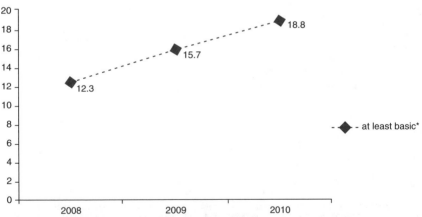

*Without physician notes and Nursing Assessments, as defined in Jha AK, et al. Use of Electronic Health Records in U.S. Hospitals. N Engl J Med. 2009 360;16.

FIGURE 3-7 Adoption of "Basic" Electronic Health Records Among Nonfederal Acute Care Hospitals.
Source: Reproduced from ONC report to Congress. Update on the Adoption of Health Information Technology and Related Efforts to Facilitate the Electronic Use and Exchange of Health Information: A Report to Congress. Jan 2012, Page 9.

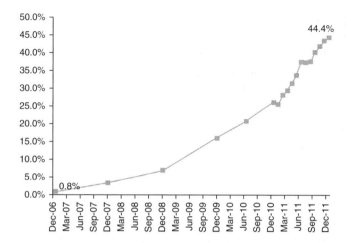

FIGURE 3-8 Adoption of Electronic Prescribing Through and Electronic Health Record Among Non-Hospital-Based Physicians.
Source: Reproduced from ONC report to Congress. Update on the Adoption of Health Information Technology and Related Efforts to Facilitate the Electronic Use and Exchange of Health Information: A Report to Congress. Jan 2012, Page 10.

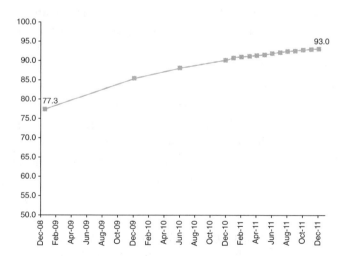

FIGURE 3-9 Adoption of Electronic Prescribing Among Retail Community Pharmacies.
Source: Reproduced from ONC report to Congress. Update on the Adoption of Health Information Technology and Related Efforts to Facilitate the Electronic Use and Exchange of Health Information: A Report to Congress. Jan 2012, Page 11.

Future Challenges

Although there is mounting evidence supporting the value of EHRs with CPOE and CDSS in several well-defined areas such as improving preventative care delivery, the extensive meta-analyses only report the combined average results. There have been several inconclusive and negative studies, and some that have actually shown patient harm associated with the installation of CPOE. In one of the most extensively reported, the mortality rate in a neonatal intensive care unit more than doubled after a CPOE system was installed at the University of Pittsburgh.[65] Much has been written about the reasons for this negative result and despite the finger pointing, there is virtually universal agreement that HIT can be very disruptive to work processes and work cultures resulting in significant harm to patients.[66] Some have called for more HIT standards and regulation to prevent these negative consequences in the same way as the U.S. Food and Drug Administration regulates medical devices.[67,68]

Due to the administrative and technical difficulties of achieving the Nationwide Health Information Network, proprietary entities have offered alternate approaches to develop "personal health records" (PHRs) through which patients create their own records in a standardized format. In these approaches, patients may physically carry records or make them available to caregivers via the Internet. Microsoft, Google, and many others have built such systems but with little marketing success. Google Health announced its shutdown on June 24, 2011, after only 3 years of operation. Google joins other lesser known firms that have decided to close down PHR services.[69] Design of existing PHRs requires patients to have a high level of health literacy and computer savvy. A major reason analysts believed Google Health failed was the newness of the concept for most people and the fact that PHRs are difficult to use and that many people find the necessary amount of data entry work necessary to complete their record to be too laborious.[70] One survey of patients found that only 7% had tried using a PHR and only about 3% continued to use them in 2011.[70] Other barriers to patient adoption include lack of personal health management tools (PHMT), the difficulty in achieving semantic interoperability such that PHMTs could be useful, problems vetting the identity of PHR users, patient privacy concerns, and perhaps most importantly, the lack of a business model to support the long-term operation of PHRs.[69]

In addition to physicians and patients affected by development and implementation of HIT, there are many other health care professionals and venues with significant complexities and characteristics that make HIT implementation challenging. Many of the same issues previously discussed in this chapter apply to these venues such as standardized data formats to facilitate data portability, work culture barriers, system expense, training issues, and other matters. For example, some emergency medical service (EMS) providers have begun to use a variety of portable EHRs to collect data at the scenes of patient incidents with systems designed to transmit data to receiving hospitals. The same issues that complicate the ease of universal HIE between health care institutions apply to the data exchange between EMS and hospital systems and will not be easily resolved.

To achieve the HIT goals of improving health care quality and reducing costs, extensive and rigorous work remains in the research and implementation arenas. After 50 years of efforts and most notably in the past 5 years, government, industry, and academia are only now recognizing the critically important and interdependent roles that standardization, administrative processes, and work cultures play in the HIT desired outcomes.

Key Terms for Review

Computerized Decision Support System (CDSS)
Computerized Physician Order Entry (CPOE)
Federated Model of Health Information Exchange
Health Information Exchange (HIE)
Health Information Technology for Economic and Clinical Health Act (HITECH Act)

Meaningful Use
Monolithic Model of Health Information Exchange
Office of The National Coordinator for Health Information Technology (ONC)
Regional Health Information Organization (RHIO)

References

1. Bush GW. Executive Order: Incentives for the Use of Health Information Technology and Establishing the Position of the National Health Information Technology Coordinator. 2004; http://georgewbush-whitehouse.archives.gov/news/releases/2004/04/20040427-4.html. Accessed September 25, 2012.

2. One Hundred Eleventh Congress of the United States of America. *The American Recovery and Reinvestment Act.* Washington, DC; U.S. Government Printing Office; 2009.

3. The Life Sciences Panel of the President's Science Advisory Committee. *Some New Technologies and their Promise for the Life Sciences.* Washington, DC: The White House; January 23, 1963.

4. Duke Evidence-based Practice Center. *Enabling Health Care Decisionmaking through Clinical Decision Support and Knowledge Management.* Rockville, MD: Agency for Healthcare Research and Quality, U.S. Department of Health and Human Services; 2012.

5. McDonald CJ. Protocol-based computer reminders, the quality of care and the non-perfectability of man. *N Engl J Med.* 1976;295(24):1351–1355.

6. Yount RJ, Vries JK, Councill CD. The Medical Archival System: an Information Retrieval System Based on Distributed Parallel Processing. *Info Proces Management.* 1991;27(4):1–11.

7. Gardner RM, Pryor TA, Warner HR. The HELP hospital information system: update 1998. *Int J Med Inform.* 1999;54(3):169–182.

8. Pryor TA, Gardner RM, Clayton PD, Warner HR. The HELP system. *J Med Syst.* 1983;7(2):87–102.

9. Higgins SB, Jiang K, Swindell BB, Bernard GR. A graphical ICU workstation. *Proc Annu Symp Comput Appl Med Care.* 1991; 783–787.

10. Giuse DA, Mickish A. Increasing the availability of the computerized patient record. *Proc AMIA Annu Fall Symp.* 1996; 633–637.

11. Stead WW, Hammond WE. Computer-based medical records: the centerpiece of TMR. *MD Comput.* 1988;5(5):48–62.

12. Greenes RA, Pappalardo AN, Marble CW, Barnett GO. Design and implementation of a clinical data management system. *Comput Biomed Res.* 1969;2(5):469–485.

13. United States Department of Health and Human Services. Certified Health IT Product List. 2012; http://oncchpl.force.com/ehrcert?q=CHPL. Accessed September 28, 2012.

14. HITECH Programs and Advisory Committees. Health IT Adoption Programs. http://www.healthit.gov/policy-researchers-implementers/health-it-adoption-programs. Accessed January 20, 2012.

15. Campbell EM, Guappone KP, Sittig DF, Dykstra RH, Ash JS. Computerized provider order entry adoption: implications for clinical workflow. *J Gen Intern Med.* 2009;24(1):21–26.

16. Bloomrosen M, Starren J, Lorenzi NM, Ash JS, Patel VL, Shortliffe EH. Anticipating and addressing the unintended consequences of health IT and policy: a report from the AMIA 2009 Health Policy Meeting. *J Am Med Inform Assoc.* 2011;18(1):82–90.

17. Ash JS, Stavri PZ, Dykstra R, Fournier L. Implementing computerized physician order entry: the importance of special people. *Int J Med Inform.* 2003;69(2–3):235–250.

18. Chaudhry B, Wang J, Wu S, et al. Systematic review: impact of health information technology on quality, efficiency, and costs of medical care. *Ann Intern Med.* 2006;144(10):742–752.

19. Ash JS, Bates DW. Factors and forces affecting EHR system adoption: report of a 2004 ACMI discussion. *J Am Med Inform Assoc.* 2005;12(1):8–12.

20. Connolly C. Cedars-Sinai Doctors Clinic to Pen and Paper. *The Washington Post.* March 21, 2005:A01. Available from http://gunston.gmu.edu/health-science/740/Presentations/cedars-sinai%20cpoe%20washpost%203-21-05.pdf. Accessed April 21, 2013.

21. Dexter PR, Perkins S, Overhage JM, Maharry K, Kohler RB, McDonald CJ. A computerized reminder system to increase the use of preventive care for hospitalized patients. *N Engl J Med.* 2001;345(13):965–970.

22. Weiner M, Callahan CM, Tierney WM, et al. Using information technology to improve the health care of older adults. *Ann Intern Med.* 2003;139(5 Pt 2): 430–436.

23. Dexter PR, Perkins SM, Maharry KS, Jones K, McDonald CJ. Inpatient computer-based standing orders vs physician reminders to increase influenza and pneumococcal vaccination rates: a randomized trial. *JAMA.* 2004;292(19):2366–2371.

24. Overhage JM, Dexter PR, Perkins SM, et al. A randomized, controlled trial of clinical information shared from another institution. *Ann Emerg Med.* 2002;39(1):14–23.

25. One Hundred Eleventh Congress of the United States of America. Health Information Technology for Economic and Clinical Health Act. 2009; http://www.hhs.gov/ocr/privacy/hipaa/understanding/coveredentities/hitechact.pdf. Accessed September 25, 2012.

26. The Office of the National Coordinator for Health Information Technology (ONC). About ONC. 2012; http://healthit.hhs.gov/portal/server.pt/community/healthit_hhs_gov_onc/1200. Accessed November 24, 2012.

27. The Office of the National Coordinator for Health Information Technology (ONC). ONC Organizational Structure. 2012; http://healthit.hhs.gov/portal/server.pt/community/healthit_hhs_gov__organization/1512. Accessed November 24, 2012.

28. United States Department of Health and Human Services. HITECH Programs & Advisory Committees. http://www.healthit.gov/policy-researchers-implementers/federal-advisory-committees-facas. Accessed September 24, 2012.

29. Centers for Medicare and Medicaid Services. Eligible Hospital Information. 2012; http://www.cms.gov/Regulations-and-Guidance/Legislation/EHRIncentivePrograms/Eligible_Hospital_Information.html. Accessed October 30, 2012.

30. Centers for Medicare and Medicaid Services. EHR Incentive Program for Medicare Hospitals. 2012; http://www.cms.gov/Outreach-and-Education/Medicare-Learning-Network-MLN/MLNProducts/downloads/EHR_TipSheet_Medicare_Hosp.pdf. Accessed October 30, 2012.

31. Centers for Medicare and Medicaid Services. Medicaid Hospital Incentive Payments Calculations. 2012; http://www.cms.gov/Outreach-and-Education/Medicare-Learning-Network-MLN/MLNProducts/downloads/Medicaid_Hosp_Incentive_Payments_Tip_Sheets.pdf. Accessed October 30, 2012.

32. Centers for Medicare and Medicaid Services. Flow Chart to Help Eligible Professionals (EP) Determine Eligibility for the Medicare and Medicaid Electronic Health Record (EHR) Incentive Programs. 2012; https://www.cms.gov/Regulations-and-Guidance/Legislation/EHRIncentivePrograms/downloads/eligibility_flow_chart.pdf. Accessed December 21, 2012.

33. Centers for Medicare and Medicaid Services. EHR Incentive Programs. 2012; http://www.cms.gov/Regulations-and-Guidance/Legislation/EHRIncentivePrograms/index.html?redirect=/ehrincentiveprograms/. Accessed September 24, 2012.

34. Centers for Medicare and Medicaid Services. Medicare Electronic Health Record Incentive Program for Eligible Professionals. 2012; http://www.cms.gov/Outreach-and-Education/Medicare-Learning-Network-MLN/MLNProducts/Downloads/CMS_eHR_Tip_Sheet.pdf. Accessed December 22, 2012.

35. Centers for Medicare and Medicaid Services. An Introduction to the Medicaid EHR Incentive Program for Eligible Professionals. 2012; http://www.cms.gov/Regulations-and-Guidance/Legislation/EHRIncentivePrograms/Downloads/EHR_Medicaid_Guide_Remediated_2012.pdf. Accessed December 22, 2012.

36. Centers for Medicare and Medicaid Services. An Introduction to the Medicare EHR Incentive Program for Eligible Professionals. 2012; http://www.cms.gov/Regulations-and-Guidance/Legislation/EHRIncentivePrograms/Downloads/Beginners_Guide.pdf. Accessed December 22, 2012.

37. Centers for Medicare and Medicaid Services. Medicaid Electronic Health Record Incentive Payments for Eligible Professionals. 2012; http://www.cms.gov/Outreach-and-Education/Medicare-Learning-Network-MLN/MLNProducts/Downloads/EHRIP_Eligible_Professionals_Tip_Sheet.pdf. Accessed December 22, 2012.

38. Centers for Medicare and Medicaid Services. Meaningful Use. 2012; http://www.cms.gov/Regulations-and-Guidance/Legislation/EHRIncentivePrograms/Meaningful_Use.html. Accessed September 24, 2012.

39. Centers for Medicare and Medicaid Services. Medicare and Medicaid EHR Incentive Program Basics. 2012; http://www.cms.gov/Regulations-and-Guidance/Legislation/EHRIncentivePrograms/Basics.html. Accessed October 30, 2012.

40. United States Department of Health and Human Services. Meaningful Use. 2012; http://www.healthit.gov/policy-researchers-implementers/meaningful-use. Accessed December 21, 2012.

41. Centers for Medicare and Medicaid Services. Eligible Professional Meaningful Use Table of Contents Core and Menu Set Objectives. 2012; https://www.cms.gov/Regulations-and-Guidance/Legislation/EHRIncentivePrograms/downloads/EP-MU-TOC.pdf. Accessed October 30, 2012.

42. Centers for Medicare and Medicaid Services. Eligible Hospital and CAH Meaningful Use Table of Contents Core and Menu Set Objectives. 2012; http://www.cms.gov/Regulations-and-Guidance/Legislation/EHRIncentivePrograms/downloads/Hosp_CAH_MU-TOC.pdf. Accessed October 30, 2012.

43. United States Department of Health and Human Services. Stage 1 vs. Stage 2 Comparison Table for Eligible Professionals. 2012; http://www.cms.gov/Regulations-and-Guidance/Legislation/EHRIncentivePrograms/Downloads/Stage1vsStage2CompTablesforEP.pdf. Accessed September 24, 2012.

44. United States Department of Health and Human Services. Stage 1 vs. Stage 2 Comparison Table for Eligible Hospitals and CAHs. 2012; http://www.cms.gov/Regulations-and-Guidance/Legislation/EHRIncentivePrograms/Downloads/Stage1vsStage2CompTablesforHospitals.pdf. Accessed September 25, 2012.

45. Dukette D, Cornish D. *The Essential 20: Twenty Components of an Excellent Health Care Team.* Pittsburgh, PA: RoseDog Books; 2009: 72–74.

46. Parthasarathy S. Sleep and the medical profession. *Curr Opin Pulm Med.* 2005;11(6):507–512.

47. Institute of Medicine. *Free Executive Summary: Beyond Expert-Based Practice. IOM Annual Meeting Summary: Evidence-Based Medicine and the Changing Nature of Healthcare.* Washington, DC: The National Academies Press; 2008: 18–19.

48. Friedman CP. What informatics is and isn't. *J Am Med Inform Assoc.* 2012;0:1–3.

49. Evans RS, Pestotnik SL, Classen DC, et al. A computer-assisted management program for antibiotics and other antiinfective agents. *N Engl J Med.* 1998;338(4):232–238.

50. Tierney WM, Dexter PR, Gramelspacher GP, Perkins AJ, Zhou XH, Wolinsky FD. The effect of discussions about advance directives on patients' satisfaction with primary care. *J Gen Intern Med.* 2001;16(1):32–40.

51. Gardner RM. Computerized clinical decision-support in respiratory care. *Respir Care.* 2004;49(4):378–386; discussion 386–378.

52. Tierney WM, Miller ME, Overhage JM, McDonald CJ. Physician inpatient order writing on microcomputer workstations. Effects on resource utilization. *JAMA.* 1993;269(3):379–383.

53. Kho AN, Dexter P, Lemmon L, et al. Connecting the dots: creation of an electronic regional infection control network. *Stud Health Technol Inform.* 2007;129(Pt 1):213–217.

54. Kho A, Dexter P, Warvel J, Commiskey M, Wilson S, McDonald CJ. Computerized reminders to improve isolation rates of patients with drug-resistant infections: design and preliminary results. *AMIA Annu Symp Proc.* 2005; 390–394.

55. Rosenman M, Wang J, Dexter P, Overhage JM. Computerized reminders for syphilis screening in an urban emergency department. *AMIA Annu Symp Proc.* 2003; 987.

56. Kroth PJ, Dexter PR, Overhage JM, et al. A computerized decision support system improves the accuracy of temperature capture from nursing personnel at the bedside. *AMIA Annu Symp Proc.* 2006; 444–448.

57. Agency for Healthcare Research and Quality. Evidence Report/Tecghnology Assessment Number 203: Enabling Health Care Decisionmaking Through Clinical Decision Support and Knowledge. 2012; http://www.ahrq.gov/clinic/tp/knowmgttp.htm. Accessed October 29, 2012.

58. Markle Foundation. The Common Framework: Technical Issues and Requirements for Implementation. 2006; http://www.markle.org/sites/default/files/T1_TechIssues.pdf. Accessed December 21, 2012.

59. Lin MC, Vreeman DJ, McDonald CJ, Huff SM. Auditing consistency and usefulness of LOINC use among three large institutions - using version spaces for grouping LOINC codes. *J Biomed Inform.* 2012;45(4):658–666.

60. National Library of Medicine. UMLS Quick Start Guide. 2012; http://www.nlm.nih.gov/research/umls/quickstart.html. Accessed January 11, 2013.

61. Sorrell WH. Supreme Court Strikes Down Vermont Prescription Privacy Law. 2011; http://www.atg.state.vt.us/news/supreme-court-strikes-down-vermont-prescription-privacy-law.php. Accessed November 24, 2012.

62. The Supreme Court of the United States. Sorrell, Attorney General of Vermont, et al. vs. IMS Health Inc. et al. 2011; http://www.supremecourt.gov/opinions/10pdf/10-779.pdf. Accessed January 12, 2013.

63. Hsiao CJ, Hing E, Socey TC, Cai B. Electronic health record systems and intent to apply for meaningful use incentives among office-based physician practices: United States, 2001–2011. *NCHS Data Brief.* 2011;79:1–8. Available from http://www.cdc.gov/nchs/data/databriefs/db79.htm. Accessed April 19, 2013.

64. The Office of the National Coordinator for Health Information Technology (ONC). Update on the Adoption of Health Information Technology and Related Efforts to Facilitate the Electronic Use and Exchange of Health Information: A Report to Congress. January 2012; http://healthit.hhs.gov/portal/server.pt/gateway/PTARGS_0_0_4383_1239_15610_43/http%3B/wci-pubcontent/publish/onc/public_communities/p_t/resources_and_public_affairs/reports/reports_portlet/files/january2012__update_on_hit_adoption_report_to_congress.pdf. Accessed September 29, 2012.

65. Han YY, Carcillo JA, Venkataraman ST, et al. Unexpected increased mortality after implementation of a commercially sold computerized physician order entry system. *Pediatrics.* 2005;116(6):1506–1512.

66. Sittig DF, Ash JS, Zhang J, Osheroff JA, Shabot MM. Lessons from "Unexpected increased mortality after implementation of a commercially sold computerized physician order entry system." *Pediatrics.* 2006;118(2):797–801.

67. Miller RA, Gardner RM. Summary recommendations for responsible monitoring and regulation of clinical software systems. American Medical Informatics Association, The Computer-based Patient Record Institute, The

Medical Library Association, The Association of Academic Health Science Libraries, The American Health Information Management Association, and The American Nurses Association. *Ann Intern Med.* 1997;127(9):842–845.

68. Miller RA, Gardner RM. Recommendations for responsible monitoring and regulation of clinical software systems. American Medical Informatics Association, Computer-based Patient Record Institute, Medical Library Association, Association of Academic Health Science Libraries, American Health Information Management Association, American Nurses Association. *J Am Med Inform Assoc.* 1997;4(6):442–457.

69. Rishel W, Booz RH. Google Health Shutdown Underscores Uncertain Future of PHRs. 2011; http://www.gartner.com/resources/214600/214682/google_health_shutdown_under_214682.pdf. Accessed October 29, 2012.

70. Lohr S. Google Is Closing Its Health Records Service. *The New York Times.* June 24, 2011.

CHAPTER 4

Hospitals: Origin, Organization, and Performance

This chapter's overview of the genesis of U.S. hospitals provides a basis for understanding their characteristics, organization, and major private and governmental insurance initiatives that contributed to their growth and centrality in the health care system. The chapter discusses the diverse functions of hospitals and their staff and management structures, and important aspects of quality of care and the relationship between staff and patients. The chapter reviews and summarizes hospital marketplace activities in response to health reform and pertinent major elements of the Patient Protection and Affordable Care Act as they directly affect hospitals.

Of all the familiar institutions in U.S. society, the hospital is, at the same time, the most appreciated, most maligned, and least understood. Besides serving as a place for the treatment of the sick and injured, it may function as a research laboratory, an educational institution, and a major employer within the community. In the era of health care reform, these core functions can be expected to remain intact. However, virtually everything about the way in which hospitals have operated including their ownership structures and financing and their relationships with physicians, other health care providers and their communities will continue to undergo vast change. Hospitals are focal points in market reforms and changes required by the Patient Protection and Affordable Care Act (ACA). Subsequent sections of this chapter outline the nature of the changes affecting hospitals, and significant challenges and opportunities presented by reforms to improve the quality of care, increase patient satisfaction, improve the health of populations, and reduce costs.

Historical Perspective

The often strained relationship between patients and hospital personnel dates back to the earliest history of health care in the United States. The indifference to patients' needs for information, comfort, and humane contact that is a common complaint about hospital care is rooted not only in the overall history of medical care but also—and especially—in the history of hospitals.

Hospitals in early America were founded to shelter older adults, the dying, orphans, and vagrants and to protect the inhabitants of a community from the contagiously sick and the dangerously mentally ill.

During the 18th century, Boston was the largest city in the new democracy, with about 7,000 citizens. Philadelphia and New York each had about 4,000 people. Whatever passed for medical care in those days was provided in the home. It was necessary, however, in these and other seaport towns to provide refuge for sailors and other shipboard victims of contagious diseases who often were unceremoniously left ashore when the ships departed. The town responded by organizing pest houses, quarantine stations, or isolation hospitals to segregate the sick from the town inhabitants and to prevent the spread of disease. Because these facilities were not intended to be used by the local citizenry, they were usually located well outside the city limits.

As populations grew, mental illness became an additional problem. Individuals whose behavior offended or frightened the townspeople came to the attention of the town board. It was common in those days for the town board to order relatives or friends to build a small stronghouse, or cell, on their property to contain a person with mental illness. If the individual had no relatives or friends, the town might lease him or her at an auction to the lowest bidder, who would take responsibility for confining that individual for 1 year, usually in exchange for his or her labor.

The existence of pest houses, or isolation hospitals, also provided the towns with a solution for dealing with other individuals whose presence posed a risk to or offended its inhabitants. Over time, people with mental illness or those in poor health, the homeless, and the petty criminal joined the contagious ill that occupied those facilities.

Bellevue Hospital was originally the Poor House of New York City, established in 1736 to house the "poor, aged, insane, and disreputable." In 1789, the Public Hospital of Baltimore was established for low-income populations, people with mental or physical illness, and the seafaring of Maryland. One hundred years later, in 1889, it became the now prestigious the Johns Hopkins Hospital.

Eventually, almost every city of any size in early America had a pest house to isolate patients during epidemics. Most cities also had an almshouse for low-income populations, sometimes with an added infirmary. Many of today's county or municipal hospitals were originally combinations of almshouses and infirmaries.

The largest county institution, Eloise Hospital in Wayne County, Michigan, was started in 1835 to serve the "old, young, deaf, dumb, blind, insane, and destitute." It grew to 6,000 beds to care for acute and chronic illness and mental diseases and to provide domiciliary services to low-income populations. The Kings County Hospital in Brooklyn, Philadelphia General Hospital, and Cleveland City Hospital are similar examples.

Most hospitals in the United States in the 19th century were dirty, unventilated, and contaminated with infections. They were overcrowded and offered little or no medical care. The only nurses available were former prison inmates or women who could get no other work. The public, however, knew little of these conditions. Because visiting was restricted, patients were effectively cut off from the outside world. Persons with family or the means to obtain home medical or nursing care shunned hospitals.

Certain religious orders saw the hospitals' clients as so helpless, so miserable with incurable disease, or so maimed by accident that they presented an opportunity for spiritual outlet for those seeking salvation through good works. Thus began the close relationships of the Protestant and Catholic religions with hospitals and hospital nursing. Religious nursing groups played a major role in the evolution of hospital care. Catholic religious orders were the first groups responsible for kindly and humane nursing performed by fairly well-educated, sincere, and devoted "sisters." The American branch of St. Vincent de Paul Sisters of Charity, founded by Mother Elizabeth Seton in 1809, established hospitals that still stand in cities across the United States.

The Protestant nursing movement began in Germany and was brought to Pennsylvania in 1850. It was based on the formal training of nurses in religion, nursing, and nursing education. The nurse teachers were called deaconesses. The Protestant church hospital, or deaconess movement, had an important influence on nursing.

Ironically, it was the Civil War of the 1860s that brought about public appreciation of the work of women in nursing. When sick or wounded soldiers were returned to their hometowns attended by obviously dedicated and capable nurses, it was the first time that relatives of those soldiers encountered women as nurses outside of their own homes. Nursing gained a much more positive image and came to be viewed as a respectable career option for women.

All this early hospital care was focused on only the most unfortunate of the population with physical and mental illness. Although provided in the most deplorable conditions, hospital care nonetheless reflected the early American concept of charity and public responsibility, which required that provision be made for low-income populations, people with physical or mental illness, vagrants, and criminals. Institutions originally classified as almshouses provided refuge for all of them. Later, physicians realized the efficacy of separating the sick population from the rest of the needy and putting them in facilities more properly called hospitals. The Pennsylvania Hospital in Philadelphia, the New York Hospital in New York City, and the Massachusetts General Hospital in Boston were founded by physicians who obtained citizen funding for charitable hospitals. Their motives for establishing hospitals also included providing a place to practice surgery and obstetrics, centrally locating patients to serve their instruction of medical students, and protecting the well population from people with physical or mental illness.

Sources That Shaped the Hospital Industry

Health Insurance

The transformation of hospitals from simple, charitable institutions to complex, technical organizations was accompanied by a parallel growth of private hospital insurance. In 1940, only 9% of U.S. population had hospital insurance.

By the 1960s, billions of dollars were flowing into hospitals from insurance companies, such as Blue Cross/Blue Shield, medical society plans, and other plans sponsored by unions, industry, physicians, and cooperatives. The availability of hospital insurance removed an important cost constraint from hospital charges. The ability of insurers to cope with ever-rising hospital costs by distributing relatively small premium increases over large numbers of subscribers opened the floodgates to hospital admissions. Expanding hospital services and relatively unrestrained reimbursement rates created an inflationary spiral that was to persist for decades.

In addition, medical advances and medical specialization encouraged hospitalization, and the hospital industry expanded to meet the demand. After World War II, the American Hospital Association (AHA) convinced Senators Lister Hill and Harold Burton to sponsor legislation that provided federal monies to the states to survey hospitals and other health care facilities and to plan and assist construction of additional facilities. The Hill–Burton Hospital Construction Act was signed as Public Law 79–75 in 1946 and became a major influence in the expansion of the hospital industry.[1] Over 4,600 projects to expand existing facilities or construct new ones were initiated within 20 years after its passage. That federal support of hospital construction was critically important to the location of hospitals in underserved rural areas.

Medicare and Medicaid

In 1966, the hospital industry was the recipient of another major legislative contribution to its fiscal well-being by the passage of Medicare, Title XVIII of the Social Security Act. The legislation provided the growing population of Americans over age 65 years with significant hospital and medical benefits. In one decisive legislative action, the large population of older Americans, the group most likely to need hospitalization, was ensured hospital care, and the hospitals were ensured to be reimbursed on the basis of "reasonable costs."

The companion program, Medicaid, Title XIX of the Social Security Act, was established at the same time to support medical and hospital care for persons classified as medically indigent. Unlike Medicare, Medicaid required the states to establish joint federal–state programs that covered persons receiving public assistance and, if they wished, others of low income. Because the states had broad discretion over eligibility, benefits, and reimbursement rates, the programs that developed differed widely among the 50 states.

Medicare, and to a lesser extent Medicaid, had enormous impact on hospitalization rates in the United States. In a little over 10 years after the implementation of Medicare, persons over 65 years old were spending well over twice as many days in the hospital as those aged 45–64 years.[1] Because the rising Medicare rates became the standards for establishing hospital reimbursement rates in general, Medicare probably did more to fuel the rising costs of hospital care than any other factor.

The Medicare and Medicaid programs also had another effect. Because these programs provided government funding for the hospital care of low-income population and older adults, they altered the long-standing nature or mission of hospitals by diminishing the traditional charitable or social role of those voluntary institutions. It was not long after the implementation of those programs that hospitals became increasingly focused on profit, maximizing the more lucrative activities, and closing or reducing services that operated at a loss. In the 1980s, hospitals along with most of U.S. industry became market oriented and aggressively enterprising. The monetary incentives built into the Medicare system favored entrepreneurial, short-term financial interests.

Rosemary Stevens, author of *In Sickness and in Wealth: American Hospitals in the Twentieth Century*, wrote this: "One effect was to bring hospitals into prominence as enterprises motivated by organizational self-interest, by the excitement of the game, by greed."[1] She concluded with this statement:

> Medicare and Medicaid, supposedly designed to promote egalitarianism, fostered sharp inequities in the health-care system while disarming criticism from low-paid American workers and the poverty population. The stage was set for today's struggles to rethink, once again, the American health-care system—and to redefine the relative roles of voluntarism, government, and business for the last few years of the twentieth century.[1]

Growth and Decline in Numbers of Hospitals

The number of hospitals in the United States increased from 178 in 1873 to 4,300 in 1909. In 1946, at the close of World War II, there were 6,000 American hospitals, with 3.2 beds available for every 1,000 persons.

That year, Congress passed the Hill–Burton Hospital Construction Act to fund expansion of the hospital system to achieve the goal of 4.5 beds per 1,000 persons.[2] The system grew thereafter to reach a high of approximately 7,200 acute care hospitals.

During the 1980s, however, medical advances and cost-containment measures moved many procedures that once required inpatient hospitalization to outpatient settings. Outpatient hospital visits increased by 40% with a resultant decrease in hospital admissions. Fewer admissions and shortened lengths of stay for patients resulted in a significant reduction in the number of hospitals and hospital beds. Health care reform efforts and the emergence of managed care as the major form of insurance for U.S. health care resulted in hospital closings and mergers that reduced the number of governmental and community-based hospitals in the United States to approximately 5,700.

Types of Hospitals

Acute care hospitals are distinguished from long-term care facilities such as nursing homes, rehabilitation centers, and psychiatric hospitals by the fact that the average length of stay for patients is less than 30 days. Such hospitals have one of three basic sponsorships:

1. Voluntary not-for-profit entities
2. Owned and managed by profit-making corporations
3. Public facilities, supported and managed by governmental jurisdictions

Hospitals may also be divided into teaching and nonteaching hospitals. Teaching hospitals are affiliated with medical schools and provide clinical education for medical students and medical and dental residents. They, and many hospitals not affiliated with medical schools, also provide clinical education for nurses, allied health personnel, and a wide variety of technical specialists.

According to the Association of American Medical Colleges, only about 6% of U.S. hospitals (about 400 hospitals) are teaching facilities affiliated with one or more of the allopathic and osteopathic medical schools in the United States.[3] Most teaching hospitals are voluntary not-for-profit institutions or government-sponsored public hospitals.

The most recently published survey of this country's hospitals conducted by the AHA concluded that there were 2,903 voluntary not-for-profit hospitals sponsored by religious groups or other community-based organizations. They constitute just over 50% of the 5,724 registered hospitals in the United States.[4]

They include large numbers of small community general hospitals and smaller numbers of large tertiary care facilities. These large tertiary care facilities are usually affiliated with medical schools. The presence of medical school faculty with strong research interests and the availability of medical residents to assist in the collection of clinical data put teaching hospitals in the forefront of clinical research on medical conditions and treatments.

The federal government, through the U.S. Department of Veterans Affairs (VA) or the U.S. Public Health Service, operates 208 public hospitals. In addition, state and local governments maintain over 1,000 public hospitals.[4] These public hospitals are usually large teaching hospitals with a heavy preponderance of economically disadvantaged patients.

Public hospitals in many localities deliver the fiscally problematic, but essential, community services that other hospitals are reluctant to provide. These high-cost, low-fiscal return services include sophisticated trauma centers, psychiatric emergency services, alcohol detoxification services, other substance abuse treatment, and burn treatment. In addition, there are 421 nonfederal psychiatric hospitals.[4]

Investor-owned, for-profit hospitals grew from a few physician-owned facilities before the 1965 Medicare and Medicaid legislation to 1,025 in 2011.[4] Most for-profit hospitals belong to one of the large hospital management companies that dominate the for-profit hospital network. An increasing number, however, are physician-owned specialty hospitals. Such hospitals usually limit their services to treatments in one of three major specialty categories: orthopedics, surgery, or cardiology.

Although these new specialty hospitals are typically upscale facilities with many patient amenities, they usually operate with greater efficiency and provide excellent care in their few targeted services. Nevertheless, they have raised a series of concerns about their performance and their effect on community hospitals.

First, it is clear that specialty hospitals treat the less complex, more profitable cases, leaving the more difficult, less profitable, or uninsured patients to be served by community hospitals. Second, because physician-owners of specialty hospitals profit directly by the value of services provided by their hospitals, there are concerns that clinical decisions may be influenced by financial incentives.[5]

Supporters of physician-owned specialty hospitals point out that the physician-owners take great pride in the quality of care provided in their hospitals, that they also work in community hospitals, and that their facilities enhance their communities by paying taxes as for-profit companies.[6]

The number of beds in not-for-profit, state and local government, and federal hospitals decreased in the last decade, whereas the much smaller number of beds in for-profit facilities increased slightly. The most recent annual survey by the AHA counted 924,333 staffed beds among all U.S. registered hospitals in the United States.[4]

Financial Condition of Hospitals

In the wake of pressures from managed care market penetration beginning in the 1990s, thousands of hospitals were involved in mergers, acquisitions, and other multihospital deals in an effort to capture and solidify market shares and gain economies of scale.

Hospitals' economic problems resulted from a combination of factors over which the hospitals had little control. The Balanced Budget Act of 1997, which reduced payments for Medicare patients below the costs of treating them, wreaked havoc on U.S. hospitals. At the same time, hospital changes were held in check by hard-bargaining managed care organizations. In this period, in contrast to the restraints on revenues, costs were rising at an unprecedented pace. Costly new technology, pharmaceuticals, and services, as well as inflation, combined with declining occupancy to significantly reduce operating margins. According to a survey by the AHA published in 2000, 90% of the responding hospitals reported serious financial problems that required cost-cutting measures, and many had reduced staff.[7] The development of private specialty hospitals and diagnostic centers owned by physicians, which compete with community hospitals for their most profitable services only added to the continuing losses of community hospitals.

Market reforms of the 2000s and impacts of the ACA continue to press hospitals forward into altered patterns of ownership, operation, and reimbursement. Ongoing changes and challenges are outlined and discussed in later sections of this chapter.

Academic Health Centers, Medical Education, and Specialization

Medical, dental, nursing, pharmacy, and allied health schools and their teaching hospitals are the principal sources of education and training for most health care providers. An academic health center is an accredited, degree-granting institution that consists of a medical school, one or more other professional schools, or programs such as dentistry, nursing, pharmacy, public health and allied health sciences that has an owned or affiliated relationship with a teaching hospital, health system, or other organized care provider.

Much of the basic and clinical research in medicine and other health care disciplines is conducted in these health centers and their related hospitals. The teaching hospitals usually provide the most technologically advanced care in their communities and also offer inpatient and ambulatory care for economically disadvantaged populations. Thus, the three objectives of academic health centers—education, research, and service—are fulfilled most adequately by teaching hospitals.

The influence of these health centers on health care during the last few decades has been extraordinary. The advances that occurred in the medical sciences and technology that resulted in the introduction of life-saving drugs, anesthetics, surgical procedures, and other therapies and the development and use of sophisticated computerized diagnostic techniques increased both the use and the costs of hospital services. This increased intervention resulted in increases in both the life expectancy of most Americans and the proportion of the gross national product devoted to health care; however, these advances also significantly expanded the knowledge base and performance skills required of physicians to practice up-to-date clinical medicine.

Academic health centers responded by increasing the number of physicians with in-depth expertise in increasingly narrow fields of clinical practice. Specialization and subspecialization grew, subdivided, and grew more. More and more physicians limited their activities to narrower and narrower fields of practice. In doing so, they greatly increased the overall technologic sophistication of hospital practice along with the number of costly consultations that take place among specialist hospital physicians; the amount of expensive equipment, supplies, and space maintained by hospitals to serve specialist needs; and, in general, the complexity of patient care. The contributions of highly specialized clinical practice to the quality of hospital care have been both extraordinarily beneficial and regrettably negative. Although the superspecialists of U.S. medicine have given the profession its justified reputation for heroic medical and surgical achievements, specialization also has fragmented and depersonalized patient care and produced a plethora of often questionable tests, procedures, and clinical interventions.

Academic health centers have contributed admirably to the advancement of medicine, and especially hospital-delivered medical and surgical care, but they have not brought their impressive expertise to bear effectively on solving delivery system problems that have plagued their industry. Rather, the commitments of academic medicine to high-technology research and patient care and its adherence to traditional organizational structures and professional roles have prevented it from taking the lead in correcting health care system problems that emanate from fragmented and piecemeal approaches to care delivery. As the technology of medicine advanced, population health and medical care diverged into the separate disciplines of public health and clinical medicine.[8] As a result, medical education and medical organizations in general did not position themselves to lead health care system reforms. As vast reforms with a population health focus begin to take shape, academic medicine is in the position of accommodation and faced with numerous challenges to prepare for ongoing changes.[9]

Hospital System of the Department of Veterans Affairs

The tax-supported, centrally directed Veterans Health Administration of the VA is the country's largest health care system and a significant component of America's medical education system. The VA owns and operates 153 hospitals, most of which are affiliated with medical schools. The VA also operates 135 nursing homes, 47 residential rehabilitation facilities, and over 900 outpatient clinics.[10] With its large number of hospitals and other facilities—over 12,000 full-time salaried physicians, over 900 dentists, and 33,000 nurses—the medical care program of the VA would be expected to be a prime target for the congressional cost cutters of large and expensive federal programs. With the conflicts in Iraq and Afghanistan, however, the VA escaped the competitive pressures of the rest of the system. Instead, with broad bipartisan political support, the VA has received an annual congressional appropriation consistently higher each year than requested in the president's budget. Apparently, the strong political advocacy for veterans in the United States restrains any congressional initiative to give up VA hospitals in favor of subsidizing the care of veterans in the private sector.

Like the rest of the hospital industry, the VA is reorganizing its facilities to lower costs, improve the quality of its care, and better integrate its patients throughout the system. Its major change has been the creation of 22 networks called Veterans Integrated Service Networks, each of which functions as a vertically integrated delivery system.[11]

An important part of the VA's organizational transition is its Health Services Research and Development Service. It works to improve the quality of health care for veterans by examining the impact of the organization, financing, and management of health services on their quality, cost, access, and outcomes. The latter activities are especially important because the VA is not only facing rising costs but also an influx of more severely traumatized patients and an aging and sicker veteran population of past wars.

Structure and Organization of Hospitals

The hospital organizational structure is a complex maze of committees, departments, personnel, and services. In addition to being a caring, people-oriented institution, it is at the same time a many-faceted, high-tech business. It operates just like any other large business, with a hierarchy of personnel, channels of authority and responsibility, and constant concern about its bottom line.

Likewise, the people who work in hospitals exhibit the same range of human characteristics as their counterparts in other businesses. Patients and their families trying to obtain the best possible results from the services of a hospital, therefore, should base their approach on the same principles they use in dealing with other service entities. They need to determine who is in charge, what services to expect from whom and when, with what results, and at what cost to them.

The following description of hospital structure and organization uses the voluntary not-for-profit community hospital as the example because this type of institution has historically provided the model for hospital organization. The direction, control, and governance of the hospital are divided among three influential entities: the medical staff, the administration, and the board of directors or trustees. The major operating divisions of a hospital represent areas of the hospital's functions. Although they may use different names, the usual units are medical, nursing, patient therapy, diagnosis, fiscal, human resources, hotel services, and community relations.

Medical Division

The medical staff is a formally organized unit within the larger hospital organization. The president or chief of staff is the liaison between the hospital administration and members of the medical staff. Typically, the medical staff consists primarily of medical physicians, but it also may include other doctoral-level professionals, such as dentists and psychologists.

A major role of the medical staff organization is to recommend to the hospital board of directors the appointment of physicians to the medical staff. The board of directors approves and grants various levels of hospital privileges to physicians. Such privileges commonly include the right to admit patients to the hospital, to perform surgery, and to provide consultation to other physicians on the hospital staff. Another medical staff function is to provide oversight and peer review of the quality of medical care in the hospital. It performs this function through a number of medical staff committees, which coordinate their efforts closely with the hospital's administration and committees of the hospital's board of directors. Additional roles of the hospital's board of directors in monitoring quality are discussed later in this chapter.

Members of the medical staff who have completed their training and are in practice are referred to as attending physicians. In addition, the hospital usually has a house staff of physicians who are engaged in post-medical school training programs under the supervision of attending staff members. These members of the house staff or residents rotate shifts to provide 24-hour coverage for the attending medical staff's patients in the specialty departments to which they are assigned.

There is no universal rule as to how a hospital's medical departments or divisions are organized. Most often, the types of practice of the hospital's medical staff determine the specialty components within the medical division. Medicine, surgery, obstetrics and gynecology, and pediatrics are usually major departments. In larger hospitals and in most teaching hospitals, the subspecialty areas of medical practice are represented by departments as well. In the internal medicine specialty, subspecialty departments might include cardiology or cardiac care, ophthalmology, urology, oncology, gastroenterology, pulmonary medicine, endocrinology, otolaryngology, and a variety of others. In the surgical area, subspecialties might include orthopedics, thoracic, neurosurgery, cardiac surgery, and plastic and reconstructive surgery. Each medical department or division in a hospital is headed by a physician department head or chairman who is charged with overseeing the practice and quality of medical services delivered in the department. In a teaching hospital, either the department head or another designated attending physician is responsible for coordinating the required educational experiences of medical students and residents.

Nursing Division

The nursing division usually comprises the single largest component of the hospital's organization. It is subdivided by the type of patient care delivered in the various medical specialties. These nursing units are composed of a number of patient beds grouped within a certain area to allow centralization of the special facilities, supplies, equipment, and personnel pertinent to the needs of patients with particular conditions. For example, the kinds of equipment and skills and the level of patient care needs vary considerably between an orthopedic unit and a medical intensive care unit.

A head nurse, often carrying the title of "nurse manager," has overall responsibility for all nursing care in his or her unit. Such care includes carrying out the attending physician's and house staff physician's orders for medications, diet, and various types of therapy. In addition, the nurse manager supervises the unit's staff, which may include nurses' aides and orderlies. The nurse manager is also responsible for coordinating all aspects of patient care, which may include services provided by other hospital units, such as the dietary department, physical therapy department, pharmacy, and laboratories. The nurse manager also has the responsibility of coordinating the services of departments such as social work, discharge planning, and pastoral care for the patients in the unit.

Because nursing services are required in the hospital at all times, staff is usually employed in three 8-hour shifts, although 12-hour shifts are increasing in popularity as a cost-saving measure by many hospitals as the total number of nurses employed with benefits can be reduced by that staffing pattern. Normally, the nurse manager of a unit works during the day shift, and two other members of the nursing staff assume what is referred to as charge duty on the other two shifts of the day. Charge nurses report to the nurse manager.

A nursing supervisor may have management responsibility for a number of nursing units. These nursing supervisors in turn report to a member of the hospital's administration, who is usually a vice president for nursing or an assistant administrator.

It is also common to find an individual with the title of ward clerk or unit secretary on each nursing unit. The ward clerk assists the nurse manager with paperwork and helps to schedule and coordinate the other hospital services related to patient care.

Allied Health Professionals

Not as well known as the physicians and nurses who are central to the care and treatment of patients in hospitals is the wide array of personnel who provide other hospital services that support the work of the physicians and nurses and the others who operate behind the scenes to make the facility run smoothly.

Staff members in an increasingly diverse array of health care disciplines are classified as allied health personnel. These professionals support, complement, or supplement the functions of physicians, dentists, nurses, and other professionals in delivering health care to patients. They contribute to environmental management, health promotion, and disease prevention.

Allied health occupations encompass as many as 200 types of health careers within 80 different allied health professions, and advancing medical technology is likely to create the need for even more personnel with highly specialized training and relatively unique skills. Those who are responsible for highly specialized or technical services that have a significant impact on health care are prepared for practice through a wide variety of educational programs offered at colleges and universities.

The range of allied health professions may be best understood by classifying them by the functions they serve in the delivery of health care. Some disciplines may serve more than one of these functions:

1. *Laboratory technologists and technicians* play a major role in the diagnosis of disease, the monitoring of physiologic function, and the effectiveness of medical interventions. Medical technologists, nuclear medical technologists, radiologic technologists, and cytotechnologists are but a few of the specialists on whom hospitals depend.

2. *Allied health practitioners of the therapeutic sciences* are essential to the treatment and rehabilitation of patients with a wide variety of injuries and medical conditions. Examples include physical, occupational, and speech therapists and physician assistants.

3. *Behavioral scientists* are crucial to the social, psychological, and patient education activities related to health maintenance, disease prevention, and accommodation to disability. Professionals in this category include social workers, health educators, and rehabilitation counselors in mental health, alcoholism, and drug abuse.

4. *Specialist support service personnel* include those who perform administrative and management functions and others with special expertise that often work closely with the actual providers of patient care. Health information administrators, formerly called medical record administrators, food service administrators, dietitians, and nutritionists are examples of personnel in this category.

The following descriptions of some of the key hospital services reflect the close functional relationships among the various kinds of highly specialized individuals required to staff hospital services.

Diagnostic Services

Every hospital either maintains or contracts with laboratories to perform a wide array of tests to help physicians diagnose illness or injury and monitor the progress of treatment. One such laboratory is the pathology laboratory, which examines and analyzes specimens of body tissues, fluids, and excretions to aid in diagnosis and treatment. These laboratories are usually supervised by the hospital's pathologist, who is a physician specialist.

Grouped under the rubric "diagnostic imaging services," in addition to basic radiographic images (x-rays), a wide array of more sophisticated imaging equipment that incorporates computer technology is found in these departments, including ultrasonography, computed tomography, magnetic resonance imaging, and positron emission tomography (PET). Unlike radiograph technology, which is limited to providing images of the body's anatomic structures, these imaging advances have unique abilities to visualize structures in several planes and, with PET, even quantify complex physiologic processes occurring in the human body. Thus, they add immeasurably to the understanding and treatment of major ailments, including heart disease, stroke, cancer, epilepsy, and other conditions.

A variety of other diagnostic services also may be available through specific medical specialty or subspecialty departments, such as cardiology and neurology. For example, a noninvasive cardiac laboratory administers cardiac stress testing to assess a patient's heart function during exercise. Obstetricians commonly use an imaging capability called ultrasonography to visualize the unborn fetus.

Rehabilitation Services

Rehabilitation or patient support departments provide specialized care to assist patients in achieving optimal physical, mental, and social functioning after resolution of an illness or injury. One such department is physical medicine, where diagnosis and treatment of patients with physical injuries or disabilities are conducted. This department is headed by a specialist physician called a physiatrist who usually works with a team of physical therapists, occupational therapists, and speech therapists. Other health-related specialists, such as social workers, may provide additional services to support the rehabilitation of patients with complex problems.

Other Patient Support Services

The hospital pharmacy purchases and dispenses all drugs used to treat hospitalized patients. The department is headed by a licensed pharmacist, who is also responsible for pharmacy technicians and others who work under his or her supervision.

Among other functions, the social services department helps patients about to be discharged to arrange financial support and coordinate needed community-based services. Generally, the social services department assists patients and their families to achieve the best possible social and domestic environment for the patients' care and recovery. Such services are available to all hospital patients and their families.

Discharge planning services (discussed in more detail later in this chapter) may or may not be a part of the social services department. Frequently, staffing includes both nurses and social workers who are responsible for planning posthospital patient care in conjunction with the patients and their families. The discharge planning department becomes involved when the patient requires referral for one or more community services or placement in a special care facility after discharge.

Nutritional Services

The nutritional services department includes food preparation facilities and personnel for the provision of inpatient meals, food storage, and purchasing and catering for hospital events. It may also operate a cafeteria for employees and, in larger hospitals, may sponsor educational programs for student dietitians. An important function of this department's staff is educating patients on dietary needs and restrictions. This department usually is headed by a chief dietitian who has a degree in nutritional science, and it may be staffed by any number of other dietitians and clinical nutrition specialists with specific expertise in dietary assessment and food preparation.

Administrative Departments

Hospitals contain other professional units that provide a wide variety of nonmedical services essential to the management of the hospital's physical plant and business services. Patients are certainly aware of two of them: the admissions department, through which a hospital stay is initiated, and the business office, through which a hospital stay is terminated. These units are two of the many components of the hospital's complex management structure.

The general administrative services of the hospital are headed by a chief executive officer or president who has the day-to-day responsibility for managing all hospital business. He or she is the highest ranking administrative officer and oversees an array of administrative departments concerned with financial operations, public relations, and personnel. Most larger hospitals have a chief operating officer, who oversees the operation of specific departments, and a chief financial officer, who directs the many and varied fiscal activities of the hospital. Those key administrative officers are commonly positioned as corporate vice presidents. The large number of employees and the wide array of individual skills required to staff a hospital competently call for a personnel or human resources department with highly specialized labor expertise. That department is also usually headed by a vice president for human resources. Because nursing is such a large component of the hospital's service operations, the larger facilities also maintain a chief nursing executive at the vice presidential level.

Hotel Services

Hotel services are generally associated with the hospitality functions common to hotels. They include building maintenance, security, laundry, television, and telephone services.

Information Technology's Impact on Hospitals

Although overall rates of adoption of health information technology throughout the health care industry have been slow, hospitals have implemented technologies at faster rates than physician offices. A recent survey conducted by the AHA found that the percentage of U.S. hospitals that adopted health information technology, specifically electronic health record (EHR) capability more than doubled from 16% to 35% between 2009 and 2011.[12]

In the past, hospitals were primarily motivated to adopt new health information technology to lower costs, reduce medical errors, and meet The Joint Commission requirements.[13] The technology allowed hospitals to reduce information duplication and improve the utilization of laboratory and radiology results.[14] Administratively, new health information technology increased the efficiency of coding and billing[15,16] and provided health care personnel with quicker access to patient records.[17]

In 2004, President Bush signed an executive order that called for "the development and nationwide implementation of an interoperable health information technology infrastructure to improve efficiency, reduce medical errors, raise the quality of care, and provide better information for patients, physicians, and other health care providers."[18] The long-range sequence of goals has been to establish:

1. Electronic medical records in medical offices and hospitals
2. Regional health information organizations for information analysis and exchange
3. Statewide information networks for data mining, knowledge gains, and information exchange
4. A national information network for public health monitoring and population statistics

Congress has continued to encourage health information technology with a steady flow of bills promoting a national health information network, overall health information technology adoption, physician grants for electronic medical records purchases, and, recently, the HITECH Trust Act. Under this act, the Centers for Medicare and Medicaid Services (CMS) are providing reimbursement incentives for eligible professionals and hospitals that are successful in becoming "meaningful users" of certified EHR technology. "Meaningful use" was defined as "not only the adoption of the technology, but the implementation and exchange of health information to improve clinical decision making at the point of care." The incentive payments began in 2011 with penalties under Medicare for noncompliance beginning in 2015.

As of mid-2012, over 4,000 hospitals had enrolled in the Medicare and Medicaid EHR Incentive Programs and eligible hospitals had received almost $5 billion in "meaningful use" incentive payments.[19] Of additional note, 85% of hospitals have reported that by 2015 they intend to take advantage of the incentive payments made available through the Medicare and Medicaid EHR Incentive Programs.[12]

Complexity of the System

Almost three-fourths of U.S. hospitals employ more than 1,000 workers.[20] Major hospital systems may have thousands of employees and an accompanying maze of communication challenges. The newer diagnostic and therapeutic methods that are increasingly effective are also increasingly complex.

Thus, even this very limited description of the hospital's complex structure and organization should make it clear that with so many different kinds of employees and so many interrelated systems and functions, it is a small wonder that hospitals function as well as they do. With the multitude of tasks performed every day by the hundreds of employees in a busy hospital, misunderstandings and information breakdowns in patient care are inevitable. In acknowledgment of this fact, the majority of this country's hospitals have patient representatives, sometimes called patient advocates, to serve as ombudspersons for the patients. They are prepared to intervene on behalf of the patients in a wide variety of situations. Contact information for those patient representatives is usually provided to patients in materials at admission or left conspicuously in patients' rooms.

Types and Roles of Patients

In the early development of hospitals, the patient was considered an unavoidable burden to society. In its mercy, society provided the hospital as a refuge. Patients receiving this charity were expected to be grateful for the shelter and nursing care and even for the opportunity to lend their bodies and illnesses for medical students' instruction and practice.

By 1900 proper training in nursing, effective anesthetic agents, modern methods of antisepsis and sterilization, and other medical advances had revolutionized hospital practices. Hospitals changed from merely supplying food, shelter, and meager medical care to the unfortunate needy and contagious to providing skilled medical, surgical, and nursing care to everyone; however, the belief persisted that patients in the hospital, removed from their usual social environment, were in a dependent relationship with charitable authorities. Remnants of the idea that these professionals have the knowledge and authority to decide what is best for grateful and uncomplaining patients have persisted to this day, regardless of the expense to the patient or the merit of the services.

Unfortunately, the behavior of many patients and their families has been conditioned to reinforce this philosophy. In the hospital otherwise assertive, independent individuals tend to assume a passive and dependent "sick role." Numerous sociologic studies of patients' behavior have concluded that the patients who behave in the traditional submissive sick role help to preserve the authoritarian attitude of health care providers that most health care consumers now consider patronizing and inappropriate.[21]

Rights and Responsibilities of Hospitalized Patients

Patients in hospitals have individual rights, many of which are protected by state statutes and regulations. The constitution of the United States and, in particular, its Bill of Rights is not suspended when a citizen enters a hospital. In fact, since 1972 the AHA has published a "Statement on a Patient's Bill of Rights" that is displayed prominently in every hospital in the country. In addition, hospitals are required by their accrediting body to make this information known to every patient admitted. Very importantly, the statement recognizes that the hospital, in addition to the physician, has a responsibility for the patient's welfare. In fact, the ultimate responsibility for everything that happens within the hospital, including the medical care provided, lies with the hospital institution and its board of directors.

Many hospitals, other institutions, and government agencies have modified the language of the original AHA Statement on a Patient's Bill of Rights to represent more accurately their individual interpretations of their responsibilities or to better communicate with special populations. In addition to posting these statements on the walls of the facility, hospitals also distribute their modified versions under their own organization title with the admission documents provided to patients.

The following description of major patients' rights is a synthesis of the statements posted by several hospitals. Patients have the right to:

1. Receive respectful and considerate treatment, including respect for their personal privacy, during examinations, tests, and all forms of interaction with their physicians, staff members, and others involved in their care.
2. Know the names and titles of all individuals providing their care and the name of the physician responsible.
3. Complete and understandable explanations of their diagnosis, treatment, and prognosis. They also have the right to designate another individual to receive such explanations on their behalf.
4. Receive from the physician all the information necessary to give informed consent before any procedure or treatment. Such

information should include a description of the procedure or treatment, the estimated period of convalescence, the risks involved, the risk of not accepting the treatment or procedure, and any alternative options.

5. Request and receive consultation on their diagnosis and treatment or obtain a second opinion.

6. Set limits on the scope of treatment that they will permit or refuse treatment and be informed of the consequences of such refusal.

7. Leave the hospital, unless unlawful, even against the advice of their physicians and receive an explanation of their responsibilities in exercising that right.

8. Request and receive information and assistance in discharging financial obligations to the hospital, and review a complete bill, regardless of the source of payment.

9. Access their records on demand and to have access to someone capable of explaining anything that is confusing or difficult to understand (since April 2004, a requirement of the federal Health Insurance Portability and Accountability Act law for hospitals, physicians, and clinics).

10. Receive assistance in planning and obtaining necessary support after discharge.

Patients are also expected to assume certain reciprocal individual responsibilities. Patients are obligated to act responsibly toward physicians and hospitals by cooperating with all reasonable requests for personal and family information. It is to their own benefit that patients inform medical or hospital personnel if they do not understand or do not wish to follow instructions. If a patient would like a family member or other advocate to be involved in treatment decisions, that individual should be identified to the physician and the hospital, and contact information should be provided.

It is also incumbent on patients to recognize that hospitals are highly stressful institutional settings and that other patients, as well as the hospital personnel, deserve consideration and respect. In no other institutional setting are individual rights at greater risk of being compromised than in a hospital; however, the risks do not arise from a purposeful disregard for patients by physicians or the hospital staff or from their individual or collective determination to subject patients to treatment against their will.

The personal integrity of patients may be unintentionally violated as a result of certain institutional circumstances and factors unique to the hospital setting. These institutional circumstances arise from the fact that the hospital, like most large complex organizations, has a life of its own, which pulses with an infinite array of daily scheduled events that pervade every aspect of its functioning. There are schedules for changing beds, bathing patients, serving meals, administering medications, obtaining specimens, providing therapy, checking vital signs, performing surgery, housekeeping, admitting, discharging, doing rounds, receiving visitors, performing examinations, and, finally, preparing patients for the night.

The vast number of tasks that evolve from the care needs of up to several hundred ill people each day requires the planning and scheduling of every activity if they are all to be accomplished in a timely manner. The pressure of the daily schedule often makes it difficult for hospital personnel to pay attention to the special needs of individual patients. Even though a patient's particular schedule of tests, procedures, treatments, and examinations is uniquely related to his or her condition and the physician's orders, it also is influenced by the needs of fellow patients and the schedules of the physicians, and numerous others involved directly or indirectly in the patient's care.

A patient's treatment may also be modified by the schedule of institutional events, which although unrelated to his or her treatment can have an impact on the care delivered. Such institutional events include inspections, grand rounds, nursing in-services, unplanned staffing shortages, and an array of technical problems with any of the hundreds of the pieces of medical equipment required by the functions of a sophisticated hospital.

A second reason why patient rights may be in jeopardy in the hospital setting is that physicians are likely to spend only a few minutes a day with each patient. This means that patients depend heavily on the nursing staff and other support personnel for the medical and personal care they should receive. Ideally, nurses are able to continuously monitor each patient's condition and alert the physician to any change in a patient's status; however, the number of patients for whom a nurse is responsible and the number of tasks that the nurse is required to perform during a single work shift make it extremely difficult, or sometimes impossible, to fulfill that obligation. In addition, the increasing number of caregivers involved with each patient provides additional opportunities for failures of communication and subsequent mistakes in the treatment programs for individual patients. Although hospitals continuously strive to develop fail-safe systems to protect patients against the possibility of human error in the delivery of their care, mistakes can happen. One patient can receive a medication intended for another. The report of a laboratory test can get lost and require the repeat of a procedure. A physician's instructions can be overlooked, and the patient may be deprived of something that he or she was supposed to receive or the patient may continue receiving something that was supposed to be stopped. A nurse's note alerting the physician to a change in the patient's condition may be missed, and the patient may fail to receive something that he or she requires.

Progressive hospital systems encourage patients to recognize their vulnerability during hospitalization and urge them or their family members to function as active participants in, rather than passive recipients or observers of, hospital care. In addition, state health departments, which license hospitals, ensure the right of patients to make complaints about hospital care and services. Hospitals are required by law to investigate patient complaints and respond to them. In fact, a hospital must provide a written response if a patient so requests.

Informed Consent and Second Opinions

No description of the structure and processes of hospitals is complete without mention of the very important personal decisions regarding medical care that patients are asked to make, often under circumstances that are stressful if not intimidating. A cornerstone of the personal rights of hospitalized patients is the right to know:

- What is being done to them and why
- What the procedure entails
- How the procedure can be expected to benefit them
- What risks or consequences are associated with a procedure
- What is the probability of risks and consequences

In short, in almost all cases the doctrine of informed consent ensures that patients have ultimate control over their own bodies. This doctrine, first recognized legally in 1914, has been reaffirmed repeatedly over the years and is now generally recognized to encompass not only all the previously mentioned elements but also the right to receive information about alternative forms of treatment to the one recommended.

A physician has no legal right to substitute his or her judgment for the patient's in matters of consent. This principle means that the patient has the absolute right to reject or question a physician's recommendation. For these reasons, it is considered appropriate for patients to obtain second opinions to satisfy concerns about the necessity for various tests and other procedures. Many insurers now require a confirming second opinion before agreeing to pay for certain surgical or other procedures. Medicare and many private health plans cover most of the costs of second opinions.[22,23]

Diagnosis-Related Group Hospital Reimbursement System

Until 1983, a patient stayed in the hospital until the physician decided that he or she was well enough for discharge. Each hospital monitored its own situation through a utilization review committee composed of physicians and administrators who reviewed the lengths of stay of hospitalized patients to ensure that neither the quality of care nor the efficiency of the hospital was being compromised by physicians' decisions.

During the 1970s and early 1980s, however, the cost of hospital care rose so fast that health insurance companies and corporations that paid huge insurance premiums to cover the hospitalization costs of their workers increased the pressure on federal agencies to find a way to stem the rising tide of hospital expenses.

Two factors made change imperative. First, hospitals were paid a set amount for each day that a patient stayed in the facility. That amount was determined retrospectively by determining what it cost per day per bed to operate the hospital the year before. Under that arrangement, the hospital had no incentive to keep costs down. In fact, if it did, it would receive a smaller daily reimbursement rate the next year than if it spent freely. Furthermore, it became clear to the government and the insurance companies that they were paying not only for uncontrolled costs per hospital day but also for hospital days that were not necessary. On a national scale hundreds of thousands of hospital days that did not benefit the patients, at a cost of several hundred dollars per day, amounted to a huge and valueless financial burden. Hospital costs were forcing the Medicare program to exceed all financial projections.

Second, there was another concern. Not only were unnecessarily long hospital stays expensive but they also could be dangerous to patients' health. Patients are exposed to infections in hospitals that they would not face at home. In addition, many older patients lose the ability to do some of the basic activities of daily living, such as dress, feed, or toilet themselves, during a long stay in a hospital. Those patients emerge from the hospital less able to function than when they went in. Shortened stays in hospitals, especially for older patients, can often be beneficial as well as less expensive.

In 1983, the federal government radically changed the way hospitals would be reimbursed for the costs of treating Medicare patients. The new payment system, referred to as diagnosis-related groups (DRGs), was designed to provide hospitals with a financial incentive to discharge patients as soon as possible. As a prospective payment system, the patient's diagnosis predetermines how much the hospital will be paid, and the hospital knows that amount in advance. The payment is a set amount based on the average cost of treating that particular illness or condition. If the patient requires less care or fewer days in the hospital than the DRG average, the hospital is paid the average cost regardless, and the hospital makes money. If the patient requires a longer stay or more care than the DRG average, the hospital loses money.

This carrot-and-stick system was adopted quickly by almost all states and insurance companies and became the standard for insurance reimbursement of hospital costs. It quickly changed hospital behavior. In addition, medical staff became much more conservative about ordering tests and procedures of marginal value in diagnosis and treatment. In most cases, the incentive to discharge patients as soon as possible did not result in negative consequences for patients.[24]

Discharge Planning

The hospital is responsible for discharge planning functions to help patients arrange for safe and appropriate accommodations after a hospital stay. Using information provided by the patient or the patient's family, a discharge planner must see to it that the patient who needs follow-up services obtains them. The planner must then help make the necessary specific arrangements. If the patient requires a transfer to another level of institutional care, such as a nursing home, it is the responsibility of the discharge planner to arrange that transfer before the patient can be discharged from the hospital.

The hospital's financial incentive to discharge patients as soon as possible should never cause patients to be discharged before they are medically ready to leave and before arrangements have been made to ensure that they will receive the necessary posthospital care. Medicare-covered patients who believe that either of these two conditions will not be met by their anticipated discharge date have the right to appeal that date. A hospital's discharge notice must include instructions on how a Medicare-covered patient can have the hospital's decision reviewed by a Medicare quality improvement organization (QIO). A QIO's function under contract with the federal government is to ensure that hospitals and physicians follow Medicare rules. Every geographic area in the United States is covered by a federally designated QIO. A QIO may reverse the decision to discharge and require Medicare to cover the costs of additional hospital days with evidence that the patient is in need of continuing hospital care. Medicare also provides a mechanism to appeal the QIO's decision.[25]

Post-DRG and Managed Care Early Market Reforms

With consumers, employers, government, and commercial payers intensifying their demands for lower costs, higher quality, better access, and more information about outcomes, in the 1990s, most hospitals undertook a series of competitive efforts to improve their market positions. Many engaged in mergers and consolidations intended to effect economies of scale and acquire stronger positions to negotiate with managed care organizations and other payers. Others, in communities with excess hospital capacity, either closed or converted to other uses, such as ambulatory or long-term care facilities.

Between the inception of DRGs in the mid-1980s and 2000s, approximately 2,000 U.S. hospitals closed, hospital inpatient days declined by one-third, and many hospitals consolidated into local, regional, or national multihospital systems. By 2001, more than half of U.S. hospitals operated as part of merged multihospital systems in contrast to just over 30% functioning within such multihospital systems in 1979.[26] Furthermore, with an increasing number of medical services occurring in ambulatory settings, hospitals reduced inpatient capacity and refocused their service efforts on intensive care and other inpatient essentials.[27]

One of the consequences of high-technology hospital care was the industrialization of patient care activities. The corporate thinking that swept the hospital industry in the 1970s and 1980s brought production line concepts to what formerly had been very personal, high-touch, rather than high-tech, relationships between patients and caregivers, primarily nurses.

Rather than being patient oriented, the care became task oriented, with every chore identified and delegated to the person at the lowest skill level who was capable of carrying it out. The result for patients was a succession of relatively anonymous caregivers, and none of whom had a knowledgeable relationship with individual patients. Responsibility and accountability for the total care of patients became increasingly diffuse. Opportunities for patients to fall into the cracks between the many caregivers increased, and more midlevel managers were necessary to oversee operations. Any questionable gains in efficiency were achieved at the costs of patient satisfaction, communication, and personal care.

Patient satisfaction studies reflected an increase in patient complaints about the loss of identity, dignity, and respect for them as individuals that characterized their hospital stay. For most, the lack of communication between hospital staff, including physicians and the patients, and their families was the most irritating aspect of the hospital experience.

After an extensive survey of over 6,000 hospital patients and 2,000 individuals who accompanied patients during their hospital stays as well as research drawn from field visits and focus groups, the Picker/Commonwealth Program for Patient-Centered Care, established in 1987, was able to identify a series of patient care failings common among hospitals.[28] One devastating research finding was that as many as 20% of patients concluded that no one was in charge of their hospital care.[29] Clearly, advances in medical care and the industrialization of many, if not most, hospitals caused the medical system to lose touch with its essential constituency—its patients—and its essential mission to serve their needs.[30]

The trend has moved away from the industrial model of hospital care that eroded public trust and confidence in hospital care and toward small team responsibility for the quality of patient services. To attract patients who now have more options, hospitals focus on friendlier staff, better food, and more amenities. Many hospitals have eliminated visiting hour restrictions and invite patients' visitors to stay as long as they like. Hospitals even accommodate visitors who stay the night with reclining chairs and delivered breakfasts.[31]

Horizontal Integration

Under the general business definition, horizontally integrated organizations are aggregations that produce the same goods or services. They may be separately or jointly owned and governed, operated as subsidiary corporations of a parent organization, or exist in a variety of other legal or quasi-legal relationships. According to Roger Kropf[32]:

> In the hospital industry, horizontal integration was viewed as potentially advantageous because a chain of hospitals might be able to purchase supplies and services at a volume discount, would be able to hire specialized staff at the corporate level to increase expertise, would be able to raise capital less expensively on the securities markets, and would be able to market hospital services under a single brand name in a number of communities.

Both for-profit and not-for-profit hospitals engaged in horizontal integration in an effort to meet the economic imperatives of the changing industry climate. The horizontal integration strategy spawned large numbers of hospital mergers and acquisitions and significant growth in the number of multihospital systems during the 1980s. As the trend in inpatient utilization and lengths of stay continued their declines throughout the 1980s, managed care organizations and other large purchasers of health care were increasing demands for the availability of comprehensive, continuous care housed within discrete, accountable systems. For this and other reasons, horizontal integration as a primary strategic initiative declined in favor.

The initial wave of hospital consolidations crested in the mid-1990s and a period of relative calm ensued over the next decade.[33] However, anticipating effects of new health care reform measures, the pace of both mergers and acquisitions has quickened rapidly since 2002.[33] As is discussed later in this chapter, in communities across the United States, consolidations of facilities, staff, and other resources of previously separate organizations are viewed as critical to survival in the reformed system.

Vertical Integration

Vertically integrated organizations are ones that operate a variety of business entities, each of which is related to the other. In health care, a vertically integrated system includes several service components, each of which addresses some dimension of a population's health care needs. The system may be fully comprehensive, with a complete continuum of services ranging from prenatal to end-of-life care. Other systems may contain some, but not all, of the services required by a population. A fully comprehensive vertically integrated system in its ideal form includes all facilities, personnel, and technologic resources to render the complete continuum of care, which comprises (1) all outpatient primary care and specialty diagnostic and therapeutic services, (2) inpatient medical and surgical services, (3) short- and long-term rehabilitative services, (4) long-term chronic institutional and in-home care, and (5) terminal care. Such a system also includes all required support services such as social work and health education. In theory, vertically integrated systems offer attractive benefits to their sponsoring organizations, patients, physicians, and other providers, as well as payers.

Sponsors of vertically integrated organizations gain the advantage of an increased market share across a mixture of high-profit, loss-generating, and break-even revenue sources. They benefit from an increased likelihood of retaining patients for many or all their service needs. In addition, they are advantageously positioned to negotiate with managed care organizations by ensuring the availability of comprehensive, continuous care for an insured population at competitive prices. For patients, the most obvious benefit is continuity of care throughout the various system components and improved case management. Physicians and other providers benefit from both greater certainty about the flow of patients to their practices and improved ease of referrals. Managed care organizations and other large purchasers view integrated organizations favorably because of the relative ease of negotiating pricing with one organization instead of several. In addition, quality monitoring, patient case management, and physician and other provider activity can be managed and monitored more efficiently when they are all part of the same organization. Vertical integration is a cornerstone of the seamless process of patient care sought in the reformed health care system.[34]

Quality of Hospital Care

It has always been easier to evaluate the quality of the medical care provided in hospitals than that provided in medical offices or other delivery sites because of the availability of comprehensive medical records and other sources of clinical information, systematically collected and stored for later recovery. The definition of quality, however, derives from both various operational factors and the measures or indicators of quality selected and the value judgments attached to them. For many years, quality was defined as "the degree of conformity with preset standards" and encompassed all the elements, procedures, and consequences of individual patient–provider encounters. Most often, however, the standards against which care was judged were implicit rather than explicit and existed only in the minds of peer evaluators.

The peer review technique had both benefits and failings. A common peer review quality assurance process used in hospitals until the 1970s was the chart audit. Periodically, an audit committee made up of several providers appointed by the hospital medical staff would review a small sample of patient records and make judgments as to the quality of care provided.

Such audits were ineffective for several reasons. First, the evaluators used internalized or implicit standards to make qualitative judgments. Second, there was no rational basis for chart selection that would permit the evaluators to extrapolate the sample findings to the broader patient population. Third, even if deficiencies were identified, the auditors were reluctant to take corrective action because their deficient colleagues might be on the next audit committee reviewing their patient care.

Avedis Donabedian of the University of Michigan made an important contribution to quality-of-care studies by defining the three basic components of medical care—structure, process, and outcome. Structural components are the qualifications of the providers, the physical facility, equipment, and other resources, and the characteristics of the organization and its financing.[35] Until the 1960s, the contribution of structure to quality was the primary, if not the only, quality assurance mechanism in health care. Traditionally, the health care system relied on credentialing mechanisms, such as licensure, registration, and certification by professional societies and specialty boards, to ensure the quality of clinical care.

Hospital reviews for accreditation by the Joint Commission were also based almost exclusively on structural criteria. Judgments were made about physical facilities, the equipment, the ratios of professional staff to patients, and the qualifications of the various personnel. The underlying assumption of structural quality reviews was that the better the facilities and the qualifications of the providers, the better the quality of the care rendered.

The past focus on structural criteria assumed quite erroneously that enough was known about the relationship of the structural aspects of care to its processes and outcomes to identify the critical or appropriate structural indicators. It was much later that hospital accreditation involved process criteria and, more recently, outcomes.

The process components are what occur during the encounters between patients and providers. Process judgments include what was done, how appropriate it was, and how well performed, as well as what was omitted that should have been done. The assumption underlying the use of process criteria is that the quality of the actions taken during patient encounters determines or influences the outcomes.

The outcomes of care are all the things that do or do not happen as a result of the medical intervention. Only recently has quality assurance in the hospital field focused on the relationships among structure, process, and outcomes. In the past, it had always been argued by providers that so many different variables influence the outcomes of medical care that it is inappropriate and unfair to providers to attribute patient outcomes solely to medical interventions. That argument was dismissed, however, with the introduction of computerized information systems and sophisticated analytical techniques that permit the collection and analysis of data on most or all the potential intervening influences and allow the findings to be adjusted for patient differences. Now, quality-of-care data are routinely standardized to account for age, gender, severity of illness, accompanying conditions, and other variables that might influence outcomes.

Variations in Medical Care

In 1973 two researchers, John Wennberg and Alan Gittlesohn, published what would be the first of a series of papers documenting the variations in the amounts and types of medical care provided to patients with the same diagnoses living in different geographic areas.[36] Those publications emphasized that the amount and cost of hospital treatment in a community had more to do with the number, specialties, and individual preferences of the physicians than the medical conditions of the patients.

With persistent concerns about improving the quality of hospital care and containing soaring costs, various groups formed to survey and report on the quality of hospital care. Chief among them has been the Leapfrog Group. It was founded in 2000 by the Business Roundtable with support from The Robert Wood Johnson Foundation. Members include more than 160 Fortune 500 corporations and other large private and public sector health benefits purchasers who represent more than 36 million enrollees.

The Leapfrog Group fields the Leapfrog Hospital Quality and Safety Survey, a voluntary online survey that tracks hospitals' progress toward implementing all 30 of the safety practices endorsed by the National Quality Forum. The Leapfrog Website[1] displays each hospital's results and is updated each month with data from additional hospitals; anyone can review the results at no charge. Leapfrog has also compiled the first free online database of programs across the country that offer financial or nonfinancial rewards and incentives for improved performance.[37]

Hazards of Hospitalization

Medical errors have been a serious problem in hospitals for years, but improving patient safety did not become a serious national concern until recently. Although those in the health professions and more knowledgeable members of the public have long been aware of the error-prone nature of hospital care, it was not until the November 1999 release of a report prepared by the prestigious National Academy of Science's Institute of Medicine (IOM) on medical mistakes that the magnitude of the risks to patients receiving hospital care became common public knowledge.

By extrapolating the findings of several well-conducted studies of adverse events occurring in hospitals to the 33.5 million hospital admissions in the United States during 1997, the IOM report concluded that as few as 44,000 and as many as 98,000 deaths occur annually because of medical errors.[38] The report put the magnitude of the problem in the context of comparable concerns by noting that more people die from medical errors each year than motor vehicle accidents or breast cancer and that medication errors alone kill more people than workplace injuries.

---

1. www.leapfroggroup.org.

Errors are defined as "the failure to complete a planned action as intended or the use of a wrong to achieve an aim."[38] Those errors may be attributed to failures in diagnostic, treatment, or surgical procedures; selection or doses of medication; delays in diagnosis or treatment; and a host of other procedural lapses, including communication or equipment failures.

There is general agreement that system deficiencies are the most important factor in the problem and not incompetent or negligent physicians and other caregivers. Modern medicine with its highly effective but extremely complex diagnostic and therapeutic methods can be formidably risky. Extensive surgical procedures are error prone, as are increasingly powerful therapeutic drugs. Miscommunication among overstressed employees is common in busy hospitals. With so many steps and so many people involved in the care of hospital patients, the potential for error grows with every patient day, and small lapses develop into large tragedies.[38]

The IOM report presented a series of recommendations to improve the quality of care over a 10-year period with a comprehensive strategy for reducing medical errors through a combination of technologic, policy, regulatory, and financial strategies intended to make health care safer. Better use of information technology such as bedside computers, avoidance of similar-sounding and look-alike names and packages of medications, and standardization of treatment policies and protocols would help to avoid confusion and reliance on memory and handwritten communications. The most controversial of the recommendations, however, was the call for a nationwide mandatory reporting system that would require states to report all "adverse events that result in death or serious harm".[38]

The health care system and its practicing physicians need to make radical changes in cultural attitudes and individual prerogatives, however, before the necessary system changes and reporting requirements can be institutionalized. The IOM report, which moved awareness of the magnitude of medical errors from the anonymity of the hospitals to the nation's media and subsequently to the halls of Congress, has already produced vociferous debate over issues of mandatory or voluntary reporting. Questions of liability, confidentiality, and avoidance of punishment must be settled before any mandatory reporting legislation can be passed. In the meantime, other recommendations for more focus on patient safety by professional groups, medical societies, health care licensing organizations, and hospital administrations could be followed with more immediate benefits.

Nurse Shortage Staffing Crisis

Over the past two decades, three factors combined to drive a hospital nursing shortage to crisis proportions. First, increasing dissatisfaction with staffing reductions, overwork, and inadequate time to maintain the quality of patient care drove nurses out of hospitals into early retirement or into home or ambulatory care. Second, with the heavy work responsibilities of nursing as a career and many other more attractive options, fewer young people were entering the nursing field. Last, aging of the nurse workforce accelerated staffing losses. With one-third of the employed nurses over 50 years of age, only an increasing pool of new nurses entering the pipeline could rescue hospital nursing from its critical shortage.[39]

The consequences are serious. There is increasing evidence that nurse staffing is related to patient outcomes in both medical and surgical cases. Studies indicate a direct link between the number of registered nurses and the time they spend with patients and the number of serious complications and patient deaths. Low nurse staffing increases the likelihood that some patients will suffer pneumonia, shock and cardiac arrest, and gastrointestinal bleeding, and some patients will die as a result.[40]

Although the nursing shortage is projected to be far from over, the situation has improved. In the last few years pay increases, relatively high national unemployment rates, and private initiatives aimed at encouraging men and women to become nurses have resulted in an increase in the supply of employable registered nurses. The period between 2002 and 2009 saw the number of full-time equivalent registered nurses increase by 62%.[41] However, variables such as the shortage of primary care physicians and the impact of the ACA confound accurate predictions of whether future supply will be sufficient to meet future demand.[41]

Research Efforts in Quality Improvement

After The Joint Commission recognized the development of multi-institutional hospital networks, it produced a new and quantitatively measurable definition of quality with a focus on results. The new definition characterizes the quality of a provider's care as the degree to which the care delivered increases the likelihood of desired patient outcomes and reduces the likelihood of undesired outcomes, given the current state of medical knowledge.

This objective and quantitative definition of quality contrasted sharply with the previous subjective and qualitative definition that required estimates of adherence to somewhat nebulous performance standards. It also left room for nonclinical outcomes, such as accessibility (the ease with which patients can avail themselves of services) and acceptability (the degree to which health care satisfies patients).

Hospitals now conduct regular patient satisfaction studies to obtain patients' views about the services they receive. Such studies encompass several aspects of care, including access, convenience, information received, financial coverage, and perceived quality. Patient satisfaction studies add a new dimension to the definition of quality. "Quality" becomes what the patient receives as judged by the patient rather than what the facility provides as judged by the providers.

Closely related to the cost and quality dilemma associated with high technology was the problem that some patients received too many procedures, tests, and/or medications that were inappropriate, useless, or even harmful.

A large number of studies have examined the appropriateness of the use of various medical tests and procedures. Using similar methods, researchers compared medical records against well-established criteria for performing specific medical procedures. Those procedures were then rated as performed for "appropriate," "inappropriate," or "equivocal" reasons. The RAND Corporation summarized the findings of a number of RAND-supported research studies, as shown in Figure 4-1.[42]

Overall, it appears that a significant proportion of hospital procedures is performed for inappropriate reasons. The proportion of all procedures judged to be questionable or equivocal also shows wide-ranging variation. "On average, it appears that one-third or more of all procedures performed in the United States are of questionable benefit".[38]

Responsibility of Governing Boards for Quality of Care

Although medical staffs and other professional providers of patient care in hospitals make the decisions and carry out the procedures that lead to the patient care outcomes, hospital governing boards are ultimately

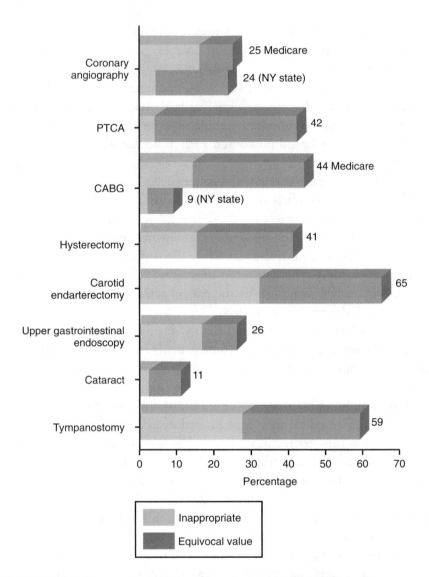

FIGURE 4-1 Proportion of Procedures Judged Either "Clinically Inappropriate" or "Of Equivocal Value": Summary of Selected Studies. *Source:* Reprinted with permission from: RAND Health Research Highlights, "Assessing the Appropriateness of Care: How Much is Too Much?" RB-4522, RAND.

responsible for the quality of the care provided. The board is responsible for the hospital's quality assurance and risk management programs, all quality improvement programs, and the oversight of the medical staff.

The latter responsibility is discharged primarily through its oversight of and final decisions regarding appointments and privilege delineations of medical staff members. Otherwise, oversight of the medical staff is delegated to the various committees of the medical staff organization.

The board oversees the hospital's quality assurance programs and related functions by monitoring specific information regarding program effectiveness in the identification and resolution of patient care problems and of the medical staff in quality assurance. Some of the indicators that hospital boards regularly review are:

- Mortality rates by department or service
- Hospital-acquired infections
- Patient complaints
- Patient falls
- Adverse drug reactions
- Unplanned returns to surgery
- Hospital-incurred traumas

Needless to say, only the most diligent and dedicated lay board members are capable of interpreting these data and then formulating clear and understandable explanations for their occurrence. Health care reforms will refocus hospitals' quality assessment criteria and as such can be expected to require a reorientation of hospital boards of directors' roles in what has been a historically important set of functions. Details of these changes for boards' quality monitoring functions will await many future stages of health care reform implementation.

Hospitalists: A Rapidly Growing Innovation

Physicians called "hospitalists" are rapidly taking over the care of inpatients in U.S. hospitals. Hospitalists, usually internists by training, assume responsibility for the care of inpatients from admission to discharge. They substitute for the patient's primary physician for the period of the hospital stay and provide and/or coordinate all patient care by staff and specialists. Because hospitalists are based in the hospitals, they are able to provide more responsive and continuous care than patients' primary physicians, whose hospital visits are brief and less frequent.

Because it is generally accepted that the presence of hospitalists shortens lengths of stay, improves the continuity and quality of hospital care, and has economic advantages to hospitals, hospitalist medicine is rapidly becoming the preferred model of inpatient care.[43]

Forces of Reform

The performance benchmarks of cost, quality, and access that with few exceptions, hospitals addressed for decades with moderate enthusiasm and little, if any, effect have become the survival criteria for the future. Provisions of the ACA will radically alter virtually all dimensions of hospitals' institutional perceptions of themselves, their relationships with providers, payers, and health care consumers. A detailed description of all aspects of how the ACA will impact hospitals is beyond the scope of this text. It also is noted that proposed federal rules and regulations to implement the ACA are being revised as the implementation process proceeds. However, four areas of major significance for hospitals in the reformed system are described later in the belief that these, regardless of subsequent regulatory or rule revisions, will remain as foundational elements of the reformed system. The four elements are (1) population focus, (2) market consolidations through mergers and acquisitions, (3) accountable care organizations (ACOs), and (4) reimbursement and payment revisions. For purposes of explanation, these elements are discussed separately. However, as readers will realize, they are in fact interdependent and closely linked by the reformed system's overall goals of increasing the quality of care by encouraging improved coordination and continuity that will result in reduced costs.

Population Focus

Perhaps the most enveloping changes of health reform for hospitals come with the new "population focus" of health care delivery, which enacts a radical shift from fee-for-service payments based on episodes of care to payment that rewards providers for keeping patients healthy and averting costly hospitalization.[44] These changes are causing hospitals to reorient strategic planning about how they will measure success based on value delivered in terms of patient outcomes, rather than volume of services delivered. Since medicine and public health parted directions in the 1940s,[45] "population health" was not embraced by individual providers and hospitals as providers and hospitals were reimbursed on a piecemeal, procedure-by-procedure basis, with no accountability for the overall health status of populations they treated. Health system reforms now require a population focus in which groups composed of many levels of health care providers including hospitals take responsibility for managing the total health spectrum of a group of patients "to achieve the best possible quality at minimum necessary cost."[46] This population focus is understandably foreign to hospitals accustomed to accountability for individual patient outcomes only within their institutions. *Modern Health Care* noted in its January 21, 2013 edition, "Hospitals can no longer live in a four–walls, brick and mortar world. Community-based care will be the future metric against which providers will be measured. That is, their reimbursement will be based on performance of care rendered in multiple provider sites by various types of caregivers, including in-home settings."[47]

Market Consolidations: Mergers and Acquisitions

Facing a new reimbursement environment emphasizing the quality and continuity of care and now with collaborations mandated by provisions of the ACA, consolidation activities through mergers and acquisitions have accelerated at a feverish pace in the industry. As hospitals anticipated vastly increasing numbers of older Americans entering Medicare, continuing reductions in Medicare and commercial reimbursements, and state and federal budget crises, they initiated innovative consolidations and mergers well ahead of the passage of the ACA.[48] Already financially stressed, hospitals in addition to declining reimbursements also anticipate increases in operating costs due to increased regulatory compliance, new technology requirements, and the desirability of increased employment of physicians.[48,49] To positively position for evolving market trends, in the past several years and in unprecedented numbers, hospitals have joined with each other and with physician groups to create new or larger integrated systems of care to expand market share and accompanying negotiating power with payers and suppliers as the providers for ever larger population groups.[48,50] Hospital merger and acquisition transactions increased by 18% in 2012 over 2011 with 109 deals affecting 352 facilities.[50] These transactions included one deal in which 10 not-for-profit hospitals agreed to change the ownership of 160 hospitals.[50] In certain markets, insurers are purchasing hospitals and physician practices with the goals of wielding greater control over the costs of care.[51] All these developments underscore that previously accepted tenets of competition and collaboration among providers and payers are changing significantly. As models of integrated care delivery continue gaining traction to align with reimbursement incentives for population-based health outcomes, forging of new and different relationships between and among components of the delivery and reimbursement systems can be expected to continue.

Accountable Care Organizations

The ACA adopted the ACO model, consisting of groups of providers and suppliers of health care, health-related services, and others involved in patient care that work together to coordinate care for the patients they serve under the original Medicare (not Medicare Advantage managed care) program.[52] ACOs are intended to address the well-acknowledged fragmentation of the health care system by ensuring care coordination across multiple providers for the entire spectrum of needs so that all patients receive timely and appropriate care, avoiding unnecessary duplication of services, medical emergencies, and hospitalizations.[53] As early as 1998, private and state ACO-type demonstration projects began and ultimately reported measureable cost reductions and quality improvements.[54] However, information on the impact of ACOs is limited with numerous questions remaining as the private and public sectors engage in widespread experimentation with the adoption of this model.[54]

Under the ACA, an ACO may include the following types of provider groups and suppliers of Medicare-covered services[52]:

- ACO professionals: physicians and hospitals in group practice arrangements
- Networks of individual practices of ACO professionals
- Partnerships or joint venture arrangements between hospitals and ACO professionals, or hospitals employing ACO professionals
- Other Medicare providers and suppliers as approved by the U.S. Department of Health and Human Services

Each ACO must be a legally constituted entity within its state and include health care providers, suppliers, and Medicare beneficiaries on its governing board[55] and must take responsibility for at least 5,000 Medicare beneficiaries for a period of 3 years. To qualify for support under the ACA, ACOs must also meet Medicare-established quality measures of care appropriateness, coordination, timeliness, and safety.[55]

Providers' participation in an ACO is voluntary and Medicare recipients participating in ACOs are not restricted from using physicians outside of their ACO.[52]

The payment structure for ACOs combines fee-for-service payments with shared savings and bonus payments linked with specific quality performance standards for which all providers in an ACO are accountable.[56] Quality performance standards for ACOs will be assessed using a scoring methodology in five key areas: (1) patient and caregiver experience of care, (2) care coordination, (3) patient safety, (4) preventive health, and (5) at-risk population/frail elderly health.[52] ACOs' required collaborations with physicians and diverse providers and suppliers offer hospitals opportunities to combine their patient care expertise with the actuarial data analysis and risk management prowess of payers to develop, monitor, and manage effective and efficient systems of patient care.[34] ACO opportunities will also entail many challenges including abilities to provide effective and efficient care across multiple settings from outpatient settings to hospitals, the ability to plan and control budgets, and the ability to maintain dynamic and current communication among participating providers and patients.[34,57]

Reimbursement and Payment Revisions

Various ACA provisions that affect hospitals use a combination of payment reforms to support the intentions of improving patient care quality, decreasing costs and improving population health. This section summarizes major provisions.

ACO Medicare Fee-for-Service Shared Savings Program

The ACA enables ACOs to share in savings to the federal government based on ACO performance in improving quality and reducing health care costs.[58] Medicare provider participation in this program is voluntary, but if selected, participation requires a 3-year commitment.[59] The basis for the shared savings incentive is an ACO's performance in reducing per capita Medicare expenditures below a benchmark determined by the CMS. Shared-savings payments equal the difference between the estimated per capita Medicare expenditures and the benchmark.[60] Participating ACOs continue to receive the same fee-for-service payments as in the past, but can earn additional shared-savings amounts based on the quality performance standards discussed earlier in the "Accountable Care Organizations" section. A distinct feature of this program is that it allows ACOs to determine the level of financial risk (directly correlated with potential financial reward) it wishes to assume. The program offers providers a financially risk-free, "one-sided risk" option that can earn a maximum of 50% of savings realized each year and a "two-sided risk" option in which participants are at financial risk of losses for each of the 3-year contract period but can earn up to 60% of savings realized each year.[59]

Hospital Value-Based Purchasing (VBP) Program

CMS began implementing VBP pilot projects in 2003; this model has been replicated by private insurers as well, structured to provide incentives to discourage inappropriate, unnecessary, and costly care.[61] Now mandated by the ACA, the VBP program applies to over 3,000 acute care Medicare participating hospitals, enabling them to earn incentive payments based on clinical outcomes and patient satisfaction. Hospitals with low case volumes and ones that offer only specific specialties such as psychiatry, long-term treatment, rehabilitation, and cancer treatment are exempted.[62] The VBP uses 12 "clinical processes of care measures" and 8 "patient experience of care measures" to assess hospital performance on the parameters of "achievement" and "improvement."[63] The program is funded by annual percentage reductions in the standard reimbursement that Medicare pays all hospitals.[64] The first wave of revised payments will occur in 2013. As reported in December 2012, 1,557 hospitals had earned incentive payments and 1,427 had incurred payment reductions of up to 1% of their standard reimbursement as a result of performance during the prior year.[62] For some hospitals, incentive payments and reductions are inconsequential and for others, result in material financial.

Readmissions Reduction Program

Beginning October 1, 2012, the ACA requires the CMS to reduce payments to hospitals for the readmission of patients with specified diagnoses within 30 days of a prior hospitalization. The ACA also requires that readmission information be made public on the CMS "Hospital Compare" Website.[65] Annually, Medicare spends $17 billion or 20% of all Medicare fee-for-service payments for unplanned readmissions.[66]

The intent of the program is to encourage hospitals to improve the quality and continuity of care beyond the acute episode that resulted in the initial hospitalization. Penalty determinations are based on 3 prior years' hospital discharge data.[65] Payment reductions are based on a CMS formula that assigns each hospital a benchmark for excess readmissions for heart attack, heart failure, and pneumonia. In 2013, Medicare payments to more than 2,200 hospitals will be reduced by up to 1%, a loss of $300 million for the affected hospitals. Hospitals that do not improve will be penalized by up to 2% in 2014 and 3% in 2015.[67] Recommendations to extend the program to readmissions of Medicare patients for all-causes are under deliberation.[68] The program continues to generate significant debate with hospitals contending that many factors contributing to readmissions are not in their control.[67]

Bundled Payments for Care Improvement Initiative

The Bundled Payments for Care Improvement Initiative (BPCI) was developed by the CMS Center for Medicare & Medicaid Innovation (CMMI) that was created by the ACA. The BPCI recognizes that separate Medicare fee-for-service payments for individual services provided during a beneficiary's single illness often result in fragmented care with minimal coordination across providers and settings and results in rewarding service quantity rather than quality. The BPCI is designed to test whether, as prior research has shown, bundled payments can align incentives for hospitals, post-acute care providers, physicians, and other health care personnel to work closely together across many settings to achieve improved patient outcomes at lower cost.[69] Approval for participation in the BPCI is determined through an application process administered by the CMMI. ACOs and other collaboratives of hospitals, physicians, and community-based providers are eligible to apply. The BPCI offers four broadly defined models of care linking payments for multiple services delivered to beneficiaries during an episode of care.[69] Model 1 defines an episode of care as an inpatient stay in an acute care hospital. In this model, Medicare pays the hospital an amount discounted from standard Medicare reimbursement and continues to pay physicians their usual fee-for-service amounts. Under defined circumstances, hospitals and physicians are permitted to share in Medicare savings that result from their redesigned care strategies.[69] In Models 2, 3, and 4, participants may select among 48 different clinically defined episodes of care. Models 2 and 3 use a retrospective bundled payment arrangement where expenditures are settled against a Medicare-determined discounted target price based on a participant's historical fee-for-service payments for the selected episode of care. Any reduction in expenditures beyond the discount reflected in the target price is paid to participants. Under Model 4, CMS makes a prospectively determined, single lump sum payment to a hospital that encompasses all services furnished during an inpatient stay. Physicians and other practitioners are reimbursed by the hospital from the bundled, lump sum payment.[70,71] In January 2013, CMS announced that over 450 health care organizations including not-for-profit and for-profit hospitals, academic medical centers, physician-owned facilities, and postacute providers had joined the BPCI program.[71]

The foregoing descriptions of how the ACA affects hospital performance provide only a snapshot of initiatives. For more in-depth information, readers are strongly encouraged to access the Websites included in the references to this chapter.

Continuing Change

U.S. hospitals will retain their core roles as the purveyors of the most technologically sophisticated care in the world, the educational practice platforms of physicians and other health professionals, and the sites of clinical research. In the frenetic environment of health system reforms, hospitals now assume yet another role as one component of an integrated system and continuum of community-based care.

Debates and analyses will continue regarding hospitals' roles in the reformed system and health care marketplace. Results of government and private entity experiments with the reconfigured roles of hospitals in a new population-focused, value-driven delivery system will yield numerous opportunities for continued refinements that affect both the quality and costs of care. There are reasons for optimism in the prospect of ACOs with hospitals as major participants, providing excellent patient-centered coordination of care that successfully addresses the negative hallmarks of the health care delivery system—fragmentation, duplication, medical errors, and excessive costs. Observers are expressing concern however, that the newly established ACOs are joining health care organizations that otherwise would compete with each other, thus creating networks with dangerous market power.[72] Health care market analysts also have pointed out that hospital mergers can actually increase costs that are passed on to consumers.[73] Ongoing market restructuring through hospital mergers and consolidations will test the impacts of reshuffling providers' and payers' relative positions and can also be expected to spawn ongoing antitrust and related legal issues.[74] Nonetheless, positive reports of the impacts of hospital consolidations on quality are emerging.[75] In a study of 2,791 short-term, general, nonfederal hospitals comparing performance on the five parameters of risk-adjusted mortality rate, risk-adjusted complications index, risk-adjusted patient safety index, CMS "Hospital Compare" indicators, and 30-day mortality rates for selected admission diagnoses, findings indicated that hospitals that are members of systems "significantly outperform and improve significantly faster than independent hospitals."[75] While hospitals of the future will no longer be the axis on which the rest of the system turns as they were in the past, they will be essential components of integrated systems of community-based care.

Recent evidence bears out that there will be great variation in the capability of America's thousands of hospitals to adjust to radical reversals of form and function required by the ACA and other reforms. It is likely that the Darwinian law of nature, survival of the fittest, will determine which hospitals remain to serve the American public in the future.

Key Terms for Review

Academic Health Center	Hospitalist
Accountable Care Organization (ACO)	Informed Consent
Bundled Payments for Care Improvement Initiative (BPCI)	Population Health Focus
Diagnosis-Related Group (DRG) Reimbursement	Readmissions Reduction Program
	Teaching Hospital
Hill–Burton Act	Value-Based Purchasing (VBP)
Horizontal Integration	Vertical Integration

References

1. Stevens R. *In Sickness and in Wealth: American Hospitals in the Twentieth Century.* New York, NY: Basic Books, 1989.
2. Teisberg EO, Vayle EJ. *The Hospital Sector in 1992.* Boston, MA: Harvard Business School, 1991.

3. Association of American Medical Colleges. Teaching hospitals. Available from https://www.aamc.org/about/teachinghospitals/. Accessed December 29, 2012.

4. American Hospital Association. Fast Facts on U.S. Hospitals. Available from http://www.aha.org/research/rc/stat-studies/101207fastfacts.pdf. Accessed February 2, 2013.

5. Rohr R. The paradox of specialty hospitals. *Hospitalist Leadership Connection*, May 12, 2009. Available from http://www.HCPRO.com. Accessed December 23, 2012.

6. Greenwald L, Cromwell J, Adamache W, et al. Specialty versus community hospitals: referrals, quality, and community benefits. *Health Aff.* 2006;25:106–118.

7. Bellandi D. Spinoffs, big deals dominate in '99. *Mod. Healthc.* 2000;30:36.

8. Association of American Medical Colleges. After reform, more medical schools emphasize public health. Available from https://www.aamc.org/newsroom/reporter/170156/public_health.html. Accessed January 14, 2013.

9. Shomaker, S. Preparing for health care reform: ten recommendations for academic health centers. *Acad. Med.* 2011;86:555–558. Available from http://journals.lww.com/academicmedicine/Fulltext/2011/05000/Commentary__Preparing_for_Health_Care_Reform__Ten.11.aspx. Accessed January 14, 2013.

10. Facts About the Department of Veterans Affairs. January 2009. Available from http://www.va.gov/opa/publications/factsheets/fs_department_of_veterans_affairs.pdf. Accessed December 24, 2012.

11. Gilles RR, Shortell SM, Young GJ, et al. Best practices in managed organized delivery systems. *Hosp Health Serv Admin.* 1997;42:299–321.

12. HSS Secretary Kathleen Sebelius announces major progress in doctors, hospital use of health information technology. February 17, 2012. Available from http://www.hhs.gov/news/press/2012pres/02/20120217a.html. Accessed December 26, 2012.

13. Ewing T, Cusick D. Knowing what to measure. *Health Financ Manage.* 2004;58:60–63.

14. Wang SJ, Middleton B, Prosser LA, et al. A cost-benefit analysis of electronic medical records in primary care. *Am J Med.* 2003;114:397–403.

15. Shmitt KF, Wofford DA. Financial analysis projects clear returns from electronic medical records. *Health Financ Manage.* 2002;56:52–57.

16. Manchemi N, Brooks RG. Reviewing the benefits of electronic health records and associated patient safety technologies. *J Med Syst.* 2006;30:159–168.

17. Sandrick K. Calculating ROI for CPRs. *Health Manage Technol.* 1998;19:16.

18. White SV. Interview of David Brailer. *J Healthc Qual.* 2004;26:20–24.

19. Conn, J. CMS: $7.7 billion in EHR payments through September. *Mod. Healthc.* Available from www.modernhealthcare.com/article/20121106/NEWS/311069955. Accessed December 26, 2012.

20. Health Career Choices. The ever growing health care industry. Available from http://healthcareerchoices.com/articles/ever-growing-healthcare-industry/. Accessed December 26, 2012.

21. Faulkner M, Anyard B. Is the hospital sick role a barrier to patient participation? *Nurs. Times.* 2002;98:35–36.

22. U.S. Department of Health and Human Services. Centers for Medicare & Medicaid Services. Clarification of evaluation and management payment policy. CMS Manual System, Pub 100–02 Medicare Benefit Policy, Transmittal 147, August 26, 2011. Available from http://www.cms.gov/regulations-and-guidance/guidance/transmittals/downloads/R147BP.pdf. Accessed January 14, 2013.

23. Patient Advocate Foundation. Second opinions. Available from http://www.patientadvocate.org/index.php?p=691. Accessed January 14, 2013.

24. Thorpe KE. Health care cost containment: results and lessons from the past 20 years. In: Shortell SM, Reinhardt UE, Eds. *Improving Health Policy and Management.* Ann Arbor, MI: Health Administration Press, 1992, p 246.

25. Federal Register. U.S. Department of Health and Human Services. Centers for Medicare and Medicaid Services. Medicare program: notification of hospital discharge appeal rights; final rule. November 27, 2006. Available from http://www.canhr.org/factsheets/misc_fs/PDFs/Medicare_HosDis_Notice_Regs07.pdf. Accessed January 13, 2013.

26. Federal Trade Commission. U.S. Department of Justice. Improving health care: a dose of competition. Available from http://www.justice.gov/atr/public/health_care/204694/chapter3.htm#1. Accessed December 28, 2012.

27. Shortell SM. *The Future of Hospitals and Health Care Management.* Washington, DC: VA Office of Research and Development, 1996.

28. Delbanco TL, Stokes DM, Cleary PD, et al. Medical patients' assessments of their care during hospitalization: insights for internists. *J Gen Intern Med.* 1995;10:679–685.

29. Gerteis M, Leviton SE, Daily J, et al. *Through the Patient's Eyes: Understanding and Promoting Patient-Centered Care.* San Francisco, CA: Jossey-Bass, 1993.

30. Sunshine L, Wright JW. *The Best Hospitals in America.* New York, NY: Henry Holt and Company, 1987.

31. Rundle RL. We hope you enjoy your stay. *Wall St. J.* November 22, 2004: R5.

32. Kropf R. Planning for health services. In: Kovner AR, Ed. *Health Care Delivery in the United States.* New York, NY: Springer, 1995, p 353.

33. Healthcare Financial Management Association. What's your organization's position in the next mergers and acquisitions wave? March 1, 2009. Available from http://www.hfma.org/content.aspx?id=2465. Accessed January 14, 2013.

34. Cognizant. Five key trends reshaping the future of healthcare. Available from http://www.cognizant.com/InsightsWhitepapers/Five-Key-Trends-Reshaping-the-Future-of-Healthcare.pdf. Accessed January 24, 2013.

35. Donabedian A. Evaluating the quality of medical care. *Millbank Mem Fund Q.* 1966;44:166–206.
36. Wennberg JE, Gittlesohn A. Small area variation in health care delivery. *Science.* 1973;182:1102–1108.
37. The Leapfrog Group. The Leapfrog Incentive and Reward Compendium. Available from http://www.leapfroggroup.org/compendium2. Accessed December 28, 2012.
38. Kohn LT, Corrigan JM, Donaldson MS, et al. *To Err Is Human: Building a Safer Health System.* Washington, DC: Institute of Medicine, 1999.
39. Dworktn RW. Where have all the nurses gone? *Pub. Int.* 2002;148:23–36.
40. Needleman J, Buerhaus PI, Stewart M, et al. Nurse staffing in hospitals: is there a business case for quality? *Health Aff.* 2006;25:204–211.
41. Auerbach DI, Buerhaus PI, Staiger DO. Registered nurse supply grows faster than projected amid sure in new entrants ages 23–36. *Health Aff.* 2011:30:2286–2290.
42. RAND Health Research Highlights. *Assessing the Appropriateness of Care: How Much Is Too Much?* Santa Monica, CA: Rand Corporation, 1998.
43. Glabman M. *Hospitalists: The Next Big Thing.* American Hospital Association, Center for Healthcare Governance, Trustee. Chicago, IL: Health Forum, Inc., 2005, 7–11.
44. Becker's Hospital Review. 5 ways population health is transforming hospital strategy. Available from http://www.beckershospitalreview.com/hospital-physician-relationships/5-ways-population-health-is-transforming-hospital-strategy.html. Accessed January 14, 2013.
45. Association of American Medical Colleges. After reform, more medical schools emphasize public health. Available from https://www.aamc.org/newsroom/reporter/170156/public_health.html. Accessed January 14, 2013.
46. Becker's Hospital Review. The road to population health: key considerations. Available from http://www.beckershospitalreview.com/hospital-physician-relationships/the-road-to-population-health-key-considerations.html. Accessed January 14, 2013.
47. Nahm S, Mack G. Goodbye, post-acute care. *Mod. Healthc.* 2013;43:26. Available from http://www.modernhealthcare.com/article/20130119/MAGAZINE/301199993/goodbye-post-acute-care. Accessed January 24, 2013.
48. Ahlquist GL, Bailey C, Saxena SB, et al. Healthcare reform and hospitals systems: preparing for the future means structural transformation. Booz & Co. Available from http://www.booz.com/media/uploads/BoozCo-Healthcare-Reform-Hospital-Systems-Structural-Transformation.pdf. Accessed January 16, 2013.
49. Brown TC, Werling KA, Walker BC, et al. Current trends in hospital mergers and acquisitions. *Healthc. Financ. Manage.* 2012;66:114.
50. Barr PS. Taking a different path. *Mod. Healthc.* 2013;43:S1. Available from http://www.modernhealthcare.com/article/20130126/

MAGAZINE/301269951/taking-a-different-path. Accessed February 3, 2013.

51. Becker's Hospital Review. Hospital M & A outlook 2012: 5 key trends. Available from http://www.beckershospitalreview.com/hospital-transactions-and-valuation/hospital-maa-outlook-2012-5-key-trends.html. Accessed January 22, 2013.

52. HealthCare.gov. Accountable care organizations: improving care coordination for people with Medicare. Available from http://www.healthcare.gov/news/factsheets/2011/03/accountablecare03312011a.html. Accessed January 15, 2013.

53. Centers for Medicare & Medicaid Services. Accountable care organizations. Available from http://www.cms.gov/medicare/medicare-fee-for-service-payment/aco/index.html?redirect=/aco. Accessed January 15, 2013.

54. American Hospital Association. Accountable care organizations: AHA research synthesis report. Available from http://www.aha.org/research/cor/content/ACO-Synthesis-Report.pdf. Accessed January 11, 2013.

55. Centers for Medicare & Medicaid Services. More doctors, hospitals partner to coordinate care for people with Medicare. Available from http://www.cms.gov/apps/media/press/release.asp?Counter=4501&intNumPerPage=10&checkDate=&checkKey=&srchType=1&numDays=3500&srchOpt=0&srchData=&keywordType=All&chkNewsType=1%2C+2%2C+3%2C+4%2C+5&intPage=&showAll=&pYear=&year=&desc=&cboOrder=date. Accessed January 9, 2013.

56. Baxley L, Borkan J, Campbell T, et al. In pursuit of a transformed health care system: from patient centered medical homes to accountable care organizations and beyond. *Ann Fam Med.* 2011;9:467. Available from http://www.annfammed.org/content/9/5/466.full. Accessed January 14, 2013.

57. Page AE. The future of health care delivery? *American Academy of Orthopaedic Surgeons.* Available from http://www. aaos.org/news/aaosnow/oct10/advocacy3.asp. Accessed January 9, 2013.

58. Accountable Care Facts. Top questions about ACOs: what are the real cost savings that can be anticipated by an ACO and how will they be achieved? Available from http://www.accountablecarefacts.org/topten/what-are-the-real-cost-savings-that-can-be-anticipated-by-an-ACO-and-how-will-they-be-achieved-1. Accessed January 10, 2013.

59. American College of Physicians. Detailed summary—Medicare shared savings/accountable care organization (ACO) program. Available from http://www.acponline.org/running_practice/delivery_and_payment_models/aco/aco_detailed_sum.pdf. Accessed January 11, 2013.

60. Rawlings RB, Stallings TJ, Riley JB, et al. Health reform for hospitals and health systems. McGuire Woods. Available from http://www.mcguirewoods.com/news-resources/publications/health_care/health%20reform%20for%20hospitals.pdf. Accessed January 9, 2013.

61. Deloitte Development LLC. Value-based purchasing: a strategic overview for health care industry stakeholders. Available from http://www.deloitte.com/assets/Dcom-UnitedStates/Local%20Assets/Documents/Health%20Reform%20Issues%20Briefs/US_CHS_ValueBasedPurchasing_031811.pdf. Accessed January 20, 2013.

62. The Henry J. Kaiser Family Foundation. Kaiser Health News. Medicare discloses hospitals' bonuses, penalties based on quality. Available from http://www.kaiserhealthnews.org/stories/2012/december/21/medicare-hospitals-value-based-purchasing.aspx?p=1. Accessed January 20, 2013.

63. U.S. Department of Health and Human Services. Centers for Medicare & Medicaid Services. Hospital value-based purchasing program. Available from http://www.cms.gov/Outreach-and-Education/Medicare-Learning-Network-MLN/MLNProducts/downloads/Hospital_VBPurchasing_Fact_Sheet_ICN907664.pdf. Accessed January 19, 2013.

64. U.S. Department of Health and Human Services. Centers for Medicare & Medicaid Services. Frequently asked questions: hospital value-based purchasing program. Available from http://www.cms.gov/Medicare/Quality-Initiatives-Patient-Assessment-Instruments/hospital-value-based-purchasing/Downloads/FY-2013-Program-Frequently-Asked-Questions-about-Hospital-VBP-3-9-12.pdf. Accessed January 14, 2013.

65. CMS.gov. Readmissions reduction program. Available from http://www.cms.gov/Medicare/Medicare-Fee-for-Service-Payment/AcuteInpatientPPS/Readmissions-Reduction-Program.html. Accessed January 14, 2013.

66. Silow-Carrrol S, Edwards JN, Lashbrook A. Reducing hospital readmissions: lessons from top-performing hospitals. *The Commonwealth Fund*. Available from http://www.commonwealthfund.org/~/media/Files/Publications/Case%20Study/2011/Apr/1473_SilowCarroll_readmissions_synthesis_web_version.pdf. Accessed January 11, 2013.

67. Fiegel C. 2,200 hospitals face Medicare pay penalty for readmissions. *American Medical Association*. Amednews. Available from http://www.ama-assn.org/amednews/2012/08/27/gvsb0827.htm. Accessed January 19, 2013.

68. O'Reilly KB. National quality forum upholds rehospitalization measure. *American Medical Association*. Amednews. Available from http://www.ama-assn.org/amednews/2012/07/16/prsb0716.htm. Accessed January 19, 2013.

69. U.S. Department of Health and Human Services. Centers for Medicare & Medicaid. Center for Medicare & Medicaid Innovation. Bundled payments for care improvement (BPCI) initiative: general information. Available from http://innovation.cms.gov/initiatives/bundled-payments/index.html. Accessed January 19, 2013.

70. U.S. Department of Health and Human Services. Centers for Medicare & Medicaid Fact sheets, details for: bundled payments for care improvement initiative. Available from http://www.cms.gov/apps/media/press/factsheet.asp?counter=4068. Accessed January 19, 2013.

71. Zigmond JA. More than 450 provider organizations join payment-bundling initiative. *Modern Health Care*. Available from http://www.modernhealthcare.com/article/20130131/news/301319949/more-than-450-provider-organizations-join-payment-bundling-initiative. Accessed February 3, 2013.
72. Richman BD, Schulman KA. A cautious path forward on accountable care organizations. Available from http://jamanetwork.com/article.aspx?articleid-645471. Accessed January 19, 2013.
73. Roy A. How hospital mergers increase health costs, and what to do about it. *Forbes*. Available from http://www.forbes.com/sites/aroy/2012/03/01/how-hospital-mergers-increase-health-costs-and-what-to-do-about-it. Accessed January 29, 2013.
74. Pear R. Trade commission challenges a hospital merger. *New York Times*. Available from http://www.nytimes.com/2011/08/22us/22health.html?_r=0. Accessed January 29, 2013.
75. Foster D. 100 top hospitals research: hospital system membership and performance. Truven Health Analytics. Available from http://www.100tophospitals.com/assets/health_system_hospitals_perform_better.pdf. Accessed February 3, 2013.

CHAPTER 5

Ambulatory Care

This chapter reviews the major elements of ambulatory (outpatient) care and discusses changes supported by the Patient Protection and Affordable Care Act (ACA) and the American Reinvestment and Recovery Act. Ambulatory care encompasses a diverse and growing sector of the health care delivery system. Physician services are the chief component; however, hospital outpatient and emergency departments, community health centers, departments of health, and voluntary agencies also contribute important services, particularly for the uninsured and vulnerable populations. Ambulatory surgery is a continuously expanding component of ambulatory care, as new technology allows an increasing number of procedures to be performed safely and efficiently outside the hospital in other types of outpatient facilities.

Overview and Trends

Ambulatory care comprises health care services that do not require overnight hospitalization. Once largely consisting of visits to private physicians' offices and hospital outpatient clinics and EDs, ambulatory care today encompasses a broad and expanding array of services.

New medical and diagnostic procedures and technologic advancements allow procedures previously requiring hospitalization to be performed on an outpatient basis. Surgical procedures that commonly warranted a hospital stay several decades ago are now routinely performed on a same-day, ambulatory basis.

In addition to the numerous new diagnostic and treatment tools available in the outpatient setting and the advanced technology that makes outpatient treatment safe and effective, financial mandates also have driven services into the ambulatory arena. Beginning in the 1980s, prospective hospital reimbursement replaced retrospective payment on a national scale through Medicare's initiation of the diagnosis-related group (DRG) payment system. The new payment system provided financial incentives intended to decrease the duration of inpatient stays and to increase service delivery efficiency. Hospitals responded to the new payment system by shifting procedures and services amenable to outpatient delivery from the more expensive inpatient environment to less expensive and more efficient ambulatory delivery systems.

Both DRGs and increasing pressures from health care purchasers to control costs contributed to the rapid expansion of managed care. With the goal of providing services in the least expensive, most effective manner possible, managed care organizations exerted a powerful influence that compelled a shift toward the appropriate use of ambulatory services to replace more expensive inpatient care.

Ambulatory care capacity has expanded in both the hospital-based and non-hospital-based, or "freestanding," settings. Historically, hospitals operated virtually all ambulatory or outpatient clinics within the hospital's main facilities or in contiguous facilities on the hospital campuses. Many hospitals still operate clinic services on-site, and many have retained ambulatory surgical services within the main facility in response to community need, physician demand, and teaching activity. The conversion of underused inpatient units also provided a cost-effective means for hospitals to accommodate the shift to ambulatory surgical services and other ambulatory procedures within the hospital.

Beginning in the 1980s, hospitals expanded their service networks to include geographically distributed freestanding facilities throughout their service areas, both for routine diagnosis and treatment and for ambulatory surgical services. In addition to cost considerations, two other factors influenced this trend for hospitals. First, the 1980s and 1990s saw increased consumer demand for conveniently located, easily accessible facilities and services, two factors frequently lacking on hospital campuses. This is particularly true for large teaching hospitals, which are often located in congested urban centers and are perceived as inconvenient locations to access by patients. Second, with the growing concerns of inner-city hospitals about competition with other institutions for market share of profitable outpatient services and referrals for inpatient care, hospitals recognized the need to expand their service distribution network to larger segments of the community by establishing conveniently located facilities. Hospitals also recognized that some ambulatory services, such as surgery, could be operated most efficiently off-site and be removed from the scheduling complexities and other requirements of a system that must accommodate a vast array of physician and patient needs.

Independent of hospital organizations, for-profit corporations' freestanding facilities providing ambulatory, primary, specialty, and surgical services have proliferated. In addition to profitability and cost-control features attractive to insurers, responsiveness to consumer preferences was also a primary driver in these developments.

The decade of the 1990s saw a continuing upward trend in the total number of ambulatory care facilities owned and operated by hospitals, physicians, and independent chains. Services provided by these facilities are diverse and represent a response to population demographics in their respective service areas as well as reimbursement opportunities. A partial listing of the array of ambulatory care facilities includes cancer treatment, diagnostic imaging of many different types, renal dialysis, pain management, physical therapy, cardiac and other types of rehabilitation, outpatient surgery, occupational health, women's health, and wound care.

A significant corollary to developments in ambulatory care delivery for hospital-operated and independent organizations has been the entry of physicians into the business of outpatient diagnostic, treatment, and surgical services previously available to their practices in only the hospital setting. The same factors operative in the larger industry—technologic advances making the purchase, maintenance, and operation of the required equipment feasible and cost effective in freestanding facilities; consumer demand for convenient, user-friendly environments; and profitability—have compelled this development.

Physician involvement in this arena has paralleled that of hospitals in practice areas, such as ophthalmologic surgery for lens replacement and laser therapy, certain types of gynecologic surgery, fiber-optic gastrointestinal diagnosis, chemotherapy, renal dialysis, computed tomography, magnetic resonance imaging, and more. The implications of this trend for hospitals' business volume and revenue have been significant as physicians and hospitals emerge as competitors engaged in the same lines of business. These developments are permanently, and in the view of some, negatively altering the long-standing relationships between physicians and their affiliated hospitals.[1–3]

The ambulatory care delivery system is changing and growing rapidly as its various organization models evolve, including new efforts to measure quality relative to costs. The service constellation also is growing rapidly and becoming more diverse. Numerous service delivery hybrids continue to develop in the ambulatory care arena. With the implementation of the Patient Protection and Affordable Care Act (ACA) and accompanying proliferation of new care delivery models such as patient-centered medical homes (PCMHs) and accountable care organizations (ACOs) that emphasize population health, the roles of both primary and specialty ambulatory services are evolving rapidly along with their respective reimbursement systems. This chapter provides a framework for understanding the origins, development, and future direction of this important sector of the health care delivery system that continues on the growth trajectory shown by Figures 5-1 and 5-2.[4]

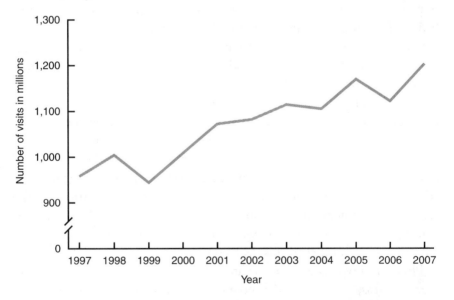

FIGURE 5-1 Annual Number of Ambulatory Care Visits in Millions, United States, 1997–2007.
Source: Reproduced from CDC/NCHS, National Ambulatory Medical Care Survey and National Hospital Ambulatory Care Survey. *Vital and Health Statistics, 13*:169: April 2011.

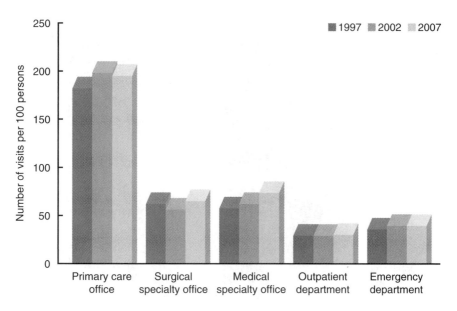

FIGURE 5-2 Age-Adjusted Ambulatory Care Visit Rates by Setting: United States, 1997, 2002, and 2007.
Source: Reproduced from CDC/NCHS, National Ambulatory Medical Care Survey and National Hospital Ambulatory Care Survey. *Vital and Health Statistics,13*:169: April 2011.

Private Medical Office Practice

Private physician office practices constitute the predominant mode of ambulatory care in the United States. In 2009, the most recent year for which data are available, the National Center for Health Statistics estimated that patients made more than 1 billion visits to physician offices: more than 586 million to primary care physicians, more than 257 million to medical specialists, and more than 193 million to surgical specialists.[5] Figure 5-3 provides a snapshot of physician office visits by specialty. In more than 50% of reported office visits, electronic medical records were used, either used exclusively or in part as documentation. Claims for payment were submitted electronically at more than 86% of visits.[5]

The way physicians organize and operate their private practices has evolved from a variety of factors.

Physician group practice can be traced to the Mayo Clinic in the late 19th century. The Mayo Clinic group practice generated considerable

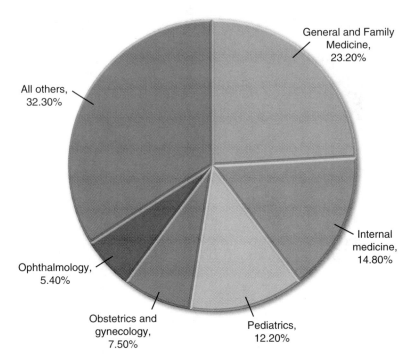

FIGURE 5-3 Percent Distribution of Office Visits by Physician Specialty: United States, 2009.
Source: Reproduced from CDC/NCHS, National Ambulatory Medical Care Survey Summary Tables, 2009.

controversy among physicians. A 1932 report by a New York private foundation's Committee on the Costs of Medical Care endorsed organized group practices and the use of insurance payments. The American Medical Association (AMA) had long opposed the group practice model and condemned the report, declaring that group and salaried physicians were unethical. The controversy erupted into a legal battle when Group Health Insurance was organized in Washington, DC in 1937. The AMA expelled all Group Health Insurance–salaried physicians. Hospitals received lists of so-called "reputable physicians" who were not part of group practices. The Washington, DC Medical Society and the AMA were subsequently indicted, found guilty, and fined for having conspired to monopolize medical practice."[6] For the next few decades negative confrontations occurred as physicians sought participation in developing group health plans. Participating physicians were socially ostracized and denied hospital privileges. By the 1950s, because of effective legal challenges against organized medicine and an ongoing physician shortage, opposition to group practice subsided.

Before 1950, most physicians operated solo practices. Since then, specialization, changing economics, and the desire for more control over their lifestyles caused physicians to group together, either in single fields, such as primary care, or into multispecialty groups. Group practice involves several physicians practicing together in some type of coordinated arrangement. In contrast to an individual physician, fee-for-service payment basis, most groups pay their members a salary augmented with a percentage of the group practice's net profits.

The old solo-practice model made the physician responsible for his or her entire patient caseload 24 hours a day, every day of the year. Before the proliferation of specialties, these physicians normally provided all medical care required by their patients, with the exception of surgery or occasional consultation. The demands on their time and stamina were enormous. Aside from occasional coverage arrangements with a colleague to allow for brief time off, their schedules were relentless and unpredictable.

Beginning in the 1960s, several factors influenced a major shift from the solo mode of private practice to group practice. Social movements in the United States produced a heightened awareness of lifestyle adaptations that allowed healthy accommodation for personal growth and balance between professional and personal responsibilities. In the same period, medical specialization burgeoned as the growth in medical knowledge and technologic advances increased exponentially. Rapidly advancing knowledge in every field of medicine and the resulting specialization created new challenges for the solo generalist and the specialist. Most obvious were increasing demands on physicians to maintain a command of an exponentially growing body of diagnostic and therapeutic knowledge in virtually every field of practice.

The introduction of Medicare reimbursement in 1966 dramatically altered the private medical office and its billing and reimbursement processes. Before this development, physician reimbursement came from largely two sources—personal patient payments or third-party private insurance. Blue Cross/Blue Shield and a relatively small number of other private indemnity carriers comprised most of the third-party payments. Billing and collection were relatively simple. When Medicare began providing coverage for everyone above the age of 65 years, private physicians' offices found themselves dealing with a vast array of new government regulations and fee schedules. In addition, many Medicare recipients also carried supplemental private insurance contracts to reimburse the balance that Medicare did not cover. For the private physician's office the regulation, complexity, and volume of billing requirements burgeoned. Solo-practice office administration, once the province of the physicians themselves, with possibly a receptionist and bookkeeper, now required an increased level of sophistication and a great deal more time.

Other factors also influenced the shift to group practice. Malpractice insurance costs began to rise dramatically in the 1970s. Inflation fueled rising office lease and rental expenses. The need for more sophisticated administrative support services increased with advancing technology and more complex billing and record-keeping requirements. As technology advanced and diagnostic equipment became available for in-office use, groups could benefit from sharing equipment acquisition costs and ensuring the volume necessary to justify ongoing staffing and maintenance. Physicians recognized that group practice could provide other economies of scale through shared administrative overhead.

Group practice evolved in two forms. One consisted of groups of physicians in the same discipline, usually primary care, surgery, obstetrics, or pediatrics. The other form was multidisciplinary specialty practices, usually including primary care physicians in collaboration with several major specialties or subspecialties. There were important features that both generalist and specialist physicians found more attractive in group practice than solo practice. First, although typically each physician carried his or her own caseload of patients, physicians could arrange a routine, pre-planned schedule of after-hours on-call and weekend and vacation coverage. Another attractive dimension of group practice was that it provided a professionally supportive environment.

With the continuing growth of medical information and knowledge required to maintain state-of-the-art competencies and an ever-expanding range of diagnostic and therapeutic alternatives available, group practice enabled physicians to access each other's knowledge and experience in an informal consultative environment. This interchange of information not only provided professional support but also introduced an informal system of peer review to each physician's practice, which, in theory, could contribute to patient care quality. Group practice also enabled patient orientation to alternative coverage arrangements, and thus, their expectation of seeing or contacting another physician in the absence of their own could be established in advance.

Multispecialty group practices evolved for many of the same reasons as single-specialty groups. For specialists, a major benefit was that group membership reduced reliance on patient referrals from other community physicians because economic incentives made keeping the business inside the group beneficial to all members. Patients also benefited by having diagnosis, treatment, and consultation services available at one location. The arrangement also facilitated communication and coordination of results and findings and sped up the turnaround of information.

Surgical group practices evolved similarly to those in the general and other specialty medical fields for similar reasons; however, surgeons have tended to avoid multispecialty grouping. Instead, most are either general surgeons or specialists in such areas as gastrointestinal, cardiothoracic, vascular, or orthopaedic surgery. Economies of scale afford the same advantages in these practices as those in general medical and multispecialty practices with respect to sharing operating costs.

In 2007, approximately 20% of medical practices with three or more physicians contained about one-half of all office-based physicians.[7] By 2009, almost 70% of surveyed physicians were working in group practices, ranging in size from 2 to more than 11 physicians per group practice.[5] On average, approximately one-half of all physicians' practice revenue was derived from public sources with about 31% from Medicare and 17% from Medicaid.[8] Today, an increasing number of physicians are choosing employment by hospitals over private practice. The American Hospital Association reported in 2012 that the number of physicians employed by hospitals has grown by 32% since 2000.[9] From physicians' perspectives, hospital employment has become desirable due to factors such as flat reimbursement rates, complex insurance and health information technology requirements, high malpractice premiums, and the desire for greater work–life balance. For hospitals, employing physicians provides opportunities to gain market share for admissions, the use of diagnostic testing and other outpatient services, and referrals to high-revenue specialty services.[10]

In the 1990s, many hospitals acquired physician practices with the goals of capturing new market share, ensuring inpatient admissions, bringing new volume to ancillary departments such as laboratory and radiology, and improving service delivery efficiency to meet the demands of managed care. In succeeding years, hospitals divested from these arrangements due to financial losses resulting from low physician productivity and high overhead expense.[11] However in the past decade, hospital acquisitions of physician practices have accelerated rapidly as hospitals prepare to position for health reform by creating physician networks that are well positioned to negotiate with health plans, manage coordination of care, monitor quality, and contain costs.[12] There is strong indication that hospital leaders will continue active physician recruitment in the foreseeable future.[11] In the past, hospitals targeted primary care physicians for employment but now are also seeking employment from specialists in anticipation of creating "closed integrated health care delivery systems."[11] In addition to physicians, staff of hospital-owned physician practices may include registered nurses, nurse practitioners, physician assistants, medical office assistants, laboratory personnel, receptionists and clerical support, information technology personnel, and case management staff. Given the uncertainties of health reform, with the acquisition of physician practices hospitals are preparing to cope with a spectrum of scenarios that range from continuing fee-for-service payment to population health management and financial risk-based reimbursement.[11]

Integrated Ambulatory Care Models

The current models of ambulatory care derive reimbursement for services on a piecework basis, without requirements for coordinating care or services between or among providers. Such piecework reimbursement promotes using a high volume of interventions, offers providers no compensation for effort to efficiently coordinate services on behalf of patient needs, and lacks methods to aggregate information on patient outcomes.[13] Historically, these models have been service focused rather than patient focused and as a result, highly fragmented and inefficient. ACA system reforms include health care delivery and reimbursement principles that make patient health outcomes the primary focus, rather than only delivery of discrete services. In addition, reforms place new emphasis on providers' responsibilities for the overall health outcomes of their total population of patients, not just individuals. This emphasis requires integration and coordination of care across the spectrum of patient needs and among multiple providers in all sectors of the health and human services delivery system. The ACA provides resources to support the development and testing of two service delivery and reimbursement models, PCMHs and ACOs. The overarching goals of these models are to make medical care more effective and efficient and thereby to improve the health of populations and reduce costs, while increasing both patient and provider satisfaction. The timely, coordinated, and efficient delivery of ambulatory primary care and specialty services is central to both of these models.

Patient-Centered Medical Home

The PCMH described as the "main policy vehicle to reinvigorate U.S. primary care"[14] "is a team-based model of care led by a personal physician who provides continuous and coordinated care throughout a patient's lifetime to maximize health outcomes."[15] The PCMH is responsible for providing all of a patient's health care needs or appropriately arranging a patient's care with other qualified professionals. This includes the provision of preventive services, treatment of acute and chronic illness, and assistance with end-of-life issues. The PCMH applies to all ages of patients with a distinctive orientation toward individual patients' partnership with the provider team, in all aspects of their care. The model recognizes that the current reimbursement system fails to meaningfully address multiple patient needs and provider demands for a comprehensive, coordinated, and integrated approach to managing all aspects of an individual's health. As such, the PCMH embodies recommendations for major reimbursement reforms that compensate physicians for the time required to provide and arrange for the holistic care necessary to meet the full spectrum of patient needs, not only for in-office, face-to-face encounters.[13] As described in "Joint Principles of the Patient-Centered Medical Home" by the American Academy of Family Physicians (AAFP), American Academy of Pediatrics, American College of Physicians, and American Osteopathic Association, the PCMH embodies seven principles, summarized below[16]:

1. Every patient has an ongoing relationship with a personal physician trained to provide first-contact, continuous care.
2. The personal physician leads a team of individuals in the practice who take responsibility for the ongoing care of patients.
3. The personal physician is responsible to provide for all the patient's health care needs or takes responsibility for appropriately arranging care with other qualified professionals, including acute care, chronic care, preventive services, and end-of-life care.

4. Care is coordinated and/or integrated across all elements of the complex health care system (subspecialty, hospital, home, nursing home) and is facilitated by transferable electronic registries to ensure patients get care where and when they need it.

5. Quality and safety are hallmarks: Physicians create care plans with their patients, engage in voluntary quality improvement activities, and use information technology to support optimal care; patients actively engage in decision making, and physicians seek feedback to ensure that expectations are being met; and practices voluntarily obtain recognition by a nongovernment entity to demonstrate capabilities to provide patient-centered services consistent with the medical home model.

6. Enhanced patient access includes open scheduling, expanded hours, and new options for communication between practice staff and patients (e.g., e-mail).

7. Payment for services recognizes the added value provided to patients in the PCMH and includes reimbursement for time required by physicians and other team members for face-to-face and other types of interactions with patients, care coordination, follow-up, documentation, and other responsibilities central to holistic health care for every patient.

The PCMH model is not new; it was described in 1967 by the American Academy of Pediatrics and in 2004 by the American College of Physicians and the AAFP.[17] However, with increasing recognition of the health care delivery systems' stark inadequacies of care continuity, safety, and quality, and increasing pressures to reduce costs and waste, the model has gained widespread support and presently has formal support from all major primary physician groups and 19 additional physician organizations.[18] In 2006, the Patient-Centered Primary Care Collaborative (PCPCC) was created to advocate for improvement in the primary care delivery model and now consists of more than 1,000 member organizations, including patient advocate groups, several large national employers, most of the nation's primary care physician associations, health benefits companies, trade associations, academic health centers, and health care quality improvement associations.[18] The PCPCC report "Benefits of Implementing the PCMH: A Review of Cost and Quality Results: 2012" cites growing support for the PCMH by "90 commercial insurance plans, numerous employers, 42 state Medicaid programs, numerous federal agencies, the Department of

Defense, hundreds of safety-net clinics and thousands of small and large clinical practices."[19] The ACA includes numerous provisions that support continuing development of the PCMH model; a detailed description of all provisions is beyond the scope of this text. However, major provisions affecting the development of the PCMH model may be categorized under the broad headings of expanded Medicaid coverage eligibility, additional payment opportunities, workforce development, and innovations in access and care coordination. Examples of provisions include[20]:

- Medicaid eligibility expanded to all Americans under age 65 with incomes up to 133% of the federal poverty level, resulting in new coverage for approximately 16 million previously uninsured individuals.
- Medicare and Medicaid payment rate increases for primary care services. Additional Medicare and Medicaid funding for designated preventive services.
- Dedicated funding to place 15,000 primary medical, nursing, and dental providers in health care provider shortage areas.
- Reallocation of the number of graduate medical education training positions with priorities given to primary care and general surgery.
- Support for health professional training through scholarships and loans with priority for programs focusing on primary care models such as PCMHs, team management of chronic disease, and those integrating physical and behavioral health services.
- Establishment of the Center for Medicare and Medicaid Innovation to test various payment and service delivery models to improve care and lower costs.

To successfully promote adoption and sustainability of the PCMH model, the fee-for-service payment model must be changed and new payment models must provide support for required practice infrastructure enhancements as well as incentives for participation.[20] A number of payment models have been proposed with a variety of possible variations based on PCMH characteristics. These include increased fee-for-service payments combined with other types of reimbursement or grants that address costs associated with required infrastructure improvements. Other models incorporate shared savings provisions that reward PCMHs based on meeting preestablished performance measures.[21]

Experts studying the transition of primary care practices to the PCMH model report significant challenges inherent to this change, in addition to payment reform. A Commonwealth Fund report notes, "To become a PCMH, most practice organizations must undergo wrenching cultural and system changes."[22] The nation's first large-scale demonstration project for PCMHs was launched in 2006 by the AAFP and concluded in 2008. An analysis of this project concluded that transformation to this new model of care is a long-term endeavor requiring in addition to substantial payment reforms, "highly motivated physicians, a redesign of staff roles and care processes, investment in health information technology, and other financial and non-financial support."[23] Numerous pilot and demonstration projects testing characteristics of the PCMH model have been conducted, are currently underway or planned, supported by private foundations, state governments, industry groups, and the Centers for Medicare and Medicaid Services.[24–26] The National Committee for Quality Assurance (NCQA) has developed educational materials and guidelines for primary care practices to earn "PCMH Recognition" through adherence to a set of standards; by 2012, a total of 5,000 PCMHs had earned this recognition[27] and NCQA recognition has become the de facto standard for designation as a PCMH.[28] In 2013, NCQA launched a credentialing program for "Patient-Centered Medical Home Content Expert" offering certification to professionals who complete prescribed educational requirements and pass a comprehensive examination.[27]

Accountable Care Organization

The ACA adopted the ACO model, which is a group of providers and suppliers of health care, health-related services, and others involved in patient care that work together to coordinate care for the patients they serve under the original Medicare (not Medicare Advantage managed care) program.[29] Ideally, PCMHs will be the primary care component of ACOs for the Medicare population. Like PCMHs, ACOs are designed to ensure care coordination so that all patients receive timely and appropriate care, and avoid unnecessary duplication of services, medical emergencies, and hospitalizations.[30] An ACO may include the following types of provider groups and suppliers of Medicare-covered services[29]:

- ACO professionals: physicians and hospitals in group practice arrangements
- Networks of individual practices of ACO professionals

- Partnerships or joint venture arrangements between hospitals and ACO professionals or hospitals employing ACO professionals
- Other Medicare providers and suppliers as approved by U.S. Department of Health and Human Services

Each ACO must be a legally constituted entity within its state and include health care providers, suppliers, and Medicare beneficiaries on its governing board[31] and must take responsibility for at least 5,000 Medicare beneficiaries for a period of 3 years. To qualify for support under the ACA, ACOs must also meet Medicare-established quality measures of care appropriateness, coordination, timeliness, and safety.[32] Providers' participation in an ACO is voluntary and Medicare recipients participating in ACOs are not restricted from using physicians outside their ACO.[29]

The ACA provides a payment structure for ACOs that combines fee-for-service payments with shared savings and bonus payments linked with specific quality performance standards for which all providers in an ACO are accountable.[33] Quality performance standards for ACOs are assessed using a scoring methodology in five key areas: patient and caregiver experience of care, care coordination, patient safety, preventive health, and at-risk population/frail elderly health.[29] Like the payment structure for PCMHs, the ACO payment structure shifts the orientation of patient care from a series of fee-for-service reimbursed interventions toward financial reward for maintaining patients' health. In January 2013, the Centers for Medicare and Medicaid Services announced that 250 ACOs are serving over 4 million Medicare beneficiaries.[33]

Other Ambulatory Care Practitioners

In addition to physicians, a number of other licensed health care professionals conduct practices in ambulatory settings. Among the most common are dentists, podiatrists, social workers, psychologists, physical therapists, and optometrists. Like physicians, they may practice singly or in single-specialty or multispecialty groups. For example, there are general solo-practice dentists and multispecialty dental groups who provide general preventive and curative services, as well as services in specialties such as periodontics and orthodontics. Likewise, psychologists in a group may include both generalists and specialists in forensic, child, and other types of psychological interventions.

Ambulatory Care Services of Hospitals: History and Trends

Acute-care not-for-profit hospitals have operated outpatient clinics since the 19th century. The early ones were located predominantly in urban centers whose indigent populations lacked access to private medical care. At that time the provision of outpatient services was largely a function of government-sponsored public hospitals. With the proliferation of the not-for-profit hospitals beginning in the early 20th century, outpatient clinics provided a means for those hospitals to fulfill part of their charitable mission by serving low-income populations who had little, if any, access to private physicians. Hospital outpatient clinics also provided a teaching setting for university-affiliated hospitals, which trained physicians as part of their community mission.

Historically, hospital outpatient clinics were a low-status component of the hospital. J. H. Knowles, who was then director of the Massachusetts General Hospital, wrote in 1965, "Turning to the outpatient department of the urban hospital, we find the stepchild of the institution. Traditionally, this has been the least popular area in which to work, and as a result, few advances in medical care and teaching have been harvested here for the benefit of the community."[34] Because they provided care for a low-income population, hospital outpatient clinics addressed complex medical and social problems, poor compliance with treatment, and discontinuity in care. Hospitals did not support the outpatient clinics with equipment and staff. Medical students and hospital-affiliated physicians of lowest rank agreed to staff the clinics, often in return for earning hospital admitting privileges.

Today, hospital outpatient clinics in urban and rural areas still function as the community's safety net for the medically needy population; however, the status of those services within the hospital and the roles and positions of physicians working in them have changed radically. The change has been most dramatic since the early 1980s when an array of factors converged to increase both the volume and scope of available hospital outpatient services. Far from the stepchild image characterized by Knowles, hospitals now view outpatient clinical services as helping to ensure a source of inpatient admissions and generating revenue from the use of hospital ancillary services.

Today's hospital outpatient clinics are organized along the lines of private physician group practices and are generally aesthetically pleasant, well equipped, and customer oriented. With respect to the hospitals' financial picture, the direction is clear. In 1990, outpatient services revenue constituted 23% of total U.S. voluntary hospital revenues.[35] This figure has continued to rise over succeeding decades, with the outpatient share of total hospital revenue reaching 42% in 2010.[36]

Because traditionally, in addition to serving a community's needy population, hospital clinic services were designed to provide teaching and research opportunities, they have been organized in relation to human organ systems and the diseases affecting those organ systems. For example, medical clinics, in addition to general medicine, might include clinics for dermatology (skin), cardiology (heart), gastroenterology (digestive tract), rheumatology (bone and connective tissue), and other specialties. In addition to general surgery, surgical clinics might include such specialties as orthopaedics (bone), vascular (circulatory system), and others. This type of organizational structure was attractive to attending specialists, researchers, and educators because it allowed focused concentration on particular patient complaints and illnesses. Beyond this benefit, however, the complex interactions among physicians and patients inherent in this anatomic organization of services have both positive and negative implications for both.

For patients, specialty clinics provide a focused approach to diagnosis and treatment by physicians with interests and training in their particular conditions. Also, medical teaching responsibilities in clinics often result in thorough and exhaustive patient physical examination and case review for the health care students' benefit, which might not otherwise occur in a nonteaching setting.

Hospital-based specialty clinic treatment also has drawbacks for patients. Often, specialty clinics treat patients only on certain days each week or are only scheduled 2 to 3 days per month, depending on the demand for the service. Patients with multiple conditions may have to visit several specialty clinics, necessitating many return visits during which a number of different physicians examine them. Because communication among physicians in different specialty clinics can prove to be uncertain, patients may receive conflicting advice or instruction, may be medicated inappropriately with drugs prescribed by several different specialists, or may "fall through the cracks" when a complaint arises that does not fit the specialty area of one of their providers. Similarly for the physician, this type of categorical treatment environment requires a high degree of initiative to maintain accurate, current information on patients treated by multiple specialists. Such communication challenges among clinical settings are ripe for the implementation of PCMHs.

Beginning in the early 1980s, several influences began to have an impact on how hospital outpatient clinic services were organized and delivered. One major influence was the adoption of the DRG hospital reimbursement method, which emphasized decreased lengths of stay. For hospitals, an anticipated result was declining inpatient revenues. Another major factor was the growing influence of managed care and its emphasis on the role of primary medical care. These issues also brought a heightened realism to several years of growing concern on the part of medical educators. The uncontrolled proliferation of specialists at the expense of maintaining a balanced supply of general physicians would have to be addressed to respond to payer and rising consumer demands for more cost-effective, efficient, and coordinated care.

Facing declining inpatient revenue, increasing fiscal pressures, and shifting medical education emphasis to primary medicine, hospitals initiated reorganization and expansion plans for outpatient clinic services that focused heavily on primary care areas. Teaching hospitals planned jointly with their affiliated medical schools, and nonteaching facilities followed suit to pursue expansion of both the volume and array of outpatient services with primary care as the core. Teaching hospitals also undertook outpatient clinic reorganizations, creating primary care centers under the direction of paid, full-time faculty department heads with administrative, clinical, and teaching oversight responsibility.

Hospitals hired full-time and part-time physicians as employees who, with medical school faculty appointments, undertook ongoing responsibility for day-to-day patient care, teaching, and supervision of students and medical residents. Primary care physician employees were organized into practice group models along the lines of private group practices. This primary care model provided a rational structure for the general medical care of clinic patients and helped ensure appropriate referrals and coordination of patient care within and among outpatient clinic specialty units.

The group model of outpatient primary care also supported the hospitals' teaching mission by alleviating reliance on voluntary physician staffing of clinic sessions and student supervision responsibilities. Medical students and medical residents were provided a more supportive and consistent learning environment by continuously interacting with members of the practice group instead of interacting with different mentors over the course of their rotations. Patients benefited from improved coordination of their care and the opportunity to develop a relationship with an individual provider, who functioned as their private attending physician. Developments in the organization of primary care in hospital-based clinics have made a major contribution to the coordination and appropriate delivery of health care to consumers of hospital-based outpatient clinic services.

Although major changes have occurred in the organization and delivery of hospital outpatient clinics over the past 30+ years, fiscal and operational challenges remain for hospitals' outpatient clinics. Some have enjoyed considerable success in attracting new patients with private insurance and self-pay capability and have succeeded in achieving a healthier balance in their previously predominant caseload of Medicaid or charity-care patients. Trends in the volume of hospital outpatient clinic caseloads and payment sources will be subjects of great interest as hospital markets continue to consolidate and the ACA legislation continues to be implemented over the next several years.

Hospital Emergency Services

In 2006, U.S. hospitals operated 3,833 hospital EDs, 186 fewer than those in 1996.[37] During that same 10-year period, the annual number of ED visits increased by 32%, from 90.3 million to 119.2 million; on average about 227 visits every minute.[37] The increase in ED visits was attributed to overall population growth, a decrease in the number of available EDs, increases in the numbers of older Americans, constrained capacity in other outpatient settings, and increasing numbers of uninsured patients.[37]

According to the most recently published data from the National Ambulatory Medical Care Survey: 2009 Emergency Department Summary Tables, approximately 15.8% of patients arrived at EDs by ambulance, and about 12.6% of visits resulted in hospitalization.[38] Per capita ED use was heaviest for infants under 1 year of age; persons 75 years of age and older had the next highest per capita rate of visits.[38]

The number of ED visits rose from 124 million in 2008 to just more than 136 million in 2009, a 10% increase, which was described as the "steepest single-year upsurge on record."[39] More than 136 million visits worked out to 45.1 visits per 100 people, up from 41.4 per 100 in 2008 and 39.4 in 2007. There were 19% uninsured patients and 39% privately insured patients in 2009, compared with 15.4% and 41.9%, respectively, in 2008.[39] The number of uninsured patients' emergency room (ER) visits continues to reflect the EDs' safety-net function.

In 2011, a continued reduction in the number of urban hospital-based EDs in the United States was reported in a research study published in the *Journal of the American Medical Association* which found that from 1990 to 2009, the total number of urban hospital EDs had declined by 27%.[40] For-profit ownership, location in a competitive market, and low profit margin are some of the primary factors associated with increased risk of urban ED closure.[40]

The reasons for ED visits encompass a broad spectrum, ranging from life-threatening conditions to those treatable in primary care settings. The Centers for Disease Control and Prevention reports that almost half of metropolitan center hospitals routinely experience ED crowding and that one-third of hospitals report the need to divert ambulances to other EDs because of a lack of capacity.[41–43]

EDs in most hospitals are high-technology facilities staffed by emergency medicine specialists 24 hours a day, 365 days a year. Although designed to care for life-threatening illness or injury, the public increasingly looks to them for medical care that ranges from the unnecessary to the routine. Almost 8% of ED visits were deemed to be nonurgent in 2009[38] (Figure 5-4), which when viewed in terms of number of total nonurgent ED visits, equates to well over 10 million visits in that year alone.

One contributing factor to this level of inappropriate ED use is patients' self-interpretation of symptoms. Also, when physicians receive after-hours calls or calls regarding potentially serious complaints and it is neither practical nor seems appropriate for the patient to be seen in the private office, physicians may direct patients to the ED for immediate care. Physicians may also use the EDs to perform certain tests or examinations requiring equipment not available in their offices. Because state and

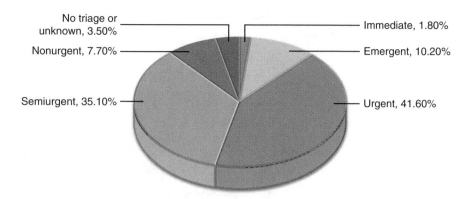

No triage or unknown, 3.50%
Nonurgent, 7.70%
Semiurgent, 35.10%
Immediate, 1.80%
Emergent, 10.20%
Urgent, 41.60%

FIGURE 5-4 Percent Distribution of Emergency Department Visits by Immediacy with which Patients should be Seen.
Source: Reproduced from CDC/NCHS, National Ambulatory Medical Care Survey: Emergency Department 2009 Summary Tables.

federal regulations require that hospitals turn no one away from the ED without an appropriate assessment, patients know that EDs are a guaranteed source of care regardless of their ability to pay or the nature of their complaint.

In terms of payment source, in 2006 Medicaid patients represented the highest ED visit rate and privately insured persons the lowest.[37] However by 2009 this had altered considerably, with privately insured persons having the highest percentage of visits (38.6%), followed by Medicaid and Children's Health Insurance Program (CHIP), which comprised 29.3% visits (Figure 5-5).[38]

More than one-third of annual ER visits were for injuries, poisoning, and adverse effects of prior medical treatment (45.4 million visits in 2009). The latter included complications of medical and surgical procedures and adverse effects of medication.[38]

EDs are organized to treat episodes of serious illness and injury and are, therefore, not a good choice for routine care. First, care is much more expensive than in an appropriate ambulatory setting because it consumes the time of specialist personnel for conditions in which that level of personnel is unnecessary. Second, waiting times are often long because life-threatening cases appropriately have priority. Third, the ED, by its

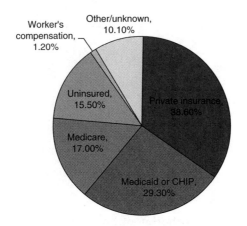

FIGURE 5-5 Percent of Emergency Department Visits by Expected Source(s) of Payment: United States, 2009.
Source: Reproduced from CDC/NCHS National Ambulatory Medical Care Survey: 2009 Emergency Department Summary Tables.

nature, is not organized or staffed to provide follow-up care for routine illnesses. To promote appropriate care for patients who inappropriately present at the ED, staff will refer them, when possible, to ambulatory primary care services. Initially, managed care organizations attempted to curb inappropriate ED use by requiring their members to obtain telephone preauthorization before going to the ED and by imposing financial disincentives through co-pays of ED fees when the visit did not result in hospitalization; however, the consumer backlash against such restrictions resulted in most states passing "prudent layperson" legislation, which requires insurance companies to reimburse costs based on care that a reasonable layperson would consider necessary.[44]

Despite the recognition that inappropriate ED use drives up costs and results in inadequate continuity of care, many individuals who lack resources to pay for care or are unaware of other sources of care find the ED the most accessible source of care. Until the health care system successfully reduces financial barriers to care and achieves a universal, basic level of access to routine medical care, a large volume of inappropriate ED visits can be expected to persist.

In the past, like other teaching hospital outpatient clinics, the ED was a place of indenture for medical interns or medical residents who were required to provide coverage as a component of their training. Often, to earn extra income, medical residents would contract to "moonlight" extra hours for their assigned hospital or for other hospital EDs. Nonteaching hospitals also often hired medical residents on a contracted basis to cover the ED or required attending staff to provide rotating coverage.

From both the physicians' and patients' perspective, these staffing configurations were less than ideal. Under these arrangements, physicians working in EDs often had little training or experience with the illnesses and injuries encountered there. This type of haphazard ED staffing was abandoned by the mid-1980s. Expanded knowledge, techniques, and equipment available for the care of critically ill and injured patients and concerns about liability resulted in dramatic changes in how EDs are staffed and organized. Since 1979, emergency medicine has been recognized as a medical specialty with accompanying requirements for extended specialty training and experience to attain board certification, as in the other medical specialty fields.[45] Now, physicians qualified by training and experience in emergency medicine staff most hospital EDs. Several corporations employ groups of board-qualified or board-certified emergency medicine physicians and contract their services to hospitals. Medical schools with accredited training programs in emergency medicine may staff their affiliated hospitals' EDs as a faculty practice group and provide clinical training for department medical residents, similar to the organization of other outpatient clinics.

In addition to physicians, EDs are staffed by nurses with advanced education and training in the triage and care of critically ill or injured patients. EDs also employ an array of other personnel who provide medical and nursing assistance and clerical support. Depending on the needs of the population served by the hospital, ED staff may also include mental health professionals and social workers. On-call arrangements with hospital staff members of other departments or with contracted professionals assist ED staff to meet other needs of patients presenting at the ED.

Freestanding Facilities

Non-hospital-based, or freestanding, ambulatory care facilities may be owned and operated by hospitals, hospital systems, or physician groups or by independent, for-profit, or not-for-profit single entities or corporate chains. Many hospital systems, independent entities, and chains operate multiple ambulatory care facilities that provide a wide array of services, including ambulatory surgery, occupational health services, physical rehabilitation, substance abuse treatment, renal dialysis, cancer treatment, diagnostic imaging, cardiovascular diagnosis, sports medicine, and urgent/emergent care. Technology advances, entrepreneurial business opportunities, cost-reduction initiatives, and consumer preferences for convenient services continue to advance freestanding services as major components of the health care delivery system.

The following provides an overview of the major types of freestanding facilities that play roles in the rapid expansion of ambulatory care services.

Urgent Care Centers

The first urgent care centers opened in the 1970s. The Urgent Care Association of America (UCAOA) describes urgent care center services as "providing walk-in, extended hour access for acute illness and injury care that is either beyond the scope or availability of the typical primary care practice or retail clinic."[46] Urgent care centers may also provide other health care services such as occupational medicine, travel medicine, and sports and school physicals. In most states, urgent care centers do not require licensure separate from that of a typical physician office that operates under the physician's license auspices.[46] The UCAOA emphasizes that urgent care centers neither treat the life-threatening emergencies appropriate for hospital EDs nor assist with labor and delivery. The UCAOA also distinguishes urgent care centers from in-store retail clinics, in that urgent care centers provide a broader scope of services to a wider age range of health care consumers and use a staffing model primarily composed of physicians rather than of nurse practitioners.[46] (See discussion in section "Retail Clinics.")

The American Academy of Urgent Care Medicine defines this medical discipline as "provision of immediate medical service (no appointment necessary) offering outpatient care for the treatment of acute and chronic illness and injury."[47] The UCAOA estimates that there are more than 8,700 such facilities in the United States providing more than 150 million visits annually.[46] The UCAOA reports that 55% of centers are located in suburban communities, 25% in urban areas, and 20% in rural areas.[46] Ownership is diverse, including for-profit corporate chains, single entities, hospitals, private physician groups, and managed care organizations.

By operating for extended hours, including evenings, weekends, and holidays, and accepting patients on a walk-in basis, they meet consumer needs for convenient care for episodic illness or injury. Some centers enable patients to register online with a brief medical history in advance to expedite their visit. Physician staff members are usually specialists in internal, family, or emergency medicine.

Established in 1997, the American Board of Urgent Care Medicine offers certification in the field of urgent care medicine to qualified candidates who have successfully completed an Accreditation Council for Graduate Medical Education residency in emergency medicine, family practice, general surgery, internal medicine, obstetrics and gynecology or pediatrics; meet several other requirements for experience in the field and continuing medical education; and pass a certification examination.[48]

In addition to physicians, urgent care centers may employ registered nurses, nurse practitioners, physician assistants, reception or other support staff, and may provide radiology and basic laboratory services. Acceptable payment typically includes all forms of insurance, cash, and credit cards. Individual urgent care centers may be granted certification by the UCAOA upon meeting specific criteria for staffing models, facility equipment, hours of operation, and other requirements.[49]

From the consumer standpoint, urgent care centers fill gaps in the delivery system created by the inflexibility of private physician appointment scheduling and unavailability during nonbusiness hours. The centers provide a much more convenient and user-friendly alternative to a hospital ED during hours when private physicians are unavailable. In addition, for individuals who are new to a community and have not had the opportunity to establish a physician relationship, the centers can meet immediate needs in a convenient, economical manner without incurring the long waits and expense of the hospital ED. Typically located in highly visible facilities, such as storefronts in commercial areas, they offer valued convenience and ease of accessibility to their consumers. Because they are a less expensive alternative to the hospital ED, health plans usually fully reimburse members' use of urgent care facilities when their physicians are not available.

Urgent care centers emphasize to patients that they do not provide ongoing care for chronic conditions, although they may be the site where a chronic condition such as diabetes or hypertension is initially diagnosed. If patients do not have a routine source of care, center personnel may encourage them to establish a patient relationship with a primary doctor and may provide information about area physicians or primary care centers that are accepting new patients to encourage continuity. The UCAOA recommends that "all individuals have a primary care physician and supports the American Academy of Family Physician's concept of a 'medical home'."[46] To maintain positive relationships with physicians whose patients they have treated, the centers may forward records of treatment to the patients' physicians.

Hospitals have expressed concern that urgent care centers may attract significant numbers of paying patients, leaving to hospital EDs a disproportionate share of the most ill and expensive-to-treat patients. In areas where the centers have proliferated, the private physician community also has voiced concerns about the availability of such facilities affecting patients' motivation to develop a relationship with a primary physician. Nonetheless, the growth in numbers of urgent care centers is a clear indication that consumers perceive them as a positive alternative to the hospital ED, and for those without a primary physician's availability, they can meet nonemergency needs in a convenient and consumer-friendly manner.

Retail Clinics

Clinics operated at retail sites such as pharmacies and supermarkets are a rapidly emerging form of ambulatory care. The first retail clinics opened in 2000 in the Minneapolis–St. Paul area in grocery stores.[50] Expanding from approximately 300 retail clinic sites in 2007, by the end of 2010, there were approximately 1,200 retail sites.[51] Between 2007 and 2009, the number of retail clinic visits quadrupled, from 1.48 million visits in 2007 to 5.97 million visits in 2009.[51] Forty-four percent of patients use retail clinics in evenings and on weekends and 64.5 percent report that they have no primary physician.[51] Known by consumer-friendly names, such as "MinuteClinic" and "TakeCare," the clinics operate in CVS pharmacies, Walgreens, Wal-Mart, and Target stores, and many other retail locations. Retail clinics represent an entrepreneurial response to consumer demand for fast, affordable treatment of easy-to-diagnose, acute conditions. Staffed by nurse practitioners or physician assistants, a physician is not required on-site, although many clinics have physician consultation available by phone. Market analysts are forecasting more than a doubling of the current number of retail clinics to 2,800 by 2018.[52]

The clinics' lower cost has captured health plans' attention. Many health plans are contracting with retail clinics to allow patients to pay only co-pays. Some employers are encouraging retail clinic use by waiving the co-pay entirely.[53] At least 85% or more of clinic sites accept insurance and co-payments; a recent survey noted that 62% of all visits derived some part of payment from an insurance carrier and that some retail clinics have partnered with integrated systems such as the Cleveland Clinic and Allina Health.[51,54]

Reactions to the clinics from the organized medical community vary from acceptance of this development as a consumer choice to strong opposition. Primary care physicians have many concerns about quality and continuity of care as well as competition. The AAFP has the retail clinic phenomenon under continuing study and in 2013 issued a policy affirming its belief that the PCMH is best suited to improving the quality of care. In this policy, the AAFP opposed expansion of retail clinic services beyond minor acute illness and chronic medical conditions and agreed that retail clinics can be a component of patient-centered care while coordinating with primary care physicians to avoid fragmentation.[55] A past president of a state medical society noted, "MinuteClinic has exposed an Achilles' heel of office-based practice; there is an access problem. If there were not, care options such as 'MinuteClinic' or similar counterparts would not be venturing in for-profit medicine."[53]

In 2007, the AMA petitioned federal and state regulators to investigate retail clinics for possible conflicts of interest, noting that its petitions were prompted by retail stores' admissions that the retail clinics increased prescription drug sales and help increase other sales. The AMA also took issue with health insurers allowing retail clinics to waive or lower patient co-payments while continuing to require physicians to collect the fees, arguing that this practice may actively influence patients to choose the clinic over a physician visit on the basis of cost rather than quality.[56]

As retail clinics continue proliferating, more research is required to learn about how these entities will fit into the reformed delivery system. Researchers have suggested that the ACA may further increase retail clinic utilization as demand for primary care may outstrip physician availability.[51] This growing ambulatory care enterprise is under close observation by employers, insurers, retailers, investors, and the medical and consumer communities. It is clear that retail clinics are in the mainstream of primary health care delivery and will likely continue to influence the future primary care delivery system.

Ambulatory Surgery Centers

Ambulatory or outpatient surgery accounted for almost two-thirds of all surgeries performed in 2006.[57] In the decade between 1996 and 2006 the rate of visits to freestanding ambulatory surgery centers (ASCs) increased approximately 300%, whereas the rate in hospital-based centers was flat[57] (Figure 5-6). In 2006, an estimated 53.3 million surgical and nonsurgical procedures were performed during 34.7 million ambulatory surgery visits.[57] Approximately 19.9 million ambulatory surgery visits occurred

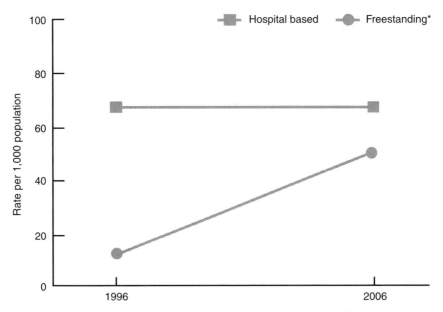

*The rate of ambulatory visits includes ambulatory surgery patients admitted to hospitals as inpatients for both 1996 and 2006. As a result, the data differ from those presented in the 1996 report.

FIGURE 5-6 Rates of Ambulatory Surgery Visits by Facility Type, United States, 1996 and 2006.
Source: Reproduced from CDC/NCHS National Ambulatory Medical Care Survey, 2006.

in hospitals, and 14.9 million occurred in freestanding settings.[57] The National Center for Health Statistics defines ambulatory surgery as "surgical and nonsurgical procedures performed on an ambulatory (outpatient) basis in a hospital or freestanding center's general operating rooms, dedicated ambulatory surgery rooms, and other specialized rooms such as endoscopy units and cardiac catheterization labs."[57] Outpatient surgery continues to be a major contributor to the overall growth trend in ambulatory care.

Since the 1990s the number of ASCs has more than doubled, with more than 5,000 ASCs currently in operation in the United States. Almost 57 million outpatient surgical and nonsurgical procedures are performed annually in the United States. Total surgical center ASC payments have increased from $1.2 billion in 1999 to $3.2 billion in 2009, an increase of 167%.[58]

In the 1970s, physicians led the development of freestanding ASCs because they saw opportunities created by advancing technology to establish quality and cost-effective alternatives to inpatient surgery. ASCs were physicians' solutions to frustration with in-hospital bureaucracy, operating room schedule difficulties, and patient inconvenience. Today, physicians have either complete or partial ownership of approximately 96% of freestanding ASCs, hospitals have some level of ownership interest in 25% of all ASCs, and 2% are owned entirely by hospitals.[59] Between 2000 and 2007 the number of Medicare-certified ASCs increased at an average annual rate of 7.3%; by 2008 there were more than 5,000 Medicare-certified ASCs in the United States.[60]

Hospitals responded to the demand for outpatient surgery when faced with competition from physician-run freestanding facilities and insurer demands for lower costs. In 1982, Medicare expanded coverage to include ambulatory surgical procedures, and the Medicare hospital prospective payment system subsequently created strong incentives for hospitals to shift surgery to outpatient settings.[59] Between 1982 and 1992, outpatient surgeries in community hospitals had increased by more than 200%, whereas inpatient procedures declined by more than 32%.[61]

Advancements in medical technology and changes in reimbursement criteria were the two primary drivers promoting the increase in ambulatory surgical procedures as alternatives to inpatient surgery. One of the most significant factors was new general anesthetics that resolved safely and quickly, enabling surgical patients to return to normal functioning within a few hours. Advancements in surgical equipment and techniques reduced or eliminated the invasiveness of many procedures and their complications and risks. With these and other technologic advances making outpatient surgery increasingly feasible and safe, mounting financial pressures resulted in Medicare, insurance companies, and managed care organizations requiring that certain procedures be performed in the less costly ambulatory setting unless physicians were able to document the necessity of hospitalization. The initial years of the shift from inpatient to ambulatory surgery provided opportunities for hospitals to convert underused facility space into efficient, cost-effective care delivery areas, encouraging the development of separate surgical management systems for ambulatory and complicated cases, and well-managed ASCs quickly became profitable.

Freestanding ambulatory surgical facilities owned and operated by hospitals, physicians, or independent entities offer several advantages over similar types of in-hospital services, including enhanced aesthetics, ease of accessibility, and the opportunity to customize the scheduling of service delivery independent of hospital bureaucracy. It is not surprising that ASCs were embraced rapidly by physicians. Patients view freestanding facilities as far more user friendly and responsive to their needs than their hospital-based counterparts, with 98% reporting a high degree of satisfaction with services.[62]

ASCs are among the most highly regulated health care providers. Forty-three states require licensure of ASCs with explicit criteria for licensure approval.[59] Medicare also requires rigorous inspection of ASCs to qualify for reimbursement.[59] Many ASCs also voluntarily submit to accreditation reviews by The Joint Commission, the Accreditation Association for Ambulatory Health Care, the American Association for the Accreditation of Ambulatory Surgery Facilities, or the American Osteopathic Association.[59]

Patient care quality has benefited significantly from improved technology and advanced, less traumatic surgical techniques applied in the ambulatory setting. Patients experience fewer complications, much faster recovery, and less disruption to normal activity from ambulatory than from hospital inpatient surgery. Continuing advances in surgical and anesthetic procedures, postoperative management, and other evolving technology provide future opportunities to move even more types of inpatient surgery into the ambulatory setting.

Federally Qualified Community Health Centers

Federally funded, community-based primary care centers originated during Lyndon Johnson's presidency in the mid-1960s and represented a facet of that administration's social reform movement labeled the "war on poverty." Originally authorized by the Office of Economic Opportunity, coordinating responsibility was transferred to the Public Health Service in the mid-1970s. Funded under Section 330 of the Public Health Service Act, the organization and staffing patterns of these facilities drew from earlier models of public health services oriented toward the needs of underserved communities.[63] Centers were initially established in cities and in rural communities across the country, and although differing from each other with respect to size and the scope of available services, they had common characteristics rooted in federal funding requirements, including focus on needs of the underserved, comprehensive primary care, professional staffing, community involvement, and partnerships between the public and private sectors. Subsequent amendments to Section 330 established specialized primary care programs for migrant workers, the homeless, and residents of public housing.[63]

Federally qualified health centers (FQHCs) are typically staffed by multidisciplinary teams that include physicians, nurses, social workers, nutrition science professionals, and support personnel. The staffing pattern reflects a commitment to a comprehensive service approach to address the multidimensional nature of health and health-related needs of underserved populations. Target populations are minorities, women of childbearing-age, infants, persons with HIV/AIDS, substance abusers, and individuals and families who experience health service access barriers for any reason. In addition to primary care, preventive care, and dental services, community health centers assist patients to link with other supportive programs and services such as public assistance; Medicaid; the supplemental nutrition program for Women, Infant, and Children (WIC); and the CHIP. Many community health centers also offer on-site laboratory testing, pharmacy services, and radiology services, and may provide transportation, translation, and health education services as specific population needs dictate. To facilitate access to services, community health centers may also employ outreach workers drawn from the centers' service areas. These workers receive training in health and social service needs assessment and advocacy for early intervention and continuity of care.

FQHC grants are administered by the Health Resources and Services Administration of the U.S. Department of Health and Human Services. Fees for services are based on income and many services are offered without charge for the health care of the neediest patients. The program has grown substantially over the years from 104 centers in the early 1970s. In 2011, more than 1,100 community health centers operated more than 8,500 sites providing care to approximately 20.2 million patients in every state, the District of Columbia, Puerto Rico, U.S. Virgin Islands, and the Pacific Basin. Nearly two-thirds of the patients served were members of ethnic and minority groups. Nearly 40% had no health insurance.[64]

FQHCs are the provider of choice for Medicaid beneficiaries. Although Medicaid beneficiaries account for only 16% of the general population, they represent almost 40% of health center patients.[65]

The number of Medicaid beneficiaries receiving services from FQHCs increased by 39% in just the 5 years from 2007 to 2011 (Figure 5-7).[65] Medicaid has been the FQHCs' largest revenue source, representing 38% of total revenue.[65] However, since 2007, Medicaid reimbursement has declined at a time when FQHCs are serving increasing numbers of Medicaid patients (Figure 5-7).[65]

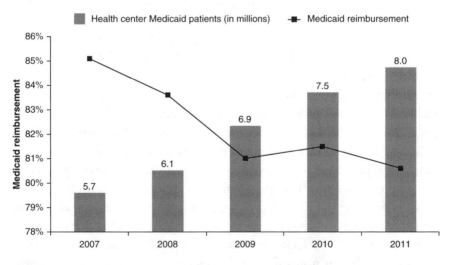

FIGURE 5-7 Medicaid Reimbursement Declines as Health Center Medicaid Patients have Increased in Number.
Source: Reproduced from Bureau of Primary Health Care. HRSA. DHHS 2007-2011. Uniform Data System.

The Medicaid payment structure, as enacted by the Congress in recent years, was intended to help ensure that FQHC grant revenues were dedicated to the uninsured rather than subsidizing care for Medicaid patients. The widening gap between decreasing reimbursement and increasing numbers of Medicaid patients threatens FQHCs' capacity to serve both uninsured and insured patients and diminishes their rate of return. Given the fundamental interrelationship between FQHCs and Medicaid, changes in one profoundly impact the other.[65]

FQHCs may be organized under the aegis of local health departments (LHDs), as part of larger not-for-profit human service organizations, or as stand-alone, not-for-profit corporations. All FQHCs must meet fundamental parameters that include[63]:

- Location in a high-need community designated as a medically underserved area or population
- Governance by a community board of directors composed of 51% or more health center patients who represent the population served
- Provision of comprehensive primary health care services and supportive services (education, translation, transportation, etc.) that promote access to health care
- Provision of services available to all with fees adjusted on ability to pay
- Meeting other performance and accountability requirements regarding administrative, clinical, and financial operations

FQHCs continue to be a critically important source of primary care for the nation's most vulnerable and underserved citizens. In recognition of their crucial role, in 2009 the Obama administration earmarked $600 million in the ARRA to support major construction and renovation projects at 85 FQHCs and to support their adoption of electronic health records and other health information technology systems.[66] The ACA also contains important provisions for FQHCs including funds for program expansion and construction of new FQHC sites.[20] Also, under a provision of the ACA, in 2011, the Centers for Medicare and Medicaid Services launched a 3-year pilot program to test the PCMH model for FQHC Medicare beneficiaries.[67]

Public Health Ambulatory Services

The delivery of ambulatory health services by state, county, or municipally supported governmental entities has its roots in the early American ethic of community responsibility for care of needy community residents. Since the colonial period, altruistic citizens sought the charity of the community to provide for the less fortunate by supporting the development of almshouses or "poor houses" to care for the needy and for orphaned children. Many of these institutions became the precursors of community hospitals.

With the evolution of state and local governments' roles in providing welfare services and the development of the public health discipline in the late 19th and early 20th centuries, tax-supported state and LHDs began providing ambulatory personal health services. The public health community's successful campaigns in controlling childhood and other communicable diseases were rapidly followed by the recognition of the emergence of chronic disease by the medical care community. This recognition resulted in major shifts of resources toward specialized medical care, to the detriment of public health's preventive agenda.[68] In addition to maintaining its basic mission to promote and protect the public's health and safety, the public health community was expected to mount new initiatives to promote healthy lifestyles, provide safety-net services to needy populations, and expand regulatory oversight to accommodate the rapidly expanding medical care industry.[68]

Ambulatory health services that became the domain of health departments included the administration of preventive public health measures, such as cancer and chronic disease screening, immunization, high-risk maternal and infant care, family planning, tobacco control, and tuberculosis and sexually transmitted disease screening and treatment. Some LHDs also established federally qualified or other types of community health centers to provide a range of primary care services to needy individuals of all ages.

Today, the scope of ambulatory care services delivered by public health departments ranges across a wide spectrum from prevention-oriented programs, such as immunizations, well-baby care, smoking cessation, and cancer and chronic disease screening and education, to a full range of personal health services offered through ambulatory care centers. Historically, support for ambulatory public health services has included combinations of city, county, and state funding, plus federal and state disease-specific or block grant funds.

Public health ambulatory services staff may include physicians, nurses, aides, social workers, public health educators, community health workers, and clerical and administrative staff, who function under the overall administrative direction of a local health officer. This health officer may or may not be a physician, depending on the population size of the jurisdiction and individual state or municipal requirements. Depending on the geographic area, the governmental aegis may be state, county, or city.

Findings of the National Association of County and City Health Officials (NACCHO) 2010 *National Survey of Local Health Departments* reveal the extent to which LHDs are providing ambulatory services.[69] With responses from 2,107 LHDs of 2,565 surveyed, the survey reported that a significant proportion of local public health agencies continue to directly provide an array of ambulatory services. As examples of the services most frequently provided, adult and child immunizations top the list at 92% of respondents. Seventy-five percent of LHDs reported services to treat tuberculosis and 59% reported services to treat sexually transmitted diseases other than HIV/AIDS. Fifty-five percent of respondents reported that they provide family planning services.[69] The NACCHO launched its next survey of LHDs in January 2013.[70]

The September 11, 2001 terrorist attacks and threats of bioterrorism brought a renewed focus to the role of the federal, state, and local public health agencies in providing public protection and supporting national security. In response, in 2002 the federal government transferred $5 billion to the states to improve public health and medical emergency preparedness to strengthen the existing public health infrastructure.[71] Experts acknowledge that the infusion of federal funds improved local and state level emergency preparedness across several parameters.[71] However, the new funding occurred when states were encountering the sharpest revenue shortfalls in recent decades. And "Instead of building more capacity, public health agencies found themselves having to support ongoing services and the new preparedness mission with very little extra funding."[71] The 2009 threat of an H1N1 (swine flu) influenza pandemic tested the capacity of state and local public health agencies to identify and mobilize personnel and other resources to meet ambulatory services demands for mass immunizations. A report on state and LHDs' timeliness of communication using Websites following the declaration of a national public health emergency in response to the H1N1 outbreak found considerable variability in local level performance. Further study will help to determine the causes of variability, including Internet access, staffing constraints, and patterns in media use.[72] An in-depth guide for public health agencies' responsibilities in strategic planning at all levels of government in meeting immunization demands and any other infectious, occupational, or environmental incidents or threats is provided by a U.S. Department of Health and Human Services/CDC 2011 document, "Public Health Preparedness Capabilities: National Standards for State and Local Planning."[73]

Not-for-Profit Agencies

Not-for-profit agencies operate a variety of ambulatory health care services throughout the United States. Services have evolved from many sources, often cause related, to address needs of population groups afflicted by specific diseases or types of conditions. Asthma, diabetes, multiple sclerosis, and cerebral palsy are a few of the conditions addressed. As not-for-profit organizations, many are chartered by states as charitable organizations and maintain tax-exempt status with the Internal Revenue Service. These designations allow them to solicit charitable contributions for which their donors may receive tax deductions. Governed by boards of directors who receive no compensation for their services, these organizations may be operated by a totally volunteer staff or employ numerous paid professionals and have annual operating budgets of several million dollars.

Characteristically, voluntary ambulatory health care agencies were established through the advocacy of special interest groups that desired to address the health care or health-related needs of a population group whose needs were not being adequately met by existing community services. Some operate as single entities, others as independent affiliated agencies of national organizations. Planned Parenthood Federation of America is an example of one such organization. Its clinics provide preventive care, education, and direct services for gynecologic care and contraception in numerous locations throughout the United States. Another example is the Alzheimer's Association, which provides or assists affected individuals and their caregivers with specialized education and social support and promotes research into causes of and treatment for the disease. Frequently, legislative advocacy related to the organization's interests at the federal, state, and local levels is a major component of not-for-profit organization activity.

Financial support for voluntary ambulatory health care agencies is diverse. Sources may include charitable contributions, private payment, third-party insurance reimbursement (including Medicare and Medicaid), and federal, state, or local government grants. In many agencies, a large proportion of clients is uninsured or underinsured and lacks personal resources, making financial subsidies crucial to continued viability. Agencies with missions to serve the neediest members of the community continue meeting challenges posed by the ebb and flow of government grant dollars and community economic conditions that affect philanthropic support through efficient business practices and a variety of private fundraising activities.[74] Although voluntary agencies provide only a small fraction of the ambulatory care services, as compared with hospitals and other ambulatory care organizations, they are important as repositories of community values, as symbols of community charity and volunteerism, and as advocates for populations with special needs.

Continued Future Expansion and Experimentation

The focus of U.S. health care delivery system has shifted from hospitals to expanded use of ambulatory care services. This shift will continue with advances in medical technology and diagnostic and treatment modalities that allow more services to be provided safely and effectively in the outpatient setting, cost-reduction initiatives by private and government payers, and consumer demands for more convenient, accessible services. The roles of urgent care centers and retail clinics in the ambulatory care landscape will continue to evolve as experience is acquired and evidence is analyzed about patient outcomes, satisfaction, costs, and profitability As reforms continue to impact the health care marketplace, The PCMH and ACO models will continue to be subjects of numerous federal and state government and industry-sponsored demonstration programs and pilot projects in the years ahead. The results and analyses will provide fertile opportunities for health services research to inform practitioners and policymakers about the effectiveness of system reforms in achieving the goals of higher quality care and reduced costs.

Key Terms for Review

Accountable Care Organization (ACO)
Ambulatory Care
Federally Qualified Health Center
(FQHC)
Patient-Centered Medical Home
(PCMH)

Retail Clinic
Urgent Care Center
Voluntary Ambulatory Health Agency

References

1. Goldsmith J. Hospitals and physicians: not a pretty picture. *Health Affairs.* 2007;26:w72–w75. Available from http://content.healthaffairs.org/content/26/1/ w72.full.pdf+html. Accessed December 30, 2012.
2. Berenson RA, Ginsburg PB, May JH. Hospital–physician relations: cooperation, competition, or separation? *Health Affairs.* 2007;26(1):w31–w43. Available from http://content.healthaffairs.org/content/26/1/w31.full. pdf+html. Accessed December 30, 2012.
3. MacNulty A, Reich J. Surveys and interviews examine relationships between physicians and hospitals. *The Physician Executive.* 2008. Available from http://www.noblis.org/MissionAreas/HI/ThoughtLeadership/Documents/articleACPESurvey.pdf. Accessed December 30, 2012.
4. Schappert SM, Rechtsteiner EA. Ambulatory medical care utilization estimates for 2007. National Health Statistics Reports. *Vital and Health Statistics.* 13. April 2011(169):3. Available from http://www.cdc.gov/nchs/data/series/sr_13_169.pdf. Accessed December 30, 2012.
5. CDC, NCHS. National Ambulatory Medical Care Survey: 2009 summary tables. Available from http://www.cdc.gov/nchs/data/ahcd/namcs_summary/2009_namcs_web_tables.pdf. Accessed December 30, 2012.
6. Raffel MW, Raffel NK. *The U.S. health system: origins and functions, 4th ed.* Albany, NY: Delmar Publishers; 1994:36–44.
7. Hing E, Burt CW. *Office-based medical practices: methods and estimates from the National Ambulatory Medical Care Survey: advance data.* March 12, 2007, No. 383. Available from http://www.cdc.gov/nchs/data/ad/ad383.pdf. Accessed December 31, 2012.
8. Center for Studying Health System Change. A snapshot of U.S. physicians: key findings from the 2008 health tracking study physician survey. Available from http://www.hschange.com/CONTENT/1078. Accessed December 31, 2012.
9. Hospitals and Health Networks Daily. Hospital statistics chart rise in physician employment. Available from http://www.hhnmag.com/hhnmag/HHN Daily/HHNDailyDisplay.dhtml?id=1970001363. Accessed January 12, 2013.

10. Center for Studying Health System Change. Rising hospital employment of physicians: better quality, higher costs? Available from http://www.hschange.com/CONTENT/1230/. Accessed January 12, 2013.

11. Kocher R, Sahni R. Hospitals' race to employ physicians—the logic behind a money-losing proposition. *New England Journal of Medicine*. 2011;364:1791. Available from http://www.nejm.org/doi/full/10.1056/NEJMp1101959. Accessed January 20, 2013.

12. Endres A, Good C, Stansberry M. Health Care Institutional Management. Hospital-owned physician practices: comeback of the 21st century. Available from http://www.trinity.edu/eschumac/HCAD5320/Departmental%20Papers/Fall%202011/Hospital%20owned%20physician%20practices%20Inst%20Mgmt.pdf. Accessed January 3, 2013.

13. American College of Physicians. Enhance care coordination through the patient centered medical home (PCMH). Available from http://www.acponline.org/running_practice/delivery_and_payment_models/pcmh/understanding/pcmh_back.pdf. Accessed January 9, 2013.

14. Reid RJ, Coleman K, Johnson EA, et al. The group health medical home at year two: cost savings, higher patient satisfaction, and less burnout for providers. *Health Affairs*. 2010;29:835. Available from http://content.healthaffairs.org/content/29/5/835.full.html. Accessed January 9, 2013.

15. American College of Physicians. The patient-centered medical home. Available from http://www.acponline.org/running_practice/delivery_and_payment_models/pcmh/. Accessed December 31, 2012.

16. American Academy of Family Physicians. Joint principles of the patient-centered medical home. 2007. Available from http://www.aafp.org/online/etc/medialib/aafp_org/documents/membership/pcmh/joint.Par.0001.File.tmp/PCMHJoint.pdf. Accessed December 31, 2012.

17. American College of Physicians. The advanced medical home: a patient-centered, physician-guided model of health care. Position paper. Philadelphia, PA: American College of Physicians; 2006. Available from http://www.acponline.org/advocacy/where_we_stand/policy/adv_med.pdf. Accessed December 31, 2012.

18. American College of Physicians. Who supports the PCMH model? Available from http://www.acponline.org/running_practice/delivery_and_payment_models/pcmh/understanding/who.htm. Accessed December 31, 2012.

19. Patient-Centered Primary Care Collaborative. Benefits of implementing the PCMH: a review of cost and quality results. 2012. Available from http://www.pcpcc.net/files/benefits_of_implementing_the_primary_care_pcmh_0.pdf. Accessed January 12, 2013.

20. Safety Net Medical Home Initiative. Health reform and the patient-centered medical home: policy provisions and expectations of the Patient Protection and Affordable Care act. Available from http://www.safetynetmedicalhome.org/sites/default/files/policy-brief-2.pdf. Accessed January 9, 2013.

21. Safety Net Medical Home Initiative. Paying for the medical home: payment models to support patient-centered medical home transformation in the safety net. Available from http://www.safetynetmedicalhome.org/sites/default/files/policy-brief-1.pdf. Accessed January 9, 2013.

22. The Commonwealth Fund. *Guiding transformation: how medical practices can become patient-centered medical homes.* Available from http://www.commonwealthfund.org/~/media/Files/Publications/Fund%20Report/2012/Feb/1582_Wagner_guiding_transformation_patientcentered_med_home_v2.pdf. Accessed January 14, 2013.

23. Rosenberg CN, Peele P, Keyser D, et al. Results from a patient-centered medical home pilot at UPMC health plan hold lessons for broader adoption of the model. *Health Affairs.* 2012;31:2423. Available from http://content.healthaffairs.org/content/31/11/2423.full.html. Accessed January 14, 2013.

24. American College of Physicians. Grant-funded activities. Available from http://www.acponline.org/running_practice/delivery_and_payment_models/pcmh/understanding/grant_activities.htm. Accessed December 31, 2012.

25. National Academy for State Health Policy. Medical home and patient-centered care. Available from http://www.nashp.org/med-home-map. Accessed January 14, 2013.

26. Bitton A, Martin C, Landon BE. A nationwide survey of patient centered medical home demonstration projects. *Journal of General Internal Medicine.* 2010;25:584. Available from http://www.ncbi.nlm.nih.gov/pmc/articles/PMC2869409/. Accessed January 14, 2013.

27. National Committee for Quality Assurance. NCQA certification program identifies medical home experts. Available from http://www.ncqa.org/newsroom/2013newsarchive/newsreleaseJanuary172013.aspx. Accessed January 18, 2013.

28. Stange KC, Miller WL, Nutting PA, et al. Context for understanding the national demonstration project and the patient-centered medical home. *Annals of Family Medicine.* 2010;8:S4. Available from www.annfammed.org/content/8/Suppl_1/S2.full.pdf. Accessed January 11, 2013.

29. HealthCare.gov. Accountable care organizations: improving care coordination for people with Medicare. Available from http://www.healthcare.gov/news/factsheets/2011/03/accountablecare03312011a.html. Accessed January 15, 2013.

30. Centers for Medicare and Medicaid Services. Accountable care organizations. Available from http://www.cms.gov/medicare/medicare-fee-for-service-payment/aco/index.html?redirect=/aco. Accessed January 15, 2013.

31. Longworth D. Accountable care organizations, the patient-centered medical home, and health care reform: what does it all mean? *Cleveland Clinic Journal of Medicine.* 2011;78:578. Available from http://www.ccjm.org/content/78/9/571.full.pdf. Accessed January 16, 2013.

32. Centers for Medicare and Medicaid Services. More doctors, hospitals partner to coordinate care for people with Medicare. Available from http://www.cms.gov/apps/media/press/release.asp?Counter=4501&intNumPerPage=10&checkDate=&checkKey=&srchType=1&numDays=3500&srchOpt=0&srchData=&keywordType=All&chkNewsType=1%2C+2%2C+3%2C+4%2C+5&intPage=&showAll=&pYear=&year=&desc=&cboOrder=date. Accessed January 9, 2013.

33. Baxley L, Borkan J, Campbell T, et al. In pursuit of a transformed health care system: from patient centered medical homes to accountable care organizations and beyond. *Annals of Family Medicine*. 2011;9:467. Available from http://www.annfammed.org/content/9/5/466.full. Accessed January 14, 2013.

34. Knowles JH. The role of the hospital: the ambulatory clinic. *Bulletin of the New York Academy of Medicine*. 1965;41:68–70.

35. Fraser I, Lane L, Linne E. Ambulatory care: a decade of change in health care delivery. *The Journal of Ambulatory Care Management*. 1993;16:1–8.

36. American Hospital Association Trendwatch Chartbook 2012. Table 4.2: distribution of inpatient vs. outpatient revenues, 1990–2010. Available from http://www.aha.org/research/reports/tw/chartbook/2012/table4-2.pdf. Accessed January 16, 2013.

37. Pitts SR, Niska RW, Xu J, Burt CW. National hospital ambulatory medical care survey: 2006, emergency department summary. *National Health Statistics Reports*. August 6, 2008;(7). Hyattsville, MD: National Center for Health Statistics. Available from http://www.cdc.gov/nchs/data/nhsr/nhsr007.pdf. Accessed January 5, 2013.

38. CDC. Ambulatory and Hospital Care Statistics Branch. National ambulatory medical care survey: 2009 emergency department summary tables. Available from http://www.cdc.gov/nchs/data/ahcd/nhamcs_emergency/2009_ed_web_tables.pdf. Accessed January 1, 2013.

39. Berry E. Emergency department volume rises as office visits fall. *American Medical Association amednews.com*. Available from http://www.ama-assn.org/amednews/2012/01/16/bisb0116.htm. Accessed December 31, 2012.

40. Hsia RY, Kellermann AL, Shen Y. Factors associated with closures of emergency departments in the United States. *JAMA*. 2011;305(19):1978–1985. doi:10.100.1001/jama.2011.620. Available from http://jama.jamanetwork.com/article.aspx?articleid=1161864. Accessed December 31, 2012.

41. Cunningham PJ. What accounts for differences in the use of hospital emergency departments across U.S. communities? *Health Affairs*. 2006;25:w324–w336.

42. U.S. Government Accounting Office. *Report to the Chairman, Committee on Finance, U.S. Senate. Hospital emergency departments: crowding continues to occur and some patients wait longer than recommended time frames*. Available from http://www.gao.gov/new.items/d09347.pdf. Accessed December 31, 2012.

43. CDC National Center for Health Statistics. Media brief. Almost half of hospitals experience crowded emergency departments. Available from http://www.cdc.gov/nchs/pressroom/06facts/hospitals.htm. Accessed December 31, 2012.

44. Kongstvedt PR. *Essentials of managed health care, 5th ed.* Sudbury, MA: Jones and Bartlett; 2007:14.

45. American Board of Emergency Medicine. ABEM history. Available from https://www.abem.org/PUBLIC/portal/alias_Rainbow/lang_en-US/tabID_3573/DesktopDefault.aspx. Accessed January 1, 2013.

46. Urgent Care Association of America. Urgent care industry information kit. 2011. Available from http://www.ucaoa.org/docs/UrgentCareMediaKit.pdf. Accessed January 1, 2013.

47. American Academy of Urgent Care Medicine. Available from http://aaucm.org/default.aspx. Accessed January 1, 2013.

48. American Board of Urgent Care Medicine. Board Certification brochure: eligibility requirements. Available from http://aaucm.org/Resources/370/FileRepository/ABUCM%20Brochure.pdf. Accessed January 2, 2013.

49. Urgent Care Association of America. Certified urgent care criteria. Available from http://www.ucaoa.org/recognition_certification_criteria.php. Accessed January 1, 2013.

50. Scott MK. *Health care in the express lane: retail clinics go mainstream.* Oakland, CA: HealthCare Foundation; September 2007. Available from http://www.chcf.org/~/media/MEDIA%20LIBRARY%20Files/PDF/H/PDF%20HealthCareInTheExpressLaneRetailClinics2007.pdf. Accessed January 2, 2013.

51. Mehrotra A, Lave JR. Visits to retail clinics grew fourfold from 2007–2009, although their share of overall outpatient visits remains low. *Health Affairs.* 2012;31:2126–2127. Available from http://www.health affairs.org/content/31/9/2123.full.html. Accessed January 14, 2013.

52. GBI Research. *Retail clinics: 2012 Yearbook.* Available from http://gbiresearch.com/report.aspx?ID=retail-clinics-2012-yearbook&companyID=jr.

53. Sullivan D. Retail health clinics are rolling your way. *Family Practice Management.* 2006;13(5):65–72. Available from http://www.aafp.org/fpm/2006/0500/p65.html. Accessed January 2, 2013.

54. Laws M, Scott MK. The emergence of retail-based clinics in the United States: early observations. *Health Affairs.* 2008;27:1293–1297. Available from http://content.healthaffairs.org/content/27/5/1293.full.html. Accessed January 2, 2013.

55. American Academy of Family Physicians. Retail clinics. Available from http://www.aafp.org/online/en/home/policy/policies/r/retailhealth.html. Accessed January 12, 2013.

56. Medical News Today. AMA calls for investigation of retail health clinics. 2007. Available from http://www.medicalnewstoday.com/articles/75308.php Accessed January 2, 2013.

57. Cullen KA, Hall MJ, Golosinskiy A. Ambulatory surgery in the United States, 2006. *National Health Statistics Reports*. 2009;(11). Revised. Hyattsville, MD: National Center for Health Statistics. Available from http://www.cdc.gov/nchs/data/nhsr/nhsr011.pdf. Accessed January 2, 2013.

58. Manchikanti L, Parr AT, Singh V, Fellows B. Ambulatory surgery centers and interventional techniques: a look at long term survival. *Pain Physician*. 2011;14(2):E177–E215. Available from http://www.painphysicianjournal.com/linkout_vw.php?issn=1533-3159&vol=14&page=E177. Accessed January 2, 2013.

59. Ambulatory Surgery Center Association. Ambulatory surgery centers: a positive trend in health care. Update 2011. Available from http://www.ascassociation.org/ASCA/Resources/ViewDocument/?DocumentKey=7d8441a1-82dd-47b9-b626-8563dc31930c. Accessed January 3, 2013.

60. KNG Health Consulting LLC. An analysis of recent growth of ambulatory surgical, centers. Final report. June 2009. Available from http://209.235.210.229/pdf/kng_health-asc_growth_factors-final-report.pdf. Accessed January 3, 2013.

61. Casalino LP, Devers KJ, Brewster LR. Focused factories? Physician-owned specialty facilities. *Health Affairs*. 2003;22:56–67.

62. Ambulatory Surgery Center Association. What is an ASC? Quality, Customer Service and Cost. Available from http://www.ascassociation.org/ASCA/AboutUs/WhatisanASC/. Accessed January 3, 2013.

63. U.S. Department of Health and Human Services, Health Resources and Services Administration, Bureau of Primary Health Care. The health center program: program requirements. Available from http://bphc.hrsa.gov/about/requirements/index.html. Accessed January 4, 2013.

64. U.S. Department of Health and Human Services, Health Resources and Services Administration, Bureau of Primary Health Care. The Affordable Care Act and health centers. Available from http://bphc.hrsa.gov/about/healthcenterfactsheet.pdf. Accessed January 4, 2013.

65. National Association of Community Health Centers, Inc. Snapshot: health Centers face declining Medicaid reimbursement. October 2012. Available from http://www.nachc.com/client/documents/MedicaidReimbursement.pdf. Accessed January 4, 2013.

66. The White House Office of the Press Secretary. President Obama announces Recovery Act awards to build, renovate community health centers in more than 30 states. December 9, 2009. Available from http://www.whitehouse.gov/the-press-office/president-obama-announces-recovery-act-awards-build-renovate-community-health-cente. Accessed January 4, 2013.

67. U.S. Department of Health & Human Services. New Affordable Care Act support to improve care coordination for nearly 200,000 people with Medicare. Available from http://www.hhs.gov/news/press/2011pres/06/20110606a.html. Accessed January 16, 2013.

68. McGinnis M. Can public health and medicine partner in the public interest? *Health Affairs*. 2006;25:1048–1049.

69. National Association of County and City Health Officials. NACCHO 2010 national profile of local health departments. Available from http://www.naccho.org/topics/infrastructure/profile/resources/2010report/upload/2010_Profile_main_report-web.pdf. Accessed January 23, 2013.

70. National Association of County and City Health Officials. The national profile of local health departments study series. Available from http://www.naccho.org/topics/infrastructure/profile/index.cfm. Accessed January 23, 2013.

71. Salinsky E, Gursky E. The case for transforming governmental public health. *Health Affairs*. 2006;25:1019–1028.

72. Ringel JS, Trentacost E, Lurie N. How well did health departments communicate about risk at the start of the swine flu epidemic in 2009? *Health Affairs*. 2009;28:w743–w759.

73. U.S. Department of Health and Human Services/CDC. *Public health preparedness capabilities: national standards for state and local planning. March 2011.* Available from http://www.cdc.gov/phpr/capabilities/dslr_capabilities_july.pdf. Accessed January 4, 2013.

74. Alliance for Advancing Nonprofit Health Care. The value of nonprofit health care. Available from http://www.nonprofithealthcare.org/reports/5_value.pdf. Accessed January 4, 2013.

CHAPTER 6

Medical Education and the Changing Practice of Medicine

This chapter provides an overview of the evolution in medical education from the colonial apprentice system to today's high-technology, specialty-oriented instruction in the basic sciences and clinical fields. It includes discussions of the HITECH and Affordable Care Acts and resulting impacts on medical education and practice. Developments such as evidence-based clinical practice guidelines, the introduction of specialty physicians called "hospitalists," physician report cards, health information technology (HIT), and new ethical issues are reviewed. The chapter concludes with a discussion of the future direction of medical education and practice.

Medical Education: Colonial America to the 19th Century

There were no medical schools in colonial America. Women treated the sick at home with the help of medicinal herbs, the advice of friends, and some self-help publications of questionable credibility. Only a few of the university-trained physicians in Europe came to the colonies. Those European physicians trained other physicians in an apprentice relationship. Because there was no formal method of testing or licensing new physicians after they concluded their apprenticeship, they were free to practice with no regulation.

The first medical school in America was established in 1756 at the College of Philadelphia (later the University of Pennsylvania). In 1768, a second was founded at King's College (later Columbia University). Both schools graduated only a small number of students each year.

Training under a single physician remained the most common method of physician education until the founding of hospitals in the mid-18th century. Physicians brought their own apprentices to the hospital, and they encouraged other students to observe patient treatment. This practice became so popular that the Philadelphia Hospital began charging a fee to students who were not apprenticed to physicians on the staff. By 1773, the hospital felt it had become necessary to regulate this training system and initiated a program whereby an aspiring physician would pay a fee to the hospital and be formally apprenticed to the institution for 5 years.[1] Physicians were granted a certificate on the completion of their apprenticeship.

By 1800, only four new U.S. medical schools had been added. Harvard University established a medical school in 1783 and Dartmouth College in 1797. The schools were small, with three or four faculty members teaching all courses and there were still very few restrictions on who could practice medicine. The first law concerning medicine in the colonies was enacted in Virginia in 1639 to control physician fees.[2] Various states attempted to enact medical licensing legislation during the 18th and early 19th centuries, but "by the time of the Civil War, not a single state had a medical licensure act in effect."[2] As the number of medical schools grew, their diplomas came to be viewed as licenses to practice.

In 1821, Georgia became the first state to restrict medical licenses to graduates of medical schools. Opposition was strong, especially from the apprentice-trained physicians. However, as physicians from medical schools began to outnumber those from the apprentice system, the Doctor of Medicine (MD) degree became the standard of competence. The endorsement of formal medical education over apprenticeship training encouraged an increase in the number of medical schools.

Many of the new medical schools had weak programs and no hospital affiliations. In 1892, Harvard became the first medical school to require 4 years of training. In 1893, Johns Hopkins initiated a 4-year curriculum as part of a pioneering effort to improve medical education. The Johns

Hopkins model became the standard for the subsequent reform of all medical education.[1]

Many medical schools during this period operated without strict admission requirements, a well-trained faculty, or a place for clinical observation and practice. As a consequence, the quality of medical degree varied greatly from school to school. Medical societies were organized to improve the quality of education and practice. The first such society was the Medical Society of Boston, organized in 1736.[2]

By the mid-19th century, most states had medical societies. In 1847, most of the state societies were affiliated with the newly formed American Medical Association (AMA). The goal of the AMA at the time was to improve medical education. The AMA's early attempts to reform or close some of the weaker medical schools were often ineffective; many AMA members were professionally associated with weaker schools and had a vested interest in keeping them open.[1] As a result, attempts to establish a national standard for medical teaching floundered for a few decades.

The Association of American Medical Colleges (AAMC), founded in 1876 by 22 medical schools, supported a 4-year curriculum such as the one introduced by the medical schools of Harvard and Johns Hopkins. However, it lacked the influence at that time to accomplish the desired medical education reforms.

Flexner Report and Medical School Reforms

In 1904, the AMA created a new Council on Medical Education and also began the *Journal of the American Medical Association*. The AMA used the journal to publish medical school failure statistics on state board licensing examinations and to group schools in categories by their failure rates.

The most important educational reform accomplishment of the AMA began in 1905 when it enlisted the Carnegie Foundation to investigate and rate medical schools. Abraham Flexner of the Foundation led a study of the medical schools in the United States and Canada. He proposed to examine the entrance requirements at each institution, the size and training of the faculty, endowment fees, the quality of laboratories, and the relationship between the medical schools and hospitals.

Flexner started his educational survey of all 155 medical schools in the United States and Canada in 1909. He visited each school, interviewing the dean and faculty members and inspecting laboratories and equipment. He summarized the facts observed during each visit and mailed his summary to the dean for verification. The deans and faculty of each school cooperated happily with Flexner in the mistaken belief that Carnegie was contemplating a contribution to their school.

Flexner's full report, "Medical Education in the United States and Canada," was published by the Carnegie Foundation in 1910. The report was an accurate description of the assets and liabilities of each medical program and their teaching facilities. Overall the report was a searing indictment of most medical schools of the time. Some were referred to as a "disgrace" and a "plague spot." The report recommended corrective measures. In the aftermath of this criticism, some schools closed while others consolidated. Soon after, some attempted to make improvements based on the report's recommendations. Flexner had proposed that the number of schools be reduced from 155 to 31, but a decade later the number had only been reduced to 85.[1]

Not all observations in Flexner's report were negative. Dartmouth, Yale, and Columbia were able to make alterations that improved the quality of their programs. Schools that received praise for excellent performance in the United States and Canada included Harvard; Western Reserve; McGill; the University of Toronto; and especially Johns Hopkins, which was described as a "model for medical education."

Formulated by an independent body, the Flexner Report gave increased leverage to medical reformers. Licensing legislation was pursued more vigorously, and new requirements for the length of medical training and for the quality of laboratories and other facilities were established. The AMA and the AAMC accelerated their efforts at reform and, in 1942, established the Liaison Committee on Medical Education to serve as the official accrediting body of medical schools.

One of the most important outcomes of Flexner's report was its stimulation of financial support for medical education from foundations and wealthy individuals. Schools that received the most favorable ratings from Flexner shared most of the money. Because most were associated with universities, the university-affiliated medical schools gained significant influence over the direction of medical education.[1]

Transition from Academic Medical Centers to Academic Health Centers

Federal research grants of the 1950s and 1960s encouraged research-oriented medical schools and their teaching hospitals to become the country's centers of scientific and technologic advances in health care. Most of the large tertiary-care hospitals affiliated with the approximately 80 medical schools operating at that time attracted patients with complicated medical conditions and were getting better results than their smaller unaffiliated counterparts.

Because university medical complexes were increasingly recognized as leading the way toward a more sophisticated and effective health care system, the federal government assisted in extending that expertise through the regional medical program legislation of 1965 and associated funding. One of many federal grant programs of the 1960s, the regional medical program legislation supported the development of programs across the United States to upgrade medical knowledge about the leading causes of death: heart disease, cancer, and stroke. The regional medical programs supported research, continuing professional education, service innovation, and regional networking among hospitals and other health care facilities. By 1974, however, the university-based regional medical programs had lost their political support and disbanded.

However, by 1974 university-based academic medical centers were well established as the proponents of cutting-edge advances in research and clinical medicine. By the early 1980s, federal support had increased the number of medical schools to 127.

Academic medical centers broadened into academic health centers by adding to their complexes professional health care programs such as nursing, pharmacy, dentistry, and allied health. Together with their large teaching hospitals and other clinical facilities, these academic health centers became a powerful force in the health care arena.

Academic health centers became the principal places of education and training for physicians and other health care personnel, the sites for most basic research in medicine, and the clinical settings in which many of the advances in diagnosis and treatment were tested and perfected. Today, the teaching hospitals of academic health centers are also major providers of the most sophisticated patient care required by trauma centers, burn centers, and neonatal intensive care centers, and the technologically advanced treatment of cancer, heart disease, and neurologic and other acute and chronic conditions. In addition to their complex tertiary-care services, teaching hospitals also provide much of the primary care for the economically disadvantaged populations in their geographical regions. While the teaching hospitals of the 126 academic health centers represent only 6% of the nation's hospitals, they provide more than one-half of the nation's care to indigent and underserved populations.[3]

The highly specialized, high-technology nature of academic health centers makes them the most expensive type of facility in America's health care system. Care provided at the teaching hospitals is often more expensive because student physicians order more diagnostic tests and procedures and often must consult with senior doctors regarding diagnoses and treatment procedures. As health care has shifted from an era of abundant resources to one of more stringent economic constraints, academic health centers have been under increasing pressure to reduce high-cost activities or face ballooning deficits that could threaten their survival.[4]

Medical schools' diverse research, teaching, and patient care responsibilities require them to generate revenues from multiple sources. A major source of revenue is the clinical practice of faculty who provide care to patients in addition to their responsibilities for teaching medical students. In 2011, the largest proportion, 37%, of the total revenue of the 126 reporting U.S. medical schools came from their faculty practice plans in which medical school faculty provided medical care to patients[5] Federally supported research grants and contracts contributed about 20%. Medical schools receive relatively smaller proportions of their total revenue from state and local government appropriations, hospital programs, tuition and fees, federal and other grants and contracts, and endowments.[5]

For many years, the federal government subsidized the training of resident physicians through the Medicare program and over half of the total patient revenues of academic health center hospitals came from Medicare and Medicaid payments. Therefore, any reduction in the support from these programs affects academic health centers. By scaling back subsidies for graduate medical education and encouraging beneficiaries to enroll in managed care plans, the government decreased academic health centers' revenue and reduced the number of patients available for clinical training and research.[6]

Graduate Medical Education Consortia

There are two types of physicians: the MD and the Doctor of Osteopathic Medicine (DO). MDs are also known as allopathic physicians. Although both MDs and DOs may use all accepted methods of treatment, including drugs and surgery, DOs place special emphasis on the body's musculoskeletal system. As of September 2012, there were 138 accredited schools of allopathic medicine[7] and 29 accredited colleges for degrees in osteopathy.[8]

No one national agency grants licenses to practice medicine. Instead, after completing a residency a physician must obtain a license from the medical board of the state where they plan to practice. Each state has independent requirements about who may practice within the state and may have special requirements or restrictions for licensure. To provide direct patient care, physicians are required to complete a 3- to 7-year graduate medical program accredited by the Accreditation Council for Graduate Medical Education (ACGME) in one of the recognized medical specialties. The ACGME is an independent, not-for-profit organization established in 2000 to "improve health care by assessing and advancing the quality of resident physicians' education through exemplary accreditation."[9]

There are currently almost 9,000 U.S. residency programs accredited by the ACGME. Given the large number of programs, over many years questions have arisen about program quality and responsiveness to personnel supply and specialty distribution issues. Reflecting these concerns, U.S. residency programs were described at the 1992 Macy Foundation conference, "Taking Charge of Graduate Medical Education: To Meet the Nation's Needs in the 21st Century," as "responsive principally to the service needs of hospitals, the interests of the medical specialty societies, the objectives of the residency program directors, and the career preferences of the medical students."[10]

In February 2012, ACGME announced major changes in how the nation's medical residency programs will be accredited in future years through the establishment of an outcomes-based evaluation system. Expected to be fully implemented by 2014, the new system will measure medical residents' competencies in performing essential tasks necessary for clinical practice in the 21st century.[11] Concerns regarding medical residency program quality and balancing the supply and demand for medical specialists in the United States have also been addressed with varying success by a number of graduate medical education consortia. These consortia are formal associations of medical schools, teaching hospitals, and other organizations involved in the training of residents. The consortia provide centralized coordination and direction that encourages the members to function collectively. The major aims of graduate medical education consortia are to improve the structure and governance of residency programs, to increase the ambulatory care training experiences, and to address imbalances in physician specialty and location.[12] As noted earlier, Medicare supports hospitals' residency training programs in recognition of the added expenses entailed by training requirements. However, Medicare limits the number of residents per hospital. Among other health workforce–related provisions, the Patient Protection and Affordable Care Act (ACA) of 2010 will increase the number of residency training positions by authorizing the Medicare administration to redistribute available residency training slots from hospitals that have underutilized their slots to hospitals in need of additional residents.[13] In this redistribution, priority is given to primary care and general surgery in states with the lowest physician to population ratios.[14] The ACA also promotes residency training in outpatient settings and in rural and underserved areas by increasing flexibility in the laws and regulations that govern Medicare's residency program funding.[14]

Whether the consortia and provisions of the ACA will succeed in ameliorating the imbalances in both the medical specialty and primary care workforces to meet American society's medical care needs and whether the ACGME outcome-based evaluation system will successfully be implemented to assist in that endeavor remain open questions. As in so many other aspects of health care, it is likely that market forces combined with policy decisions will determine the outcomes.

Delineation and Growth of Medical Specialties

In its early history, the AMA resisted the development of medical specialties due to concerns about fragmenting care. The AMA's slow response to specialty interests prompted specialists to form their own societies and associations. In the last half of the 19th century, physicians interested in ophthalmology, otology, gynecology, obstetrics, and pediatrics formed their own specialty groups. In the early 1900s, with specialization increasing among physicians, specialty hospitals were founded in some cities, and general practitioners found themselves eased out of hospitals by specialists. In response, the American Academy of General Practice was formed in 1947 to advocate general practice departments in hospitals. It was not until 1969, however, that general practice, now called family medicine, became a recognized specialty.

Deficient Training of Medical Specialists

Despite the growth in the number of specialists, at the time of the Flexner Report there was no standard for adequate specialty training. The length of specialty training required by various medical schools and hospitals ranged from just a few weeks to 3 years, and the quality of graduating specialists could vary from excellent to incompetent. A physician with almost any level of training could practice as a specialist.

In 1917, the U.S. Army, in need of physicians, examined the qualifications of physicians who wished to be classified as specialists, and the results were shocking. Though many had practiced as specialists for years, very high percentages of self-declared physician specialists were rejected by the service as unfit to practice as specialists and some were deemed unfit to practice in any branch of medicine at all.

As improved technology and the development of safer and more effective anesthesia and antiseptic techniques made surgery a more acceptable medical option, the demand for surgery grew and the numbers of surgeons and hospitals increased in response. The American College of Surgeons, established in 1912, set up an oversight board and established practice standards in 1917 for certifying specialist surgeons. At the same time, the AMA started inspecting internship sites and produced a list of approved hospital internship sites.

Although both the AMA and the American College of Surgeons began to rate the quality of postgraduate training, they quickly realized that they could not make their findings public and the results were suppressed. In 1924, the AMA Council on Medical Education began to approve hospitals for residency specialty training programs. For the next 40 years, residency programs were initiated in hospitals with little regard for the quality of the training experience. Often poorly planned and supervised, residents' educational experiences were deemed secondary to their obligations as medical house staff to serve whatever patient load they were assigned. Assigned to single departments, the opportunities for developing expert clinical knowledge and skills varied with the interest and teaching skills of a few attending physicians in the department. Educational standards and reform were needed, and half a century after the Flexner Report was published the AMA again requested an outside examination of the medical education process. The AMA commissioned a Citizens Committee on Graduate Medical Education, chaired by John S. Mills, who issued his report in 1966. Key recommendations of the report included the elimination of independent internships and the awarding of accreditation of residency training programs to institutions rather than to individual medical departments. In 1970, the AMA endorsed the inclusion of the first year of graduate medical education in a program approved by an appropriate residency review committee (RRC). The term internship was dropped, and by 1980 the AMA had issued recommendations for broad training in the first postdoctoral year.

The current curriculum requirements for becoming a specialist are well defined and standardized. The physician must graduate from a medical school, serve in a residency program in an approved setting, and pass a qualifying specialty examination. The appropriate specialty board then certifies the physician. The boards are sponsored by the major specialty society in the specific area of study and the appropriate specialty section of the AMA.

Specialty Boards and Residency Performance

Boards were formed for each specialty to ensure a proper instructional program and training period followed by an examination and certification to practice. The American Board of Ophthalmology, established in 1933, was the first specialty board. In the same year, an advisory board for medical specialties, the American Board of Medical Specialties (ABMS), was established as an independent, not-for-profit organization. The mission of ABMS is "to maintain and improve the quality of medical care by assisting the member boards in their efforts to develop and utilize professional and educational standards for the certification of physician specialists in the United States and internationally."[15] By 1991, there were 24 member boards, each representing a specific medical specialty.

As of 2012, ABMS member boards certify physicians in 24 medical specialties and 130 subspecialties. The number of subspecialties is increasing as different kinds of specialists train in similar subspecialties. For instance, the specialties of family medicine, internal medicine, and pediatrics all have subspecialties in sports medicine. In addition, advancing technology is creating new subspecialties each year. Table 6-1 provides a partial list of the current specialty and subspecialty certifications offered by ABMS member boards.[16]

The usual procedure for subspecialization is for specialists to complete their residency training and to first become certified by the board in their specialty. Then they take another period of training, called a fellowship, which prepares them to subspecialize or conduct research in a specific area.

Each specialty board has an RRC charged with the responsibility of preserving the quality of graduate medical education. In 1928, the AMA

Table 6-1 Medical Specialties and Subspecialty Areas

American Board of Allergy and Immunology

Allergy and Immunology	No subspecialties

American Board of Anesthesiology

Anesthesiology	Critical Care Medicine
	Hospice and Palliative Medicine
	Pain Medicine
	Pediatric Anesthesiology[1]
	Sleep Medicine[1]

American Board of Colon and Rectal Surgery

Colon and Rectal Surgery	No subspecialties
American Board of Dermatology	
Dermatology	Dermatopathology
	Pediatric Dermatology

American Board of Emergency Medicine

Emergency Medicine	Critical Care Medicine
	Emergency Medical Services[2]
	Hospice and Palliative Medicine
	Medical Toxicology
	Pediatric Emergency Medicine
	Sports Medicine
	Undersea and Hyperbaric Medicine

(continues)

Table 6-1 Medical Specialties and Subspecialty Areas (continued)

American Board of Family Medicine

Family Medicine

Adolescent Medicine
Geriatric Medicine
Hospice and Palliative Medicine
Sleep Medicine
Sports Medicine

American Board of Internal Medicine

Internal Medicine

Adolescent Medicine
Advanced Heart Failure and Transplant
Cardiology
Cardiovascular Disease
Clinical Cardiac Electrophysiology
Critical Care Medicine
Endocrinology, Diabetes, and Metabolism
Gastroenterology
Geriatric Medicine
Hematology
Hospice and Palliative Medicine
Infectious Disease
Interventional Cardiology
Medical Oncology
Nephrology
Pulmonary Disease
Rheumatology
Sleep Medicine
Sports Medicine
Transplant Hepatology

American Board of Medical Genetics

Clinical Biochemical Genetics*
Clinical Cytogenetics*
Clinical Genetics (MD)*
Clinical Molecular Genetics*

Medical Biochemical Genetics
Molecular Genetic Pathology

American Board of Neurological Surgery

Neurological Surgery

No subspecialties

American Board of Nuclear Medicine

Nuclear Medicine

No subspecialties

American Board of Obstetrics and Gynecology

Obstetrics and Gynecology

Critical Care Medicine
Female Pelvic Medicine and Reconstructive
Surgery[1]
Gynecologic Oncology
Hospice and Palliative Medicine
Maternal and Fetal Medicine
Reproductive Endocrinology/Infertility

American Board of Ophthalmology

Ophthalmology

No subspecialties

American Board of Orthopedic Surgery

Orthopedic Surgery

Orthopedic Sports Medicine
Surgery of the Hand

Table 6-1 Medical Specialties and Subspecialty Areas (continued)

American Board of Otolaryngology

Otolaryngology

Neurotology
Pediatric Otolaryngology
Plastic Surgery Within the Head and Neck
Sleep Medicine

American Board of Pathology

Pathology–Anatomic/Pathology–Clinical*
Pathology–Anatomic*
Pathology–Clinical*

Blood Banking/Transfusion Medicine
Clinical Informatics[1]
Cytopathology
Dermatopathology
Neuropathology
Pathology–Chemical
Pathology–Forensic
Pathology–Hematology
Pathology–Medical Microbiology
Pathology–Molecular Genetic
Pathology–Pediatric

American Board of Pediatrics

Pediatrics

Adolescent Medicine
Child Abuse Pediatrics
Developmental–Behavioral Pediatrics
Hospice and Palliative Medicine
Medical Toxicology
Neonatal–Perinatal Medicine
Neurodevelopmental Disabilities
Pediatric Cardiology
Pediatric Critical Care Medicine
Pediatric Emergency Medicine
Pediatric Endocrinology
Pediatric Gastroenterology
Pediatric Hematology–Oncology
Pediatric Infectious Diseases
Pediatric Nephrology
Pediatric Pulmonology
Pediatric Rheumatology
Pediatric Transplant Hepatology
Sleep Medicine
Sports Medicine

American Board of Physical Medicine and Rehabilitation

Physical Medicine and Rehabilitation

Brain Injury Medicine[1]
Hospice and Palliative Medicine
Neuromuscular Medicine
Pain Medicine
Pediatric Rehabilitation Medicine
Spinal Cord Injury Medicine
Sports Medicine

American Board of Plastic Surgery

Plastic Surgery

Plastic Surgery within the Head and Neck
Surgery of the Hand

(continues)

Table 6-1 Medical Specialties and Subspecialty Areas (continued)

American Board of Preventive Medicine*
Aerospace Medicine*
Occupational Medicine*
Public Health and General Preventive
Medicine*

Clinical Informatics[1]
Medical Toxicology
Undersea and Hyperbaric Medicine

American Board of Psychiatry and Neurology
Psychiatry*
Neurology*
Neurology with Special Qualification in Child
Neurology*

Addiction Psychiatry
Brain Injury Medicine[1]
Child and Adolescent Psychiatry
Clinical Neurophysiology
Epilepsy[3]
Forensic Psychiatry
Geriatric Psychiatry
Hospice and Palliative Medicine
Neurodevelopmental Disabilities
Neuromuscular Medicine
Pain Medicine
Psychosomatic Medicine
Sleep Medicine
Vascular Neurology

American Board of Radiology
Diagnostic Radiology*
Interventional Radiology and Diagnostic
Radiology*
Radiation Oncology*
Medical Physics*

Hospice and Palliative Medicine
Neuroradiology
Nuclear Radiology
Pediatric Radiology
Vascular and Interventional Radiology

American Board of Surgery
Surgery*
Vascular Surgery*

Complex General Surgical Oncology[1]
Hospice and Palliative Medicine
Pediatric Surgery
Surgery of the Hand
Surgical Critical Care

American Board of Thoracic Surgery
Thoracic Surgery

Congenital Cardiac Surgery

American Board of Urology
Urology

Female Pelvic Medicine and Reconstructive
Surgery[1]
Pediatric Urology

*Specific disciplines within the specialty where certification is offered.

[1]Approved 2011; first issue yet to be determined

[2]Approved 2010; first issue to be determined

[3]Approved 2010; first issue 2013

Source: Reprinted with permission from the American Board of Medical Specialties (ABMS),
© 2013, www.abms.org.

published the guidelines for approved residencies and fellowships that set
educational standards for residencies. The ACGME, formed in 1972 by
the ABMS, the American Hospital Association, the AMA, the AAMC,

and the Council of Medical Specialty Societies, extends authority to RRCs to determine the standards for its residencies. The ACGME supervises and receives reports from each RRC.

In addition to the controls of ACGME and its five parent organizations, numerous influences affect different aspects of residency content and training. These include the 24 specialty boards, RRCs, hospital directors, medical school deans, program directors, training directors, faculty, house staff, and specialty societies. The problems inherent in this complex system of control will intensify as legislated health care reforms require changes to accommodate specialty imbalance, physician supply, reductions in funding, shifts from inpatient to ambulatory care, and the reconfigurations of practice and reimbursement taking shape in the health care industry.

A fast-growing field of medical practice has been developing outside the aforementioned system of control over specialty training. Hospitalists are physicians whose sole responsibility is the care of hospitalized patients, and their number is growing. As of 2012, there were more than 30,000 physicians employed as hospitalists in the United States and about 70% of hospitals now have hospitalists on their staff.[17]

Several benefits are attributed to the use of hospitalists. Hospitalists are dedicated to hospital care and thus are familiar with the hospitals' systems to expedite care. They can provide continuous observation of patients and respond rapidly to crises and changes in patient condition. In general, hospitalists coordinate all care during hospital stays and are expected to care for hospitalized patients in consultation with each patient's primary care physician.

The burgeoning hospitalist movement reflects hospitals' efforts to reduce costs and medical errors and improve the quality of care. Studies confirm that hospitalists reduce costs by shortening hospital stays, preventing complications, and reducing readmissions. In addition, hospital patients seem more satisfied with hospitalist care than with primary physicians who are able to spend only a few minutes a day with each of their inpatients as they fit hospital visits into their busy office schedules.

Because there are no specific training requirements for hospitalists, most are trained in internal medicine or in pediatrics as in the case of providing hospital inpatient children's services. For personal reasons, physicians who are employed as hospitalists have chosen to forego private practice and have become employees of one or more hospitals or of companies that contract to provide hospitalist services to several hospitals.

Physician Workforce Supply and Distribution

By the mid-1960s, the federal government predicted that there would be a national shortage of physicians in the United States. New policies and programs were established to increase the number of physicians by increasing medical school funding. In the 20 years between 1980 and 2000, the total number of physicians in the United States increased from 467,679 to 813,770—an increase of 74%. The overall physician to population ratio during the same period increased from 207 to 296 per 100,000 people. In 2011, the AAMC reported an overall active physician to population national median of just over 244 physicians per 100,000 people in the United States.[18] In November 2012, the Kaiser Family Foundation reported 834,769 professionally active physicians in the United States.[19]

The absence of a national, comprehensive methodology has made accurate predictions of physician supply needs extremely challenging and has resulted in continuing debates between those who predict physician shortages and those who warn of a physician oversupply. In addition, the wide geographic variation in physician practice location rather than the actual number of physicians remains a pressing problem in the current health care delivery system. The number of active physicians providing patient care per 100,000 people in each state varies from a high of over 415 per 100,000 people in Massachusetts to a low of just over 176 per 100,000 people in Mississippi, with the states having the highest ratio of physician per population concentrated regionally in the northeastern states.[18] The low supply of physicians in both the more rural and inner-city areas especially continues to create a medical care delivery crisis to populations living in those underserved areas.

Almost one-fourth of all hospital residencies are filled by International Medical Graduates (IMGs) and, consequently, they represent approximately one-fourth of the active physician workforce in the United States.[20] Most foreign medical graduates gained entry to U.S. health care system by completing an accredited medical residency in the United States. More than 6,000 IMGs enter medical and surgical residency programs in the United States annually.[20] Most of the hospitals in the United States depend on IMGs to help fill their residency positions, as more residency programs are available than the number of available U.S. medical school graduates each year.

Due to concerns about a lack of basic clinical and communication skills among some IMGs, since 1998 IMGs have been required to pass a clinical skill assessment prior to entering a U.S. residency. Although there was a surge of IMG entrants immediately before the requirement went into effect, there was a significant drop in IMG entrants after the requirement was initiated.[21] However, the quality of the applicants has improved while still providing enough IMGs to fill the residency positions not taken by U.S. medical graduates.[22]

Ratios of Generalist to Specialist Physicians and the Changing Demand

Primary care or generalist physicians are widely defined as those who practice family medicine, general internal medicine, and general pediatrics. Physicians practicing obstetrics and gynecology are also sometimes included as primary care practitioners. For years, the numbers of generalist physicians have been considered too low to meet the basic health care needs of large segments of the general population. Additionally, the emphasis on medical diagnosis and treatment by combinations of specialist and subspecialist physicians has been criticized as contributing significantly to the complexity and rising costs of medical care.

In the early 1990s, the growth of managed care raised concerns that the long-standing 60:40 ratio of medical specialists to primary care physicians would leave the United States with an inadequate number of primary care physicians and an oversupply of specialists. Those forecasts led to a number of federal and state policies that encouraged the training of more primary care practitioners. There followed a significant increase in the number of physicians practicing in the primary care fields of family medicine and pediatrics.

The adequacy of the supply of primary care physicians and the number of training programs for medical students, which had appeared to meet population needs for primary care in years past, have recently been reexamined during the current era of health care delivery reform.[23] Health care legislation, including the passage of the ACA, is expected to extend health care coverage to 16 million presently uninsured Americans by 2014. A 2012 *Annals of Family Medicine* report on the primary care physician workforce projects the need for approximately 52,000 additional primary care physicians by 2025. The report notes that the largest contributor to this need, 33,000 physicians, will be sheer population growth with another 10,000 primary care physicians needed for the aging population and 8,000 more to accommodate newly insured individuals.[24] A number of provisions of the ACA are aimed at improving access to primary health care and addressing the urgent need for the additional primary care workforce. Expansion of the primary care workforce depends in large part on increased recruitment and retention of medical students and medical residents who will train as primary care providers.[25] Other national legislations such as the 2009 American Recovery and Reinvestment Act (ARRA) funded the National Health Service Corps to recruit primary care providers to work in underserved areas and over $200 million in grants are being awarded to community-based "teaching health centers" to establish more primary care residency programs.[25]

In contrast to earlier predictions, the marketplace demand for medical specialists also has not decreased, due to factors such as general population growth and the aging of the baby-boom population, who as they age require additional and more complex medical care provided by specialists.[26]

The current ratio of specialists to generalist physicians is estimated to be 67:33.[27] The ratio favoring specialty practice results from individual career choices made by medical students before graduation. One of the most important influences of academic health centers is the socialization process that shapes the skills, values, and attitudes of future physicians and other health care professionals. Other factors that influence the choice of specialty include significant income differentials between primary care and specialty practice, life–work balance preferences, and the types of outpatient clinical practice sites in which residents receive training. These outpatient sites are often overcrowded hospital outpatient clinics serving large numbers of poor and medically difficult patients with overburdened teaching faculty. In addition, hospitals often favor specialty training because it generates significantly more revenue than primary care.[27] Considering the origins of the specialist–generalist imbalance, it is significant that until very recently almost every aspect of most medical school and teaching hospital experiences favored the practice of specialty medicine. Many medical students who intended to become generalist physicians at the onset of their medical education were induced by exposure to the medical education environment to change their minds in favor of becoming specialists.

Preventive Medicine

In 1991, the Pew Charitable Trusts published a report that outlined factors expected to drive future health care. They concluded that an approach that stresses disease prevention would characterize future health care systems. The report emphasized that health concerns should be addressed at a community level and that medical schools should require physician training learning in community environments. The need to focus on preventive care and treatment techniques that use technology to the patient's advantage was a challenge facing new physicians, which was also recognized many years ago.[28]

The practice of medicine and medical education, however, has a history of poor results in establishing health promotion and disease prevention as a high priority in U.S. health care system, largely because the delivery system and its reimbursement incentives have evolved as an acute illness complaint–response system. Provider payment incentives have always favored intervention after the fact rather than prevention, in spite of strong evidence of the cost-effectiveness of primary prevention. As a result, the United States currently spends most of its health care dollars treating diseases that could have been prevented. Parameters for prevention are clearly established in many areas, but past studies have shown that only a small percentage of physicians actually adhere to the guidelines.[29]

More recently, however, rising public awareness, media pressure, and enlightened leadership have produced some innovative and productive collaborations between clinical and preventive medicine. In addition to their participation in the public health measures to prevent vaccine-preventable childhood diseases, sexually transmitted diseases, and HIV infection that depend on physician case reporting, immunization, and education, practicing physicians have continued to collaborate in community prevention campaigns for problems such as childhood obesity, diabetes, smoking cessation, cholesterol education, and early cancer detection. For these collaborations to expand and grow, there is strong recognition of the need for significant changes in all areas of medical education, accountability measures, and health care financing.[30] A 2012 report of the Institute of Medicine, "Primary Care and Public Health: Exploring Integration to Improve Population Health", offers new perspectives on how the primary care and public health sectors can leverage health care workforce and provisions in the ACA to advance a population-based, prevention-oriented mind-set in the health care delivery system. The report offers several suggestions for community-level linkages of academic health centers' strengths with provider and community resources to research, develop, and implement sustainable delivery system changes that will result in improved health status of populations.[31]

Changing Physician–Hospital Relationships

Historically, physicians and hospitals maintained unique relationships that brought both of them profits from a single source—patient admission. The independence and autonomy of physicians were respected, and their financial relationship with the hospital in the care of patients was overlooked by paying physicians separately on a fee-for-service basis and the hospital on the basis of costs incurred. Because hospitals were dependent on physicians to admit patients and make use of the hospitals' resources, hospitals courted physicians by providing them with equipment, staff, and other perquisites with little regard for the effects on hospital costs.

Physicians had responsibilities to the hospital as an institution and to the patients they admitted to the hospital. As a component of a hospital's governance structure, the medical staff organization was responsible to the board of trustees and the hospital administration for many organizational activities that required medical expertise. Through the medical staff organization and its committees, physicians have been obligated to provide the knowledge and authority to establish clinical policies and procedures, perform utilization review, ensure quality, and determine the credentialing standards for admission to the hospital's medical staff.[32]

The roles and responsibilities of physicians have changed from the time when physicians were the sole determinants of hospital admission criteria, the ordering of diagnostic tests and therapeutic procedures, the establishment of the length of hospital stays, decisions on the use of hospital-owned services and other resources, and referrals. In the current environment of constrained and reconfigured reimbursement systems, heightened accountability, and physician entrepreneurship, the relationships between physicians and hospitals are now different and often strained.

Under the prospective payment system, hospitals are at financial risk if physicians allow lengths of inpatient stays to exceed insurer criteria. New payment criteria also financially penalize hospitals if treatment results in costly complications or the need for readmission.[33,34] As a result, hospitals must monitor and question physician decisions. Another reason why physicians can no longer ignore the financial consequences of their clinical decisions includes health plans selecting hospitals to serve their members based on operating efficiency and cost-effectiveness. Physicians who are not sensitive to the impact of their practice patterns on the financial burden of the hospitals where they have privileges and who do not cooperate in keeping the hospital financially competitive will likely not be viewed favorably by hospital administration.

In addition to these stresses on the internal relationships of hospitals and physicians, there are external conflicts. Advanced technology and the economic environment cause hospitals and physicians to become competitors for patient business. Group practice growth and advanced technologies that permit many procedures that formerly required hospitalization to be performed in ambulatory settings have given physicians the financial resources and patient volume to acquire the necessary equipment and trained staff that allow physicians to independently own and operate ambulatory centers. These entrepreneurial activities have placed physicians in direct competition with hospitals.

In addition to the aforementioned hospitalist employment, increasing employment of primary care and specialist physicians by hospitals has been one response to the changing health care system environment. The American Hospital Association reported in 2012 that the number of physicians employed by hospitals has grown by 32% since 2000.[35] This trend is the result of changing interests on the part of both physicians and hospitals. From physicians' perspectives, employment has become desirable due to factors such as flat reimbursement rates, complex insurance and health information technology (HIT) requirements, high malpractice premiums, and a desire for greater work–life balance. For hospitals, employing physicians provides opportunities to gain market share for admissions, the use of diagnostic testing and other outpatient services, and referrals to high-revenue specialty services.[36] In addition, hospital executives cite physician–hospital integration as an important strategy to prepare for payment reforms such as accountable care organizations and penalties for hospital readmissions.[36] The AMA has raised concerns about the potential effects of employment requirements on the physician–patient relationship. In a policy issued in late 2012, the AMA reminds physicians that "in any situation where the economic or other interests of the employer are in conflict with patient welfare, patient welfare must take priority." The AMA statement also notes that physicians should inform patients about any financial incentives that may impact treatment options.[37] Clearly, the competition for patients in the reformed environment has vastly changed traditional hospital–physician relationships.[38]

Evidence-based Clinical Practice Guidelines

Clinical practice guidelines are systematically developed protocols used to assist practitioner and patient decisions about appropriate health care by defining the roles of specific diagnostic and treatment modalities in patient diagnosis and management. The protocols contain recommendations that are based on scientific evidence gathered from a rigorous systematic review and synthesis of the published medical literature and are therefore described as evidence based.[39]

Clinical practice guidelines evolved in the late 1970s and early 1980s after the publication of data showing wide variations in the applications of medical procedures in different regions of the United States and increased use of questionable, inappropriate, and unnecessary services that added significantly to the increasing costs of health care. It is important to note that the variations in the level of health care interventions were so great as to suggest that physicians were unaware of the relative effectiveness of various procedures and that patients were not benefiting from much of the care they received.

Health care researchers conjectured that assessments of the outcomes or relative effectiveness of various medical procedures would lead to practice guidelines and eliminate ineffective, unnecessary, or inappropriate procedures and their related costs. To this end, Congress created the Agency for Health Care Policy and Research in 1989, now renamed the Agency for Healthcare Research and Quality (AHRQ). The agency was directed to fund outcomes research and to start developing practice guidelines. After a slow start, the agency began releasing practice guidelines for specific conditions. Although fewer than two dozen guidelines had been released by 1995, the agency's efforts sparked a great deal of guideline development by other institutions and agencies. The RAND Corporation, medical specialty societies, health maintenance organizations, insurers, and many other professional health care organizations have produced clinical practice guidelines that have subsequently been reviewed and evaluated by the following specific AHRQ criteria:

- "The guideline must contain systematically developed recommendations, strategies, or other information to assist health care decision making in specific clinical circumstances.
- The guideline must have been produced under the auspices of a relevant professional organization (e.g., medical specialty society, government agency, health care organization, or health plan).
- The guideline development process must have included a verifiable, systematic literature search and review of existing evidence published in peer-reviewed journals.
- The guideline must be current and the most recent version (i.e., developed, reviewed, or revised within the last 5 years) must be available upon request in print or electronic format (for free or for a fee), in the English language."[40]

Over 14,000 evidence-based clinical practice guidelines that have met these AHRQ evaluation criteria have been collected in a database, organized by searchable topics, and made available online at the AHRQ's National Guideline Clearinghouse.[41]

The widespread application of evidence-based clinical practice guidelines is expected to continue to have a significant effect on medical practice. Evidence-based clinical practice guidelines are considered to be the most objective and least biased clinical practice guidelines that serve as a means to assist in preventing the use of unnecessary treatment modalities and in avoiding negligent events, with patient safety and the delivery of consistent high-quality care as foremost priorities.[42] With government agencies, health systems, third-party payers, and specialty societies promoting the use of evidence-based clinical practice guidelines, they have become an integral part of current medical practice.

Physician Report Cards and Physician Compare

In the 1970s, the AMA code of ethics explicitly prohibited "information that would point out differences between doctors." Thirty-two states passed laws supporting the AMA's position. The laws were intended to prevent misleading or competitive advertising of office hours, charges, or services. The position of organized medicine, however, reflected a long history of protecting physician performance from public scrutiny.[43]

Subsequently, the state laws supporting the AMA's position were determined to be violations of the First Amendment. Passage of freedom of information acts that prohibited governments from hiding information from the public removed the barriers that prevented the public from comparing the performance of physicians. In 1986, when the Health Care Financing Administration released hospital-specific mortality rates for Medicare patients, the information dam was broken. In December 1991, the publication *Newsday* reported the first information regarding physician performance ever made public.[43] Never again would the public be denied access to government data about the quality of medical care. The publication was based on New York state's pioneering effort to compare and publish hospital-specific, severity-adjusted heart surgery mortality rates. Although New York state had intended to publish only the names of the hospitals involved, a *Newsday* freedom of information request, supported by the State Supreme Court, forced the release of the rankings of the heart surgeons involved.[43]

Within less than a decade, the contentious matter of exposing the comparative performance of physicians on a wide spectrum of variables has been resolved in favor of the consumers of medical care.

Many states have passed legislation that gives the public access to physician information, including disciplinary records, malpractice actions, and whether a physician has lost privileges at a hospital.

Medical societies in general support physician-profiling programs that report a physician's education, training, licensure, and membership in professional societies, state disciplinary actions, and serious misdemeanor convictions. They have, however, objected strongly to the inclusion of medical malpractice and hospital disciplinary information out of concern that such information would be taken out of context, possibly misinterpreted by the consumer, and possibly not adequately reflect the quality of care provided by the physician. Now, as a component of the ACA, the Centers for Medicare and Medicaid Services is launching a "Physician Compare" Web site that will be a companion to its previously established "Hospital Compare" site. The site, which must be populated with quality-related data by 2014, will allow Medicare beneficiaries to search for physicians and other health professionals who serve Medicare patients and participate in Medicare's Physician Quality Reporting System and Electronic Prescribing Incentive Program.[44] Concerns will continue about data collection methods and the fairness, accuracy, and objectivity of the comparative data used in all types of reports about physician performance. Therefore, although it is expected that increased transparency will contribute to the quality of care, it is likely that physician performance reports will have significant limitations for both the medical provider and the consumer.[45]

Health Information Technology and Physician Practice

The introduction of HIT into the practice of medicine has signaled a new era in clinical practice to both new and established physicians. Advances in health informatics supported by the ARRA, the Health Information Technology for Electronic and Clinical Health (HITECH) Act, and the ACA are educating physicians to track, transfer, and share medical knowledge and patient information in electronic format and communicate with other physicians. The recent focus on the role of HIT to improve health quality and lower costs has created momentum for its adoption both in the practices of established physicians and in medical school education.

Medical schools and teaching hospitals have responded by introducing medical informatics training into their coursework.[46] Curricula include technology-enabled team communication and care, centralized electronic health records (EHRs), digital access to relevant data sources and medical libraries, real-time reporting of data, and support for decisions through evidence-driven care protocols. For example, students can be trained in the use of EHRs, wireless technologies, and personal digital assistants used for accessing medical information, placing medication prescription orders (eRX), and transmitting alerts that serve as reminders to order timely preventative health testing for patients. A study of third-year medical students reported generally positive attitudes toward the use of EHR in an ambulatory setting. They noted that they received more feedback on their electronic charts than on paper charts. Students were concerned, however, about the potential impact of EHRs on their ability to conduct the doctor–patient encounters.[47]

The American Board of Medical Specialties has also recently approved physician subspecialty certification in "clinical informatics" within several established medical specialties, as listed in Table 6-1, a recognition of the importance of HIT in the practice of the established physician.

The expanding use of EHRs in hospitals and physician practices as a replacement for paper charts, paper medical reports, and even paper prescriptions for tests and medications is another exciting change made possible through continuing advances in electronic information technology.

The use of EHRs has been given much impetus through the ARRA. Although this law had a primary economic focus on saving and creating jobs in the United States, important secondary objectives included the investment of billions of dollars in programs related to health care, education, and "green" energy.

As part of the ARRA, the HITECH Act was enacted to stimulate the adoption and the use of EHRs in a variety of health care settings and by specific categories of health care occupations. Over $25 billion was made available through the EHRs Incentive Payment Program under HITECH Act to be paid out through the Medicare and Medicaid programs to eligible health care providers who demonstrated that they were using EHRs in a meaningful way by meeting specific criteria and objectives "Meaningful use" criteria requires that EHRs capture specific health information that improves the coordinated delivery of care to patients and also that EHRs are designed and utilized in ways that improve communication among health care providers and also between health care providers and their patients.[48]

Eligible providers who can participate in the EHR Incentive Payment Program under reimbursement for care provided to Medicare patients include physicians, dentists, optometrists, podiatrists, chiropractors, and hospitals. Under the Medicaid program, physicians, certified nurse midwives, dentists, nurse practitioners, physician assistants, and hospitals are considered to be eligible providers in the EHR Incentive Payment Program once they register in the program. All registered eligible providers must have met the very specific participation standards and percentage of use criteria for meaningful use of EHRs before incentive payments are made.[49]

A second stage of meaningful use criteria approved in August 2012 is expected to encourage EHR system participants to actively elicit more consumer engagement in the health care provider–patient communication process. The overall participation rate for all categories of eligible health care providers has more than met program expectations under both Medicare and Medicaid. As the various forms of information technology become established in medical practice, traditional diagnostic mechanisms will rely more on assisted decision making for physicians through computer decision support systems, evidence-based medicine, EHR systems, computerized physician order entry, and electronic prescribing as the medical practice norm.

Escalating Costs of Malpractice Insurance

The steeply rising costs of medical liability insurance are a continuing concern for practicing physicians, medical schools, and teaching hospitals. In the last decade, schools of medicine and hospitals have seen their liability premium costs increase from 6 to 10 times—from thousands to millions. In some states, physicians, especially specialists, have seen their premiums triple or quadruple in just a few years.

Rising liability insurance costs reflect steep increases in the amount of malpractice jury awards. Also, during an economic downturn insurance companies that depended on investment income are forced to raise premiums to keep their businesses viable.

In any case, the effect has been demoralizing to many physicians. Media reports indicate that physicians are leaving high-premium states, choosing to retire early, or reducing high-risk aspects of their practice to lower their insurance costs.[50]

Ethical Issues

Two developments have focused attention on a number of issues in medical ethics. Rather than concerns about unethical or unprofessional conduct, these ethical issues reflect the practice dilemmas faced by physicians working in the rapidly changing health care environment. The first set of ethical concerns relates to the policies promoted by health insurers. Efforts of such organizations to manage the financing, costs, accessibility, or quality of the care delivered cause them to subject physicians to a range of guidelines, treatment parameters, peer reviews, and financial incentives and penalties. Cost-avoidance policies that require preauthorization for the more expensive procedures, substitution of less expensive tests and medications, and restraint of hospitalization in favor of alternative ambulatory services raise questions about increased risks to patients.

An opposite set of ethical concerns could be raised about the risk to patients subjected to the practices of fee-for-service traditional medicine, which the health insurers try to avoid—unnecessary hospitalizations, needless or inappropriate tests and procedures, ineffective treatments, and uncoordinated care provided by multiple providers. There is no question, however, that particular control strategies of health insurers present related ethical issues. Increasingly, physicians admit that they may have to exaggerate the severity of an illness in order to help patients get necessary care. Systems that encourage deceitful practices detract from the professional standards of medicine.

The second development creating vexing ethical issues is the remarkable advance in technologic capability. Medicine's ability to prolong the lives of severely brain-injured patients, increasingly premature infants, terminally ill or brain-dead patients, and others with no promise of functional survival has increased the need for ethical guidelines. At present, individual physicians decide how they will advise the families of such patients. If the family and the physician cannot agree about treatment, there is no set procedure for deciding what to do. These and other ethical dilemmas brought about by the technologic advances in medicine present formidable challenges to the ethics committees of hospitals and professional organizations.

Among the most critical of future ethical issues are those related to advances in the field of molecular biology and gene manipulation and therapy. International research efforts, such as the Human Genome Project and the discovery and characterization of molecular correlates of human health and disease, with all their potential use and abuse ramifications present a mind-boggling ethical challenge. The future use of individual genetic blueprints for diagnosis and treatment as well as for predicting future medical events has scientists, policy makers, and ethicists concerned about potential runaway applications of technology. Amid all the potential benefits of these amazing scientific advances are fears of the unethical applications of such technology.

Physicians and the Internet

A survey estimates that 86% of physicians use the Internet to gather health, medical, or prescription drug information. Among physicians who use the Internet for health information, 92% reported that they accessed it from their office and 21% said they did so with a patient in the examination room.[51] Physicians themselves have developed personal Web sites to establish their credentials, explain their practice specialties, and attract patients and referrals. In addition, it can be expected that patients' and physicians' use of email and other sharing of information electronically will continue to increase and with it a variety of issues related to confidentiality, patient expectations, and potential liability.[52]

In addition to information on professional meetings and seminars and the latest developments in clinical practice, physicians currently can obtain the latest data from more than 132,000 clinical trials in 179 countries from the National Institutes of Health Web site, www.ClinicalTrials.gov.[53] Information is provided about the research locations, design, purpose, criteria for participation, and diseases or treatments under study for each listed clinical trial.

Future Perspectives

Medicine has made astounding progress in the last half century. An increasing number of highly specialized physicians and support personnel have achieved marvels of technical accomplishment. Yet the overall success of U.S. health care system as reported in 2010 by the Commonwealth Fund, a private U.S. foundation whose mission is to promote a high-performing equitable health care system, indicated that the United States underperforms the six other industrialized countries included in their study (Australia, Canada, Germany, the Netherlands, New Zealand, and the United Kingdom) in key areas of quality of care, access to care, efficiency of care, equity of care, and a healthy lifestyle, despite the United States having the most costly health care system.[54] According to the Central Intelligence Agency's World Factbook 2012, the United States ranks 50th in the world in the country comparison of life expectancy at birth.[55]

Advances in information technology and the expansion of the primary care workforce are seen by the Commonwealth Fund as some of the areas that hold promise for an improved performance of U.S. health care system in the future.[56] Initiatives of the HITECH Act to advance the use of HIT and the ACA to promote robust development of the primary care workforce are causes for optimism.

Over almost three decades since the introduction of prospective payment systems and four decades since the inception of managed care, physicians and their professional organizations have navigated enormous shifts in the medical care delivery environment. Major changes in regulation, reimbursement, fiscal and quality accountability, technology, hospital relationships, patient demographics, patient expectations, and a host of other factors have impacted physician practices. As a group, physicians have accommodated and weathered these changes with resilience and creativity. They have responded to market forces and seized the opportunities of new technologies with entrepreneurial endeavors that replaced services previously restricted to hospitals with their own outpatient enterprises such as diagnostic imaging and ambulatory surgery centers. They have created networks to leverage negotiating power to secure health plan subscriber populations for their practices and collaborated with health plans to implement new disease management protocols. More recently, recognizing the impacts of continuing health system consolidations, growing numbers of physicians are accepting employment by hospitals as an alternative to the rigors of managing private practices and are creating new partnerships with hospitals that supplant their prior voluntary medical staff roles.[57] The new health care reform era via the HITECH Act and the ACA will demand numerous additional and unprecedented accommodations in both medical education and practice to ensure physicians' effectiveness in the evolving health care marketplace. Changes in physician medical practice will be far reaching as reimbursement transitions from the individual patient fee-for-service model to models that are population based.[58]

Given the U.S. medical care system's history of individually focused patient care, its "complaint–response" orientation, and its fee-for-service reimbursement, most physicians and other health care professionals have not been sufficiently educated about or imbued with values for their potential to prevent disease, ways to address the problems of disparities in access to care, and accountability for the effectiveness of therapies for population groups under their care. As a result, system participants—providers, consumers, and payers—tried and understandably failed to solve the health care system's problems with fragmented approaches. The dilemmas of trying to ensure balance among the parameters of access, cost, and quality of health care that provoked market-driven reforms evolved from an entrepreneurial system that constantly improved the technical ability to diagnose and treat the ills of individual patients, without addressing the health status of community populations and the larger society.

It is ironic that when medicine's scientific and technologic capabilities are poised to make their greatest contributions to the prevention and treatment of disease, the most daunting challenges arise from dysfunctions in the system that should exist to support, rather than impede, improving population health. The health care system's problems of limited access for large segments of the population, high cost, and variable quality have demonstrated at great expense that it is not sufficient for physicians and other health professionals to serve one patient at a time. Addressing societal issues of population health requires much more than a complaint–response system and a piecework-oriented reimbursement system. It is this recognition that several of the ACA's provisions intend to address, which among other initiatives discussed earlier include support for the patient-centered medical home (PCMH) and accountable care organization (ACO) models.

Both PCMH and ACO entail physician-led multidisciplinary team-based approaches that coordinate the full spectrum of patient care with appropriate community resources. Examples of community resources include assisting patients with obtaining additional health services, communicating with specialists, or obtaining transportation or housing assistance that are crucial to well-being. Both models have the goal of improving the health care of individual patients and the health status of defined population groups and, ideally, use blended fee-for-service reimbursement with prospective payment.[59] "No longer will physicians be rewarded for working downstream—responding to patients' symptoms and diseases—many of which could have been prevented. Rather, they will need to move upstream—emphasizing wellness and prevention and mobilizing the services of inter-professional teams to facilitate health care."[60] These reforms will be enormous shifts from the traditional medical practice reimbursement models to models in which physicians deliver value to patients through efficient and effective services that drive financial reward.[61] In summary, the reforming health care system will affect every dimension of physician practice with new reimbursement methodologies, new expectations for evidence of population health improvements through the use of EHRs and electronic reporting, requirements for a team-based approach to patient management that necessitates linkages with community resources and participation in public reporting of quality measures. "The point is that health care is being reformed not just by federal legislation and new regulations. It is changing at virtually every point of interaction that physicians have: between physicians and their patients, physicians and their peers, physicians and other clinicians, physicians and technology, physicians and payers . . . the list goes on."[62] The success of medical care will now be defined in the parlance of public health by the health status parameters of population groups.

Noted in a report by the AAMC director of public health and prevention projects, the separation of the disciplines of medicine and public health dates to the late 19th century when medical schools' focus shifted from community-based care and prevention to hospital care and scientific research.[63] Succeeding decades saw continuing interest and efforts to include more emphasis on population-based medicine in medical school curricula. An AAMC bibliography lists journal articles on this subject that begin in 1938.[64] In 1999, the AAMC and the Centers for Disease Control and Prevention established a cooperative agreement "to strengthen collaborations between academic medicine and public health."[65] In 2002, the AMA partnered with the U.S. Department of Health and Human Services to develop an educational program, "Roadmaps for Clinical Practice," which included "A Primer on Population-Based Medicine," and subsequent case studies on disease prevention and health promotion.[66] Medical education reforms in population and public health have continued with recent changes in medical school accreditation standards that identify "health of populations, public health sciences and preventive medicine as part of required curricular content."[65] In 2012, U.S. medical licensing examination began testing students on public health principles with more emphasis on public health planned for future examinations.[63] The challenges of including substantial additions on public health subject matter in the already full medical school curricula are broadly recognized and include factors such as the value systems and expertise of faculty and students' perceptions that public health lacks relevance to their future practice.[67] Nonetheless, it is abundantly clear that the success of future physicians' practices make it essential, not optional, for medical schools to include both education on the fundamental tenets of population health and training opportunities that will develop skills to manage patient care in the reformed delivery system. "Efforts to develop health professionals who can improve health, and not just deliver care, should be a continuing priority for the academic medicine and public health communities."[65]

In his landmark report of 1910, Abraham Flexner presaged the situation of today:

> His (the physician's) relationship was formerly to his patient—at most to his patient's family, and it was almost altogether remedial. If the patient had something wrong with him the doctor was called in to cure it. Payment of a fee ended the transaction. But the physician's function is fast becoming social and preventive, rather than individual and curative. Upon him society relies to ascertain, and through measures essentially educational, to enforce the conditions that prevent disease and make positively for physical and moral well-being.[68]

Historically, medicine responded to the American public's desire to have the best and the most of medical services, but medicine now has a new responsibility to help the American public understand that the challenges of improving health status and its costs are beyond the sole grasp of traditional system "insiders." Collaborative partnerships of medicine, medical education, other health- and community-serving professionals and organizations, citizens, and their elected officials must assume the responsibility for carefully and deliberately creating a new form of health care organization that ensures a coherent, efficient, and effective health care delivery system for all Americans.

Key Terms for Review

Academic Health Center

Accreditation Council for Graduate Medical Education (ACGME)

Agency for Healthcare Research and Quality (AHRQ)

American Board of Medical Specialties (ABMS)

Evidence-based Clinical Practice Guidelines

Flexner Report

Graduate Medical Education Consortia

Hospitalist

Physician Compare

References

1. Barsukiewicz CK, Raffel MW, Raffel NK. *The U.S. health system: origins and functions, 6th ed.* Clifton Park, NY: Delmar/Cengage Learning; 2010.
2. Jones RS. Organized medicine in the United States. *Ann Surg.* 1993;217: 423–429.

3. Newton WP, DuBard CA. Shaping the future of academic health centers: the role of departments of family medicine. *Ann Fam Med.* 2006;4(Suppl 1): S2–S11.

4. The Consequences of current financing methods for the future roles of AHCs. In: *Academic health centers: leading change in the 21st century.* Kohn, L. ed. The National Academies Press. 2004. Available from http://www.nap .edu/openbook.php?record_id=10734&page=92. Accessed September 5, 2012.

5. Association of American Medical Colleges. Fully accredited medical school revenue by source, 126 schools, FY2011. Available from https://www.aamc .org/download/285860/data/fy11msrev_pie.pdf. Accessed September 8, 2012.

6. Association of Academic Health Centers. Health workforce. 1400 Sixteenth Street, NW, Suite 720, Washington, DC. Available from http://www.aahcdc .org/Policy/Issues/HealthWorkforce.aspx#fi. Accessed September 6, 2012.

7. Association of American Medical Colleges. Medical schools. Available from http://www.aamc.org/about/medicalschools/. Accessed September 6, 2012.

8. American Association of Colleges of Osteopathic Medicine. U.S. colleges of osteopathic medicine. Available from http://www.aacom.org/about/colleges/ Pages/default.aspx. Accessed September 6, 2012.

9. Accreditation Council for Graduate Medical Education. ACGME mission, vision and values. Available from http://www.acgme.org/acgmeweb/About/ Mission,VisionandValues.aspx. Accessed January 12, 2013.

10. Morris TQ, Sirica CM. *Taking charge of graduate medical education to meet the nation's needs in the 21st century.* New York, NY: Proceedings of a conference sponsored by the Josiah Macy, Jr. Foundation; June 1992.

11. Accreditation Council for Graduate Medical Education. ACGME announces plan to transform how medical residency programs will educate future physicians for a changing health care system. February 22, 2012. Available from http://www.prnewswire.com/news-releases/acgme-announces-plan-to-transform-how-medical-residency-programs-will-educate-future-physicians-for-a-changing-health-care-system-140051823.html. Accessed September 5, 2012.

12. Kelly JV, Larned FS, Smits HL. Graduate medical education consortia: expectations and experiences. *Acad Med.* 1994;12:931–943.

13. AAMC-Association of American Medical Colleges. AAMC summaries of DGME and IME Sections of the health reform bill and CMS proposed rules implementing these provisions, section 5503: redistribution of unused residency slots (DGME and IME). July 28, 2010. Available from https://www .aamc.org/download/163590/data/summaries_of_gme_sections_of_health_ reform_bill_.pdf. Accessed January 11, 2013.

14. The Henry J. Kaiser Family Foundation. Summary of new health reform law. Available from http://www.kff.org/healthreform/upload/8061.pdf. Accessed August 25, 2012.

15. American Board of Medical Specialties. *Who we are and what we do.* Available from http://www.abms.org/about_ABMS/who_we_are.aspx. Accessed January 12, 2013.

16. American Board of Medical Specialties. Specialties and subspecialties. Available from http://www.abms.org/who_we_help/physicians/specialties .aspx. Accessed September 6, 2012.

17. Wachter RM, Bell D. Renaissance of hospital generalists. *BMJ.* 2012;344:e652 doi:1136/bmj.e652. Available from http://hospitalmedi-cine.ucsf.edu/downloads/renaissance_of_hospital_generalist _wachter.pdf. Accessed September 6, 2012.

18. American Association of Medical Colleges. *Center for Workforce Studies. 2011 State physician workforce data book.* Available from https://www.aamc.org/download/263512/data/statedata2011.pdf. Accessed September 9, 2012.

19. The Henry J. Kaiser Family Foundation. United States: Total professionally active physicians. Available from http://www.statehealthfacts.org/profileind .jsp?ind=934&cat=8&rgn=1&cmprn=2. Accessed January 11, 2013.

20. American Medical Association. International medical graduates in ameri-can medicine: contemporary challenges and opportunities. January 2010. Available from http://www.ama-assn.org/ama1/pub/upload/mm/18/ img-workforce-paper.pdf. Accessed September 9, 2012.

21. Whelan GP, Gary NE, Kostis J, et al. The changing pool of international medical graduates seeking certification training in US graduate medical edu-cation programs. *JAMA.* 2002;288:1079–1084.

22. U.S. Government Accountability Office. GAO 10-412, Foreign medical schools: education should improve monitoring of schools that participate in federal student loan program. June 2010. Available from http://gao.gov/new .items/d10412.pdf. Accessed September 9, 2012.

23. Peccoralo LA, Callahan K, Stark R, Decherrie LV. Primary care training and the evolving healthcare system. *Mt Sinai J Med.* 2012;79:451–463.

24. Petterson SM, Liaw WR, Phillips RL, et al. Projecting US primary care phy-sician workforce needs. *Ann Fam Med.* 2012;10:503–509. Available from http://www.medscape.com/viewarticle/774675. Accessed January 11, 2013.

25. KaiserEDU.org. Primary care shortage: background brief. April 2011. Available from http://www.kaiseredu.org/Issue-Modules/Primary-Care-Shortage/Background-Brief.aspx. Accessed September 10, 2012.

26. Harris S. Physician shortage spreads across specialty lines. *AAMC Reporter.* 2010. Available from https://www.aamc.org/newsroom/reporter/ oct10/152090/physician_shortage_spreads_across_specialty_lines.html. Accessed September 10, 2012.

27. Tucker L, Johnson-Fleece M. Medical education and training: a policy update. 2010 American Board of Internal Medicine Foundation Forum. Available from http://www.abimfoundation.org/Events/2010-Forum/~/med ia/1F1F3D3C4A97401B9942EF797A53E630.ashx. Accessed September 10, 2012.

28. O'Neil EH. Education as part of the health care solution. *JAMA*. 1992;268:1146.

29. Inwald SA, Winters FD. Emphasizing a preventive medicine orientation during primary care/family practice residency training. *J Am Osteopath Assoc*. 1995;95:268.

30. Association of Academic Health Centers. *Out of order, out of time: the state of the nation's workforce*. 2008. Available from http://www.aahcdc.org/policy/AAHC_OutofTime_4WEB.pdf. Accessed September 10, 2012.

31. Institute of Medicine. *Primary care and public health, exploring integration to improve population health*. March 28, 2012. Available from http://www.iom.edu/Reports/2012/Primary-Care-and-Public-Health/Briefing-Slides.aspx. Accessed June 28, 2012.

32. Kovner AR. *Health care delivery in the United States, 5th ed*. New York, NY: Springer; 1995:429–430.

33. Henry J. Kaiser Family Foundation. Medicare revises hospitals' readmissions penalties. Available from http://www.kaiserhealthnews.org/stories/2012/October/03/medicare-revises-hospitals-readmissions-penalties.aspx. Accessed January 12, 2013.

34. American Medical Association. Amednews. Medicare's no-pay events: coping with complications. Available from Accessed January 12, 2013.

35. Hospitals and Health Networks Daily. Hospital statistics chart rise in physician employment. Available from http://www.hhnmag.com/hhnmag/HHNDaily/HHNDailyDisplay.dhtml?id=1970001363. Accessed January 12, 2013.

36. Center for Studying Health System Change. Rising hospital employment of physicians: better quality, higher costs? Available from http://www.hschange.com/CONTENT/1230/. Accessed January 12, 2013.

37. Pear R. Doctors warned on "divided loyalty." *New York Times*. Available from http://www.nytimes.com/2012/12/27/health/27doctors.html?ref=health&_r=0. Accessed December 27, 2012.

38. Casalino LP, November EA, Berenson RA, Pham HH. Hospital-physician relations: two tracks and the decline of the voluntary medical staff. *Health Affairs*. 2008;27:1305–1307. Available from http://content.healthaffairs.org/content/27/5/1305.full.html. Accessed January 8, 2013.

39. U.S. Department of Health and Human Services, National Institutes of Health, National Heart Lung and Blood Institute. About clinical practice guidelines. Available from http://www.nhlbi.nih.gov/guidelines/about.htm#what. Accessed September 12, 2012.

40. U.S. Department of Health and Human Services, Agency for Healthcare Research and Quality. The National Guideline Clearinghouse™. Fact Sheet. AHRQ Publication No. 12-M052-EF. August 2012. Available from http://www.ahrq.gov/clinic/ngcfact.htm. Accessed September 14, 2012.

41. U.S. Department of Health and Human Services, Agency for Health Care Research and Quality. Guidelines by Topic. Available from http://guideline .gov/browse/by-topic.aspx. Accessed September 15, 2012.

42. Shea KG, Sink EL, Jacobs JC Jr. Clinical practice guidelines and guideline development. *J Pediatr Orthop*. 2012;32(Suppl 2):S95–S100.

43. Special report, docs fight to hide lawsuits. *New York Daily News*, Sports Final. April 17, 2000:12.

44. U.S. Department of Health and Human Services, Centers for Medicare & Medicaid Services. Physician compare initiative. Available from https://www .cms.gov/Medicare/Quality-Initiatives-Patient-Assessment-Instruments/ physician-compare-initiative/index.html. Accessed January 12, 2013.

45. Christianson JB, Volmar KM, Alexander J, Scanlon DP. A report card on provider report cards: current status of the health care transparency movement. *J Gen Intern Med*. 2010;25:1235–1241.

46. Kushniruk OT. Incorporation of medical informatics and information technology as core components of undergraduate medical education—time to change! *Stud Health Technol Inform*. 2009;143:62–67.

47. Chumley RE, Dobbie AE. Electronic health records in outpatient clinics: perspectives of third year medical students. *BMC Med Educ*. 2008;8.

48. Centers for Medicare and Medicaid. Meaningful Use. Available from http://www.cms.gov/Regulations-and-Guidance/Legislation/ EHRIncentivePrograms/Meaningful_Use.html. Accessed September 16, 2012.

49. Centers for Medicare and Medicaid, Services. EHR Incentive Program. July 2012 Monthly Report. Available from http://www.cms.gov/Regulations- and-Guidance/Legislation/EHRIncentivePrograms/Downloads/July2012_ MonthlyReports.pdf. Accessed September 20, 2012.

50. Henry J. Kaiser Family Foundation. Medical malpractice policies. Available from http://www.kaiseredu.org/Issue-Modules/Medical-Malpractice-Policy/ Background-Brief.aspx. Accessed January 12, 2013.

51. American Medical Association. Amednews. 86% of physicians use internet to access health information. Available from http://www.ama-assn.org/ amednews/2010/01/04/bisc0104.htm. Accessed January 13, 2013.

52. Kassirer JP. Patients, physicians, and the internet. *Health Affairs*. 2000;19:115–123. Available from http://content.healthaffairs.org/content/19/6/115. Accessed January 9, 2013.

53. U.S. National Institute of Health. ClinicalTrials.gov. Available from http:// clinicaltrials.gov/. Accessed September 15, 2012.

54. Davis K, Schoen C, Stremikis K. *Mirror, mirror on the wall: how the performance of the U.S. health system compares internationally*. The Commonwealth Fund; 2010 update. Available from http://www.commonwealthfund.org/ Publications/Fund-Reports/2010/Jun/Mirror-Mirror-Update.aspx?page=all. Accessed September 14, 2012.

55. Central Intelligence Agency. *World factbook 2012*. Life expectancy at birth. Available from https://www.cia.gov/library/publications/the-world-factbook/rankorder/2102rank.html?countryName=United%20States&countryCode=us&regionCode=noa&rank=50#us. Accessed September 14, 2012.

56. The Commonwealth Fund. U.S. ranks last among seven countries on health system performance based on measures of quality, efficiency, access, equity, healthy lives. 2010. Available from http://www.commonwealthfund.org/News/News-Releases/2010/Jun/US-Ranks-Last-Among-Seven-Countries.aspx. Accessed September 16, 2012.

57. Casalino LP, November EA, Berenson RA, Pham HH. Hopsital-physician relations: two tracks and the decline of the voluntary medical staff. *Health Affairs*. 2008;27:1308–1312. Available from http://content.healthaffairs.org/content/27/5/1305.full.html. Accessed January 8, 2013.

58. Health Care Financial Management Association. The return of capitation: preparing for population-based health care. Available from http://www.hfma.org/Content.aspx?id=3234. Accessed January 13, 2013.

59. Baxley L, Borkan J, Campbell T, et al. In pursuit of a transformed health care system: from patient centered medical homes to accountable care organizations and beyond. *Ann Fam Med*. 2011;9:466–467. Available from http://www.annfammed.org/content/9/5/466.full. Accessed January 15, 2013.

60. Garr DR, Margalit R, Jameton A, Cerra FB. Educating the present and future health care workforce to provide care to populations. *Acad Med* 2012;87:1159–1160. Available from http://journals.lww.com/academicmedicine/Fulltext/2012/09000/Commentary___Educating_the_Present_and_Future.11.aspx. Accessed December 27, 2012.

61. National Health Care Reform Magazine. Accountable care organizations and PPACA after November 2nd 2010. Available from http://www.healthcarereformmagazine.com/article/accountable-care-organizations0.html. Accessed January 15, 2013.

62. Jacobs LP. 10 ways market changes will reshape physician practices. Available from http://www.medscape.com/viewarticle/773905. Accessed January 9, 2013.

63. Association of American Medical Colleges. After reform, more medical schools emphasize public health. Available from https://www.aamc.org/newsroom/reporter/170156/public_health.html. Accessed January 14, 2013.

64. Association of American Medical Colleges. Public health and medical education bibliography. Available from https://www.aamc.org/download/64930/data/publichealthbibliography_web_v011110.pdf.pdf. Accessed January 16, 2013.

65. Maeshiro R, Koo D, Keck CW. Integration of public health into medical education. Available from http://download.journals.elsevierhealth.com/pdfs/journals/0749-3797/PIIS0749379711005113.pdf. Accessed January 14, 2013.

66. American Medical Association. *Roadmaps for clinical practice: a primer on population-based medicine.* Available from http://www.ama-assn.org/resources/doc/public-health/roadmaps_rev.pdf. Accessed January 9, 2013.

67. Mahoney JF, Fox MD, Chheda SG. Overcoming challenges to integrating public health and population health into medical curricula. *Am J Prev Med.* 2011;41:S173. Available from http://download.journals.elsevierhealth.com/pdfs/journals/0749-3797/PIIS0749379711004090.pdf?refuid=S0749-3797(11)00511-3&refissn=0749-3797&mis=.pdf. Accessed January 14, 2013.

68. Flexner A. *Medical education in the United States and Canada.* New York, NY. Carnegie Foundation for the Advancement of Teaching; 1910. Bulletin No.4. Available from http://www.ama-assn.org/resources/doc/public-health/roadmaps_rev.pdf. Accessed January 9, 2013.

CHAPTER 7

The Health Care Workforce

This chapter defines the major health care professions, with particular emphasis on their educational preparation, credentials, numbers, and roles in the health care delivery system. Factors that influence demand for the various health care providers are also reviewed. The chapter concludes with a discussion of health workforce policy developments in light of the Patient Protection and Affordable Care Act of 2010 and some expectations for the future.

As one of the nation's largest and most important industries, health care is also one of the largest employment sectors. The Department of Labor estimates that 16.4 million people, or approximately 11.4% of U.S. workforce, are employed in the health care industry. In the next decade, more new jobs, about 5.6 million, will be created in health care than in any other industry.[1]

Although hospitals are still a major employer, recent employment growth has been primarily among health maintenance organizations, ambulatory clinics and services, home health providers, and offices of health practitioners.

Health Professions

There are more than 200 occupations and professions among the more than 16 million workers in the health care field. As the system continues to change, making use of new technology, expanding in some sectors and contracting in others, additional occupations and professions will appear. The personnel of those new occupations and professions will be required to possess more specialized knowledge and more sophisticated skills.

Specialization to attain higher levels of technical competence also reduces the flexibility of providers to develop more efficient staffing patterns. Specialization among the workforce increases personnel costs, as additional employees are required to perform specific tasks. Smaller service facilities, especially in rural areas, are burdened most by the need for infrequently used specialists.

As a result, there is growing acceptance of multiskilled health practitioners. Hospitals, in particular, are employing individuals trained in more than one skill. A large number of combinations are feasible: Occupational therapy assistants are also serving as physical therapy assistants, radiologic technologists are performing ultrasound, and a variety of nonclinical personnel are performing phlebotomy.

Table 7-1 shows the distribution of health care workers.

Table 7-1 Percent Distribution of Health Care Employment by Setting

Offices and Clinics of	Percent Distribution
Physicians	17.0
Dentists	6.2
Other Practitioners	4.7
Outpatient care centers	4.0
Home health care services	7.2
Other ambulatory health care services*	1.8
Medical and diagnostic laboratories	1.6
Hospitals	34.6
Nursing and residential care facilities	22.8
All health service sites	100.0

*Ambulance services, blood banks, diagnostic centers, and others.

Source: Reprinted from U.S. Department of Labor, Bureau of Labor Statistics, Career Guide to Industries, 2010–2011.

Credentialing and Regulating Health Professionals

Government regulation of the health professions is considered necessary to protect the public from incompetent and unethical practitioners. Because each state assumes and exercises most of that responsibility for itself, how health care occupations are regulated and the manner in which regulation is carried out vary from state to state. About 50 health occupations are regulated throughout the United States.

Regulatory restrictions limit health care service agencies in how they may use personnel and limit their ability to explore innovative ways to provide patient care. Similarly, regulatory restrictions influence educational programs to focus curricula on what has been prescribed by regulatory boards and their related accrediting bodies. Many states have taken steps to revise their credentialing systems to provide greater flexibility and responsiveness to fast-changing health care technology.[2]

The health care occupations have been regulated by one of three procedures: state licensure, state or national certification, or state or national registration. In licensure, the state law defines the scope of practice to be regulated and the educational and testing requirements that must be met to engage in that practice. Licensure, the most restrictive of the three types of regulation, is intended to restrict entry or practice in certain occupations and to prevent the use of professional titles by those without predetermined qualifications. For example, it is illegal for individuals to perform procedures defined in the statutes as medicine or dentistry or to call themselves physicians or dentists without the appropriate license.

Most licensure boards are composed primarily of practitioners whose concern is for setting standards and assessing competence for initial entrance into the field. Except by requiring attendance at continuing education courses, licensure boards have done very little about ensuring continuing competence, dealing with impaired practitioners, or disciplining wayward members of their professions; however, they do have the power to censure, warn members, or even revoke licenses.

Certification is the regulating process under which a state or voluntary professional organization, such as a national board, attests to the educational achievements and performance abilities of persons in a health care field of practice. It is a much less restrictive regulation than licensing and means that the individual has obtained advanced or specialized training in that area of practice. When applied to such fields as psychology and social work, certification does not make it illegal for unqualified individuals to engage in activities within the scope of practice in those fields as long as they do not claim or use the titles of certified psychologist or social worker. Certification allows the public, employers, and third-party payers to determine which practitioners are appropriately qualified in their specialty or occupation.

Certification generally has no provision for regulating impaired or misbehaving practitioners other than putting them on probation or dropping them from certification. Unlike the licensed professions, the certified occupations have no legal basis for preventing an impaired or professionally delinquent individual who is uncertified from practicing. It is left to third-party payers or employers to insist on only certified practitioners.

Registration began as a mechanism to facilitate contacts and relationships among members of a profession and potential employers or the public. It is the least rigorous of regulatory processes, ranging from simple listings or registries of persons offering a service, such as private duty nurses, to national registration programs of professional or occupational groups that require educational and testing qualifications. Because most registration programs are voluntary, they have little to do with continuing competence or disciplinary actions.[3]

Health Care Occupations

Space does not allow for the description of all of the occupations in health care, but several major health care occupations are outlined.

Physicians

There are 137 accredited medical schools in the United States that award the doctor of medicine (MD) degree. The 17,364 graduates of U.S. medical schools in 2011 reflects an increase of 529 over the number graduated during the previous year. The number of women enrolled in U.S. medical schools has more than doubled in the past 20 years. In 2011, the graduating medical class was 48% female.

The number of minority students enrolled in medical schools now constitutes more than one-third of medical school enrollees. In 2011, 62% of the medical school graduates were white, 6.5% black, 7.7% Hispanic,

21.7% Asian, and 4.7% either foreign, Native American, or of mixed or unknown race.[4]

There are 26 accredited colleges of osteopathy that offer the doctor of osteopathy (DO) degree. In the last two decades their enrollment has nearly doubled, and they now graduate about 4,200 students per year. Doctors of medicine and doctors of osteopathy share the same privileges in most of U.S. hospitals. The 63,000 doctors of osteopathy practicing in the United States make up about 7% of all the physicians in the country.[5]

Although medical education in the United States begins in undergraduate medical school, it continues intensively for as many as 8 years of graduate medical training. Most states require 1 year of graduate medical education before a physician can be licensed. That year, which used to be called an internship, is now considered the first of 3 years of residency training regarded by the medical profession as the minimum needed to practice medicine.

Residency training prepares a physician to practice a medical specialty. In a period of 3–8 years, depending on the specialty, residency qualifies a physician for certification in 1 of 24 medical specialty boards. Further residency training, often called a fellowship, can lead to a certificate in 1 of over 100 subspecialties. Because U.S. medical schools consistently graduate about 5,000 fewer new physicians per year than are employed as first-year residents, physicians trained in medical schools outside of the United States fill the gap. The responsibility for evaluating the credentials of international medical graduates (IMGs) entering the United States to enter residency programs lies with the Educational Commission for Foreign Medical Graduates, a private nonprofit organization sponsored by major U.S. medical organizations, including the American Association of Medical Colleges. Approximately 6,000 IMGs enter the United States each year to meet the annual shortfall of U.S. medical school graduates.[6]

The impetus for this influx is the demand for resident house officers in both teaching and nonteaching hospitals. Many hospitals, particularly those in rural or inner-city areas, depend heavily on foreign medical graduates to staff their clinical services.

After finishing residency training, most IMGs remain in the United States to practice. As a result, IMGs now constitute about one-fourth of the active U.S. physician workforce. Also, a relatively stable group of about 1,350 U.S. citizens attend medical schools outside the country and return to the United States to practice each year.

About 35% of more than 700,000 practicing physicians in the United States are in primary care, general pediatrics, general or family practice, or general internal medicine practice. Almost two-thirds of this country's physicians limit their practice to one of the many medical specialties. Employment of physicians and surgeons is projected to grow by 24% from 2010 to 2020, as the expanding population of baby boomers will increase demand for physician services.[7]

Nevertheless, there are serious shortages in certain medical specialties that affect the efficiency and quality of medical care in some geographic areas. Depending on the region of the country, several of a wide range of medical specialists may be in short supply.[8]

Nursing

Nursing was a common employment position for women during the 19th century through association with a religious or benevolent group. A physician, Ann Preston, organized the first training program for nurses in the United States in 1861 at Women's Hospital of Philadelphia. Training was open to all women "who wished greater proficiency in their domestic responsibilities."[9]

At the turn of the 20th century, hundreds of new hospitals were built under the aegis of religious orders, ethnic groups, industrialists, and elite groups of civic-minded individuals. Because student nurses were a constantly renewable source of low-cost hospital workers even some of the smallest hospitals maintained nursing schools.[10] Hospital nursing school programs, therefore, were primarily sequences of on-the-job training rather than academic courses. As the programs evolved, stronger academic components were introduced, eventually leading to baccalaureate degrees instead of hospital diplomas.

Before World War I, nursing was divided into three domains—public health, private duty, and hospital. Public health nursing was considered the elite pursuit and was recognized as instrumental in the campaign against tuberculosis and promoting infant welfare. Few nurses worked for hospitals. In 1920, more than 70% of nurses worked in private duty, about half in patients' homes and half for private patients in hospitals.

The war emphasized the effectiveness of hospitals, and they soon became the center of nursing education in the increasingly specialized acute-care medical environment. The social medicine and public health aspects of nursing were subjugated to the image of nursing as a symbol of patriotism, national sacrifice, and efficiency. The war experience established nurses as dedicated associates in hospital science. Nursing leaders promoted the idea of upgrading nursing through high-quality hospital nursing schools, preferably associated with universities. The choice to idealize the role of the nurse as dedicated and deferential to the physician specialist in the hospital marginalized the independent role of the nurse in social medicine and public health.[11]

Registered Nurses

Different levels of nursing education were developed at a variety of educational institutions. A registered nurse (RN) could be trained in a 2-year associate degree program at a community college or a junior college, a 2- to 3-year diploma program offered through a hospital, or a 4- to 5-year bachelor's of science degree program at a university or college.

The increasing complexity in health care forced specialization in nursing as it did in medicine. Nurses with a bachelor's degree may undertake advanced studies in several clinical areas to develop the needed competence for teaching, supervision, or advanced practice. Clinical nurse specialists in hospitals play important liaison roles between the medical practitioners in narrow and highly technical subspecialties, the patients, and supportive nursing services. By the 1960s, master's degree and doctoral programs were developed for nurses who wished to specialize.

The number of RNs in the United States increased by almost 1.5 million between 1980 and 2008. The latest available survey of the RN population conducted in 2008 and reported in 2010 indicated a new high of over 3 million RNs in the United States and that 84.8% of those nurses were actively employed. The average age for RNs had climbed to 46 years by 2004, the highest average age for the RN population since record keeping began in 1960. By 2008, the median age had leveled off at 46 years. This plateau in the aging trend in the nursing workforce has been primarily due to an increase in the number of RNs under age 30 who are currently entering the workforce as graduates of bachelor's degree programs that traditionally have a younger student population. In 2008, 10.8% of RNs were less than 30 years old, an increase over the 8% reported in 2004 but still much less than the 25% reported in 1980.[12]

It has been estimated that about one-third of the increase in the number of nurses in the United States since the 1990s was due to the influx of nurses born outside of the country.[13] Nurses are encouraged to leave their home countries and work in the United States for the opportunities that provide foreign-born nurses with higher earnings, a higher standard of living, and advanced education. As reported in 2008, Internationally Educated Nurses (IENs) from the Philippines continue to constitute the largest group of IENs in the United States, followed in numbers by IENs from Canada.[12]

One of the major changes occurring in nursing is in the type of program that nurses enter to obtain their basic education. Almost 90% of nurses now receive their basic education in an institution of higher education compared with 20% in 1960. The associate degree in nursing (ADN) from an institution of higher learning, often a community college, is reported to be the initial nursing degree obtained by over 45% of currently licensed RNs. RNs with master's or doctorate degrees rose from 376,901 in 2004 to 404,163 in 2008. Licensed RNs with graduate degrees currently comprise 13.2% of all licensed RNs, twice what was reported in 1988.[12]

Nurses began to specialize during the 1950s. After World War II, nurses were in short supply, and hospitals began to group the least physiologically stable patients in one nursing unit for intensive care. The more competent nurses cared for the sickest patients, but instead of lowering the need for nurses the critical care nurse specialty began, and the need for staff nurses continued to grow.

There are now more than 180 U.S. schools that have at least one of the three types of doctoral programs in nursing. The doctor of nursing is the first professional doctoral degree building on the liberal arts or scientific education that had prepared students to take the state licensing exam to practice as an RN. The doctors of nursing science degrees are professional doctorates that prepare the nurse for advanced clinical practice. The nursing PhD is an academic degree with requirements similar to PhD in other fields—extensive preparation in a narrow field and a dissertation.[14] Table 7-2 shows the distribution of employed RN nurses by setting.

Men comprise a small percentage of the nurse population, although their numbers are increasing. In 2008, the number of male RNs licensed after the year 2000 reached 9.6%. This percentage is expected to continue

Table 7-2 Percent Distribution of Employed Registered Nurses by Setting in 2008

Setting	Percent Distribution
Hospital	62.2
Nursing home	5.3
Ambulatory care setting	10.5
Home health	6.4
Community/Public Health*	8.0
Nursing education	3.8
Other	3.8
Total	100.0

*Includes: schools and occupational health.
Source: Data from U.S. Department of Health and Human Services, Health Resources and Service Administration, Bureau of Health Professions, National Center for Health Workforce Analysis, 2008 National Sample Survey of Registered Nurses.

to increase as the more recently enrolled male nursing student population graduates and becomes licensed.[2]

Increases are also occurring in the number of RNs identifying themselves as members of a racial/ethnic minority group. The number of RNs from minority racial/ethnic groups has increased by over 180,000 during the years 2000 to 2008. The trend for increased minority racial/ethnic group RNs in the workforce is expected to advance even more rapidly in the future as minority racial/ethnic groups are increasingly represented in the recently graduated nurse population currently entering the health care workforce.[12]

Hospital consolidations in response to market forces affect nursing employment in several ways. Hospital workforces have been reorganized to adjust to fiscal restraints, reductions in the number of admissions, and shortened lengths of stay. At the same time, increases in the intensity of nursing care required by the more complicated illnesses of the patients who are admitted to hospitals suggest the need for higher nurse-to-patient ratios. Thus, although many hospitals employ fewer nurses for inpatient care, those retained are expected to maintain clinically sophisticated nursing skills, monitor lesser trained persons employed to provide direct patient care, and manage units with high proportions of seriously ill patients.

Fewer nurses taking care of more severely ill patients, combined with the need to supervise nonprofessional and unlicensed personnel performing nursing tasks, has increased nursing workloads and affected morale.[14]

Not surprisingly, concerns for the quality of care, frustration with workplace issues such as burnout and poor management, unresponsive hospital managers, and burnout from working in understaffed facilities have made hospital nursing a less attractive career. As a result, many nurses have retired or sought employment in non-inpatient settings.[15]

Although there remain important concerns about the continued aging of the currently employed RN population and the difficulty that schools of nursing are experiencing in expanding nursing enrollment due to lack of faculty, there are promising developments. There has been a recent increase in the number of nursing graduates taking the licensure exam, and hospitals are developing innovative ways to increase enrollment in schools of nursing. Some facilities offer attractive sign-on bonuses to recruit new graduates. In addition, many schools of nursing are adding accelerated programs as a way to bring nurses to the workforce more quickly.[16] The Robert Wood Johnson Foundation, which has a long history of supporting nurses, is addressing one of the roots of the problem. Its projects are directed at changing the frustrating nursing work environment through alterations of both physical facilities and hospital cultures. The changes are intended to decrease the amount of time nurses spend on non-nursing tasks to permit them to focus on the more satisfying responsibilities of maintaining the quality of patient care.[17] Figure 7-1 illustrates

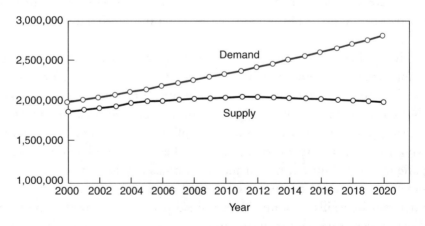

FIGURE 7-1 National Supply and Demand Projections of FTE Registered Nurses, 2000 and 2020.
Source: U.S. Department of Health and Human Services, Health Resources and Service Administration, Bureau of Health Professions, RN Supply and Demand Projections.

the supply and demand projections for the nursing profession published in a 2002 government report. As of 2012, discussion continues regarding future projections of supply and demand for the nursing profession, the extent of the projected nursing shortage, and ways to countermand the projected nursing shortages.

Licensed Practical Nurses

A licensed practical nurse (LPN) works under the direct supervision of an RN or physician. One-year LPN training is offered at about 1,100 state-approved technical or vocational schools or community or junior colleges. Programs include both classroom study and supervised clinical practice. Like RNs, LPNs must pass a state licensing examination.

Between 2002 and 2010, employment in hospitals for more than 750,000 LPNs has decreased from 28% to 22%. The reduction in inpatient hospital days and the substitution of unlicensed personnel have contributed to this decrease. The demand for LPNs in other work settings, however, is increasing and employment overall in this occupation is expected to increase by 22% from 2010 to 2020. Nursing homes and residential care facilities that provide assisted living employ almost 36% of the currently licensed LPNs, and another 12% are employed in physician offices. The remainder work in home health care, government agencies, schools, and varied types of outpatient care centers.[18]

Nurse Practitioners

Nurse practitioners are RNs with advanced education and clinical experience. Nurse practitioners provide primary and specialty care and in almost all states they are allowed to prescribe medicine. Each state specifically defines practice requirements and allowed parameters for this type of advanced practice nursing role.[19] Most nurse practitioners specialize. Neonatal nurse practitioners work with newborns. Pediatric nurse practitioners treat children from infancy through adolescence. School nurse practitioners serve students in elementary and secondary schools, colleges, and universities. Adult and family nurse practitioners are generalists who serve adults and families. Occupational health nurse practitioners work in industry providing on-the-job care. Psychiatric nurse practitioners serve people with mental or emotional problems. Geriatric nurse practitioners care for older adults.

The earliest nurse practitioners were nurse midwives and nurse anesthetists. A nurse midwife is usually an RN who completes a 1- or 2-year master's degree program in nurse midwifery. They are licensed by the state and may also be required to be certified by the American College of Nurse Midwives. Currently, almost all midwife-assisted births take place in a hospital or birthing clinic.

The roots for the nurse anesthetist specialty go back to more than a century, when nurses administered anesthesia in Catholic hospitals. Early training was provided in hospitals, but in 1945 the American Association of Nurse Anesthetists established a certification program. Nurse anesthetists are now required to have a master's degree from an accredited school and must pass the national certification examination. Most nurse anesthetists work with physician anesthesiologists in hospitals, ambulatory surgery centers, and urgent care centers providing comprehensive care to patients who need anesthesia.[20]

The current nurse practitioner movement began in the 1960s because of the shortage of physicians. The goal was to have specially prepared nurses augment the supply of physicians by working as primary care providers in pediatrics, adult health, geriatrics, and obstetrics. Nurse practitioners had to overcome some resistance from organized medicine and legal difficulties caused by restrictions in most state nurse practice acts, which prohibited nurses from diagnosing and treating patients. Nurse practitioners sought state-by-state changes in nurse practice acts, and by 1975 most states had started certifying or accepting the national certification of nurse practitioners, nurse midwives, and nurse anesthetists.[21]

Two-thirds of the first 131 nurse practitioner programs were relatively short certificate programs, and one-third were master's programs. The programs primarily trained for practice in pediatrics, midwifery, maternity, family medicine, adult health, or psychiatry. As in most ventures into uncharted territory, several approaches to nurse practitioner preparation were tested. Eventually, it was accepted that a nurse practitioner should be an RN with a master's degree. National certification and recertification are necessary.[22]

Efforts at health care cost containment have increased the demand for cost-effective nurse practitioners. Rural hospitals, with limited reserves of physicians, make substantial use of nurse practitioners and physician assistants and consider them to be a cost-effective means to an expanded scope of service to primary care.[23]

Nurse practitioners and physician assistants also are heavily involved in emergency department care, managing a wide range of conditions either independently or in collaboration with a physician. As reported in the National Hospital Ambulatory Medical Survey of 2009, 4.4% of emergency department visits were handled by nurse practitioners and almost 10% were handled by physician assistants.[24]

The high regard for nurse practitioners among both other medical personnel and the public is evidenced by the fact that there are now more than 400 accredited master's and more than 100 post-master's programs in the United States for the preparation of nurse practitioners.[25]

Clinical Nurse Specialist

A different, but related, type of advanced nursing practice role is the clinical nurse specialist. This specialty role was developed in response to the specific nursing care needs of increasingly complex patients.[26] Like specialist physicians, clinical nurse specialists are advanced practice specialists with in-depth knowledge and skills that make them valuable adjunct practitioners in specialized clinical settings. As a result, there are now more than 200 master's programs for the advanced preparation of clinical nurse specialists.[27]

Dentistry

Dentistry in early America was primitive. Tooth extraction was performed by itinerant tooth drawers, the neighborhood doctor or barber, or sometimes the local blacksmith. Because there were no regulations, anyone could practice dentistry, and skilled craftsmen and artisans turned their talents to dental practice.

Until about 1850 almost all prominent dentists were medical doctors who had chosen dentistry rather than general medicine as their vocation.[28] It was also in the 19th century that dentistry began its emergence from a trade to a profession. Dental schools were established to replace preceptorships, and dental practitioners participated in developing laws to regulate the profession.[29]

In 1840, the State of Maryland chartered the first dental school, the Baltimore College of Dental Surgery. The course of study lasted 2 years, the same as that required for a medical degree. By 1884, 28 dental colleges existed. Although a few were affiliated with universities, most were privately owned. New York took the lead in regulating the profession by licensure. In 1868, New York established a board of censors to examine candidates, which later became the State Board of Dental Examiners. By the end of the century, most other states also had passed licensure laws.

The mix of university-affiliated and independent dental schools resulted in significant variations in the quality of dental education. In 1922, 12 years after the Carnegie Foundation for the Advancement of Teaching had issued the Flexner Report evaluating U.S. medical education, the foundation created a commission to examine dental education. The commission's report appeared in 1926 and resulted in a complete reorganization of dental education in the United States.[30]

World War II brought about profound changes in Americans' attitudes toward dentistry. Citizens were shocked to learn that the dental health of the nation's young men was deplorable. Among the first 2 million draftees summoned by the Selective Service System, one of five lacked even the minimum standard of 12 functioning teeth. The Selective Service had to eliminate all dental standards to avoid mass disqualification of selectees. As a consequence, after the war the United States made a vigorous effort to improve the dental health of the country's population.

Before World War II, dentists were not involved in public health, and few dental schools taught anything on the subject. A decade after the first graduate course of study in dental public health was established in the 1940s by the University of Michigan, the new field of public health dentistry emerged in the United States. Today, a number of schools have established courses leading to advanced degrees in the field, and there is an American Board of Dental Public Health to certify public health dental specialists.

The U.S. Public Health Service established the National Institute of Dental Research in 1948. Ultimately incorporated into the National Institutes of Health, the National Institute of Dental Research played a major role in advancing basic and applied dental research.

Also beneficial to dentistry during the postwar years was the increase in insurance group plans that provide payment for routine dental care and, in certain instances, more extensive dentistry at an additional premium. By 1980, almost 100 million Americans were covered, to some degree, by a dental insurance plan; today, it is a common employee benefit.

The overall number of dentists per U.S. citizen reached its highest point in 1987 but will continue to decrease in the coming decades. There have been major decreases in the annual number of dental graduates, whereas the general population continues to increase.

Dentistry currently includes nine practice specialties:

1. Dental public health
2. Endodontics
3. Oral and maxillofacial pathology
4. Oral and maxillofacial radiology
5. Oral and maxillofacial surgery
6. Orthodontics and dentofacial orthopedics
7. Pediatric dentistry
8. Periodontics
9. Prosthodontics

Recognition of Dental Anesthesiology as an additional dental specialty is currently under consideration by the American Dental Association (ADA) 2012 House of Delegates.

In contrast to the predominance of specialization in the practice of medicine, more than 83% of the over 155,000 practicing dentists in the United States are general practitioners.[31] There are 64 accredited dental schools in the United States. The class of 2010 had 4,996 graduates. Graduates receive a Doctor of Dental Surgery degree or its equivalent, a Doctor of Dental Medicine.

Increased recruitment outreach efforts to racial/ethnic minority dental school applicants have been made over the last three decades; however, the ADA reports that only 12% of currently enrolled dental students are of a minority racial/ethnic background. Efforts to increase the racial/ethnic diversity of U.S. dental profession are a current focus of several ongoing initiatives of the ADA. Education scholarships made available for minority dental students, early career recruitment tactics such as outreach through job shadowing opportunities, and mentorship from currently enrolled minority dental students provided to potential dental school minority applicants are several of the recent innovations sponsored by the ADA.[32] Women are more prominent in dental school enrollment. Female dental students, once a rarity, now comprise nearly one-half of dental school graduates each year.[33]

Overall, dentists are working fewer hours for increased earnings. Dentistry has successfully resisted managed care and capitated payments and remains a "cottage industry." With most dentists in solo practice choosing to serve only those with dental insurance or the fiscal means to pay prevailing fees, many of the population groups with the greatest need for dental services continue to be underserved. While neither dental education nor the dental practice model have traditionally placed a high priority on the creation of a dental safety net for underserved populations, more recent interest in the delivery of dental health care to underserved populations and geographic areas has generated additional recruitment efforts to address this dental care delivery crisis.[32]

Pharmacy

Pharmaceutical practice dates back to ancient Egypt, Rome, and Greece. The first apothecaries appeared in Europe during the 12th century. By 1546, the Senate of the city of Nuremberg, Germany, recognized the value of standardizing drugs to ensure uniformity in filling prescriptions.[34]

Hospital pharmacists were apprentice physicians in early America. In the early 1800s, medicine and pharmacy separated, and by 1811 the New York Hospital had a full-time pharmaceutical practitioner. The American Pharmaceutical Association was organized in 1852. Professional training programs were developed for pharmacists, and by 1864 there were eight colleges of pharmacy in the United States.[35]

One hundred twenty-seven colleges of pharmacy are now accredited to confer degrees by the American Council on Pharmaceutical Education. Pharmacy programs grant a Doctor of Pharmacy (PharmD) degree after at least 6 years of postsecondary study. The PharmD degree has replaced the Bachelor of Pharmacy degree, which is no longer awarded. Many colleges of pharmacy also offer a master's or PhD degree after completion of a PharmD program for pharmacists who want more laboratory or research experience to do research for pharmaceutical companies or teach at a university. After graduation, each pharmacist is licensed by passing a state examination and completing an internship with a licensed pharmacist. Schools of pharmacy graduate about 12,000 students annually. The number of active pharmacists in the United States now exceeds 275,000, an increase of more than 100,000 since 1980.[36]

In 1976, the American Pharmaceutical Association created the Board of Pharmaceutical Specialties. It has since approved nuclear pharmacy, nutrition support pharmacy, oncology pharmacy, pharmacotherapy, psychiatric pharmacy, ambulatory care pharmacy (added in 2011), critical care pharmacy (added in 2013), and pediatric pharmacy (added in 2013) as the eight specialties in which pharmacists may be certified.[37]

Forty-three percent of pharmacists work in community pharmacies and drugstores, many of which are owned by large commercial chains. There, they may supervise other employees, manage overall business needs, computerize patients' records, and advise physicians and patients about drug dosage, side effects, and interaction with other medications. Twenty-three percent of pharmacists work in hospitals, and the balance are employed by clinics, nursing homes, health maintenance organizations, and the federal government.

Employment of pharmacists is expected to grow faster than the average for all occupations because of the increased pharmaceutical needs of an aging population and the increased use of medications. The need for pharmacists is increasing as they also become more involved in drug therapy decision making and patient counseling. Although enrollment in pharmacy programs is growing as students are attracted by high salaries and good job prospects, employment opportunities are expected to exceed applicants through the year 2020.[36]

Podiatric Medicine

Podiatric medicine is concerned with the diagnosis and treatment of diseases and injuries of the lower leg and foot. Podiatrists can prescribe drugs; order radiographs, laboratory tests, and physical therapy; set fractures; and perform surgery. They also fit corrective inserts called orthotics, design plaster casts and strappings to correct deformities, and design custom-made shoes.

As of 2011, there were nine accredited schools in the United States where students can apply after graduating from college. Graduates obtain a Doctor of Podiatric Medicine degree. The 4 years of professional training is similar to that for physicians. Most podiatrists spend 3 or more years completing a residency in a hospital after they graduate.[38] Podiatrists may also take postgraduate training and become board certified in the specialties of primary care in podiatric medicine, diabetic foot wound care and footwear, limb preservation and salvage, or podiatric surgery. All doctors of podiatric medicine are licensed by the state in which they practice. Podiatric care is more dependent on disposable income than other medical services. Medicare and most private health insurance programs cover acute medical and surgical foot services, as well as diagnostic radiographs and leg braces; however, routine foot care ordinarily is not covered.

Chiropractors

Chiropractors treat the whole body without the use of drugs or surgery. Special care is given to the spine, because chiropractors believe that misalignment or irritations of spinal nerves interfere with normal body functions. Today, there are 15 accredited chiropractic programs and two accredited chiropractic institutions in the United States. Students need at least 90 credit hours of previous undergraduate education before applying to one of the accredited programs or institutions. After completion of the Doctor of Chiropractic Degree, all states require licensure. The U.S. Department of Labor estimates that currently there are more than 52,000 chiropractic practitioners. Projections to 2020 indicate that this number will increase to more than 67,000. An expected growth rate of 28% for chiropractic employment over the 2010–2020 decade will help to meet the increasing demand for chiropractic care as the aging population in the United States becomes more likely to experience musculoskeletal and joint problems and seek chiropractic care.[39] Patients are generally satisfied with chiropractic care, and for specific conditions causing back pain, chiropractors achieve outcomes comparable with those of physicians.[40]

Chiropractic practice has strong public support, and chiropractors have used that patronage to make significant gains in legal and legislative areas. Regardless of medicine's questions about chiropractic's lack of scientifically proven effectiveness, chiropractors achieved Medicare coverage and participate in most managed care, and many other insurance policies contain some form of chiropractic coverage.

Optometry

A Doctor of Optometry examines patients' eyes to diagnose vision problems and eye disease, prescribes drugs for treatment, and prescribes and fits eyeglasses and contact lenses. An optometrist should not be confused with an ophthalmologist or an optician. An ophthalmologist is a physician who specializes in the treatment of eye diseases and injuries and uses drugs, surgery, or the prescription of corrective lenses to correct vision deficiencies. An optician is a licensed health professional who fits eyeglasses or contact lenses to individual patients as prescribed by ophthalmologists.

Optometrists must graduate from 1 of the 20 accredited 4-year colleges of optometry and pass both written and clinical examinations of the state board to obtain a license to practice. More than 1,300 students graduate each year to swell the current number of active optometrists to over 34,000.

One-year residency programs are available for optometrists who wish to specialize in family practice optometry, pediatric optometry, geriatric optometry, low-vision rehabilitation, cornea and contact lenses, refractive and ovular surgery, vision therapy and rehabilitation, ocular disease, and community health optometry.

Optometrists usually work in private practice, but many are now forming small group practices. Optometrists may hire opticians and optometric assistants to help them increase their productivity and thus care for more patients. Persons above 45 years of age visit optometrists and ophthalmologists more frequently because of the onset of vision problems in middle age and the increased likelihood of cataracts, glaucoma, diabetes, and hypertension in old age. Employment opportunities in the field of optometry are projected to increase by 33% by 2020. Factors leading to this projected growth include: more than half of the people in the United States wearing glasses or contact lenses, a continuing need for eye care by the majority of the aging population, and an increasing number of health insurance plans, including Medicare and Medicaid providing some vision care coverage.[41]

Health Care Administrators

Like any other business, health care needs good management to keep it running smoothly. Health care administrators are managers who plan, organize, direct, control, or coordinate medicine and health services in hospitals, clinics, nursing care facilities, and physicians' offices. Many health care administrators are employed in hospital settings, and others work for insurers, clinics, or medical group practices. Employment opportunities are numerous with over a quarter of a million jobs for health care administrators.

Bachelor's, master's, and doctoral degree programs in health care administration are offered by a variety of colleges and universities. At least 70 schools have accredited programs leading to a master's degree in health services administration. There are also short certificate or diploma programs, usually lasting less than 1 year, in health services administration or in medical office management, however, a bachelor's degree in medical administration is currently considered the minimum entry-level educational degree required for higher level management positions.[42]

Allied Health Personnel

Unlike professionals in medicine, dentistry, nursing, and pharmacy, allied health personnel represent a varied and complex array of health care disciplines. Allied health personnel support, complement, or supplement the professional functions of physicians, dentists, or other health professionals in delivering health care to patients, and they assist in environmental health control, health promotion, and disease prevention. A number of more recent categories of health care specialists were created to implement the new procedures, equipment, and diagnostic, surgical, and therapeutic techniques that proliferated during the last three decades. Allied health occupations encompass as many as 200 types of health careers within 80 different allied health professions.[43]

The range of allied health professions may be understood best by classifying them according to the functions they serve, grouped into the following four categories:

1. Laboratory technologists and technicians
2. Therapeutic science practitioners
3. Behavioral scientists
4. Support services

It should be recognized, however, that some allied health disciplines should be included in more than one of these functional classifications.

Technicians and Technologists

There are a rapidly growing number of technicians and technologists, including such major categories as cardiovascular technicians and technologists, clinical laboratory technicians, emergency medical technicians, health information technicians, nuclear medicine technologists, cytotechnologists, histologic technicians and technologists, surgical technologists, occupational safety and health technicians, pharmacy technicians, and many more. Because space does not allow for a discussion of all of these important health vocations, the following descriptions include only several representative disciplines in this allied health category.

Laboratory Technologists and Technicians

Clinical laboratory technologists and technicians have a critically important role in the diagnosis of disease, monitoring of physiologic function and the effectiveness of intervention, and application of highly technical procedures. Technologists, also known as clinical laboratory scientists or medical technologists, usually have a bachelor's degree in one of the life sciences. Clinical laboratory technicians, also known as medical technicians or medical laboratory technicians, generally need an associate's degree or a certificate.

Among their roles, clinical laboratory personnel analyze body fluids, tissues, and cells checking for bacteria and other microorganisms; analyze chemical content; test drug levels in blood to monitor the effectiveness of treatment; and match blood for transfusion.

The National Accrediting Agency for Clinical Laboratory Sciences currently approves/accredits 581 programs for clinical laboratory technologists and technicians. Employed graduates of those programs number over 330,000. More than 50% of those employed work in hospitals. Most of the others work in physician offices or diagnostic laboratories. Employment growth in the next decade is projected to remain steady as the aging of the general population is expected to lead to an increased need for diagnosis through testing of medical conditions such as type 2 diabetes and cancer, and the development of new laboratory tests.[44]

Radiologic Technology

A radiologic technologist works under the supervision of a radiologist, a physician who specializes in the use and interpretation of radiographs. The radiologic technologist uses radiographs, fluoroscopic equipment, and high-tech imaging machines such as ultrasonography, computed tomography, magnetic resonance imaging, and positron emission tomography to produce films that allow physicians to study the internal organs and bones of their patients. Formal training programs in radiography range in length from 1 to 4 years and lead to a certificate, associate's degree, or bachelor's degree. Two-year associate's degrees are most prevalent. The Joint Review Committee on Education in Radiology accredited over 700 formal programs in 2012.

Prior to 2003, the vacancy rate for radiologic technologists was reported by the American Association of Radiologic Technologists to be the highest in any field of health care. Over subsequent years the vacancy rate, representing the number of unfilled positions that are open and actively being recruited, has steadily fallen from a high in 2003 of 10.3% to a current rate of 2.1%, signaling a tightening job market for radiologic technologists. However, technologic advances and the growth and aging of the nation's population will increase the demand for diagnostic imaging and the skilled technologists required to perform diagnostic imaging. The U.S. Department of Labor predicts that employment opportunities for radiologic technologists will grow faster than the average for all occupations through 2020.[45]

Nuclear Medicine Technology

Nuclear medicine technologists use diagnostic imaging techniques to detect and map radioactive drugs in the human body. They administer radioactive pharmaceuticals to patients and then monitor the characteristics and functions of tissues or organs in which they localize. Abnormal areas show higher or lower concentrations of radioactivity than do normal ones.

Nuclear medicine technologists are prepared in 1-year certificate programs offered by hospitals to those who are already radiologic technologists, medical technologists, or RNs or who are in 2- to 4-year programs offered in university schools of allied health. Nuclear medicine technologists must meet the minimum federal standards on the administration of radioactive drugs and the operation of radiation detection equipment. In addition, about half of all states require technologists to be licensed. Technologists also may obtain voluntary professional certification or registration.[46]

Therapeutic Science Practitioners

Practitioners of the therapeutic sciences are essential to the treatment and rehabilitation of patients with diseases and injuries of all kinds. Physical therapists, occupational therapists, speech pathology and audiology therapists, radiation therapists, and respiratory therapists are only some of the allied health disciplines in this category.

Physical Therapy

Physical therapists provide services that help restore function, improve mobility, relieve pain, and prevent or limit physical disabilities of patients suffering from injuries or disease. They restore, maintain, and promote overall fitness and health. They review patients' medical histories and measure patients' strength, range of motion, balance, coordination, muscle performance, and motor function. They then develop and implement treatment plans that include exercises to develop flexibility, strength, and endurance. They also may give patients exercises to do at home.

Physical therapists may also use electrical stimulation, hot or cold compresses, and ultrasound to relieve pain and reduce swelling. They also teach patients to use assistive and adaptive devices, such as crutches, prostheses, and wheelchairs. Physical therapists supervise physical therapy assistants to aid them in meeting the needs of an increasing number of patients. Physical therapy assistants earn associate's degrees and take a national certifying examination. Physical therapists may practice as generalists or specialize in areas such as pediatrics, geriatrics, orthopedics, sports medicine, neurology, or cardiopulmonary physical therapy. Physical therapists most often work in the offices of other health practitioners or in hospitals. Clinics, nursing homes, and home health care are other typical work settings where physical therapists are employed.[47]

According to the Commission on Accreditation in Physical Therapy Education (CAPTE), there were 211 accredited physical therapy programs in 2012. Of those, 5 offered master's degrees and 196 offered doctoral degrees. CAPTE no longer accredits physical therapy programs that do not provide at least master's level degrees. Employment opportunities have grown rapidly in the physical therapy field, and the demand now exceeds the supply.

Occupational Therapy

Occupational therapists assist patients in recovering from accidents, injuries, or diseases, to improve their ability to perform tasks in their daily living and working environments. Occupational therapists work with a wide range of patients, from those with irreversible physical disabilities to those with mental disabilities or disorders. Occupational therapists assist patients in caring for their daily needs such as dressing, cooking, and eating. They also use physical exercises and other activities to increase strength and dexterity, visual acuity, and hand–eye coordination. Occupational therapists instruct in the use of adaptive equipment such as wheelchairs, splints, and aids for eating and dressing. They may also design or make special equipment needed by patients at home or at work to perform activities of daily living or work responsibilities. Therapists may collaborate with clients and employers to modify work environments so that clients can maintain employment.

A bachelor's degree in occupational therapy was the minimum requirement for entry into this field, but beginning in 2007, a master's degree or higher is now required.

Occupational therapists work in offices, nursing homes, community mental health centers, adult daycare programs, rehabilitation centers, and residential care facilities. Private practice is currently the fastest growing sector of this profession. As the population ages and patients with critical problems survive more frequently, the demand for occupational therapists will continue to increase.[48]

Speech-Language Pathology

Speech-language pathologists, sometimes called speech therapists, treat patients with speech problems, swallowing, and other disorders in hospitals, schools, clinics, and private practice. About one-half of all speech pathologists are employed in the education system—from preschools to universities.

About 253 colleges and universities offer graduate programs in speech-language pathology. A master's degree is the standard practice requirement. Speech-language pathologists use written and oral tests and special instruments to diagnose the nature of the impairment and develop an individualized plan of care. They may teach the use of alternative communication methods, including automated devices and sign language.

The number of speech-language pathologists, now numbering about 123,000, is expected to grow in the next decade as the general population ages with increased instances of health conditions such as strokes, brain injuries, and hearing loss, requiring speech-language therapy intervention.[49]

Physician Assistant

The emergence of physician assistants (PAs) closely parallels the creation of nurse practitioners. In the 1960s, there was a shortage of health care providers. Duke University initiated the first PA program in 1961. It was a new provider model designed to benefit from the experience and expertise of the many hospital corpsmen and medics that were discharged from the armed forces. As the flow of returning corpsmen and medics tapered off, individuals without prior health care training were accepted into PA programs.

Today, there are at least 165 accredited education programs for PAs. Most offer a master's degree, some offer a bachelor's, and a few offer associate's degrees. PAs provide health care services under the supervision of a physician. Unlike medical assistants who perform routine clinical and clerical tasks, PAs are formally trained to provide diagnostic, preventive, and therapeutic health care services as delegated by the physician. PAs take medical histories, order and interpret laboratory tests and x-rays, make diagnoses, and prescribe medications as allowed by law in the 50 states and the District of Columbia.

Many PAs are employed in specialties such as internal medicine, pediatrics, family medicine, orthopedics, and emergency medicine. Others specialize in surgery and may provide preoperative and postoperative care and act as first or second assistants during major surgery.

The U.S. Department of Labor projects a significant increase in the employment of PAs because of an expected expansion of the health care industry and an emphasis on cost containment.[50]

Behavioral Scientists

Behavioral scientists are crucial in the social, psychological, and community and patient educational activities related to health maintenance, prevention of disease, and accommodation of patients to disability. They include professionals in social work, health education, community mental health, alcoholism and drug abuse services, and other health and human service areas.[51]

Social Work

Social workers counsel patients and families to assist them in addressing the personal, economic, and social problems associated with illness and disability. They arrange for community-based services to meet patient needs after discharge from a health facility. A bachelor's degree is required; however, a master's degree from an accredited graduate school of social work is often the standard for employment.

Social workers provide social services in hospitals and other health-related settings. Medical and public health social workers provide patients and families with psychosocial support in cases of acute, chronic, or terminal illnesses. Mental health and substance abuse social workers assess and treat persons with mental illness or those who abuse alcohol, tobacco, or other drugs.

The most recent tally (2012) by the Council on Social Work Education listed 480 accredited bachelor's program, and 218 accredited master's in social work degree programs. There are over 100 doctoral programs that prepare social workers for advanced clinical practice and research in social work. Employment of social workers is expected to grow faster than the average of other occupations, especially for those social workers with backgrounds in gerontology, substance abuse treatment, and mental health.[52]

Rehabilitation Counselor

A rehabilitation counselor gives personalized counseling, emotional support, and rehabilitation therapy to patients limited by physical or emotional disabilities. Patients may be recovering from illness or injury, have psychiatric problems, or have intellectual deficits. After an injury or illness is stabilized, the rehabilitation counselor tests the patient's motor ability, skill level, interests, and psychological makeup and develops an appropriate training or retraining plan. The goal is to maximize the patient's ability to function in society.

A master's degree is often required to be licensed or certified as a rehabilitation counselor. The Commission on Rehabilitation Counselor Certification offers voluntary certification. The need for rehabilitation counselors is expected to grow as the population ages and advanced medical care saves more lives. In addition, legislation requiring equal employment rights for persons with disabilities will increase the demand for counselors to prepare disabled people for employment.[53]

Support Services

Support services are necessary for the highly complex and sophisticated system of health care to function. Service specialists perform administrative and management duties and often work closely with direct providers of health care services. Health information administrators, dental laboratory technologists, electroencephalographic technologists, food service administrators, surgical technologists, and environmental health technologists are some of the allied health professionals in this category, and they serve to illustrate the diverse nature of the required support disciplines in allied health.

Health Information Administrators

Health information administrators are responsible for the activities of the medical records departments of hospitals, skilled nursing facilities, managed care organizations, rehabilitation centers, ambulatory care facilities, and a number of other health care operations. They plan and maintain information systems that permit patient data to be received, recorded, stored, and retrieved easily to assist in diagnosis and treatment. These data may also be used to track disease patterns, provide information for medical research, assist staff in evaluating the quality of patient care, and verify insurance claims. Health information administrators supervise the staff in the medical records department and are responsible for maintaining the confidentiality of all the information within their departments.

A bachelor's degree in health information administration is the entry-level credential. The Council of Certification of the American Health Information Management Association gives a national accreditation examination for Registered Health Information Administrator. Currently, there are more than 50 programs preparing health information administrators and more than 150 programs training medical records and health information technologists/technicians. In addition, in 2010, with support from the American Recovery and Reinvestment Act, the Office of the National Coordinator for Health Information Technology established a Workforce Development Program with the goal of rapidly training a new workforce of skilled health information technology (HIT) professionals to assist providers with implementing electronic health records. The program includes university-based and community college-based training through curricula developed by five university grantees funded by the program. Training programs are 6 months to 1 year in duration and designed for individuals with prior HIT or health care work experience. With a target of 1,500 graduates, nine university-based training centers focus on preparation for professional roles as clinician and public health leader, health information management and exchange specialist, health information privacy and security specialist, research and development scientist, programmer and software engineer and HIT subspecialist. Eighty-two community colleges in all 50 states are participating in a consortium with a target of 10,500 graduates with training focused on professional roles as practice workflow and information management redesign specialists, clinician/practitioner consultants, implementation support specialists, implementation managers, technical/software support and trainers.[54] The U.S. Department of Labor estimates further vigorous growth in the employment of health information personnel by 2020.[55]

Career Advancement in Allied Health

Because the allied health fields offer so diverse an array of programs, the opportunity for career advancement through educational "laddering" is probably without equal.

It is commonplace for graduates of allied health programs to practice for a period of time and then advance their careers by entering higher level programs that award advanced degrees.

Alternative Therapists

Rather than diminishing the public's interest in alternative forms of health care, the increasing sophistication of scientific medicine has fostered a receptive climate for alternative forms of therapy. Across the country, there is widespread interest in complementary and alternative medicine (CAM). CAM is defined as "a group of diverse medical and health care systems, practices, and products that are not presently considered to be part of conventional medicine." Complementary medicine and alternative medicine differ from each other. Complementary medicine is used together with conventional medicine. Alternative medicine is used in place of conventional medicine.[56]

In 1992, with one-third of Americans resorting to alternative medical therapies, the National Institutes of Health created an Office of Alternative Medicine to examine the efficacy of alternative therapies. The more perplexing question of how alternative therapies work was to be investigated later. In 1998, when more than 40% of Americans reported the use of alternative or complementary therapies, the Office of Alternative

Medicine was elevated to the National Center for Complementary and Alternative Medicine and its mandate expanded.

The 2007 National Health Interview Survey (NHIS), which included a comprehensive survey of the use of CAM by Americans, reported that 38% of adults were using CAM. Several mind and body approaches ranked among the top 10 CAM practices reported by adults. The survey found that 12.7% of adults had used deep-breathing exercises, 9.4% had practiced meditation, and 6.1% had practiced yoga; use of these three CAM practices had increased significantly since the previous (2002) NHIS. Progressive relaxation and guided imagery were also among the top 10 CAM therapies used by adults; deep-breathing and yoga ranked high among children. The NHIS also found that in 2007, adults in the United States spent nearly $34 billion "out of pocket" on visits to CAM practitioners and purchases of CAM products, classes, and materials. Nearly two-thirds of the "out of pocket" costs that adults spent on CAM were for self-care purchases of CAM products and classes (22.0 billion), compared with about one-third spent on visits to CAM practitioners (nearly 12 billion). Despite this emphasis on self-care therapies, it was estimated that over 38 million adults in the United States made more than 354 million visits to CAM practitioners.[57]

The Center previously had also engaged in the first international study of traditional medicines, including ancient Chinese and Native American medicines. The Center proposed the first National Institutes of Health study of botanicals to sort through 1,500 medicinal herbs for evaluation. Unusual therapies, such as telepathic distance healing, considered to be on the far fringes of medical practice, were also investigated.[58]

Along with alternative techniques came new classes of alternative practitioners. To name a few, there are certified Trager practitioners, who rock and cradle the patient's body for relaxation and mental clarity; doctors of naturopathy, who use natural healing methods that include diet, herbal medicine, and homeopathy; advanced certified Rolfers, who use deep massage to restore the body's natural alignment; and registered polarity practitioners, who use touch and advice on diet, self-awareness, and exercise to balance energy flow. Although professional medical societies strongly oppose naturopathy, considering the practice "unscientific" and "irrational," naturopathic doctors have made great strides in the last few years. Although they do not have medical degrees and are trained in loosely monitored schools, they are able to generate strong public support within state legislatures.[59]

The gains of alternative practitioners reflect the public's frustrations with conventional medicine, high drug prices, and media reports of disproved treatments. The interest of insurance companies in alternative forms of medicine is also important. Many insurers have taken the position that when traditional medicine is ineffective and an alternative form of therapy, such as acupuncture for a condition such as chronic pain, costs less and satisfies the patient, they will pay for it. As a result, several states now require insurance companies to cover naturopathic procedures and other techniques, such as acupuncture.[60]

Factors That Influence Demand for Health Personnel

Without attempting to include all interrelated factors that influence demand for various types of health personnel, it is important to recognize some major determinants of the size and nature of the health care employment sector. Regardless of the potential for legislatively mandated reforms of the health care system, the number and skill requirements of each discipline within the health care workforce depend on the interdependence of the following factors.

Changing Nature of Disease, Disability, and Treatment

The aging of the population and advances in the treatment of acute and life-threatening conditions result in an increased survival of people with chronic illness or disabilities. The growing number of patients with deteriorating mental capacities, cardiac conditions, cancer, stroke, head and spinal cord injuries, neonatal deficits, and congenital disorders significantly increase the demand for workers who provide and support prolonged medical treatment, rehabilitation, and nursing home or custodial care.

Physician Supply

Although many categories of health personnel perform independently of physicians, most of the decisions regarding the use of health care resources, the acceptance of other therapeutic modalities, and the treatment provided by nonphysicians, are made by physicians. It is therefore important to recognize that the anticipated changes in the numbers and types of physicians have a direct impact on the demand for many other types of health care personnel.

Technology

Medical and nonmedical technology used in the provision of health care has important implications for the number and skill requirements of the health care workforce. Advances in digital image transmission, and laser technology have the potential to both increase and decrease the demand for various kinds of personnel. Some technologies, such as transluminal coronary angioplasty and positron emission tomography, have led to the elimination of more laborious medical interventions. Others, such as sophisticated remote patient monitoring systems, have facilitated shifts to new service settings, such as ambulatory surgical centers. Also, automation of clinical laboratory testing has reduced the need for laboratory personnel. Thus, the mix of skills and the numbers of personnel ebb and flow with the discovery and application of new service modalities.

Expansion of Home Care

Health care reforms will continue the shift in health service delivery sites from acute-care hospitals to ambulatory, home care, and long-term care settings. With the emphasis on cost containment and an array of high-technology devices that contribute to more efficient techniques for providing nursing care and occupational, physical, and respiratory therapy in the home, the home care component of the health care industry is expected to expand significantly in the next decade. In addition, there is a growing body of evidence that therapy provided in the home helps patients recover faster and reduces hospital readmissions.

Corporatization of Health Care

Solo practice among health professionals is becoming a practice pattern of the past. The increase in group practices, the development of several forms of provider organizations, increasing hospital employment of physicians, the assembly of vertically integrated systems that link hospitals, nursing homes, home care, and other services; and the diversification of health providers into various health-related corporate ventures all reflect the corporatization of health care.

It is significant that since the beginning of the most recent U.S. recession, employment in health care continued to rise in ambulatory care, nursing, and residential care. While overall nationwide employment dropped steadily during the recent 2007–2009 economic recession, the health care industry showed continued growth by adding almost half of a million jobs. Historically, this has also been the case during previous economic recessions in 1990 and 2001. As demand for health care is expected to increase steadily during the years ahead, the health care industry is expected to continue to serve as a leading contributor to overall employment growth in the future.[61] Figure 7-2 depicts the projected increases in employment of selected health care personnel for the period through 2016.[62]

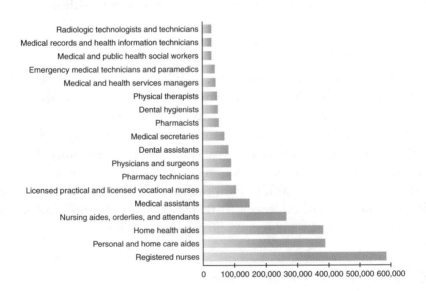

FIGURE 7-2 Projected Change in Total Employment, Selected Health Care Occupations, 2006–2016.
Source: U.S. Department of Labor, Bureau of Statistics, Employment Projections Chart Data.

Health Care Workforce Issues and the Patient Protection and Affordable Care Act

Policy makers at every level of government, insurers, educators, providers, and consumers have a vested interest in the issues that pertain to the health care workforce. The Association of Academic Health Centers clearly defined those issues in a 1994 publication.[63] Those issues remained central to the ACA's workforce initiatives and the establishment of a new National Health Care Workforce Commission (NHCWC):

- The adequacy of supply of health professionals, such as nurses, allied health professionals, primary care physicians, and geriatricians
- The geographic distribution of health professionals, especially shortages in rural and underserved urban areas
- The underrepresentation of minorities in all health professions
- The potential supply and poor distribution of specialty physicians
- The questions about the appropriate scope of practice for various health professionals and concern about legal restrictions on scope of practice for nonphysician practitioners
- The concern about the quality and relevance of the health professions' educational programs; whether educational institutions are producing the health professionals needed for an effective and productive workforce in the 21st century
- The costs associated with educating health professionals. The competency testing of health care professionals
- The redefinition of health professions as technology and the delivery system change, as various professions reconsider the credentials needed to practice within the profession
- The concern about the supply of faculty to train health professionals

The following summarize the ACA's provisions to address workforce issues in addition to establishment of the Commission[64,65]:

- Increasing workforce supply by enhancing federal student loans for several health professions including primary care and geriatric physician, nurses, allied health personnel, public health workers and those working in underserved areas
- Enhancing workforce education and training, including cultural competency through grants for primary care, dental health,

mental health, nursing, public health personnel, community health personnel and those working with disabled individuals and those working in rural settings

- Supporting the existing health care workforce through increased funding for minority applicants to the health professions and a primary care extension program to educate providers about evidence-based therapies, health promotion, chronic disease management and mental health
- Strengthening primary care through redistributions of unfilled residency positions to address shortages, increased funding for primary care residency training programs at teaching health centers and establishing a demonstration program to increase graduate nurse training
- Improving access to health care services through increased funding for federally qualified health centers, state and medical school support to improve and expand emergency services for children, new support for coordinating and integrating primary and specialty care in community-based mental health settings

The NHCWC's required composition includes 15 representatives from the areas of health care workforce and health professionals, educational institutions, employers, third-party payers, health care services and health economics research, consumers, labor unions, and state or local workforce investment boards. The NHCWC has an overall mandate to evaluate and make recommendations for numerous dimensions of the nation's health care workforce including education and training support for existing and potential new workers at all levels, efficient workforce deployment, professional compensation, and coordination among different types of providers. The Commission is also charged with monitoring grants awarded under ACA workforce development initiatives and must submit two reports to Congress each year. The NHCWC has been recognized as potentially having the most significant influence on shaping the nation's future health care workforce policies.[66]

The Future: Complexities of National Health Care Workforce Planning

The United States has never planned comprehensively or strategically for the development and deployment of its health care workforce and as a result, "the preparation of each generation of health workers is just as fragmented and confusing as the health care system they will one day join."[64] Federal and state governments, educational institutions, professional organizations, insurers, and provider institutions have had separate and often conflicting interests in health workforce education and training, regulation, financing, entry-level preparation, and scope of practice. The various levels at which policy decisions have been made and the disparate interests that influence those decisions have presented major obstacles to ensuring a coherent, efficient, and rational health workforce in the United States. Complex supply and demand factors influence workforce requirements and the prediction of future requirements is severely confounded by the lack of uniform data at national and state levels across the professions.[67] Supply factors include variables such as income variations among professions, licensure requirements, and transferability of skills. Demand is affected by factors such as population demographic characteristics, consumer expectations, and payment systems. In the upcoming years, the current workforce shortages in professions such as generalist physicians, nurses, and mental health workers; the disproportionate geographic distribution of many types of providers in urban and rural areas; and underrepresentation by minorities in the health professions are major focal points of the ACA and the NHCWC. The aging population, the shifting nature of diseases, health care delivery and reimbursement reforms, new technology, and economic factors will continue to change consumer demands and provider expectations, all lending more complexity to the challenges of planning for future workforce requirements. The expected influx of previously uninsured individuals as a result of the ACA alone will put unprecedented stresses on delivery system personnel.[68] It will be necessary to modify the roles and scope of practice of many of the health care professions to adapt to changing service patterns.

New health care system reforms and a far more cost- and consumer-conscious health care market combined with an aging population and technologic advances will require health services personnel to adapt to different work settings and service responsibilities. The ACA and its workforce-related provisions include many opportunities to take actions with potential to result in meaningful improvements in national workforce planning, development, and deployment. Already one of the nation's largest industries, health care employment will continue to experience significant growth.[69] The centrality of the health care workforce to the quality, costs, and accessibility of the health care delivery system makes these improvements critical to the future of health care delivery in the United States.

Key Terms for Review

Behavioral Scientist

Certification

Health Information Administrator

International Medical Graduates (IMGs)

Laboratory Technologists and
Technicians

Licensure

National Institute for Complementary
and Alternative Medicine

Nurse Practitioner

Osteopathic Medicine

Physician Assistant (PA)

Registration

Therapeutic Science Practitioner

References

1. U.S. Department of Labor, Bureau of Labor Statistics. Monthly labor review. January 2012. Industry employment and outlook projections to 2020. Available from http://www.bls.gov/opub/mlr/2012/01/art4full.pdf. Accessed July 1, 2012.

2. Finocchio LJ, Dower CM, McMahon T, et al. Policy considerations for the 21st century. San Francisco, CA: Per Health Professions Commission. December, 1995:9–13. Available from http://www.soundrock.com/pdf/ Reforming %20Health%20Care%20Workkforce%20Regulation.pdf. Accessed December 29, 2012.

3. Finocchio LJ, Dower CM, McMahon T, et al. Policy considerations for the 21st century. San Francisco, CA: Per Health Professions Commission. December, 1995:1–4. Available from http://www.soundrock.com/pdf/ Reforming %20Health%20Care%20Workkforce%20Regulation.pdf. Accessed December 29, 2012.

4. American Association of Medical Colleges. Total graduates by U.S. medical school and race and ethnicity. 2011. Available from https://www.aamc.org/ download/145668/data/table30-gradsschlraceeth2011.pdf. Accessed July 2, 2012.

5. American Association of Colleges of Osteopathic Medicine. Osteopathic medicine and medical education in brief. Available from http://www.aacom .org/about/osteomed/Pages/default.aspx. Accessed July 3, 2012.

6. Bouldet JR, Morcini JJ, Whelan GP, et al. The international medical graduate pipeline: recent trends in certification and residency training. *Health Affairs*. 2006;25:469–477.

7. U.S. Department of Labor, Bureau of Labor Statistics. *Occupational Outlook Handbook*. 2012–2013 edition, physicians and surgeons. Available from http://www.bls.gov/ooh/healthcare/physicians-and-surgeons.htm. Accessed July 4, 2012.

8. Association of American Medical Colleges. Recent studies and reports on physician shortages. Washington, DC; April 2009. Available

from http://www.aamc.org/www.aamc.org/download/100598/data/recentworkforcestudiesnov09.pdf. Accessed September 1, 2012.

9. O'Brien P. All a woman's life can bring: the domestic roots of nursing in Philadelphia, 1830–1885. *Nursing Res.* 1987;36:12–17.

10. Stevens R. *In Sickness and in Wealth: American Hospitals in the Twentieth Century.* New York: Basic Books; 1989:96–98.

11. Kovner C. Nursing. In: Kovner AR, Ed. *Health Care Delivery in the United States.* New York: Springer; 1995:101–121.

12. U.S. Department of Health and Human Services, Health Resources and Services Administration. The registered nurse population: initial findings from the 2008 National Survey of Registered Nurses. March, 2010. Available from http://bhpr.hrsa.gov/healthworkforce/rnsurveys/rnsurveyinitial2008.pdf. Accessed July 5, 2012.

13. Buerhaus PI, Staiger DO, Auerbach DI. Is the current shortage of hospital nurses ending? *Health Affairs.* 2003;22:191–198.

14. U.S. Department of Health and Human Services, Health Resources and Services Administration, Bureau of Health Professions. The registered nurse population: findings from the 2008 national sample survey of registered nurses. September, 2010. Executive Summary. Available from http://bhpr.hrsa.gov/healthworkforce/rnsurveys/rnsurveyfinal.pdf. Accessed December 29, 2012.

15. U.S. Department of Health and Human Services, Health Resources and Services Administration, Bureau of Health Professions. The registered nurse population: findings from the 2008 national sample survey of registered nurses. September, 2010:171. Available from http://bhpr.hrsa.gov/healthworkforce/rnsurveys/rnsurveyfinal.pdf. Accessed December 29, 2012.

16. Hassmiller SB, Cozine M. Addressing the nurse shortage to improve the quality of care. *Health Affairs.* 2006;1:268–274.

17. Robert Wood Johnson Foundation. A new era of nursing: transforming care at the bedside. April, 2007. Available from http://www.rwjf.org/pr/product.jsp?id=18662. Accessed July 8, 2012.

18. U.S. Department of Labor, Bureau of Labor Statistics. Occupational outlook handbook, 2012–2013 edition, licensed practical and licensed vocational nurses. 2012. Available from http://www.bls.gov/ooh/healthcare/licensed-practical-and licensed-vocational-nurses.htm. Accessed July 9, 2012.

19. U.S. Department of Labor, Bureau of Labor Statistics. Occupational outlook handbook, 2012–2013 edition, registered nurses. 2012. Available from http://www.bls.gov/ooh/healthcare/registered-nurses.htm. Accessed July 9, 2012.

20. Bullough B, Bullough VI. *Nursing Issues for the Nineties and Beyond.* New York: Springer; 1994:15.

21. Sultz HA, Henry OM, Sullivan JA. *Nurse Practitioners, USA.* Lexington, MA: Lexington Books; 1979:215–229.

22. Dunn I. A literature review of advanced clinical nursing in the United States of America. *J Adv Nursing.* 1997;25:814–819.

23. Krein SL. The employment and use of nurse practitioners and physician assistants by rural hospitals. *Rural Health*. 1997;13:45–58.

24. U.S. Department of Health and Human Services. Centers for Disease Control and Prevention, National Center for Health Statistics. National hospital ambulatory medical care survey: 2009 emergency department summary tables. 2012. Available from http://cdc.gov/nchs/ahcd/web_tables .htm#2009. Accessed July 9, 2012.

25. American Association of Colleges of Nursing, One Dupont Circle, NW Suite 530, Washington DC 20036. Accredited programs. Available from http:// www.aacn.nche.edu/ccne-accreditation/accredited-programs. Accessed July 16, 2012.

26. National Association of Clinical Nurse Specialists, 100 North 20th Street, 4th Floor, Philadelphia, Pennsylvania 19103. What is a clinical nurse specialist? 2012. Available from http://www.nacns.org/html/cns-faq.php. Accessed July 8, 2012.

27. National Association of Clinical Nurse Specialists, 100 North 20th Street, 4th Floor, Philadelphia, Pennsylvania 19103. CNS program directory. 2012. Available from http://www.nacns.org/html/educators. php. Accessed July 8, 2012.

28. Ring M. *Dentistry: An Illustrated History*. New York: Harry N. Abrams; 1985:203.

29. Loevy HT, Kowitz AA. Dental development in the midwest of America. *Int Dental J*. 1992;12:157–164.

30. Ring M. *Dentistry: An Illustrated History*. New York: Harry N. Abrams; 1985:283–284.

31. U.S. Department of Labor, Bureau of Labor Statistics. *Occupational Outlook Handbook*, 2012–2013 edition, dentists. 2012. Available from http://www. bls.gov/ooh/healthcare/dentists.htm. Accessed July 8, 2012.

32. American Dental Association, 211 East Chicago Avenue, Chicago, Illinois 60611. Available from http://www.ada.org/sections/educationAndCareers/ pdfs/minority_dentist_brochure.pdf. Accessed July 9, 2012.

33. American Dental Association, 211 East Chicago Avenue, Chicago, Illinois 60611. Frequently asked questions. 2012. Available from http://www.ada .org/1444.aspx. Accessed September 1, 2012..

34. Gable FB. *Opportunities in Pharmacy Careers*. Lincolnwood, IL: NTC Publishing Group; 1993:10–14.

35. Higby GJ. American hospital pharmacy from the Colonial Period to the 1930s. *Am J Hosp Pharm*. 1994;51:2817–2823.

36. U.S. Department of Labor, Bureau of Labor Statistics. *Occupational Outlook Handbook*, 2012–2013 edition, pharmacists. 2012. Available from http:// www.bls.gov/ooh/healthcare/pharmacists.htm. Accessed July 10, 2012.

37. Board of Pharmacy Specialties, Division of the American Pharmacists Association. Current specialties. 2013. Available from http://www.bpsweb. org. Accessed April 29, 2013.

38. U.S. Department of Labor, Bureau of Labor Statistics. *Occupational Outlook Handbook*, 2012–2013 edition, podiatrists. Available from http://www.bls.gov/ooh/healthcare/podiatrists.htm. Accessed July 10, 2012.

39. U.S. Department of Labor, Bureau of Labor Statistics. *Occupational Outlook Handbook*, 2012–2013 edition, chiropractors. 2012. Available from http://www.bls.gov/ooh/healthcare/chiropracters.htm. Accessed July 10, 2012.

40. Shekelle MM, Rachel L. An epidemiologic study of episodes of back pain care. *Spine*. 1995;20:1668–1673.

41. U.S. Department of Labor, Bureau of Labor Statistics. *Occupational Outlook Handbook*, 2012–2013 edition, optometrists. 2012. Available from http://www.bls.gov/ooh/healthcare/optometrists.htm. Accessed July 11, 2012.

42. U.S. Department of Labor, Bureau of Labor Statistics. *Occupational Outlook Handbook*, 2012–2013 edition, medical and health services managers. 2012. Available from http://www.bls.gov/ooh/Management/Medical-and-health-services-managers.htm. Accessed July 11, 2012.

43. Explorehealthcareers.org. Field profile: Allied health professions. 2013. Available from http://explorehealthcareers.org/en/Field/1/Allied_Health_Professions.aspx. Accessed April 29, 2013.

44. U.S. Department of Labor, Bureau of Labor Statistics. *Occupational Outlook Handbook*, 2012–2013 edition, medical clinical laboratory technologists and technicians. 2012. Available from http://www.bls.gov/ooh/healthcare/medical-and-clinical-laboratory-technologists-and-technicians.htm. Accessed July 11, 2012.

45. U.S. Department of Labor, Bureau of Labor Statistics. *Occupational Outlook Handbook*, 2012–2013 edition, radiologic technologists. 2012. Available from http://www.bls.gov/ooh/healthcare/radiologic-technologists.htm. Accessed July 12, 2012.

46. U.S. Department of Labor, Bureau of Labor Statistics. *Occupational Outlook Handbook*, 2012–2013 edition, nuclear medicine technologists. 2012. Available from http://www.bls.gov/ooh/healthcare/nuclear-medicine-technologists.htm. Accessed July 12, 2012.

47. U.S. Department of Labor, Bureau of Labor Statistics. *Occupational Outlook Handbook*, 2012–2013 edition, physical therapists. 2012. Available from http://www.bls.gov/ooh/healthcare/physical-therapists.htm. Accessed July 12, 2012.

48. U.S. Department of Labor, Bureau of Labor Statistics. *Occupational Outlook Handbook*, 2012–2013 edition, occupational therapists. 2012. Available from http://www.bls.gov/ooh/healthcare/occupational-therapists.htm. Accessed July 12, 2012.

49. U.S. Department of Labor, Bureau of Labor Statistics. *Occupational Outlook Handbook*, 2012–2013 edition, speech-language pathologists. 2012. Available from http://www.bls.gov/ooh/healthcare/speech-language-pathologists.htm. Accessed July 14, 2012.

50. U.S. Department of Labor, Bureau of Labor Statistics. *Occupational Outlook Handbook*, 2012–2013 edition, physician assistants. 2012. Available from

http://www.bls.gov/ooh/healthcare/physician-assistants.htm. Accessed July 14, 2012.

51. Sultz HA. *Allied Health Personnel. Consultant Report to the Labor-Health Industry Task Force on Health Personnel.* Albany, NY: New York State Department of Health; 1987.

52. U.S. Department of Labor, Bureau of Labor Statistics. *Occupational Outlook Handbook*, 2012–2013 edition, social workers. 2012. Available from http://www.bls.gov/ooh/community-and-social-service/social-workers.htm. Accessed July 14, 2012.

53. U.S. Department of Labor, Bureau of Labor Statistics. *Occupational Outlook Handbook*, 2012–2013 edition, rehabilitation counselors. 2012. Available from http://www.bls.gov/ooh/community-and-social-service/rehabilitation-counselors.htm. Accessed July 14, 2012.

54. Health IT.gov. Health IT Adoption Programs: Workforce Development Program. Available from http://www.healthit.gov/policy-researchers-implementers/workforce-development-program. Accessed December 30, 2012.

55. U.S. Department of Labor, Bureau of Labor Statistics. *Occupational Outlook Handbook*, 2012–2013 edition, medical and health services managers. 2012. Available from http://www.bls.gov/ooh/management/medical-and-health-services-managers.htm. Accessed July 14, 2012.

56. National Center for Complementary and Alternative Medicine, National Institutes of Health. What is complementary and alternative medicine? 2012. Available from http://nccam.nih.gov/health/whatiscam. Accessed July 15, 2012.

57. National Center for Complementary and Alternative Medicine, National Institutes of Health. Health statistics reports, number 18, July 30, 2009. Costs of complementary and alternative medicine (CAM) and frequency of visits to CAM practitioners, United States 2007. Available from http://www.cdc.gov/nchs/data/nhsr/nhsr018.pdf. Accessed July 15, 2012.

58. National Center for Complementary and Alternative Medicine. National Institutes of Health, Draft minutes of the tenth meeting. January 28, 2002. Available from http://nccam.nih.gov/about/naccam/minutes/2002jan.htm. Accessed July 15, 2012.

59. Petersen A. States grant herb doctors new powers. *Washington Post.* August 22, 2002:D1.

60. Rubenstein S. Alternative health plans widen. *Wall Street Journal.* September 22, 2004:D7.

61. U.S. Bureau of Labor Statistics, Monthly labor review. Employment in health care: a crutch for the ailing economy during the 2007–09 recession. April 2011. Available from http://www.bls.gov/opub/mlr/2011/04/art2full.pdf. Accessed July 15, 2012.

62. U.S. Department of Labor, Bureau of Labor Statistics. Spotlight on Statistics. Projected change in total employment, selected health care occupations.

2006–2016. Available from http://www.bls.gov/spotlight/2009/health_care/. Accessed January 1, 2013.

63. McLaughlin CJ. Health work force issues and policy-making roles. In Larson PF, Osterweis M, Rubin ER, Eds. *Health Work Force Issues for the 21st Century.* Washington, DC: Association of Academic Health Centers; 1994:1–3.

64. Hahn A, Sussman J. Foundations and health care reform 2010: policy brief: improving workforce efficiency. Brandeis University: The Heller School for Social and Policy Management. July 14, 2010. Available from http://sillermancenter.brandeis.edu/PDFs/Workforce%20Policy%20Brief%20in%20conf%20template%20v2.pdf. Accessed December 27, 2012.

65. Congressional Research Service. Public Health, Workforce, Quality, and Related Provisions in the Patient Protection and Affordable Care Act (PPACA); 9–26. June 7, 2010. Available from https://www.aamc.org/download/130996/data/ph.pdf.pdf. Accessed December 27, 2012.

66. American Academy of Family Physicians. Commission is likely to set nation's health workforce policies, say experts. August 18, 2010. Available from http://www.aafp.org/online/en/home/publications/news/news-now/government-medicine/20100818workforcecommission.html. Accessed December 21, 2012.

67. Bipartisan Policy Center. The complexities of national health care workforce planning:executive summary. October 18, 2011. Available from http://bipartisanpolicy.org/sites/default/files/Workforce%20study_Public%20Release%20040912.pdf. Accessed December 31, 2012.

68. American Medical News. Influx of newly insured a prompt for practices to rethink patient flow. October 22, 2012. Available from http://www.ama-assn.org/amednews/2012/10/22/bil21022.htm. Accessed December 27, 2012.

69. U.S. Department of Labor, Bureau of Labor Statistics. Monthly labor review. January 2012. Industry employment and outlook projections to 2020. Available from http://www.bls.gov/opub/mlr/2012/01/art4full.pdf. Accessed July 15, 2012.

CHAPTER 8

Financing Health Care

This chapter reviews the most currently available data on national health care expenditures and sources of payment and provides a historical overview of the developments that played major roles in creating the national health care financing infrastructure. Major factors that affect health care costs are identified and discussed. Significant trends in health care spending are reviewed, along with underlying reasons for changes. The roles of the private sector and government as payers are presented. The chapter concludes with a review of major features of the Patient Protection and Affordable Care Act (ACA) that affect the financing of health services.

Overview

As implementation of the Patient Protection and Affordable Care Act (ACA) continues, it is important to recognize that although it has had significant immediate effects particularly with respect to health insurance regulation, the effects of its policy changes on the financing of health care will unfold over many succeeding years well beyond the implementation of its final provisions in 2019. The ACA does not change the fundamental structure of U.S. health care financing system. As in the past, health care expenditures in the United States will continue to be financed through a combination of private and public sources.

In 2007, a majority of working Americans under the age of 65 had private health insurance coverage provided by their employers.[1] However, an underlying trend during the last two decades, especially during the years of economic recession and contraction of U.S. job market and slowed economic recovery, has been a decline in employment-based health insurance coverage of the nonelderly U.S. population, as fewer workers have access to job-based health care insurance coverage.[1,2] The primary sources of public funding for health care expenditures are

Those individuals privately buying their own health insurance coverage has remained relatively stable at approximately 4%–6%.[1] The number of Americans without health insurance coverage has increased steadily, but for the first time in several years, in 2011, it was reported the number of uninsured Americans dropped by over one million, primarily because of an influx of newly insured young adults, who benefited from a provision in the 2010 health care reform legislation that required health care insurers to allow parents to keep adult children on their health insurance plans up to age 26.[3]

The primary sources of public funding for health care expenditures are Medicare, covering health care services for most individuals over 65 years and disabled individuals; and Medicaid, which supports services for the low-income population. The number of those with such public health insurance has increased, with Medicare and Medicaid picking up some of the slack left by the continued erosion of employment-based health insurance coverage that had been previously available for employed workers and work retirees.[3]

Financing of U.S. health care system continues to evolve from a variety of influences, including provider, employer, purchaser, consumer, and political factors. As pointedly reflected in the national health care reform debates, these influences produced major tensions about the role and responsibility of the government as payer, the financial responsibilities of employers as the primary purchasers of health insurance, the relationships of costs to quality, and the impacts of payment systems on quality. Controlling the rising costs of health care and dealing with the estimated over 48.6 million uninsured or underinsured Americans continue as two of the most challenging issues.[4]

Health Care Expenditures in Perspective

National health expenditures and trends are reported annually by the National Center for Health Statistics of the Centers for Disease Control and Prevention; the Office of the Actuary, National Health Statistics Group; and the U.S. Department of Health and Human Services, (DHHS), Centers for Medicare & Medicaid Services (CMS). Expenditures are reported and tracked over time using a standard format that identifies both the private and public sources of funds and the objects of expense. Table 8-1 provides

Table 8-1 National Health Expenditures, 2011, by Type of Expenditure and Source of Funds (in billions)

Year and Type of Expenditure	Total	Out-of-Pocket	Health Insurance	Private Health Insurance	Medicare	Medicaid	Other Health Insurance Programs	Other Third-Party Payers**	Public Health Activity	Investment
National Health Expenditures ($)	2,700.7	307.7	1,960.1	896.3	554.3	407.7	101.8	200.5	79.0	153.5
Health Consumption Expenditures ($)	2,547.2	307.7	1,960.1	896.3	554.3	407.7	101.8	200.5	79.0	—
Personal Health care ($)	2,279.3	307.7	1,779.1	786.1	521.6	374.5	97.0	192.5	—	—
Hospital Care ($)	850.6	28.1	742.4	306.9	231.3	151.0	53.3	80.0	—	—
Professional Services ($)	723.1	116.4	550.8	328.5	140.2	56.9	25.2	55.8	—	—
Physician and Clinical Services ($)	541.4	52.3	440.3	249.1	124.0	44.8	22.5	48.8	—	—
Other Professional Services ($)	73.2	19.0	47.7	26.7	15.9	4.9	0.2	6.5	—	—
Dental Services ($)	108.4	45.1	62.8	52.7	0.3	7.3	2.5	0.5	—	—
Other Health, Residential, and Personal Care ($)***	133.1	7.5	84.5	6.4	5.1	69.3	3.8	41.1	—	—
Home Health care ($)	74.3	5.6	66.5	5.1	32.9	27.6	0.9	2.2	—	—
Nursing Care Facilities and Continuing Care Retirement Communities ($)****,*****	149.3	39.9	100.4	12.4	37.6	46.1	4.3	9.0	—	—
Retail Outlet Sales of Medical Products ($)	348.9	110.2	234.4	126.7	74.6	23.6	9.5	4.3	—	—
Prescription Drugs ($)	263.0	45.0	214.3	122.2	63.7	19.0	9.4	3.7	—	—
Durable Medical Equipment ($)	38.9	21.3	17.0	4.6	7.7	4.6	0.1	0.6	—	—
Other Nondurable Medical Products ($)	47.0	43.8	3.2	—	3.2	—	—	0.0	—	—
Net Cost of Health Insurance ($)*******	156.4	—	149.9	110.3	24.5	14.2	0.9	6.5	—	—
Government Public Health Activities ($)	79.0	—	—	—	—	—	—	—	79.0	—

(continues)

Table 8-1 National Health Expenditures, 2011, by Type of Expenditure and Source of Funds (in billions) *(continued)*

| Year and Type of Expenditure | Total | Out-of-Pocket | Health Insurance | Health Insurance | | | | Other Third-Party Payers** | Public Health Activity | Investment |
				Private Health Insurance	Medicare	Medicaid	Other Health Insurance Programs			
Investment ($)	153.5	—	—	—	—	—	—	—	—	153.5
Research ($)*********	49.8	—	—	—	—	—	—	—	—	49.8
Structures and Equipment ($)	103.7	—	—	—	—	—	—	—	—	103.7

*Includes Children's Health Insurance Program (Titles XIX and XXI), Department of Defense, and Department of Veterans Affairs.

**Includes worksite health care, other private revenues, Indian Health Service, workers' compensation, general assistance, maternal and child health, vocational rehabilitation, other federal programs, Substance Abuse and Mental Health Services Administration, other state and local programs, and school health.

***Includes expenditures for residential care facilities (NAICS 623210 and 623220), ambulance providers (NAICS 621910), medical care delivered in nontraditional settings (such as community centers, senior citizens centers, schools, and military field stations), and expenditures for Home and Community Waiver programs under Medicaid.

****Includes freestanding facilities only. Additional services of this type provided in hospital-based facilities are counted as hospital care.

*****Includes care provided in nursing care facilities (NAICS 6231), continuing care retirement communities (623311), state and local government nursing facilities, and nursing facilities operated by the Department of Veterans Affairs (DVA).

******Includes all administrative costs (federal, state, and local employees' salaries; contracted employees including fiscal intermediaries; rent and building costs; computer systems and programs; other materials and supplies; and other miscellaneous expenses) associated with insuring individuals enrolled in the following health insurance programs: Medicare, Medicaid, Children's Health Insurance Program, Department of Defense, Department of Veterans Affairs, Indian Health Service, workers' compensation, maternal and child health, vocational rehabilitation, Substance Abuse and Mental Health Services Administration, and other federal programs.

*******Net cost of health insurance is calculated as the difference between CY incurred premiums earned and benefits paid for private health insurance. This includes administrative costs, and in some cases, additions to reserves, rate credits and dividends, premium taxes, and plan profits or losses. Also included in this category is the difference between premiums earned and benefits paid for the private health insurance companies that insure the enrollees of the following programs: Medicare, Medicaid, Children's Health Insurance Program, and workers' compensation (health portion only).

********Research and development expenditures of drug companies and other manufacturers and providers of medical equipment and supplies are excluded from "research expenditures" but are included in the expenditure class in which the product falls.

Note: Numbers may not add to totals because of rounding. The figure 0.0 denotes amounts less than $50 million. Dashes (—) indicate "not applicable." Dollar amounts shown are in current dollars.

Source: Centers for Medicare and Medicaid Services, Office of the Actuary, National Health Statistics Group.

an example of one recent report for 2011.[5] National health care expenditures recently (2010) totaled over $2.6 trillion, 17.9% of the gross domestic product (GDP), or $8,402 per person (Figure 8-1).[6] By 2011, national health care expenditures increased, by almost 4% from the previous year, to over $2.7 trillion, or $8,680 per person.[5,7]

Expenditures for personal health care services in 2011 represented over 84.3%, or $227.6 billion of the national total.[6] The three top expenses in 2011 for personal health care in overall national health care expenditures are hospital care at approximately $850.6 billion, physician services at approximately $541.4 billion, and prescription drugs at approximately $263 billion[5,7,8] (Figure 8-2).[8] Private health insurance in 2011 was the primary source of payment for health care services, with an outlay of $891 billion. Medicare, with expenditures of $567 billion, is the next highest source, and Medicaid ranks as third highest at $405 billion.[8] Together, all public sources of funding represented over 40% of total payments in that year (Figure 8-3).[8]

Historically, the rate of growth in health care expenditures has been an overarching concern of both the private and government sectors as health care expenditure growth outstripped general inflation by

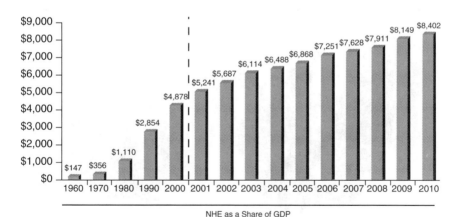

NHE as a Share of GDP

5.2%   7.2%   9.2%   12.5%   13.8%   14.5%   15.4%   15.9%   16.0%   16.1%   16.2%   16.4%   16.8%   17.9%   17.9%

Note: According to CMS Population in the U.S. Bureau of the Census resident-based population, less armed forces overseas.

FIGURE 8-1 National Health Expenditures per Capita and Their Share of the Gross Domestic Product, 1960–2010.
Source: Centers for Medicare and Medicaid Services, Office of the Actuary, National Health Statistics Group.

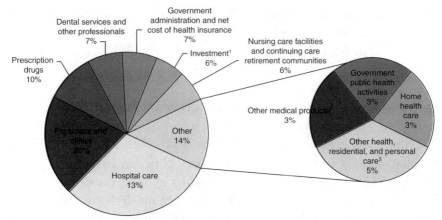

[1] Includes research (2%) and structures and equipment (4%).
[2] Includes durable (1%) and nondurable (2%) goods.
[3] Includes expenditures for residential care facilities, ambulance providers, medical care delivered in nontraditional settings (such as community centers, senior citizens centers, schools, and military field stations), and expenditure for Home and Community Waiver programs under Medicaid.

FIGURE 8-2 The Nation's Health Care Dollar ($2.7 Trillion), Calendar Year 2011: Where It Went.
Source: Centers for Medicare and Medicaid Services, Office of the Actuary, National Health Statistics Group.

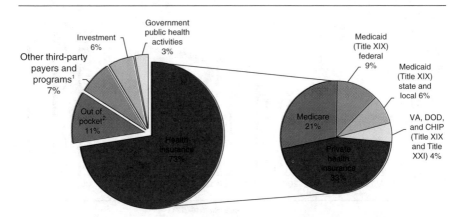

[1] Includes worksite health care, other private revenues, Indian Health Service, workers' compensation, general assistance, maternal and child health, vocational rehabilitation, Substance Abuse and Mental Health Services Administration, school health, and other federal and state local programs.
[2] Includes co-payments, deductibles, and any amounts not covered by health insurance.

Note: Sum of pieces may not equal 100% due to rounding.

FIGURE 8-3 The Nation's Health Care Dollar, Calendar Year 2011: Where It Came From.
Source: Centers for Medicare and Medicaid Services, Office of the Actuary, National Health Statistics Group.

significant margins.[9,10] And although insured Americans view U.S. health care delivery system as superior to that of other developed nations, all of which have some form of universal health care, serious questions have loomed regarding the value returned for U.S. costs that are much higher, while the citizens of those other nations experience better health outcomes.[10] Despite the largest increase in its percentage of GDP devoted to health care among 29 Organization for Economic Cooperation and Development (OECD) countries in the period 1970–2005, the United States had a lower life expectancy than predicted, based on per capita income, and was just as likely to rank in the bottom half as in the top half on a series of health status indicators.[10] According to these data published by the OECD, the United States spent more than double the median spending per person among OECD countries in 2005, and despite having the third highest level of public source spending for health care, public insurance covered only 26.5% of U.S. population.[10] The United States also has had lower health care utilization rates in terms of factors such as hospital days and physician visits per capita than most other OECD countries and a lower supply of expensive technology. Extensive comparative studies have concluded that U.S. higher per capita income and much higher U.S. prices for medical care have accounted for much of the spending differences, not superior health care that yields better health outcomes.[11]

Studies indicate that 30%–40% of U.S. health spending is "waste" in that it provides services of no discernible value and inefficiently produces valuable services; this is another important dimension of U.S. health care spending.[12] One of these studies was reported in a mid-2008 statement by Peter R. Orszag, then Director of the Congressional Budget Office (CBO) at the Health Reform Summit of the Committee on Finance of the U.S. Senate, "Opportunities to Increase Efficiency in Health Care."[13] In his statement, Mr. Orszag noted that "future health care spending is the single most important factor determining the nation's long-term fiscal condition" and that changing physician practice norms through the use of evidence-based practices to decrease variability in costs and revised economic incentives are needed to decrease waste.[13]

It is no surprise that a $2-trillion-plus enterprise invites fraud and abuse. The Federal Bureau of Investigation estimated that "fraudulent billings to public and private health care programs were 3–10%

of total health spending, or $75–250 billion in fiscal year 2009."[14] There has been a decade-long history of collaboration among the U.S. Department of Justice and the Office of the Inspector General of the DHHS to fight health care fraud, which has had impressive results with hundreds of convictions and exclusions of providers from federal health care programs.[14] However, development of complex, sophisticated criminal schemes involving providers, patients, drug dealers, and others continues to evolve.[14] Recognizing that fraud and abuse drain critical and substantial resources from the health care delivery system, in 2009, the U.S. Attorney General and DHHS Secretary announced a multifaceted new approach to curbing fraud and abuse through creation of a Health Care Fraud Prevention and Enforcement Action Team that would use "cutting edge technology to identify and analyze suspected fraud and to build complex health care fraud cases quickly and efficiently."[14]

A well-rounded perspective on health care financing in the United States requires a grasp of much more than just the numbers. It requires an appreciation for the complexity of the human aspects of the multiple players in the health care delivery system; the financing system's historical roots; and the many social, political, and economic characteristics that now interplay in an industry that currently encompasses more than one-sixth of the total U.S. economy and is predicted to reach 20% of the total U.S. economy by 2021.[15]

Drivers of Health Care Expenditures

Major drivers of health care expenditures include advancing medical and diagnostic technology, growth in the population of older adults, emphasis on specialty medicine, uninsured and underinsured, labor intensity, and reimbursement system incentives.

Beginning in the 1950s, health care technology expanded rapidly. Hospitals became high-technology centers, consuming increasing resources in care delivery and capital to expand capacity and add technology. In 1960, national hospital care expenditures totaled $9.0 billion; by 1970, they had increased more than threefold to $27.2 billion,[5] a growth rate vastly outstripping overall inflation and growth in the GDP.

Diagnostic, therapeutic, and surgical techniques have caused changes in health care delivery and costs that resulted from the availability of new equipment and computer-aided technologies. Such advances come at a high price.[16] Information technology and computer-aided innovations have required expensive software and hardware, new patient care equipment, and highly trained personnel. The large capital investments needed to finance innovations in technology have driven the economic and professional imperatives for their use. Historically, the health care reimbursement system did not require documentation regarding the necessity for the use of technologic interventions nor analysis of their benefit. The tendency to favor broad, rather than discretionary, use has grown with the number of interventions available.

The addition of new pharmacologic agents; increased access to drug coverage through Medicare and managed care; and "direct to consumer" marketing of prescription drugs via television, radio, print, and online media have combined to make the rise in prescription drug spending a focal point of national attention.[17] Recent data indicated that growth in prescription drug spending had slowed because of several factors, including the economic recession, fewer new product introductions, and safety concerns.[18] However, spending for prescription drugs remains among the top three expenses in total national health care expenditures.[8]

Growth in the number of older adults is another major factor in rising health care expenditures. Current estimates place the population 65 years and older at 40.4 million, 13.1% of the population, or about one of every eight Americans.[19] The population 85 years and older is expected to grow from 5.5 million in 2010 to 6.6 million by 2020.[19] The number of persons aged 65 or older is expected to grow to 19.3% of the population by 2030, totaling 72.1 million.[20]

Persons over the age of 65 are the major consumers of inpatient hospital care. These individuals account for more than one-third of all hospital stays and nearly one-half of all days of care in hospitals.[21,22] In addition, the aging of the baby boomers born between 1946 and 1964 is expected to have a profound effect on health care services consumption beginning with the second decade of the 21st century.[23]

Growth in specialized medicine occurred as medical science and technology advanced. Americans' preference for specialty care resulted in high utilization and rapidly rising costs. Unlike other developed nations, where physician specialists represent half or fewer of physicians in general practice, nearly 60% of practicing physicians in the United States are specialists.[24] Since the 1940s, when employers offset post–World War II wage controls with fully paid health insurance benefits, working Americans were insulated from health care costs. They grew to expect and demand what they perceived as the "best" care, placing a high value on the use of specialists and advanced technology, sometimes resulting in inappropriate use and expense. For most, the costs of treatment were irrelevant, and physicians' recommendations were uninhibited by economic considerations for their well-insured patients. Historically, U.S. health insurance models carried no prohibitions against patient self-referrals to specialty care. Patients freely referred themselves to specialists based on their own interpretations of symptoms. Initially, managed care plans placed strong restrictions on patient self-referrals to specialists. However, consumer backlash in subsequent years significantly loosened restrictions against such self-referrals.

According to U.S. Census Bureau, among all developed countries of the world, the United States has the highest proportion of population without health insurance coverage.[25] Lacking health insurance or having insufficient coverage carries major consequences by affecting the ability of individuals to receive timely preventive, acute, and chronic care. A lack of insurance coverage drives individuals to seek care in hospital emergency departments at costs higher than care provided at the physician's office or other ambulatory settings. Furthermore, uninsured or underinsured individuals tend to be low users of preventive services and are known to delay seeking care, even for acute conditions. These behaviors often result in increased illness severity and more complications, adding to diagnostic and treatment costs. Uninsured Americans are much more likely than insured individuals to enter care in the late stages of disease and require avoidable hospitalizations.[6] Providers absorb increased costs as free care. Insurers pass costs on to the insured in the form of higher premiums, and citizens pay higher taxes to support public hospitals or public insurance programs.[26]

Health care is a labor-intensive industry. It is one of the largest industries in the United States, employing approximately 16.4 million workers, many of whom represent some of the most highly educated, trained, and compensated individuals in the workforce.[27] In the next decade, more new jobs, approximately an additional 5.6 million, will be created in health care than in any other industry.[27] Among the most important factors that continue to produce high employment demands are technologic advances and continued growth in the aging population with more intense and diverse health care needs.

Both private and government health care financing mechanisms are major contributors to rising costs. Until the widespread introduction of prospective payment and managed care in the 1980s, government and private third-party payers reimbursed largely on a piecework, fee-for-service, retrospective basis. This system created economic incentives favoring high utilization among both physicians and hospitals. In combination with other factors, the economic incentives created by the health care financing system played major roles in the rapid rate of expenditure growth. Later sections of this chapter review the history of attempts to change the health care financing system, which provided a foundation for managed care's emergence as the predominant form of health care financing in the United States.

Evolution of Private Health Insurance

As early as the mid-1800s, a movement began to insure workers against lost wages resulting from work-related injuries. Later, insurance to cover lost wages resulting from catastrophic illness was added to accident policies. It was not until the 1930s that health insurance began paying part or all costs of medical treatment to providers. The basic concept of health insurance is antithetical to the central premise by which "insurance" was historically defined. Whereas insurance originally guarded against the low risk of rare occurrences such as premature death and accidents, the health insurance model that evolved provided coverage for predictable and discretionary uses of the health care system as well as unforeseen and unpredictable health events. Known as indemnity insurance because it protected individuals from financial risk associated with the costs of care, the insurance company set allowable charges for services, and providers could bill the patient for any excess.[28] Coverage for routine health care services added a new dimension to the concept of insurance. Indemnity coverage prevailed until the advent of managed care in the 1970s.

Development of Blue Cross and Blue Shield and Commercial Health Insurance

In 1930, a group of Baylor University teachers contracted with Baylor Hospital in Dallas, Texas, to provide coverage for hospital expenses.[29] This arrangement created a model for the development of what was to become Blue Cross, a private, not-for-profit insurance empire that grew over the succeeding four decades into the dominant form of health insurance in the United States. The Blue Shield plans providing physician payments began shortly after Blue Cross, and by the early 1940s, numerous Blue Shield plans were operating across the country. In 1946, the American Medical Association (AMA) financed the Association Medical Care Plans, which later became the National Association of Blue Shield Plans.

The establishment and subsequent growth of the "Blues" signaled a new era in U.S. health care delivery and financing. They played a significant role in establishing hospitals as the centers of medical care proliferation and technology, and by reimbursing for expensive services, they put hospital care easily within the reach of middle-class working Americans for the first time. The insulation from costs of care provided by the Blues had a major impact on utilization. By the late 1930s, annual hospital admission rates for Blue Cross enrollees were 50% higher on average than for the nation as a whole.[30] In addition to contributing to increased utilization of hospital services by removing financial barriers, the Blue Cross movement had other lasting impacts on national policy making. Rosemary Stevens noted, "In the United States, the brave new world of medicine was specialized, interventionist, mechanistic and expensive—at least as interpreted, through prepayment, for workers in major organizations" (p. 190).[30] By 1940, the Blue Cross movement represented a major financing alternative that countered forces that had long lobbied politically for a form of national health insurance, a concept opposed vehemently by private medicine.[30]

Uniform features of all Blue Cross plans included not-for-profit status; supervision by state insurance departments; direct payments through contract arrangements with providers; and the use of community rating, in which all individuals in a defined group pay single premiums without regard to age, gender, occupation, or health status. Community rating helped ensure nondiscrimination against groups with varying risk characteristics to provide coverage at reasonable rates for the community as a whole; however, as commercial insurers entered the health care insurance marketplace, using "experience rating" and basing premiums on historically documented patterns of utilization, Blue Cross plans, to remain competitive, began offering a variety of benefit packages. Ultimately, the Blue Cross plans were compelled to switch to experience-rating schemes to avoid attracting a disproportionate share of high-risk individuals for whom commercial insurance was prohibitively expensive.[30] During a period of insurance consolidations and mergers, beginning in the mid-1990s, Blue Cross plans in several states converted from not-for-profit to for-profit status. The effects of these conversions on costs of coverage and access to care have long remained under study.[31]

For-profit commercial health insurers entered the market in significant numbers in the decade after start-up of Blue Cross and Blue Shield. Unbounded by the requirement for community rating by the not-for-profit Blues, they used experience rating to charge higher premiums to less healthy individuals and successfully competed for the market of healthier individuals by offering lower premiums than the Blues. By the early 1950s, commercial insurers had enrolled more subscribers than the Blues.[32]

Managed Care

By the 1960s, rapidly increasing Medicare expenditures accompanied by quality concerns captured the attention of health and government policy makers and of industry as the major purchasers of health care benefits, and a proposal was designed by the Nixon administration and Congress that resulted in enactment of the Health Maintenance Organization (HMO) Act of 1973.[30] Although many employer groups had used principles of managed care for prior decades through contracts with health care providers to serve employees on a prepaid basis, provisions of the HMO Act opened participation to the employer-based market, allowing the rapid proliferation of managed care plans.[30]

The HMO Act of 1973 provided loans and grants for the planning, development, and implementation of combined insurance and health care delivery organizations and required that a comprehensive array of preventive and primary care services be included in the HMO arrangement.

The legislation also mandated that employers with 25 or more employees offer an HMO option if one was available in their area and required employers to contribute to employees' HMO premiums in an amount equal to what they contributed to indemnity plan premiums. Initially, this employer mandate helped stimulate the growth of HMO membership in regions where federally funded and qualified plans were first established.

As authorized by the 1973 legislation, HMOs were organizations that combined providers and insurers into one organizational entity. As originally established, members of HMOs usually were required to obtain all their medical care within the organization.

Initially, there were two major types of HMOs. The first was a staff model and was the type most commonly established from the initial HMO legislation. It employed groups of physicians to provide most health care needs of its members. HMOs often provided some specialty services within the organization or contracted for services with community specialists. In the staff model, the HMO also operated the facilities in which its physicians practiced, providing on-site ancillary support services, such as radiology, laboratory, and pharmacy services. The HMO usually purchased hospital care and other services for its members through fee-for-service or prepaid contracted arrangements. Staff model HMOs were referred to as "closed panel" because they employed the physicians who provided the majority of their members' care, and those physicians did not provide services outside the HMO membership. Similarly, community-based physicians could not participate in HMO member care without authorization by the HMO.

The second type of HMO stimulated by the 1973 legislation was the individual practice association (IPA). IPAs are physician organizations composed of community-based independent physicians in solo or group practices that provide services to HMO members. An IPA HMO, therefore, did not operate facilities in which members received care but rather provided its members services through private physician office practices. Like the staff model HMO, the IPA HMO purchased hospital care and specialty services not available through IPA-participating physicians from other area providers on a prepaid or fee-for-service basis. Some IPA HMOs allowed physicians to have a nonexclusive relationship that permitted treatment of nonmembers as well as members; however, HMO relationships with an IPA also could be established on an exclusive basis. In this scenario, an HMO took the initiative in recruiting and organizing community physicians into an IPA to serve its members. Because the HMO was the organizing force in such an arrangement, it was common for the HMO to require exclusivity by the IPA, limiting its services only to that HMO's membership.[33]

The staff model and IPA-type organizations illustrate two major types of HMOs, but each type spawned several hybrids. Other forms of managed care organizations (MCOs) emerged throughout the 1980s in response to national cost and quality concerns. Peter Kongstvedt identified three additional HMO models as the most common: group practice, network, and direct contract.[33] In a group practice model, an HMO contracts with a multispecialty group practice to provide all the physician services required by HMO enrollees. The physicians remained independent—employed by their group rather than the HMO. In the network model, the HMO contracts with more than one group practice and maintains contracts with several physician groups representing both primary care and specialty practices. The direct contract model HMOs maintain contractual relationships with individual physicians, in contrast to the physician groups as in the IPA and network models. The direct contract approach gives the HMO the advantages of maintaining a higher level of control over fee arrangements by reducing physicians' negotiating power to an individual basis and avoiding the risk of lost services to its members by contractual termination of a large group of providers.

All forms of managed care entail interdependence between the provision of and payment for health care. Managed care is population, rather than individual, oriented. It is a system through which care-providing groups or networks take responsibility and share financial risk with an insurer for a specified population's medical care and health maintenance. The population basis enables the insurer to determine actuarially projected use of services related to age, gender, and other factors. Service utilization estimates provide a basis for expected costs over a defined period. Estimates enable the insurer to establish premiums for benefit coverage.

By linking the insurance and delivery of services, managed care reverses the financial incentives of providers in the fee-for-service model. Fee-for-service is essentially a piecework, pay-as-you-go system in which the care provider is financially rewarded for high service utilization. Managed care uses the concept of prepayment, in which providers are paid a preset amount in advance for all services their insured population is projected to need in a given period. Capitation, a method that pays providers for services on a per-member-per-month basis, is a common form of prepayment. The provider receives payment whether or not services are used. If a physician exceeds the predetermined payment level, he or she may suffer a financial penalty. Similarly, if the physician uses fewer resources than predicted, he or she may retain the excess as profit.

Withholds are another form of payment device that seek to provide financial incentives for efficient resource management. In the withhold scheme, a percentage of the monthly capitated fee is withheld from payment to accommodate potential cost overruns for referrals or hospitalizations; all, part, or none of the withholds may be returned to the physician at the end of an annual period, depending on financial performance.[28] The key element of all physician prepayment arrangements is to encourage cost-conscious, efficient, and effective care.

Managed care plans also rely on transferring some measure of financial risk from the insurers to beneficiaries. Transfers of financial risk to beneficiaries most commonly take the form of co-payments and deductibles. Co-payments require that beneficiaries pay a set fee each time they receive a covered service, such as a co-payment for each physician office visit. A deductible requires beneficiaries to meet a predetermined, out-of-pocket expenditure level before the MCO assumes payment responsibility for the balance of charges.

Today, managed care is synonymous with health insurance in the United States, and its principles have been adopted by the Medicare and Medicaid programs. Employers provide the primary source of health insurance, covering approximately 149 million Americans under age 65.[34] Sixty-one percent of employers offered health benefits in 2012.[34] Most employees in companies offering health care coverage subscribe to one or more managed care plans, with only 1% now enrolled in conventional plans.[34]

As enrollment in managed care accelerated throughout the 1980s and 1990s, concerns emerged about MCO restrictions on consumer choice of providers and services. In response, MCOs spawned point-of-service (POS) plans that allow members to use providers outside the MCOs' approved provider networks. To exercise this choice, POS members are charged co-payments and deductibles higher than those charged for in-network services. In 2012, POS plans represented 9% of covered employee enrollment.[34] Another form of managed care arrangement, preferred provider organizations (PPOs), were formed by physicians and hospitals to serve the needs of private, third-party payers and self-insured firms. Through these arrangements, PPOs guarantee a certain volume of business to hospitals and physicians in return for a negotiated discount in fees. PPOs offer attractive features to both physicians and hospitals. Physicians are not required to share in financial risk as a condition of participation, and PPOs reimburse physicians on a fee-for-service basis. By providing predictable admission volume, PPOs help hospitals to shore up declining occupancy rates and attenuate the competition for admissions with other hospitals. To control costs, PPOs use negotiated discount fees, requirements that members receive care exclusively from contracted providers (or incur financial penalty), requirements for preauthorization of hospital admission, and second opinions for major procedures. PPOs maintain systems of utilization review to control costs and advocate for more efficient service utilization by hospitals and physicians. Currently, PPOs are the most popular managed care plans, encompassing 56% of employer-covered workers in 2012.[34]

The organizational forms of managed care have continued to evolve because of changing marketplace conditions, including purchaser preferences, beneficiary demands, and other factors. The emergence of PPOs as the most popular employee choice and the decline of staff model HMOs are notable trends. PPOs represented a means to involve payers and providers in negotiating fees and monitoring utilization while giving beneficiaries more choice. The decline of the staff model HMO resulted from many factors, including beneficiary demands for more choice among providers, large capital outlays associated with facility maintenance and expansion, and increased competition from IPA models. In 1988, staff models constituted about 42% of MCO membership. Ten years later, they represented less than one-half percent of managed care enrollment.[35] Another notable trend has been MCOs' increased use of evidence-based clinical practice guidelines contained in programs of disease management for subscribers with potentially medically high-risk and high-cost conditions. The Disease Management Association of America has described disease management as a system of coordinated health care interventions and communications for populations in which patient self-care efforts are significant.[28] Candidates for these programs are identified from claims data and enrolled in services through which they are periodically contacted by professional staff of the insurer or a contracted disease management company to ensure compliance with physician orders and monitor condition status between physician visits. The goal is to prevent complications, thereby controlling costs.[28] For very-high-risk conditions such as heart failure, disease management programs may equip subscribers with electronic devices connected to the Internet that allow real-time condition monitoring from the subscribers' homes.[28]

All MCOs encourage avoidance of unnecessary use of high-cost services by appropriate and timely treatment at the primary level and, when indicated, participation in disease management programs.

Managed Care Backlash

In what is termed the managed care "backlash" that began in the late 1990s, organized medicine, other health care providers, and consumers railed against MCO policies on choice of providers, referrals, and other practices that were viewed as unduly restrictive.[28] A federal commission was established to review the need for guidelines in the managed care industry.[36] In 1998, President Clinton signed legislation that imposed patient protection requirements on private insurance companies providing health coverage to federal workers.[37] Public dissatisfaction with constraints over the right to receive care deemed necessary and the freedom of physicians to refer patients to specialists received wide publicity. Public concerns driving sentiments toward more government regulation of the managed care industry included the belief that managed care was hurting the quality of patient care and that the managed care industry was not doing as good a job for patients as other sectors of the health care industry. Ultimately, the states took the lead in the patients' rights arena. Beginning in 1998, state legislatures have enacted over 900 laws and regulations addressing both consumer and provider protections.[38]

In another response to the managed care backlash, increasing numbers of employers began offering health insurance plans that allowed employees who entered such a plan to make personal decisions about their coverage, dubbed consumer-driven health plans (CDHPs). The ultimate goals of the CDHPs were to have employees take more responsibility for health care decisions and exercise more cost consciousness. The typical CDHP consists of either a health reimbursement arrangement (HRA) or a health savings account (HSA). Among employers that offered CDHPs in 2012, HSAs outpaced HRAs by two to one.[39] Eligibility for a HSA requires the employee's enrollment in a high-deductible health insurance plan. Employers and employees may contribute to the HSA up to a qualified amount. CDHPs provide comparative information to employees in web-based and traditional formats to increase knowledge about their health care choices and associated costs. In the HSA high-deductible arrangement, the employee draws on the HSA to purchase care until the account is exhausted, when the policy's major medical provision activates. The second type of plan allows employees to design their own provider networks and benefits, based on anticipated needs and costs. The third uses web-based information to enable employees to choose from established groupings of provider networks and benefits to "customize" coverage. In 2006, less than one-fifth of those obtaining health benefits from their employers participated in CDHPs.[40] Although more employers are now offering such plans to their employees, participation rates have remained relatively unchanged,[39] and predictions vary widely regarding the growth of such arrangements in the health insurance marketplace.[34,39]

Trends in Managed Care Costs

Beginning in the 1980s, restrictions imposed on hospital and physician practices through prospective payment and restrictive fee schedules contributed to a decline in health care expenditure growth. Throughout the 1990s, market factors that enabled large health insurance purchasers to aggressively negotiate provider arrangements contributed to the impact of expenditure-cutting managed care initiatives.

The surge in managed care enrollment in the 1990s with decreases in premiums significantly contributed to a decline in the average annual growth of national health care expenditures[41]; however, after 4 years of decline, health insurance premiums increased 8.2% in 1998, more than double the increase of the previous 3 years.[42] The insurance "underwriting cycle," in which insurers underprice during periods of market development and then increase premiums later to restore profitability, was noted as a major reason for increases.

Since 2002, average premiums for employment-based family health care coverage have increased by 97% to a 2012 level of $15,745.[34] On average in 2012, covered workers contributed approximately 18% of premium for single coverage[34] and approximately 28% for family coverage (Figure 8-4).[34]

Higher premiums and requirements for increased employee contributions have caused some workers to drop coverage. This effect increases in severity as the annual earnings of employees decrease, meaning that lower wage workers who can least afford the risk of high health care costs are the most likely to become uninsured. Employers also seek to control costs through "benefit buy-downs." Such methods include reducing the scope of benefits, increasing co-payments and/or co-insurance, and increasing

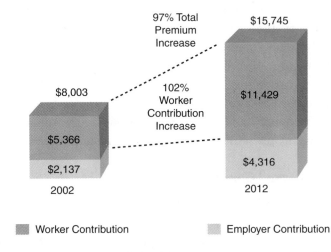

FIGURE 8-4 Average Annual Health Insurance Premiums and Worker Contributions for Family Coverage, 2002–2012.
Source: Employer Health Benefits 2012 Annual Survey-Summary of Findings (#8346), The Henry J. Kaiser Family Foundation, 2012. This information was reprinted with permission from the Henry J. Kaiser Family Foundation. The Kaiser Family Foundation, a leader in health policy analysis, health journalism, and communication, is dedicated to filling the need for trusted, independent information on the major health issues facing our nation and its people. The Foundation is a non-profit private operating foundation, based in Menlo Park, California.

co-pays for prescription drugs.[43] Some experts have estimated that every 1% increase in premiums produces a net increase of 164,000 uninsured individuals.[44]

In 2011, PPO enrollment was reported as 108.3 million, HMO enrollment as 68.1 million, high-deductible health plan enrollment as 24.1 million, and POS as 9.5 million, totaling 210 million enrollees in MCO plans.[45]

Since the mid-1990s, MCOs have undergone many changes. Company mergers and consolidations have been among the most prominent. A 5-year literature analysis of MCO performance indicated that MCOs overall did not accomplish their early promises to change clinical practice and improve quality while lowering costs. Findings suggested that a systematic revamping of information systems, coupled with appropriate incentives and revised clinical processes, were required to produce the desired changes in cost and quality performance.[46] Changes in managed care company operating policies have more recently responded to provider and consumer demands reflected by state-enacted patient protection legislation, a loosening of early restrictions on patient provider choice and specialty referrals, and patient access to information about operating policies, especially regarding denials of payment.[28]

MCOs and Quality

The most influential managed care quality assurance organization is the National Committee on Quality Assurance (NCQA). The NCQA was formed in 1979 as two managed care trade organizations, the American Managed Care and Review Association and the Group Health Association of America, merged under the title of the American Association of Health Plans. The organization title was later changed to the NCQA in 1990, when the NCQA became an independent, not-for-profit organization deriving its revenue primarily from fees for accreditation services.[47] The organization publishes and markets an online searchable compendium of quality indicators on nearly 500 health plans serving over 107 million Americans.[48]

The NCQA evaluates participating organizations on a voluntary request basis. NCQA programs include accreditation for MCOs, PPOs, managed behavioral health care organizations, new health plans, and disease management programs. The NCQA also provides certification for organizations that verify provider credentials, physician organizations, utilization management organizations, patient-centered medical homes, and disease management organizations and programs. It also provides physician recognition programs for performance excellence in several areas of condition management such as back pain, diabetes, or heart disease/stroke.[49] Accreditation of MCOs entails rigorous reviews of all aspects of the respective organizations, including online surveys and on-site reviews of key clinical and administrative processes. The review focuses on several major areas: quality management, physician credentialing, member rights and responsibilities, and utilization management.[50] Beginning in 1999, the NCQA began including outcomes of care and measures of clinical processes in accreditation reviews, increasing the likelihood that accreditation status accurately reflects the quality of care delivered.[51]

In 1989, a partnership among the NCQA, health plans, and employers developed the Health Plan Employer Data and Information Set (HEDIS).[52] The HEDIS (now called the Healthcare Effectiveness Data and Information Set) provides a standardized method for MCOs to collect, calculate, and report information about their performance to allow employers, other purchasers, and consumers to compare different plans. The HEDIS has evolved through several stages of development and continuously refines its measurements through a rigorous review and independent audits. The data set contains measures of MCO performance, divided among eight domains[53]:

1. Effectiveness of care
2. Access/availability of care
3. Satisfaction with the experience of care
4. Health plan stability
5. Use of services
6. Cost of care
7. Informed health care choices
8. Health plan descriptive information

The CMS requires that all Medicare managed care plans publicly report HEDIS data, and the NCQA requires all accredited plans to allow public reporting of their clinical quality data. A number of states also require plans providing Medicaid managed care to report HEDIS data.[54]

The NCQA/HEDIS data provide an important avenue of accountability to the employer purchasers and consumers of health care and provide feedback to its providers that is critical in efforts to achieve improvement. The 2012 NCQA report "The State of Health Care Quality" noted an all-time high submission of audited HEDIS data representing 125 million Americans.[55] Benchmarked against the performance of the top 10% of all participating health plans, that data disclosed quality disparities and gaps that were used to inform purchasers, plan administrators, and policy makers. Comparisons allowed the calculation of number of avoidable illnesses and deaths for several of the most common, costly, and life-threatening health conditions.[55]

MCOs also apply several internal techniques to manage quality, many of which directly or indirectly relate to physician performance. They focus attention on the quality of the institutional providers, especially on the hospitals with which they contract for services. Data systems that monitor claims information track the use of services to provide feedback to monitor resource use and quality. Through disease management programs, MCOs attempt to control costs and improve care quality for individuals with chronic and costly conditions through methods such as the use of evidence-based clinical guidelines, patient self-management education, disease registries, risk stratification, proactive patient outreach, and performance feedback to providers. Programs may also use clinical specialists who provide monitoring and support to patients with disease management issues. Employer purchasers, a number of states, and the federal government have endorsed disease management programs for their employees and Medicaid and Medicare recipients.[56,57]

Self-Funded Insurance Programs

Since the late 1970s, self-funding (full or partial) and self-insurance of employee health benefits have become increasingly common among large employers.[58] Through the self-funded mechanism, the employer (or other group, such as a union or trade association) collects premiums and pools these into a fund or account that it uses to pay for medical benefit claims instead of using a commercial carrier. Self-funded plans often use the services of an actuarial firm to set premium rates and a third-party administrator to administer benefits, pay claims, and collect data on utilization.[59] Many third-party administrators also provide case management services for potentially extraordinarily expensive cases to help coordinate care and control employer risk of catastrophic expenses.

Self-funded plans offer significant advantages to employers, such as avoiding additional administrative and other charges made by commercial carriers. By self-funding benefits, employers can also avoid premium taxes and accrue interest on the cash reserves held in the benefit account. A major stimulus to the development of self-insurance programs has been their exemption from the Employee Retirement and Income Security Act of 1974 (ERISA), which mandates minimum benefits under state law. This exemption allowed employers much greater flexibility in designing benefit packages and provided one mechanism to control benefit costs.

Major controversies continue to arise from the ERISA exemption of self-insured employer plans. One controversy is based on states' interpretation of their responsibilities for consumer protection through regulation of the types and scope of required coverage in employer-provided plans. ERISA has historically preempted such regulation. Another major area of dispute centers on the states' losses of premium revenue taxes as they struggle with growing financial burdens of uncompensated care and caring for uninsured populations. An additional area of controversy and legal actions surrounding ERISA is its prohibition against employees suing employer-provided health plans over matters involving coverage decisions. Under ERISA, organizations that administer employer-based health benefit plans maintain a degree of legal immunity from litigation and liability for withholding coverage or failing to provide necessary care. In 2004, the U.S. Supreme Court upheld an Appeals Court decision that beneficiaries of employment-related managed care plans cannot hold the plans accountable for damages when injured as a result of coverage denial decisions.[60]

Government as a Source of Payment: A System in Name Only

Federal and state governments and, to a lesser extent, local government, finance health care services. Federal funding originally focused on specific population groups, providing health care for those in government service, their dependents, and particular population groups, such as Native Americans. Today, a combination of public programs, chief among them the federal Medicare program and joint federal–state Medicaid program, constitutes nearly 40% of total national care expenditures.[5,6]

Government payment for health services includes federal support of U.S. Public Health Service hospitals, the Indian Health Service, state and local inpatient psychiatric and other long-term care facilities, services of the Veterans Affairs hospitals and health services, services provided by the Department of Defense to military personnel and their dependents, workers' compensation, public health activities, and other government-sponsored service grants and initiatives.

In the absence of a comprehensive national health and social services policy, government's role in financing health care services can be described as a system only in the loosest interpretation of that term. It may be more accurate to describe government's various roles in health care financing as a mosaic of individual programs of reimbursement, direct payments to vendors, grants, matching funds, and subsidies.

As a source of health care service payments, the system of financing operates primarily in a vendor–purchaser relationship, with government contracting with health care services providers rather than providing services directly. A prime example is the Medicare program in which the federal government purchases hospital, home health, nursing home, physician, and other medical services under contract with suppliers. The Medicaid system operates similarly.

America's history of fierce resistance from the private sector, both organized medicine and, to an extent, the voluntary medicine and hospital systems, has prevented enactment of a comprehensive national health care system. Although the ACA creates federally supported programs to enable coverage of the majority of the nation's uninsured, it does not result in anything that could be characterized as a national system of health care.

Medicare and Medicaid, comprising the majority of public spending on health, are discussed in the following sections.

Medicare

Were it not for the successful opposition of the private sector led by the AMA, the Social Security Act of 1935, the most significant piece of social legislation ever enacted by the federal government, would have included a form of national health insurance. It took another 30 years, during which time many presidential and congressional acts for national health insurance had been proposed and defeated, that Congress enacted Medicare, "Health Insurance for the Aged," Title XVIII of the Social Security Act, in 1965. Medicare became only the second mandated health insurance program in the United States, after workers' compensation. When Medicare was enacted, approximately only one-half of the elderly had any type of health insurance. Such health insurance usually covered only inpatient hospital costs, and much of health care spending was paid for out-of-pocket.[61] Today, the Medicare program covers 50 million Americans, including most 65 years and older, younger individuals who receive Social Security Disability Insurance benefits, and individuals with end-stage kidney disease and Lou Gehrig's disease following their eligibility for Social Security Disability Insurance. In 2012, expenditures totaled $550 billion and are projected to grow to 1.1 trillion by 2022.[62]

The enactment of Medicare legislation was an historical benchmark, signaling government's entry into the personal health care financing arena. The Medicare program was established under the aegis of the Social Security Administration, and hospital payment was contracted to local intermediaries chosen by hospitals. Over 90% of hospitals chose their local Blue Cross association as the intermediary. In response to organized medicine's opposition to government certification, the Social Security Administration agreed to accreditation by the private Joint Commission on Accreditation of Hospitals (now The Joint Commission) as meeting the certification requirement for Medicare participation. Describing the enactment of Medicare as a "watershed," Rosemary Stevens wrote the following (pp. 281–282)[30]:

> Thus with the stroke of a pen, the elderly acquired hospital benefits, the hospitals acquired cost reimbursement for these benefits, the Blue Cross Association was precipitated into prominence as a major national organization (since the national contract was to be with the association, with subcontracting to local plans), and the Joint Commission was given formal government recognition.

The Medicare amendment stated that there should be "prohibition against any federal interference with the practice of medicine or the way medical services were provided" (pp. 286–287).[30] Ultimately, however, the government's acceptance of responsibility for payment for the care of older adults generated a flood of regulations to address cost and quality control of the services and products for which it was now a major payer.

As originally implemented, the Medicare program consisted of two parts, which differed in sources of funding and benefits. Part A provided benefits for hospital care, limited skilled nursing care, short-term home health care after hospitalization, and hospice care. This portion of coverage was mandatory and was funded by Social Security payroll taxes.[63] Part B, supplementary medical insurance, was structured as a voluntary program covering physician services and services ordered by physicians, such as outpatient diagnostic tests, medical equipment and supplies, and home health services. This portion was funded from beneficiary premium payments, matched by general federal revenues.[63]

The Balanced Budget Act of 1997 added Part C, Medicare + Choice, allowing private health plans to administer Medicare contracts, with beneficiary enrollment on a voluntary basis. In 2003, the Medicare Prescription Drug, Improvement, and Modernization Act changed Part C to "Medicare Advantage," revising the administration of Medicare managed care programs to entice additional participation.[64] Since passage of the Medicare Prescription Drug, Improvement, and Modernization Act, beneficiary enrollment in private Medicare health plans has increased substantially[64] (Figure 8-5).

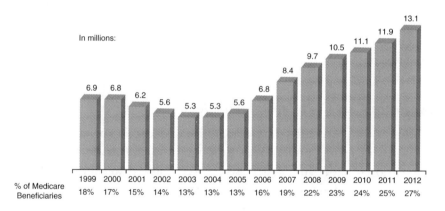

Note: Includes local HMOs, PSOs, PPOs, regional PPOs, PFFS plans, 1876 Cost Plans, Demonstrations, HCPP and PACE Plans.

FIGURE 8-5 Total Medicare Private Health Plan Enrollment, 1999–2012.
Source: Medicare Advantage Fact Sheet (#2052-16), The Henry J. Kaiser Family Foundation, December 2012. This information was reprinted with permission from the Henry J. Kaiser Family Foundation. The Kaiser Family Foundation, a leader in health policy analysis, health journalism, and communication, is dedicated to filling the need for trusted, independent information on the major health issues facing our nation and its people. The Foundation is a non-profit private operating foundation, based in Menlo Park, California.

Today, 13.1 million beneficiaries participate in private Medicare health plans.[64] The Medicare Prescription Drug, Improvement, and Modernization Act also added a Part D for prescription drug coverage to provide financial relief from these costs, particularly for low-income individuals.[65]

From its inception, Medicare coverage was not fully comprehensive, and that remains true today. Beneficiaries are required to share costs through a system of deductibles and coinsurance, and there is no limit on out-of-pocket expenditures. For Part A, the deductible requires beneficiaries to reach a set amount in personal outlays for hospitalization in each 12-month period, and co-insurance requires that patients cover 20% of hospitalization costs for services received during hospitalization that are not covered by Part A.[66] The program also limits total compensated days of hospital care on a lifetime pool of days. For Part B coverage, monthly premiums are deducted from Social Security payments. These limitations gave rise to the availability of a variety of private supplemental, or "Medi-gap," policies, designed to assist with cost-sharing requirements and benefit gaps.[62] Also, the prescription drug benefit contained a gap in which beneficiaries are fully exposed to costs between designated levels of expenditures.[65]

Medicare Cost Containment and Quality Initiatives

Within a few years after implementation, Medicare spending was significantly exceeding projections. Although hospital costs for the growing population of older adults increased more rapidly than expected, the rise over projected Medicare expenses could not be explained by that phenomenon alone. A 1976 study by the U.S. Human Resources Administration reviewed the first 10 years of Medicare hospital expenses and attributed less than 10% of increases to utilization by the older adult population. Almost one-fourth of the increase over projected hospital costs was attributed to general inflation and two-thirds to huge growth in hospital payroll and non-payroll expenses, including profits.[30]

Like Blue Cross, Medicare's hospital reimbursement mechanism was cost-based and retrospective on a per-day-of-stay basis. Although facilitating the rapid incorporation of almost 20 million beneficiaries into the new benefit system, cost-based reimbursement also fueled utilization of services in an era of rapidly advancing medical technology. Paid on a retrospective basis for costs incurred, hospitals had a strong incentive to use services with no incentives for efficiency.

In the decade after Medicare enactment, several amendments to the Social Security Act made significant changes. In general, amendments during the first 5 years increased the types of covered services and expanded the population of eligible participants. During a later period, amendments addressed concerns about the rising costs and questionable quality of the program.

Many such initiatives attempted to slow spiraling costs and address quality concerns. They were largely unsuccessful. In 1966, Congress enacted the Comprehensive Health Planning Act to support states in conducting local health planning to ensure adequate facilities and services and avoid duplications.[67] In 1974, the Health Planning Resources and Development Act replaced the Comprehensive Health Planning Act with health systems agencies to develop plans for local health resources based on quantified population needs. The Act also required all states to obtain approval from a state planning agency before starting any major capital project, and several states adopted certificate-of-need legislation for this purpose. Congress repealed the federal mandate in 1987, but most states still maintain some form of certificate-of-need program, focused on development of physician-owned facilities such as ambulatory surgery and diagnostic imaging centers.[68] Health systems agencies were unsuccessful in materially influencing decisions about service or technology expansion because decisions were dominated by institutional and economic interests. Concurrent with attempts to slow cost increases through a planning approach, a number of other legislative initiatives took shape that were directly related to concerns over Medicare costs and service quality.

Professional standards review organizations, established in 1972, signaled the first federal attempt to review care provided under Medicare, Medicaid, and certain other federally funded health care programs.[69] Each local professional standards review organization was a not-for-profit organization composed of a group of local physicians who performed record reviews and made payment recommendations to the local Medicare intermediary. Plagued by questionable effectiveness and high administrative costs, professional standards review organizations were replaced by peer review organizations in 1982. Peer review organizations were given more specific and measurable cost and quality standards than their predecessor professional standards review organizations.[70] In 2001, peer review organizations were renamed "quality improvement organizations" as part of broad, quality improvement initiatives of the CMS.

Both not-for-profit and investor-owned for-profit hospitals saw the opportunity for expansion offered by Medicare's guarantee of full-cost reimbursement. Between 1970 and 1980, there was over a 200% increase in the number of hospitals involved in multihospital systems of both types.[71]

The federal budgets of 1980 and 1981 again amended the Medicare legislation with a strong focus on reducing the number and length of hospitalizations. Amendments advocated home health services as a hospital alternative by eliminating the limit on annual number of home health care visits, a 3-day hospitalization requirement for home health visit coverage eligibility, and occupational therapy as a requirement for initial entitlement to home health care services. Budget provisions also lifted exclusion from Medicare participation of for-profit home health care agencies in states that did not require agency licensure.

Diagnosis-Related Groups

The unsuccessful efforts at Medicare cost containment and quality control of the 1970s and 1980s culminated in Medicare's 1983 enactment of a case payment system that radically changed hospital reimbursement. The new payment system shifted hospital reimbursement from the retrospective to prospective mode. Using diagnosis-related groups (DRGs) developed for the Health Care Financing Administration, the new system provided a patient classification method to relate the type of patients a hospital treated (i.e., age, sex, gender, diagnoses) to costs.[72] The DRG payment system based hospital payments on established fees for services required to treat specific diagnoses rather than on discreet units of services. The DRGs group the over 10,000+ International Classification of Disease codes into well over 500 patient categories. Patients within each category are grouped for similar clinical conditions and expected resource use.[73] DRGs form a manageable, clinically coherent set of patient classes that relate a hospital's case mix to the resource demands and associated costs experienced by the hospital. The payment an individual hospital receives under this system is ultimately calculated using input from a variety of other data known to impact costs, such as hospital teaching status and wage data for its geographic location.

The DRG system provided incentives for the hospital to spend only what was needed to achieve optimal patient outcomes. If outcomes could be achieved at a cost lower than the preset payment, the hospital received an excess payment for those cases. If the hospital spent more to treat cases than allowed, it absorbed the excess costs. The DRG system also financially provided for cases classified as "outliers" because of complications. The DRG system did not build in allowances to the payment rate for direct medical education expenses for teaching hospitals, hospital outpatient expenses, or capital expenditures. These continued to be reimbursed on a cost basis.

The principle of case-based prospective payment soon was adopted in varying forms by numerous states and private third-party payers as their reimbursement basis. The prospective payment system raised many concerns among hospitals, health care providers, and consumers about its possible effects, including fears about premature hospital discharges, hospitals' questionable ability to streamline services to conform to preset payments, and the home health care industry's capacity to accommodate an increased caseload.

"Quicker and sicker" was the slogan popularized by the media during the first years of the prospective payment system to characterize the drive for shorter hospital stays. The media also popularized the term "patient dumping," referring to numerous documented instances of hospitals' transferring patients who were at high risk of expensive and potentially unprofitable service needs to other hospitals.

Subsequent research on the impact of the prospective payment system demonstrated that many early concerns were unfounded and that DRGs did have a measurable impact on slowing the overall growth rate of Medicare spending.[74] Extensive research also compared quality indicators before and after DRG implementation. The federal Prospective Payment Assessment Commission was established to monitor the effects of the prospective system. Studies revealed few effects on Medicare patient readmission rates attributable to the DRG system.[75] The RAND Corporation also conducted several studies of another indicator of patient care quality, in-hospital mortality rates. The studies reviewed almost 17,000 records of Medicare patients admitted to hospitals for five common diagnoses. Findings included a drop of 24% in the average length of hospital stay for these conditions and an overall improvement in mortality rates among the diagnoses studied.[75]

Concerns about patient dumping were formally addressed in the 1985 federal budget by the Emergency Medical Treatment and Labor Act of 1986 (EMTALA), which required hospitals to treat everyone who presented in their emergency departments, regardless of ability to pay. Stiff financial penalties, as well as risk of Medicare certification loss by hospitals inappropriately transferring patients, accompanied the EMTALA provisions.[76]

Evidence indicates that the prospective payment system slowed hospital cost growth during the early years after implementation through reductions in lengths of stay, hospital personnel, and new medical technologies; however, total Medicare cost growth later reaccelerated, in part because of increased volume in outpatient spending and other factors whose impacts have not been clearly determined.[75] Concerns about the capacity of the home health care industry to meet anticipated increases in demand dissipated quickly. Both the not-for-profit and the proprietary sectors of the industry responded by creating new or expanding existing home health care services as components of vertically integrated systems. In the early years of the prospective payment system, hospitals did not experience the predicted negative financial impact, and they actually posted substantial profits.[75] In fact, the federal government partially justified subsequent reductions in prospective payment on the basis that early payments were too high relative to costs.[75,76] It has even been suggested that the large surpluses generated by not-for-profit hospitals in the early years of prospective payment fueled hospital costs by making new surpluses available for investment.[75]

From the outset, the prospective payment system's cost-containment effectiveness was limited by its application to only inpatient hospital care for Medicare recipients. Aggressive shifting of Medicare-covered services to the outpatient setting and shifting hospital costs onto private pay patients were two major reactions that dampened the prospective payment system's cost-containment results.

Medicare Physician Reimbursement

Medicare Part B physician reimbursement was established as fee-for-service, based on prevailing fees within geographic areas. The Medicare physician payment rate increase averaged 18% annually between 1975 and 1987 and provoked legislative action.[77] Medicare first enacted a temporary price freeze for physician services.[77] Assessments of the price freeze suggested that physicians offset the lower fees by increasing the volume of services.[77] This raised the issue of whether physicians respond to fee pressures by using more services to compensate for lower reimbursement. Concerns over absolute cost increases and overuse of costly specialty care prompted additional congressional cost-containment action.

The 1989 Federal budget established a new method of Medicare physician reimbursement that became effective in 1992, using a resource-based relative value scale to replace the fee-for-service reimbursement system.[78] The resource-based relative value scale was intended to control cost growth by instituting the same payments for the same services, whether performed by a generalist or specialist physician, reducing the number of expensive procedures and lowering the incentive for physicians to specialize. Relative value units were adjusted for geographic area variations in costs. The resource-based relative value scale continues to be used with a committee of the AMA and national medical specialty societies recommending annual updates.[78]

The Health Insurance Portability and Accountability Act of 1996 and the Balanced Budget Act of 1997

Medicare reforms enacted by the DRG prospective payment system, managed care influences, market competition, technology advances, and consumerism produced unprecedented changes in hospital and physician reimbursement, hospitals' affinity for technology, and consumer expectations of hospital care. The Medicare prospective payment system had succeeded in demonstrating that "more is not necessarily better," as lengths of stay and service intensity declined to accommodate the DRG framework, with no demonstrable negative impact on the quality of patient care. Then, in the early 1990s, the nation witnessed vigorous debates regarding the Clinton administration's National Health Security Act. Although the Act never reached a congressional vote, many months of debate thrust national concerns about Medicare spending, lack of access to services, beneficiary costs, and provider choice into the public spotlight. Popular and political sensitivities rose against the backdrop of escalating national predictions about potential insolvency of the Hospital Insurance Trust Fund.[79]

Several trends supported the need for major changes in the Medicare system. First, CBO projections indicated that Medicare cost growth could not be sustained without cuts in other government programs, major increases in taxes, or larger budget deficits.[80]

Second, Medicare's fee-for-service indemnity structure was becoming rapidly outmoded, as employer-sponsored plans, Medicaid, and private insurance were rapidly embracing managed care principles.

Third, Medicare coverage left significant gaps requiring co-pays and coinsurance that many beneficiaries were unable to fill with supplemental "Medi-gap" insurance policies. Although some Medicare beneficiaries were eligible for Medicaid subsidies of these expenses, subsidies created additional financial burdens for the states.

Acknowledging the President's and Congress's discord on a national health reform program, in 1995 Congress focused on slowing Medicare cost growth and achieving broader choices for Medicare beneficiaries through managed care plans as models of cost containment and consumer satisfaction.[80]

The presidential and congressional campaigns of 1996 frequently focused on the health care issues brought to light during debate on the National Health Security Act and consumer concerns about managed care. This political environment supported the rapid formulation and passage of the bipartisan Health Insurance Portability and Accountability Act of 1996 (HIPAA), also called the Kassebaum–Kennedy Bill. Among its important health insurance features, HIPAA included the prohibition of insurance companies from denying coverage due for preexisting medical conditions or denying sale of personal insurance policies to individuals who were previously covered in group plans. It also established a pilot program to enable workers to save tax-free dollars for future medical expenses through medical savings accounts.[81] Although the Act accomplished important beneficial outcomes, it fell far short of addressing the pervasive problems of the overall health care system in general or the Medicare and Medicaid programs in particular.

The 1998 federal budget process reflected pressures to produce a balanced budget and to respond meaningfully to national health issues from both the consumer and cost-containment perspectives. The resulting Balanced Budget Act (BBA) created major new policy directions for Medicare and Medicaid and took important incremental steps in extending health care coverage through an initiative to insure uninsured children through a $16 billion allocation for a new State Children's Health Insurance Program (SCHIP).[82]

The Act was characterized as containing "some of the most sweeping and significant changes to Medicare and Medicaid since their inception in 1965."[82] Overall, the BBA proposed to reduce growth in Medicare and Medicaid spending by $125.2 billion in 5 years through regulatory changes and payment changes to hospitals, physicians, post–acute-care services, and health plans. It also increased beneficiary premiums for Medicare Part B and required new prospective payment systems for hospital outpatient services, skilled nursing facilities, home health agencies, and rehabilitation hospitals. It also reduced allowances for the medical education expenses of teaching hospitals and funded incentives to hospitals for voluntarily reducing the numbers of medical residents. As the largest Medicare spender, the BBA targeted hospitals as the source of more than one-third of total anticipated savings. Decreased Medicare spending growth in the period 1998–2002 demonstrated the immediate impact of the BBA. After growing at an average annual rate of 11.1% for the 15 years before 1997, the average annual rate of spending growth between 1998 and 2000 dropped to 1.7%, resulting in approximately $68 billion in savings.[83]

Among the most significant policy shifts of the BBA was opening the Medicare program to private insurers through the Medicare + Choice Program, for the first time allowing financial risk sharing for the Medicare program with the private sector through managed care plans. The participation of private insurers was intended to increase both the impact of competitive market forces on the program and consumer awareness of alternatives to the fee-for-service system.

The BBA constituted federal commissions to carry out monitoring and recommendation functions during implementation, including the Medicare Payment Advisory Commission and an independent National Bipartisan Commission on the Future of Medicare whose functions entailed analyzing numerous dimensions of Medicare's financial condition and benefits design over time.[84]

Implementation of the Medicare BBA provisions experienced widespread challenges and delays drawing fire from industry advocacy groups, professional organizations, and consumers. Just before several of the BBA's provisions took effect, President Clinton signed the Balanced Budget Refinement Act of 1999, providing $17.5 billion to restore cuts to industry sectors negatively impacted by the BBA and outlining delayed implementation schedules for many of the BBA's original mandates.[85]

The Medicare + Choice program enrollment initiative experienced serious challenges. Because of reduced Medicare reimbursement, costs of working with federal bureaucracy, and market shifts reducing profitability, MCOs lost their early enthusiasm for participation. Plan withdrawals resulted in a decline from 6.3 million beneficiaries in 2000 to 4.6 million in 2003.[86] In response, in 2000, Congress enacted the Benefits Protection and Improvement Act that increased participating health plans' and provider payments.[87]

Medicare Cost Containment and Quality Improvement

In 2001, the CMS inaugurated the "Quality Initiative," encompassing every dimension of the health care delivery system. The Quality Initiative includes nursing homes, hospitals, home health care agencies, physicians, and other facilities.[88] The program collects and analyzes data to monitor conformance with standards of care and performance. In addition to the Quality Initiative, the Medicare Quality Monitoring System "processes, analyzes, interprets and disseminates health-related data to monitor the quality of care delivered to Medicare fee-for-service beneficiaries."[89] Since 2003, the Medicare administration has also continued to experiment with hospital pay-for-performance plans designed to improve quality and avoid unnecessary costs. A 2011 report on the outcomes of a 5-year Medicare pay-for-performance demonstration project in 260 hospitals matched with 780 controls suggested several possible strategies for improving quality and containing costs.[90]

With the goal of providing public, valid, and user-friendly information about hospital quality, in 2005, Medicare launched the Website "Hospital Compare," in a collaboration with the Hospital Quality Alliance, a public–private partnership organization. Hospital Compare encompasses common conditions and criteria that assess individual hospitals' performance consistency with evidence-based practice; reporting is required for hospitals to qualify for Medicare rate updates.[91] Data from the "Hospital Consumer Assessment of Healthcare Providers and Systems" surveys has been added to the Hospital Compare information, providing patient perspectives on their hospital experience.[92] In 2007, the Medicare administration announced that beginning in 2008 it would no longer pay for procedures resulting from hospital-acquired infections, an aggressive step in using quality standards as a basis for public reporting and payment.[93] In consultation with the Hospital Quality Forum and many other expert organizations, Medicare also identified categories of untoward hospital-acquired events, dubbed "never happen events," for which it would not reimburse hospitals for resulting patient treatment.[94] On an ongoing basis, the CMS maintains a list of hospital-acquired conditions (HACs) [95] for which it will not make reimbursement payments for any patient treatment required following a "never happen event." Some examples of HAC include catheter-acquired urinary tract infections, foreign objects retained after surgery, falls or trauma during hospitalization, and manifestations of poor blood sugar control while hospitalized. The CMS updates this list at intervals on an as-needed basis.[96]

Medicaid and the SCHIP

In 1965, Medicaid legislation was enacted as Title XIX of the Social Security Act. Medicaid is administered by the CMS and is a mandatory joint federal–state program in which federal and state support is shared based on the state's per capita income. Before Medicaid's implementation, health care services for the economically needy were provided through a patchwork of programs sponsored by state and local governments, charitable organizations, and community hospitals.

Today, Medicaid provides health and long-term care coverage to more than 62 million low-income Americans including 31 million low-income children, 16 million adults, and 16 million elderly and people with disabilities.[97] The program represents a major source of health care system funding, accounting for approximately 19% of $2.7 trillion in personal health services spending and almost 31% of spending for nursing home care in 2011.[5] The Medicaid program is the third largest source of health insurance in America after employer-based programs and Medicare.[8]

The federal government establishes broad program guidelines, but program requirements are the prerogative of state governments. Medicaid requires states to cover certain types of individuals or groups under their plans, and states may include others at their discretion. The program provides three types of coverage:

1. Health insurance for low-income families with children
2. Long-term care for older Americans and individuals with disabilities
3. Supplemental coverage for low-income Medicare beneficiaries for services not covered by Medicare, including Medicare premiums, deductibles, and coinsurance[98]

Until the more recent enactment of Medicare Part D, the third type of coverage also paid for prescription drugs.

Medicaid federal guidelines established a mandated core of basic medical services for state programs and included inpatient and out-patient hospital services, physician services, diagnostic services, and nursing home care for adults. Later Medicaid amendments expanded mandated benefits to include home health care, preventive health screening services, family planning services, and assistance to recipients of Supplemental Security Income. State Medicaid programs currently must extend benefits to all pregnant women who meet federal income level guidelines and children whose family incomes fall below specified federal income guidelines. Individual states have broad discretion to include additional services in their Medicaid programs, and many have elected extended benefits beyond the core of mandated benefits.

Medicaid funding sources are distinct from those for Medicare. Medicare, funded from contributions of payroll taxes matched by employers, is an entitlement because individuals have contributed to their cost of coverage. Medicaid, which is funded by personal income and corporate and excise taxes, is a transfer payment representing funds transferred from more economically affluent individuals to those in need.[99]

Unlike Medicare, which reimburses providers through intermediaries such as Blue Cross, Medicaid directly reimburses service providers. Rate-setting formulas, procedures, and policies vary widely among states. Because of the variations in benefits and reimbursement policies, Medicaid has been described as "50 different programs."[99]

Throughout the 1980s, as costs grew rapidly, states tested various prepaid, managed care approaches, and some implemented prospective payment systems modeled on DRG reimbursement. Several states experimented with voluntary Medicaid managed care enrollment, contracting with HMOs to provide some or all of their Medicaid benefits under federally approved demonstration projects. Through a provision of the BBA, the federal government allowed states to mandate managed care enrollment for their Medicaid beneficiaries, and today all 50 states offer some type of Medicaid managed care plans.

Two-thirds of Medicaid enrollees now receive most or all of their benefits in managed care, and many states are expanding their use of managed care to additional geographic areas and Medicaid populations.[100] All states are struggling with the burden of rising Medicaid costs.

The 2008 economic recession accelerated Medicaid enrollment, spending, and growth,[101] but in a recent sign of an improved national economy, Medicaid spending growth slowed to 2% and enrollment slowed for the third consecutive year.[102] Medicaid spending increased by nearly 10%, but this was the smallest increase since 2006, based on a 50-state survey by the Kaiser Family Foundation's Commission on Medicaid and the Uninsured, an editorially independent program of the Henry J. Kaiser Family Foundation (Figure 8-6).[97]

SCHIP Evolved into the Children's Health Insurance Program

The Balanced Budget Act of 1997 contained a child health initiative originally named the SCHIP that built on the underlying Medicaid program by targeting uninsured children whose family income was too high to

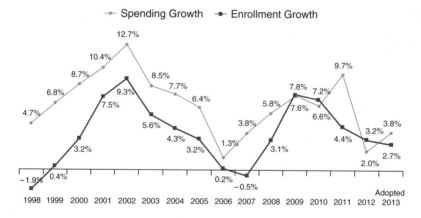

Note: Enrollment Percentage changes from June to June of each year; spending growth percentages changes in state fiscal year.

FIGURE 8-6 Percent Change in Total Medicaid Spending and Enrollment, FY 1998-FY 2013.
Source: Medicaid Today; Preparing for Tomorrow (#8380). The Henry J. Kaiser Family Foundation, October 2012. This information was reprinted with permission from the Henry J. Kaiser Family Foundation. The Kaiser Family Foundation, a leader in health policy analysis, health journalism, and communication, is dedicated to filling the need for trusted, independent information on the major health issues facing our nation and its people. The Foundation is a non-profit private operating foundation, based in Menlo Park, California.

qualify for Medicaid and yet too low to afford purchasing private health insurance. At its creation in 1997, SCHIP was the largest expansion of health insurance coverage for children in the United States since Medicaid began in the 1960s.[103] SCHIP targeted enrollment of 10 million children through federal matching funds for states beginning in 1998.[104] In 1999, all 50 states were receiving federal support from BBA allocations under the SCHIP. By 2010, almost eight million children had been enrolled in the program since its inception (Figure 8-7).[105,106] However, in 2010–2011, over 9.8 million or approximately 9.8% of all American children, defined as under the age of 18, still remained uninsured.[107] The SCHIP program was renamed the "Children's Health Insurance Program" (CHIP), and was reauthorized in succeeding years and again in 2010 for the period through 2015 by the ACA.[104]

Medicaid Quality Initiatives

The CMS and State Operations has the principle responsibility for developing and carrying out Medicaid and CHIP quality initiatives through working partnerships with the respective state's programs. The CMS describes five broad criteria for assessing the quality of Medicaid services for adults[108]:

1. Prevention and health promotion
2. Management of acute conditions

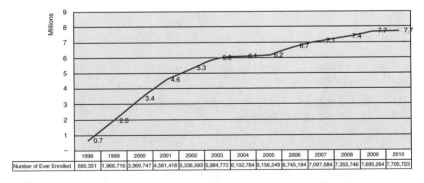

FIGURE 8-7 Number of Children Ever Enrolled in the Children's Health Insurance Program, 1998–2010.
Source: Children's Health Insurance Statistical Enrollment Data System (SEDS) 2/1/11.

3. Management of chronic conditions
4. Family experience of care
5. Availability of services

A Division of Quality, Evaluation, and Health Outcomes has focused on providing technical assistance to states in their quality improvement initiatives.[109] The ACA has mandated a "National Quality Strategy" that focuses on three broad goals to improve the delivery of health care services, improve patient health outcomes, and general U.S. population health by focusing on quality monitoring efforts.[110]

Prelude to Passage of the ACA

A 2007 Henry J. Kaiser Family Foundation's health tracking poll on 2008 presidential election issues indicated that health care was the top domestic issue, behind only the Iraq war in voter priority for candidates' attention.[111]

By the 2012 election, health care policy issues remained as one of the top voter concerns, as indicated in a recent Henry J. Kaiser Family Foundation voter tracking poll completed shortly before the 2012 election.[112] Voter concerns regarding Medicare and Medicaid and the ACA were eclipsed only by voter concerns about the state of the overall economy.[112]

In 2007, presidential candidate Barack Obama had campaigned with strong promises of swift, major health reform legislation to address the continuing issues of costs, quality, and access. Almost 1 year to the date of his inauguration as President, and after many months of acrimonious dialogue as the Senate and House constructed reform bills, in January 2010, the cover of Modern Health care headlined, "Requiem for Reform," following the election of a Republican Massachusetts senator to replace the late Democrat and health care reform proponent, Edward Kennedy.[113] Democrats lost their filibuster-proof Senate majority and, with it, hopes for passing a comprehensive reform bill dimmed. However, the improbable occurred and the ACA was signed into law on March 23, 2010.

Passage of the ACA represented an unprecedented combination of political will, fortitude, and compromise on the parts of health care reform proponents that had not been seen since the passage of Medicare and Medicaid 45 years earlier.

Health Care Financing Provisions of the ACA

Provisions of the ACA encompass various forms of financial implications such as new direct and indirect federal expenses related to health coverage expansions and other initiatives. The ACA also includes mechanisms to generate new federal revenues through penalties, fees, and excise taxes levied on firms and individuals that are intended to help offset ACA expenses. In addition, the ACA provides funding for experimentation with new reimbursement approaches for hospitals and health providers with longer-term goals of reducing costs and improving quality. Recognizing the significance of Medicare cost growth in the long-term fiscal viability of the program, the ACA required the establishment of an Independent Payment Advisory Board (IPAB) with the authority to curb Medicare spending if growth exceeds preset targets.

The review of the ACA financial implications that follows is not comprehensive, but rather intended to address some of the most significant ACA provisions. Cost and revenue projections are in a continuous state of refinement as the ACA is implemented. For more information and current details, readers are encouraged to consult references at the conclusion of the chapter and periodic updates provided by the CBO, the Congressional Research Service, and federal agencies participating in the implementation process.

Individual Mandate and Insurance Expansion

Beginning in 2014, the ACA requires most Americans to carry health insurance coverage or pay a penalty. This requirement is known as the "individual mandate." Groups exempt from the penalty include individuals for whom the cost of insurance would exceed 8% of their income, people with incomes below the federal requirement for tax filing, religiously exempt individuals, undocumented immigrants, incarcerated individuals, and members of Indian tribes. Coverage may include employer-provided insurance, Medicaid, or personally purchased policies.

Medicaid Expansion

Under the ACA, states may expand Medicaid eligibility levels for non-elderly individuals, including low-income parents and childless adults with incomes up to 133% of the federal poverty line (FPL).[114] The federal government provides states with expansion funding at 100% for 2014 through 2016, 95% for 2017, 94% for 2018, 93% for 2019, and 90% for 2020 and subsequent years.[115] As a result of the expansion, the number of Medicaid enrollees is expected to increase by 14.9 million in 2014 and by 25.9 million by 2019.[114] As initially legislated by the ACA, states' participation in the expansion was mandatory. However, a 2012 U.S. Supreme Court decision made states' participation optional. By February 2013, 22 states and the District of Columbia had agreed to participate, 13 states rejected participation, and 15 states remained undecided.[116]

Health Insurance Exchanges

The ACA requires states to establish health benefit exchanges (American Health Benefit Exchanges) and create separate exchanges for small employers (Small Business Health Options Program) with up to 100 employees. The exchanges intend to create a competitive health insurance market by providing web-based, easily understandable, comparative information to consumers on plan choices and to standardize rules regarding health plan offers and pricing.[117] To participate in exchanges, health plans must meet federal requirements for minimum coverage known as "essential health benefits." Essential health benefits that were developed with input from the Institute of Medicine, the DHHS, the Department of Labor, and citizens include services in the following 10 categories[118]:

1. Ambulatory patient services
2. Emergency services
3. Hospitalization
4. Maternity and newborn care
5. Mental health and substance use disorder services, including behavioral health treatment
6. Prescription drugs
7. Rehabilitative and habilitative services and devices
8. Laboratory services
9. Preventive and wellness services and chronic disease management
10. Pediatric services, including oral and vision care

Recognizing variations across states in the availability of services in the required categories, the DHHS includes considerable flexibility in the implementing procedures.[119]

Federal support is available to states for establishment of exchanges until 2015, after which they are expected to be financially self-sustaining. The exchanges must be governmental or not-for-profit entities.[117,120] For individuals, eligibility to purchase insurance through an exchange is open to American citizens and legal immigrants whose employers do not provide health insurance, and those for whom the cost of employer-sponsored coverage is prohibitive. Consumers are guaranteed acceptance into their choice of plans. To help make coverage affordable, the federal government provides varying levels of premium and cost-sharing subsidies based on personal income ranging between 100% and 400% of the FPL. Subsidies are provided in the forms of advance and refundable tax credits.[117]

Penalties, Taxes, and Fees

Under the ACA, employers are not required to offer health insurance. However, employers with more than 50 employees will be assessed a fee of $2,000 per full-time employee (in excess of 30 employees) if they do not offer coverage and if they have at least one employee who receives a premium credit through a health insurance exchange. Employers with 50 or more employees that do offer coverage but have at least one employee who receives a premium credit through a health insurance exchange are required to pay the lesser of $3,000 for each employee who receives a premium credit or $2,000 for each full-time employee (in excess of 30 employees). Large employers that offer coverage will be required to automatically enroll employees into the employer's lowest cost premium plan if the employee does not enroll in employer coverage or does not opt out of coverage.[121]

Table 8-2 lists other new taxes and fees imposed on firms by the ACA beginning in 2010 with projections of their contribution of $146.9 billion to federal revenues through 2019.[122]

In addition to the new revenues derived from firms, ACA provisions affecting individuals that include requirements such as increased Medicare payroll taxes, modifications to tax-advantaged HSAs and flexible spending accounts, and an increase in the floor for tax deductions of itemized medical expenses are projected to add $248.8 billion in federal revenues by 2019 resulting in combined new projected revenues by 2019 of $391.7 billion.[122] The CBO's projection of the total costs of the ACA insurance expansion initiatives is just under $1.1 trillion.[123]

Table 8-2 Health-Related Revenue Projections for ACA Provisions Affecting Firms

Provisions Affecting Firms		
Excise Taxes and Fees	Effective Date, Taxable Years Beginning	Increase in Revenues (FY 2010–FY 2019)
40% Excise Tax on High-Cost Plans	2018	$32.0 billion
Impose Annual Fee on Health Insurance Providers	2014	$60.1 billion
Annual Fee on Manufacturers and Importers of Branded Drugs	2011	$27.0 billion
Annual Fee/Excise Tax on Manufacturers and Importers of Certain Medical Devices	2013	$20.0 billion
10% Excise Tax on Indoor Tanning Services	July 1, 2010	$2.7 billion
Limitation on Employer Deductions		
Eliminate Deductions for Expenses Allocable to Medicare Part D subsidy	2013	$4.5 billion
Limit Deduction for Compensation to $500,000 for Executives of Health Insurance Companies	2013	$0.6 billion

Source: Adapted from Joint Committee on Taxation, March 20, 2010, JCX-17-10. Available from http://www.coburn.senate.gov/public//index.cfm?a=Files.Serve&File_id=9e7f8345-d811-4ccc-87c1-52d6b477d193.

Reimbursement Experimentation

Pilot programs newly authorized or expanded by the ACA and conducted over several years following the law's implementation will experiment with approaches to payment reforms with the dual goals of slowing the rate of spending growth and improving the quality of patient care. Learning from the outcomes of these programs is intended to provide valuable information for continuing and refining future initiatives targeted at the same goals. Examples of four far-reaching pilot programs are described briefly below. Readers are encouraged to consult the references at the end of this chapter for more details and for links to information on other reimbursement-oriented pilot programs enacted by the ACA.

Accountable Care Organizations

The ACA adopted the accountable care organization (ACO) model, consisting of groups of providers and suppliers of health care, health-related services, and others involved in caring for Medicare patients to voluntarily work together to coordinate care for the patients they serve under the original

Medicare (not Medicare Advantage managed care) program.[124] ACOs are intended to address the costly results of health care system fragmentation by ensuring care coordination across multiple providers for the entire spectrum of needs so that all patients receive timely and appropriate care, avoiding unnecessary duplication of services, medical emergencies, and costly hospitalizations.[125] The ACA enables ACOs to share in savings to the federal government based on ACO performance in improving quality and reducing health care costs.[126] The basis for the shared savings incentive is an ACO's performance in reducing per capita Medicare expenditures below a benchmark determined by the CMS. The reimbursement structure for ACOs combines fee-for-service payments with shared savings and bonus payments linked with specific quality performance standards for which all providers in an ACO are accountable.[127] Although the subject of experimentation in the private sector since 1998, information on the impact of ACOs is limited with numerous questions remaining about effectiveness in reducing costs and improving the quality of care.[128]

Hospital Value-Based Purchasing Program

The CMS began implementing Value-Based Purchasing (VBP) Program pilot projects in 2003; this model has been replicated by private insurers, structured to provide incentives to discourage inappropriate, unnecessary, and costly care.[129] Now mandated by the ACA, the VBP program applies to over 3,000 acute care Medicare participating hospitals, enabling them to earn incentive payments based on clinical outcomes and patient satisfaction.[130] The program is funded by annual percentage reductions in the standard reimbursement that Medicare pays all hospitals.[131]

Bundled Payments for Care Improvement Initiative

The Bundled Payments for Care Improvement Initiative (BPCI) was developed by the CMS Center for Medicare & Medicaid Innovation (CMMI) that was created by the ACA. The BPCI recognizes that separate Medicare fee-for-service payments for individual services provided during a beneficiary's single illness often result in fragmented care with minimal coordination across providers and settings and results in rewarding service quantity rather than quality. The BPCI is designed to test whether, as prior research has shown, bundled payments can align incentives for hospitals, post-acute care providers, physicians, and other health care personnel to work closely together across many settings to achieve improved patient outcomes at lower cost.[132]

Independent Payment Advisory Board

Even with major reductions in Medicare spending authorized by the ACA, projections of continued cost growth predict that Medicare will consume 5.7 % of the nation's GDP by 2035. Trustees of Medicare funds have assessed projected growth as unsustainable.[133] To address Medicare spending growth, the ACA created the IPAB, housed in the Executive Branch, with authority to curb rising Medicare spending if per beneficiary spending exceeds preset targets. The IPAB is constituted by 15 individuals appointed by the President and confirmed by the Senate. Its mission is to recommend policies to Congress to curb Medicare spending including suggestions to improve coordination of care, eliminate waste, encourage best practices, and prioritize primary care. The IPAB is specifically prohibited from recommending policies that ration care, raise taxes, increase Medicare premiums or cost-sharing, restrict benefits, or modify eligibility.[134] The need for the new IPAB recognized that historically, Congress has found it "extremely challenging to enact policies that curtail the growth of Medicare spending."[135] The IPAB was established in part to offset political influences of interest groups by giving authority to outside experts, rather than congressional members in recommending cost savings.[136] As described in the ACA, the IPAB recommendations will be made in the form of proposed legislation, with deadlines for congressional action. The ACA provides that in the absence of congressional action on IPAB proposed legislation, the Secretary of Health and Human Services is empowered to implement IPAB proposals that cannot be reversed by the Executive Branch or the courts.[135] Effective in 2014, the IPAB is required "to produce an annual public report with standardized information on system-wide health care costs, access to care, utilization of services, and quality of care, including comparisons by region, types of services, and types of providers for Medicare and private payers."[136] Beginning in 2015 and every other year thereafter, the ACA requires the IPAB to submit recommendations to the President and Congress to slow overall growth in national health care expenditures.[136]

Continuing Challenges

U.S. health care spending and implementation of the ACA will continue to confront policy makers with a daunting array of issues, demanding creativity and courage to enact meaningful changes. Paying for required changes may be the least of all challenges. Rather, breaking loose from old philosophies, value systems, and the politics that have brought U.S. health care enterprise to its present paradoxical state of superior technology entrenched in a profit-driven reward system with little regard for the value of services, will pose overarching challenges. As journalist Steven Brill stated in a searing 2013 review of U.S. health care delivery system costs, "Bitter Pill: Why Medical Bills are Killing Us," "When we debate health care policy, we seem to jump right to the issue of who should pay the bills, blowing past what should be the first question: Why exactly are the bills so high?"[137] As noted in this chapter, U.S. health care costs compared with other developed nations are unjustifiable, given comparison of this country's health status with other developed nations who spend far less. In the immediate and post-ACA reform era, Mr. Brill's query may be the quintessential issue for U.S. citizens and their policy makers. The ACA holds out much hope for achieving meaningful change that will improve U.S. citizens' health status, but only if system changes succeed in replacing the existing volume-driven system with one driven by values that have consumer health outcomes as the primary focus.

Key Terms for Review

Accountable Care Organization (ACO)
Balanced Budget Act of 1997 (BBA)
Bundled Payment for Care Initiatives (BPCI)
Capitation
Community-rated Insurance
Consumer-Driven Health Plan (CDHP)
Diagnosis-Related Groups (DRGs)
Disease Management Programs
Emergency Medical Treatment and Labor Act (EMTALA)
Experience-Rated Insurance
Financial Risk Sharing
Health Insurance Exchange
Health Insurance Portability and Accountability Act of 1996 (HIPAA)

Healthcare Effectiveness Data and Information Set (HEDIS)
HMO Act of 1973
Indemnity Insurance
Independent Payment Advisory Board (IPAB)
Individual Mandate
Managed Care Backlash
Medicaid
Medicare
National Committee on Quality Assurance (NCQA)
Preferred Provider Organizations
Self-Funded Health Insurance
Value-Based Purchasing

References

1. Congressional Budget Office. Long-term outlook for health care spending: overview of the U.S. health care system. November, 2007. Available from http://www.cbo.gov/sites/default/files/cbofiles/ftpdocs/87xx/doc8758/11-13-lt-health.pdf. Accessed January 25, 2013.

2. Fronstin P. Employee Benefit Research Institute Issue Brief No. 370. Employment-based health benefits: trends in access and coverage 1997–2010. April 2012. Available from http://www.ebri.org/pdf/briefspdf/EBRI_IB_04-2012_No370_HI-Trends.pdf. Accessed January 25, 2013.

3. Aizenman NC. Number of uninsured Americans drops by 1.3 million, census report shows. *The Washington Post.* September 12, 2012. Available from http://articles.washingtonpost.com/2012-09-12/national/35494577_1_young-adults-number-of-uninsured-americans-employer-sponsored-coverage. Accessed January 23, 2013.

4. U.S. Department of Health and Human Services, Assistant Secretary for Planning and Evaluation, Todd SR, Sommers BD. Overview of the uninsured in the United States: a summary of the 2012 current population survey report. September 12, 2012. Available from http://aspe.hhs.gov/health/reports/2012/uninsuredintheus/ib.shtml. Accessed January 26, 2013.

5. U.S. Department of Health and Human Services, Centers for Medicare & Medicaid Services. National health expenditures tables, 2011. Available from http://www.cms.gov/Research-Statistics-Data-and-Systems/Statistics-Trends-and-Reports/NationalHealthExpendData/downloads/tables.pdf. Accessed January 26, 2013.

6. The Henry J. Kaiser Family Foundation. *Health care Costs: A Primer, Key Information on Health care Costs and their Impact.* May 2012. Available from http://www.kff.org/insurance/upload/7670-03.pdf. Accessed January 26, 2013.

7. U.S. Department of Health and Human Services, Centers for Medicare & Medicaid Services. NHE Fact sheet. 2011. Available from http://www.cms.gov/Research-Statistics-Data-and-Systems/Statistics-Trends-and-Reports/NationalHealthExpendData/NHE-Fact-Sheet.html. Accessed January 26, 2013.

8. U.S. Department of Health and Human Services, Centers for Medicare & Medicaid Services. Office of the Actuary. National Statistics Group. The nation's health dollar, calendar year 2011: where it came from; where it went. Available from http://www.cms.gov/Research-Statistics-Data-and-Systems/Statistics-Trends-and-Reports/NationalHealthExpendData/Downloads/PieChartSourcesExpenditures2011.pdf. Accessed January 26, 2013.

9. Altman S, Tompkins C, Eliat E, et al. Escalating health care spending: is it desirable or inevitable? *Health Affairs.* January-June 2003;Suppl Web Exclusives:W3-1–14. Available from http://content.healthaffairs.org/content/suppl/2003/12/04/hlthaff.w3.1v1.DC1. Accessed January 26, 2013.

10. Anderson GF, Frogner BK. Health spending in OECD countries: obtaining value per dollar. *Health Affairs.* November 2008;27:1718–1727. Available from http://content.healthaffairs.org/content/27/6/1718.full .pdf+html?sid=c36a93f4-1fd6-4a8d-b8ec-fd02705138f9. Accessed January 26, 2013.

11. Anderson GF, Reinhardt UE, Hussey PS, et al. It's the prices, stupid: why the United States is so different from other countries. *Health Affairs.* 2003;22:89–105. Available from http://content.healthaffairs.org/content/22/3/89.full.pdf. Accessed January 26, 2013.

12. Milstein A, Gilbertson E. American medical home runs. *Health Affairs.* 2009;28:1317–1326. Available from http://content.healthaffairs.org/content/28/5/1317.full.pdf+html?sid=85d64e7c-6451-4b89-bbbb-dc5e2d744c0c. Accessed January 26, 2013.

13. Orszag PR, Congressional Budget Office. *Opportunities to Increase Efficiency in Health care.* June 2008. Available from http://www.cbo.gov/sites/default/files/cbofiles/ftpdocs/93xx/doc9384/06-16-healthsummit.pdf. Accessed January 26, 2013.

14. Morris L. Combating fraud in health care: an essential component of any cost containment strategy. *Health Affairs.* 2009;28:1351–1356. Available from http://content.healthaffairs.org/content/28/5/1351.full .pdf+html?sid=fe75a902-60fe-4869-a43e-460f8f75ffd6. Accessed January 26, 2013.

15. Torres C. Health spending will climb to nearly one-fifth of GDP. *Kaiser Health News.* June 12, 2012. Available from http://capsules.kaiserhealthnews .org/index.php/2012/06/report-health-spending-will-climb-to-nearly-one-fifth-of-gdp/. Accessed January 26, 2013.

16. Chernew ME, Jacobson PD, Hofer TP, et al. Barriers to constraining health care cost growth. *Health Affairs.* 2004;23:122–128. Available from http://content.healthaffairs.org/content/23/6/122.full.pdf+html?sid=c05493a7-22d5-4df7-8759-c049fadb089d. Accessed January 26, 2013.

17. Levit K, Smith C, Cowan C, et al. Inflation spurs health spending in 2000. *Health Affairs.* 2002;21:179. Available from http://content.healthaffairs .org/content/21/1/172.full.pdf+html?sid=49a8c0c7-3f71-4cb7-acda-8229eb6a1e42. Accessed January 26, 2013.

18. Hartman M, Martin A, Nuccio O, et al. Health spending growth at a historic low in 2008. *Health Affairs.* 2010;29:147–152. Available from http://content.healthaffairs.org/content/29/1/147.full.pdf+html?sid=d19da8dc-e4d6-4ddd-9c9b-64e74a539a76. Accessed January 26, 2013.

19. U.S. Department of Health and Human Services, Administration on Aging. *Profile of older Americans.* 2011. Available from http://www.aoa.gov/aoaroot/aging_statistics/Profile/2011/docs/2011profile.pdf. Accessed January 27, 2013.

20. U.S. Department of Health and Human Services, Administration on Aging. Population 65 and over by age: 1900–2050. August 14, 2008. Available from

http://www.aoa.gov/AoARoot/Aging_Statistics/future_growth/docs/By_Age_65_and_over.xls. Accessed January 27, 2013.

21. Coile RC Jr, Trusko BE. Healthcare 2020: challenges of the millennium. *Health care Management Technology*. 1999;20:37.

22. Centers for Disease Control and Prevention. 2010 National hospital discharge survey, number and rate of hospital discharges, average length of stay and days of care, number and rate of discharges by sex and age, 2010. July 2010. Available from http://www.cdc.gov/nchs/data/nhds/2average/2010ave2_ratesexage.pdf. Accessed January 27, 2013.

23. Smith S, Heffler S, Freeland M, et al. The next decade of health care spending: a new outlook. *Health Affairs*. 1999;18:89–90. Available from http://content.healthaffairs.org/content/18/4/86.full.pdf+html?sid=54b3934e-b45b-450c-93cc-b240b400f8a6. Accessed January 27, 2013.

24. Hing E, Schappert SM, Centers for Disease Control and Prevention. National Center for Health Statistics No. 105. September 2012. Generalist and specialty physicians; supply and access, 2009–2010. Available from http://www.cdc.gov/nchs/data/databriefs/db105.htm. Accessed January 27, 2013.

25. DeNavas-Walt C, Proctor BD, Smith JC. *U.S. Census Current Population Reports, P60–236, Income, Poverty, and Health Insurance Coverage in the United States: 2008*. Washington, DC: U.S. Government Printing Office; 2009. Available from http://www.census.gov/prod/2009pubs/p60-236.pdf. Accessed January 27, 2013.

26. American College of Physicians and American Society of Internal Medicine. The cost of the lack of health insurance. 2004. Available from http://www.acponline.org/advocacy/where_we_stand/access/cost.pdf. Accessed January 27, 2013.

27. U.S. Department of Labor, Bureau of Labor Statistics. Monthly labor review, January 2012. Industry employment and outlook projections to 2020. Available from http://www.bls.gov/opub/mlr/2012/01/art4full.pdf. Accessed January 27, 2013.

28. Kongstvedt PR. *Essentials of Managed Health care*, 6th ed. Sudbury, MA: Jones and Bartlett; 2012.

29. Wilson F, Neuhauser D. *Health Services in the United States*, 2nd ed. Cambridge, MA: Ballinger; 1982.

30. Stevens R. *In Sickness and in Wealth: American Hospitals in the Twentieth Century*. New York, NY: Basic Books; 1989.

31. Conover CJ, Hall MA, Ostermann J. The impact of Blue Cross conversions on health spending and the uninsured. *Health Affairs*. 2005;24:473–482. Available from ttp://content.healthaffairs.org/content/24/2/473.full.pdf+html?sid=8f0e08b0-df4c-41dc-a44e-49b9bee6c8f3. Accessed January 27, 2013.

32. Thomasson M. Economic History Association. Health insurance in the United States. Available from http://eh.net/encyclopedia/article/thomasson.insurance.health.us. Accessed January 27, 2013.

33. Kongstvedt PR. *The Managed Health care Handbook*, 4th ed. Gaithersburg, MD: Aspen; 2000.
34. The Henry J. Kaiser Family Foundation and Health Research and Educational Trust. Employer health benefits 2012, summary of findings. 2013. Available from http://ehbs.kff.org/pdf/2012/8346.pdf. Accessed January 27, 2013.
35. Trespacz KL. Staff-model HMOs: don't blink or you'll miss them. *Managed Care Magazine*. July 1999. Available from http://www.managedcaremag.com/archives/9907/9907.staffmodel.html. January 27, 2013.
36. Blendon RJ, Brodie M, Benson JM, et al. Understanding the managed care backlash. *Health Affairs*. July1998;17:80. Available from http://content.healthaffairs.org/content/17/4/80.full.pdf+html?sid=d0c8ee29-8f23-4089-b481-3d60dc6039f3. Accessed January 27, 2013.
37. White House Backgrounder. President Clinton releases report documenting actions federal government is taking to implement a patients' bill of rights and urges voters to send back a Congress that shares his commitment to pass legislation to assure protections for all health plans. November 2, 1998. Available from http://archive.hhs.gov/news/press/1998pres/981102.html. Accessed January 27, 2013.
38. National Conference of State Legislatures. Managed care state laws and regulations including consumer and provider protections. September, 2011. Available from http://www.ncsl.org/issues-research/health/managed-care-state-laws.aspx. Accessed January 27, 2013.
39. Insurance Journal. September 17, 2012. More employers offering consumer-driven health plans: survey. Available at http://www.insurancejournal.com/news/national/2012/09/17/263225.htm. Accessed January 28, 2013.
40. Gabel JR, Pickreign JD, Witmore HH, et al. Behind the slow growth of employer-based consumer-driven health plans. *Center for Studying Health System Change*. December 2006. Available from http://www.hschange.com/CONTENT/900/. Accessed January 28, 2013.
41. Smith S, Heffler S, Freeland M, et al. The next decade of health spending: a new outlook. *Health Affairs*. 1999;18:4. Available from http://content.healthaffairs.org/content/18/4/86.citation. Accessed February 25, 2013.
42. Levit K, Cowan C, Lazenby H, et al. Health spending in 1998: signals of change. *Health Affairs*. 2000;19:131. Available from http://content.healthaffairs.org/content/19/1/124.full.pdf+html?sid=8ce595ad-4322-4533-9ad5-f329bde5be88. Accessed January 28, 2013.
43. Strunk BC, Ginsburg PB, Gabel JR. Tracking health care costs: growth accelerates again in 2001. *Health Affairs*. Available from http://content.healthaffairs.org/content/early/2002/09/25/hlthaff.w2.299.citation. Accessed February 25, 2013.
44. Chernew M, Cutler D, Keenan P, et al. University of Michigan, Economic Research Institute on the Uninsured. Increasing health insurance costs and

the decline in insurance coverage. March 2005. Available from http://www .rwjf-eriu.org/pdf/wp8.pdf. Accessed January 28, 2013.

45. MCOL. Current national managed care enrollment. 2011. Available from http://www.mcol.com/current_enrollment. Accessed January 28, 2013.

46. Miller RH, Luft HS. HMO plan performance update: analysis of the literature, 1997–2001. *Health Affairs*. 2002;21:81. Available from http://content .healthaffairs.org/content/21/4/63.full.pdf+html?sid=f4bb6878-6406-4fdd-9505-eecdbb709182. Accessed January 28, 2013.

47. Iglehart JK. The National Committee for Quality Assurance. *The New England Journal of Medicine*. 1996;335:995.

48. National Committee for Quality Assurance. NCQA 'Gold Standard' Accreditation Fact Sheet. NCQA_'Gold_Standard'_Accreditation_10. 20.12.pdf. 2012 Available from http://www.ncqa.org/Consumers/ AccreditingandRankingHealthPlans.aspx. Accessed January 28, 2013.

49. National Committee for Quality Assurance. Programs. December 19, 2012. Available from http://www.ncqa.org/Programs.aspx. Accessed January 28, 2013.

50. National Committee for Quality Assurance. NCQA Health Plan Accreditation brochure. Available from http://www.ncqa.org/Portals/0/ HPA%20Brochure%20Web.pdf. Accessed January 29, 2013.

51. Pawlson LG, O'Kane ME. Professionalism, regulation, and the market: impact on accountability for quality of care. *Health Affairs*. 2002;21:202. Available from http://content.healthaffairs.org/content/21/3/200.full.pdf+html?sid=b3acc50f-b4d6-4230-b4ca-5fcb7603784c. Accessed January 28, 2013.

52. Epstein M. The role of quality measurement in a competitive marketplace. In: Altman SH, Reinhardt UE, eds. *Strategic Choices for a Changing Health care System*. Chicago, IL: Health Administration Press; 1996:217.

53. National Committee for Quality Assurance. HEDIS compliance audit program. 2013. Available from http://www.ncqa.org/ HEDISQualityMeasurement/NCQASurveyorsVendorsAuditors/ HEDISComplianceAuditProgram/HEDISComplianceAuditProgram. aspx. Accessed January 29, 2013.

54. National Committee for Quality Assurance. NCQA Medicaid managed care toolkit, 2012 health plan accreditation standards. March 2012. Available from http://www.ncqa.org/Portals/0/Public%20Policy/2012_NCQA_ Medicaid_Managed_Care_Toolkit_Summary_-_March_2012_Final.pdf. Accessed January 29, 2013.

55. National Committee for Quality Assurance. The state of health care quality. 2012. Available from http://www.ncqa.org/Portals/0/State%20of%20Health%20 Care/2012/SOHC%20Report%20Web.pdf. Accessed January 29, 2013

56. Fireman B, Bartlett, J, Selby J. Can disease management reduce health care costs by improving quality? *Health Affairs*. 2004;23:63–64. Available from ttp:// content.healthaffairs.org/content/23/6/63.full.pdf+html?sid=6831112e-e269-4122-8fe7-1b6826f8e8d5. Accessed January 29, 2013.

57. Mays GP, Au M, Claxton G. Convergence and dissonance: evolution in private sector approaches to disease management and care coordination. *Health Affairs*. 2007;20:1683–1691. Available from http://content.healthaffairs.org/search?fulltext=convergence+and+dissonance&submit=yes&x=0&y=0. Accessed January 29, 2013.

58. Moran DW. Whence and whither health insurance? A revisionist history. *Health Affairs*. 2005;24:1415–1425. Available from http://content.healthaffairs.org/content/24/6/1415.full.pdf+html?sid=31828a32-25bc-4906-b996-9c2f95ab59c6. Accessed January 30, 2013.

59. Health Insurance On-line. Information on self-funded insurance plans. Available from http://www.online-health-insurance.com/health-insurance-resources/part2/page94.php. http://www.online-health-insurance.com/health-insurance-resources/part2/page94.php? http://www.online-health-insurance.com/health-insurance-resources/part2/page94.php? iframe=true&width=100%&height=100%. Accessed January 30, 2013.

60. Butler PA. ERISA update: the Supreme Court Texas decision and other recent developments National.Academy for State Health Policy. State Coverage Initiatives Issue Brief. 2004. Available from http://www.statecoverage.org/node/180. Accessed January 30, 2013.

61. U.S. Congressional Budget Office. The long-term outlook for health care spending: Medicare and Medicaid: an overview. 2007. Available from http://www.cbo.gov/publication/41646. Accessed January 30, 2013.

62. The Henry J. Kaiser Family Foundation. Medicare at a glance, fact sheet 2012. November 2012. Available from http://www.kff.org/medicare/upload/1066-15.pdf. Accessed January 30, 2013.

63. Good T. History of Medicare: beginning to now. *Medicare Pathways*. January 27, 2013. Available from http://www.medicarepathways.com/2013/01/history-of-medicare-beginning-to-now/. Accessed January 30, 2013.

64. The Henry J. Kaiser Family Foundation. Medicare Advantage fact sheet. (#2052-16). December 2012. Available from http://www.kff.org/medicare/upload/2052-16.pdf. Accessed January 30, 2013.

65. The Henry J. Kaiser Family Foundation. The Medicare prescription drug benefit, updated fact sheet. (#7044-13). November 2012. Available from http://www.kff.org/medicare/upload/7044-13.pdf. Accessed January 30, 2013.

66. American Association of Retired Persons. Medicare made clear. 2012. Available from http://www.aarphealthcare.com/content/dam/aarphealthcare/docs/medicare-made-clear.pdf. Accessed January 30, 2013.

67. Arrowood WD. The urban planner in health planning: a report by the American Society of Planning Officials. *The Social Service Review*. 1970;44:491–492. Available from http://www.jstor.org/stable/30021773. Accessed January 30, 2013.

68. National Conference of State Legislatures. Certificate of need: state health laws and programs. March, 2012. Available from http://www.ncsl.org/issues-research/health/con-certificate-of-need-state-laws.aspx. Accessed January 30, 2013.

69. Congressional Budget Office. Testimony on the professional standards review organizations program. June 27, 1979 Available from http://www .cbo.gov/sites/default/files/cbofiles/ftpdocs/52xx/doc5226/doc23.pdf. Accessed January 30, 2013.

70. Compilation of the Social Security Laws: Social Security Online. April 26, 2013. Functions of quality improvement organizations. Available from http://www.ssa.gov/OP_Home/ssact/title11/1154.htm. Accessed April 29, 2013.

71. Sloan FA, Vraciu RA. Investor-owned and not-for-profit hospitals: addressing some issues. *Health Affairs.* 1983;2:26. Available from http://content .healthaffairs.org/content/2/1/25.full.pdf+html?sid=6b6d6a75-923a-4a5a-b459-9af281801faa. Accessed January 31, 2013.

72. 3M Health Information Group. The history of the development of the diagnosis-related groups (DRGs). In: *All Patient Refined Diagnosis Related Groups (APR-DRGs) Version 20.0,* 3M Health Information Group, 2003. Available from http://www.hcup-us.ahrq.gov/db/nation/nis/APR-DRG sV20MethodologyOverviewandBibliography.pdf. Accessed February 1, 2013.

73. Mistichelli J. National Reference Center for Bioethics Literature. Diagnosis-related groups and the prospective payment system: forecasting social implications. 1984 Available from http://bioethics.georgetown.edu/publications/ scopenotes/sn4.pdf. Accessed January 30, 2013.

74. Russell LB, Manning CL. The effect of prospective payment on Medicare expenditures. *The New England Journal of Medicine.* 1989;320:439. Available from http://www.nejm.org/doi/pdf/10.1056/NEJM198902163200706. Accessed February 1, 2013.

75. Thorpe KE. Health care cost containment: results and lessons from the past 20 years. In: Shortell SM, Reinhardt UE, eds. *Improving Health Policy and Management.* Ann Arbor, MI: Health Administration Press; 1992:246.

76. American Academy of Emergency Physicians. EMTALA. March 26, 2012. Available from http://www.aaem.org/em-resources/regulatory-issues/emtala. Accessed February 25, 2013.

77. Kovner A. *Jonas' Health care Delivery in the United States,* 5th ed. New York, NY: Springer; 1995.

78. American Medical Association. The resource-based relative value scale: overview of the RBRVS. 2013. Available from http://www.ama-assn.org/ama/pub/ physician-resources/solutions-managing-your-practice/coding-billing-insurance/medicare/the-resource-based-relative-value-scale/overview-of-rbrvs .page. Accessed February1, 2013.

79. Board of Trustees, Federal Hospital Insurance Trust Fund. 1995 *Annual Report of the Board of Trustees of the Hospital Insurance Trust Fund.* Washington, DC: U.S. Government Printing Office; 1995.

80. Reischauer RD. Medicare: beyond 2002, preparing for the baby-boomers. *Brookings Review.* 1997;15:24.

81. U.S. Department of Labor. The health insurance portability and accountability act (HIPPA), fact sheet. December 2004. Available from http://www.dol .gov/ebsa/newsroom/fshipaa.html. Accessed February 1, 2013.

82. The Balanced Budget Act of 1997, Public Law 105-33. *Medicare and Medicaid Changes*. Washington, DC: Deloitte & Touche LLP and Deloitte & Touche Consulting Group LLC; 1997:1.

83. Medicare Payment Advisory Commission. Report to the Congress: Medicare payment policy (March 2003), chapter 1, context for Medicare spending. Available from http://www.medpac.gov/publications%5Ccongressional_ reports%5CMar03_Ch1.pdf. Accessed February 1,2013.

84. National Bipartisan Commission on the Future of Medicare Task Forces. Available from http://rs9.loc.gov/medicare/task.html. Accessed February 1, 2013.

85. U.S. Department of Health and Human Services. Balanced Budget Refinement Act of 1999: Highlights, November 18, 1999. Available from http://archive.hhs.gov/news/press/1999pres/19991118b.html. Accessed February 1, 2013.

86. The Henry J. Kaiser Family Foundation. Fact sheet: Medicare, Medicare + Choice. April 2003. Available from http://www.kff.org/medicare/upload/ Medicare-Choice-Fact-Sheet-Fact-Sheet.pdf. Accessed February 1, 2013.

87. Ross MN. Paying Medicare + Choice plans: the view from MedPAC. *Health Affairs*. Available from http://content.healthaffairs.org/content/ early/2001/11/28/hlthaff.w1.90.full.pdf+html?sid=89df9e35-d945-4d02- bcd3-2f62274be415. Accessed February 1, 2013.

88. Centers for Medicare & Medicaid Services. Quality initiatives— general information. April 3, 2013. Available from http://www.cms. gov/Medicare/Quality-Initiatives-Patient-Assessment-Instruments/ QualityInitiativesGenInfo/index.html?redirect=/qualityinitiativesgeninfo/. Accessed February 1, 2013.

89. Leavitt MC. Report to congress: improving the Medicare quality improve- ment organization program—response to the Institute of Medicine study. Available from http://www.cms.gov/Medicare/Quality-Initiatives-Patient- Assessment-Instruments/QualityImprovementOrgs/downloads/QIO_ improvement_RTC_fnl.pdf. Accessed February 25, 2013.

90. Werner R, Kolstad JT, Stuart EA, et al. The effect of pay-for-performance in hospitals: lessons for quality improvement. *Health Affairs*. 2011;30:690– 696. Available from http://content.healthaffairs.org/content/30/4/690.full .html. Accessed February 26, 2013.

91. U.S. Department of Health and Human Services, Centers for Medicare & Medicaid Services. *Hospital Compare*. Available from http://www.medicare .gov/hospitalcompare/. Accessed February 1, 2013.

92. HCAHPS on line. Hospital Consumer Assessment of Healthcare Providers and Systems. HCAHPS fact sheet. 2010. Available from http://www.hcahp- sonline.org/files/HCAHPS%20Fact%20Sheet%202010.pdf. Accessed February 1, 2013.

93. Pear R. Medicare won't cover hospital errors. *New York Times*. August 19, 2007. Available from http://www.nytimes.com/2007/08/19/washington/19hospital.html?pagewanted=all&_r=0. Accessed February 1, 2013.

94. U.S. Department of Health and Human Services, Centers for Medicare and Medicaid Services. Letter to State Medicaid Directors. Available from http://downloads.cms.gov/cmsgov/archived-downloads/SMDL/downloads/SMD073108.pdf. Accessed February 26, 2013.

95. U.S. Department of Health and Human Services. Centers for Medicare and Medicaid Services. Proposals for improving quality of care during inpatient stays in acute care hospitals in the fiscal year 2011 notice of proposed rulemaking. April 19, 2010. Available from http://www.cms.gov/Medicare/Medicare-Fee-for-Service-Payment/AcuteInpatientPPS/downloads/FSQ09_IPLTCH11_NPRM041910.pdf. Accessed February 1, 2013.

96. U.S. Department of Health and Human Services. Centers for Medicare and Medicaid Services. Hospital-acquired conditions (HAC) in acute patient prospective payment system (IPPS) hospitals. October, 2012. Available from http://www.cms.gov/Medicare/Medicare-Fee-for-Service-Payment/HospitalAcqCond/downloads/hacfactsheet.pdf. Accessed February 3, 2013.

97. Henry J. Kaiser Family Foundation. Medicaid today preparing for tomorrow, a look at state Medicaid spending, enrollment and policy trends for results from a 50-state Medicaid budget survey for state fiscal years 2012 and 2013(# 8380). October 2012. Available from http://www.kff.org/medicaid/upload/8380.pdf. Accessed February 2, 2013.

98. Almanac of Policy Issues. Medicaid: An Overview. September 2000. Available from http://www.policyalmanac.org/health/archive/hhs_medicaid.shtml. Accessed February 2, 2013.

99. Koch AL. Financing health care services. In: Williams SJ, Torrens PK, eds. *Introduction to Health care Services*, 4th ed. Albany, NY: Delmar; 1993:309.

100. The Henry J. Kaiser Family Foundation. Medicaid managed care: key data, trends and issues (#8046). February 2012. Available from http://www.kff.org/medicaid/upload/8046-02.pdf. Accessed February 2, 2013.

101. The Henry J. Kaiser Family Foundation. The crunch continues: Medicaid spending, coverage and policy in the midst of a recession, results from a 50-state Medicaid budget survey for state fiscal years 2009 and 2010, (#7985). Available from http://www.kff.org/medicaid/upload/7985_ES.pdf. Accessed January 30, 2013.

102. Galewitz.P. Medicaid spending growth drops as enrollment slows. *Kaiser Health News*. October 25, 2012. Available from http://www.kaiserhealthnews.org/stories/2012/october/25/state-medicaid-spending-study.aspx. Accessed January 30, 2013.

103. American Medical Association. What is SCHIP? September, 2009. Available from http://www.ama-assn.org/resources/doc/rfs/schip.pdf. Accessed February 2, 2013.

104. Shi L, Singh DA. *Delivering Health care in America: A Systems Approach.* Burlington, MA: Jones & Bartlett Learning; 2012:222–223.

105. Centers for Medicare and Medicaid FY 2011 Annual Enrollment Report. February 10, 2012. Available from http://www.medicaid. gov/Medicaid-CHIP-Program-Information/By-Topics/Childrens-Health-Insurance-Program-CHIP/Downloads/Enrollment-Reports/ FY2011StateCHIPTotalTableFinal.pdf. Accessed February 1, 2013.

106. Centers for Medicare and Medicaid. CHIP enrollment trends. February 1. 2011. Available from http://www.medicaid.gov/Medicaid-CHIP-Program-Information/By-Topics/Childrens-Health-Insurance-Program-CHIP/ Downloads/CHIPEverEnrolledYearGraph.pdf. Accessed February 1, 2013.

107. U.S. Department of Health and Human Services. ASPE. Overview of the uninsured in the United States: a summary of the 2011 current population survey. September 2011. Available from http://aspe.hhs.gov/health/ reports/2011/cpshealthins2011/ib.shtml. Accessed February 2, 2013.

108. Federal Register. Medicaid program: initial core set of health quality measures for Medicaid-eligible adults. December 30, 2010. Available from https://www.federalregister.gov/articles/2010/12/30/2010-32978/medicaid-program-initial-core-set-of-health-quality-measures-for-medicaid-eligible-adults. Accessed February 26, 2013.

109. U.S. Department of Health and Human Services, Centers for Medicare & Medicaid Services. Quality strategy tool kit for states. April 1, 2013. Available from http://www.medicaid.gov/Medicaid-CHIP-Program-Information/ By-Topics/Quality-of-Care/Downloads/Quality-Strategy-Toolkit-for-States. pdf. Accessed April 29, 2013.

110. U.S. Department of Health and Human Services, Centers for Medicare & Medicaid Services. Medicaid.gov. Quality of care. March, 2011. Available from http://www.medicaid.gov/Medicaid-CHIP-Program-Information/ By-Topics/Quality-of-Care/Quality-of-Care.html. Accessed February 2, 2013.

111. The Henry J. Kaiser Family Foundation. *Kaiser Health Tracking Poll: Election 2008* (#7709). October, 2007. Available from http://www.kff.org/kaiserpolls/ upload/7709.pdf. Accessed February 2, 2013.

112. The Henry J. Kaiser Family Foundation. *Kaiser Health Tracking Poll* (#8381), October 2012. Available from http://www.kff.org/kaiserpolls/upload/8381-F.pdf. Accessed February 2, 2013.

113. Lubell J, DoBias M. Looking for a pulse. *Modern Health care.* 2010;40: 6–7, 16.

114. U.S. General Accountability Office. States' implementation of the patient protection and affordable care act. August 1, 2012. Available from http:// www.gao.gov/products/gao-12-821. Accessed February 26, 2013.

115. The Henry J. Kaiser Family Foundation. Summary of new health reform law. April 15, 2011. Available from http://www.kff.org/healthreform/ upload/8061.pdf. Accessed January 11, 2013.

116. Modern Health care. Health care Business News. Christie agrees to expand Medicaid. February 26. 2013. Available from http://www.modernhealthcare .com/article/20130226/INFO/302269983/christie-agrees-to-expand-medicaid. Accessed February 28, 2013.

117. The Henry J. Kaiser Family Foundation. Explaining health care reform: questions about health insurance exchanges. April, 2010. Available from http://www.kff .org/healthreform/upload/7908-02.pdf. Accessed February 26, 2013.

118. U.S. Department of Health and Human Services. Essential health benefits: HHS informational bulletin. February 24, 2012. Available from http://www .healthcare.gov/news/factsheets/2011/12/essential-health-benefits 12162011a.html. Accessed February 27, 2013.

119. EQUAL Health Network. HHS essential health benefits bulletin. December 17, 2011. Available from http://www.equalhealth.info/index.php/2011/12/ hhs-essential-health-benefits-bulletin/. Accessed February 26, 2013.

120. Oxman, M. CMS approves 3 more health exchanges: many states opt out. December 18, 2012. *Wolters Kluwer Law and Health*. Available from http://health.wolterskluwerlb.com/2012/12/cms-approves-3-more-health-exchanges-many-states-opt-out/. Accessed February 18, 2013.

121. The Henry J. Kaiser Family Foundation. Summary of coverage provisions in the affordable care act. July 17, 2012. Available from http://www.kff.org/ healthreform/upload/8023-r.pdf. Accessed February 26, 2013.

122. Mulvey J. Health-related revenue provisions in the patient protection and affordable care act. April 8, 2010. *Congressional Research Service*. Available from http://www.coburn.senate.gov/public//index.cfm?a=Files.Serve&File_ id=9e7f8345-d811-4ccc-87c1-52d6b477d193. Accessed February 24, 2013.

123. Congressional Budget Office. Updated estimates for the insurance coverage provisions of the affordable care act. March, 2012. Available from http:// www.cbo.gov/sites/default/files/cbofiles/attachments/03-13-Coverage%20 Estimates.pdf. Accessed February 15, 2013.

124. Healthcare.gov. Accountable care organizations: improving care coordination for people with Medicare. March 12, 2012. Available from http://www .healthcare.gov/news/factsheets/2011/03/accountablecare03312011a.html. Accessed January 15, 2013.

125. Centers for Medicare & Medicaid Services. Accountable care organizations. Available from http://www.cms.gov/medicare/medicare-fee-for-service-payment/aco/index.html?redirect=/aco. Accessed April 29, 2013.

126. Accountable Care Facts. Top questions about ACOs: what are the real cost savings that can be anticipated by an ACO and how will they be achieved? 2011 Available from http://www.accountablecarefacts.org/topten/what-are-the-real-cost-savings-that-can-be-anticipated-by-an-ACO-and-how-will-they-be-achieved-1. Accessed January 10, 2013.

127. Baxley L, Borkan J, Campbell T, et al. In pursuit of a transformed health care system: from patient centered medical homes to accountable care organizations and beyond. *The Annals of Family Medicine*. 2011;9:467. Available

from http://www.annfammed.org/content/9/5/466.full. Accessed January 14, 2013.

128. American Hospital Association. Accountable care organizations: AHA research synthesis report. June, 2010. Available from http://www.aha.org/research/cor/content/ACO-Synthesis-Report.pdf. Accessed January 11, 2013.

129. Deloitte. Value-based purchasing: a strategic overview for health care industry stakeholders. 2011. Available from http://www.deloitte.com/assets/Dcom-UnitedStates/Local%20Assets/Documents/Health%20Reform%20Issues%20Briefs/US_CHS_ValueBasedPurchasing_031811.pdf. Accessed January 20, 2013.

130. The Henry J. Kaiser Family Foundation. Medicare discloses hospitals; bonuses, penalties based on quality. December 20, 2012. *Kaiser Health News*. Available from http://www.kaiserhealthnews.org/stories/2012/december/21/medicare-hospitals-value-based-purchasing.aspx?p=1. Accessed January 20, 2013.

131. U.S. Department of Health and Human Services. Centers for Medicare & Medicaid. Frequently asked questions: hospital value-based purchasing program. March 9, 2012. Available from http://www.cms.gov/Medicare/Quality-Initiatives-Patient-Assessment-Instruments/hospital-value-based-purchasing/Downloads/FY-2013-Program-Frequently-Asked-Questions-about-Hospital-VBP-3-9-12.pdf. Accessed January 14, 2013.

132. U.S. Department of Health and Human Services. Centers for Medicare & Medicaid. Center for Medicare & Medicaid Innovation. Bundled payments for care improvement (BPCI) initiative: general information. January 31, 2013. Available from http://innovation.cms.gov/initiatives/bundled-payments/index.html. Accessed January 19, 2013.

133. Social Security. Status of the social security and Medicare programs: a summary of the 2012 annual reports. November 9, 2012. Available from http://www.ssa.gov/oact/trsum/index.html. Accessed February 26, 2013.

134. The White House. The facts about the independent payment advisory board. Available from http://www.whitehouse.gov/blog/2011/04/20/facts-about-independent-payment-advisory-board. Accessed February 28, 2013.

135. Health Policy Brief. The independent payment advisory board. April 5. 2012. *Health Affairs*. Available from http://www.healthaffairs.org/healthpolicybriefs/brief.php?brief_id=59. Accessed February 27, 2013.

136. The Henry J. Kaiser Family Foundation. Explaining health reform: Medicare and the new independent payment advisory board. May 2010. Available from http://www.kff.org/healthreform/upload/7961-02.pdf. Accessed February 26, 2013.

137. Brill S. Bitter pill: why medical bills are killing us. *Time*. March 4, 2013. Available from http://healthland.time.com/2013/02/20/bitter-pill-why-medical-bills-are-killing-us/. Accessed March 6, 2013.

CHAPTER 9

Long-Term Care

Long-term care needs are not confined only to older Americans, but the fastest growing proportion of the population is older Americans who are the major consumers of long-term care services. Advances in medical care have made a longer life span possible, with accompanying challenges presented by chronic disease and physical limitations. This chapter provides an overview of the major components of the diverse array of long-term care services presently available in institutional, community-based, and home-based settings to individuals in all age groups who require long-term care. This chapter also reviews components of the Patient Protection and Affordable Care Act that affect long-term care services.

Each individual life span, from birth to death, can be seen as a connected flow of events—a continuum. The unrelenting progression of time is the one constant that expresses the diverse range of life's possibilities. An infant may be born with a birth defect, a young adult may suffer a head injury from an automobile accident, or an older adult may have a stroke. Such unanticipated events as these have a profound long-term impact on an individual's capacity to develop or to maintain abilities for self-care and independence. These individuals may require very different kinds and intensities of personal care assistance, health care services, and/ or psychosocial and housing services over an extended segment of their life span.

The age, diagnosis, and ability to perform personal self-care and the sites of care delivery vary widely for recipients of long-term care.

Thus, long-term care requires diversified, yet coordinated, services and flexibility within the service system to respond to recipients' changing needs over time.

The ideal health care delivery system provides participants with comprehensive personal, social, and medical care services. This ideal delivery system requires mechanisms that continually guide and track individual clients over time through the array of services at all levels and intensities of care that they require.[1] Because it generates a continuous flow of high costs over an extended period, long-term care has a particular need to use what the American Hospital Association calls a seamless continuum of care[2] that promotes the highest quality of life but still responds to growing public concerns about cost-effectiveness.[3] The particular package of services provided to each person should be tailored to meet his or her needs. Service needs vary from assistance with personal care and basic needs for food and safe shelter, to rehabilitation when possible, and socialization opportunities. Additionally, the type and extent of physical disability and the intensity of services required determine the location of long-term care. For example, an older individual with paralysis after a stroke may be able to remain at home with services that dovetail with family caregivers in the home. Another with a similar disability may require nursing home placement because that environment best meets the particular requirements of the situation.

Configuring a package of services that promotes independence and maintains lifestyle quality as far as possible within personal, community, and national resources makes the variety of long-term care services complex and sometimes confusing. Concern about cost-effectiveness and the desire to accommodate personal and family desires, finances, and reimbursement eligibility result in the need for both the availability of an array of services and coordination of those services to meet individual needs in the most effective way.

Within the last 50 years, extensive changes in demographics and the types and availability of health care services have occurred in the United States. The economic ramifications of a rapidly increasing population of older Americans, advances in medicine that have made many heretofore unknown life-sustaining measures available for use by health care professionals, and an emphasis on preventive care and healthy lifestyle all have had an impact on the continued growth of the population who presently require or potentially will require long-term care services. Older adults represent the largest population group requiring long-term care services. Current estimates place the population 65 years of age and older at 40.4 million, 13.1% of the population, or about one in every eight Americans.[4] The number of persons aged 65 years or older is expected to grow to 19.3% of the population by 2030, totaling 72.1 million.[4] The population 85 years of age and older is expected to grow from 5.5 million in 2007 to 6.6 million by 2020 (Figures 9-1 and 9-2).[4,5]

Many will grow old alone because of smaller family size, single parenting, and divorce. The increasing economic need for family members to delay retirement and work outside the home also reduces the availability of family caregivers to participate in the informal family caregiving system.

Development of Long-Term Care Services

The colonists who emigrated from Europe to the New World brought with them many of the social values and institutional models of their native countries. One of these, the almshouse, was a place where people who were sick or disabled or older adults who lacked adequate family or financial support could be cared for in a communal setting. Charitable

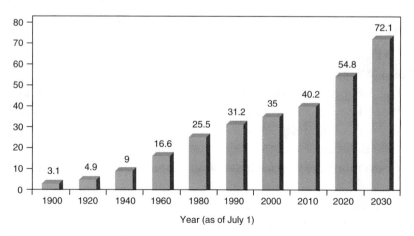

FIGURE 9-1 Projected Number (In Millions) of Persons 65 Years of Age or Older by 2030.
Source: U.S. Bureau of the Census.

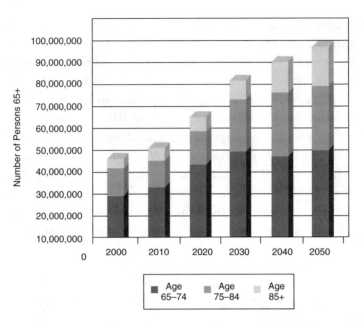

FIGURE 9-2 Projected Population, Age 65 Years and Older, 2000–2050.
Source: U.S. Bureau of the Census.

community members purchased private homes and converted them to almshouses that operated as communal residences. Municipal and county governments also created homes and "infirmaries" to care for impoverished older adults. These early models were the basis for "homes for the elderly," which existed until the economic upheavals of the Great Depression and the restructuring of the social welfare system after World War II.

The economic devastation experienced during the Great Depression of the 1930s affected the availability of long-term care services, especially homes for older adults, in several ways. Operating small private nursing homes became attractive to people in financial danger of losing their homes to mortgage foreclosure because taking in outsiders and providing care generated a new source of income. After the Great Depression, many local charitable agencies could no longer afford to provide care based on the almshouse tradition and the federal government became more involved in developing, overseeing, and paying for long-term care services as part of the social welfare reforms, such as the 1935 Social Security Act.[6] The Social Security Act provided financial assistance for particular categories of older Americans and people with disabilities. Additionally, the

Social Security Act established a form of old age and survivor's insurance that allowed workers and their employers to contribute to a fund that could supplement retirement income. This form of income security reduced the extent of indigence frequently found in the older population and increased the amount of secure income that older Americans could spend on services and care in later years. Government lending programs available to not-for-profit organizations beginning in the 1950s spurred the development of nursing homes in this sector; major growth in the proprietary sector did not occur until after the passage of Medicare and Medicaid legislation in 1965. The Centers for Medicare & Medicaid Services (CMS) reported the ownership basis of nursing homes in the *Nursing Home Data Compendium, 2010*. More than two-thirds are operated on a for-profit basis (Figure 9-3).[7]

Public and private homes for older adults often varied in the adequacy of care and the kinds of services provided. Nursing homes often were thought of as homes where minimal custodial care required to meet the basic needs of food, clothing, and shelter was provided, sometimes in very unhygienic and inhumane environments. Nursing homes often were places where older and frail adults, some of society's most vulnerable members, were taken to die and were not seen as residence options where they could receive needed care to prolong or enhance the quality of their lives. Physical care often was substandard, and emotional,

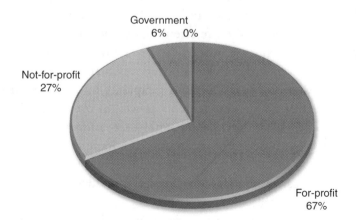

FIGURE 9-3 Percent Distribution of Nursing Homes by Type of Ownership.
Source: Data from CMS Nursing Home Data Compendium, 2010.

spiritual, and social needs were ignored. Because many frail, older people suffer from perceptual and cognitive disabilities in addition to physical disabilities their behavior in a group setting was often considered by nursing home staff to be a problem, and sometimes it led to the overuse of physical restraints or chemical restraints such as sedatives and mood-altering drugs.

The provision of home nursing care also has a long tradition in the United States as an alternative to institutional care provided in hospitals and nursing homes. Family members traditionally have provided home care to their own relatives. An interest in providing formal professional home care services began in the late 19th century as a social response to the unhealthy living conditions of immigrants residing in urban tenements. Such crowded and unsanitary conditions became a public health concern because they were frequently implicated in the spread of contagious diseases, such as tuberculosis, typhoid, and smallpox. Agencies such as the Visiting Nurses Association were established to provide trained nurses to tend to the sick in their homes. Their role quickly expanded to include preventive education regarding hygiene, nutrition, and coordination of social welfare intervention, especially in caring for society's most vulnerable populations of people with illnesses, low incomes, or disabilities.[8]

The passage of Medicare and Medicaid legislation in 1965 provided more stable sources of reimbursement than were previously only available through private pay and charitable funding and promoted the expansion of the long-term care industry. Medicare and Medicaid affected the long-term care industry in several overt ways. They established minimal standards of care and services that were required to be provided to Medicare and Medicaid recipients in order for providers of care to qualify for reimbursement, as well as provision of funding sources for older Americans, people with disabilities, and those lacking the means to pay for care. This funding simultaneously attracted both the scrupulous and the unscrupulous into the long-term care industry, as it quickly became apparent that being a provider of long-term care could be very profitable.

The long-term care industry came under increasing scrutiny in the early 1970s during congressional hearings on the nursing home industry, after several hundred exposés published in newspapers and additional publications such as the Nader Report and Mary Adelaide

Mendelson's book, *Tender Loving Greed*. The litany of nursing home corruption and abuses that were exposed during that period included the following[9,10]:

- Care that did not recognize the right to human dignity
- A lack of activities for residents
- Untrained and inadequate staff, including untrained administrators
- Unsanitary conditions
- Theft of residents' belongings
- Inadequate safety precautions (especially fire protection)
- Unauthorized and unnecessary use of restraints
- Both overmedication and undermedication of patients
- Failure to act in a timely manner on complaints and reprisals against those who complained
- Discrimination against patients who were members of minority groups
- A lack of dental and psychiatric care
- Negligence leading to injury and death
- Ineffective inspections and nonenforcement of laws that were meant to regulate the nursing home industry
- Reimbursement fraud

These congressional hearings and simultaneous public outcry resulted in more strict enforcement of Medicare and Medicaid guidelines and credentialing, increased establishment and enforcement of nursing home and home care licensure, more active accreditation procedures by the Joint Commission, laws related to the reporting of elder abuse, federal guidelines regulating the use of physical restraints, and establishment of ombudsman programs. All these measures have led to a much more regulated and responsive long-term care industry. More vocal and astute consumers also have provided economic and social mandates for high-quality standards of care—which had previously not been adhered to in any meaningful, organized quality assurance process—to be maintained in the long-term care industry overall. The Omnibus Budget Reconciliation Act of 1987 legislated new guidelines and restrictions on the use of physical and chemical restraints, established a nursing home resident bill of rights, mandated quality assurance standards, established a standard survey process, and mandated training and educational requirements for nursing home staff.[11]

Modes of Long-Term Care Service Delivery

Long-term care facilities (LTCFs) are institutions such as nursing homes and skilled nursing facilities (SNFs) that provide health care to people who are unable to manage independently in the community. This care may represent custodial or chronic care management or short-term rehabilitative services.[12] The site of care delivery categorizes long-term care programs. Institution-based services are those long-term care services provided within an institution such as a nursing home, hospital with inpatient extended care or rehabilitation facility, or inpatient hospice. Community-based services coordinate, manage, and deliver long-term care services such as adult day care programs, residential group homes, or care in the recipient's home.

Skilled Nursing Care

An SNF that is Medicare and Medicaid certified is defined as "a facility, or distinct part of one, primarily engaged in providing skilled nursing care and related services for people requiring medical or nursing care, or rehabilitation services."[13] Skilled nursing care is provided by or under the direct supervision of licensed nursing personnel, such as registered nurses and licensed practical nurses, and emphasis is on the provision of 24-hour nursing care and the availability of other types of services.

In 2010, the CMS reported that 3.3 million Americans resided in 15,884 SNFs.[7] One of seven or approximately 14% of SNF residents are under the age of 65 years and 86% are 65 years of age and older.[14] Because SNFs are only one portion of the array of types of long-term care facilities, and an LTCF may provide more than one level of service in the same facility, an exact number of residents in skilled nursing care have been much more difficult to ascertain. However, the forthcoming National Study of Long-Term Care Providers (NSLTCP) sponsored by the Centers for Disease Control and Prevention/National Center for Health Statistics (NCHS) is expected to provide an integrated initiative for data collection with regard to long-term care. NCHS plans to release their first overview report in late 2013, combining both survey and administrative data. The first NSLTCP report will include nursing homes, home health care agencies, hospices, residential care facilities, and adult day services centers. It is expected that this study will provide detailed statistical data about residents and participants receiving long-term care, agencies that provide those services, and descriptions of services provided.[15]

Annual national expenditures for care in a nursing home in 2008 alone totaled $138.4 billion. Medicare, Medicaid, and other public funds paid the largest portion (62%), and 38% was funded by out-of-pocket, private insurance, and other private funds (Table 9-1).[16] At $248 per day for a private room and $222 per day for a semiprivate room, the 2012 national average cost per resident had reached $90,520 per year for a private room and $81,030 per year for a semiprivate room.[17] The nursing home industry remains a dominant sector of the long-term care industry, with expenditures for care in a nursing home reported as double those for home care.[16]

Despite the burgeoning numbers of older Americans, national nursing home occupancy rates have declined from 84.5% occupancy in 1995 to 82% occupancy in 2010.[18] Many factors are believed to be contributing to the steady decline in occupancy rates. Today's older adults are healthier, delaying the need for skilled nursing services. The vastly increased availability of assisted-living facilities and the availability of other community-based assistance through day care and home care are also playing roles in delaying the need for skilled, institutional care.

Nursing home residents can be of any age, although most are adults in their later years. The typical nursing home resident is an older woman with cognitive impairment who was living alone on a limited income before nursing home placement. The decreased ability to function independently and a lack of family caregivers are additional factors associated with an increased risk of nursing home admission.

Table 9-1 Sources of Payment for Nursing Home Care[*], 2011

Source of Payment	Amounts in Billions[*]	Percentage
Total	149.3	100
Medicare	37.6	25.2
Medicaid	46.1	30.9
Other third party/other health insurance	13.3	8.9
Private (out of pocket, other private funds)	39.9	26.7
Private insurance	12.4	8.3

Note: [*]Care in nursing home care facilities and in CCRCs. Numbers may not add to totals due to rounding.

Source: Centers for Medicare and Medicaid Services.

Typical staffing in SNFs includes a physician medical director, a nursing home administrator, a director of nursing, at least one registered nurse on the day and evening shifts, and either a registered nurse or a licensed practical nurse on the night shift. Certified nursing assistants provide direct custodial care under the supervision of licensed nursing personnel and represent the majority of all nursing staff employed by SNFs.[19] SNFs use the services of an array of ancillary professionals who may be employed by the SNFs or contracted. These services include physical therapy, occupational therapy, pharmacy, nutrition, recreational therapy, podiatry, dentistry, laboratory, and hospice.[19] Support staff, including dietary, laundry, housekeeping, and maintenance workers, complete the employee complement. The licensed nursing home administrator, along with the owner/operator, is responsible for carrying out the regulatory mandates regarding the mix and ratio of licensed and unlicensed personnel and the availability of licensed nursing personnel on an around-the-clock basis to provide skilled care and supervision.

Nursing homes are highly regulated by both state licensure and federal certification. The 1987 Omnibus Budget Reconciliation Act increased government involvement in nursing home industry regulation by[11]:

- Mandating regularly scheduled comprehensive assessments of the functional capacity of residents in nursing homes
- Establishing training standards for nursing home aides
- Placing restrictions on the use of physical restraints and psychoactive drugs
- Establishing a nursing home resident bill of rights
- Setting guidelines for the role of the medical director, including continuing education, involvement, and responsibility

States license nursing home administrators. Individual states set criteria for licensure in relationship to minimum age, educational requirements, passing examination scores, and continuing education requirements. In 2006, the National Association of Boards of Examiners of Long-Term Care Administrators announced the endorsement of a uniform set of "principles of interstate licensure" that allows reciprocity between and among states' licensing requirements. This new interstate licensure endorsement intends to assist mobility of administrators across states while ensuring maintenance of the highest entry-level standards in the profession.[20] A lack of nursing home compliance with state and federal mandates can lead to penalties such as direct fines, exclusion from Medicare and Medicaid certification, and withdrawal of nursing home licensure. Accreditation through The Joint Commission provides an additional quality check. Although highly desirable, Joint Commission accreditation remains voluntary.

A 1986 report by the Institute of Medicine, "For Profit Enterprise in Health Care," synthesized research on the quality of nursing home care based on for-profit and not-for-profit ownership noting that for-profit and investor-owned nursing homes tend to provide care of lower quality than their not-for-profit counterparts.[21] These findings have been replicated by other studies over the years.[22] In 2011, the Government Accountability Office reported findings of a first-ever analysis of the 10 largest for-profit nursing home chains, which noted among other findings that these facilities had "the lowest staffing levels; the highest number of deficiencies identified by public regulatory agencies and the highest number of deficiencies causing harm or jeopardy to residents."[22] It is important to note that research findings do not necessarily apply to an individual nursing home as "some for-profit nursing facilities give excellent care and some not-for-profit nursing facilities give poor care, but the general rule is documented in study after study: not-for-profit nursing facilities generally provide better care to their residents."[22] In response to concerns such as these, the Patient Protection and Affordable Care Act (ACA) will require Medicare- and Medicaid-certified SNFs to publicly disclose detailed ownership information, accountability requirements, expenditures, and other information related to quality indicators. It will also require these facilities to publish standardized information on a website to enable Medicare enrollees to compare facilities.[23]

Assisted-Living Facilities

Assisted-living facilities are appropriate for long-term care for individuals who do not require skilled nursing services and whose needs lie more in the custodial and supportive realm. The American Association of Homes and Services for the Aging defines assisted living as a "program that provides and/or arranges for daily meals, personal and other supportive services, health care and 24-hour oversight to persons residing in a group residential facility who need assistance with the activities of daily living."[24]

Estimates in 2010 placed the number of professionally managed assisted-living communities at 6,315 nationwide with approximately 475,500 apartments.[25] The average assisted-living resident is described as an 87-year-old female widow who requires assistance with two or more activities of daily living. The average resident stays in assisted living for 28 months and has an average annual income of $27,260.[25] The assisted-living population is expected to grow to almost 2 million individuals by 2025 (Figure 9-4).

Assisted-living facilities vary significantly in size, ranging from just a few residents to several hundred. They may take the form of small to large homes with just a few residents or large multi-unit apartment complexes with several hundred residents. Available services also vary but generally include, in addition to housing, congregate meals, 24-hour monitoring for emergencies, medication supervision, and assistance with one or more activities of daily living such as bathing, dressing, and personal grooming. Assisted-living facilities also typically provide scheduled activities, including communal recreation and group transportation for medical appointments and for social and cultural events. Many assisted-living facilities contract with home health agencies to provide skilled nursing care and with hospice service providers when such services are needed by individual residents.

States carry out oversight and regulation of assisted-living facilities at varying levels. These variations in laws and regulations create a diverse operating environment as well as a wide range of terminology and available services for consumers.[25] The quality of facilities, care, and services

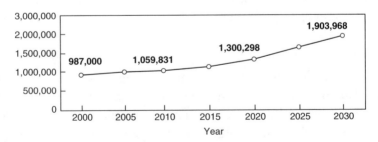

FIGURE 9-4 Projected Growth of Assisted Living Beds Based on Population Growth for Those 75 Years and Older.
Source: National Center for Assisted Living, reprinted with permission.

therefore may be an exclusive function of the policies of the owner organization or a combination of owner and organization policies coupled with state regulatory oversight.

Costs of assisted living are borne largely from private resources, although in certain circumstances supplemental social security income, private health insurance, long-term care insurance (LTCI), or special government rent subsidies for low-income older adults may apply. Estimates place the average monthly cost at $3,326, but costs can range across a broad continuum depending on the level of amenities desired in a facility and the types of services required. Residents fund accommodations from personal resources or from LTCI policies.[16–17,25]

Residential institutions such as adult homes, board and care homes, and group homes for people with mental or developmental disabilities also represent assisted-living arrangements. Care provided in adult homes has been available only to people who are for the most part healthy but limited in their ability to do their own housekeeping, household maintenance, and cooking. Residents must be able, for the most part, to meet their own personal care needs for dressing, eating, bathing, toileting, and ambulation unassisted. Oversight of residents may include services such as supervision of medications to the extent of reminding residents to take their medication or providing some assistance with bathing, grooming, transportation, laundry, and simple housekeeping. If provided at all, direct nursing care can be provided only in the case of minor illness of a temporary nature. Staffing levels in adult homes are state defined, with the ratio determined by the number of beds.

Home Care

Home care is community-based care provided to individuals in their own residences. Home care may be either a long-term provision of supportive care and services to chronically ill clients to avoid institutionalization or short-term intermittent care of clients after an episode of illness or hospitalization. Home care may be provided through the formal system of agency-employed professional home care providers, such as registered nurses, licensed practical nurses, home health aides, physical therapists, occupational therapists, speech-language pathologists, social workers, personal care aides, and homemakers, who make home visits. A considerably smaller number of home care staff may be self-employed individuals who contract privately with clients. An informal system also provides home care through caregivers consisting of family, neighbors, and friends of people in need of health care support services. Very often, a combination of both formal and in formal systems delivers home care.

Professional home care services originated in social welfare initiatives in the early 20th century in public response to the horrific living conditions of immigrants in U.S. industrialized cities. Public health concerns also gained impetus at that time as the germ theory of disease became accepted, and the control of contagious disease using preventive measures of hygiene and sanitation became a public health concern and mandate of local, state, and national health departments and agencies.

After Medicare's enactment of reimbursement for home care services in 1965, between 1967 and 1985 the number of Medicare-certified home health agencies grew more than threefold to 5,983, with public health agencies dominating the home care industry.[22] In the late 1980s, significant additional growth in the number of agencies ceased due to Medicare reimbursement issues.[26] However, with Medicare reimbursement changes since the 1990s, the number of Medicare-certified, hospital-based, and freestanding for-profit home health agencies grew rapidly.[26] The home care industry expanded its scope of services in response to demographic, economic, and legislative changes that include:

- An increase in the number of older persons and their expressed desire to remain in their own homes for care whenever possible
- Decreased numbers of informal caregivers that are available to provide in-home care to their relatives
- Increased innovations in high-technology home care that have redefined and expanded the categories of diseases and chronic conditions that can be cared for effectively in the home
- Medicare and Medicaid reimbursement that supported expanded coverage
- The 1999 Olmstead decision of the Supreme Court upholding the right of citizens to receive care in the community

In 2011, about 3.4 million Medicare beneficiaries received home health services from 11,900 home health agencies.[27] Approximately 70% of the freestanding home health care agencies were classified as proprietary or for-profit[28]; Medicare remains the largest payer for home health care services, accounting for just over 44% of total annual home care expenditures in 2011 (Table 9-2).[16]

Eligibility for Medicare reimbursement of home care services originally included four criteria:

1. Home care must include the provision of skilled nursing care; physical, occupational, and speech therapies; and medical social services as warranted by the patient's condition.
2. The person must be confined to the home.
3. A physician must order that home care services are required.
4. The home care agency must meet the minimum quality standards as outlined by Medicare and must be Medicare certified.

Under the ACA, in April 2011, Congress added more criteria for eligibility for Medicare reimbursement for home care to those listed above. Additional criteria included a requirement for Medicare beneficiaries receiving home care to have a face-to-face office visit encounter or a telehealth visit with a physician or nurse practitioner when home health care is ordered. This change was intended to ensure that beneficiaries receive a complete evaluation when home health care is ordered. Tighter supervision of therapy services provided under the home health benefit was also included. Under the new requirement, patients must be assessed by a qualified therapist at specific therapy intervals. The additional review was intended to serve as a safeguard against manipulation of therapy visits to garner increased payment.[28]

Table 9-2 Sources of Payment for Home Care, 2011

Source of Payment	Amount in Billions[*]	Percentage
Total	74.3	100
Medicare	32.9	44.3
Medicaid	27.6	37.1
Other third party/other health insurance	3.1	4.2
Private (out of pocket, other private funds)	5.6	7.5
Private insurance	5.1	6.9

Note: [*]Numbers may not add to totals due to rounding.

Source: Centers for Medicare and Medicaid Services.

In 2006 the Centers for Medicare & Medicaid Services had recommended a "postacute care" (PAC) reform plan that emphasized a consumer-centered approach giving more choice and control of post-hospitalization services to patients and caregivers, providing a seamless continuum of care through better service coordination and ensuring quality services in the most appropriate setting.[29] The reform plan, called "Medicaid Money Follows the Person" (MFP), sets demonstration projects in motion through 2011 by providing grants to states for additional federal matching funds for Medicaid beneficiaries making the transition from an institution back to their homes or to other community settings. The ACA extended the MFP demonstrations through 2016, and by 2011 43 states and the District of Columbia had received federal grants under the program. Over 16,000 persons had made the transition from institutions to home or other community settings by mid-2011.[30] Grants enable state Medicaid programs to fund home- and community-based services for individuals' needs such as personal care assistance to enable their safe residency in the community.

Other long-term care provisions under the ACA include "Community First Choice Option in Medicaid," which provides states with an increased federal Medicaid matching rate to support community-based attendant services for individuals who require an institutional level of care[31,32]; "State Balancing Incentive Program," which enhances federal matching funds to states to increase the proportion of Medicaid long-term services and support dollars allocated toward home and community-based services[32]; and establishment of the "Federal Coordinated Health Care Office," which is charged to improve the integration of benefits and increase coordination between federal and state governments for individuals receiving both Medicare and Medicaid benefits. This office has launched state demonstration projects to identify and evaluate delivery system and payment models for individuals eligible for both Medicare and Medicaid that can be rapidly tested and, if successful, replicated in other states.[33]

Research published between 2000 and 2010 in the *New England Journal of Medicine*, the *American Journal of Managed Care*, *Journal of the American Geriatrics Society*, *Health Care Financing Review*, and other sources notes the significant cost-effectiveness of home care when compared with the higher costs of providing institutional care for a variety of conditions such as the need for intravenous antibiotic therapy, diabetes, chronic obstructive pulmonary disease, and congestive heart failure.[34]

Medicare certification of home care agencies requires state licensing.[35] Most states issue a license for 1 year and require resubmission of an application and an annual state reinspection performed by a survey team. The state licensing agency has the right to investigate complaints and to conduct periodic reviews of all licensure requirements. The few agencies that treat only private pay or private insurance patients may not require a license; however, most home health care agencies want to participate in Medicare and Medicaid, so they maintain certification standards. Participation in voluntary accreditation indicates that home care agencies have a commitment to continuous quality improvement. Organizations that are actively engaged in the accreditation process for home health care agencies include the Community Health Accreditation Program, an independent, consumer-based subsidiary of the National League for Nursing; The Joint Commission; and the National Association for Home Care and Hospice.

Until the proliferation of social programs in the 1960s and 1970s, individuals requiring long-term health care were almost always cared for by family members and/or friends in the family home. This informal care system provided a valuable social service at little or no public cost. This arrangement is still the most used system of long-term care as family members care for more than 80% of the older adults needing some level of assistance. The informal care system offers significant savings to the public; however, the potential for caregivers to suffer physical and emotional burnout and the growing inability of family caregivers to fully manage care without outside assistance have begun to diminish these savings.

Recent estimates place the number of family caregivers at over 61 million. Most caregivers assist family members, most commonly their mothers. The majority of caregivers are females, 75% of whom, in addition to providing caregiving to a family member, also are employed outside the home.[36] Family caregivers are frequently required to make major compromises in their finances, lifestyles, and personal freedom to care for another family member. The costs can be high. Stresses experienced by the caregiver can lead to exhaustion, illness, and depression.[37] In addition, with increased longevity, middle-aged individuals often find themselves caring for their children and their aged parents simultaneously. Dubbed the "sandwich generation,"[38] these caregivers suffer even more stress from this dual role, which in many cases becomes a triple role for those who also provide care for their grandchildren as well. Employers also experience losses because of the demands of caregiving on their employees. One study estimated the annual costs of lost productivity for U.S. businesses due to caregiving at nearly $34 billion.[39] Employer costs are associated with worker replacement, absenteeism, workday interruptions, elder care crises, and supervisory time.[36,39] Some larger employers are responding with flexible scheduling and other considerations to help accommodate their employees' caregiving responsibilities for family members.[39]

Estimates place the market value of long-term care delivered by unpaid family members and friends at more than $450 billion per year, more than double the annual national health care expenditures for nursing home and home care combined.[40] Both the economic and personal contributions of the informal caregiving system form the bedrock of the nation's chronic care system and require more policy-level attention and support. The federal government took an important first step to assist family caregivers through the Family Medical Leave Act (FMLA) of 1993. The FMLA provides up to 12 workweeks of unpaid leave per year for the birth of a child or adoption of a child, or for employees to care for themselves or a sick family member, while ensuring continuation of health benefits and job security. In 2009, the FMLA was amended to specifically ensure 26 workweeks of unpaid, job-protected leave for active military service members and their families who might require care.[40] FMLA has serious shortcomings, however. It provides only for unpaid leave, a condition that makes its use financially unfeasible for many individuals. Also, the FMLA does not cover workers in companies of 50 or fewer employees, effectively excluding approximately half of America's workers.[41]

Several states have implemented programs to assist caregivers by expanding paid leave provisions. California was a leader in this regard when it enacted the Paid Family Leave Law in 2002, allowing workers up to 6 weeks of partially paid leave to bond with a new biological, adopted, or foster child or to care for a seriously ill family member.[41] While only a handful of additional states have enacted paid leave legislation or regulations for private sector employees, several additional states have such legislation under consideration. Similar provisions now exist for public employees in at least 40 states.[41] As discussed earlier, provisions of the ACA have potential to lessen the burden on informal caregivers by enabling increased Medicaid payment flexibility to support home- and community-based services. Particularly relevant to family caregivers, the ACA also created an "Independence at Home Medical Practice Pilot Program" to provide Medicare beneficiaries with multiple chronic conditions with home-based primary care services and a "Community Care Transitions Program" for high-risk Medicare beneficiaries following hospital discharge. The ACA also requires federally funded geriatric education centers to provide free or low-cost training for family caregivers.[42]

Historically, home health care services have been vulnerable to breaches in operational integrity. In the 1990s, the Clinton administration and Congress responded to dramatic increases in Medicare and Medicaid home care services spending and concerns about service quality and fiscal integrity.[43] One major response was the authorization of an antifraud and abuse pilot project, Operation Restore Trust, which investigated home health agencies, nursing homes, hospice organizations, and medical product suppliers in five states with the highest rates of use. Subsequently, Operation Restore Trust was expanded to selected home health care agencies in 12 states and included training for agency surveyors in identifying care improperly billed to Medicare.[43]

The Balanced Budget Act of 1997 also contained provisions to enable the Health Care Financing Administration to control costs and address service quality issues more effectively in Medicare-certified home health care agencies. Provisions targeted reducing unnecessary and inappropriate services, including dividing Medicare home health services funding into separate streams for posthospital and chronic health problems to enhance accountability. Other provisions of the Balanced Budget Act contained several measures to thwart fraudulent practices by home health clients and agencies.[44] The Clinton administration also proposed revisions in the federal standards that home health care agencies must meet to continue participation in the Medicare program. Revisions included criteria such as requiring criminal background checks of home health aides as a condition of employment, requiring agencies to discuss expected treatment outcomes with patients, and requiring coordination of care when patients are being served by multiple providers.[44]

Also in 1997, the Department of Health and Human Services promulgated new regulations requiring home health agencies to implement a standardized reporting system, the Outcomes and Assessment Information Set, to monitor patients' conditions and satisfaction with services.[45]

Vigorous antifraud and abuse initiatives continue in the Medicare program through its partnerships with the Department of Justice, the Federal Bureau of Investigation, the Office of the Inspector General, and several other federal and state law enforcement agencies.[46] Home health care services are an integral component of the health care delivery system's continuum, which can provide an effective, safe, and humane alternative to institutional care for the medical treatment and personal care of individuals of all ages. Ideally, lessons learned from continuing initiatives to thwart abuses and improve quality and the ACA provisions that support expanded home- and community-based services will help to ensure that home health care fulfills its purposes in ensuring the highest possible quality of life for all recipients of these services.

Hospice Care

Hospice is a philosophy supporting a coordinated program of care for the terminally ill. The most common criterion for admission into a hospice is that the applicant has a diagnosis of a terminal illness with a limited life expectancy of 6 months or less. Aggressive medical treatment of the patient's disease may no longer be medically feasible or personally desirable. The disease may have progressed despite available medical treatments, making continuance of curative treatment futile or intolerable, or the patient may elect to discontinue such treatment for a variety of personal reasons, such as continued deterioration of quality of life related to treatment side effects.

The term "palliative care" often is used synonymously with hospice care. Palliative care is care or treatment given to relieve the symptoms of a disease rather than attempting to cure the disease. Pain, nausea, malaise, and emotional distress caused by feelings of fear and isolation are only some of the difficulties that patients encounter during the stages of a terminal illness. Hospice treatment is directed toward maintaining the comfort of the patient and enhancing the patient's quality of life and sense of independence for as long as possible.

Hospice has its historical roots in medieval Europe. Hospices were originally way stations where travelers on religious pilgrimages received food and rest. Over time, the concept evolved into sanctuaries where impoverished people or those who were sick or dying received care.

English physician Dame Cicely Saunders established St. Christopher's, a hospice located in a London suburb, in 1967, and it became a model for the modern hospice. Here, terminally ill patients received intensive symptom management, modern techniques of pain control, and psychological and emotional support. She brought the founding concepts of the modern hospice to the United States in a lecture tour in the late 1960s, during which she emphasized that dying patients were also on a kind of pilgrimage and needed a more responsive environment than could be provided in high-technology, impersonal, cure-oriented hospitals.

U.S. hospice movement began as a consumer-based grassroots movement supported by volunteer and professional members of the community. Today, 34% of hospice organizations are operating as not-for-profit entities, whereas for-profit hospice organizations have multiplied over the years and now represent about 60% of hospice organizations (Figure 9-5).[47]

U.S. founders shared the belief that the hospice concept was a more humane alternative to the technology-driven, curative emphasis in

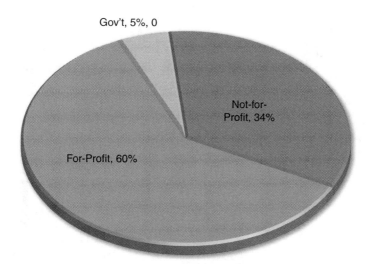

FIGURE 9-5 Tax Status of Medicare-certified Hospice Agencies.
Source: Adapted from *NHPCO Facts and Figures: Hospice Care in America.* Alexandria, VA: National Hospice and Palliative Care Organization, October 2012.

hospitals. Because the medical system can view choosing to discontinue aggressive medical treatment as a failure, terminally ill patients can feel depersonalized and isolated inside a traditional hospital setting. Ideally, the physician, the patient, and the patient's family jointly recognize the need to refer the patient to a hospice when deciding to stop curative treatment.

The first U.S. hospice was established in New Haven, Connecticut, in 1974. The number of hospices has increased steadily every year, with over 5,300 hospices now serving over 1.6 million individuals annually (Figures 9-6 and 9-7).[47]

Major growth in the availability of hospice care followed the enactment of 1982 legislation that extended Medicare coverage to hospice services, allowing the movement to escape its prior dependency on grant support and philanthropy. A 73-fold increase in the number of hospice providers occurred between 1984 and 1998. In 2011, approximately 44.6% of all U.S. deaths occurred in hospice care.[47]

Consistent with the hospice philosophy, a multidisciplinary team of nurses, social workers, counselors, physicians, and therapists provides

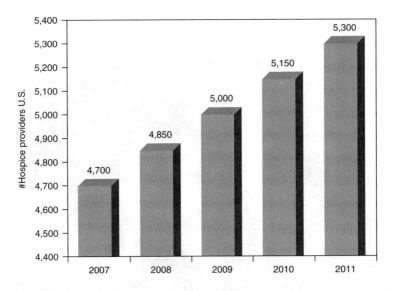

FIGURE 9-6 Total Hospice Providers by Year.
Source: Reproduced with permission from *NHPCO Facts and Figures: Hospice Care in America.* Alexandria, VA: National Hospice and Palliative Care Organization, October 2012.

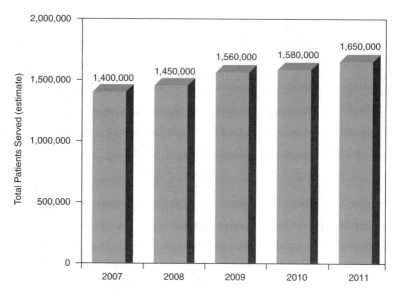

FIGURE 9-7 Total Hospice Patients Served by Year.
Source: Reproduced with permission from *NHPCO Facts and Figures: Hospice Care in America.* Alexandria, VA: National Hospice and Palliative Care Organization, October 2012.

services. Hospices also provide necessary drug therapies and medical appliances and supplies. Bereavement services for surviving family members continue for a year or longer after the patient's death. Most hospice organizations also provide bereavement services for the larger community.[47]

A variety of different settings accommodates hospice care, including the home, hospitals, SNFs, assisted-living facilities, or hospice inpatient facilities. The most important unifying concept about hospice is that no matter where the care is delivered, a specialized multidisciplinary team of health care professionals works together to manage the patient's care. A physician directs the team, coordinated by a nurse. The team members can include physicians, nurses, respiratory and physical therapists, pharmacists, pastoral care providers, social workers, psychologists, home health aides, and homemakers. Each team member contributes his or her particular skills and expertise to assist in managing pain, alleviating emotional distress, promoting comfort, and maintaining the independence of the hospice patient. Hospice care strongly encompasses the patient's family and routinely includes counseling (including bereavement counseling), spiritual support, and respite care for family members.

The hospice philosophy emphasizes volunteerism, and it is the only health care provider whose Medicare certification requires that at least 5% of total patient care hours are contributed by volunteers. In 2011, the National Hospice and Palliative Care Organization estimated that over 450,000 volunteers assisted hospice organizations with 21 million contributed hours of service.[47,48] Volunteers from the community are actively encouraged to participate in a wide range of hospice activities, including direct services to patients and families, clerical services, and other support services and assistance with fundraising.

Hospice care has demonstrated its cost savings in care for the terminally ill. The unique blend of care provided by a specialized team, use of volunteers, and frequent use of family members as primary caregivers in the home all decrease expenses. The focus on palliative care rather than on cure-oriented care also decreases the cost. A number of research studies have examined the savings from the use of hospice care. Similar to Medicare, annual Medicaid expenditures for hospice care represent only a small fraction of total expenditures.[47]

Managed care organizations and traditional health insurers recognize both the human and economic benefits of hospice care and typically include hospice in their benefit packages. Insurers may have their own team of hospice-type providers within their respective networks or may contract with community hospice organizations to provide hospice care. Medicare-eligible subscribers of Medicare-participating health plans are automatically eligible for hospice care, and services must be provided through a Medicare-certified hospice organization. The patient is not required to obtain a referral from their health plan or to discontinue their managed care contract in order to receive hospice care.

A basic tenet of the hospice philosophy is that hospice care should be available regardless of the ability to pay. When the patient does not have health insurance and does not qualify for Medicare or Medicaid, hospice services may still be available. A hospice may offer a sliding payment scale to the patient, with the hospice drawing on internal funds garnered through its fundraising activities to supplement available patient payments.

Ongoing quality assurance to monitor care quality is an inherent concept in hospice care. Three standards used most frequently are licensure, certification, and accreditation. Licensure is based on state-imposed statutes as part of the consumer protection code of a state. Not all states have such licensing statutes. States that have licensing statutes require that all hospices within their jurisdiction meet the standards set forth in the law. Certification means that hospices have been examined on the federal level and have been found to at least minimally meet the mandated requirements for Medicare and Medicaid reimbursement. A hospice program that is not certified may still operate legally but is ineligible to bill Medicare or Medicaid for its services.

Respite Care

Family caregivers continue to be a key factor in providing care for many long-term care recipients in their communities, rather than placing them in institutions. Providing care up to 24 hours a day can place enormous physical and emotional stress on family caregivers.

Respite care is temporary surrogate care given to a patient when that patient's primary caregiver must be absent. In the 1970s, formal respite-care programs originated to meet the increasing need for assistance after the rapid deinstitutionalization of individuals who had developmental disabilities or mental illness. Since then, the respite-care model has expanded to include any family-managed care program that helps to avoid or forestall the placement of a patient in a full-time institutionalized environment by providing planned, intermittent caregiver relief. Respite care offers an organized, reliable system in which both patient and primary caregiver are the beneficiaries.

Respite care may be offered in a variety of settings: the home; a day care situation; or institutions with overnight care, such as hospitals, nursing homes, or group homes. Respite-care auspices may include private, public, and voluntary not-for-profit agencies. The length of respite care varies, but it is intended to be short term and intermittent.

Respite-care services are highly differentiated. Some are very structured and self-contained; others are highly flexible and exist in a more casual support capacity. A number of services are oriented to treating only patients with a particular ailment, but, for many, the only criterion the patient must meet for admission is that he or she requires supervised medical treatment and nursing care, which usually has been provided by family or friends as primary caregivers. Respite models include:

- Alzheimer's disease care on an inpatient basis with admissions lasting for several weeks
- Community-based, adult day care centers that offer nursing, therapeutic, and social services
- In-home assistance, where visiting homecare or personal care aides supply services
- Temporary patient furloughs to a hospital or nursing home at regular intervals

Respite-care program staffing varies widely, deploying both professionals and nonprofessionals. For example, respite care could be as informal as having a member from the caregiver's church come into the home for a few hours while the caregiver goes out or as professional as a specialized dementia day care program where nurses, aides, and recreational and physical therapists are specifically educated to care for dementia patients in a structured, caregiving environment. When respite care entails overnight care in an institutional setting, such as a nursing home, hospital, or group home, the staff providing care is the same staff employed by the institution to provide care to their regular patients in the institution.

Formal respite programs in the United States that are financially accessible to all in need have remained sparse. One of the greatest barriers limiting the expanded use of respite care is cost. Family caregivers operating on a limited budget may have difficulty finding funds to compensate a respite provider. Although some respite providers offer care on a sliding scale, almost any fee may exceed the financial means of the family. In these situations, not-for-profit organizations may assist by providing respite assistance at a tolerable cost for patients who meet certain financial or medical parameters.

Historically, there have been few provisions in the Medicare and Medicaid programs to support formal respite care. Medicare contains no allowances for respite, unless services are provided by a Medicare-certified hospice, Medicare-certified hospital, or Medicare-certified nursing home and co-pay fees are required. The person receiving respite care may be responsible for 5% of the Medicare-approved amount for respite care. For example, if Medicare pays $100 per day for inpatient respite care, the co-pay would be $5 per day.[49] Each time a patient receives respite care,

Medicare covers up to 5 days. There is no limit to the number of times that a patient can receive respite care. The amount paid for respite care can change each year.[49] Medicaid has stringent requirements regarding the specific type and length of care provided as well as financial eligibility for services and does not pay for respite care directly but often states use waivers to apply federal funds to offset respite costs for eligible Medicaid recipients. Some states allow family members to receive a wage subsidy for respite services for persons over the age of 60 with very low incomes, but eligibility, types of care, and funding vary on a state-by-state basis.[50] Available respite programs offered by voluntary agencies as the result of federal grants often provide service for only specific medical conditions, such as Alzheimer's disease. Both proprietary and not-for-profit organizations are developing specialized dementia and connected respite-care programs in response to recent federal legislation. Many specialized dementia respite-care programs currently are developed and marketed to private pay customers, but such programs often are beyond the financial capability of many families.

One of the major barriers to responsive changes in reimbursement for respite care has been that funding mechanisms have viewed respite care as meeting a social need but not an acute medical care need. In addition, community systems of respite care can be difficult to organize because the level of need is intermittent and unpredictable. Family caregivers often are viewed as the most direct beneficiaries of respite care, rather than the patients who actually receive the health care. With the indisputable conclusion that respite-care programs offer society value and cost savings through postponement or avoidance of costly institutionalization, bipartisan federal legislation was developed in 2003 to address respite-care issues. Entitled the Lifespan Respite Care Act, over 200 national, state, and local organizations advocated its passage, culminating in its signing into law in 2006.[51] The law authorized $289 million over 5 years for state grants to develop respite programs. According to the National Family Caregivers Association (now renamed Caregiver Action Network or CAN), the 2006 Act defined respite programs as "coordinated systems of accessible, community-based respite care services for family caregivers of children and adults with special needs."[51] Passage of this legislation was a landmark because it provided a nationwide acknowledgment of the inherent economic value of the informal family-provided care system. In addition, as a major thrust of federal initiatives, the U.S. Administration on

Aging (AoA) has continued to pilot several different types of demonstration programs targeted at determining the cost-effectiveness and consumer acceptability of various combinations of community-based services that support older persons' ability to continue living independently. In its adoption of the 2010 AoA budget, Congress authorized a $7 million increase for home- and community-based services for older Americans, emphasizing the federal government's role in assisting older Americans to remain independent members of their communities.[52] For the fiscal year 2013, AoA has requested Congress to fund $3.7 million for home- and community-based services, which is equal to the amount that was enacted by Congress in 2012.[53]

Adult Day Care

An adult day care center may provide a supervised program of social activities and custodial care (social model), medical and rehabilitative care through skilled nursing (medical model), or specialized services for patients with Alzheimer's disease or other forms of dementia. An adult day care center operates during daytime hours in a protective group setting located outside the recipient's home. The primary intent of adult day care is to prevent the premature and inappropriate institutionalization of older adults by providing socialization, health care, or both. Older adults maintain their mental and physical well-being longer and at a higher level when they continue to reside in their homes and their communities. Furthermore, for those who depend on the services of a regular family caregiver, an adult day care center can provide respite for the caregiver and therapeutic social contacts for the care recipient.[54]

The concept of adult day care grew out of social concern for the quality of life and care of older adults based on the work of Lionel Cousins, who in the 1960s established the first adult day care center in the United States to "prepare patients for discharge by teaching and promoting independent living skills."[55] Originally, development and growth in such programs were slow because there was no national policy to support the idea and no permanent funding base, as the prototype Medicare and Medicaid programs supported and encouraged institutionalization; however, as the cost of institutionalization, the inhumanity of many nursing homes, and the burden placed on family caregivers were recognized, the focus of long-term care has been redirected toward support of community-based care as a preferred alternative to institutionalization whenever possible. Since then, the growth in the number of adult day care programs has been rapid. In 1978, only 300 adult day care centers existed nationwide; but according to the National Adult Day Services Association, by 2010, 4,000 were in operation, 80% of which were operated by not-for-profit organizations.[56] The number in operation had increased to over 4,600 adult day care centers by 2012, a 35% increase in the number of centers since 2002.[57]

The services that adult day care centers offer are similar, but the emphasis varies with the model they follow. Most adult day care centers offer a variety of medical, psychiatric, and nursing assessments; counseling; physical exercises; social services; crafts; and rehabilitation in activities of daily living skills. Special-purpose adult day care centers serve particular populations of clients, such as veterans, older persons with mental health problems, the blind, people with Alzheimer's disease, or people with cerebral palsy, for example.

Staffing patterns of adult day care programs vary from program to program and are directly related to the type of program and specific services offered. The mix of unskilled to skilled employees also depends on the kinds of services being offered. Programs based on the medical model are more likely to employ more registered nurses, occupational therapists, and physical therapists to provide skilled assessment, direct care, and rehabilitative therapies than in a social model, where aides may perform most of the custodial care and a recreational therapist may be employed to plan and deliver recreational and socialization activities. The number of clients enrolled in a day care program varies according to the staffing pattern and facility size. The cost of care may vary widely depending on the range and scope of services provided. Medicare generally does not provide reimbursement for day care services. Medicaid may provide reimbursement for services in a medical model day care program, but this practice varies from state to state. Often, services are paid for through private fees or through programs supported by grant funds or by charitable or religious organizations.

Most centers are licensed by the states in which they operate.[56] Most also are certified by the particular community agency that is funding the day care center. Licensure and credentialing ensure that the day care center meets at least the minimum standards and guidelines set by the overseeing agency that provides grant funding to the community agency and ensure that the overseeing agency has thereby met all criteria for obtaining underlying federal government grants. In 1999, the Commission on Accreditation of Rehabilitation Facilities, along with the National Adult Day Services Association, published adult day care standards, which include organizational measurement and quality and information systems and outcomes quality. The new standards provided an enhanced level of quality guidance to adult day care management, as well as more recognition of the value of adult day care services in the overall continuum of long-term care.[58]

Innovations in Long-Term Care

Innovative long-term care services that meet the diverse medical needs, personal desires, and lifestyle choices of older Americans have made important strides over the years. The continuum of care model recognizes the complex configuration of individual needs and encourages the implementation of programs and services of adequate variety, intensity, and scope to provide the best configuration of care to any individual. Concepts such as aging in place, life care communities, naturally occurring retirement communities, and high-technology home care are some of the changes that offer enriched alternatives to long-term care recipients.

Aging in Place

Moving to a nursing home or dependent care facility is seen by many as a change in lifestyle to be steadfastly avoided for as long as possible. Most people prefer to remain actively engaged in their own support and care, in their own residence, and within the context of their own family. Research indicates enhanced quality of life and longevity when older adults are able to remain in their own residences. The term "aging in place" in the context of older and frail persons refers to at least partial fulfillment of this desire. An aging-in-place health care system allows older adults to maintain their health while living as independently as possible in their own homes, without a costly, and in many cases traumatic, move to an institutional setting. At the federal, state, and local governmental levels, as evidenced by legislation, and at the grassroots level, an increasingly favorable light is shining on the well-documented cost-effectiveness of health care programs that encourage the aging-in-place concept and the concurrent maintenance of independent living.

Aging-in-place programs bring together a variety of health and other supportive services to enable participants to live independently in their own residences for as long as that is safely possible. Services that participants receive most frequently include:

- Nursing services provided by registered and licensed nurses
- Home care aide assistance
- Homemaker services to assist with meals and housekeeping
- A 24-hour emergency response system
- Home-delivered groceries
- Transportation to health care appointments

In 1972, a model of aging-in-place service delivery, called On Lok Senior Health Services, was established as a demonstration project to provide health services to a selected population of frail older people in San Francisco. The term "On Lok" derives from the Chinese language, meaning "peaceful and happy abode."[59] Participants in the On Lok program live in their own residences with an interdisciplinary team of health care professionals managing their health care. When institutional care is required (either in a nursing home or hospital) or ancillary diagnostic or specialty physician services are needed, they are provided through contractual arrangements with outside providers. The prototype program was so successful that Congress mandated replication of this model by the establishment of demonstration programs, called the Program for All-Inclusive Care for the Elderly, or PACE, in other parts of the country. The early success of PACE was evidenced by the fact that although its clients were certified as eligible for nursing home placement, only 6% were placed in nursing homes; the rest were able to remain in their homes.[60] Also impressive was the low hospitalization rate of participants when compared with typical Medicare beneficiaries with similar health status. Through provisions of the Balanced Budget Act, PACE earned a permanent status as a Medicare-approved benefit.[60]

Continuing Care Retirement and Life Care Communities

Continuing care retirement communities (CCRCs) are available for those Americans who do not wish to stay in their own homes as they get older yet are essentially well enough to avoid institutionalization. Estimates have placed the number of licensed CCRCs at well over 2,200, accommodating more than 725,000 older Americans,[61] with the numbers of both the licensed facilities and their residents increasing every year. Over 80% of CCRCs have been operated by not-for-profit organizations and nearly 50% have been faith based.[61] CCRCs provide residences on a retirement campus, typically in apartment complexes designed for functional older adults. Unlike ordinary retirement communities that offer only specialized housing, CCRCs offer a comprehensive program of social services, meals, and access to contractual medical services in addition to housing. There are three types of CCRCs[62]:

- Life care or extended contract/continuing life care community (CLCC): This is the most expensive option. It offers unlimited assisted living, medical treatment, and skilled nursing care without any additional charges as the resident's needs change over time.
- Modified contract: This contract offers a set of services provided for a specified length of time. When that time is expired, other services can be obtained, but will have higher monthly fees.
- Fee-for-service contract: The initial enrollment fee may be lower, but assisted living and skilled nursing are paid for at their market rates.

According to the American Association of Retired Persons (AARP), CCRCs provide the most expensive of all long-term care options and require an entrance fee as well as monthly charges.[62] Fees depend on a variety of factors including the resident's health status, the type of housing chosen, the size of the facility, and the type of service contract.[62] Cost varies widely, and such programs require upfront entrance fees that can range from $100,000 to $1 million. Monthly charges can range from $3,000 to $5,000, but they may increase as needs change.[62] However, as advocates for this lifestyle point out, many Americans approaching their retirement years have sufficient equity in their homes and investment income to pay the required entrance and monthly maintenance fees.

CLCCs achieve financial viability by using an insurance-based model and, as such, are regulated by state insurance departments as well as other regulatory agencies to which their services may be subject in their respective states. The program administrators establish eligibility criteria for participants using actuarial data from the insurance industry. The future lifetime medical costs of participants are anticipated, and rates and charges are set accordingly. Prospective CLCC residents are provided a contract outlining what the CLCC provides in terms of home accommodations, social activities, services and amenities, and access to on-site levels of health care. Most CLCCs require a one-time entrance fee and a monthly fee as previously mentioned. There are many variations to the types of contracts offered.[63] In general, services may include the following:

- Meals
- Scheduled transportation
- Housekeeping services
- Housing unit maintenance
- Linen and personal laundry
- Health monitoring
- Wellness programs
- Some utilities
- Social activities
- Home health care
- Skilled nursing care

A life care community offers more comprehensive benefits and support systems for older persons than any other option available today in the United States. Less than 1% of older citizens have taken advantage of this option in the past, in great part because of the expense and the requirement of an extended contractual commitment.

Naturally Occurring Retirement Communities

A "naturally occurring retirement community" (NORC) is a term coined by Professor Michael Hunt of the University of Wisconsin–Madison in the 1980s to describe apartment buildings where most residents were 60 years of age or older. Now, the NORC acronym is widely used to describe apartment complexes, neighborhoods, or sections of communities where residents have opted to remain in their homes as they age.[64] Today, numerous communities throughout the United States formally recognize NORCs.

The U.S. AoA recognized NORCs through the development of a competitive grant awards program for demonstration projects designed to test and evaluate methods to assist older Americans in their desire to age in place. Community centers and other not-for-profit organizations could compete for grant funding, and demonstration projects were enacted in several states.[64] NORC programs use a combination of services such as case management, nursing, social and recreational activities, health education, transportation, nutrition, and referral linkages to enhance quality of life and safety for older adults who wish to remain in their homes during their aging process. NORCs appear to hold much potential as a positive alternative to institutionalization and possible cost savings for individuals and government.[65]

High-Technology Home Care: Hospitals without Walls

Traditionally, home health care focused on providing supportive care to persons with long-term disability and chronic disease. Changes in reimbursement mechanisms to a prospective payment system based on diagnosis-related groups (DRGs) have led to the more rapid discharge of all patients from hospitals after episodes of hospitalization for acute illness, exacerbation of chronic disease, progression of disability, or surgery. Patients frequently are discharged home while they still require advanced intensive therapeutic treatments and rely on complex, high-technology services such as ventilators, kidney dialysis, intravenous antibiotic therapy, parenteral nutrition, or cancer chemotherapy.

The delivery of high-technology home care not only is more cost-effective than hospitalization or institutionalization in a nursing home but also allows the client to move from the more dependent patient role to the more autonomous role as a client in their own residence. Home health care agencies have accommodated this trend toward provision of advanced high-technology therapy in the home setting through innovations in the type and organization of the specialty services they provide. Improvements and innovations have taken place in the portability, mobility, reliability, and cost of medical devices such as intravenous therapy pumps, long-term venous access devices, continuous ambulatory peritoneal dialysis equipment, and ventilators. Innovative teams of skilled practitioners in specialized areas such as intravenous therapy and kidney dialysis and the concurrent development of innovative support teams of pharmacists and specialty technicians who prepare and deliver necessary intravenous, parenteral nutrition, and dialysis fluids and medications have made the home setting an appropriate environment for the delivery of high-technology therapies.

Long-Term Care Insurance

Long-term care insurance (LTCI) is one financing option for the various components of long-term care. The earliest long-term care policies were first offered in the 1970s and covered only care in nursing homes.[66] In 2010, the AARP estimated that between 7 and 9 million Americans owned LTCI policies, and 95% of those policies provided coverage for long-term care in a variety of setting options such as nursing homes, assisted living, or in the home.[67] Individuals purchase the majority of policies, but an increasing number of employers are now offering coverage through group purchase plans. The federal government has encouraged the purchase of long-term care policies by offering tax deductions to employers who offer long-term care insurance as a benefit. Almost all long-term care insurance policies sold today meet federal standards, specified by the Health Insurance Portability and Accountability Act of 1996, for favorable tax treatment. Many states also now offer incentives to individuals in the form of income tax deductions for the purchase of tax-qualified long-term care policies.[67]

The ACA included a provision, the Community Living Assistance Services and Supports Act (CLASS Act), to establish a national voluntary long-term care insurance program funded through payroll deductions by persons at least 18 years of age. After 5 years of enrollment, the program would have allowed participants who became functionally impaired to receive benefits to purchase a variety of basic assistive services. However, by late 2011, amid much controversy, the Department of Health and Human Services abandoned the program. Analysts noted that the CLASS ACT suffered from "serious design flaws," including the act's voluntary enrollment, which would not provide an adequate population base over which to spread financial risk, and its dual purposes of providing benefits to disabled young people capable of working as well as older persons with age-related disabilities. Advocates have lamented the withdrawal of the Act as losing an opportunity to shift costs from the Medicaid program to private insurance.[68]

The benefits of LTCI policies vary across a broad spectrum. The most desirable policies cover services across the continuum of potential long-term care needs, with maximum subscriber flexibility. Specialists counsel buyers to be wary of limitations relative to inflationary factors in the costs of coverage, renewal clauses, limits on payments for various modes of long-term care, requirements for prior hospitalization for eligibility for home care, cancellation features of policies, and lifetime benefit limits. As with life insurance, the premium cost reflects age at purchase of the policy. LTCI companies also use underwriting criteria and may reject applicants or increase premiums for individuals with preexisting conditions that render them at high risk for future long-term care services.

Insurance industry advocates and other analysts contend that individuals and society will benefit in the future from the proliferation of LTCI. In this view, public dependency, especially on Medicaid, to fund long-term care needs would decrease, and individuals would have the ability to access the highest quality long-term care services without risk of impoverishment.[69]

The decision to invest in an LTCI product is very personal and depends on many factors, primarily on the level of assets the individual has or expects to have at risk if long-term care is required. Other alternatives to LTCI, such as transferring assets to children to become financially eligible for Medicaid, using the equity in a home in a reverse mortgage, selecting special living arrangements, and using personal savings, are not universally applicable. All these options must be carefully assessed against the cost of LTCI to make viable and appropriate future plans.

Future of Long-Term Care

The United States will need more and diverse long-term care programs in the future to serve increasing needs, especially of older adults. Some of the causes underlying the intensifying need for diverse long-term care service options are as follows:

- Changes in the demographics of U.S. population
- Social and economic changes in families
- Increasingly sophisticated medical technology
- Greater consumer sophistication and demands
- Increasing scrutiny of federal and state government financial involvement in support of long-term health care

The future configuration of the long-term care service delivery system is difficult to predict, although an analysis of current trends suggests certain directions.

Long-term care services have become increasingly diversified and specialized, which allows programs and providers to focus on becoming experts in meeting specific needs of specialized populations such as people with Alzheimer's disease or AIDS. One danger to be avoided would be to allow specialization to lead to fragmentation, duplication of services, and pressure to categorize participants into narrow service niches. Services such as subacute care and the provision of transitional health care after hospitalization for medically complex long-term care patients are responding as the drive to discharge patients from hospitals quickly results in a greater need for more intense supportive care environments beyond hospital walls. Service delivery systems that function within the managed care environment are becoming increasingly common, and the bundling of posthospitalization care with hospitalization into one episode of care provided through one integrated service provider is occurring more frequently. Demonstrated cost-effectiveness and expressed client preferences for community-based care are reflected in the ACA provisions. As discussed earlier, the ACA promotes increased consumer choice, flexibility, care coordination, and community-based rather than institutional care, holding promise for a more rational, less costly, and more coordinated long-term care system. In addition, ACA supports for patient-centered medical homes and accountable care organizations that take full responsibility for the continuum of care should complement long-term care reform initiatives.

Long-term care employees have traditionally been paid less and given less status than workers in acute-care health services. The long-term care industry is enduring an employment crisis with an inadequate number and quality of applicants to fill vacancies in direct caregiver positions across all industry sectors. Factors contributing to the long-term care employment crisis include the following[70]:

- The growing need for services
- Competition among employers
- Workload and working conditions
- Employee turnover
- Wages and benefits constrained by reimbursement policies
- A lack of social supports for workers, including child care and transportation
- A lack of opportunities for education and career mobility

Staffing shortages seriously affect the quality of long-term care services. The industry's ability to develop innovative approaches to attracting and retaining staff will have important implications as service demands swell with the aging of the baby-boom generation. Supported by government, not-for-profit organizations, and major philanthropies, identifying solutions to the staffing crises in long-term care has been the subject of ongoing research at academic and policy development institutions throughout the country.[69]

Until recently, the needs of the informal caregiver system were virtually ignored. Significant legislative action at the federal and state levels only recently began to recognize these needs in terms of employer allowances and other programmatic and economic considerations at the federal and state levels.

An undercurrent of concern continues to run beneath all aspects of long-term health care delivery, especially with regard to the development of responsive, patient-centered, quality-driven, accessible, affordable, and cost-effective health care services for all citizens—including the society's most vulnerable: people with chronic disabilities and frail older adults. Experimentation with ACA programs and demonstrations are in their early stages. As exemplified by the demise of the CLASS Act, no one can yet predict if or how Congress and the long-term care industry will establish solutions to the crises in meeting present and future long-term care needs for our nation's aging population or how SNFs and other long-term care options will be affected, including the extent of the effects of suggested legislation in relation to Medicare. Possible compromises include certain Medicare reductions and a suggested increase in the eligibility age for Medicare beneficiaries from 65 to 67 years, among many other proposals that will have a direct effect on the provision of long-term care.[71] Insurance industry experts suggest the need for a national long-term care strategy that incorporates four primary components: education and awareness, caregiving, healthy aging, and long-term care financing (Figure 9-8).

Given the industry's current unmet needs and rising demands, future years will continue to be a period of experimentation, innovation, and change in the long-term health care system.

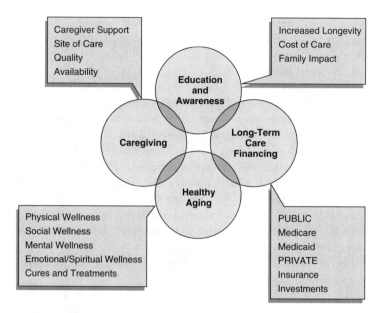

FIGURE 9-8 Components of a National Long-term Care Strategy.
Source: Genworth Financial, reprinted with permission.

Key Terms for Review

Assisted Living
Continuing Care Retirement
   Community (CCRC)
Continuing Life Care Community
   (CLCC)
Hospice

Naturally Occurring Retirement
   Community (NORC)
Palliative Care
Respite Care
Skilled Nursing Facility (SNF)

References

1. Evashwick CJ. Strategic management of a continuum of care. *J Long-Term Care Admin.* 1993;21:13–24.
2. Shortell SM. *Transforming Health Care Delivery: Seamless Continuum of Care.* Chicago, IL: American Hospital Publishing; 1994:1–7.
3. Jack CM, Paone DL. *Toward Creating a Seamless Continuum of Care: Addressing Chronic Care Needs.* Chicago, IL: Section for Aging and Long-Term Care Services of the American Hospital Association; 1994:3–5.

4. U.S. Department of Health and Human Services, Administration on Aging. *Profile of older Americans: 2011.* 2012. Available from http://www.aoa.gov/aoaroot/aging_statistics/Profile/2011/docs/2011profile.pdf. Accessed January 5, 2013.

5. U.S. Department of Health and Human Services, Administration on Aging. Population 65 and over by Age: 1900–2050. August 14, 2008. Available from http://www.aoa.gov/AoARoot/Aging_Statistics/future_growth/docs/By_Age_65_and_over.xls. Accessed January 5, 2013.

6. Shore HH. History of long-term care. In: Goldsmith SB, ed. *Essentials of Long-Term Care Administration.* Gaithersburg, MD: Aspen; 1994:5–6.

7. U.S. Department of Health and Human Services. Centers for Medicare & Medicaid Services. CMS Nursing Home Data Compendium, 2010. Available from http://www.cms.gov/Medicare/Provider-Enrollment-and-Certification/CertificationandComplianc/downloads/nursinghomedatacompendium_508.pdf. Accessed January 5, 2013.

8. Pavri JM. Overview: one hundred years of public health nursing: visions of a better world. *Imprint.* 1994;4:43–48.

9. Glasscote RM, Beigel A, Butterfield A, et al. *Old Folks at Homes: A Field Study of Nursing and Board and Care Homes.* Washington, DC: American Psychiatric Association; 1976.

10. Moss FE, Halamandaris VJ. *Too Old, Too Sick, Too Bad.* Gaithersburg, MD: Aspen; 1977:15–37.

11. Evans JM, Fleming KC. Medical care of nursing home residents. *Mayo Clin Proc.* 1995;70:694.

12. Centers for Disease Control and Prevention. Long-term care settings. November 24, 2010. Available from http://www.cdc.gov/HAI/settings/ltc_settings.html. Accessed January 6, 2013.

13. Long-Term Care Education.com. Definition of the skilled nursing facility. 2007. Available from http://www.ltce.com/learn/skilledcare.php. Accessed January 6, 2013.

14. National Center on Elder Abuse. Fact Sheet: Abuse of residents of long term care facilities. February 2012. Available from http://www.centeronelderabuse.org/docs/Abuse_of_Residents_of_Long_Term_Care_Facilities.pdf. Accessed January 8, 2013.

15. Centers for Disease Control and Prevention. National study of long term care providers: an introduction. Available from http://www.cdc.gov/nchs/data/nsltcp/NSLTCP_FS.pdf. Accessed January 8, 2013.

16. Centers for Medicare & Medicaid Services. National health expenditures; aggregate and per capita amounts, annual percent change and percent distribution, by type of expenditure: selected calendar years 1960–2011 (Table 2). Nursing care facilities and continuing care retirement communities expenditures; levels, annual percent change and percent distribution, by source of funds: selected calendar years 1970–2011 (Table 15). Home health care services expenditures; levels, annual percent change and percent distribution, by source of funds: selected calendar years 1970–2011 (Table 14). 2013.

Available from http://www.cms.gov/Research-Statistics-Data-and-Systems/
Statistics-Trends-and-Reports/NationalHealthExpendData/downloads/
tables.pdf. Accessed January 13, 2013.

17. MetLife Mature Market Institute. The 2012 MetLife market survey of nursing
home, assisted living, adult day services, and home care costs. November 2012.
Available from https://www.metlife.com/mmi/research/2012-market-sur-
vey-long-term-care-costs.html#keyfindings; and from https://www.metlife.
com/assets/cao/mmi/publications/studies/2012/studies/mmi-nursing-
home-costs-table.pdf. Accessed January 6, 2013.

18. National Center for Health Statistics. *Health, United States, 2011: With
Special Feature on Socioeconomic Status and Health*. Hyattsville, MD:
2012., Table 120. Nursing homes, beds, residents and occupancy rates,
by state: United States, selected years 1995–2010. Available from http://
www.cdc.gov/nchs/data/hus/hus11.pdf#glance. Accessed January 6, 2013.

19. Jones AL, Dwyer LL, Bercovitz AR, et al. The National Nursing Home
Survey:2004 overview. National Center for Health Statistics. *Vital Health
Stat*. 2009;13(167). Percent distribution of nursing homes, according to
type of ownership. Available from http://www.cdc.gov/nchs/data/series/
sr_13/sr13_167.pdf. Accessed January 5, 2013.

20. Association of Boards of Examiners of Long Term Care Administrators.
NAB urges states to approve nationwide standards for nursing home administrator licensing. March 8, 2006. Available from http://www.nabweb.org/
nabweb/uploadedfiles/News_Alerts/Endorsement%20Release%203-8-06.
pdf. Accessed January 6, 2013.

21. The National Academy of Sciences. *For-profit Enterprise in Health Care*.
Washington, DC: National Academy Press; 1986:510–515.

22. Center for Medicare Advocacy. Is there a difference in care? 2012. Available
from http://www.medicareadvocacy.org/2012/03/15/non-profit-vs-for-profit-
nursing-homes-is-there-a-difference-in-care. Accessed January 19, 2013.

23. Center for Medicare Advocacy. Health reform: the nursing home provisions. 2010. Available from http://www.medicareadvocacy.org/print/2010/
reform_10_06.17snfprovisions.htm. Accessed January 19, 2013.

24. Long-term Care Education.com. Definition of assisted living. Available from
http://www.ltce.com/learn/assistedliving.php. Accessed January 9, 2013.

25. Assisted Living Federation of America. Assisted living. 2012. Available
from http://www.alfa.org/alfa/Assisted_Living_Information.asp. Accessed
January 9, 2013.

26. National Association for Home Care and Hospice. Basic statistics about home
care: updated 2010. 2010. Available from http://nahc.org/facts/10hc_stats
.pdf. Accessed January 13, 2013.

27. Medicare Payment Advisory Commission. MEDPAC report to Congress:
Medicare payment policy. March 2012. Available from http://www.medpac
.gov/documents/Mar12_EntireReport.pdf. Accessed January 11, 2013.

28. L & M Policy Research report prepared for Centers for Medicare and
Medicaid Services. Home health study report. January 11, 2011. Available

from http://www.cms.gov/Medicare/Medicare-Fee-for-Service-Payment/ HomeHealthPPS/downloads/HHPPS_LiteratureReview.pdf. Accessed January 13, 2013.

29. Centers for Medicare & Medicaid Services. Post acute care reform plan: policy council document. September 28, 2006. Available from http:// www.cms.gov/Medicare/Medicare-Fee-for-Service-Payment/SNFPPS/ Downloads/pac_reform_plan_2006.pdf. Accessed January 13, 2013.

30. The Henry J. Kaiser Family Foundation. Kaiser Commission on Medicaid and the Uninsured. Money follows the person: A 2011 survey of transitions, services and costs. Executive summary. December 1, 2011. Available from http:// www.kff.org/medicaid/upload/8142-02-2.pdf. Accessed January 19, 2013.

31. American Association of Retired Persons. Health care reform improves access to Medicaid home and community-based services. June 2010. Available from http://assets.aarp.org/rgcenter/ppi/ltc/fs192.hcbs.pdf. Accessed January 19, 2013.

32. The Henry J. Kaiser Family Foundation. Medicaid long-term services and supports: key changes in the health reform law. June 4, 2010. Available from http://kff.org/health-reform/issue-brief/medicaid-long-term-services-and-supports-key/#./?&_suid=136769128304009136120831925913. Accessed January 19, 2013.

33. Reinhard SC, Kassner E, Houser A. How the affordable care act can help move states toward a high-performing system of long-term services and supports. *Health Aff.* 2011;30:447–450. Available from http://content .healthaffairs.org/content/30/3/447.full.html. Accessed January 20, 2013.

34. American Association for Homecare. Cost effectiveness of homecare. Available from https://www.aahomecare.org/issues/cost-effectiveness-of-homecare. Accessed January13, 2013.

35. Centers for Medicare & Medicaid Services. Home health agencies, certification and compliance, home health providers. April 9, 2013. Available from http://www.cms.gov/Medicare/Provider-Enrollment-and-Certification/ CertificationandComplianc/HHAs.html. Accessed May 4, 2013.

36. National Alliance for Caregiving. Caregiving in the U.S.: a focused look at those caring for someone age 50 or older. November 2009. Available from http://www.caregiving.org/data/2009CaregivingAARP_Full_Report.pdf. Accessed January 14, 2013.

37. Family Caregiver Alliance. Caregiving. 2009. Available from http://www .caregiver.org/caregiver/jsp/content_node.jsp?nodeid=2313. Accessed January 14, 2013.

38. Pierret CR. The "sandwich generation": women caring for parents and children. *Mon. Labor Rev.* September 2006:1–9. Available from http://www.bls .gov/opub/mlr/2006/09/art1full.pdf. Accessed January 14, 2013.

39. MetLife Mature Market Institute and National Alliance for Caregiving. The MetLife caregiving cost study: productivity losses to U.S. businesses. July 2006. Available from http://www.caregiving.org/data/Caregiver%20 Cost%20Study.pdf. Accessed January 14, 2013.

40. Feinberg L, Reinhard SC, Houser A, Choula R. *Valuing the Invaluable: The Growing Contributions and Costs of Family, 2011 Update*. AARP Public Policy Institute, 2011. Available from http://assets.aarp.org/rgcenter/ppi/ltc/i51-caregiving.pdf. Accessed January 14, 2013.

41. Family Caregiver Alliance. Health Reform and Family Caregivers. 2010. Available from http://caregiver.org/caregiver/jsp/content/pdfs/HCR%20provisions%20for%20caregivers-2010.pdf. Accessed January 21, 2013.

42. Family Caregiver Alliance. Health Reform and Family Caregivers. 2010. Available from http://caregiver.org/caregiver/jsp/content/pdfs/HCR%20provisions%20for%20caregivers-2010.pdf. Accessed January 21, 2013.

43. U.S. Department of Health and Human Services. Secretary Shalala launches new "Operation Restore Trust": expanded initiative builds on 23–1 recovery success. May 20, 1997. Available from http://archive.hhs.gov/news/press/1997pres/970520.html. Accessed January 14, 2013.

44. U.S. Department of Health and Human Services, Assistant Secretary for Legislation. Testimony on the Balanced Budget Act Home Health Provisions by Nancy-Ann Min DeParle, Administrator, Health Care Financing Administration. March 31, 1998. Available from http://www.hhs.gov/asl/testify/t980331a.html. Accessed January 14, 2013.

45. Centers for Medicare & Medicaid. OASIS and outcome-based quality improvement in home health care: research and demonstration findings, policy implications, and considerations for future change. March 2002. Available from http://www.cms.gov/Medicare/Quality-Initiatives-Patient-Assessment-Instruments/HomeHealthQualityInits/downloads/HHQIOASISReportSummary.pdf. Accessed January 14, 2013.

46. U,S. Department of Health and Human Services. Centers for Medicare & Medicaid Services. Medicare fraud and abuse: prevention, detection and reporting. November 2012. Available from http://www.cms.gov/Outreach-and-Education/Medicare-Learning-Network-MLN/MLNProducts/downloads/Fraud_and_Abuse.pdf. Accessed January 21, 2013.

47. National Hospice and Palliative Care Organization. NHPCO facts and figures: hospice care in America, 2012. Available from http://www.nhpco.org/sites/default/files/public/Statistics_Research/2012_Facts_Figures.pdf. Accessed January 15, 2013.

48. Hospice Foundation of America. Volunteering and hospice. 2013. Available from http://www.hospicefoundation.org/pages/page.asp?page_id=171081. Accessed January 15, 2013.

49. Medicare.com. Medx publishing. Respite care: what respite care does Medicare cover? Available from http://www.medicare.com/assisted-living/respite-care.html. Accessed January 16, 2013.

50. Helpguide.org. *Respite Care*. April 2013. Available from http://www.helpguide.org/elder/respite_care.htm. Accessed May 4, 2013.

51. Mental Health Association in New York State. President signs critical respite bill for family caregivers. January 3, 2007. Available from

https://mhanys.org/publications/mhupdate/update070103.htm. Accessed January 17, 2013.

52. U.S. Administration on Aging. AoA FY 2010 budget signed into law. Available from http://www.aoa.gov/AoARoot/Press_Room/News/2009/12_18_09. aspx. December 18, 2009. Accessed January 17, 2013.

53. Department of Health and Human Services. Administration on Aging. Fiscal year 2013; justification of estimates for appropriations committee. p. 42. Available from http://www.aoa.gov/aoaroot/about/Budget/DOCS/ FY_2013_AoA_CJ_Feb_2012.pdf. Accessed January 16, 2013.

54. Cefalu CA, Heuser M. Adult day care for the demented elderly. *Am Fam Phys.* 1993;47:723–724.

55. Lamden RS, Tynan CM, Warnke J, et al. Adult day care. In: Goldsmith SB, ed. Long-Term Care Administration Handbook. Sudbury, MA: Jones and Bartlett; 1993:395–396.

56. National Respite Network and Resource Center. Adult day care: one form of respite for older adults. August 18, 2010. Available from. http://archrespite.org/ images/docs/Factsheets/fs_54-adult_day_care.pdf. Accessed January 16, 2013.

57. National Adult Day Services Association. About adult day services. Available from http://www.nadsa.org/learn-more/about-adult-day-services/. Accessed January 16, 2013.

58. MacDonnell C. CARF accredits adult day care. *Nurs Homes.* 1999;48:53.

59. Miller JA. *Community-Based Long-Term Care.* New York, NY: Sage; 1991.

60. Deloitte & Touche, LLP, and Deloitte & Touche Consulting Group, LLC. *The Balanced Budget Act of 1997, Public Law 105–33 Medicare and Medicaid Changes.* Washington, DC: Deloitte & Touche, LLP; 1997.

61. National Commission for Quality Long-Term Care. Long-term care in America, an introduction. January 2007. Available from http://www. avalerehealth.net/research/docs/The_US_Long_Term_Care_System_An_ Introduction.pdf . Accessed January 17, 2013.

62. American Association of Retired Persons. Continuing care retirement communities: what they are and how they work. Available from http://www.aarp .org/relationships/caregiving-resource-center/info-09-2010/ho_continuing_ care_retirement_communities.html. Accessed January 17, 2013.

63. Senior Resource for Continuing Care Retirement Communities. Continuing care retirement communities (CCRCs) and life care. Available from http:// www.seniorresource.com/hccrc.htm. Accessed January 17, 2013.

64. The NORC Aging in Place Initiative. All about NORCs. June 21, 2005. Available at http://www.norcs.org/page.aspx?id=119552. Accessed January 17, 2013.

65. U.S. Department of Health and Human Services Assistant Secretary for Planning and Evaluation, Office of Disability, Aging and Long Term Care Policy. Supportive services programs in naturally occurring retirement communities. November 2004. Available from http://aspe.hhs.gov/daltcp/ reports/Norcssp.pdf. Accessed January 17, 2013.

66. National Care Planning Council. Overview of the long term care insurance industry. Available from http://www.longtermcarelink.net/eldercare/long_term_care_insurance.htm#overview. Accessed January 17, 2013.

67. Ujvari K, AARP Public Policy Institute. *Long-Term Care Insurance: 2012 Update*. Available from http://www.aarp.org/content/dam/aarp/research/public_policy_institute/ltc/2012/ltc-insurance-2012-update-AARP-ppi-ltc.pdf. Accessed January 17, 2013.

68. Gleckman H. Requiem for the CLASS Act. *Health Aff.* 2011;30:2231–2232. Available from http://content.healthaffairs.org/content/30/12/2231.full.html. Accessed January 20, 2013.

69. Merlis M. *Financing Long Term Care in the Twenty-first Century: The Public and Private Roles*. Institute for Health Policy Solutions. New York, NY: The Commonwealth Fund; 1999:20.

70. Institute for the Future of Aging Services. The long-term care workforce: can the crisis be fixed? January 2007. Available from http://www.leadingage.org/uploadedFiles/Content/About/Center_for_Applied_Research/Center_for_Applied_Research_Initiatives/LTC_Workforce_Commission_Report.pdf. Accessed January 17, 2013.

71. The Long Term Living editors. What President Obama's re-election means for the future of long-term care. Long Term Living Magazine. 2012. Available from http://www.ltlmagazine.com/article/what-president-obamas-reelection-means-future- long-term-care. Accessed January 17, 2013.

CHAPTER 10

Mental Health Services
Susan V. McLeer, MD, MS

This chapter provides an overview of mental health services in the United States. It examines historical trends and the forces affecting the distribution and kinds of mental health services, compared with epidemiologic data on the prevalence of psychiatric disorders to hypothesize whether national needs for mental health care are being met. Anticipated changes in organization and fiscal structures expected with implementation of the Patient Protection and Affordable Care Act are examined. States' fiscal burdens for mental health services are highlighted. This chapter also addresses opportunities for improvement and evidence of the impact of health insurance and service financing on effective mental health service delivery.

Current Background

The United States is in the midst of cataclysmic changes in health care with enormous political controversy regarding how the nation and individual states should proceed to address the issues of cost, quality, and access to health care services. As this book goes to press, President Obama is midway through the first year of his second term, virtually assuring that the Patient Protection and Affordable Care Act (ACA) will be implemented. Following the 2012 Presidential election, the majority of seats in the House are occupied by Republicans and the majority of seats in the Senate are occupied by Democrats. How this balance of power will play out in developing and funding federal health care policy is far from certain, given that the Congress has been gridlocked for much of the last

2 years. Moreover, definitive efforts at restructuring health care delivery and financing are being initiated at a time when the nation is just beginning to emerge from a major recession. Although improving, unemployment is still too high and revenues, particularly at the state-level, remain low, secondary to continued high unemployment, closure of domestic businesses, lack of a complete recovery of markets, as well as reductions in other sources of revenue. In spite of all of this, change is happening. The paradigms used for providing care and the mechanisms for funding programs and individual care are undergoing rapid change.

In the midst of this change process, a new lexicon has emerged, requiring definitions. "Mental health care" now is often referred to as "behavioral health care," with psychiatric care, a medical subspecialty, being but one aspect of an integrated approach to needed services. Usage of terms is not uniform throughout the country. Some jurisdictions such as states or counties have departments of mental health, whereas others have departments of behavioral health. The term "mental health service," can be considered interchangeable with "psychiatric and behavioral health services" throughout the chapter and use within the chapter will depend upon the historical and political context. The concept of "patient" has been replaced with "consumer" or "person/people" with a "psychiatric or substance abuse disorder" or "mental health issue." The paradigm for service provision has shifted from a treatment plan model, which formerly used a diagnosis-anchored, "problem-based" list, to a model that is "strength-based." The "Recovery Movement" has been well underway since 2004 and advocates for the provision of holistic care within the obvious context that a psychiatric illness or mental health issue is but one aspect of a person's life. The task of recovery is self-directed, individualized, and person-centered. It is founded on the principles that consumers have opportunities for choice, self-direction, and empowerment. The model is similar to that used in working with individuals with other disabilities for several decades. More will be discussed about this later in the chapter.

Historical Overview

In the early years of our nation, the mentally ill were confined at home, in jails, or in almshouses, where they suffered severely. The Quakers, in the first half of the 19th century, were the first to adopt the principles, which evolved from a European movement for the "moral treatment" of the mentally ill. Consequently, in 1814, in the City of Philadelphia, the Quakers established the first free-standing "asylum" where people with mental illness could receive kind, but firm, treatment while engaged in work, education, and recreation.[1] Effective biological treatments were nonexistent. Unfortunately, the vast majority of ill people did not have access to moral treatment; rather, they were confined under the most adverse circumstances in overcrowded asylums and hospitals that housed the mentally ill, criminals, alcoholics, and low-income, homeless people.

A heightened awareness of mental illness resulted from World War I when thousands of soldiers returned suffering from "war neurosis," also called "shell shock," a condition synonymous with current criteria for posttraumatic stress disorder. In the 1930s, the first effective biological treatments emerged in the forms of insulin coma, drug-induced convulsions, electroconvulsive therapy, and psychosurgery. With the advent of World War II, the federal government became active in the mental health field, passing the National Mental Health Act in 1946, which resulted in the establishment of the National Institute of Mental Health (NIMH). Federal, state, and county public funds were allocated for mental health training, research, and service. The Department of Veterans Affairs recognized the need for increased services and established psychiatric hospitals and clinics.

During the 1940s and 1950s, psychiatric care remained focused on inpatient services. By the mid-1950s, over half a million people were hospitalized in state or county mental hospitals. Fortuitously, this corresponded with the development of the first psychoactive medications specifically targeting psychiatric disorders. These agents included chlorpromazine (Thorazine) and reserpine, used for the treatment of schizophrenia and other psychotic disorders. These pharmaceutical advances profoundly changed patterns of care, reducing the need for convulsive therapies and psychosurgery and provided patients with effective interventions that allowed them to live outside of a psychiatric hospital. Concurrently, new outpatient services were developed along with nonhospital transitional residential facilities, or halfway houses, for the mentally ill.

In 1955, Congress established the Joint Commission on Mental Illness and Health. The Commission attacked the quality of care and inadequate patient access to care in large state and county psychiatric hospitals. This was the first time a federal body had considered managing the allocation of resources for the mentally ill. The Commission's report stimulated a substantial shift in sites for the provision of mental health services from inpatient state and county psychiatric hospitals to outpatient facilities. The Commission's recommendations fell on fertile ground and were reiterated by President Kennedy in his first message to Congress.

By the early 1960s, the winds of change had been whipped up not only by the Commission, but also by the development of new psychotropic medications and psychosocial treatments that could provide effective intervention outside the hospital. Congress passed the Mental Retardation Facilities and Community Mental Health Centers Construction Act, resulting in new federal support for community-based services. Large entitlement programs became accessible to the mentally ill, mainly Medicaid, Medicare, Supplemental Security Income (SSI), Social Security and Disability Insurance, and housing subsidies, among others.

Throughout the 1960s and 1970s, the federal government became even more involved in financing mental health care. Community mental health centers developed and expanded, and more health professionals entered the mental health field. Federal and state funding, originally targeted for severely mentally ill people, was shunted through the community mental health systems to provide services for those with less severe illness.[2,3] This shift in service was based on two untested assumptions: (a) psychiatric disorders lie on a quantitative continuum, with severe mental illness not differing qualitatively from lesser forms of mental distress, and (b) early intervention could prevent the development of major psychiatric disorders. Over time, neither assumption has been shown to be valid. Nonetheless, based on these assumptions, money was invested and services were provided to people with mild to moderate dysfunction and "problems in living," with the hope that the incidence of severe mental illness would be reduced through primary prevention.[4]

Treatment of less severe mental health problems was handled through psychosocial interventions without proven efficacy and without systematic and standardized evaluations of outcome. Payment for mental health services was allocated on the basis of units of service provided; hence, there was no incentive for limiting the duration of treatment. Patients were provided with nonspecific, psychosocial interventions for years. From 1955 to 1980, the number of patient care episodes delivered in organized mental health settings increased fourfold, from 1.7 million to 7 million.[5] Few of these patients were severely mentally ill.[6] Insurers became rightly concerned that psychiatric treatment was an uncontrolled health care cost and started limiting coverage for the diagnosis and treatment of mental illness by way of limits on the amount of service that would be reimbursed, irrespective of the nature of the illness, such as lifetime limits, and by developing discounted fee-for-service contracts with the costs of care of the mentally ill being reimbursed as a percentage of cost, a system that used different metrics than those used for reimbursement of the cost for nonpsychiatric illnesses. In addition, insurers were concerned that psychiatric care would drain their coffers and started issuing contracts that outsourced coverage for mental health care, a process referred to as "carve outs." Another process that was developed in an effort to control costs was the use of "capitation," a process through which a set amount was paid for care of a defined population, irrespective of the amount of service provided. Through these financing initiatives, nonparity of insurance coverage for the mentally ill was born and once that had happened, the mental health system was defined as "different" from other health systems, needing a "different," nonequal payment system. The issue of nonparity has plagued the financing mechanisms for mental health care for decades.

Simultaneously, with the development of new insurance structures and with the shift in focus toward ambulatory care within the community mental health centers, many severely mentally ill patients, who formerly had been warehoused in large state or county psychiatric hospitals, were discharged from institutions to community boarding and nursing homes. The deinstitutionalization movement was presented as important to the rehabilitation of those with severe mental illness. Emphasis was placed on the necessity of providing service in community settings. States, through Medicaid, received financial incentives to move patients from inpatient settings to boarding houses. This transfer, coupled with the changes in the staffing and programs at community mental health centers, resulted in many severely mentally ill patients finding limited access to care. Treatments provided at the mental health centers no longer targeted the vulnerable group of people with severe disabilities. Advocacy groups such as the National Alliance on Mental Illness emerged, directing their efforts to channel public dollars reallocated so that services and biomedical research could target severe and persistent mental illness. Advocates maintained that the pivotal issue was the treatment of psychiatric illness, not the maintenance of mental health. Through the efforts of advocacy groups and the National Institutes of Health and clinical researchers, the assumptions fueling the staffing and programming of mental health centers during the 1970s and early 1980s were shown to be erroneous. These were breakthrough developments. Psychiatric disorders were no longer viewed as being on a quantitative continuum, but rather viewed as discontinuous in development. Psychiatric disorders were no longer viewed as originating from intrapsychic conflict, but seen as biologically based illnesses, often precipitated and exacerbated by psychosocial stressors. These disorders and their symptoms became more clearly defined and were viewed as disorders requiring specific targeted treatments, not unfocused "talk" therapies.

By the late 1970s, health care costs had soared, and the federal government became concerned with identifying mechanisms for restraining health-related spending. President Carter, recognizing that new research findings presented opportunities for improving care to the mentally ill, appointed a Presidential Commission on Mental Health. Because of fiscal constraints and political infighting both in Washington and in the field of psychiatry itself, the majority of the Commission's findings and recommendations were never operationalized; however, the Commission's work quietly filtered down to the Department of Health and Human Services, resulting in substantial changes of great importance to those with severe mental illness. Psychosocial rehabilitation programs were expanded under Medicaid. Medicaid payment for outpatient mental health care was expanded; co-payment requirements for case management services were reduced. Patients with severe and persistent mental illness became eligible for SSI funding. These changes resulted in a substantial shift in quality-of-life for this population; however, by the mid-1980s, programs were sharply curtailed again, with cutbacks in housing subsidies, social services, and increased exclusion of people with mental illness from SSI benefits.

By 1990, the locus of mental health care in the United States had definitely shifted from inpatient to outpatient settings. Of the 1.7 million episodes of mental health services delivered in 1955, 77% were in inpatient settings and 23% in outpatient programs. By 1990, 67% of the 8.6 million episodes of mental health services delivered were provided in outpatient programs, 7% in partial hospitalization settings (not 24-hour facilities), and 21% in inpatient services.[7]

Since the 1990s, because of constant and rigorous pressure placed on Congress and legislative bodies by advocacy groups, the focus on severe mental illness returned. Through block grants, state departments of mental health refocused their energies and reallocated resources to ensure the provision of services to the most vulnerable, those afflicted with severe and persistent mental illness. Federal money was reallocated for research and training, with efforts focused on treatment, not prevention.

Financing mechanisms also changed during the 1990s. The Medicare Prescription Drug, Improvement, and Modernization Act expanded drug coverage for older Americans; the Child Health Insurance Program (CHIP), financed jointly by federal and state governments, increased the number of insured children in low-income families, and the Wellstone–Domenici Parity Act of 2008 advanced the cause of insurance parity for mental health services.[8]

In 2010, the ACA provided the opportunity for health care reform and improved access to health services through new provisions for insurance coverage for people who were uninsured, either because of lack of access, secondary to pre-existing illness, or an inability to pay for health insurance. The ACA supported and reinforced the concept of insurance parity.[9]

Recipients of Psychiatric and Behavioral Health Services

Mental illness is widespread in U.S. population. Well-designed epidemiologic studies, conducted by the Epidemiologic Catchment Area (ECA) Program, the National Comorbidity Survey, and the National Comorbidity Survey Replication, estimate that 26.2% of Americans aged 18 and older, approximately one in four adults, suffers from a diagnosable mental disorder in a given year, approximately 57.7 million people.[10,11] However, many of these disorders are temporary and have minimal effects on personal functioning. A subgroup of people having a diagnosable mental illness is classified as having a "serious mental illness" (SMI), that is, they have at least one disorder that meets diagnostic criteria, excluding substance use disorders, and symptoms that have been present for at least 12 months. This subgroup, 6% of adults in the United States, is viewed as being at greatest risk and having the greatest need for service.[10]

Neuropsychiatric disorders are the leading cause of disability in the United States and Canada, surpassing cardiovascular disease, cancer, and unintentional injuries as measured in units encompassing the total burden of disease and defined as disability-adjusted life years (DALYS). DALYS represent the total number of years lost to illness, disability, or premature death within a given population. They are calculated by adding the number of years of life lost to the number of years lived with disability for a certain disease or disorder. Figure 10-1 depicts World Health Organization estimates of categories of diseases and disorders and the percentage each category contributes to the total DALYS for the United States and Canada. As shown, neuropsychiatric disorders contribute nearly twice as many DALYS as cardiovascular diseases and cancers (Figure 10-1).

People and their families suffer immeasurably from mental illness. Studies of the measurable costs for mental illness have examined both direct costs for behavioral health services and treatment as well as expenditures and losses secondary to disability. Estimates based on a 2002 database indicate that at least $300 billion in costs are accrued each year, comprised of disability benefits payments, health care expenditures, and lost earnings[10,12,13] (Figure 10-2).

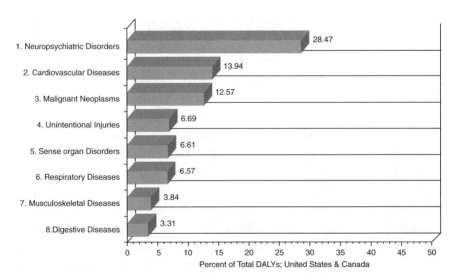

FIGURE 10-1 Burden of Disease: Leading Contributing Disease Categories to DALYs.
Source: Reprinted from National Institute of Mental Health, http://www.nimh.nih.gov/statistics/2LEAD_CAT.shtml.

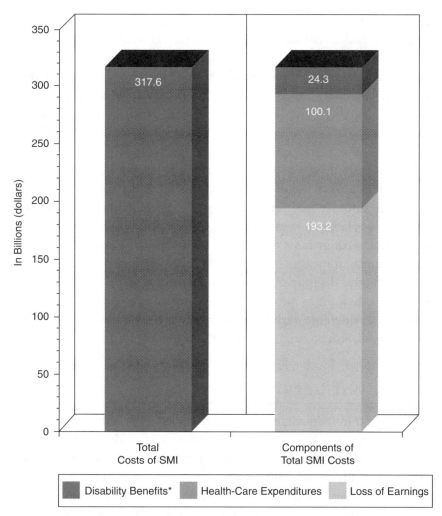

FIGURE 10-2 Annual Total Direct and Indirect Costs of Serious Mental Illness (SMI) in 2002.
Source: Reprinted from National Institute of Mental Health, "Annual Total Direct and Indirect Costs of Serious Mental Illness (2002)," nimh.nih.gov/statistics/4COST_TOTAN.shtml.

In contrast to widely held assumptions, psychiatric disorders can now be diagnosed and treated as effectively as physical disorders. They are classified according to criteria that provide predictability regarding the natural history of the illness and its treatment. Currently, there are 17 diagnostic categories in the *American Psychiatric Association's Diagnostic and Statistical Manual of Mental Disorders (DSM-IV)*, and within these categories, the specific diagnostic criteria for over 450 conditions are delineated.[14] Criteria for specific diagnoses in each of these categories have been subjected to extensive field testing for diagnostic reliability and validity. The DSM-IV is currently undergoing revision and new, research-based revisions to the diagnostic criteria will be forthcoming over the next year.

The co-existence of two diagnoses is called "co-morbidity." According to the National Institute of Mental Health, nearly half of those with any psychiatric disorder meet criteria for two or more disorders, with severity strongly related to comorbidity.[15] ECA studies in both clinical and nonclinical settings have determined that the prevalence of substance abuse comorbidity ranges between 23% and 80% depending on the specific psychiatric diagnosis.[16] In addition, clinical studies of people with intellectual disabilities, formerly referred to as mental retardation, have revealed considerable variation in prevalence estimates of co-morbid psychiatric disorders, ranging from 30% to 60%.[17]

Treatment Services

In 2011, 45.6 million adults, of age 18 or older, 19.6% of the adult population, met criteria for at least one psychiatric disorder in the previous 12-month period; of these, 17.5% also met criteria for a substance abuse disorder. An additional 5.8% of adults in the United States were found to have a substance abuse disorder, but no other mental illness. Among the 45.6 million known to have a mental illness, only 38.2% were able to access mental health treatment services. Among the subgroup with greatest need for treatment, those diagnosed with a SMI, only 59.6% received some form of treatment.[18] These data do not take into consideration whether or not treatment was of adequate duration or quality. Those with SMI are most often treated within the mental health sector; however, others, less severely afflicted, receive services and treatment in other settings. For example, within a 12-month period, of those who were diagnosed with a mental health problem, 41.1% received some treatment, including 12.3% treated by a psychiatrist, 16.0% treated by a nonpsychiatrist mental health specialist, 22.8% treated by a general medical provider, 8.1% treated by a human services provider, and 6.8% treated by a complementary and alternative medical provider.[19] The lack of care was greatest in traditionally underserved groups, such as the elderly, racial–ethnic minorities, as well as people with low incomes or no health insurance. Another notably underserved group was those living in rural areas where mental health or behavioral health services were not available.

Barriers to Care

There are multiple factors associated with lack of access to care. These include (a) provider distribution, (b) financial limitations, (c) lack of or inadequate health insurance, (d) stigma, (e) misunderstandings about the treatability of conditions, (f) personal and provider attitudes, (g) cultural issues, and (h) a poorly organized delivery system of care. Patients with a mental illness and a substance use disorder experience additional barriers secondary to the stigma associated with substance abuse. Substance abuse is a chronic brain disease, like many of the other psychiatric disorders, but the general community and, more disturbingly, providers tend not to view substance abuse and addiction as a chronic illness, but often attribute causality to moral issues. Furthermore, if there is a relapse, rather than seeing the relapse within the structure of a chronic illness, the person who has relapsed is apt to be removed from the treatment program with providers failing to recognize or realize that substance abuse, by its very nature as a chronic illness, is subject to fluctuations that include improvements in function, periods of stabilization, and relapses.[20]

Children and Adolescents

Data on service use by children and adolescents with diagnoses of mental disorder first became available in 1999 following a NIMH survey of children and adolescents between age 9 and 17. Only 9% of children and adolescents had been able to access and receive some mental health services in the general medical and specialty mental health delivery sectors. This accounted for less than half of those with a diagnosed mental illness. The study found that the largest provider of services to children and youth was the school system.[21] In 2009, results from a larger study indicated that the prevalence of mental health disorders in children aged 4–17 had increased more than 40% between the mid-1990s and 2006, with 7% of the population being diagnosed with at least one psychiatric illness.

Increased sensitivity and use of screening tools by primary care physicians appeared to have a major effect on findings with the rate of diagnosis of a mental illness doubling in primary care offices.[22] Access to care still remains problematic.

Clinical research involving children and adolescents suffering from mental illness has lagged considerably behind that for adults. Although diagnostic techniques have been highly refined through standardized diagnostic interviews and symptom rating scales that facilitate accurate identification of those in need of service, research funding for treatment of mental illness in childhood and adolescence has not kept pace. The effects of a mental disorder on the developmental process of children are only beginning to be appreciated, but clearly impact development in emotional, social, and cognitive domains. Moreover, few practitioners access research findings regarding treatment efficacy, and there are inadequate numbers of well-trained child and adolescent psychiatrists available for the population at risk. The need for expanding the workforce, developing early interventions, providing treatment and rehabilitation services, and seeking enhanced funding for research is critical.

Older Adults

Although many advances have been made in the treatment of mental disorders, a crisis looms in providing behavioral health services to the older population. People 65 years old and older represented 12.9% of the population in 2009, but are expected to increase in number and represent 19% of the population, over 72.1 million people, by 2030.[23] In addition to this increase in sheer volume, epidemiologic studies have indicated that baby-boomer cohorts have high-prevalence rates for depression, suicide, anxiety, and alcohol and drug abuse.[24]

Studies have indicated that one in four older Americans have a significant psychiatric disorder, with depression and anxiety disorders being most common. The prevalence of psychiatric disorders in the aging population is expected to more than double over the next 25 years with numbers increasing from 7 to 15 million people. In addition, there looms yet another problem regarding the abuse of alcohol and substances, particularly the abuse and misuse of prescription medication. In 2000–2001, estimates were that 1.7 million older adults abused substances and alcohol and that the prevalence is expected to increase to 4.4 million by 2020.[25]

The implications of these findings on future resource allocation decisions are enormous.

Although older adults suffer from many of the same mental disorders as their younger counterparts, diagnosis and treatment are complicated by medical conditions that mimic or mask psychiatric disorders. Older adults are also more likely to be reluctant to report symptoms and tend to emphasize physical complaints, minimizing complaints about their mental status. Stereotypes about aging predispose older adults to believe that adverse mental changes are to be expected, contributing to a tendency to minimize the symptoms associated with a psychiatric disorder. Fears of developing dementia are omnipresent and add to reluctance in symptom disclosure. Such concerns make assessment and accurate diagnosis challenging.[26]

The Organization of Psychiatric and Behavioral Health Services

Psychiatric disorders and behavioral health problems are treated by an array of providers representing multiple disciplines working in both public and private settings. The loose coordination of facilities and services has resulted in the mental health delivery system being referred to as a "de-facto mental health service system,"[27] with four sectors characterized by poor communication among them.[28]

The psychiatric and behavioral health sector consists of behavioral health professionals, such as psychiatrists, psychologists, psychiatric nurses, psychiatric social workers, and behavioral health clinicians. More recently, providers are hiring peer specialists, people with a psychiatric or substance abuse disorder, who are trained to help others in accessing care and developing a recovery plan. Early reports suggest that peer specialists are particularly helpful in enhancing treatment compliance and community integration. The psychiatric and behavioral health sector provides the majority of care in outpatient settings, such as private office practices or private or public clinics. Most acute care is provided in psychiatric units of general hospitals or beds located throughout hospitals. Intensive treatment for adults and children is provided in private psychiatric hospitals, with residential treatment centers being available for children and adolescents. Public sector facilities include state and county mental hospitals and multiservice facilities that provide or coordinate a wide range of outpatient, intensive case management, partial hospitalization, or inpatient services. Very few long-term care inpatient facilities remain with most care being provided within the community. Currently, there is a movement away from large community residential facilities for the mentally ill and an increased focus on independent living accommodations such as apartments for mentally ill people in need of housing. Case managers work with people to enhance their daily living skills, their use of the public transportation systems, and their ability to access care as well as other resources within the community.

The primary care sector consists of health care professionals, such as internists, family practitioners, pediatricians, and nurse practitioners in private office-based practices, clinics, hospitals, and nursing homes. This sector often is the initial point of contact and may be the only source of mental health services for a large proportion of people with psychiatric or behavioral health disorders. The rates of mental health diagnosis in the primary care setting have increased materially in the past decade, doubling for children and increasing by almost 30% for adults.[8]

The human services sector consists of social service agencies, school-based counseling services, residential rehabilitation services, vocational rehabilitation services, criminal justice/prison-based services, and religious professional counselors. With the advent of the recession of 2008, the role of this sector has shifted as many states have faced significant challenges in balancing their budgets. With increased unemployment and business closures, state revenues are deficient. Consequently, many states have decreased services within the human service and mental health sectors. This has resulted in people with mental illness facing even greater financial and resource barriers to accessing care. In addition, many have experienced significant losses in welfare benefits that have resulted in an inability to pay insurance co-pays for service visits and more importantly, an inability to pay co-pays for medication. Decreased personal revenues, including state-supported general assistance, have resulted in an increase in the homeless population and an increased feeling of desperation among those mentally ill people who have limited financial resources. These economic circumstances and resulting barriers to care have caused exacerbations of symptoms among mentally ill persons who had been previously stable and productive. Co-morbid substance use and abuse has increased as well as petty crimes. As a consequence, many people with SMI have transitioned from the psychiatric and behavioral health sector into the human service sector, specifically into the criminal justice and prison system. Compounding the tragedy of imprisonment is the limited and variable quality of treatment programs for substance abuse and mental illness within the prisons. Costs for prisons far exceed the costs for treating and supporting people with a psychiatric disability within the community. The old adage of "a penny wise, a pound foolish" appears to apply to those states where budget cuts have shifted care from programs specifically designed to care for people with mental illness and substance abuse disorders into the criminal justice and prison systems.

The volunteer support network sector consists of self-help groups and family advocacy groups. This sector has been invaluable in shifting public attention to people with persistent and severe mental illness. Advocacy groups have also had a major impact on Congress in its appropriations for funding research focused on mental illness and substance abuse disorders through the National Institutes of Health. More recently, advocates have been vigorous in lobbying state legislators to minimize cuts to service programs and general assistance for people with mental illness.

Paradigm Shifts

Within the last 5 years, there have been three paradigm shifts directed toward turning the "de facto" mental health system into a more integrated and effective system of care.

Recovery Oriented Systems of Care

The recovery transformation of the mental health system was first introduced in 2002 by the Freedom Commission on Mental Health, established by executive order of President George W. Bush.[29] In 2004, there was a National Consensus Conference on Mental Health Recovery and Mental Health Systems Transformation.[30] This invitational conference was sponsored by the U.S. Department of Health and Human Services and the Interagency Committee on Disability Research in partnership with six other Federal agencies. At this conference, recovery was cited as the single most important goal for transforming mental health care in America. The focus on choice, strength-based empowerment of the consumer, and the establishment of hope for a better life culminated in a true paradigm shift for both assessment and treatment planning.

Recovery is the process of pursuing a fulfilling and contributing life, regardless of the difficulties one has faced. The Recovery Oriented Systems of Care (ROSC) provides a holistic and integrated approach to care, seeking to enhance a person's positive self-image and identity. The overarching goals in ROSC are to empower mentally ill people through the provision of choices and a vision of a hopeful future. Evaluations, which formerly were focused on establishing a diagnosis and a list of problems, are now through the ROSC, person-centered and strength-based. Diagnoses and specific problems remain important, but are now viewed as issues that must be managed within the context of life goals that have the potential to enhance the person's quality-of-life and self-identity. Actively linking a person's strengths with family and community resources are critical steps. Peer specialists facilitate initial contacts between a person and the providers of care, and facilitate a person's connections with resources in the community. Resources may be illness related, but also may be related to the planning of leisure activities, shopping, and other normalizing activities. The ROSC shifts care from the old episodic care model to one that emphasizes continuity. Choice is provided through the treatment planning process. Both providers and individuals are encouraged to focus beyond symptoms of mental illness and articulate needs and desires for housing, utilization of public transportation systems, employment, leisure activities or even a weight-reduction strategy. In ROSC, the traditional treatment plan targeting symptom reduction shifts to that of a "hope plan" for the individual's future.[31]

The Patient Protection and Affordable Care Act

The ACA provides the mechanisms and funding for massive expansion of insurance coverage through private health insurance exchanges and Medicaid expansion. Under the ACA, the individual mandate of health insurance coverage must provide psychiatric and behavioral health benefits as well as provide for coverage parity. In addition, the ACA's targeted improvements of health outcomes through improved quality of care and efficiencies through Accountable Care Organizations and their integration and coordination of health services will benefit mental health services. The impact of the ACA on insurance coverage will be discussed later in this chapter, but the impact of increased integration and coordination of services most notably affects mental health care through integration with primary care services.

Integration of Primary Care and Behavioral Health Services

People with mental illness, particularly those with SMI, die 15–20 years earlier than people without mental illness.[32] Moreover, many of the medications used to treat SMI pose an increased risk for the development of Type 2 Diabetes, whereas others have complex interactions with other medications that the person may be taking for nonpsychiatric conditions. As a result, it is crucial that behavioral health services become increasingly integrated with primary care services. From the perspective of the primary care providers, there is great need for consultation from psychiatrists and behavioral health specialists, particularly given that primary care providers carry much of the burden for early diagnosis of mental illness and substance abuse disorders. Yet, psychiatrists and other behavioral health professionals have traditionally not been involved with the primary care treatment team. Finances have been a major barrier to involvement, particularly the problems posed by insurance nonparity, which has made it difficult, if not impossible, for the behavioral health clinicians to cover costs within a primary care setting. With the ACA's new parity provision for insurance coverage, newer models of care are emerging that emphasize the integration of behavioral health services with primary care. Multiple models for facilitating such integration are being studied, the most prominent model being that of the patient-centered medical home. Funding for establishing such models of integrated care has been provided by the federal government and some of the states. Early reports suggest that this integrative methodology improves health outcomes and, in the long run, will decrease health care costs.[33,34]

Financing Psychiatric and Behavioral Health Services

Mental health services are funded in many ways, including private health insurance, Medicaid, Medicare, state and county funding as well as contracts and grants. As noted in the historic review of mental health services, the history of insurance coverage for behavioral health services has been one of unequal coverage for psychiatric and behavioral health disorders when compared to coverage for nonpsychiatric medical illnesses. The term, "nonparity" has been used to describe insurance inequalities. Insurance inequalities have taken many forms and imposed severe limitations on the amount and kind of care people with chronic and severe mental illness, such as schizophrenia, have been able to access. Recognizing that schizophrenia is a chronic illness not unlike some of the nonpsychiatric chronic illnesses, such as multiple sclerosis, diabetes, stroke, and heart disease, it becomes blatantly apparent that the insurers have produced huge inequities biased against people with mental illness.

The Mental Health Parity Act of 1996 was approved by the U.S. Congress with overwhelming bipartisan support. Enacted in 1998, this legislation equated aggregated lifetime limits and annual limits for mental health services with aggregate lifetime and annual limits for medical care; however, the law allowed many cost-shifting loop holes, such as setting limits on psychiatric inpatient days, prescription drugs, outpatient visits; raising coinsurance and deductibles; and modifying the definition of medical necessity.[35] The Act did not require employers to offer mental health coverage, nor did it impose any limits on insurance co-payments, deductibles, days, or visits. Furthermore, coverage was not required for people suffering from substance use and abuse disorders, which are psychiatric disorders with substantial public health significance.

In 2008, contained within the Emergency Economic Stabilization Act, Senators Paul Wellstone (D-Minnesota) and Pete Domenici (R-New Mexico) proposed the Mental Health Parity and Addiction Equity Act to build upon the Mental Health Parity Act of 1996. Enacted in 2008 with bipartisan support, the law took effect in October 2009. It was intended to end health insurance benefit inequity between mental health and substance abuse benefits and medical/surgical benefits for group health plans with more than 50 employees. Unfortunately, there was a 2-year delay in releasing the Federal regulations for implementation of this Act and the regulations were not released until January of 2010. Significant features of the legislation include the following:

- Equity coverage applicable to all deductibles, co-payments, co-insurance, and out-of-pocket expenses and to all treatment limitations including frequency of treatment, numbers of visits, days of coverage or other similar limits

- Parity coverage for annual and lifetime dollar limits with medical coverage
- Broad definition of mental health and substance abuse benefits
- If a plan offers two or more benefit packages, the parity requirements apply to each package
- Mental health/substance abuse benefit coverage is not mandated, but if a plan offers such coverage, it must be provided at parity with other medical/health benefits coverage
- A group health plan or coverage that provides out-of-network coverage for medical/surgical benefits must also provide out-of-network coverage, at parity, for mental health/substance use disorder benefits
- Preserves existing state parity laws and would only preempt a state law that "prevents the application" of the federal act. Therefore, state parity laws applicable to health insurance coverage continue in effect unless the state laws conflicts with Act's ban on inequitable financial requirements and treatment limitations.[36]

However, as of the end of 2012, it was clear that the intent of the Parity Act can still be avoided by use of nonquantitative treatment limitations (NQTL) for almost all of the psychiatric and substance abuse disorders, whereas applying few of NQTLs to nonpsychiatric illnesses. Clearly, regulators need to develop (a) standards for disclosure of criteria for the medical/surgical benefit, (b) standards that plans should use in establishing that the plan has applied NQTLs in a "comparable and no more stringent manner," (c) standards for determining what constitutes "recognized clinically appropriate standards of care," and (d) standards for delineating parity in scope of service.[37]

Public Funding of Mental Health Care

Because many U.S. citizens have lacked adequate or even basic health insurance coverage for the treatment of psychiatric or substance abuse disorders, most people with severe mental illness have coverage through publically funded insurance, such as Medicaid or Managed Medicaid. These programs are funded by the states, with state monies matched by the federal government through a preset formula.

As previously noted, the 2008 recession had a profoundly negative impact on revenues for the states secondary to increased unemployment and the closure of businesses. Moreover, costs for states have increased significantly. In a 50-state study conducted by the Kaiser Family Foundation Commission on Medicaid and the Uninsured, it was reported that despite additional federal assistance through the American Recovery and Reinvestment Act (ARRA), state budgets were being severely challenged as Medicaid enrollment increased sharply, resulting in the need to decrease other costs, mainly in the human services sector and public welfare systems, despite increased federal funding.

Across the country, states' estimated Medicaid enrollment grew by an average of 5.4% in state fiscal 2009, the highest rate in 6 years, surpassing the projected 3.6% increase at the start of the year. Similarly, total Medicaid spending growth averaged 7.9% in 2009, the highest rate in 5 years, well above the 5.8% projected growth. For 2010, states' estimated Medicaid enrollment grew by 6.6% over 2009 levels.[39] However, for the first time since the advent of the recession of 2008, Medicaid enrollment decreased for 2011.[40] These findings, before the Presidential election, were interpreted as reflecting an increase in employment. However, it does appear that other more problematic factors may be contributing to this trend, mainly the fact that many states have requested and received waivers that allow more restrictive eligibility requirements for Medicaid enrollment.

In a separate study, conducted by the Nelson A. Rockefeller Institute of Government, an even bleaker picture has emerged regarding state budgets. It was noted that the 2008 federal stimulus package would provide fiscal relief to state governments exceeding $150 billion between 2008 and 2011. Although such aid was massive, it was temporary and based on the assumption that with economic recovery, state tax revenues would rise sharply. But in studying the course of past recessions, it is clear that states usually lag considerably behind in recovery (Figure 10-3).

The Institute developed models based on past recessions using a "low gap" scenario and a "high gap" scenario for determining budgets when the ARRA monies ceased in 2011–2012. Assuming a low prestimulus gap, states could face a 4% fiscal gap in general expenditures, which would approximate $70 billion (Figure 10-4). If a higher gap scenario is assumed with prestimulus approximating $370 billion, then states would face a 2011–2012 fiscal gap of more than 7% of general expenditures accounting for more than $100 billion (Figure 10-5). It is clear from these analyses that states face substantial budget dilemmas and they cannot assume that "recovery" of the economy will prevent the need for restructuring, such as cutting expenditures and increasing tax revenues.[41] In response to their current budget shortfalls and not yet even planning for future budget gaps, states have sharply reduced their funding of psychiatric and behavioral health services and costs have been shifted "downstream" to county and community levels, which also suffer from inadequate budgets secondary to the recession and its impact on the local tax base. Many psychiatric hospitals and community-based programs have been closed, and more are closing. Some states have declared their mental health programs to be in shambles. People with severe and persistent mental illness appear to be disproportionately affected. It is clear, however, that monies are inadequate and that health care services at state levels will be affected adversely for at least another 2 years. Compounding these, adverse financial issues affecting people with severe mental illness is the process by which states can apply to the Department of Health and Human Services for waivers to allow changes in state requirements for Medicaid eligibility. These waivers almost always result in changes that cause significant numbers of people to lose their Medicaid benefit in order for states to achieve

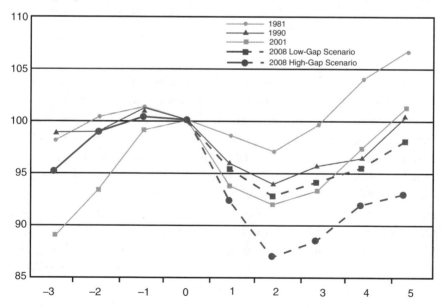

FIGURE 10-3 State Tax Revenue Takes Several Years to Recover After a Recession.
Source: D.J. Boyd, The Nelson A. Rockefeller Institute of Government, reprinted with permission.

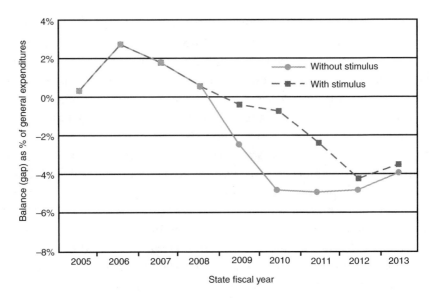

FIGURE 10-4 After Stimulus Wanes, Gaps Could Approximate 4% of Spending or $70 Billion, Even Under the Low Gap Scenario.
Source: D.J. Boyd, The Nelson A. Rockefeller Institute of Government, reprinted with permission.

balanced budgets. Guidelines are needed for approval of waivers that consider the waivers' impact on patients with chronic conditions.

With regard to financing mental health services, the ACA is clearly a "game changer," through its appropriation of an estimated $100 billion over a 10-year period (2010–2019) in mandatory funding and authorization of another $100 billion over the same time period in discretionary funding, subject to the Congress' annual appropriation process. Insurance reform as mandated by the ACA is expected to have a major impact on the financing of psychiatric and behavioral health care. In July 2012, the Congressional Budget Office estimated that 55 million Americans under the age of 65 (20% of those under age of 65) were uninsured.[42] Most uninsured people, because of limited finances, are less likely to seek care for symptoms of mental illness. Fortunately, under the ACA, the pool of insured people will be expanded considerably by two mechanisms: (a) the establishment of state-based affordable health insurance exchanges and (b) the expansion of Medicaid.

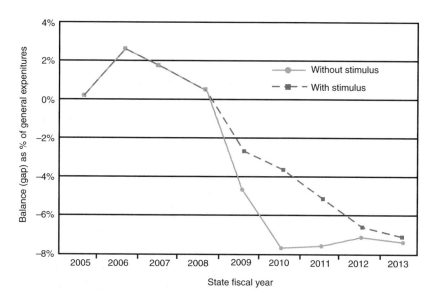

FIGURE 10-5 After Stimulus Wanes, Gaps Could Approximate 7% of Spending or $120 Billion, Under the High Gap Scenario.
Source: D.J. Boyd, The Nelson A. Rockefeller Institute of Government, reprinted with permission.

State-based affordable health insurance exchanges are structures designed to provide a competitive and transparent private purchasing arrangement through which insurers offer individuals and small businesses the opportunity to purchase health insurance. Under the ACA exchanges are supported, in part, by the federal government through grants to the states. The states can manage the exchanges in collaboration with the federal government, or have the federal government manage the exchanges, and must have the exchanges in place by 2014. Another provision in the ACA is that people will be required to be insured with at least an approved basic level of coverage and, for most people, the state-based exchanges will provide opportunities for accessing affordable, lower cost insurance. In setting up the exchanges, decisions must be made regarding what constitutes basic coverage. As noted earlier, under the ACA, coverage for mental health services is mandated and parity of coverage is required. However, the level of coverage has not been specified and, as has been discussed elsewhere in this chapter, there still remain mechanisms for restricting benefits for mental health services through NQTLs. Nonetheless, by 2014, it is reasonably certain that many more people will be insured with at least basic coverage for psychiatric and behavioral health services.[43]

By January 1, 2014, Medicaid will be expanded to provide eligibility to nearly all low-income people under the age of 65 with income below 138% of the Federal Poverty Line (FPL). This expansion will affect millions of low-income adults, with and without children, and in some instances children currently covered through the CHIP. It is anticipated that by 2020, if all states participate in the expansion of Medicaid, there will be an additional 20 million people covered by Medicaid.[44] Theoretically, this should improve access to psychiatric and behavioral health services. However, the decision of the U.S. Supreme Court on June 28, 2012 made it possible for states to opt out from Medicaid expansion. This decision will probably decrease the number of people covered under Medicaid, but those individuals, still being mandated to carry insurance, will be eligible to purchase basic insurance through the state health insurance exchanges and will be eligible for a subsidy to make the purchasing of insurance affordable. In addition, as noted earlier, states can now also decrease the number of people on Medicaid by seeking Medicaid federal waivers. Waivers are having a particularly adverse impact on people with SMI.

Currently, the federal government covers from 50% to 76% of the costs of providing care to Medicaid beneficiaries, with each state's "match rate" depending on its per capita income. CHIP is financed by both the state and the federal government, with the federal match being a capped amount determined by block grants; however, the match rate for CHIP is significantly higher than that for Medicaid and ranges from 65% to 83%. The expansion of Medicaid under the ACA entails three processes: (a) the financing of newly-eligible Medicaid beneficiaries, (b) moving children from CHIP to Medicaid, and (c) offering an early expansion option. For newly eligible Medicaid beneficiaries, the federal government will cover 100% of costs from 2014 to 2016. The match rate will be progressively decreased after that, but will not drop below 90%. Currently, states under the CHIP regulations must provide Medicaid to children under the age of 6 with family incomes up to 138% of the FPL and children 6 years old to 18 years old with family income up to 100% of the FPL. Under the ACA, in 2014, all children regardless of age with family income at 138%

of the FPL will be Medicaid beneficiaries. Estimates are that 24% of children currently in the CHIP will be moved to Medicaid, accounting for approximately 700,000 children. Finally, with the early expansion option, states can expand coverage to childless adults and receive the current Medicaid match without having to seek a waiver. In 2014, the federal match will be expanded in accord with the metrics noted earlier. Under the ACA, millions of low-income people and their children will have access to Medicaid coverage, removing yet another financial barrier to accessing psychiatric and behavioral health care services.[45]

Cost Containment Mechanisms

As in other health care sectors, managed care programs were designed to control costs through financial incentives which reward outcomes of care, not service utilization. Today, over 176 million Americans, 58.5% of the adult population, receive their health coverage through their employer.[46] Employer surveys indicate that 99% of all workers covered by employer benefits are enrolled in some type of managed care plan.[47] Managed care systems for people with mental illness tightly control utilization and closely monitor heavy users of mental health services. Before the passage of the Parity Act of 2008, managed care firms often did not incorporate coverage for mental illness in their basic contracts because of concerns about the costs of chronic care. If coverage was provided, it was "carved out," and outsourced to a subcontractor, known as a "Managed Behavioral Healthcare Organization" (MBHO), which would assume the financial risk as well as the benefits of managing budgets and authorization for access to mental health services. The past practice of limiting mental health benefits to a greater extent than general health care benefits is no longer permitted under the federal parity laws, and the U.S. Department of Labor has been charged with monitoring and insuring compliance with parity laws and regulations.

Public sector initiatives have paralleled private sector efforts in using MBHOs to control costs. Recent research indicates that MBHOs, both within the public and private sector, have facilitated access and coordinated care for those in greatest need as more people with SMI are now more likely to receive mental health specialty services than in the past.[48,49]

The Future of Psychiatric and Behavioral Health Services

As previously noted, there have been significant paradigm changes in psychiatric and behavioral health care and service organization. Qualitatively, the shift to a recovery model of care provides for a strength-based system, individualized in accord with client-directed life goals and objectives, with the psychiatrist being but one component of an array of providers. This is a substantial shift from the practitioner or provider-driven system focused on diagnosis-anchored problems. Secondly, the move toward fully integrating psychiatry and behavioral health services with primary care is also a substantial shift away from a separate and more isolated model of care. Both of these shifts are transforming events, which will qualitatively change the face of mental health care, if not all health care nationally. However, the real "game changer" is the ACA, which, for vast numbers of Americans, will assure access to affordable health insurance and mandate parity of mental health benefits. As these new initiatives and health care laws are implemented, it is expected that overall health services will be improved by assuring increased access to needed psychiatric and behavioral health services, and by increasing the likelihood that those with SMI will be able to access primary care services. Integration of mental health with primary care services will go a long way in reducing untoward effects from drug interactions as well as early interventions for illnesses that are more likely to occur in those with psychiatric illness and on psychotropic medications, such as Type II Diabetes Mellitus. It is a time of great change and promise in the health care delivery system as a whole and for the mental health services sectors in particular. It is also a time that will require practitioners to be extraordinarily flexible in embracing change.

Key Terms for Review

"Carve-out"	Mental Health Parity
Co-morbidity	National Alliance on Mental Illness
Deinstitutionalization	Nonquantitative treatment limitations
Disability-Adjusted Life Years (DALYS)	(NQTLs)
Managed Behavioral Healthcare Organization (MBHO)	Recovery-Oriented Systems of Care (ROSC)

References

1. Bockoven JS. *Moral Treatment in Community Mental Health*. New York: Springer; 1972.
2. Morrissey JP, Goldman HH. Cycles of reform in the care of the chronically mentally ill. *Hosp Community Psychiatry*. 1984;35:785–789.
3. Gronfein W. Incentives and intentions in mental health policy: a comparison of the Medicaid and community mental health programs. *J Health Social Behav*. 1985;26:192–206.
4. Mechanic D. *Mental Health and Social Policy*. 3rd ed. Englewood Cliffs, NJ: Prentice Hall; 1989:27–46.
5. Klerman GL. The psychiatric revolution of the past 25 years. In: Gove WR, ed. *Deviance and Mental Illness*. Newbury Park, CA: Sage Publishing; 1982:180.
6. Mechanic D. Establishing mental health priorities. *Milbank Q*. 1994;72: 501–514.
7. Redick RW, Witkin MJ, Atay JE, et al. The evolution and expansion of mental health care in the United States between 1955 and 1990. In: *Mental Health Statistical Note 210*. Washington, DC: U.S. Department of Health and Human Services; 1994.
8. Glied SA, Frank RG. Better but not best: recent trends in the well-being of the mentally ill. *Health Aff*. 2009;28:637–638.
9. 111th U.S. Congress. Public Law 111-148. *The Patient Protection and Affordable Care Act*. Washington, DC: U.S. Government Printing Office; March 23, 2010.
10. Kessler RC, Chiu WT, Demler O, Walters EE. Prevalence, Severity, and Comorbidity of Twelve-month DSM-IV Disorders in the National Comorbidity Survey Replication (NCS-R). *Arch Gen Psychiatry*. June 2005;62(6):617–627.
11. National Institute of Mental Health. The numbers count: mental disorders in America. 2008. Available from http://www.nimh.nih.gov/health/publications/the-numbers-count-mental-disorders-in-america/index.shtml. Accessed December 22, 2012.
12. Substance Abuse and Mental Health Services Administration. *National Expenditures for Mental Health Services and Substance Abuse Treatment, 1986-2005*. DHHS Publication No. (SMA) 10-4612. Rockville, MD: Center for Mental Health Services and Center for Substance Abuse Treatment, Substance Abuse and Mental Health Services Administration; 2010. Available from http://store.samhsa.gov/shin/content/SMA10-4612/SMA10-4612.pdf. Accessed December 19, 2012.
13. Mark TL, Coffey RM, McKusick DR, et al. *National Estimates of Expenditures for Mental Health Services and Substance Abuse Treatment, 1991–2001* SAMHSA Publication No. SMA 05-3999. Rockville, MD: Substance

Abuse and Mental Health Services Administration; 2005. Available from http://www.samhsa.gov/spendingestimates/SEPGenRpt013105v2BLX.pdf. Accessed January 3, 2013.

14. American Psychiatric Association. *Diagnostic and Statistical Manual.* 4th ed. Washington, DC: American Psychiatric Press; 1994.

15. National Institute of Mental Health. Questions and answers about the national comorbidity survey replication study. May 3, 2013. Available from http://www.nimh.nih.gov/health/topics/statistics/ncsr-study/questions-and-answers-about-the-national-comorbidity-survey-replication-ncsr-study.shtml#q6. Accessed May 4, 2013.

16. Regier DA, Farmer ME, Rae DS, et al. Comorbidity of mental disorders with alcohol and other drug abuse: results from the Epidemiological Catchment Area (ECA) Study. *JAMA.* 1991;264:2511–2518.

17. Kerker BD, Owens PL, Zigler E, Horwitz SM. Mental health disorders among individuals with mental retardation: challenges to accurate prevalence estimates. *Public Health Rep.* 2004;119(4):409–417.

18. Substance Abuse and Mental Health Services Administration, *Results from the 2011 National Survey on Drug Use and Health: Mental Health Findings,* NSDUH Series H-45, HHS Publication No. (SMA) 12-4725. Rockville, MD: Substance Abuse and Mental Health Services Administration; 2012.

19. Wang PS, Lane M, Olfson M, Pincus HA, Wells KB, Kessler RC. Twelve-month use of mental health services in the United States: results from the National Comorbidity Survey Replication. *Arch Gen Psychiatry.* 2005; 62(6):629–640.

20. National Institute on Drug Abuse. Addiction science: from molecules to managed care. July 2008. Available from http://www.drugabuse.gov/publications/addiction-science. Accessed December 4, 2012.

21. U.S. Department of Health and Human Services. *Mental Health: A Report of the Surgeon General*—Chapter 3. Rockville, MD: U.S. Department of Health and Human Services, Substance and Mental Health Services Administration, Center for Mental Health Services, National Institutes of Health, National Institute of Mental Health; 1999:409.

22. Glied SA, Frank RG. Better but not best: recent trends in the well-being of the mentally ill. *Health Aff.* 2009;28:639–640.

23. U.S. Department of Health and Human Services Administration on Aging. *Aging Statistics 2009.* September 1, 2011. Available from http://www.aoa.gov/AoARoot/Aging_Statistics/index.aspx Accessed January 3, 2013.

24. Regier DA, Boyd JH, Burke JD Jr, et al. One month prevalence of mental disorders in the United States: based on five epidemiological catchment area sites. *Arch Gen Psychiatry.* 1988;45:977–986.

25. Bartels SJ, Blow FC, Brockmann LM, et al. Substance abuse & mental health among older americans: the state of the knowledge and future directions, Older American Substance Abuse and Mental Health Technical Assistance Center, Substance Abuse and Mental Health Services Administration. 2005

Available from http://gsa-alcohol.fmhi.usf.edu/Substance%20Abuse%20 and%20Mental%20Health%20Among%20Older%20Adults-%20 The%20State%20of%20Knowledge%20and%20Future%20Directions. pdf. Accessed January 3, 2013.

26. U.S. Department of Health and Human Services. *Mental Health: A Report of the Surgeon General*—Chapter 6. Rockville, MD: U.S. Department of Health and Human Services, Substance and Mental Health Services Administration, Center for Mental Health Services, National Institutes of Health, National Institute of Mental Health; 1999:340–341.

27. Regier DA, Narrow WE, Rae DS, et al. The de facto U.S. mental and addictive disorders service system: epidemiological catchment area prospective 1-year prevalence rate of disorders and services. *Arch Gen Psychiatry.* 1995;50:85–94.

28. U.S. Department of Health and Human Services. *Mental Health: A Report of the Surgeon General*—Chapter 6. Rockville, MD: U.S. Department of Health and Human Services, Substance and Mental Health Services Administration, Center for Mental Health Services, National Institutes of Health, National Institute of Mental Health; 1999:406–407.

29. President's New Freedom Commission on Mental Health. *Achieving the Promise: Transforming Mental Health Care in America, Executive Summary, 3-4.* July 2003. Available from http://govinfo.library.unt.edu/mentalhealth-commission/reports/FinalReport/downloads/downloads.html. Accessed January 3, 2013.

30. U.S. Department of Health and Human Services. Substance Abuse and Mental Health Services Administration. Interim Report of the President's New Freedom Commission on Mental Health. October 29, 2002. Available from http://govinfo.library.unt.edu/mentalhealthcommission/reports/ Interim_Report.htm. Accessed May 4, 2013.

31. U.S. Department of Health and Human Services. Substance Abuse and Mental Health Services Administration. Transforming Mental Health Care in America: The Federal Action Agenda, 2005. Available from http:// www.samhsa.gov/federalactionagenda/NFC_execsum.aspx. Accessed January 3, 2013.

32. Newcomer JW, Hennekens CH. Early death rate for severe mental illness and risk of cardiovascular disease. *JAMA.* 2007;298(15):1794–1796.

33. Collins C, Hewson DL, Munger R, Wade T. Evolving Models of Behavioral Health Integration in Primary Care. New York: Millbank Memorial Fund, 2010.

34. Butler M, Kane RL, McAlpine D, Kathol RG et al. *Integration of Mental Health/Substance Abuse and Primary Care.* Washington, DC: Agency for Healthcare Research and Quality, U.S. Department of Health and Human Services; 2008.

35. National Alliance on Mental Illness. *The Mental Health Parity Act of 1996.* Available from http://www.nami.org/Content/ContentGroups/

E-News/1996/The_Mental_Health_Parity_Act_of_1996.htm. Accessed January 3, 2013.

36. Mental Health America. Fact Sheet: Paul Wellstone and Pete Domenici Mental Health Parity and Addiction Equity Act of 2008. Available from http://takeaction.mentalhealthamerica.net/site/PageServer?pagename=Equity_Campaign_detailed_summary. Accessed January 3, 2013.

37. US Department of Labor. Mental Health Parity and Addiction Equity Act: Sub-regulatory guidance in the form of Frequently Asked Questions (FAQs). Available at http://www.dol.gov/ebsa/faqs/faq-aca7.html. Accessed December 14, 2012.

38. The Henry J. Kaiser Family Foundation. Kaiser Commission on Medicaid and the Uninsured. The Crunch Continues: Medicaid Spending, Coverage and Policy in the Midst of a Recession: Results from a 50-state Medicaid Budget Survey for State Fiscal Years 2009-2010. Executive Summary. September 2, 2009. Available from http://kaiserfamilyfoundation.files.wordpress.com/2013/01/7985_es.pdf.2010. Accessed May 4, 2013

39. U.S. Department of Health and Human Services. Substance Abuse and Mental Health Services Administration. Projections of National Expenditures for Mental Health Services and Substance Abuse Treatment 2004-2014. November 23, 2008. Available from http://162.99.3.205/post/Projections-of-National-Expenditures-for-Mental-Health-Services-(2004-2014).aspx. Accessed May 4, 2013.

40. The Kaiser Commission on Medicaid and the Uninsured. Medicaid Today: Preparing for Tomorrow: A Look at State Medicaid Program Spending, Enrollment and Policy Trends. Results from a 50-state Medicaid Budget Survey for State Fiscal Years 2012 & 2013. October 1, 2012. Available from http://www.kff.org/medicaid/8380.cfm. Accessed December 4, 2012.

41. Boyd DJ. What will happen to state budgets when the money runs out? The Nelson A. Rockefeller Institute of Government. February 19, 2009. Available from http://www.rockinst.org/pdf/government_finance/2009-02-19-What_Will_Happen_to.pdf. Accessed January 3, 2013.

42. Congressional Budget Office. Estimates for the Insurance Coverage Provisions of the Affordable Care Act Updated for the Recent Supreme Court Decision. July 2012. Available from http://www.cbo.gov/sites/default/files/cbofiles/attachments/43472-07-24-2012-CoverageEstimates.pdf. Accessed December 5, 2012.

43. The White House. ACA. Fact Sheet: The Affordable Care Act: Secure Health Coverage for the Middle Class. June 28, 2012. Available from http://www.whitehouse.gov/the-press-office/2012/06/28/fact-sheet-affordable-care-act-secure-health-coverage-middle-class. Accessed May 4, 2012.

44. Kaiser Commission on Medicaid and the Uninsured. The Cost and Coverage Implications of the ACA Medicaid Expansion: National and State-by-State Analysis. November 2012. Available from http://www.kff.org/medicaid/8384.cfm. Accessed December 5, 2012.

45. The Henry J. Kaiser Family Foundation. Financing new Medicaid coverage under health reform, the role of the federal government and states. May 7, 2010. Available from http://www.kff.org/healthreform/8072.cfm.Accessed April 15, 2012.

46. IDeNavas-Walt C, Proctor BD, Smith JC. U.S. Census Bureau Current Population Reports, P60-236. *Income, Poverty, and Health Insurance Coverage in the United States: 2008.* Washington, DC: U.S. Government Printing Office. September 2009. Available from http://www.census.gov/prod/2009pubs/p60-236.pdf. Accessed December 21, 2012.

47. The Kaiser Family Foundation and Health Research and Educational Trust. Employer health benefits 2009 annual survey. Exhibit 5.1. Available from http://ehbs.kff.org/pdf/2009/7936.pdf. Accessed December 21, 2012.

48. Mechanic D, Bilder S. Treatment of people with mental illness: a decade-long perspective. *Health Aff.* 2004;23:93.

49. Dixon K. Implementing mental health parity: the challenge for health plans. *Health Aff.* 2009;28:663–665. Available from http://content.healthaffairs.org/cgi/reprint/28/3/663?maxtoshow=&HITS=10&hits=10&RESULTFORMAT=&fulltext=managed+behavioral+health+care&andorexactfulltext=and;&searchid=1&FIRSTINDEX=10&sortspec=date&resourcetype=HWCIT. Accessed December 19, 2012.

11

Public Health and the Role of Government in Health Care

This chapter presents the history of governmental efforts to prevent or control the problems of health and disease. Efforts to protect the public's health, begun in early European history and transferred to Colonial America, are traced with emphasis on their purpose, motivation, and success. Trends in the rise and historical challenges of America's elaborate federal, state, and local partnerships in the delivery of public health services are described, as well as the activities of private and voluntary agencies. Barriers to effective preventive services that result from the lack of a population perspective in the U.S. health care system are discussed. Specific provisions of the Patient Protection and Affordable Care Act (ACA) that impact public health are reviewed. The chapter concludes with a discussion of future public health opportunities and challenges in the reforming system.

Public Health Defined

The term "public health" is usually defined broadly as the efforts made by communities to cope with the health problems that arise when people live in groups. Community life creates the need to control the transmission of communicable diseases, maintain a sanitary environment, provide safe water and food, and sustain disabled and low-income populations.[1] Grounded in the tenets of social justice, public health applies the principles of medicine, epidemiology, statistics, social and behavioral sciences, environmental sciences, and other disciplines in order to achieve the best possible health status for populations.

Thus public health is unique in its interdisciplinary approach and methods, its emphasis on preventive strategies, its linkage with government and political decision making, and its dynamic adaptation to new problems placed on the agenda. Above all else, it is a collective effort to identify and address the unacceptable realities that result in preventable and avoidable health and quality of life outcomes, and it is the composite of efforts and activities that are carried out by people and organizations committed to these ends.[2]

In the context of its population perspective, public health has continued to adapt and apply various "ecological models" to its pursuits. These models take into account the vast number of factors or determinants that impact the health status of groups of people. Health determinants include factors such as the following:

- Physical environments in which people live and work
- Political conditions under which people live
- Human biology and genetics
- Social factors such as economic circumstances; discrimination by race, ethnicity, gender, or sexual orientation; and the availability of familial or other social supports
- Behavioral choices
- Cultural norms

The interdependence and interaction of factors such as these coalesce to produce effects on population health.[3,4] Ecological models typically explain the occurrence of a healthy state or its absence by identifying causes rooted in the physical and/or social environment and behavioral causes related to an individual. In public health, the utility of these models resides in their facilitating decisions about the most expeditious path to developing effective interventions.

A Brief Early History

The world history of public health is a fascinating study of civilized society's attempts to deal with the biologic, social, and environmental forces that have contributed to the pervasive problems of morbidity and mortality and with the unfortunate citizens who have been handicapped by illness, disability, and poverty. The following observations are presented primarily to set the stage for understanding the development of government's role in the evolution of public health in the United States.

Throughout history, public health activities have reflected the state of knowledge at the time regarding the nature and cause of the diseases that afflict humankind, the practices used for their control or treatment, and the dominant social ideologies of political jurisdictions. From the concepts of spiritual cleanliness and community responsibility codified by the ancient Hebrews for religious reasons to the systems of personal hygiene practiced by the Greeks in an effort to achieve a perfect balance between body and mind, ancient civilizations learned patterns of individual behavior they believed promoted health and reduced the risk of disease. It remained for the Romans, however, to develop public health as a governmental matter beyond individual practice.

The engineering and administrative accomplishments that provided the Romans with clean water and effective sewage and swamp drainage systems were the forerunners of politically sanctioned environmental protections of the public's health. In addition, the Roman Empire is given credit for establishing a network of infirmaries to treat illness among the disadvantaged populations. These infirmaries are considered to be the first public hospitals.

The medieval period that followed the fall of Rome was characterized by the disintegration of the cities and the return of anarchy. The overpopulated walled towns built to withstand enemy attacks crowded families together in the unhealthiest circumstances. The pest-ridden, unsanitary living conditions and the narrow, dark streets that overflowed with human waste and refuse provided fertile environments for disease epidemics that decimated large segments of those populations. Superstitious, demonic, and theological theories of epidemic disease displaced ancient concerns for personal hygiene and the quality of the environment.

The Renaissance, however, was characterized by a great revival of learning. Along with advances in art, literature, and philosophy and the rise of industry and commerce, there was a renewed interest in science and medicine. From the 16th to the 18th centuries, public health was shaped by two countervailing trends.[2] Although the administration of rudimentary medical and nursing services continued to be the responsibility of towns and other local units, the concept of the modern state was beginning to emerge.

Because only a political jurisdiction that protected and cared for its citizens could reap the continuing economic benefits of production and world trade, healthy laborers and soldiers became valuable commodities. Thus in the centralized national governments of Europe during the 16th and 17th centuries, maintaining the health of laborers and soldiers became important economic, political, and public health concerns.

Public Health in England

Poverty, illness, and disability were common problems in the towns and parishes of England during the 16th and 17th centuries, and most communities responded with some form of publicly supported medical care provided in private homes or at public infirmaries. The Elizabethan Poor Laws of 1601 addressed the issue of the "lame, impotent, old, blind, and such other among them being poor and not able to work" without dealing directly with health matters.[5] The law was expanded subsequently to include the provision of nursing and medical care.

It was also in England that the collection and analysis of national statistics regarding industrial production and demographics began in the 17th century. The work of the father of political arithmetic, William Petty (1623–1687), and the statistical analyses of his friend John Graunt (1620–1674) established the importance of vital statistics and led to such epidemiologic tools as population-specific and disease-specific morbidity and mortality rates, life tables, and the calculus of probability. Study of the vital statistics contained in the *Bills of Mortality* published weekly in London led to a better understanding of the social phenomena that were factors in the promotion of health and the occurrence of disease.

Of interest, in light of subsequent debates about the merits of national health services, was the proposal of John Bellers, a London merchant and philanthropist (1654–1725). At the turn of the century, he proposed dealing with public health problems on a national scale. In *An Essay Towards the Improvement of Physick*, Bellers suggested that people's health was too important to the community to be left to the uncertainty of individual initiative. He argued that the health of the people was the responsibility of the state, whose task it was to establish and maintain hospitals and laboratories, erect a national health institute, and provide medical care for the sick.

The Elizabethan Poor Laws obligated each parish in England to maintain its own disadvantaged citizens. Despite a variety of schemes to deal with the health problems of the low-income populations, including the widespread development of workhouses to teach the unemployed to support themselves, the fundamental economic and social problems that led to pervasive poverty remained unsolved. By the 19th century, the industrialization of England had made poverty and social distress increasingly prevalent. In that climate, the drastic Poor Law Amendment Act of 1834 was passed. The dual intent was to reduce the rates of populations' dependency and free the labor market to spur industrialization. The law required that able-bodied people and their families be given aid only in exchange for their labor in well-regulated workhouses whose conditions were to be harsher than those of the lowest paid workers.[6]

The circumstances of the new industrial society, factories, and the congested dwellings of urban environments produced new health problems. As people crowded into burgeoning towns and cities, diseases flourished and spread. It was the Poor Law Commission of 1834 under the leadership of Edwin Chadwick that developed the means to address public health problems. Motivated by the belief that it would be good economy to prevent disease, Chadwick advocated the use of carefully collected data to link population characteristics, environmental conditions, and the incidence of diseases.

After many investigations, political debates, and subsequent political compromises, England's Public Health Act became law in 1848, and a General Board of Health was created. Although the subsequent history of public health in England is a chronicle of social change, epidemics, and political machinations, it is evident that the growth of their sanitary reform movement and the creation of the General Board of Health in 1848 established the British as world leaders in public health philosophy and practice. Public health in early America was heavily influenced by the medical and administrative experience of the British.[5]

Development of U.S. Public Health and Government-Supported Services

The history of public health in the United States from the early colonial period to the end of the 19th century followed the same development pattern as that of England. Yellow fever and cholera epidemics stimulated sanitary reforms, and the early cities and towns began to assume responsibility for the collective health of their citizens. Public medical care in the United States, however, bore the stigma of its "Poor Law" legacy. The New York Poor Law of 1788 provided that any town or city could establish an almshouse, and within a few years most towns and cities had done so. Although there was a series of shocking exposés of terrible conditions in many of these facilities, the concept of the almshouse and town-employed physicians remained the mainstay of sick people among the low-income population until the Great Depression of the 1930s.

Lemuel Shattuck, a Massachusetts statistician, conducted U.S. sanitary surveys similar to those of Chadwick in England. In his Report of the Sanitary Commission, published in 1850, he documented differences in morbidity and mortality rates in different locations and related them to various environmental conditions. Consequently, he argued that the city or state had to take responsibility for the environment. Although largely ignored at the time of its release, the report has come to be considered one of the most influential documents in the evolution of public health in the United States.[7]

In 1865, emulating the Shattuck survey in Massachusetts, the New York City Council of Hygiene and Public Health published a shocking exposé of unsanitary conditions in the city. Within a year, New York City passed a public health law that created a city board of health. Creating an appropriate administrative structure for local public health efforts became a turning point for public health in the United States.

As in England and other countries, early federal public health initiatives were motivated more by economic and commercial concerns than humanitarian values. For instance, the U.S. Public Health Service was established in 1798 as the Marine Hospital Service when President John Adams signed into law an act providing for the care and relief of seamen who were sick or disabled. Because healthy sailors were a valuable commercial commodity and because the seaport towns took responsibility for only their own citizens, it was left to the federal government to provide health services to the seamen and passengers of the important shipping industry. Additionally, it was of serious concern to the citizens of seaports that the personnel of foreign ships not transmit diseases contracted elsewhere.

Soon thereafter, the first marine hospital was set up in Boston Harbor, and seamen received care in port cities along the East Coast. In 1870, the Marine Hospital Service was reorganized as a national hospital system with central headquarters in Washington, DC. The medical officer in charge, known at first as the supervising surgeon, was later given the title of "surgeon general." The title of surgeon general continues to this day for the chief medical officer of the United States. In light of the commercial motivation for its creation, the Marine Hospital Service was established as a component of the Treasury Department.

In 1889, Congress established the Public Health Service Commissioned Corps. Envisioned as a mobile force of physicians to assist the nation in fighting disease and protecting health, the Corps was set up along military lines, with titles and pay corresponding to Army and Navy grades and physicians subject to duty wherever assigned.[8] In 1891, the bacteriologic laboratory in the Staten Island Marine Hospital was moved to Washington, DC, where it was expanded to include pathology, chemistry, and pharmacology. It was the forerunner of the National Institutes of Health, which today provides two-thirds of all federal support for biomedical research. Eleven years later, in 1902, a new law changed the Marine Hospital Service's name to Public Health and Marine Hospital Service. In 1912, the name would be changed again to its present designation: the U.S. Public Health Service. From this modest start, the Public Health Service underwent a series of reorganizations and expansions until it became a major agency of the U.S. Department of Health and Human Services (DHHS) and responsible for the largest public health program in the world.[9]

In 1933, it became apparent that state and local governments with limited tax revenues required help from the federal government to provide welfare assistance, and the Federal Emergency Relief Act was passed. It provided federal aid to the states and authorized general medical care for acute and chronic illness, obstetric services, emergency dental extractions, bedside nursing, drugs, and medical supplies. Because participation by the states was optional, the act was not implemented in many parts of the country.[10]

The passage of the Social Security Act of 1935 ended the era of makeshift federal and state programs to meet the health needs of sick people among the low-income population. Title VI of the landmark Social Security Act of 1935 was instrumental in the expansion of the Public Health Service. The Act delegated to the Public Health Service the authority to assist states, counties, health districts, and other political subdivisions to establish and maintain public health services. Title VI provided the impetus for all political jurisdictions to create public health agencies and services. After 141 years, the Public Health Service was removed from the Treasury Department to become a component of the new Federal Security Agency, created in 1939 to bring together most of the health, welfare, and educational services scattered throughout the federal government. In 1946, the Federal Security Agency also was expanded to include the Children's Bureau and the Food and Drug Administration. During World War II, the Public Health Service carried out emergency health and sanitation efforts that contributed substantially to the country's defense efforts. Since 1946, the Public Health Service has provided national leadership in hospital planning, research, and operation.

In 1953, the Public Health Service with the other components of the Federal Security Agency became part of the newly created Department of Health, Education and Welfare (HEW). During the next decade, the health care industry faced the multiple challenges of coping with a rapidly expanding U.S. population, rising public expectations for health services, and a host of technologic advances in health care with an inadequate supply of health professionals.

The National Institute for Occupational Health and Safety; the National Institute on Alcohol Abuse and Alcoholism; the National Health Service Corps; and major initiatives in addressing cancer and heart, lung, and blood diseases were established in the early 1970s. In 1979, the education component of HEW was transferred to a new Department of Education, and HEW was renamed as the DHHS.[8]

Now, with a proposed 2013 budget of $941 billion,[8] the DHHS is the federal government's principal agency concerned with health protection and promotion and provision of health and other human services to vulnerable populations. In addition to administering the Medicare and Medicaid programs, DHHS includes over 300 separate programs[11] that carry out activities through the following operating divisions[12]:

1. National Institutes of Health (NIH): Established first as a laboratory in 1887, the NIH is the world's premier medical research organization and includes 18 separate health institutes, the National Center for Complementary and Alternative Medicine, and the National Library of Medicine. The NIH supports over 30,000 research projects on a variety of medical conditions and has a budget for 2013 of almost $31 billion.

2. Food and Drug Administration (FDA): This agency is responsible for ensuring the safety of foods and cosmetics and the safety and efficacy of pharmaceuticals, biologic products, and medical devices. Its proposed 2013 budget is $4.5 billion.

3. Centers for Disease Control and Prevention (CDC): Established in 1946, the CDC is the primary federal agency responsible for protecting the American public's health through monitoring disease trends, investigations of outbreaks and health and injury risks, and implementation of illness and injury control and prevention measures. The proposed 2013 budget is over $11 billion.

4. Indian Health Service (IHS): The IHS operates 38 hospitals, 56 health centers, 4 school health centers, and 44 health stations. Through transfers of IHS services operating authority, tribes also administer an additional 13 hospitals, 160 health centers, 3 school health centers, 76 health stations, and 160 Alaska village clinics. Services are provided to nearly 1.5 million Native Americans and Alaska natives of 557 federally recognized tribes in Alaska and the 48 contiguous states. The agency has a proposed 2013 budget of almost $5 billion.

5. Health Resources and Service Administration (HRSA): Established in 1982 to provide a coordinated agency for multiple programs serving low-income, uninsured, and medically underserved populations, the HRSA provides funds for comprehensive primary and preventive services through community-based health centers at more than 3,000 sites nationwide. The HRSA also supports maternal and child health programs and programs to increase diversity and numbers of health care professionals in underserved communities. It has a proposed 2013 budget of over $9 billion.

6. Substance Abuse and Mental Health Services Administration (SAMHSA): The agency works to improve the quality and availability of substance abuse prevention, addiction treatment, and mental health services through federal block grants. It provides a variety of grants to states and local communities to address emerging substance abuse trends, mental health service needs, and HIV/AIDS. The agency's proposed 2013 budget is over $3 billion.

7. Agency for Healthcare Research and Quality (AHRQ): Established in 1989, AHRQ is the lead agency for supporting research to improve the quality of health care, reduce its cost, improve patient safety, address medical errors, and broaden access to essential services. Major activities include sponsoring and conducting research to provide evidence-based information on health care outcomes with respect to quality, costs, uses, and access. The agency's proposed 2013 budget is $400 million.

8. Centers for Medicare & Medical Services (CMS), formerly the Health Care Financing Administration: This agency administers the Medicare and Medicaid programs. Medicare insures over 40 million Americans, and Medicaid, a joint federal–state program, provides coverage for over 34 million low-income persons, including 18 million children, and nursing home coverage for low-income older adults. It administers the Children's Health Insurance Program, which covers several million children. The agency's proposed 2013 budget is $869 billion.

9. Administration for Children and Families (ACF): The ACF administers over 60 programs to promote the economic and social well-being of families, children, individuals, and communities. It administers the state/federal welfare program, temporary assistance to needy families, national child support enforcement, and the Head Start program. It provides funds to assist low-income families with child care expenses, supports state programs in adoption assistance and foster care, and funds child abuse and domestic violence prevention programs. The agency has a 2013 proposed budget of over $50 billion.

10. Administration on Aging (AoA): The federal focal point and advocate agency for older persons, the AoA administers federal programs under the Older Americans Act. Programs assist older persons to remain in their own homes by supporting services such as Meals on Wheels. The AoA collaborates with its nationwide network of

regional offices and state and area agencies to plan, coordinate, and develop community-level systems of services that meet the needs of older individuals and their caregivers. The agency has a proposed 2013 budget of $2 billion.

DHHS has been the federal government's largest grant-making agency under the aegis of its various operating divisions. In recent years, however, there has been a sharp reduction in research grants with most research and demonstration activities funded through solicited contracts. Unsolicited research proposals are unlikely to be funded.[13]

Veterans Health Administration System

Initiated to provide care for Civil War veterans who were disabled or indigent, the Veterans Health Administration (VHA) system grew to become one of the world's largest health care delivery systems. It currently operates over 100 medical centers, 900 ambulatory care and community outpatient clinics, 100 nursing homes, 40 residential rehabilitation treatment programs, 200 veteran centers, and comprehensive home care programs.

The VHA maintains major affiliations with more than 100 medical schools throughout the United States. VHA medical centers also affiliate with numerous dental schools and over 1,000 other schools throughout the United States. Each year, approximately 90,000 health professionals receive training at VHA medical centers. The VHA also conducts a broad array of world-class clinical and health services research projects.[14]

Because the VHA system usually has a lifelong relationship with its patients, it has instant access to each patient's complete medical record, an advantage over private medicine that reduces both costs and medical errors. The long-term relationship also allows more preventive care, higher quality services, and greater patient satisfaction and monetary savings.

Through the Department of Defense Military Health Service program, the federal government provides both direct health care services and support for the U.S. military personnel and their dependents, military retirees and their families, and others entitled to Department of Defense benefits.[15] The Military Health Service operates hospitals and clinics worldwide, primarily servicing active-duty members of the armed forces. Most civilian care is purchased through managed care support contracts implemented under the TRICARE program. The states also play an important role in funding health care and health-related services. Each year, state and local governments contribute about 14% of total health care expenditures, including hospital, nursing home, or home health care services.[16] Many states also operate and fund state mental institutions; support medical schools; maintain health departments that provide direct preventive and primary care services; and support maternal and child health improvement, infectious disease monitoring and control, and other community health initiatives.

City and County Public Health Responsibilities

City and county government jurisdictions support and deliver general and specialty health care services through their health departments and over 1,000 hospitals and health systems that together comprise the infrastructure of many of America's metropolitan health systems. The outpatient and inpatient services of government-supported public hospitals provide a community's "safety net" for individuals who are uninsured or underinsured and cannot access care elsewhere. Public hospitals also are often the sites of major teaching programs for an area's medical school. Frequently, they provide services that are financially unattractive to other community hospitals, such as burn care, psychiatric medicine, trauma care, and crisis response units for both natural and human-made disasters.[17] In addition, city and county health departments may provide direct patient care services in clinics or health centers, referrals for care, and other services to meet community needs of their high-risk, medically underserved populations.

Decline in Influence of the Public Health Service

Over the years, many accomplishments of public health agencies have contributed to significant improvements in both the health and life expectancy of Americans. Using population-based strategies for disease and injury prevention, public health has contributed to substantial declines in morbidity and mortality and dramatically changed the profiles of disease, injury, and death in the United States. Yet, despite the centrality of public health in providing the basis for the health of Americans, its funding has always competed with other more highly valued demands in the health sector.[18]

Several reorganizations of federal public health agencies occurred in response to continuing criticism of their failure to improve access to at least minimally adequate medical care to underserved populations. Pressures emanated from public health professionals, medical care organizations, political leaders, and the popular media. Criticism of the Public Health Service rose in the 1960s when its efforts to provide incentives to state and local agencies for more innovative approaches to meeting these demands through categorical and project grants were judged ineffective. Thus when several new and important programs for improving access to medical care were passed, agencies other than the Public Health Service were assigned to administer them. Medicare was assigned to the Social Security Administration, Medicaid to Social and Rehabilitation Services, Head Start and Neighborhood Health Centers to the Office of Economic Opportunity, and the Model Cities Program to the Department of Housing and Urban Development.

The end of President Johnson's term of office in 1968 marked the end of an era in federal health policy. The Nixon administration took issue with the three-tiered system of the federal Public Health Service, state health agencies, and local public health departments, which was expected to combine local initiative with policy input and national standards for advancing access to adequate health services. In its place, a new policy, dubbed the "new federalism," was initiated. It involved the progressive removal of federal responsibilities for a uniform, cooperative national public health system and the transfer of those responsibilities to the states. It was the beginning, at the federal level, of a strategy to convert federal program support to block grants, reducing the available funds and sending them to the states for administration. Though the effort was relatively unsuccessful during the Nixon–Ford administrations, it was revived in a new and more extreme form when Ronald Reagan was elected in 1980, and public health became the primary target. The decline of the government's organized system of public health services accelerated thereafter.[18]

Responsibilities and Responses of the Public Health Sector

In 1985, the Institute of Medicine (IOM) concerned about the need to protect the nation's health through an effective, organized public health sector convened a special committee to study the status of public health in the United States. The committee reported its findings and recommendations in 1988. The report concluded thus: "Public health is a vital function that is in trouble."[7] In an analysis of the contributing factors, it noted the following:

> We have observed disorganization, weak and unstable leadership, a lessening of professional and expert competence in leadership positions, hostility to public health concepts and approaches, outdated statutes, inadequate financial support for public health activities and public health education, gaps in the data gathering and analysis that are essential to public health functions of assessment and surveillance, and lack of effective links between the public and private sectors for the accomplishment of public health objectives.[7]

The report linked the poor public image of public health and the public's lack of knowledge and appreciation for the mission and content of public health to those deficiencies and to a number of other problems. Particular emphasis was placed on the failure of sound policy development in public health as evidenced by ambiguous responses to the AIDS epidemic, the "politicization" of public health agencies, and the lack of clear delineation of the responsibilities between levels of government.

In 1988, the committee made organizational, educational, financial, and political recommendations for addressing these complex and interrelated problems. Unfortunately, its strategies depended on continuing strong financial support for existing public health agencies and stronger, more sharply focused leadership that could build increasingly productive links with the private and voluntary health care sectors. In the ensuing years, the required leadership did not materialize, financial support for public health continued to decline, and public and political support for government public health agencies further diminished.

In 1990, the DHHS published "Public Health Service: Healthy People 2000: National Health Promotion and Disease Prevention Objectives."[19] Objective 8.14 of this document called for 90% of the population to be served by local health departments that would effectively carry out the three core functions of public health: assessment, policy development, and assurance as described by the IOM's report.[7] Assessment refers to collecting and analyzing data to define population health status and quantify existing or emerging health problems. Policy development involves generating recommendations from available data to address public health problems, analyzing options for solutions and mobilizing public and community organizations through implementation plans. Assurance entails governmental public health agency responsibility to ensure that basic components of the health care delivery system are in place. These core health department functions are intended to put into operation, within the resource and other constraints extant in their respective jurisdictions, the following generally accepted 10 essential health department performance responsibilities:[20]

- Monitor health status to identify and solve community health problems
- Diagnose and investigate health problems and health hazards in the community
- Inform, educate, and empower people about health issues
- Mobilize community partnerships and action to identify and solve health problems
- Develop policies and plans that support individual and community health efforts
- Enforce laws and regulations that protect health and ensure safety
- Link people as needed with personal health services and ensure the provision of health care when otherwise unavailable
- Ensure the provision of a competent public and personal health care workforce
- Evaluate the effectiveness, accessibility, and quality of person- and population-based health services
- Research for new insights and innovative solutions to environmental health problems

Figure 11-1 depicts how the three core functions relate to the 10 essential services. It is important to note that "research" is at the center as its role is to inform the other functions.

It is through the fulfillment of these public health responsibilities that public health departments protect the public against preventable communicable diseases and exposure to toxic environmental pollutants, harmful products, and poor-quality health care. These public health practices promote healthy personal behaviors and risk factor reduction community-wide by identifying and modifying patterns of chronic disease and injury, informing and educating consumers and health care providers about appropriate uses of medical services, developing and maintaining

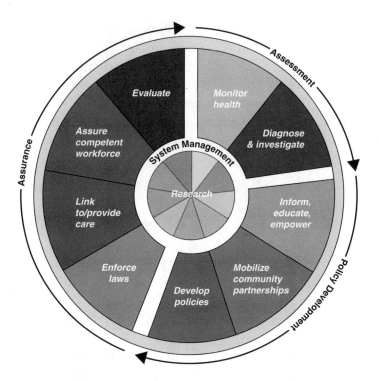

FIGURE 11-1 Three Core Functions and Ten Essential Public Health Services.
Source: Reprinted from U.S. Department of Health and Human Services, Centers for Disease Control and Prevention: Core functions of public health and how they relate to the 10 essential services. Available from http://www.cdc.gov/nceh/ehs/ephli/core_ess.htm.

comprehensive health programs in schools and child day care facilities, providing occupational safety and health programs, and ensuring that HIV and sexually transmitted disease prevention programs are implemented. These public health practices are the bedrock foundations of modern population-focused health care.

However, in 1993, a team of investigators from the School of Public Health at the University of Illinois at Chicago, working with representatives of the CDC, surveyed 208 health departments responding from a random national sample stratified by jurisdiction and population base. The findings suggested that less than 40% of U.S. population was served by a health department that effectively addressed the core functions of public health.[21]

With support for public health continuing to decline, it was not surprising that the United States failed to meet 85% of the challenging goals of *Healthy People 2000*. In the 10-year plan *Healthy People 2010* released by the DHHS in January 2000,[22] the government admitted that the nation had met only 15% of the 319 targets established in 1990. In some areas, particularly obesity, marijuana use, exercise, asthma, and diabetes, the health of Americans either stayed the same or worsened. *Healthy People 2010*, the third set of 10-year targets for health improvement in the United States, set two broad goals, supported by 467 objectives that are grouped into 28 focus areas: to increase the years and quality of health life and to eliminate health disparities.[23]

These goals and their supporting objectives were developed for the new decade by the Healthy People Consortium, a group of 650 national, professional, and voluntary organizations; the business community; and state and local public health agencies. Meetings began in 1996 and the first completed draft of 7,704 pages was posted on the Internet for public comment in September 1998. More than 11,000 comments were received. The final report on *Healthy People 2010* noted that while progress was made in meeting or moving toward 71% of the program's targets, "disparities have not changed for 80% of the health objectives and have increased for an additional 13%."[24] *Healthy People 2020*, like its predecessor, has been crafted with extensive expert and public input. In addition to encompassing the unmet 2010 objectives, it adds several topic areas including[25] the following:

- Adolescent health
- Blood disorders and blood safety
- Dementias
- Early and middle childhood
- Genomics
- Global health
- Health-related quality of life and well-being
- Health care–associated infections
- Lesbian, gay, bisexual, and transgender health
- Older adults
- Preparedness
- Sleep health
- Social determinants of health

In addition, the 2020 initiative encourages the creation of easy-to-use applications for professionals working with its objectives at state and local levels through "my healthy people" electronic applications to track progress.[25]

Although the goals and objectives of the *Healthy People* initiatives are commendable and their definition gives the agencies involved a sense of accomplishment, the lack of a cohesive, well-supported public health sector made the overall effort extremely challenging. It is particularly disconcerting that the DHHS announcement heralding the release of *Healthy People 2020* also noted that the nation falls short in "a number of critical areas."[24]

The 2001 terrorist attacks and the subsequent anthrax incidents revealed public health as ill prepared to provide an effective health defense system. A report of the CDC called for a system of "public health armaments," including a "skilled professional workforce, robust information and data systems and strong health departments and laboratories."[26]

There are serious concerns that the inadequate numbers of skilled public health professionals, such as public health nurses, epidemiologists, laboratory workers, and others, result from public sector budget restraints and competition with other sectors of the economy. As a result, many public health employees are inadequately prepared through education and training for the jobs they perform.[27]

Relationships of Public Health and Private Medicine

Public health and clinical medicine have complementary roles in caring for the health of the American people. Although they often address the same health problems, their attention is directed at different stages of disease or injury. Clinical medicine devotes its most intensive resources to restoring health or palliating disease in individuals after the fact. Public health devotes its resources to identifying and implementing strategies that promote health or prevent disease in large populations.[28]

According to the Association of American Medical Colleges' director of public health and prevention projects, "the separation of the two disciplines has its roots in the late 19th century, when medical schools began to focus more on hospital-based care and scientific research and less on community-based care and prevention. The separation has continued partly because medical schools have jam-packed curricula and insufficient medical faculty with public health expertise."[29]

Although the goals of private medicine and public health would appear to suggest obvious and strong collaborative professional relationships, these relationships have been hindered by the often contentious relationship that existed for decades between public health leadership and the private medical practitioners and their advocacy organization, the American Medical Association. Although the need for curative medicine administered to individuals and the need for preventive measures for the protection of populations have coexisted in all societies since ancient civilizations, and physicians who specialize in public health or preventive medicine have received the same basic medical education as those who pursue the diagnostic and therapeutic specialties, the ideological differences between them have produced vigorous debates. J. G. Freymann suggests that the reasons for the persistent discord include the identification of public health by practicing physicians with governmental bureaucracy, the linking of the care of low-income populations with welfare, the focus of physicians toward individuals, and the custom of being paid only for active therapy.[30] In addition, having successfully controlled many of the highly visible public health problems such as outbreaks of poliomyelitis and other vaccine-preventable diseases, much of what public health accomplishes is now invisible to the general public and therefore not politically attractive. Perhaps one of the most significant indications of this is that only about 3% of U.S. health care spending is devoted to public health activities.[31]

Historically, the different emphases of the two types of practitioners, that is, the population-based orientation of public health professionals and the individual-centered focus of private health providers, have often divided rather than enhanced public and private health services. The scientific advances of the past decades only served to heighten the value differences between practitioners with a population perspective and those focused on individual patients. Physician education increasingly emphasizing sophisticated technologies and specialization left little, if any, opportunity for education on the core topics and concepts of population health. However, the Patient Protection and Affordable Care Act (ACA), with its emphasis on population health and reimbursement incentives aligned with population rather than individual outcomes, has potential over time to begin closing the gap between public health and medicine. Changes are already beginning in accreditation standards for medical school curricula regarding the inclusion of population health and public health sciences and prevention along with revisions in national licensing examinations on these topics.[32]

Opposition to and Cooperation with Public Health Services

The history of public health is marked by struggles over the limits of its mandate. Just as the opponents of the several attempts to initiate programs of national health insurance described public health prejudicially as "socialized medicine," special interest groups are threatened by the perception that public health programs represent social change that constitutes an unjustified intrusion of government into the lives of private individuals.

The medical profession had both philosophical and economic reasons for voicing their concerns. P. Starr observed: "Doctors fought against public treatment of the sick, requirements for reporting cases of tuberculosis and venereal disease, and attempts by public health authorities to establish health centers to coordinate preventive and curative medicine."[33] Extending the boundaries of public health was regarded as the opening wedge for usurping the physicians' role. Physicians opposed disease screening and primary care services, even though they were targeted at populations with the lowest incomes, because physicians feared that public health agencies were expanding into activities they believed were rightfully their own.

There are, however, many examples of the synergistic effects of private and public medicine. The immunization of children and adults against a variety of preventable diseases is a positive example of how public health and private medical practitioners have worked together effectively. A number of screening programs, such as those for tuberculosis, lung cancer, breast cancer, and hypertension, have linked the personal services of private medicine and the population-oriented practice of public health in productive liaisons.

Resource Priorities Favor Curative Medicine Over Preventive Care

The allocation of U.S. health resources provides persuasive evidence of the public's and the professionals' fascination with dramatic high-technology diagnostic and therapeutic medicine. Despite the centrality of public health in providing basic health programs and the economic advantages of prevention as compared with cure, in recent years there has been little funding for research or practice for public health promotion or disease prevention. This is in contrast to the large sums that finance the research in and practice of remedial medical care. In fact, between 1981 and 1993 there were public health imperatives on the emergence of AIDS; the reemergence of tuberculosis and measles; and the escalating problems of substance abuse, violence, and teenage pregnancy. In this period, total U.S. health expenditures increased by more than 210%, whereas funding of public health services as a proportion of the national health care budget declined by 25%.[28]

In 2006, *Health Affairs* devoted one of its monthly issues to the "State of Public Health." In a prologue to one of its published articles, the editors wrote the following:

> Public health has always been the neglected stepchild of U.S. health care system. It subsisted on whatever funding was left over after flashier parts of the system took their cut, and it took on tasks, such as being the provider of last resort for the uninsured and indigent, that no one else was willing to perform.[34]

Public health had neither public nor political recognition as an essential and all-encompassing effort to prevent illness and promote health. Rather, it endured a continuing identity problem with people persisting in perceptions of public health as publicly funded medical care for the poor.

One might expect that with the many schools of public health in the United States that offer master's and doctorate degrees in public health there would be a continuing source of future public health officials, leaders with skills in leadership, management, and negotiation. However, most public health school graduates gravitate toward academia, forsaking public health administration for teaching and research. Thus a substantial portion of politically appointed public health officials continue to lack formal public health training.[35]

The current medical care system fails to provide effective preventive services even when they are demonstrated to be the most cost-effective procedures available. In contrast, new treatment technologies are implemented despite serious reservations about their efficacy and cost-effectiveness. Thus, with all its groundbreaking research, talented workforce, and technologic know-how, the United States has the distinction of having the world's most costly and inefficient health care system.[36]

The major investment in hospital neonatal intensive care units during the last two decades is a dramatic example of the lack of balance in the health care system. Though numerous studies have demonstrated that funds expended for prenatal care of high-risk mothers reduce the number of premature births requiring exceedingly expensive efforts to save those infants, public subsidies for prenatal care have declined while more and more costly technology has been introduced to increase the ability to salvage premature infants. For example, the federal Women's, Infant's and Children's Supplemental Nutrition Program (WIC), which provides supplemental food, nutrition, and health education to low-income pregnant and postpartum women, infants, and children, is estimated, after careful studies, to reduce low-birth-weight rates by 25% and very-low-birth-weight rates by 45%, with Medicaid savings of $4.21 for every WIC dollar spent. In contrast, neonatal intensive care, although effective in reducing neonatal mortality, is the least cost-effective strategy.[37]

Challenges of Disenfranchised Populations

Funding priorities are of critical importance in determining the effectiveness of health care in the future. Just as the preference for support of costly neonatal intensive care units rather than preventive public health prenatal care programs contributes to the unacceptably high U.S. rates of infant mortality, the focus on remedial medicine for Americans suffering from health disparities has denied the reality of system inequities. The major causes of disease and disability among the increasing numbers of disenfranchised individuals are conditions that result from multiple causes that are not amenable to technologic remedies. And while the vast majority of health spending is devoted to medical care, there is strong evidence that behavior and environment are responsible for more than 70% of avoidable mortality and that health care is just one of several determinants of health."[38] Table 11-1 reveals the magnitude of preventable mortality. In

Table 11-1 Deaths from Preventable Causes, USA, Year 2000

Cause	Number	Percentage of Total U.S. Deaths
Smoking	435,000	18.1
Poor diet/physical inactivity	400,000	16.6
Alcohol consumption	85,000	3.5
Motor vehicle crashes	43,000	1.8
Firearms	29,000	1.2
Sexual behaviors	20,000	.08
Illicit use of drugs	17,000	.07
Total preventable deaths	1,029,000	41.35

Source: Data from A. H. Mokdad et al., "Actual Causes of Death in the United States, 2000," *Journal of the American Medical Association* 291, no. 10, March 2004.

total, these causes of death account for 40% of all deaths occurring each year. Tobacco, diet, and sedentary lifestyles are major contributors to early mortality, yet effective medical interventions are not integrated into the practice standards that drive the delivery of medical services.

Thus, the traditional medical model of clinical practice has poorly served disenfranchised individuals. Disenfranchised individuals need a multidisciplinary approach that focuses on overall needs. Attention is needed to manage both acute and chronic conditions—helping patients change their lifestyles and behaviors to maintain quality of life within their social and community contexts.

The medical and public health systems that evolved from the remarkable scientific achievements since the turn of the 20th century placed emphases on tests, drugs, surgeries, vaccines, and environmental controls. Personal behaviors were considered either outside the scope of medical care system or immutable to change. Health insurance companies that rarely reimbursed providers for preventive services in general and behavioral counseling in particular, reinforced these assumptions.

Public Health Services of Voluntary Agencies

The role of volunteerism, voluntary agencies, and institutions as adjunct resources and services to those provided by government public health agencies and for-profit practices and corporations is a major theme in the evolution of health care in the United States. Private, not-for-profit institutions have been the prevailing mechanism through which health care services in the United States, with the government, share the responsibilities for meeting the needs of communities and special populations.[39]

In addition to not-for-profit hospitals, there is a host of voluntary agencies providing nursing home care, hospice care, home care, medical and vocational rehabilitation, and other personal health care services. A variety of voluntary agencies serves the special needs of persons with specific medical conditions such as AIDS, asthma, diabetes, cerebral palsy, hemophilia, and muscular dystrophy. Similar organizations support research on conditions such as cancer, heart disease, and respiratory disorders. Others, such as the American Red Cross, Planned Parenthood, and Meals on Wheels, focus on providing specific services to populations in need. Many voluntary agencies provide numerous valued and effective services that are not available in the private medical care sector. Programs directed at health education, disease prevention, disease detection, health maintenance, rehabilitation, and terminal care have been provinces of voluntary not-for-profit agencies.

The influence of large nonprofit foundations, such as the Robert Wood Johnson Foundation, the Commonwealth Fund, and the Pew Charitable Trusts, on the advancement of health care from a population perspective has been considerable. By providing funds on a competitive basis to stimulate research and innovative program demonstrations, these and other foundations have caused hospitals and other agencies, in collaboration with academic and other partners, to engage in progressive health service delivery improvements that may otherwise have been years in development.

The synergistic effect of government, private, and voluntary efforts has been both a bane and a blessing in the provision of health care in the United States. U.S. health care system's disorderly evolution as a combination of the charitable efforts of voluntary and religious organizations, multilevel government responses to community needs, and traditional U.S. free enterprise developed a complex network that is both inordinately technologically successful and plagued by costly inefficiencies, duplications, and inequities in access and quality. Nevertheless, this pluralistic approach has endured and is now confronted by changes mandated by the ACA. The pluralistic system will have numerous opportunities to test its ability to succeed in adapting to a significantly altered marketplace.

Changing Roles of Government in Public Health

For decades, all three levels of government in the United States—federal, state, and local—have played significant roles in financing and regulating public health services and in maintaining agencies and systems that directly or indirectly deliver health care. The federal government surveys the population's health status and health needs, sets policies and standards, passes laws and regulations, supports biomedical and health services research, provides technical assistance and resources to state and local health agencies, helps finance health care through support of programs (such as Medicare and Medicaid), and delivers personal health care services through networks of facilities (such as those maintained by the Department of Defense, the Department of Veterans Affairs, and the Administration on Native Americans).[7]

Public health services in the states are financed, regulated, and delivered through a variety of organizational structures. In some states, public health activities are divided among several entities, including health departments, social service, welfare, aging, and Medicaid. Many states now combine health and social service agencies to create large human service operations that join health and social services for children and youth, for people with developmental disabilities and other special populations, and for special problems such as alcoholism and drug abuse. Most states contribute heavily to the financing of Medicaid, medical education, and public health programs and to mental health through both community mental health programs and state-operated psychiatric hospitals. States also are involved in regulation through health codes, licensing of facilities and personnel, and supervision of the insurance industry.

Considerable variation exists in the organizational structure of agencies engaged in public health activities in local governmental jurisdictions. Counties, districts, and other local governments may have health, social service, environmental, and mental health departments. They can be independent or divisions of state agencies. Many cities and counties support and operate local health departments, public hospitals, clinics, and various other services. They also establish and enforce local health codes.

Rather than supporting and acknowledging the many benefits of this multilevel configuration of public health agencies that ensure safe food and water; control of epidemic diseases; and programs of care for infants, children, and adults with special needs and, in general, improve the length and quality of life in the United States, the nation has moved toward increased privatization, withdrawn support from public health activities, and allowed the system to fall into disarray. Before the terrorist attacks of 2001, the United States appeared to have lost sight of both the goals and benefits of public health.[7]

Public Health in an Era of Privatization

The market forces of the 1980s and 1990s that affected hospitals, nursing homes, voluntary agencies, and other institutions of U.S. health care system also significantly changed the financial base and functions of public health departments. The declines in public health funding and the trend toward privatization of those public health services that could be delivered more efficiently outside of local bureaucracies left many local health departments with minimal staff focused on only the most essential public health services.

Outsourcing to private providers who often had more comprehensive clinical capacity was one of several organizational strategies to contain or reduce costs while maintaining or improving the quality and efficiency of necessary public health services. Survey findings indicate that those health departments merely became smaller while cost savings were rare.[40] Health departments have maintained their responsibilities for assessing and ensuring the delivery of necessary public health services following the privatization of some services. As might be expected, however, the reduction of health department–delivered services has made it difficult for many departments to maintain a strong community presence.

Government Challenges in Protecting the Public's Health

Because the provision of medical treatment and related services accounts for most of aggregate national health expenditures, national debate and efforts to reform U.S. health care system have focused on financing, insurance, and containing the cost of treatment. Various estimates suggest that only about 10% of all early deaths can be prevented by medical treatment. In contrast, population-wide public health approaches have the potential to help prevent some 70% of early deaths in the United States through measures targeted to the social, environmental, and behavioral factors that contribute to those deaths.[41] Clearly, the value placed on high-technology clinical medicine by U.S. individuals, societies, and governments overwhelmed the consideration of the more cost-effective, but less dramatic, public health prevention strategies. Unlike pictures of heart transplant recipients, for example, images of the hundreds of thousands of children who have not been crippled and have not died from poliomyelitis due to successful immunization programs cannot be shown by the media.

State and local governments struggling with large deficits have considered it necessary to sacrifice the personnel and services of their public health agencies. The shortsightedness of those decisions, however, is becoming increasingly evident. Although there is continued general unhappiness with tax-supported programs and institutions, pressures for improving state and local public health services have developed outside the community of public health advocates. Leaders in business and industry connect a healthy and educated public to economic growth and development. Recent research underscores economic concerns related to the population's health status. A 2012 report of the Integrated Benefits Institute, a not-for-profit research group, estimated the annual costs of employees' lost productivity and absenteeism due to poor health at $344 billion.[42]

After the terrorist attacks of 2001, lawmakers, prodded by the public, recognized that a broader public health infrastructure is required to protect Americans. A number of public health defense programs were proposed that include stockpiling vaccines against anthrax, plague, and smallpox. Of particular importance is the need to prepare health care professionals, hospitals, and other agencies to respond quickly and effectively to threats or actual disasters.[43]

To that end, the largest reorganization of the federal government since World War II took place in April 2003 with the establishment of the Department of Homeland Security (DHS). Twenty-two new and existing governmental agencies that include 180,000 employees were assembled under the leadership of a newly appointed secretary of homeland security. The DHS has the broad mission of strengthening the country's borders, improving intelligence analyses, infrastructure protection, and comprehensive response and recovery operations should there be a terrorist attack with chemical or biologic weapons.

To help fulfill its mandate, the new department has a host of interlocking governmental relationships with other federal and state units. Among those are liaisons with the NIH, the CDC, the U.S. Public Health Service, the FDA, and other units of the DHHS. Most importantly, state and local health departments are expected to play principal roles in prevention of spread or in response and recovery operations should any attacks occur.[44]

Federal strategy, or lack thereof, resulted in a series of disjointed public health activities and practices across 3,000 local agencies operating under 50 state health departments. Without nationally consistent plans and systems, public health responses will, as occurred during the New Orleans hurricane Katrina experience, find it difficult to coordinate with other responders such as law enforcement and transportation during disasters that cross political jurisdictions. These experiences indicate that there has been little forethought of how national health protection activities should be organized and delivered. The objective of protecting the nation against catastrophic events may have been gravely weakened by leaving local and state health departments to construct their own goals and priorities. After 6 years of preparedness funding, states and localities still lacked the guidance and capabilities to develop effective preparedness capabilities.[45]

Public Health Ethics

Following the issuance of the 1988 IOM report, "The Future of Public Health," the National Public Health Leadership Institute (PHLI) was established by the CDC in 1990 to address the infrastructure and system deficiencies cited by the IOM report by creating a network of senior public health leaders to collaborate on meeting public health challenges.[46] The Public Health Leadership Society was created in 1993 by graduates of the PHLI.[47] In 2000, the PHLI adopted the task of writing a public health code of ethics with the intent that it first be broadly vetted throughout the public health community and then adopted by public health organizations and institutions.[48] The need for a code of ethics recognized that public health's mandate to ensure and protect the health of the public is inherently moral. As such, the code draws from several ethical concepts relevant to human rights, distributive justice for the disenfranchised, and the duty to take action as an ethical motivation.[48] Different from the code of medical ethics, which is concerned with an individual and clinical focus, public health ethics are concerned with institutions' interactions with communities. Principles of the ethical practice of public health are as follows[48]:

1. Public health should address principally the fundamental causes of disease and requirements for health, aiming to prevent adverse health outcomes.
2. Public health should achieve community health in a way that respects the rights of individuals in the community.
3. Public health policies and programs and priorities should be developed and evaluated through processes that ensure an opportunity for input from community members.
4. Public health should advocate and work for the empowerment of disenfranchised community members, aiming to ensure that the basic resources and conditions necessary for health are accessible to all.
5. Public health should seek the information needed to implement effective policies and programs that protect and promote health.
6. Public health institutions should provide communities with the information they have that is needed for decisions on policies or programs and should obtain the community's consent for their implementation.
7. Public health institutions should act in a timely manner on the information they have within the resources and mandate given to them by the public.
8. Public health programs and policies should incorporate a variety of approaches that anticipate and respect diverse values, beliefs, and cultures in the community.
9. Public health programs and policies should be implemented in a manner that most enhances the physical and social environment.
10. Public health institutions should protect the confidentiality of information that can bring harm to an individual or community if made public. Exceptions must be justified on the basis of the high likelihood of significant harm to the individual or others.

11. Public health institutions should ensure the professional competence of their employees.
12. Public health institutions and their employees should engage in collaborations and affiliations in ways that build the public's trust and the institution's effectiveness.

In 2002, the American Public Health Association became the first national organization to adopt the code; it was subsequently disseminated and adopted by numerous national organizations.[49]

ACA and Public Health—Major Provisions

In addition to increasing health system access by ultimately expanding health insurance coverage for 32 million previously uninsured Americans by 2019, the ACA includes several provisions with significant effects on public health. Specifically, Titles IV and V of the ACA legislation target an array of public health–related reforms and initiatives as summarized here. These summaries are not exhaustive and readers are encouraged to access the references cited for additional information and details.

ACA Title IV, "Prevention of Chronic Disease and Improving Public Health," required the establishment of a National Prevention, Health Promotion and Public Health Council (the Council), chaired by the U.S. Surgeon General, to develop and lead a national prevention strategy, building on existing federal programs such as *Healthy People 2020*, and to make recommendations to the President and Congress for federal policy changes that support public health goals.[50,51,52] Established by executive order in 2010, the Council currently provides leadership to and coordination of public health activities of 17 federal departments, agencies, and offices and receives[53] input from a 22-non-federal-membered presidentially appointed Prevention Advisory Group.[54] The Council announced four strategic directions in June 2011: (1) building healthy and safe community environments, (2) expanding quality preventive services in both clinical and community settings, (3) empowering people to make healthy choices, and (4) eliminating health disparities. It also established six priorities[55]:

- Tobacco-free living
- Preventing drug abuse and excessive alcohol use

- Healthy eating
- Injury- and violence-free living
- Reproductive and sexual health
- Mental and emotional well-being

In its third *Annual Status Report* delivered in June 2012, the Council outlined more than 50 key indicators aligned with evidence-based data sources that address the four strategic directions and priorities. The report also listed several programs underway in communities across the United States that address priorities of the Council's strategic directions.[56]

Title IV also created the Prevention and Public Health Fund, the nation's first mandatory funding stream dedicated to improving public health.[57] The Fund is intended to eliminate the prior shortcomings of unpredictable federal budget appropriations for public health and prevention programs. The ACA mandates the Fund's use to "improve health and help restrain the rate of growth in private and public sector health care costs" through programs at the local, state, and federal levels to "curb tobacco use, increase access to primary preventive care services, as well as to help state and local governments respond to public health threats and outbreaks."[50,57] The ACA stipulated that $7 billion be appropriated to the Fund in fiscal years 2010–2015 and that $2 billion be appropriated in each fiscal year thereafter.[58] The actual allocation for each year is set in the ACA law: however, specific uses of the Fund will be determined annually by Congress' budget appropriations process in consultation with the President.[57] In 2012, some examples of Fund allocations included the following: community-based preventive health programs such as increased funding for the operation and expansion of school-based health clinics, expanding public awareness of clinical preventive services and benefits, conducting an oral health care prevention and education campaign, enhancing local and state public health infrastructures, supporting public health workforce training, and expanding nationwide data collection on public health services.[57] Most of these initiatives are supported by federally derived grant awards administered by the states.[59]

Other examples of Title IV provisions specifically intended to increase access to clinical preventive services include providing Medicare coverage for annual wellness visits and preventive services without co-payments or deductibles, providing states with increased Medicaid matching funds for clinical preventive services recommended by the U.S. Preventive Services Task Force and for adult immunizations recommended by the Advisory Committee on Immunization Practices, and awarding grants to states to provide incentives for Medicaid beneficiaries' participation in programs that promote healthy lifestyles.[59,60] Title IV provisions that support prevention and public health innovation include funding for federal health programs to collect and report data by race, ethnicity, and other indicators of disparity; provision of an educational campaign and technical assistance to promote workplace wellness; and provision of assistance from the CDC for state, local, and tribal public health agencies to improve surveillance for and responses to infectious diseases and other conditions impacting community health.

Taken together, the Council's strategy and the Public Health Fund have the potential to significantly impact population health by creating a cohesive approach for federal agencies to coordinate efforts targeted at prevention and wellness and by targeting funding to identify high-priority areas.[52] Very importantly, the ACA requires accountability for the Council's results through annual reports and periodic evaluations and reviews by the DHHS secretary and comptroller general.[50]

The purpose of Title V of the ACA, "Health Care Workforce," is to improve access to and the delivery of health care services for all individuals, particularly low-income, underserved, uninsured, minority, health disparity, and rural populations.[60] A CDC statement, "A Shrinking Public Health Workforce," citing a report by the Council on State Governments, the Association of State and Territorial Health Officials, and the National Association of State Personnel Executives noted that "by 2012, state and federal public health agencies could lose half of their workforce to retirement, the private sector, and other factors."[61] The CDC statement also noted that "the Association of Schools of Public Health estimates the workforce shortage will reach nearly 250,000 by 2020."[61]

Title V recognizes that an adequately trained public health workforce of sufficient size required to fulfill the numerous functions of public health across its arrays of responsibilities for all Americans is a bedrock component of the nation's health. As such, many of its provisions address the long-standing concerns about a national shortage of trained public health professionals and it incorporates numerous provisions to encourage the entry of new public health professionals into the workforce and to provide for continuing professional development of the existing public health workforce.

An overarching feature of Title V mandates the establishment of a National Health Workforce Commission to review current and projected workforce needs and provide analyses and recommendations to Congress and the federal administration to align federal policies with national needs. The Title also establishes competitive grants to support state-level comprehensive workforce planning and workforce development strategies.[59] To specifically address needs of the underserved and health disparities, Title V authorizes student loan repayments to public health students and others who work for a 3-year period in health professional shortage areas and medically underserved areas or with medically underserved populations. Similar loan repayments are made available to allied health professionals to work in the areas noted earlier as employees of public health agencies. The Title also created a mandatory fund for the National Health Service Corp scholarship and loan repayment program and a "Ready Reserve Corp" within the U.S. Public Health Service to respond to national public health emergencies. An additional provision to increase workforce supply includes a $50 million grant program to support nurse-managed health clinics.[59]

Also addressing needs of underserved populations and health disparities, Title V adds support for training programs in cultural competency, prevention, public health, and working with individuals with disabilities and provides grants to promote the deployment of community health workers in medically underserved areas.[59] To encourage advanced public health training and education, Title V supports fellowship training in public health to address workforce shortages in state and local health departments in the areas of applied epidemiology, public health laboratory science, and informatics and creates a U.S. Public Health Sciences program to train physicians, dentists, nurses, mental and behavioral health specialists, public health professionals, and others in areas such as team-based service, public health epidemiology, and emergency preparedness and response.

In addition to public health workforce shortages in historically underserved areas, as in many health professions, the public health disciplines themselves suffer from significant racial and ethnic disparities.[62]

To impact these disparities, Title V reauthorizes a program for minority applicants to the health professions and expands scholarships for disadvantaged students who commit to working in medically underserved areas.[59] Recognizing the core functions that federally qualified health centers serve in meeting the needs of underserved populations, Title V authorizes new and expanded funding for the centers.[59]

In summary, ACA Titles IV and V address numerous public health issues that have a lengthy history of documentation by the IOM and scores of other research studies conducted in academia and by government and private entities. The provisions of these ACA Titles give promise of a health care system that recognizes and most importantly supports the centrality of public concepts, principles, and practices to improving the health status of all Americans.

The drive by those paying for health care (employers, organized consumers, and governments) for improved measures of health status and system performance and the emphasis on integrated health systems that focus on health improvement for defined populations effectively created pressures within the system for more cost-effective, community-driven strategies for combining the resources of public health and networks of personal care services. These pressures drove many major provisions of the ACA. The ACA, with its strong external incentives and requirements, offers opportunities to both public health leaders and organized medicine to increase their collaborative emphases on preventive services in innovative ways.

The Future

Major challenges will remain to enact the required changes in strongly held perceptions and patterns of practice. Both internal reflection and new visions for public health's role in the reformed system will be necessary to change entrenched personal behaviors and organizational commitments.

The ACA's new and overarching emphasis on prevention that is tied with reimbursement may be the impetus to galvanize change from rewarding diagnosis and remediation of existing disease to its prevention. While the complementary, if not integrated, systems of public health and medical care services pose ideal models with which to address the nation's 21st century health care problems, long-standing differences in philosophy, values, and assumptions between public health and organized medicine await resolution over the course of many years' of system changes required by the ACA. Optimistically, new and functional relationships driven by mutual needs will develop between these two sectors for the benefit of all Americans.

With support from the ACA and its National Prevention Strategy, public health systems, public health departments, and their community collaborators are positioned to achieve high performance in improving population health status.

Key Terms for Review

Assessment

Assurance

Department of Health and Human
Services (DHHS)

Ecological Models

National Prevention, Health Promotion
and Public Health Council

Policy Development

Prevention and Public Health Fund

References

1. Shindell S, Salloway JL, Oberembt CM, et al. *A Coursebook in Health Care Delivery.* New York: Appleton & Lange; 1976:304–308.
2. Turnock BJ. *Public Health, What it is and How it Works,* 5th ed. Burlington, MA: Jones & Bartlett Learning; 2012:11.
3. Longest BB. *Health Policymaking in the United States,* 5th ed. Chicago, IL: Health Administration Press; 2010:16.
4. Goldsteen RL, Goldsteen K, Graham DG. *Introduction to Public Health.* New York: Springer Publisher Company; 2011:18–23.
5. Rosen G. *A History of Public Health.* New York: MD Publications; 1957.
6. Bloy M. The Poor law amendment act: 14 August 1834. September 23, 2002. Available from http://www.victorianweb.org/history/poorlaw/plaatext.html. Accessed February 10, 2013.
7. Committee for the Study of the Future of Public Health, Division of Health Care Services, Institute of Medicine. *The Future of Public Health.* Washington, DC: National Academies Press; 1988.
8. U.S. Department of Health and Human Services. *The Public Health Service: Some Historical Notes.* Washington, DC: Public Health Service; 1988.
9. U.S. National Library of Medicine, National Institutes of Health. History of Medicine. Images from the history of medicine. January 5, 2012. Available

from http://www.nlm.nih.gov/exhibition/phs_history/intro.html. Accessed February 10, 2013.

10. Yerby AS. Public medical care for the needy in the United States. In: DeGroot LJ, Ed. *Medical Care, Social and Organizational Aspects*. Springfield, IL: Charles C. Thomas; 1966:382–401.

11. U.S. Department of Health and Human Services. About HHS. 2013. Available from http://www.hhs.gov/about/ Accessed May 10, 2013.

12. U.S. Department of Health and Human Services. Fiscal year 2013 budget in brief. Available from http://www.hhs.gov/budget/budget-brief-fy2013.pdf. Accessed February 8, 2013.

13. Tradeline Inc. Downward trend in funding: time to re-think research models and facility planning. January 7, 2009. Available from https://www.tradelineinc.com/reports/83FA3720-2B3B-B525-84D6F8181F4D0E42. Accessed February 8, 2013.

14. Department of Veterans Affairs. Veterans health administration. Aapril 24, 2013. Available from http://www.va.gov/About_va. Accessed May 10, 2013.

15. TRI-CARE 4U.COM. About TRICARE 4U. 2013. Available from http://www.tricare4u.com/apps-portal/tricareapps-app/static/beneficiaries/benefits/. Accessed February 9, 2013.

16. Monaco RM, Phelps JH. Effects of health spending on the U.S. economy. Available from http://aspe.hhs.gov/health/costgrowth/. 2005. Accessed February 8, 2013.

17. National Association of Public Hospitals and Health Systems. About NAPH. Available from http://www.naph.org/Main-Menu-Category/Our-Work/Quality-Overview/Overview.aspx. Accessed February 9, 2013.

18. Shonick W. *Government and Health Services: Government's Role in the Development of U.S. Health Services, 1930–1980*. New York: Oxford University Press; 1995.

19. U.S. Department of Health and Human Services. Healthy people 2000 educational and community-based programs progress review. 1999. Available from http://odphp.osophs.dhhs.gov/pubs/HP2000/PROGRVW/Education/Educational.htm. Accessed February 9, 2013.

20. Centers for Disease Control and Prevention. Core functions of public health and how they relate to the 10 essential services. May 25, 2011. Available from http://www.cdc.gov/nceh/ehs/ephli/core_ess.htm. Accessed February 9, 2013.

21. Turnock BJ, Handler A, Hall W, et al. Local health department effectiveness in addressing the core functions of public health. *Public Health Rep*. 1994;109:653–658.

22. Healthy People 2010, National Health Promotion and Disease Prevention Objectives, U.S. Department of Health and Human Services. Office of disease prevention and health promotion. Available from http://www.healthypeople.gov. 2013. Accessed February 9, 2013.

23. O'Hara JL. AHRQ reports outline quality shortfalls, healthcare disparities. Available from http://www.im.org/AcademicAffairs/PolicyIssues/

PatientCare/quality/Pages/AHRQReportsOutlineQualityShortfalls,Health careDisparities.aspx. May 8, 2009. Accessed February 9, 2013.

24. U.S. Department of Health and Human Services. HHS releases assessment of healthy people 2010 objectives: life expectancy rises, but health disparities remain. 2010. *HHS News.* Available from http:// healthypeople.gov/2020/about/hp2010pressreleaseOct5.doc. Accessed February 9, 2013.

25. U.S. Department of Health and Human Services. HHS announces the nation's new health promotion and disease prevention agenda. *HHS News.* December 2, 2010. Available from http://healthypeople.gov/2020/about/ defaultpressrelease.pdf. Accessed February 9, 2013.

26. Blendon RJ, Scoles K, DesRoches C, et al. Americans' health priorities revisited after September 11. *Health Affairs.* 2001. Available from http://content .healthaffairs.org/content/early/2001/11/13/hlthaff.w1.96.citation. Accessed February 10, 2013.

27. Gebbie KM, Turnock BJ. The public health workforce, 2006: new challenges. *Health Affairs.* 2006;25:923–933. Available from http://content/ healthaffairs.org/content/25/4/923.full.html. Accessed February 10, 2013.

28. U.S. Department of Health and Human Services. *Public Health Service, for a Healthy Nation: Returns on Investment in Public Health.* Washington, DC: U.S. Government Printing Office; 1994.

29. Association of American Medical Colleges. After reform, more medical schools emphasize public health. 2011. Available from https://www .aamc.org/newsroom/reporter/170156/public_health.html. Accessed February 9, 2013.

30. Freymann JG. Medicine's great schism: prevention vs. cure: an historical interpretation. *Med Care.* 1975;13:525–536.

31. Sensenig AL. Refining estimates of public health spending as measured in national health expenditures accounts: the United States experience. *J Public Health Mgmt and Pract.* 2007;13:103–114.

32. Maeshiro R, Koo D, Keck CW. Integration of public health into medical education. 2011. Available from http://download.journals.elsevierhealth .com/pdfs/journals/0749-3797/PIIS0749379711005113.pdf. Accessed January 14, 2013.

33. Starr P. Transformation in defeat: the changing objectives of national health insurance. *Am J Public Health.* 1982;72:78–88.

34. Public Health Partnerships and Reform. Editorial. *Health Affairs.* 2006;25:1016. Available from http://content.healthaffairs.org/ content/25/4/1016.full.html. Accessed January 11, 2013.

35. Robert Wood Johnson Foundation and Institute for the Future. Public health services: a challenging future. In: *Health and Health Care 2010. The Forecast, The Challenge.* San Francisco, CA: Jossey-Bass; 2003:156–157.

36. Vogt TM, Hollis JF, Lichtenstein E, et al. The medical care system: the need for a new paradigm. *HMO Pract.* 1999;12:5–12.

37. Avruch S, Cackley AP. Savings achieved by giving WIC benefits to women prenatally. *Public Health Rep.* 1995;110:27–34.
38. Institute of Medicine. *The Future of the Public's Health in the 21st Century.* Washington, DC: The National Academies Press; 2002:221. Available from http://www.nap.edu/openbook.php?record_id=10548&page=21. Accessed January 11, 2103.
39. Seay JD, Vladeck BC. *Mission Matters: A Report on the Future of Voluntary Health Care Institutions.* New York: United Hospital Fund of New York; 1988.
40. Public Health Foundation. *Privatization and Public Health: A Report of Initiatives and Early Lessons Learned, a Public Health Foundation Study Supported by the Annie E. Casey Foundation.* Washington, DC: Public Health Foundation; 1997. Available from http://www.phf.org/resourcestools/Online/Public_Health_Privatization_Report_2000.pdf. Accessed February 8, 2013.
41. Nolte E, Mckee CM. Measuring the health of nations: updating an earlier analysis. *Health Affairs.* 2008;27:58–71.
42. The Henry J. Kaiser Family Foundation. Workers' poor health costs employers $344 billion, study finds. *Capsules. The KHN Blog.* Available from http://capsules.kaiserhealthnews.org/index.php/2012/09/workers-poor-health-costs-employers-344-billion-study-finds/. September 14, 2012. Accessed February 9, 2013.
43. McGinley L. Suddenly, Public Health Administration Is Seen as Top Priority. *Wall Street Journal.* September 28, 2002:A16.
44. History Associates. Brief documentary history of the department of homeland security: 2001–2008. 2008. Available from http://www.hsdl.org/?view&did=37027. Accessed February 8, 2013.
45. Salinsky E, Gursky EA. The case for transforming governmental public health. *Health Affairs.* 2006;25:1017–1028. Available from http://content.healthaffairs.org/content/25/4/1017.full.htm. Accessed February 1, 2013.
46. UNC Gillings School of Global Public Health, National public health leadership institute. Developing leaders, building networks: an evaluation of the national public health leadership institute-1991–2006. October 10, 2011. Available from http://www.phli.org/evalreports/index.htm. Accessed February 10, 2013.
47. National Network of Health Institutes. Public health leadership society-history. Available from http://www.phls.org/home/section/1/. Accessed February 10, 2013.
48. Thomas JC, Sage M, Dillenberg J, et al. A code of ethics for public health. *Am J Public Health.* 2002;92:1057–1059. Available from http://www.ncbi.nlm.nih.gov/pmc/articles/pmc1447186/ Accessed February 9, 2013.
49. eHow. Code of ethics for the American public health association. Available from http://www.ehow.com/about_7547811_code-american-public-health-association.html. Accessed February 9, 2013.

50. Staff of the Washington Post. *Landmark*. New York: Perseus Books Group; 2002:224.

51. U.S. Department of Health and Human Services. Obama administration releases national prevention strategy. June 16, 2011. Available from http://www.hhs.gov/news/press/2011pres/06/20110616a.html. Accessed February 9, 2013.

52. Majette GR. PPACA and public health: creating a framework to focus on prevention and wellness and improve the public's health. *J Law Med Ethics*. 2011;39:373–374. Available from http://www2.law.csuohio.edu/newsevents/images/39JLME366.pdf. Accessed February 4, 2013.

53. U.S. Surgeon General. Prevention. National prevention council. 2011. Available from http://www.surgeongeneral.gov/initiatives/prevention.index.html. Accessed February 11, 2013.

54. Surgeon General. Prevention Advisory Group. Advisory group members. 2013. Available from http://www.surgeongeneral.gov/initiatives/prevention/advisorygrp/index.html. Accessed February 11, 2013.

55. National Prevention Council. National prevention strategy. October 2012. Available from http://www.surgeongeneral.gov/initiatives/prevention/strategy/national-prevention-strategy-fact-sheet.pdf. Accessed February 11, 2013.

56. Surgeon General. 2012 annual status report; national prevention, health promotion, and public health council. June 13, 2012. Available from http://www.surgeongeneral.gov/initiatives/prevention/2012-npc-status-report.pdf. Accessed February 11, 2013.

57. American Public Health Association. Prevention and public health fund. 2011. Available from http://www.apha.org/NR/rdonlyres/745B72B7-0D8F-47D2-8516-D3BA02829BA3/0/PreventionPublicHealth32212.pdf. Accessed February 9, 2013.

58. The Henry J. Kaiser Family Foundation. Summary of new health reform law. Prevention/wellness national strategy. April 25, 2013. Available from http://www.kff.org/healthreform/upload/8061.pdf. Accessed May 10, 2013.

59. Democratic Policy and Communications Center. The patient protection and affordable care act. Available from http://dpc.senate.gov/healthreformbill/healthbill52.pdf. Accessed January 8, 2013.

60. Staff of the Washington Post. *Landmark*. New York: Perseus Books Group; 2002:226–228.

61. Centers for Disease Control and Prevention. A shrinking public health workforce. September 2, 2011. Available from http://www.cdc.gov/24-7/protectingpeople/phap/shrinking.html. Accessed February 10, 2013.

62. Rosenstock L, Silver G, Helsing K, et al. On linkages: confronting the public health workforce crisis: ASPH statement on the public health workforce. *Public Health Rep*. 2008;123:395–398. Available from http://www.ncbi.nlm.nih.gov/pmc/articles/pmc2289968/. Accessed February 6, 2013.

CHAPTER 12

Research: How Health Care Advances

This chapter explains the focus of different types of research and how each type contributes to the overall advances in health and medicine. In this chapter, health services research, a newer field that addresses the workings of the health care system rather than specific problems of disease or disability, is described. The offices and goals of health services research's major funding source, the federal Agency for Healthcare Research and Quality, are listed. Finally, research into the quality of medical care, the problems being addressed, and the research challenges of the future are discussed.

The last half of the 20th century and early 21st century have seen remarkable growth of scientifically rigorous research in medicine, dentistry, nursing, and other health professions. The change from dependence on the clinical impressions of individual physicians and other health care practitioners to reliance on the statistical probability of accurate findings from carefully controlled studies is one of the most important advances in scientific medicine. No longer is health professions' literature filled with subjective anecdotal reports of treatment progress in one or more individual cases. Now readers of peer-reviewed professional journals can monitor the progress of basic science, clinical, or technologic discoveries, with confidence, knowing that published findings are, with few exceptions, based on research studies that have been rigorously designed and conducted to yield statistically credible results.

In contrast, volumes of reports of medical developments that appear in the popular media are often premature and, depending on the source, may be cause for skepticism. The imprudent publication of inadequately proved or unproved therapies, the sensationalizing of minor scientific advances, and the promotion of fraudulent devices and treatments create unrealistic consumer expectations that often result in disappointments, mistreatment, and costly deceptions.

From both professional and public perspectives, the continuing research yield of new technologies and clinical advances creates ongoing challenges of evaluation, interpretation, and potential applications.

Focus of Different Types of Research

Figure 12-1 illustrates the focus of different types of health care research. There are clear distinctions among researchers in terms of methods and the nature of their subsequent findings. Although the kinds of information derived from each type of research may be different, each knowledge gain is an essential step in the never-ending quest to create a more efficient and effective health care system.[1]

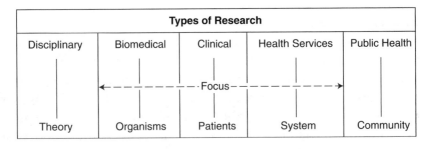

FIGURE 12-1 Variations in Research Focus.
Source: Aday et al.: *Evaluating the Healthcare System: Effectiveness, Efficiency and Equity,* 3rd edition, © 2004; permission conveyer through Copyright Clearance Center, Inc.

Types of Research

Research studies conducted by those in professional disciplines fall into several categories. Basic science research is the work of biochemists, physiologists, biologists, pharmacologists, and others concerned with sciences that are fundamental to understanding the growth, development, structure, and function of the human body and its responses to external stimuli. Much of basic science research is at the cellular level and takes place in highly sophisticated laboratories. Other basic research may involve animal or human studies. Whatever its nature, however, basic science research is the essential antecedent of advances in clinical medicine.

Clinical research focuses primarily on the various steps in the process of medical care—the early detection, diagnosis, and treatment of disease or injury; the maintenance of optimal physical, mental, and social functioning; the limitation and rehabilitation of disability; and the palliative care of those who are irreversibly ill. Individuals in all the clinical specialties of medicine, nursing, allied health, and related health professions conduct clinical research, often in collaboration with those in the basic sciences. Much of clinical research is experimental, involving carefully controlled clinical trials of diagnostic or therapeutic procedures, new drugs, or technological developments.

Clinical trials test a new treatment or drug against a prevailing standard of care. If no standard drug exists or if it is too easily identified, a control group receives a placebo or mock drug to minimize subject bias. To reduce bias further, random selection is used to decide which volunteer patients are in the experimental and control groups. In a double-blind study, neither the researchers nor the patients know who is receiving the test drug or treatment until the study is completed and the identifying code revealed.

Research studies have a number of safeguards to protect the safety and rights of volunteer subjects. Studies funded by governmental agencies or foundations are subject to scrutiny by a peer-review committee that judges the scientific merit of the research design and the potential value of the findings. Next, a hospital-based board or an institutional review board (IRB) checks for ethical considerations and patient protections. Finally, volunteer subjects must sign an informed consent form that spells out in clear detail the potential risks or side effects and the expected benefits of their participation. Volunteers must weigh any potential risks against the likelihood that by participating in research they will receive state-of-the-art care and close health monitoring that will contribute to the advancement of science.

Epidemiology

Epidemiology, or population research, is concerned with the distribution and determinants of health, diseases, and injuries in human populations. Much of that research is observational; it is the collection of information about natural phenomena, the characteristics and behaviors of people, aspects of their location or environment, and their exposure to certain circumstances or events.

Observational studies may be descriptive or analytical. Descriptive studies use patient records, interview surveys, various databases, and other information sources to identify those factors and conditions that determine the distribution of health and disease among specific populations. They provide the details or characteristics of diseases or biologic phenomena and the prevalence or magnitude of their occurrences. Descriptive studies are relatively fast and inexpensive and often raise questions or suggest hypotheses to be tested. They are often followed by analytic studies, which test hypotheses and try to explain biologic phenomena by seeking statistical associations between factors that may contribute to a subsequent occurrence and the initial occurrence itself.

Some analytic studies attempt, under naturally occurring circumstances, to observe the differences between two or more populations with different characteristics or behaviors. For example, data about smokers and non-smokers may be collected to determine the relative risk of a related outcome such as lung cancer, or a cohort study may follow a population over time, as in the case of a Framingham, Massachusetts, study. For years, epidemiologists have been studying a cooperating Framingham population to determine associations between variables such as diet, weight, exercise, and other behaviors and characteristics related to heart disease and other outcomes. These observational studies are valuable in explaining patterns of disease or disease processes and providing information about the association of specific activities or agents with health or disease effects.

Experimental Epidemiology

Observational studies are usually followed by experimental studies. In experimental studies, the investigator actively intervenes by manipulating one variable to see what happens with the other. Although they are the best test of cause and effect, such studies are technically difficult to carry out and often raise ethical issues. Control populations are used to ensure that other nonexperimental variables are not affecting the outcome. Like clinical trials, such studies may raise ethical issues when experiments involve the use of a clinical procedure that may expose the subjects to significant or unknown risk. Ethical questions also are raised when experimental studies require the withholding of some potentially beneficial drug or procedure from individuals in the control group to prove decisively the effectiveness of the drug or procedure.

Other Applications of Epidemiologic Methods

Because the population perspective of epidemiology usually requires the study and analysis of data obtained from or about large-scale population samples, the discipline has developed principles and methods that can be applied to the study of a wide range of problems in several fields. Thus, the concepts and quantitative methods of epidemiology have been used not only to add to the understanding of the etiology of health and disease but also to plan, administer, and evaluate health services; to forecast the health needs of population groups; to assess the adequacy of the supply of health personnel; and, most recently, to determine the outcomes of specific treatment modalities in a variety of clinical settings.

Advances in statistical theory and the epidemiology of medical care make it possible to analyze and interpret performance data obtained from the large Medicare and other insurance databases. Many of the research findings of seemingly inexplicable geographic variations in the amount and cost of hospital treatments and in the use of a variety of health care services have resulted from the analysis of Medicare claims data and other large health insurance databases.

Health Services Research

Until the last several decades, most research addressed the need to broaden the understanding of health and disease; to find new and more effective means of diagnosis and treatment; and, in effect, to improve the quality and length of life. For the two decades after World War II, supply-side subsidy programs dominated federal health care policy. Like other subsidy programs, Medicare and Medicaid were politically crafted solutions rather than research-based strategies. Nevertheless, these major health care subsidy programs were the driving forces behind the rise of health services research. The continuous collection of cost and utilization data from these programs revealed serious deficiencies in the capability of the health care system to efficiently and effectively deliver the knowledge and skills already at hand. In addition, evidence was growing that the large variations in the kinds and amounts of care delivered for the same health conditions represented unacceptable volumes of inappropriate or questionable care and too much indecision or confusion among clinicians about the best courses of treatment. Health services research was born of the need to improve the efficiency and effectiveness of the health care system and to determine which of the health care treatment options for each health condition produces the best outcomes.

Agency for Health Care Research and Quality

Beginning with John Wennberg's documenting large differences in the use of medical and surgical procedures among physicians in small geographic areas in the late 1980s, a number of similar studies brought the value of increasingly more costly health care into serious question. Wennberg noted that the rate of surgeries correlated with the numbers of surgeons in a geographic area and that the number of available hospital beds rather than differences among patients correlated with the rate of a population's hospitalization.

He found that per capita expenditures for hospitalization in Boston were consistently double those in nearby New Haven.[2–4] Widely varying physician practice patterns provided little direction as to the most appropriate use of even the most common clinical procedures. In addition, adequate outcome measures for specific intervention modalities generally were lacking.

The problem did not escape the attention of the 101st Congress. The development of new knowledge through research has long been held as an appropriate and essential role of the federal government, as evidenced by the establishment and proactive role of the National Institutes of Health (NIH). When it became clear that indecision about the most appropriate and effective ways to diagnose and treat specific medical, dental, and other conditions was contributing to unacceptably large variations in the cost, quality, and outcomes of health care, federal legislation was passed to support the development of clinical guidelines. The Agency for Health Care Policy and Research (AHCPR) was established in 1989 as the successor to the National Center for Health Services Research and Health Care Technology. It became one of eight agencies of the Public Health Service within the Department of Health and Human Services.

AHCPR was responsible for updating and promoting the development and review of clinically relevant guidelines to assist health care practitioners in the prevention, diagnosis, treatment, and management of clinical conditions. The authorizing legislation directed that AHCPR or public and not-for-profit private organizations convene panels of qualified experts. These panels were charged to review the literature that contained the findings of numerous studies of clinical conditions and, after considering the scientific evidence, to recommend clinical guidelines to assist practitioner and patient decisions about appropriate care for specific clinical conditions.[5]

The agency's priority activities included funding two types of research projects: patient outcome research teams and literature synthesis projects or meta-analyses. Both the patient outcome research teams and the smaller literature synthesis projects identified and analyzed patient outcomes associated with alternative practice patterns and recommended changes where appropriate. During its decade-long existence, the AHCPR supported studies that resulted in a prodigious array of publications focused on patient care and clinical decision making, technology assessment, the quality and costs of care, and treatment outcomes. Although no longer directly involved in producing clinical practice guidelines, the agency currently assists private sector groups by supplying them with the scientific evidence they need to develop their own guidelines.

Significant changes occurred in the mandate of AHCPR since its 1989 inception. The agency narrowly escaped the loss of funding and possible elimination in 1996 after incurring the wrath of national organizations of surgeons. In keeping with its original mission, AHCPR had issued clinical guidelines. One such guideline discouraged surgery as a treatment for back pain on the grounds that it provided no better outcomes than more conservative treatments. Organizations of angry surgeons led a lobbying effort that convinced key members of Congress that the agency was exceeding its authority by establishing clinical practice standards without considering the expertise and opinions of the medical specialists involved.[6]

The dispute was resolved when the AHCPR agreed to function as a "science partner" with public and private organizations by assisting in developing knowledge that could be used to improve clinical practice. The agency agreed to produce clinical guidelines that would focus on funding research on medical interventions and analyzing the data that would underlie the development of clinical guidelines.

The Health Care Research and Quality Act of 1999 retitled the AHCPR to the Agency for Healthcare Research and Quality (AHRQ). The mission of AHRQ is to (1) improve the outcomes and quality of health care services, (2) reduce its costs, (3) address patient safety, and (4) broaden effective services through the establishment of a broad base of scientific research that promotes improvements in clinical and health systems practices, including prevention of disease.[7]

While clinical practice guidelines would subsequently be generated by medical specialty and other health care organizations, the AHRQ's role would be to evaluate recommendations made in the clinical practice guidelines to ensure that they were based on a systematic literature review (evidence-based) and were revised for currency on a regular basis.

To date, over 14,000 such evidence-based clinical practice guidelines that have met the AHRQ's evaluation criteria have been collected in a database, organized by searchable topics, and made available online to health care professionals and the general public at the AHRQ's National Guideline Clearinghouse (http://www.guideline.gov/).

A top priority of the AHRQ is transmitting its sponsored research results and new health information into the hands of consumers. In addition to a number of consumer-oriented publications, the agency provides information to the public via the Internet. Its website, http://www.ahrq.gov, offers a robust array of health care information. The AHRQ is now a major collaborating organization of the Patient-Centered Outcomes and Research Institute (PCORI) established by the ACA, which is described later in this chapter.

Health Services Research and Health Policy

Health services research combines the perspectives and methods of epidemiology, sociology, economics, and clinical medicine. Applying the basic concepts of epidemiology and biostatistics, process and outcome measures that reflect the behavioral and economic variables associated with questions of therapeutic effectiveness and cost-benefit are also used. The ability of health services research to address issues of therapeutic effectiveness and cost-benefit during the nation's quest for fiscal exigency has contributed to the field's substantial growth and current value.

The contributions of health services research to health policy are impressive. Major examples include the Wennberg studies of small area variation in medical utilization, the prospective payment system based on diagnosis-related groups,[8,9] research on inappropriate medical procedures,[10] resource-based relative value scale research,[11-13] and the background research that supported the concepts of health maintenance organizations and managed care.

The RAND Health Insurance Experiment,[14,15] one of the largest and longest running health services research projects ever undertaken, began in 1971 and contributed vast amounts of information on the effects of cost-sharing on the provision and outcomes of health services. Participating families were assigned to one of four different fee-for-service plans or to a prepaid group practice. As might have been expected, individuals in the various plans differed significantly in their rate of health care use, with little measurable effect on health outcomes. The Health Insurance Experiment was followed by two large research studies: the Health Services Utilization Study and the Medical Outcomes Study. The findings of both gave impetus to the federal support of outcomes research.[16] Determining the outcomes and effectiveness of different health care interventions aids clinical decision making, reduces costs, and benefits patients.

Quality Improvement

Until the past few years, health care's impressive accomplishments had made it difficult for health care researchers, policy makers, and organizational leaders to publicly acknowledge that poor-quality health care is a major problem within the dynamic and productive biomedical enterprise in the United States. In 1990, after 2 years of study, hearings, and site visits, the Institute of Medicine issued a report that cited widespread overuse of expensive invasive technology, underuse of inexpensive "caring" services, and implementation of error-prone procedures that harmed patients and wasted money.[17,18]

Although these conclusions from this prestigious body were devastating to health care reformers, they were hardly news to health service researchers. For decades, practitioners assumed that quality, like beauty, was in the eye of the beholder and therefore was unmeasureable except in cases of obvious violation of generally accepted standards. The medical and other health care professions had promoted the image of health care as a blend of almost impenetrable, science-based disciplines, leaving the providers of care as the only ones capable of understanding the processes taking place. Thus only physicians could judge the work of other physicians. Such peer review–based assessment has always been difficult for reviewers and limited in effectiveness. Peer review recognizes that only part of medical care is based on factual knowledge. A substantial component of medical decision making is based on clinical judgment. Clinical judgment requires combining consideration of the potential risks and benefits of each physician's internal list of alternatives in making diagnostic and treatment decisions with his or her medical intuition regarding the likelihood of success based on the condition of each patient. Under these complex and often inexplicable circumstances, physicians are repelled by the notion of either judging or being judged by their colleagues.

For these reasons, until recently, quality assurance, whether in hospitals or by regulatory agencies, was focused on identifying only exceptionally poor care. This practice, popularly known as the "bad apple theory," was based on the presumption that the best way to ensure quality was to identify the bad apples or poor performers and remove or rehabilitate them. Thus, during the 1970s and 1980s, quality assurance interventions only followed the detection of undesirable occurrences. For example, flagrant violations of professional standards had to be documented before professional review organizations required physicians to begin quality improvement plans. Physicians were guaranteed due process to dispute the evidence.

Focusing on isolated violations required a great deal of review time to uncover a single case that called for remedial action. In addition, it was an unpleasant duty for reviewers to assign blame to a colleague who might soon be on a committee reviewing their records. Most importantly, such quality inspections represented a method that implicitly defined quality as the absence of mishap. Clinician dislike of quality assurance activities during the 1970s and 1980s was well founded as these processes were professionally offensive and had little constructive impact.

Specifying and striving for excellent care are very recent quality assurance phenomena in the health care arena. Hospitals and other health care organizations that had long focused on peer-review committees, incident reports, and other negative quality-monitoring activities experienced difficulty in transforming to teamwork and higher levels of transparency in quality monitoring and reporting activities.

Health services researchers had known for decades that health care quality was measurable and that excellent, as well as poor, care could be identified and quantified. In 1966, Avedis Donabedian[19] characterized the concept of health care as divided into the components of structure, process, and outcomes and the research paradigm of their assumed linkages, all of which have guided quality-of-care investigators to this day.

Donabedian suggested that the number, kinds, and skills of the providers, as well as the adequacy of their physical resources and the manner in which they perform appropriate procedures should, in the aggregate, influence the quality of subsequent outcomes. Although today the construct may seem like a statement of the obvious, at the time, attention to structural criteria was the major, if not the only, quality assurance activity in favor. It was generally assumed that properly trained professionals, given adequate resources in properly equipped facilities, performed at acceptable standards of quality. For example, for many years, the then Joint Commission on Accreditation of Hospitals made judgments about the quality of hospitals on the basis of structural standards, such as physical facilities and equipment, ratios of professional staff to patients, and the qualifications of various personnel. Later, it added process components to its structural standards and, most recently, has shifted its evaluation process to focus on care outcomes.

Early landmark quality-of-care studies used implicit and explicit normative or judgmental standards. Implicit standards rely on the internalized judgments of the expert individuals involved in the quality assessment. Explicit standards are those developed and agreed on in advance of the assessment. Explicit standards minimize the variation and bias that invariably result when judgments are internalized. More current studies judge the appropriateness of hospital admissions and various procedures and, in general, associate specific structural characteristics of the health care system with practice or process variations.

Another method for assessing the quality of health care practices is based on empirical standards. Derived from distributions, averages, ranges, and other measures of data variability, information collected from a number of similar health service providers is compared to identify practices that deviate from the norms. A current popular use of empirical standards is in the patient severity–adjusted hospital performance data collected by health departments and community-based employer and insurer groups to measure and compare both process activities and outcomes. These performance "report cards" are becoming increasingly valuable to the purchasers of care who rely on an objective method to guide their choices among managed care organizations, health care systems, and group practices. The empirical measures of quality include such variables as:

- Timeliness of ambulation
- Compliance with basic nursing care standards
- Average length of stay
- Number of home care referrals
- Number of rehabilitation referrals
- Timeliness of consultation completion
- Timeliness of orders and results
- Patient waiting times by department or area
- Infection rates
- Decubitus rates
- Medication errors
- Patient complaints
- Readmissions within 30 days
- Neonatal and maternal mortalities
- Perioperative mortalities

Normative and empirical standards are both used in studying the quality of health care in the United States. For example, empirical analyses are performed to test or modify normative recommendations. Empirical or actual experience data are collected to confirm performance and outcome improvements after the imposition of clinical guidelines derived from studies using normative standards.

Medical Errors

In 1999, the Institute of Medicine again issued a report on the quality of medical care.[20] Focused on medical errors, the report described mistakes occurring during the course of hospital care as one of the nation's leading causes of death and disability. Citing two major studies estimating that medical errors killed 44,000–98,000 people in U.S. hospitals each year, the Institute of Medicine report was a stunning indictment of the systems of hospital care at that time. The report contained a series of recommendations for improving patient safety in the admittedly high-risk environments of modern hospitals. Among the recommendations was a proposal for establishing a center for patient safety within the AHRQ. The proposed center would establish national safety goals, track progress in improving safety, and invest in research to learn more about preventing mistakes.[20] Congress responded by designating part of the increase in budget for the AHRQ for that purpose.

In 2005, the Patient Safety and Quality Improvement Act was enacted by Congress to establish patient safety organizations (PSOs) to improve the quality and safety of health care delivery by encouraging health care providers and institutions to identify, analyze, and implement prevention strategies to reduce or eliminate risks and hazards associated with the delivery of care to patients and to voluntarily report and share patient safety data without fear of legal discovery. PSOs are overseen by the AHRQ, which also maintains online access to the latest annotated links to patient safety literature and safety news at the Patient Safety Network (PSNet).[21]

Evidence-Based Medicine

Evidence-based medicine is defined as "the systematic application of the best available evidence to the evaluation of options and decisions in clinical practice, management and policy making."[22] Although this statement may appear to be a description of the way physicians and other health care providers have practiced since the inception of scientific medicine, it reflects a concern that the opposite is true. The wide range of variability in clinical practice, the complexity of diagnostic testing and medical decision making, and the difficulty that physicians have in keeping up with the overwhelming volumes of scientific literature suggest that a significant percentage of clinical management decisions are not supported by reliable evidence of effectiveness.

Although it is generally assumed that physicians are reasonably confident that the treatments they give are beneficial, the reality is that medical practice is fraught with uncertainty. In addition, the ethical basis for clinical decision making allows physicians to exercise their preferences for certain medical theories or practices that may or may not have been evaluated to link treatment to benefits.[23]

Proponents of evidence-based medicine propose that if all health services are intended to improve the health status and quality of life of the recipients, then the acid test is whether services, programs, and policies improve health beyond what could be achieved with the same resources by different means or by doing nothing at all. Evidence is the key to accountability. The decisions made by health care providers, administrators, policy makers, patients, and the public need to be based on appropriate, balanced, and high-quality evidence.[24]

The evidence-based approach to assessing the acceptability of research findings considers the evidence from randomized clinical trials involving large numbers of participants to be the most valid. Evidence-based medicine advocates dismiss outcomes research that uses large data files created from claim records, hospital discharges, Medicare, or other sources because the subjects are not randomized. "Outcomes research using claims data is an excellent way of finding out what doctors are doing, but it's a terrible way to find out what doctors should be doing," stated Thomas C. Chalmers, MD of Harvard School of Public Health, Boston.[22]

In general, most of the investigations reported in the peer-reviewed medical literature have been preliminary tests of innovations and served science rather than efforts providing guidance to practitioners in clinical practice. Only a small portion of these efforts can survive testing well enough to justify routine clinical application.[24]

The situation has changed rapidly, however. Articles on evidence-based medicine appear frequently in the medical literature.[25] Cost-control pressures that encourage efforts to ensure that therapies have documented patient benefit, growing interest in the quality of patient care, and increasing sophistication on the part of patients concerning the care that they receive have stimulated acceptance of the concepts of evidence-based medical practice.[25]

Outcomes Research and the Patient-Centered Outcomes Research Institute

Given the huge investment in U.S. health care and the inequitable distribution of its services, do the end effects on the health and well-being of patients and populations justify the costs? Insurance companies, state and federal governments, employers, and consumers look to outcomes research for information to help them make better decisions about what kinds of health care should be reimbursed, for whom, and when.

Because outcomes research evaluates results of health care processes in the real world of physicians' offices, hospitals, clinics, and homes, it contrasts with traditional randomized controlled studies that test the effects of treatments in controlled environments. In addition, the research in usual service settings, or "effectiveness research," differs from controlled clinical trials, or "efficacy research," in the nature of the outcomes measured. Traditionally, studies measured health status, or outcomes, with physiologic measurements—laboratory tests, complication rates, recovery, or survival. To capture health status more adequately, outcomes research measures a patient's functional status and well-being. Satisfaction with care also must complement traditional measures.

Functional status includes three components that assess patients' abilities to function in their own environment:

1. Physical functioning
2. Role functioning—the extent to which health interferes with usual daily activities, such as work or school
3. Social functioning—whether health affects normal social activities, such as visiting friends or participating in group activities

Personal well-being measures describe patients' sense of physical and mental well-being—their mental health or general mood, their personal view of their general health, and their general sense about the quality of their lives. Patient satisfaction measures the patients' views about the services received, including access, convenience, communication, financial coverage, and technical quality.

Outcomes research also uses meta-analyses, a technique to summarize comparable findings from multiple studies. More importantly, however, outcomes research goes beyond determining what works in ideal circumstances to assessing which treatments for specific clinical problems work best in different circumstances. Appropriateness studies are conducted to determine the circumstances in which a procedure should and should not be performed. Even though a procedure is proved to be effective, it is not appropriate for every patient in all circumstances. The frequency of inappropriate clinical interventions is one of the major quality-of-care problems in the system, and research is underway to develop the tools to identify patient preferences when treatment options are available. Although most discussions about appropriateness stress potential cost savings that could be achieved by reducing unnecessary care and overuse of services, outcomes research may be just as likely to uncover underuse of appropriate services.

It is important to recognize that the ultimate value of outcomes research can be measured only by its ability to incorporate the results of its efforts into the health care process. To be effective, the findings of outcomes research must first reach and then change the behaviors of providers, patients, health care institutions, and payers. The endpoint of outcomes research, the clinical practice guidelines intended to assist practitioners and patients in choosing appropriate health care for specific conditions, must be disseminated in acceptable and motivational ways. With the health care industry in a state of rapid change, the need to make appropriate investments in outcomes research became increasingly apparent with the inescapable conclusion that the United States cannot continue to spend almost $3 trillion each year on health care without learning much more about what that investment is buying.[26,27]

The American Recovery and Reinvestment Act (ARRA) of 2009 included $1.1 billion over a period of 2 years to expand "comparative effectiveness research" by the AHRQ and the NIH. The ARRA established a Federal Coordinating Council to recommend research priorities and create a strategic framework for research activities. The Institute of Medicine (IOM) recommended 100 priority research areas for funding by the ARRA and 10 research priority areas. Recommendations from the Federal Coordinating Council and the IOM were released in June 2009 and the ARRA required the secretary of the U.S. Department of Health and Human Services (DHHS) to consider these recommendations in directing research funds.[28,29] The goal of comparative effectiveness research is to enhance health care treatment decisions by providing information to consumers, providers, and payers to improve health outcomes by developing and disseminating evidence "on the effectiveness, benefits, and harms of different treatment options. The evidence is generated from research studies that compare drugs, medical devices, tests, surgeries, or ways to deliver health care."[29] Historically, clinical research examined the effectiveness of one method, product, or service at a time. Comparative effectiveness research compares two or more different methods for preventing, diagnosing, and treating health conditions, using methods such as practical clinical trials, analyses of insurance claim records, computer modeling, and systematic reviews of literature. Disseminating research findings in a form that is quickly useable by clinicians, patients, policy makers, health plans, and other payers about the effectiveness of treatments relative to other options is key to comparative research effectiveness goals. In addition, "identifying the most effective and efficient interventions has the potential to reduce unnecessary treatments, which may help lower costs."[29–30]

Empowering the Federal Coordinating Council, the ACA of 2010 created the PCORI, a not-for-profit, independent agency dedicated to conducting comparative effectiveness research. The PCORI is governed by a board of directors appointed by the U.S. Government Accountability Office (GAO) and is funded through the Patient-Centered Outcomes Research Trust Fund. The ACA allocated $210 million to PCORI activities for the fiscal years 2010–2012 and a total of $970 million for the years 2013–2019. Support is derived from the general U.S. Treasury fund, and fees assessed to Medicare, private health insurance, and self-insured plans.[31]

Patient Satisfaction

As reflected by the strong consumer orientation of the PCORI, patient satisfaction is recognized as an essential component of quality of care. Although the subjective ratings of health care rendered by patients may be based on markedly different criteria from those considered important by health care providers, they capture aspects of care and personal preferences that contribute significantly to perceived quality. It has become increasingly important in the competitive market climate of health care that the providers' characteristics, organization, and system attributes that are important to consumers be identified and monitored. In addition to health care providers' technical and interpersonal skills, patient concerns such as waiting times for appointments, emergency responses, helpfulness and communication of staff, and the facility's appearance contribute to patient evaluations of health services delivery programs and subsequent satisfaction with the quality of care received.

A number of instruments have been devised to measure patient satisfaction with health care, and most insurance plans, hospitals, and other health service facilities and agencies have adopted one or more to assess patient satisfaction regularly. Some, such as the Patient Satisfaction Questionnaire developed at Southern Illinois University School of Medicine, are short, self-administered survey forms. Others, such as the popular patient satisfaction instruments of the Picker Institute of Boston, Massachusetts, may be used as self-administered questionnaires mailed to patients after a health care experience or completed by interviewers during telephone surveys.[32] Whether by mail, direct contact, or telephone interview, questioning patients after a recent health care experience is an effective way to both identify outstanding service personnel and uncover fundamental problems in the quality of care as defined by patients. These activities help promote humane and effective care and are sound marketing techniques for providers.

Research Ethics

Since the 1950s, the federal government has invested heavily in biomedical research. The ensuing public–private partnership in health has produced some of the finest medical research in the world. The growth of medical knowledge is unparalleled, and the United States can take well-deserved pride in its research accomplishments.

However, many, if not most, of the sophisticated new technologies have addressed the need to ameliorate the problems of patients who already have a condition or disease. Both the priorities and the profits intrinsic to U.S. health care system have focused on remedial rather than preventive strategies. Only in the case of frightening epidemics, such as that of polio in the 1940s and AIDS in the 1990s, have there been the requisite moral imperatives to adequately fund research efforts that address public health problems. Clearly, much of the funding for medical research has failed to fulfill the generally held belief that the products of taxpayer-supported research should benefit not only the practice of medicine but also the community at large. If its intended goals are achieved, the PCORI will change the research focus to be highly inclusive of all stakeholders with a major voice from health care consumers by involving them in research topic priority determination and identifying the best mechanisms for meaningfully translating findings into clinical settings.[33]

Conflicts of Interest in Research

The increasing amount of research funding emanating from pharmaceutical and medical device companies is of serious concern. Pharmaceutical companies that pay researchers to design and interpret drug trials have been accused of misrepresenting the results or suppressing unfavorable findings. The conflicts that arise in the testing of new drugs and medical devices and publishing the results deepen as increasing numbers of studies are shifted from academic institutions to commercial research firms.[34]

For example, in 2009 the attorney general of New Jersey issued subpoenas to five prominent medical device makers for failing to disclose financial conflicts of interest among the physicians researching their products. It was learned that physicians who were testing and recommending the use of certain medical devices were being compensated with stock in the companies making those devices.[35]

To compound the problem further, the funding of the U.S. Food and Drug Administration (FDA), which regulates about a fourth of U.S. economy, has been shifted from the government to the same pharmaceutical companies it is supposed to monitor with damaging effect. Political and pharmaceutical pressures caused the FDA to stray from its science-based public health mandate. For example, the FDA has been sharply criticized for its alleged failure to adequately monitor the risks of widely advertised and commonly used drugs for the treatment of arthritis.[36] The FDA's handling of clinical trial data collected is a major problem. Although the information collected is necessary for FDA approval of a product, once the product is approved, the FDA does not provide the public with a full report of the drug's safety and efficacy. The withheld information falls into the definition of "trade secrets," and the FDA has taken the position that research data are entitled to protection as proprietary information. This explains the number of recent examples of FDA-approved drugs that were later discovered to have major safety risks.[37] Clearly, the FDA must reconsider its position that clinical trial data fall into the classification of trade secrets.

The most egregious violation of professional ethics is found in the growing body of evidence that physicians at some of the most prestigious U.S. medical schools have been attaching their names and reputations to scientific publications ghostwritten by employees of pharmaceutical companies. The publications are intended, of course, to boost the sales of pharmaceutical products.[38] The NIH, which funds much of the nation's medical research, suggests that the universities involved, rather than the government, should address the problem of ghost authorship. Because university administrators find it difficult to censure the prestigious medical faculty at their institutions, the problem remains minimally addressed with no noted measurable decline in frequency in professional biomedical literature.[39]

Future Challenges

Most U.S. health care research has been directed toward improving the health care system's ability to diagnose and treat injury, disease, and disability among those who seek care. Now, largely because of the population focus of health insurers, research studies increasingly focus on identifying and improving the health status of groups of individuals characterized by various sociodemographic and health factors. Research priorities are shifting from an individual patient perspective to a population orientation and toward continuous scrutiny of the efficiency and effectiveness of the care delivered. The ACA and its population-focused initiatives such as the PCORI are providing robust momentum to this continuing change. Experts point out that among the significant challenges to implementing changes promoted by the PCORI will be required alterations in provider behavior, cognitive biases toward rejecting new information, significant realignments of payment incentives, and inadequate resources to disseminate research findings.[40]

Basic science research will continue to contribute to the diagnostic and therapeutic efficacy of health care by adding to the knowledge about the human body and its functions. In small but critically important increments, basic science research will unlock many of the secrets of aging; cell growth regulation; mental degradation; and other mysteries of immunology, genetics, microbiology, and neuroendocrinology. The propensity of medicine to use newly obtained knowledge to alter certain physiologic processes, as in several forms of gene manipulation, will produce new ethical, legal, and clinical issues that then will require further research and adjudication.

Massive databases of gene and protein sequences and structure/function information have made possible a new worldwide research effort called bioinformatics. Bioinformatics research probes those large computer databases to learn more about life's processes in health and disease and to find new or better drugs. It is considered the future of biotechnology.

Of particular interest is research in genomics, the study of genetic material in the chromosomes of specific organisms. The sequencing of the human genome will reshape biology and medicine and lead to significant improvements in the diagnosis of disease and individual responses to drugs.[41]

Similarly, certain advances in clinical medicine and other health disciplines will result in new and disturbing ethical dilemmas. Medical achievements, such as those that permit the maintenance of life in otherwise terminal and unresponsive individuals or the transplantation of organs in short supply that require choosing among recipient candidates when those denied will surely die, generate extremely complex ethical, economic, religious, personal, and professional issues. Thus, much of the basic and clinical research that solves yesterday's problems relating to individual patient care will create new problems to be addressed in the never-ending cycle of discovery, application, and evaluation.

Medical researchers and clinicians are becoming increasingly concerned that U.S. health care is entering a "postantibiotic" era in which bacterial infections will be unaffected by even the most powerful of available antibiotics. Evidence is accumulating that a growing number of microbes, including strains of staphylococcus and streptococcus bacteria, are becoming resistant to common antimicrobials.[42] Staphylococcus bacteria are a major cause of hospital infections. According to the Centers for Disease Control and Prevention, these infections are responsible for about 13% of the 2 million infections that occur in U.S. hospitals each year. Overall, infections result in the deaths of up to 99,000 hospital patients each year.[43]

Although infectious disease epidemiologists and clinical specialists have warned for decades that the misuse and overuse of antibiotics would result in a host of deadly drug-resistant pathogens, neither physicians nor patients took the warnings seriously, with a widespread belief that the development of new antimicrobial drugs would keep medicine a step ahead of bacterial resistance.

Measures have been suggested to help maintain the efficiency of present antibiotic substances, such as limiting their use through "antibiotic stewardship" guideline development and imposing fees on antibiotic use that would cover the estimated cost of resistance inherent in antibiotic use. However, this type of fee-for-use has proved very difficult to calculate and to gain acceptance with policy makers.[44]

Limited development of new antibiotics has failed to keep step with antibiotic resistance; however, scientists now see promising alternatives in bacterial genetics to address antibiotic resistance. Economic incentives to increase the research and development of new antibiotics and a revamping of the drug approval process are some suggested remedies to increase the supply of new antibiotics brought to market.[44]

Health services research will continue to focus on the performance of the health care system as the basis for proposing or evaluating health policy alternatives. It is interdisciplinary, value-laden research concerned with the effectiveness or benefits of care, the efficiency or resource cost of care, and the equity or fairness of the distribution of care. Documenting the influence of financial incentives that affect both patient and provider, understanding the important relationships of socioeconomic status to health and health care, determining the effects of the training and experience of the health care team and the ability of the members to work together, and understanding how these many influences interact are fundamental to improving the quality of care. Reducing the monumental quandaries in medicine and health care about what works well in which situation is the challenge of health services research and the key to a more effective, efficient, and equitable health care system.

Public health research is a related research arena that deserves higher priority and significantly increased political support. If health care is ever to develop a true population perspective rather than an individual patient perspective and reap the health and economic benefits of preventive rather than only curative medicine, then epidemiology and public health research must be charged with finding ways to better understand and resolve the huge differences in health, health behaviors, health care, and health system effectiveness among communities and the population groups within them. Epidemiology, the core discipline of public health research, can assess the health problems and the provision of health care for the total population rather than just for those who are in contact with health services. Surveillance and monitoring of health conditions and assessing the effect of health care measures on the entire population are important factors in formulating health policy, organizing health services, and allocating limited resources.[45] The strategy for identifying and dealing with real or suspected biologic attacks on citizens of the United States, for example, will depend heavily on the ability of epidemiologists to identify the common source of such outbreaks, the patterns of transmission, and the outcomes of preventive and remedial efforts.

As health care adds to its traditional focus on theories, disease, and individual patient care, the performance of the health care system and the health status of populations, public health, and health services research assume increasing relevance and importance. No matter how well the health care system performs for some of the people, it cannot be fully satisfactory until it can provide a basic level of care for all.

Key Terms for Review

Analytic Studies	Empirical Quality Standards
Basic Science Research	Experimental Studies
Clinical Research	Explicit Quality Standards
Clinical Trials	Health Services Research
Comparative Effectiveness Research	Implicit Quality Standards
Descriptive Studies	Institutional Review Board (IRB)

References

1. Aday LA, Lairson DR, Balkrishnan R, et al. *Evaluating the Medical Care System: Effectiveness, Efficiency, and Equity.* Ann Arbor, MI: Health Administration Press; 1993.
2. Wennberg JE, Freeman JL, Culp WJ. Are hospital services rationed in New Haven or over-utilized in Boston? *Lancet.* 1987;1:1185–1189.
3. Wennberg JE. Which rate is right? *N Engl J Med.* 1986;314:310–311.
4. Wennberg JE, Freeman JL, Shelton RM, et al. Hospital use and mortality among Medicare beneficiaries in Boston and New Haven. *N Engl J Med.* 1989;321:1168–1173.
5. Agency for Health Care Policy and Research, U.S. Department of Health and Human Services. *AHCPR Program Note.* Rockville, MD: Public Health Service; 1990.

6. Stephenson J. Revitalized AHCPR pursues research on quality. *JAMA*. 1997;278:1557.

7. U.S. Department of Health and Human Services, Rockville, MD. *Agency for Healthcare Research and Quality*. AHRQ Profile. December 2010. Available from http://www.ahrq.gov/about/profile.htm. Accessed October 1, 2012.

8. Mills R, Fetter RB, Riedel DC, et al. AUTOGRP: an interactive computer system for the analysis of health care data. *Med Care*. 1976;14:603–615.

9. Berki SE. DRGs, incentives, hospitals and physicians. *Health Aff*. 1985;4: 70– 76.

10. Chassin MR, Kosecoff J, Park RE, et al. Does inappropriate use explain geographic variations in the use of health care services? A study of three procedures. *JAMA*. 1987;258:2533–2537.

11. Hsiao WC, Stason WB. Toward developing a relative value scale for medical and surgical services. *Health Care Finan Rev*. 1979;1:23–28.

12. Hsiao WC, Braun P, Yntema D, et al. Results and policy implications of the resource-based relative value study. *N Engl J Med*. 1988;319:881–888.

13. Hsiao WC, Braun P, Yntema D, et al. *A National Study of Resource-Based Relative Value Scale for Physician Services: Final Report to the Health Care Financing Administration*. Boston, MA: Harvard School of Public Health; 1988.

14. Newhouse JP. A design for a health insurance experiment. *Inquiry*. 1974;11:5–27.

15. Newhouse JP, Keeler EB, Phelps CE, et al. The findings of the RAND health insurance experiment—a response to Welch et al. *Med Care*. 1987;25: 157– 179.

16. Newhouse JP. Controlled experimentation as research policy. In: Ginzberg E, Ed. *Health Services Research: Key to Health Policy*. Cambridge, MA: Harvard University Press; 1991:162–194.

17. Lohr KN, The Institute of Medicine. *Medicare: A Strategy for Quality Assurance*. Vol. 1. Washington, DC: National Academy Press; 1990.

18. Surver JD. Striving for quality in health care: an inquiry into policy and practice. *Health Care Manag Rev*. 1992:17(4);95–96.

19. Donabedian A. Evaluating the quality of medical care. *Milbank Mem Fund Q*. 1966;44:166–206.

20. Kohn LT, Corrigan JM, Donaldson MS. *To Err Is Human: Building a Safer Health System*. Washington, DC: Institute of Medicine; 1999.

21. U.S. Department of Health and Human Services. *Agency for Healthcare Research and Quality*. Patient safety organizations. Available from http://www.pso.ahrq.gov/. Accessed October 1, 2012.

22. Watanabe M. A call for action from the National Forum on Health. *Can Med Assoc J*. 1997;156:999–1000. Available from http://www.cmaj.ca/content/156/7/999.full.pdf+html. Accessed October 4, 2012.

23. Marwick C. Federal agency focuses on outcomes research. *JAMA*. 1993;270:164–165.

24. Castiel LD. The urge for evidence based knowledge. *J Epidemiol Commun Health.* 2003;57:482.
25. Hooker RC. The rise and rise of evidence-based medicine. *Lancet.* 1997;349:1329–1330.
26. Reinhardt UE, Hussey PS, Anderson GF. U.S. health care spending in an international context. *Health Aff.* 2004;23:10–25.
27. Bloomberg Business Week. Healthcare spending to reach 20% of U.S. Economy by 2021. June 13, 2012. Available from http://www.businessweek.com/news/2012-06-13/health-care-spending-to-reach-20-percent-of-u-dot-s-dot-economy-by-2021. Accessed October 1, 2012.
28. Benner JS, Morrison MR, Karnes E, et al. An evaluation of recent federal spending on comparative effectiveness research: priorities, gaps and next steps. *Health Aff.* 2010;29:1768–1774.
29. Agency for Healthcare Research and Quality. What is Comparative Effectiveness Research. Available from http://effectivehealthcare.ahrq.gov/index.cfm/what-is-comparative-effectiveness-research1/. Accessed January 8, 2013.
30. The Henry J. Kaiser Family Foundation, Focus on health reform. *Explaining Health Reform: What is Comparative Effectiveness Research?* September 29, 2009. Available from http://www.kff.org/healthreform/7946.cfm. Accessed January 7, 2013.
31. Patient-centered outcomes research trust fund. How we're funded. Available from http://www.pcori.org/how-were-funded/. Accessed January 8, 2013.
32. Gerteis M, Edgman-Levitan S, Daley J. *Through the Patient's Eyes: Understanding and Promoting Patient-Centered Care.* San Francisco: Jossey-Bass; 1993.
33. Dubois RW, Graff JS. Setting priorities for comparative effectiveness research: from assessing public health benefits to being open with the public. *Health Aff.* 2011; 30:2236–2240.
34. Walker EP. HHS report slams FDA's conflict of interest oversight. January 12, 2009. Available from http://www.medpagetoday.com/PublicHealthPolicy/ClinicalTrials/12407. Accessed October 4, 2012.
35. New Jersey Office of the Attorney General. Landmark settlement reached with medical device maker synthes. May 5, 2009. Available from http://www.nj.gov/oag/newsreleases09/pr20090505a.html. Accessed October 4, 2012.
36. Miller R. Health Center Today News. University of Connecticut Health Center. FDA hearing to determine arthritis drugs' safety. February 16, 2005. Available from http://today.uchc.edu/headlines/2005/feb05/arthritisdrug.html. Accessed October 4, 2012.
37. Bodenheimer T. Uneasy alliance-clinical investigators and the pharmaceutical industry. *N Engl J Med.* 2000;342:1516–1544.
38. Singer N. Ghosts in the journals. *New York Times.* August 18, 2009:B1– B2. Available from http://www.nytimes.com/2009/08/19/

health/research/19ethics.html?_r=1&scp=1&sq=Ghosts%20in%20the%20 Journals&st=cse. Accessed January 7, 2012.

39. Wislar JS, Flanigan A, Fontanarosa PB, et al. Honorary and ghost author-ship in high impact medical journals: a cross-sectional survey. *BMJ.* 2011;343:d6128. Available from http://www.bmj.com/content/343/ bmj.d6128. Accessed October 3, 2012.

40. Timbie JW, Schneider EC, Van Busum K, et al. Five reasons that many com-parative effectiveness studies fail to change patient care and clinical practice. *Health Aff.* 2012;31:2169–2173.

41. Human Genome Project information: medicine and the new genetics. September 2011. Available from http://www.ornl.gov/sci/techresources/ Human_Genome/medicine/medicine.shtml. Accessed October 3, 2012.

42. Bren L. Battle of the bugs: fighting antibiotic resistance. 2007. Available from http://www.rxlist.com/script/main/art.asp?articlekey=85705. Accessed October 3, 2012.

43. Klevens MR, Edwards JR, Richards C, et al. Estimating health-care asso-ciated infections and deaths in U.S. hospitals, 2002. *Public Health Rep.* 2007;122:160–6. Available from http://www.ncbi.nlm.nih.gov/pmc/ articles/PMC1820440/. Accessed October 3, 2012.

44. Höjgård S. Antibiotic resistance—why is the problem so difficult to solve? *Infect Ecol Epidemiol.* 2012:2. doi: 10.3402/iee.v2i0.18165. Available from http://www.ncbi.nlm.nih.gov/pmc/articles/PMC3426322/. Accessed October 4, 2012.

45. Ibrahim MA. *Epidemiology and Health Policy.* Gaithersburg, MD: Aspen; 1985.

CHAPTER 13

Future of Health Care

This concluding chapter provides forecasts about the future of various components of U.S. health care system. It outlines the changes that have occurred and projects those trends into the future. The chapter also sketches the corporate growth in health care, the impact of technologic advances, and the Patient Protection and Affordable Care Act initiatives, and draws some tentative conclusions about the future of America's health care system.

The enactment of the Patient Protection and Affordable Care Act (ACA) is a historic achievement in expanding access to health care, promoting population health, and attempting to control short- and long-term costs. The ACA reaches into virtually every dimension of the health care delivery system with monumental changes that are unprecedented in the system's history. Predicting the future of U.S. health care system, particularly in these times of change, is highly risky at best as the nation moves into uncharted territory. The discussions that follow represent only educated conjecture about the directions the health care system will take in the coming years. Even the most thoughtful forecasts, founded on carefully studied trends and data-based projections by expert authorities, undoubtedly will be affected by unforeseeable developments in the health care environment. Trend extrapolation in the policy arena is most reliable under stable conditions.[1] The environment of the foreseeable future will be anything but stable as the system undergoes reforms. In fact, the Congressional Budget Office, as well as the Congressional Research Service, in reports on ACA implementation, points out that the scope and complexities of the legislation make predictions of fiscal and many other future outcomes extremely difficult or impossible.[2,3]

According to chaos theory, "A small change in input can quickly translate into overwhelming differences in output,"[4] and as has been demonstrated already, the health care system is particularly sensitive to input changes. In the past, every tinkering effort to address one of the three basic problems of the health care system—cost, quality, and access—has resulted in significant changes in one or both of the others. Improving access to health care for low-income populations and older adults through Medicaid and Medicare had a significant inflationary effect on costs. Attempts to contain costs through managed care raised questions about quality and access. Similarly, seemingly small changes within a health care institution, such as a leadership response to an outside financial, technologic, or market development may result in unanticipated pressures on the operations within the organization. Thus, organizational adaptations to cope with health care reforms may, in the long run, turn out to be counterproductive.

Paradox of U.S. Health Care

The extraordinary successes of U.S. health care system and the technologic accomplishments that brought worldwide acclaim to U.S. scientists have been persistently offset by the system's evident deficiencies. The policy decisions of health care leadership of the past six decades are duly credited with medicine's impressive advances, its prestige, and its wealth. Those health care policies led the National Institutes of Health and the National Science Foundation to invest heavily in the potential of our nation's universities and medical schools to develop basic and applied research and to dedicate federal and state funds to the expansion of academic medical centers. The burgeoning health care industry prompted the initiation of federal programs that significantly expanded the number and size of U.S. hospitals and led to an exponential increase in the size of the health care workforce. The policies that produced the financial incentives in the health care reimbursement system encouraged specialization among physicians and other health care practitioners.

Those policies also contributed to the long-standing problems of inequitable access, variable quality, and seemingly uncontrollable growth in costs. The success of the health care industry, the growth of its workforce, its astounding physical and technologic infrastructure, its impressive outcomes, and its unfettered revenues must be weighed against its failure to recognize a social mission broader than only addressing the individual needs of those who accessed its services. Until recently, the technology-oriented, can-do culture that pervades health care, and medicine in particular, appeared to have mesmerized the consuming public and health care providers into thinking that more dramatic medical marvels would solve the ills of the system. For many years, the public that supported the rising costs of health care had equally ascending expectations for what medicine could accomplish.

The passage of the ACA, however, represented discontent with a system that cannot deliver even a basic level of health care to significant portions of the public, that cannot control costs that have increased well beyond the rate of other commodities, and that provides services of doubtful necessity and therapeutic benefit.[5]

Continuing Challenges Facing Health Care in the Reform Era

The competitive managed care systems that took hold in the 1990s were somewhat effective in slowing the growth of health care costs. That influence was short lived however, and rising costs and several other very serious problems continued to plague the system. Those problems, described over a decade ago as major forces reshaping the health care system industry, have remained largely unaddressed and are as relevant today as they were then. Both the consumers and the providers of health care are increasingly concerned that negative consequences of social, technical, and economic forces are resulting in a more disordered and less trustworthy health care system.

U.S. health care system continues to be beset by several major forces.[6] First, the sluggish economy, receding governmental budgets, and rising health care costs have dissuaded an increasing number of middle- and upper-income people to forgo health insurance. In addition, employers, deterred by double-digit inflation in health insurance premiums, found ways to break away from paying for employee health insurance.[7] The effects of the ACA are raising new and conflicting speculations about employers dropping coverage for their employees, though the full effects will take several years to materialize.[8,9] However, a Congressional Budget Office projection in early 2013 predicted that based on changes on tax incentives, more employers than previously estimated in earlier ACA projections will drop health coverage, affecting 7 million individuals.[10] By offering health insurance exchanges and tax credits and subsidies to low- and moderate-income individuals and families, the ACA intends to encourage participation in health coverage by helping to offset health insurance premium costs and high out-of-pocket expenses.[11] In addition, the ACA provides access to separate health insurance exchanges for employers of up to 100 employees.[12]

Demand for Greater Fiscal and Clinical Accountability

The health care system, apart from the advances in clinical practice, has demonstrated a built-in inherent resistance to change. Entrenched interests; the many professions; employers; employees; and service, financial, and educational institutions have repeatedly demonstrated the capability of exercising the power necessary to maintain the status quo. As a consequence, the long and escalating problems of health care costs and rates of unacceptable clinical quality have remained unabated for decades. Because there are no single solutions to these complex problems and little likelihood that all or most of the vested interests would support a set of simultaneously applied solutions, the problems continue. Anything more than tinkering with the system would have a negative effect on at least one of the major players, capable of nullifying any of the proposed changes.

The failed attempts to address the issue of the variable quality of clinical care illustrate one facet of the problem. Concerns about the quality of health care, both anecdotally and empirically, have been expressed for decades. Because there were always small numbers of patients involved in medical errors in any individual hospital, physicians and hospital executives tended to overlook the problems. Finally, in 1999, the credible, widely publicized assessment of the problem by the Institute of Medicine (IOM), entitled "To Err Is Human: Building a Safer Health System,"[13] produced a brief flurry of discussion in Congress late in the Clinton administration and then moved far down on the list of U.S. concerns.

Now more than a decade after the report's publication, neither the health professions nor the health care industry fully prioritized patient safety and while some of the healing professions and health care delivery industries have shown a will to change in regard to prioritizing patient safety, the original IOM report's goal of reducing fatalities associated with hospital-based care by 50% within 5 years has fallen far short of being achieved.[14] When 3,000 people died on September 11, 2001, the United States went to war. When many more than 3,000 people die every 2 weeks as a result of medical errors, the silence has remained incomprehensible and discouraging.

The lack of immediate response toward improving patient safety, by physicians and policy makers detracts from the generally held assumption that the medical profession effectively polices itself. The medical profession and the vastly complex systems of personnel and organizations that support it have continued to lag behind in taking the leadership necessary to correct the long-standing system deficiencies that the IOM report identified.[14]

In fairness, physicians and other providers are beset by so many individual problems that they willingly leave the more global problems of clinical practice to their organizational leadership. They are caught between patient demands, their own uncertainties as to the best course of treatment, and the need to constrain costs. In addition, the steady production of new drugs, devices, and procedures makes current knowledge quickly obsolete. The time and effort required to remain current with clinical developments has placed a heavy burden on busy practitioners.

Although achieving system-wide improvements in health care quality depends on resolving complex, multidimensional issues, there are some hopeful signs on the horizon. Continuously rising health care costs encourage purchasers of health care coverage such as individuals, employers, and state and federal governments to become more involved in assessing and improving the quality of care. Nothing is more expensive or wasteful than the cost of inappropriate or error-prone care and its outcomes.

The federal Agency for Healthcare Research and Quality has helped to pierce the culture of silence that seems to surround medical errors by establishing the first peer-reviewed, Web-based medical journal, *Morbidity and Mortality Rounds on the Web*, to stimulate discussion of medical errors in a blame-free environment.[15] Physicians and other health professionals are encouraged to submit medical error cases to the Website for interactive discussion and analysis. Contributors may remain anonymous if they prefer.

In addition, the U.S. Department of Health and Human Services (DHHS) is participating in the Hospital Quality Information Initiative, a joint effort with the leadership of the nation's hospitals to provide the public with information on the quality of care.[16] In addition, the ACA contains several provisions that directly affect patient safety by establishing, for example, a system to track hospital medical error rates and a "carrot-and-stick approach" of reimbursement to financially reward hospitals that have improved their medical error rates. Also, a list of "never events"—particularly shocking medical errors (such as wrong-site surgery)—that should never occur has been instituted by the DHHS as one factor for reimbursement through Medicare and Medicaid. Over time, this list has been expanded to signify adverse events to patients that are unambiguous (clearly identifiable and measurable), serious (resulting in death or significant disability), and usually preventable.[17] Under the DHHS provisions, Medicare and Medicaid will not reimburse the involved health care providers for treatment required by such events.[18] Whether such financial incentives and other patient safety activities will have a material effect in significantly reducing medical error rates remains an open question.[19] A 2013 report of 6 years of data analyzed from a voluntary hospital survey established by the LeapFrog Group, an organization of Fortune 500 corporations that promotes hospital safety and quality, noted that "little progress was observed" in participating hospitals' use of public reporting of incidents, and the adoption of standards requiring the use of computerized drug order entry and hospital intensivists. The study's authors concluded: "Our study highlights the complexity of improving the quality and safety of health care in the United States through reliance on purchaser pressure and public disclosure, both of which feature prominently in the Affordable Care Act."[20]

Health Care Costs

Like the long-standing "quality of care" problem, the comparable dilemma of escalating health care costs has received only ineffective attention. The sweeping takeover of U.S. health care insurance by managed care organizations in the 1980s and 1990s had a temporary impact on the rate of national health care spending growth. The health spending growth rate reached a historic low in 2008 and remained relatively stable between 2009 and 2011, attributable to the economic recession and other factors.[21,22] However, analysts advise watchfulness about health spending acceleration in the coming 2 years as the nation continues its recovery from the recession and the ACA is implemented.[22]

The ultimate alternative to reducing excessive costs is a single-payer system that eliminates the substantial amount of health care dollars that are wasted on the administration of multiple insurance plans and the huge burden of their required paperwork. While the ACA may dampen the influence of huge corporate insurers, lacking the competitive clout of a public insurance option, large insurers will continue to exercise major influences on insurance costs.

There are reasons for optimism in the prospect of accountable care organizations (ACOs) providing coordination of care that successfully addresses the negative hallmarks of the health care delivery system— excessive costs, fragmentation, duplication, and medical errors. Observers are expressing concern, however, that the newly established ACOs are joining health care organizations that otherwise would compete with each other, thus creating networks with dangerous market power.[23] Health care market analysts also have pointed out that hospital mergers can actually increase costs that are passed on to consumers.[24] Ongoing market restructuring through hospital mergers and consolidations will test the impacts of reshuffling providers' and payers' relative positions.[25]

Growth of Home, Outpatient, and Ambulatory Care

The changes occurring in hospital care and the demographics of an aging population have produced rapid growth of home health care in recent years, with the number of home health care episodes increasing from 3.9 million in 2001 to 6.8 million in 2010. Since the implementation of the Medicare prospective payment system for home health care in 2000, the number of home health care agencies increased by 1,000 providers to reaching almost 12,000 in 2010.[26] As the population of older Americans grows, home health care services can be expected to experience corresponding expansion.

Many factors are responsible for the extraordinary growth in the number of medical and surgical procedures performed in outpatient and ambulatory settings. Advances in diagnostic technology, anesthesiology, and surgery have combined to make same-day surgery possible for procedures that formerly required hospital inpatient admissions. Third-party payers were quick to recognize the considerable cost savings of ambulatory surgery and began producing an ever-lengthening list of diagnostic and surgical procedures that would no longer be reimbursed if patients were admitted to hospitals as inpatients unless there were extenuating medical circumstances.

With federal and state incentives to encourage the development of more outpatient and ambulatory facilities and broad consumer acceptance of the use of outpatient facilities for delivery of care, almost every health care service is now being offered in outpatient or ambulatory settings. These include cancer treatment, kidney dialysis, diagnostic imaging, rehabilitation services, urgent care, wellness and preventive medicine activities, and sports medicine, in addition to surgery. With the care comparable with hospitals, far lower cost, and high consumer satisfaction and demand, it is clear that ambulatory services of all types will continue their growth trajectory.

Technology

A revealing example of the coercive power of glamorous and expensive technologic developments over thoughtful considerations of cost-benefit to patients is the medical popularity of magnetic resonance imaging (MRI). More than 7,000 of these profitable, high-technology imaging devices have been installed in hospitals and outpatient facilities across the country, costing $1–3 billion.[27,28] At an average cost of about $2 million or more each, the national investment in them is more than $14 billion. Each machine is paid for by charging patients at least $900–$1,200 per MR image, generating billions in health care costs.[29] How has this huge investment in admittedly superior diagnostic capability paid off in terms of medical care improvements? An extensive literature search published in the American College of Physicians' *Annals of Internal Medicine* in 1994 could not find a single study that documented a change in patient outcomes. Although the diagnostic information the MR image provided was considered clearer and a truer demonstration of the disease or the anatomy, neither controlled comparisons of diagnostic accuracy nor changes in therapeutic choices documented patient benefits.[30] More recent inquiries yield similar reports.[29]

It is becoming increasingly clear that technologic progress in health care has been a mixed blessing. The impersonal, if not inhumane, imposition of high-technology medicine between patients and practitioners has changed both the image and the mission of the health care enterprise. The complex social problems that affect access to health care; the geographic, economic, and other demographic disparities in the value and availability of care; and the serious discrepancies in the quality of care are issues that cannot be remedied by technologic means.

Changing Population Composition

U.S. population is not only growing older and increasing in size relative to younger population age groups, but an increasing number of older adults are surviving to a very advanced age. In addition, the number of large, intact families capable of housing and caring for aged relatives has diminished as women work outside the home, the number of single-parenting families increases, and divorce rates hover at approximately 50%. Families raise fewer children, and those children often migrate to other locations when they attain maturity. Consequently, the health care needs of the larger population of the more frail older adults are expected to place increasing demands on the health care system. Those demands will focus particularly on the chronic-care component of U.S. system, a sector that has not been particularly attractive to health care providers in the past. In addition, much of the long-term care capability in the United States is in the hands of the private, for-profit sector, which has an uneven record for the quality of its services.

The health care needs of this older adult population will also be influenced by its changing racial and ethnic diversity. The major changes occurring in the total U.S. population will be reflected in the older adult population. Minority groups and Hispanics in particular will become larger proportions of the elderly population.[31] These changes have important implications for medical care. There are significant differences in mortality rates, chronic conditions, service preferences and use, and attitudes toward medical care across racial/ethnic groups. For instance, Hispanics have lower rates of diseases such as hypertension and arthritis and higher rates of conditions such as diabetes, than the white population. Blacks are more likely to require treatment for hypertension, cerebro-vascular disease, diabetes, and obesity, and they have persistently higher mortality rates than whites.[32] The increased demands on the health care system posed by population changes coupled with the problems of health care workforce supply portend serious staffing problems. The growth in demand for nurses, nursing aides, and various types of therapists in the acute-care sector and the relative unattractiveness of long-term facilities as employment sites for those service personnel have left many chronic-care facilities dangerously understaffed. At present, there are neither the funds available in the long-term care system to attract those difficult-to-recruit service personnel nor alternative plans for meeting the residential needs of the Medicaid-dependent older population.

The chronically ill who do not require placement in a long-term care facility will continue to have difficulties interacting with a health care system that retains its historical focus on acute illness or injury and those conditions that are amenable to remediation. The current system does not deal effectively with the aged chronically ill who present persistent symptoms, increasing disability, psychosocial sequelae, and difficult life-style adjustments. Although small gains have been made by managed care organizations addressing specific chronic conditions, effective chronic illness care would require a major change in health service priorities. Simply adding new geriatric services to a system focused on acute care will not solve the basic problem.[33] Obstacles to improving the care of the chronically ill also include changing the personal values and clinical behaviors of physicians, nurses, and other health professionals. Educated for and trained in acute-care facilities, overcoming obstacles will require a major shift in mindset and practice behaviors for clinicians to accept the less dramatic, multidisciplinary nature of geriatric practice. New ACOs may help address these issues by providing care on a continuum that focuses on maintenance of optimal functionality for the chronically ill. However, the widespread changes required to move from the entrenched fee-for-service care model to one that encompasses a holistic approach to patient needs cannot be expected in the very near future.

Changing Professional Labor Supply

The economic and other forces reducing the size and services of the hospital industry, continued shifting of inpatient procedures to outpatient settings, and other organizational changes resulting from system reforms will undoubtedly result in significant disruptions in the established employment practices of many classes of health care workers. The health care industry will employ increasing numbers in the next decade,[34] and it is reasonable to predict that the kinds of employees and the sites of their employment will be in transition during the forthcoming years as the health care system continues to change. "Growth settings are expected to be in non-traditional locations such as home-based care, health practitioners' offices, and in nursing and residential care facilities. Also, an aging healthcare workforce is expected to lead to significant job openings between 2008 and 2018 through retirement and attrition."[35] For U.S. health care workforce, "The question is: how best can the U.S. health care system ensure that there are enough health professionals with the right skills to care for all who need care in the right place, at the right time?"[35]

The ACA will present formidable challenges and opportunities for U.S. health care workforce as it realigns focus from volume-driven to value-driven incentives and ushers in 30+ million newly insured patients over the next several years. The historical absence of a national health care workforce policy, particularly given the size of the workforce and variation in personnel education and training requirements, has made attempts to predict future workforce needs fraught with difficulties. In the absence of health care workforce policies or government intervention, market forces reconfigured the system on the basis of economic concerns, with little or no regard for considerations of quality or access.

The ACA proposes to address the gap in comprehensive workforce planning with a National Health Care Workforce Commission (NHCWC). The NHCWC has the mandate to evaluate and make recommendations for numerous dimensions of the nation's health care workforce including education and training support for existing and potential new workers at all levels, efficient workforce deployment, professional compensation, and coordination among different types of providers. Reporting directly to Congress, the NHCWC has been recognized as potentially having the most significant influence on shaping the nation's future health care workforce policies.[36]

Physician Supply and Distribution and Other Primary Care Practitioners

Nothing has been more dramatic during the last decade than the reduction in power, prestige, and independence of physician specialists. In the 1990s, managed care limitations on the number of specialists that could join their systems and on the frequency and circumstances of their use temporarily altered specialist physicians' positions in the health care hierarchy. In contrast, the demand for primary care practitioners increased as more people enrolled in managed care plans. There was a critical need for physicians who could provide primary care, limit access to more expensive specialists, and emphasize preventive medicine and health promotion.

Major gaps in the availability of primary care physicians have been filled by substitution of nurse practitioners and physician assistants. However, given population growth, increases in the number of older Americans, and insurance expansions resulting from the ACA, a study published in the *Annals of Family Medicine* in 2012 predicts a shortage of 52,000 primary care physicians by 2025.[37] In addition, a 2011 study reported in the *Journal of the American College of Surgeons* noted that while advanced practice nurses and physician assistants have been viewed as the means to fill the gap of primary care physicians, by 2025 the supply of these professionals will be 20% less than the numbers needed to meet demands.[38] The study's authors note that other factors may exacerbate shortages such as physicians working fewer hours and time required for care documentation responsibilities, significantly adding to the shortages.[38] While the ACA includes monetary and other incentives for training and compensating primary care physicians, experts say that the incentives will not be adequate to lure sufficient numbers to this field and that at its best, given the required period of education and training, the ACA provisions will not in themselves solve the more immediate shortage problems.[39] Predicted shortages have considerable policy implications that suggest the need to examine strategies to expand nonphysician scope of practice to assist in meeting population needs.[40] In addition to primary care physician shortages, the United States has long-term problems with the distribution of physician supply that can be expected to continue, even with ACA incentives to attract physicians to underserved areas. The persistent problem is the wide geographic variation in physician practice location rather than the actual number of physicians. The number of active physicians providing patient care per 100,000 population in each state varies from a high of over 415 per 100,000 population in Massachusetts to a low of just over 176 per 100,000 population in Mississippi, with the states having the highest ratio of physician per population concentrated regionally in the northeastern states.[41] The low supply of physicians in both the more rural and inner-city areas can be expected to continue the medical care delivery crisis to populations living in those underserved areas.

New Physician Roles

Two relatively new roles have emerged for physicians in the changing health care system. The first is the hospitalist, who provides all care to hospital inpatients of office-based physicians. Because these hospitalist physicians are constantly in hospitals and are more familiar with their inner workings, they are considered to be more efficient and more capable of continually monitoring and managing inpatient care than are non-office-based physicians. More and more hospitals are employing hospitalists to gain the benefits of shorter lengths of stay, decreased complications, and increased patient satisfaction.

The second promising role for physicians is that of medical manager or administrator. Physicians, many with additional management or administration training, are entering the medical management area through employment in pharmaceutical companies, managed care organizations, hospitals, or large group practices. The demand for physicians with advanced training in management or administration is expected to increase as the corporatization of health care continues. The emergence of ACOs as not-for-profit entities requiring executive leadership may also offer new career paths for physicians interested in health care system management. At the same time, physicians, frustrated by the changes occurring in private practice, may see health care administration as a highly regarded alternative to patient care.

Nurses

In many ways, nurses are the most qualified to respond to the changes occurring in the health system. Numbering 3 million, they represent the largest component of the health professions. Throughout the last decade, two-thirds of all nurses were employed in hospitals but the number employed in hospitals has decreased in recent years with more registered nurses seeking employment in other health care settings such as public health and ambulatory care.[42]

Nurses' training focuses more on the behavioral and preventive aspects of health care than does physician education. Their skills are as relevant to outpatient care as they are to inpatient care. As members of health care teams, nurses are experienced in managing and coordinating care with both lesser trained caregivers and professionals from other disciplines. These are characteristics that likely will be highly valued in the reformed system's integrated care scenarios.

Future of Employer-Sponsored Health Insurance

For more than 50 years, employer-sponsored health insurance protected most working Americans from overwhelming medical expenses. The insurance industry's predominant role in negotiating the parameters of the ACA reaffirmed its influential position in national policy making. The insurance industry contributed $86.2 million to the U.S. Chamber of Commerce to oppose the ACA, asserting that it would "raise costs and disrupt coverage."[43] While employers are not required to provide health benefits under the ACA, they can be monetarily penalized for not doing so, leading to possible future scenarios where employers may find it more favorable to drop coverage altogether than participate.[8] Expert analysts suggest that only a small proportion of employers will drop coverage, most likely very small firms, and that very large and medium-sized employers will retain coverage for their employees.[8,9] As noted previously in this chapter, speculation abounds about the future status of employer-sponsored health insurance programs, making it unseemly to predict how reform and market forces will combine to determine the future of this key component of the health care delivery system.

Changing Composition of the Delivery System

Hospitals, although still critically important to medical care, are no longer the hub of the health care system. The growing development of privately owned ambulatory surgery centers, urgent and immediate care facilities, diagnostic facilities, and specialty hospitals will cause traditional acute-care hospitals to become a combination of high-level intensive care units and full-service facilities for those with more serious conditions, the uninsured, and the indigent. More importantly, almost all hospitals are now or likely will become part of for-profit or not-for-profit corporate networks. Where many separate and competing hospitals once served a particular geographic area, now a smaller number of institutions divided among a few health care networks will be positioned to meet regional needs.

Health Information Technology

The growing number of new technologies for managing and transferring volumes of data should allow providers and health plans to replace voluminous and often disorganized medical records with standardized, reliable, and clinically relevant electronically delivered information. Opportunities for transcription mistakes, misinterpretation of handwriting or medication orders, and other common errors of information transfer should be minimized by new electronic health records and interoperable systems that allow easy transfer of information among care providers.

Although the technology for management of data, once collected, is advancing, there are serious obstacles to obtaining and assembling complete health information about individual patients that will be useful to treatment decisions and cost considerations. Because most patients obtain health care services from a number of providers and facilities, the information about their care is divided among various settings and sites. Originators of seamless health information systems that allow sharing of patient diagnostic, treatment, and outcome information face other problems as well. Incredibly complex confidentiality, compatibility, transferability, and organization cultural issues have challenged system designers for years.[44,45] Nevertheless, the critical role of advanced information technologies in evidence-based assessments of clinical practice, physician report cards, clinical guidelines, patient education, and a large number of other uses is recognized by everyone concerned with the future of health care. As with other obstacles to health service advances, the growing need to solve those intrinsic system problems will drive health information technology (HIT) experts to continue to develop acceptable solutions.

One of the major continuing information management challenges is dealing with fragmentation of patient information, as patients move through a disorganized treatment system.[46] A 2013 analysis of a RAND Corporation study of HIT's ability to reduce U.S. health care annual spending by $81 billion and improve the quality of care noted that HIT information systems to date are "disappointing."[47] Researchers cite poor HIT performance to date resulting from, "sluggish adoption of health IT systems, coupled with the choice of systems that are neither interoperable nor easy to use; and the failure of health care providers and institutions to reengineer care processes to reap the full benefits of health IT."[47] Researchers suggest that while government support and expert vendors are important to unlock the capabilities of HIT, future success will depend on providers embracing their central role in incorporating HIT into their care processes.[47]

Although much of the current information system development has been the result of the academic medical researchers and developers, a number of private HIT industries are engaged in the building of the technical components of that hardware and software infrastructure. Recognizing the emerging business opportunities, the free-enterprise system is augmenting years of information systems development by in-house designers employed by hospitals and academic institutions. Whether harmonious or competitive, it appears that the common interests of the clinical communities and the commercial sector will result in a new era of health care information technology. It will be a giant step forward in advancing the efficacy, efficiency, and safety of medical care.[48]

The ACA and Reemergence of Public Health: Closing the Gap

Historically, the different value systems of population health-oriented public health practitioners and individual-centered private health providers have been a great divide in the health care delivery system. The scientific advances of the past decades heightened the value differences between practitioners with a population perspective and those focused on the cure of individual patients. Physician education emphasizing sophisticated technologies and specialization left little opportunity for education on the core topics and concepts of population health. Despite the centrality of public health in providing basic health programs and the well-documented economic advantages of prevention as compared with cure, public health has had neither public nor political recognition as an essential and all-encompassing effort to prevent illness and promote health. Consequently, it has had little funding for research or practice for public health promotion or disease prevention.

Core tenets of the ACA that emphasize population health and provide reimbursement incentives aligned with population rather than individual outcomes have potential to begin closing the gap between the principles of public health and medicine. Recognizing that funding priorities are of critical importance in advancing the application of public health principles in the health care system, the ACA created the Prevention and Public Health Fund, the nation's first mandatory funding stream dedicated to improving public health.[49] The Fund is intended to eliminate the prior shortcomings of unpredictable federal budget appropriations for public health and prevention programs. The ACA mandates the Fund's use to "improve health and help restrain the rate of growth in private and public sector health care costs" through programs at the local, state, and federal levels to "curb tobacco use, increase access to primary preventive care services, as well as to help state and local governments respond to public health threats and outbreaks."[49,50]

The ACA includes several additional provisions with significant effects on public health. It established a National Prevention, Health Promotion and Public Health Council (the Council) chaired by the U.S. Surgeon General to develop and lead a National Prevention Strategy, building on existing federal programs such as *Healthy People 2020* and to make recommendations to the President and Congress for federal policy changes that support public health goals.[50–52] Established by Executive Order in 2010, the Council provides leadership to and coordination of public health activities of 17 federal departments, agencies, and offices and receives[53] input from a 22 non-federal-member, presidentially appointed Prevention Advisory Group.[54] Other ACA public health-oriented provisions increase access to clinical preventive services by providing Medicare coverage for annual wellness visits and preventive services without co-payments or deductibles, providing states with increased Medicaid matching funds for clinical preventive services recommended by the

U.S. Preventive Services Task Force and awarding grants to states to provide incentives for Medicaid beneficiaries' participation in programs that promote healthy lifestyles.[55,56] Together, the Public Health Fund and Council's Strategy have potential to significantly impact population health by creating a cohesive approach for federal agencies to coordinate efforts directed at prevention and wellness and by targeting funding to identified high-priority areas.[52]

The ACA also includes provisions to improve access to and the delivery of health care services for all individuals, particularly low-income, underserved, uninsured, minority, health disparity, and rural populations by supporting the entry of new public health professionals into the workforce and continuing professional development of the existing public health workforce.[56] To address the needs of underserved populations and health disparities, the ACA adds support for training programs in cultural competency, prevention, public health, and working with individuals with disabilities and provides grants to promote the deployment of community health workers in medically underserved areas.[55]

In summary, public health provisions of the ACA hold promise of a health care system that recognizes, and most importantly supports, the centrality of public concepts, principles, and practices to improving the health status of all Americans. Major challenges will remain to enact the required changes in strongly held perceptions and patterns of practice by both public health and private practitioners.

Summary of Predictions and Future Questions

The social and economic changes affecting society during the last decade altered public perceptions of health care and prepared many Americans for sweeping reforms in both the organization and delivery of health care services. Although tensions exist between the advocates of immediate system revisions and those who prefer more limited, incremental changes, the passage of the ACA recognized the need for significant system reforms.

Repeatedly in the history of health care in the United States, however, the public has been persuaded to instruct its representatives that health care is a "good" that should be supplied privately with as few exceptions as possible. Arguments that the system costs more and has large gaps, illogical redundancies, and inexplicable variations in quality and access were countered by prevailing beliefs that its scientific and technologic superiority offset its deficiencies.

The need for industry restructuring to remedy the deficiencies in the health care system, however, became the overriding concern of those who believe the United States should develop a more socially responsible system of health care and end its embarrassing distinction as the only Western democracy that permits a sizable percentage of its population to live without health insurance coverage. Given that health care in the United States evolved out of the professional and economic objectives of providers rather than consumer needs and has been financed by a convoluted system of private insurance augmented by inadequately managed and inflationary public sector programs, it is not surprising that the resulting system has been characterized by escalating costs and glaring gaps in coverage. Clearly, the problems could not be solved satisfactorily without major structural revisions. Solutions to the problems of huge variations in costs, treatments, and outcomes; fragmented services; episodic treatment of illness; and badly distributed overcapacity are engendered by the principles of the ACA:

- Alter the health care focus from diagnosing and treating illness to maintaining wellness and preventing illness
- Expand the health care system's accountability from the health status of individual patients to that of defined populations
- Change the health services' emphasis from acute episodic care to continuous comprehensive care and chronic disease management
- Eliminate the financial incentives to provide more services and substitute incentives to provide appropriate care at an appropriate level
- Assume universal access to health care
- Change from merely coordinating the delivery of services to actively managing the quality of processes and outcomes
- Add a serious commitment to the resolution of community and public health issues

Health care reforms can make the systems of care different, but they alone cannot make the care better. Only the health care providers working in concert with supportive systems can improve health care outcomes.

Freed from many of the disincentives of fee-for-service medicine, providers may now be better able to emphasize wellness and prevention and reduce unnecessary interventions. They may become as effective in improving the health status of entire populations as they have for patients they formerly treated on an individual basis.

Unlike the selective secrecy that has characterized health care in the past, it is expected that future health care organizations will be required to provide quality performance reports for public and purchaser scrutiny.

The relationship of hospitals to physicians will take on increasing importance as the old assumptions about medical care and surgery continue to undergo profound change in new integrated models of care delivery.

In addition, hospitals, which have long benefited from their tax-exempt status based on public and governmental assumptions that they provide substantial amounts of charity care, will, for the first time, be required to list, in public records, the exact amount they spend on subsidies for needy patients and other related activities.

The changing demographics of an aging population in the United States will compel a major expansion of long-term care facilities and services. Long-term care will become an increasingly complex array of services integrated into vertical systems. Of all the problems facing the future health care system, the aging of the population, with its attendant burden of chronic disease and disability, presents the most formidable organizational and economic challenge. Needless to say, those facilities and services striving to survive the more immediate challenges have yet to develop longer range plans to cope with that future inevitability.

The growing demand for support of chronic care is likely to continue driving major changes in the health care delivery structure in the United States. As more and more middle-aged Americans find themselves faced with the care of aged and functionally limited relatives, the demand for expanded support of chronic-care services will increase. Public awareness of the deficiencies of the current system will grow and bring considerable pressure for change in care-giving systems and supports.

Although the health care system itself is in considerable turmoil in this reform era, it is certain that the sciences within health care will continue to make progress. Clinicians and researchers will adopt advances such as devices for minimally invasive surgery, gene mapping and therapy, new vaccines, and other advances that will continue to transform the practice of medicine.

These dramatic advances, however, will be accompanied by new and vexing problems of cost, accessibility, training, and professional ethics. Practicing physicians are already overwhelmed with the profusion of new knowledge. Currently, there are 19 million citations in the computerized scientific literature database, Medline, and 2,000–4,000 more citations are added every day, 5 days a week, to this bibliographic database.[57] The availability of new knowledge also vastly exceeds the capacity of the institutions that deliver and finance health care to access and use it. The enormous potential for good that U.S. health care system enjoys comes with deep concerns. How will the recipients of new technology be chosen? Who will address the ethical dilemmas that lie behind the ability to genetically alter humans? When will the need to set stricter standards of competence when people's lives are at stake be faced by the medical profession? When will the government rein in the unlimited profits of pharmaceutical firms that price their drugs beyond the means of those who need them the most? These and many other issues are central to a constructive reformation of U.S. health care system.

The ACA represents a pragmatic approach to closing the gaps in insurance coverage by building on a mix of public and private health insurance. No matter how successful it turns out to be, the fact that any health care reform legislation was passed after the nation's long history of other attempts and failures makes this a historic landmark.

These are exciting times for students of health care. Never has so large a change in so important an industry held the potential to intimately affect so many people. It is a time for introspection regarding values, circumspection regarding advocacy for any one position, and careful inspection of any experimental changes that come about. Will the health care reforms now in progress resolve or worsen the key issues of access, costs, and quality? Can the United States possibly achieve an ideal health policy scenario, in which there is fiscal and clinical accountability for defined populations, resources allocated according to consumer needs, and transparent negotiations among all relevant parties about what services will be delivered to which people at what price? Only time and skilled leadership will tell.

Key Terms for Review

Accountable Care Organization (ACO)
National Health Care Workforce
Commission (NHCWC)

Never Events
Prevention and Public Health Fund

References

1. Longest BB. *Health Policymaking in the United States.* Chicago, IL: Health Administration Press; 2010:202.
2. Congressional Budget Office. Updated estimates for the insurance coverage provisions of the Affordable Care Act. March 2012. Available from http://www.cbo.gov/sites/default/files/cbofiles/attachments/03-13-Coverage%20Estimates.pdf. Accessed February 17, 2013.
3. Congressional Research Service. New entities created by the Patient Protection and Affordable Care Act. July 8, 2010. Available from https://www.aamc.org/download/133856/data/crsentities.pdf.pdf. Accessed January 11, 2013.
4. Gleick J. Chaos: making a new science. In: Sifonis JG, Goldberg B, Eds. *Corporation on a Tightrope: Balancing Leadership, Governance, and Technology in an Age of Complexity.* New York: Viking; 1987:9.
5. Kelley R. Where can $700 billion in waste be cut annually from the U.S. healthcare delivery system? *Healthcare Analytics,* Thomson Reuters, October 2009. Available from http://www.factsforhealthcare.com/whitepaper/HealthcareWaste.pdf. Accessed February 27, 2013.
6. Shortell SM, Reinhardt UE. Creating and executing health policy in the 1990s. In: Shortell SH, Reinhardt UE, Eds. *Improving Health Policy and Management: Nine Critical Research Issues for the 1990s.* Ann Arbor, MI: Health Administration Press; 1992:5–6.
7. Ledue C. Number of uninsured Americans could grow by 10M in five years. *Health Finance News.* Princeton, NJ; March 16, 2010. Available from http://www.healthcarefinancenews.com/news/number-uninsured-americans-could-grow-10m-five-years. Accessed October 10, 2012.
8. Deloitte. The implications of health reform on hospitals, health benefit plans, workforce and talent. Available from https://www.deloitte.com/assets/Dcom-UnitedStates/Local%20Assets/Documents/us_consulting_ImplicationsofHealthCareReform_111010.pdf. Accessed January 16, 2013.
9. Booz & Company. The future of health insurance: demise of employer-sponsored coverage greatly exaggerated. Available from http://www.booz.com/media/uploads/BoozCo-Future-of-Health-Insurance.pdf. Accessed February 6, 2013.
10. Ehley B. 7 million will lose employee coverage under Obamacare. *Financial Times.* February 5, 2013. Available from http://www.thefiscaltimes.com/Blogs/

Debt-and-Taxes/2013/02/05/Blog%20Post/7-Million-Will-Lose-Employee-Coverage-Under-Obamacare.aspx#page1. Accessed March 4, 2013.

11. The Henry J. Kaiser Family Foundation. *Explaining Health Care Reform: Questions about Health Insurance Subsidies.* July 1, 2012. Available from http://www.kff.org/healthreform/upload/7962-02.pdf. Accessed January 16, 2013.

12. The Henry J. Kaiser Family Foundation. *Explaining Health Care Reform: Questions about Health Insurance Exchanges.* April 1, 2010. Available from http://www.kff.org/healthreform/upload/7908-02.pdf. Accessed January 16, 2013.

13. Committee on Quality of Health Care in America, Institute of Medicine, Kohn LT, et al, Eds. *To Err Is Human: Building A Safer Health System.* Washington, DC: National Academy Press; 2000.

14. Wachter RM. Patient safety at ten: unmistakable progress, troubling gaps. *Health Affairs.* 2010; 29:165–168. Available from http://content.healthaffairs.org/content/29/1/165.full.html. Accessed February 27, 2013.

15. Institute for Healthcare Improvement. *AHRQ Web M&M. Morbidity & Mortality Rounds on the WEB.* October 2012. Available from http://webmm.ahrq.gov/. Accessed October 20, 2012.

16. Centers for Medicare & Medicaid Services. Hospital quality initiative overview. July 2008. Available from https://www.cms.gov/Medicare/Quality-Initiatives-Patient-Assessment-Instruments/HospitalQualityInits/downloads/HospitalOverview.pdf. Accessed February 26, 2013.

17. Meyer C. CMS issues proposed rule requiring states to implement policies for payment adjustments for provider preventable conditions. *ABA Health eSource.* April 2011. Available from https://www.americanbar.org/newsletter/publications/aba_health_esource_home/aba_health_law_esource_1104_meyer.html. Accessed March 1, 2013.

18. U.S. Department of Health and Human Services. Agency for healthcare research and quality. PSNet. Patient safety primers: never events. October 2012. Available from http://www.psnet.ahrq.gov/primer.aspx?primerID=3. Accessed October 21, 2012.

19. Grady D. Study finds no progress in safety at hospitals. NYTimes.com. November 24, 2010. Available from http://www.nytimes.com/2010/11/25/health/research/25patient.html?_r=0. Accessed October 21, 2012.

20. Moran J, Scanlon D. Slow progress on meeting hospital safety standards: learning from the Leapfrog group's efforts. *Health Affairs.* 2013;32:27–34. Available from http://content.healthaffairs.org/content/32/1/27.full.html. Accessed February 27, 2013.

21. Hartman M, Martin AB, Nuccio O, et al. Health spending growth at a historic low. *Health Affairs.* 2010;29:147–152.

22. Hartman M, Martin AB, Benson J, et al. National health spending in 2011: overall growth remains low, but some payers and services show signs of acceleration. *Health Affairs.* 2013;32:87–97.

23. Richman BD, Schulman KA. A cautious path forward on accountable care organizations. February 9, 2011. Available from http://jama.jamanetwork.com/article.aspx?articleid=645471 Accessed May 12, 2013.

24. Roy A. How hospital mergers increase health costs, and what to do about it. *Forbes*. March 1, 2012. Available from http://www.forbes.com/sites/aroy/2012/03/01/how-hospital-mergers-increase-health-costs-and-what-to-do-about-it. Accessed January 29, 2013.

25. Pear R. Trade commission challenges a hospital merger. *New York Times*. August 21, 2011. Available from http://www.nytimes.com/2011/08/22/us/22health.html?_r=0. Accessed May 12, 2013.

26. MedPac. Report to the Congress, Medicare payment policy: home health care services. March 2012. Available from http://www.medpac.gov/chapters/Mar12_ch08.pdf. Accessed March 1, 2013.

27. Centers for Disease Control and Prevention. Table 120, Number of magnetic resonance imaging (MRI) units and computed tomography (CT) scanners: selected countries, selected years, 1990–2007. February 2011. Available from http://www.cdc.gov/nchs/data/hus/2010/120.pdf. Accessed February 19, 2013.

28. eHow. How much do MRI machines cost? Available from http://www.ehow.com/about_4731161_much-do-mri-machines-cost.html. Accessed February 19, 2013.

29. Kolata G. Sports medicine said to overuse M.R.I.s. *New York Times*. October 28, 2011. Available from http://www.nytimes.com/2011/10/29/health/mris-often-overused-often-mislead-doctors-warn.html?pagewanted=all&_r=0. Accessed March 1, 2013.

30. Kent DL, Haynor DR, Longstreth WT, et al. The clinical efficacy of magnetic resonance imaging. *Ann Intern Med*. 1994;120:856–875.

31. U.S. Department of Commerce, U.S. Census Bureau. The next four decades: the older population in the United States: 2010–2050. May 2010. Available from http://www.census.gov/prod/2010pubs/p25-1138.pdf. Accessed February 17, 2013.

32. Wolf DA. Population change: friend or foe of the chronic care system? *Health Affairs*. 2001;20:64–78.

33. Wagner EH, Austin BT, Davis C, et al. Improving chronic illness care: translating evidence into action. *Health Affairs*. 2001;20:28–42.

34. U.S. Department of Labor, Bureau of Labor Statistics. Monthly labor review. January 2012. Industry employment and outlook projections to 2020. Available from http://www.bls.gov/opub/mlr/2012/01/art4full.pdf. Accessed July 1, 2012.

35. Deloitte Center for Health Solutions. Issue brief: the new health care workforce: looking around the corner to future talent management. Available from http://www.deloitte.com/assets/Dcom-UnitedStates/Local%20Assets/Documents/Health%20Reform%20Issues%20Briefs/us_chs_NewHealthCareWorkforce_032012.pdf. Accessed February 20, 2013.

36. American Academy of Family Physicians. Commission is likely to set nation's health workforce policies, say experts. August 18, 2010. Available from http://www.aafp.org/online/en/home/publications/news/news-now/government-medicine/20100818workforcecommission.html. Accessed December 21, 2012.

37. Petterson SM, Liaw WR, Phillips RL, et al. Projecting US primary care physician workforce needs: 2010–2025. *Ann Fam Med.* 2012;10:503–509. Available from http://www.annfammed.org/content/10/6/503.full. Accessed January 3, 2013.

38. Lowes R. Shortage of physicians, APNs, PAs predicted for 2025. *Medscape.* July 11, 2011. Available from http://www.medscape.com/viewarticle/746101/. Accessed January 9, 2013.

39. Lowes R. Solving primary care shortage requires more than new healthcare reform law. *Medscape.* April 26, 2010. Available from http://www.medscape.com/viewarticle/720793. Accessed January 9, 2013.

40. National Institute for Health Care Reform. Matching supply to demand: addressing the U.S. primary care workforce shortage. December 2011. Available from http://www.nihcr.org/pcp_workforce.html. Accessed February 9, 2013.

41. American Association of Medical Colleges. *Center for Workforce Studies. 2011 State Physician Workforce Data Book.* November 2011. Available from https://www.aamc.org/download/263512/data/statedata2011.pdf. Accessed September 9, 2012.

42. U.S. Department of Health and Human Services, Health Resources and Service Administration, Bureau of Health Professions, National Center for Health Workforce Analysis, 2008 National Sample Survey of Registered Nurses. 2010. Available from http://bhpr.hrsa.gov/healthworkforce/rnsurveys/rnsurveyfinal.pdf. Accessed October 21, 2012.

43. Frier S. Insurers profit from health law they fought against. *Bloomberg.* Available from http://www.bloomberg.com/news/2012-01-05/health-insurer-profit-rises-as-obama-s-health-law-supplies-revenue-boost.html. January 5, 2012. Accessed March 1, 2013.

44. Bloomrosen M, Starren J, Lorenzi NM, et al. Anticipating and addressing the unintended consequences of health IT and policy: a report from the AMIA 2009 Health Policy Meeting. *J Am Med Inform Assoc.* 2011;18(1):82–90.

45. Ash JS, Stavri PZ, Dykstra R, et al. Implementing computerized physician order entry: the importance of special people. *Int J Med Inform.* 2003;69(2–3):235–250.

46. Bell DS, Marken RS, Meili RC, et al. Rand electronic prescribing expert advisory panel. *Health Affairs.* 2004;1:305–317.

47. Kellerman AL, Jones SS. What it will take to achieve the as-yet-unfulfilled promises of health information technology. *Health Affairs.* 2013;32:63–67.

48. Menachemi N, Brooks RG. Reviewing the benefits of electronic health records and associated patient safety technologies. *J Med Syst.* 2006;30:159–168.

49. American Public Health Association. Prevention and public health fund. Available from http://www.apha.org/NR/rdonlyres/745B72B7-0D8F-47D2-8516-D3BA02829BA3/0/PreventionPublicHealth32212.pdf. Accessed February 9, 2013.

50. Staff of the Washington Post. *Landmark.* New York: Perseus Books; 2002:224.

51. U.S. Department of Health and Human Services. Obama administration releases national prevention strategy. News release. Available from http://www.hhs.gov/news/press/2011pres/06/20110616a.html.

52. Majette GR. PPACA and public health: creating a framework to focus on prevention and wellness and improve the public's health. *J Law Med Ethics.* 2011;39:373–374. Available from http://www2.law.csuohio.edu/newsevents/images/39JLME366.pdf. Accessed February 4, 2013.

53. U.S. Surgeon General. Prevention. National prevention council. Available from http://www.surgeongeneral.gov/initiatives/prevention.index.html. June 2012. Accessed February 11, 2013.

54. Surgeon General. Prevention Advisory Group. Advisory group members. Available from http://www.surgeongeneral.gov/initiatives/prevention/advisorygrp/index.html. 2013. Accessed February 11, 2013.

55. Democratic Policy and Communications Center. The patient protection and Affordable Care Act. Available from http://dpc.senate.gov/healthreformbill/healthbill52.pdf. Accessed January 8, 2013.

56. Staff of the Washington Post. *Landmark.* New York: Perseus Books Group; 2002:226–228.

57. National Library of Medicine. Medline fact sheet. February 20, 2013. Available from http://www.nlm.nih.gov/pubs/factsheets/medline.html. Accessed May 12, 2013.

Abbreviations
and Acronyms

AACN	American Association of Colleges of Nursing
AAFP	American Academy of Family Physicians
AAMC	Association of American Medical Colleges
AAN	American Academy of Nursing
AAP	American Academy of Pediatrics
AARP	American Association of Retired Persons
ACA	Patient Protection and Affordable Care Act of 2010
ACEHSA	Accrediting Commission on Education for Health Services Administrators
ACF	Administration on Children and Families
ACGME	Accreditation Council for Graduate Medical Education
ACHE	American College of Healthcare Executives
ACO	Accountable Care Organization
ACP	American College of Physicians
ACR	Advanced Certified Rolfer
ACS	American College of Surgeons
ACYF	Administration for Children, Youth, and Families

ADA	American Dental Association
ADAMHA	Alcohol, Drug Abuse, and Mental Health Administration
ADD	Administration on Developmental Disabilities
ADLs	Activities of Daily Living
AFDC	Aid to Families with Dependent Children
AFL-CIO	American Federation of Labor and Congress of Industrial Organizations
AHA	American Hospital Association
AHC	Academic Health Center
AHCPR	Agency for Health Care Policy and Research (now called Agency for Healthcare Research and Quality)
AHP	Accountable Health Plan
AHRQ	Agency for Healthcare Research and Quality (formerly Agency for Health Care Policy and Research)
AHSR	Association for Health Services Research (formerly Academy for Health Services Research and Health Policy)
AID	U.S. Agency for International Development
AIDS	Acquired Immunodeficiency Syndrome
ALOS	Average Length of Stay
AMA	American Medical Association
AMC	Academic Medical Center
ANA	Administration for Native Americans; American Nurses Association
AOA	American Osteopathic Association
AoA	Administration on Aging
APA	American Psychiatric Association; American Psychological Association
APEX/PH	Assessment Protocol for Excellence in Public Health
APHA	American Public Health Association
APTA	American Physical Therapy Association
ARRA	American Recovery and Reinvestment Act of 2009
ASAHP	Association of Schools of Allied Health Professions

ASH	Assistant Secretary for Health
ASHED	AIDS School Health Education Database
ASHP	Adolescent and School Health Programs
ASIM	American Society of Internal Medicine
ASSIST	American Stop Smoking Intervention Study
ASTHO	Association of State and Territorial Health Officials
ATF	Bureau of Alcohol, Tobacco, and Firearms
ATSDR	Agency for Toxic Substances and Disease Registry
AUPHA	Association of University Programs in Health Administration
BAC	Blood Alcohol Concentration
BBA	Balanced Budget Act of 1997
BC/BS	Blue Cross and Blue Shield
BCHS	Bureau of Community Health Services
BHP	Bureau of Health Professions
BHRD	Bureau of Health Resources Development
BIA	Bureau of Indian Affairs
BLS	Bureau of Labor Statistics
BPCI	Bundled Payment for Care Improvement Initiative
BPHC	Bureau of Primary Health Care
BRFSS	Behavioral Risk Factor Surveillance System
CAH	Critical Access Hospital
CAM	Complementary and Alternative Medicine
CAN	Caregiver Action Network (formerly National Family Caregivers Association)
CAPTE	Commission on Accreditation of Physical Therapy Education
CAT	Computerized Axial Tomography
CBER	Center for Biologics Evaluation and Research
CCN	Community Care Network; Critical Care Nurse
CCRC	Continuing Care Retirement Community

CDC	Centers for Disease Control and Prevention
CDER	Center for Drug Evaluation and Research
CDF	Children's Defense Fund
CDHP	Consumer Driven Health Plan
CDRH	Center for Devices and Radiological Health
CDSS	Computerized Decision Support System
CEO	Chief Executive Officer
CEU	Continuing Education Unit
CFO	Chief Financial Officer
CFSAN	Center for Food Safety and Applied Nutrition
CHAMPUS	Civilian Health and Medical Program of the Uniformed Services
CHC	Community Health Center
CHID	Combined Health Information Database
CHIP	Children's Health Insurance Program also known as State Children's Health Program (SCHIP)
CHP	Comprehensive Health Planning
CME	Continuing Medical Education
CMHC	Community Mental Health Center
CMMI	Center for Medicare and Medicaid Innovation
CMS	Centers for Medicare & Medicaid Services (formerly HCFA, the Health Care Financing Administration)
COBRA	Consolidated Omnibus Budget Reconciliation Act
COGME	Council on Graduate Medical Education
CON	Certificate of Need
CPI	Consumer Price Index
CPOE	Computerized Physician Order Entry
CPR	Customary, Prevailing, and Reasonable (fees); cardio-pulmonary resuscitation
CPSC	Consumer Product Safety Commission
CPT	Current Procedural Terminology
CPT-4	Current Procedural Terminology, 4th edition

CQI	Continuous Quality Improvement
CRCC	Commission on Rehabilitation Counselor Certification
CT	Computed Tomography
CTP	Certified Trager Practitioner
CVM	Center for Veterinary Medicine
DC	Doctor of Chiropractic
DDS/DMD	Doctor of Dental Surgery/Doctor of Dental Medicine
DHEW	Department of Health, Education, and Welfare
DHHS	Department of Health and Human Services
DME	Durable Medical Equipment
DNR	Do Not Resuscitate
DNS/DNSc	Doctor of Nursing Science
DO	Doctor of Osteopathy
DOE	Department of Education
DOI	Department of Interior
DOJ	Department of Justice
DOL	Department of Labor
DOT	Department of Transportation
DPM	Doctor of Podiatric Medicine
DRG	Diagnosis-Related Group
DVA	Department of Veterans Affairs
EACH	Essential Access Community Hospital
EAP	Employee Assistance Program
ECA	Epidemiologic Catchment Area
ECF	Extended Care Facility
EHR	Electronic Health Record
EMS	Emergency Medical Services
EMTALA	Emergency Medical Treatment and Labor Act
EPA	Environmental Protection Agency
EPO	Epidemiology Program Office
EPSDT	Early and Periodic Screening, Diagnosis, and Treatment

ER	Emergency Room
eRx	Electronic Prescription Order
ERISA	Employee Retirement Income Security Act
ESRD	End-Stage Renal Disease
FAHS	Federation of American Health Systems
FAS	Fetal Alcohol Syndrome
FDA	Food and Drug Administration
FDIR	Food Distribution Program on Indian Reservations
FEHBP	Federal Employee Health Benefits Program
FEMA	Federal Emergency Management Association
FFS	Fee for Service
FHSR	Foundation for Health Services Research
FHWA	Federal Highway Administration
FIC	Fogarty International Center
FMG	Foreign Medical Graduate
FMLA	Family Medical Leave Act
FNS	Food and Nutrition Service
FPL	Federal Poverty Line
FQHC	Federally Qualified Health Center
FSA	Flexible Spending Account
FTC	Federal Trade Commission
FTE	Full-Time Equivalent
FY	Fiscal Year
GDP	Gross Domestic Product
GHAA	Group Health Association of America
GHC	Group Health Cooperative
GHI	Group Health Insurance
GME	Graduate Medical Education
GMENAC	Graduate Medical Education National Advisory Committee
GNP	Gross National Product

HAC	Hospital Acquired Condition
HACCP	Hazard Analysis Critical Control Point
HANES	Health and Nutrition Examination Survey
HBCU	Historically Black Colleges and Universities
HBV	Hepatitis B Virus
HCA	Hospital Corporation of America
HCFA	Health Care Financing Administration
HCV	Hepatitis C Virus
HDHP	High Deductible Health Plan
HDL	High-Density Lipoprotein Cholesterol
HEDIS	Healthcare Effectiveness Data and Information Set
HETC	Health Education and Training Center
HEW	Health, Education, and Welfare (Department of)
HHS	Health and Human Services (Department of)
HIAA	Health Insurance Association of America
HIE	Health Information Exchange
HIP	Health Insurance Plan
HIPAA	Health Insurance Portability and Accountability Act
HIS	Health Interview Survey
HIT	Health Information Technology
HITECH	Health Information Technology for Economic and Clinical Health Act
HIV	Human Immunodeficiency Virus
HMO	Health Maintenance Organization
HNIS	Human Nutrition and Information Service
HPDP	Health Promotion and Disease Prevention
HPEAA	Health Professions Educational Assistance Act
HRA	Health Resources Administration
HRAs	Health Reimbursement Accounts
HRQL	Health-Related Quality of Life
HRSA	Health Resources and Services Administration

HSA	Health Systems Agency
HSA	Health Savings Account
HTPCP	Healthy Tomorrows Partnership for Children Program
HUD	Housing and Urban Development (Department of)
IADL	Instrumental Activity of Daily Life
ICD	International Classification of Diseases
ICD-9-CM	International Classification of Diseases, 9th Revision, Clinical Modification
ICU	Intensive Care Unit
IDDM	Insulin-Dependent Diabetes Mellitus
IEN	Internationally Educated Nurse
IHPO	International Health Program Office
IHS	Indian Health Service
IMGs	International Medical Graduates
IMR	Infant Mortality Rate
INPHO	Information Network for Public Health Officials
IOM	Institute of Medicine
IPA	Individual Practice Association
IPAB	Independent Payment Advisory Board
IPN	Integrated Provider Network
IPO	Independent Practitioner Organization
IRB	Institutional Review Board
LCME	Liaison Committee on Medical Education
LDL	Low-Density Lipoprotein Cholesterol
LIHEAP	Low-Income Home Energy Assistance Program
LOINC	Logical Observations Index Names and Codes
LOS	Length of Stay
LPN	Licensed Practical Nurse
LTC	Long-Term Care
LTCF	Long-Term Care Facility
LTCI	Long-Term Care Insurance

MBHO	Managed Behavioral Healthcare Organization
MCHB	Maternal and Child Health Bureau
MCN	Migrant Clinicians Network
MCO	Managed Care Organization
MD	Medical Doctor
MDC	Major Diagnostic Category
MDS	Minimum Data Set
MEDLARS	Medical Literature Analysis and Retrieval System
MEDTEP	Medical Treatment Effectiveness Program
MEHP	Minority Environmental Health Program
MHTS	Minority Health Tracking System
MLP	Midlevel Practitioner
MPI	Master Patient Index
MRI	Magnetic Resonance Imaging
MSA	Metropolitan Statistical Area; Medical Savings Account
MSEHP	Model State Emergency Health Powers Act
MSHA	Mine Safety and Health Administration
MSO	Management Services Organization
MVP	Medicare Volume Performance
NACAA	National Association of Consumer Agency Administrators
NACCHO	National Association of County and City Health Officials
NACHM	National Advisory Commission on Health Manpower
NAHC	National Association for Home Care
NAIEP	National AIDS Information and Education Program
NAM	National Association of Manufacturers
NAMCS	National Ambulatory Medical Care Survey
NAMHC	National Advisory Mental Health Council
NAMI	National Alliance on Mental Illness
NAPO	National AIDS Program Office

NCADI	National Clearinghouse for Alcohol and Drug Information
NCAI	National Congress of American Indians
NCCAN	National Center on Child Abuse and Neglect
NCCDPHP	National Center for Chronic Disease Prevention and Health Promotion
NCEH	National Center for Environmental Health
NCHGR	National Center for Human Genome Research
NCHS	National Center for Health Statistics
NCHSR	National Center for Health Services Research
NCI	National Cancer Institute
NCID	National Center for Infectious Diseases
NCIPC	National Center for Injury Prevention and Control
NCPIE	National Council on Patient Information and Education
NCPS	National Center for Prevention Services
NCQA	National Committee on Quality Assurance
NCRR	National Center for Research Resources
NCTR	National Center for Toxological Research
ND	Doctor of Naturopathy; Doctor of Nursing
NEI	National Eye Institute
NF	Nursing Facility
NHCWC	National Health Care Workforce Commission
NHDS	National Hospital Discharge Survey
NHE	National Health Expenditures
NHIC	National Health Information Center
NHIS	National Health Interview Survey
NHLBI	National Heart, Lung, and Blood Institute
NHSC	National Health Service Corps
NIA	National Institute on Aging
NIAAA	National Institute on Alcohol Abuse and Alcoholism
NIAID	National Institute of Allergy and Infectious Diseases

NIAMS	National Institute of Arthritis and Musculoskeletal and Skin Diseases
NICHD	National Institute of Child Health and Human Development
NIDA	National Institute on Drug Abuse
NIDCD	National Institute on Deafness and Other Communication Disorders
NIDDK	National Institute of Diabetes and Digestive and Kidney Diseases
NIDR	National Institute of Dental Research
NIDRR	National Institute on Disability and Rehabilitation Research
NIEHS	National Institute of Environmental Health Sciences
NIGMS	National Institute of General Medical Sciences
NIH	National Institutes of Health
NIMH	National Institute of Mental Health
NINDS	National Institute of Neurological Disorders and Stroke
NINR	National Institute of Nursing Research
NIOSH	National Institute of Occupational Safety and Health
NLM	National Library of Medicine
NLN	National League for Nursing
NLTN	National Laboratory Training Network
NMIHS	National Maternal and Infant Health Survey
NMR	Nuclear Magnetic Resonance
NNHS	National Nursing Home Survey
NORC	Naturally Occurring Retirement Community
NQF	National Quality Forum
NQTL	Non-Quantitative Treatment Limitation
NSLTCP	National Study of Long-Term Care Providers
NVSS	National Vital Statistics System
OAM	Office of Alternative Medicine
OASIS	Outcomes and Assessment Information Set

OBRA	Omnibus Budget Reconciliation Act
OCS	Office of Community Services
OCSE	Office of Child Support Enforcement
ODPHP	Office of Disease Prevention and Health Promotion
OECD	Organization for Economic Cooperation and Development
OEO	Office of Economic Opportunity
OFA	Office of Family Assistance
OHTA	Office of Health Technology Assessment
OIH	Office of International Health
OMB	Office of Management and Budget
OMH	Office of Minority Health
ONC	Office of the National Coordinator for Health Information Technology
ORHP	Office of Rural Health Policy
ORT	Operation Restore Trust
OSH	Office of Smoking and Health
OSHA	Occupational Safety and Health Administration
OT	Occupational Therapy
OTA	Office of Technology Assessment
OWH	Office on Women's Health
PA	Physician Assistant
PAC	Political Action Committee
PACE	Program of All-Inclusive Care for the Elderly
PAR	Preadmission Review
PCMH	Patient-Centered Medical Home
PCP	Primary Care Provider; Primary Care Physician
PCPCC	Patient Centered Primary Care Collaborative
PCORI	Patient Centered Outcomes Research Institute
PCORTF	Patient Centered Outcomes Research Trust Fund
PDA	Personal Digital Assistant
PET	Positron Emission Tomography

PGP	Prepaid Group Practice
PharmD	Doctor of Pharmacy
PHLI	Public Health Leadership Institute
PHMT	Personal Health Management Tool
PHO	Physician–Hospital Organization
PHP	Prepaid Health Plan
PHR	Personal Health Record
PHS	Public Health Service
PIRC	Preventive Intervention Research Center
PMPM	Per Member Per Month
PMPY	Per Member Per Year
POE	Point of Enrollment
PORT	Patient Outcomes Research Team
POS	Point of Service
PPA	Preferred Provider Arrangement
PPCM	Primary Care Case Management
PPHA	Pennsylvania Public Health Association
PPO	Preferred Provider Organization
PPRC	Physician Payment Review Commission
PPS	Prospective Payment System
PRO	Peer Review Organization
ProPAC	Prospective Payment Assessment Commission
PSNet	Patient Safety Network
PSO	Provider Service Organization; Provider-Sponsored Organization, Patient Safety Organization
PSQ	Patient Satisfaction Questionnaire
PSRO	Professional Standards Review Organization
PT	Physical Therapy
PTMPY	Per Thousand Members Per Year
QA	Quality Assurance
RAPs	Radiologists, Anesthesiologists, and Pathologists

RBRVS	Resource-Based Relative Value Scale
RHIO	Regional Health Information Organization
RMP	Regional Medical Program
RN	Registered Nurse
ROSC	Recovery Oriented Systems of Care
RPCH	Rural Primary Care Hospital
RPP	Registered Polarity Practitioner
RRA	Registered Records Administrator
RRC	Residency Review Committee
RSPA	Research and Special Programs Administration
RUG	Resource Utilization Group
RVS	Relative Value Scale
RVU	Relative Value Unit
SAMHSA	Substance Abuse and Mental Health Services Administration
SCHIP	State Children's Health Insurance Program also known as Children's Health Insurance Program (CHIP)
SEIU	Service Employees International Union
SHMO	Social Health Maintenance Organization
SMI	Supplemental Medical Insurance
SNF	Skilled Nursing Facility
SNOMED	Systematized Nomenclature of Medicine
SSA	Social Security Administration
SSI	Supplemental Security Income
STD	Sexually Transmitted Disease
TEFRA	Tax Equity and Fiscal Responsibility Act
Title	XVIII (of Social Security Act) Medicare
Title	XIX (of Social Security Act) Medicaid
TPA	Third-Party Administrator

TPN	Total Parenteral Nutrition
TQM	Total Quality Management
UCAOA	Urgent Care Association of America
UCR	Usual, Customary, and Reasonable Reimbursement
UMLS	Unified Medical Language System
UR	Utilization Review
USFMG	U.S. Foreign Medical Graduate
USMLE	United States Medical Licensing Examination
USPHS	U.S. Public Health Service
VA	Veterans Administration; Department of Veterans Affairs
VBP	Value-Based Purchasing
VISNs	Veterans Integrated Service Networks
VNA	Visiting Nurses Association
WHO	World Health Organization
WIC	Women's Infant's and Children's Supplemental Nutrition Program

B

Websites

U.S. Government

Agency for Healthcare Research and Quality:
http://www.ahrq.gov/

Centers for Disease Control and Prevention:
http://www.cdc.gov/

Centers for Medicare & Medicaid Services:
http://www.cms.gov/

Department of Health and Human Services:
http://www.hhs.gov/

Department of Veterans Affairs, Veterans Health Administration:
http://www.va.gov/HAC/hacmain.asp

National Center for Complementary and Alternative Medicine:
http://www.nccam.nih.gov/

National Center for Health Statistics:
http://www.cdc.gov/nchs/

National Guideline Clearinghouse:
http://guideline.gov/

National Institutes of Health:
http://www.nih.gov/

National Library of Medicine Databases:
http://clinicaltrials.gov/ and http://www.ncbi.nlm.gov/pubmed/ or
http://www.nlm.nih.gov/medlineplus/

Office of Disease Prevention and Health Promotion:
http://odphp.osophs.dhhs.gov/

Office of the National Coordinator for Health Information Technology:
http://www.healthit.gov/

State Children's Health Insurance Program (SCHIP)/Children's Health Insurance Program (CHIP):
http://www.healthcare.gov/using-insurance/low-cost-care/childrens-insurance-program/index.html

U.S. Administration on Aging:
http://www.aoa.gov/

U.S. Congressional Budget Office:
http://www.cbo.gov/

U.S. Department of Health and Human Services:
http://www.hhs.gov/ and http://healthfinder.gov

U.S. Department of Labor, Bureau of Labor Statistics:
http://bls.gov/

U.S. Food and Drug Administration:
http://www.fda.gov/

Other Organizations

American Academy of Family Physicians:
http://www.aafp.org/online/en/home.html

American Association of Retired Persons:
http://www.aarp.org/health/

American Board of Medical Specialties:
http://www.abms.org/

American Cancer Society:
http://www.cancer.org

American Health Care Association:
http://www.ahcancal.org/Pages/Default.aspx

American Heart Association:
http://www.heart.org/HEARTORG/

American Lung Association:
http://www.lung.org/

American Medical Association:
http://www.ama-assn.org/

America's Health Insurance Plans:
http://www.ahip.org/

Annals of Long-Term Care:
http://www.annalsoflongtermcare.com/

The Commonwealth Fund:
http://www.commonwealthfund.org/

Families USA:
http://www.familiesusa.org/

Health Care Careers and Jobs Center:
http://healthcarejobs.org/

The Joint Commission:
http://www.jointcommission.org/

Kaiser Family Foundation and Health Research and Educational Trust:
http://www.kff.org/

Long-Term Care Provider.com News and Analysis:
http://www.longtermcareprovider.com/

Mayo Clinic:
http://www.mayoclinic.com/

Medscape:
http://www.medscape.com/

Modern Healthcare:
http://www.modernhealthcare.com/

National Alliance for Caregiving:
http://www.caregiving.org/

National Alliance for the Mentally Ill:
http://www.nami.org/

National Association for Home Care and Hospice:
http://www.nahc.org/

National Center for Assisted Living:
http://www.ahcancal.org/ncal/

National Committee for Quality Assurance:
http://www.ncqa.org/

National Council on Aging:
http://www.ncoa.org/

Utilization Review Accreditation Commission:
http://www.urac.org

Glossary

Academic health center: A university-affiliated complex of professional academic and clinical care facilities such as medicine, nursing, pharmacy, dentistry, and allied health professions that are the principal places of education and training for physicians and other health care personnel, the sites for most basic medical research, and the settings for clinical trials. Academic health center teaching hospitals are major providers of highly sophisticated patient care required by trauma centers; burn centers; neonatal intensive care centers; and the technologically advanced treatment of cancer, heart disease, neurologic and other acute and chronic conditions. Academic health center teaching hospitals also provide much of the primary care for the economically disadvantaged populations in their geographical area.

Accountable care organization (ACO): A group of providers and suppliers of health care, health-related services, and others involved in caring for Medicare patients that voluntarily work together to co-ordinate care for the patients they serve under the original Medicare (not Medicare Advantage managed care) program. The ACA enables ACOs to share in savings to the federal government based on ACO performance in improving quality and reducing health care costs.

Accreditation Council for Graduate Medical Education (ACGME): The independent, not-for-profit professional organization that accredits 3-7 year programs of advanced education and clinical practice required by physicians to provide direct patient care in a recognized medical specialty.

Agency for Healthcare Research and Quality (AHRQ): The federal agency charged with research to develop and disseminate evidence-based practice guidelines. AHRQ is a major collaborating agency in several ACA implementation initiatives.

Ambulatory care: Services that do not require an overnight hospital stay.

American Board of Medical Specialities (ABMS): An independent, not-for-profit organization, the ABMS assists its 24 specialty member boards to develop and utilize professional and educational standards that apply to the certification of physician specialists in the United States and internationally.

Analytic studies: Test hypotheses and try to explain biologic phenomena by seeking statistical associations between factors that may contribute to a subsequent occurrence and the initial occurrence itself.

Assessment (as a core function of public health): Collecting and analyzing data to define population health status and quantify existing or emerging health problems.

Assisted living: A program that provides and/or arranges for daily meals, personal and other supportive services, health care, and 24-hour oversight to persons residing in a group residential facility who need assistance with the activities of daily living.

Assurance (as a core function of public health): Governmental public health agency responsibility to ensure that basic components of the health care delivery system are in place.

Balanced Budget Act of 1997 (BBA): The Act was characterized as containing "some of the most sweeping and significant changes to Medicare and Medicaid since their inception in 1965." The BBA took important incremental steps by extending health care coverage to uninsured children through a $16 billion allocation for a new State Children's Health Insurance Program (SCHIP). The BBA proposed to reduce growth in Medicare and Medicaid spending by $125.2 billion in 5 years. It also increased beneficiary premiums for Medicare Part B and required new prospective payment systems for hospital outpatient services, skilled nursing facilities, home health agencies, and rehabilitation hospitals. It reduced allowances for the medical education expenses of teaching hospitals and funded incentives to hospitals for voluntarily reducing the numbers of medical residents. Among the most significant policy shifts of the BBA was opening the Medicare program to private insurers through the Medicare + Choice Program, for the first time allowing financial risk-sharing for the Medicare program with the private sector through managed care plans.

Basic science research: Conducted by biochemists, physiologists, biologists, pharmacologists, and others concerned with sciences that are fundamental to understanding the growth, development, structure, and functions of the human body and its responses to external stimuli. Much basic science research is conducted at the cellular level.

Behavioral scientist: Behavioral scientists include professionals in social work, health education, community mental health, alcoholism and drug abuse services, and other health and human service areas. Bachelor's or master's level degree professionals in these fields counsel and support individuals and families in addressing the personal, economic and social problems associated with illness, addictions, employment challenges and disabilities.

Block grants: A mechanism to shift the federal government's direct support and administration of health care programs to state and local governments.

Bundled payment for care improvement initiative (BPCI): Developed by the CMS Center for Medicare & Medicaid Innovation (CMMI) that was created by the ACA; the BPCI recognizes that separate Medicare fee-for-service payments for individual services provided during a beneficiary's single illness often result in fragmented care with minimal co-ordination across providers and settings and results in rewarding service quantity rather than quality. The BPCI is designed to test whether, as prior research has shown, payments for bundled "episodes of care" can align incentives for hospitals, post–acute care providers, physicians, and other health care personnel to work closely together across many settings to achieve improved patient outcomes at lower cost.

Capitation: A managed care reimbursement method that prepays physicians for services on a per-member per-month basis whether or not services are used. If a physician exceeds the predetermined capitation amount, he or she may incur a financial penalty. If the physician uses fewer resources than predicted, he or she may retain the excess as profit.

"Carve-out": A process through which insurers outsource subscribers' mental illness care oversight to firms specializing in managing service use for mental health diagnoses.

Certification: A regulatory process, much less stringent than licensure, under which a state or professional organization attests to an individual's advanced training and performance abilities in a field of health care practice. Specific professions set certification standards for approval by their respective state or professional organizations.

Clinical research: Primarily focuses on steps in the process of medical care such as the early detection, diagnosis, and treatment of disease or injury; the maintenance of optimal, physical, mental, and social functioning; the limitation and rehabilitation of disability; and the palliative care of those who are irreversibly ill. Clinical research is conducted by a variety of professionals in medicine, nursing, and allied health, often in collaboration with basic scientists.

Clinical trials: Tests a new treatment or drug against a prevailing standard of care. Clinical trials may use control groups who receive a placebo to minimize subject bias. To further reduce bias, clinical trials may randomly assign volunteer patients to treatment and control groups. A most rigorous form of clinical trial is "double-blind" in which neither the patients nor the researchers know who is receiving a test drug or placebo until the trial's conclusion.

Community-rated insurance: Insurance plans in which all individuals in a defined group pay premiums without regard to age, gender, occupation, or health status. Community ratings helped ensure nondiscrimination against groups with varying risk characteristics to provide coverage at reasonable rates for the community as a whole.

Co-morbidity: When two disorders or illnesses occur in the same person, simultaneously or one after another, they are called co-morbid.

Comparative effectiveness research: Research designed to inform health care decisions by providing evidence on the effectiveness, benefits, and harms of different treatment options. Evidence is generated from research studies that compare drugs, medical devices, tests, surgeries, or ways to deliver health care.

Computerized decision support system (CDSS): An electronic information-based system in which individual patient data is matched with a computerized knowledge base such as evidence-based clinical practice guidelines, to assist health care providers in formulating accurate diagnoses, recommendations, and treatment plans. A CDSS may generate "hard stops" to prevent a disallowed practice or severe errors or "soft stops" that warn of less severe errors and allow physicians to choose to ignore or follow the warning.

Computerized physician order entry (CPOE): A process in which a physician enters patient treatment orders into an individual patient's electronic health record.

Consumer-driven health plan (CDHP): Developed in a reaction to the managed care backlash, the goals of CDHPs were to have employees take more responsibility for health care decisions and exercise more cost consciousness. Typical CDHPs consist of either a health reimbursement arrangement (HRA) or a health savings account (HSA). Among employers that offered CDHPs in 2012, HSAs outpaced HRAs by two to one.

Continuing care retirement community (CCRC): Residences on a retirement campus, typically in apartment complexes designed for functional older adults. Unlike ordinary retirement communities that offer only specialized housing, CCRCs offer a comprehensive program of social services, meals, and access to contractual medical services in addition to housing.

Continuing life care community (CLCC): The most expensive of CCRC options. CLCCs offer unlimited assisted living, medical treatment, and skilled nursing care without any additional charges as the resident's needs change over time.

Deinstitutionalization: The mental health movement beginning in the 1960s through which severely mentally ill patients previously confined to large state or county psychiatric hospitals were discharged to community boarding or nursing homes. The movement marked a major shift of mental health service provision from primarily inpatient settings to community-based facilities.

Department of Health and Human Services (DHHS): The federal government's principal agency concerned with health protection and promotion and provision of health and other human services to vulnerable populations. In addition to administering the Medicare and Medicaid programs, DHHS includes over 300 separate programs.

Descriptive studies: Identify factors and conditions that determine the distribution of health and disease among specific populations using patient records, interview surveys, various databases, and other information sources to provide the details or characteristics of diseases or biologic phenomena and the prevalence or magnitude of their occurrence. Descriptive studies are relatively fast and inexpensive and often raise questions or suggest hypotheses to be tested by analytic studies.

Diagnosis-related groups (DRGs): A case payment system that radically changed hospital reimbursement shifting hospital reimbursement from the retrospective to a prospective basis. The DRG system provided incentives for the hospital to spend only what was needed to achieve optimal patient outcomes. If outcomes could be achieved at a cost lower than the preset payment, the hospital received an excess payment for those cases. If the hospital spent more to treat cases than allowed, it absorbed the excess costs. This payment system was widely adopted by nongovernmental health insurers.

Disability-adjusted life years (DALYS): The total number of years of life lost to illness, disability, or premature death within a given population.

Disease management programs: MCO programs that attempt to control costs and improve care quality for individuals with chronic and costly conditions through methods such as the use of evidence-based clinical guidelines, patient self-management education, disease registries, risk stratification, proactive patient outreach, and performance feedback to providers. Programs may also use clinical specialists who provide monitoring and support to patients with disease management issues.

Ecological models: Models that identify causes of public health problems rooted in the physical and/or social environment and behavior related to an individual. Ecological models take into account the vast number of determinants that impact the health status of groups of people and facilitate decisions about the most expeditious path to developing effective interventions.

Emergency Medical Treatment and Labor Act (EMTALA): Enacted in the 1995 federal budget because of concerns about inappropriate patient transfers between hospitals prompted by payment considerations.

EMTALA requires hospitals to treat everyone who presents in their emergency departments, regardless of ability to pay. Stiff financial penalties, and as risk of Medicare decertification by hospitals inappropriately transferring patients, accompanies the EMTALA legal provisions.

Empirical quality standards: Derived from distributions, averages, ranges, and other measures of data variability, empirical quality standards compare information collected from a number of similar health service providers to identify practices that deviate from norms.

Evidence-based clinical practice guidelines: Systematically developed protocols based on extensive research that are used to assist practitioner and patient decisions about appropriate health care decisions. Guidelines define parameters for specific diagnostic and treatment modalities in patient diagnosis and management.

Experience-rated insurance: Insurance plans that use historically documented patterns of health care service utilization for defined populations of subscribers to determine premium charges.

Experimental studies: In experimental studies, the investigator actively intervenes by manipulating one variable to see what happens with the other. Although they are the best test of cause and effect, such studies are technically difficult to carry out and often raise ethical issues. Control populations are used to ensure that other nonexperimental variables are not affecting the outcome.

Explicit quality standards: Standards that are professionally developed and agreed on in advance of a quality assessment. Explicit standards minimize the variation and bias that result when judgments are internalized.

Federally qualified health center (FQHC): Community-based primary care center staffed by a multidisciplinary team of health care and related support personnel, with fees adjusted based on ability to pay. FQHCs also provide services to link patients with other community resources. Funded by the Health Resources and Services Administration to serve the neediest populations, FQHCs must meet specific operating parameters and may be organized as part of a local health department, a larger human services organization, or as a stand-alone, not-for-profit agency.

Federated model of health information exchange: An HIE design in which member institutions maintain their own data at their respective sites in the standardized format used by an HIE. In this model, individual, transinstitutional patient records are assembled in real time by searching all institutions' databases only when requested by authorized users for a particular episode of care.

Financial risk-sharing: A concept used by MCOs to transfer some measure of financial risk from insurers to beneficiaries. Such transfers of financial risk to beneficiaries commonly take the form of co-payments and deductibles. Co-payments require that beneficiaries pay a set fee each time they receive a covered service, such as a co-payment for each physician office visit. A deductible requires beneficiaries to meet a predetermined, out-of-pocket expenditure level before the MCO assumes payment responsibility for the balance of charges.

Flexner Report: The landmark report resulting from a comprehensive review of the quality of education in U.S. and Canadian medical schools, funded by the Carnegie Foundation. Issued in 1910, the report was a searing indictment of most medical schools of the time. As a result, some schools closed while others including Harvard, Western Reserve, McGill, The University of Toronto, and especially Johns Hopkins received praise. The report gave increased leverage to medical education reformers and stimulated financial support from foundations and wealthy individuals which enabled university-affiliated medical schools to gain significant influence over the direction of medical education.

Graduate medical education consortia: Formal associations of medical schools, teaching hospitals, and other organizations involved in the training of medical residents. The consortia provide centralized coordination and direction that encourages the members to function collectively with major aims to improve the structure and governance of residency programs, to increase residents' ambulatory care training experiences, and to address imbalances in physician specialty and location.

Healthcare effectiveness data and information set (HEDIS): Provides a standardized method for MCOs to collect, calculate, and report information about their performance to allow employers, other purchasers, and consumers to compare different health insurance plans. The HEDIS has evolved through several stages of development and continuously refines its measurements through rigorous reviews and independent audits.

Health information administrator: Health information administrators are responsible for the activities of the medical records departments of hospitals, skilled nursing facilities, managed care organizations, rehabilitation centers, ambulatory care facilities, and other licensed health care entities. They maintain information systems to permit patient data to be received, recorded, stored, and retrieved to assist in diagnosis and treatment and supply research data for tracking disease patterns, evaluating the quality of patient care, verifying insurance claims, and maintaining patient record confidentiality. A bachelor's degree in health information administration is the entry-level credential.

Health information exchange (HIE): A network that enables a basic level of interoperability among electronic health records maintained by individual physicians and health care organizations. HIEs are organized and governed by regional health information organizations (RHIOs).

Health Information Technology for Economic and Clinical Health Act (HITECH Act): A component of the American Recovery and Reinvestment Act of 2009 dedicated to promoting nationwide adoption and use of electronic health records.

Health insurance exchange: The ACA requires states to establish health benefit exchanges (American Health Benefit Exchanges) and to create separate exchanges for small employers (Small Business Health Options Program) with up to 100 employees. The exchanges intend to create a competitive health insurance market by providing web-based, easily understandable, comparative information to consumers on plan choices and to standardize rules regarding health plan offers and pricing.

Health services research: A research field combining perspectives and methods of epidemiology, sociology, economics, and clinical medicine. Health services research also uses process and outcome measures reflecting behavioral and economic variables associated with questions of treatment effectiveness and cost-benefit.

Health systems agencies: Organizations created by the National Health Planning and Resources Development Act of 1974 that included broad representation of health care providers and consumers on governing boards and committees to deliberate and recommend health care resource allocations to their respective federal and state governing bodies.

Hill-Burton Act: A 1946 federal law that provided funding to construct new and expand existing U.S. hospitals.

HMO Act of 1973: Federal legislation enacted by the Nixon administration that provided loans and grants for the planning, development, and implementation of combined insurance and health care delivery organizations and required that a comprehensive array of preventive and primary care services be included in the HMO arrangement. By linking the payment for services with the quality of care, the HMO Act paved the way for the proliferation of managed care principles that became the bedrock of U.S. health insurance reform in the succeeding three decades.

Horizontal integration: Consolidation of two or more hospitals or other entities under one owner through merger or acquisition.

Hospice: A philosophy supporting a coordinated program of care for the terminally ill that focuses on maintaining comfort and quality of life. The most common criterion for admission into hospice is a diagnosis of a terminal illness with a limited life expectancy of 6 months or less.

Hospitalist: A physician typically board certified in internal medicine who specializes in the care of hospital patients. A hospitalist may be an employee of one or more hospitals or an employee of one or more companies that contract with hospitals to provide services.

Implicit quality standards: Standards that rely on the internalized judgments of expert individuals conducting a quality assessment and as such are subject to variation and bias.

Indemnity insurance: A form of insurance in which the insurance company sets allowable charges for services that it will reimburse after services are delivered and allows providers to bill patients for any uncovered excess costs.

Independent Payment Advisory Board (IPAB): Created by the ACA, the mission of the IPAB is to recommend policies to Congress to curb Medicare spending including suggestions to improve coordination of care, eliminate waste, encourage best practices, and prioritize primary care. Beginning in 2015 and every other year thereafter, the IPAB is also charged with submitting recommendations to the President and Congress to slow overall growth in national health care expenditures.

Individual mandate: Under the ACA, the requirement that all American citizens (with specific exclusions) obtain health insurance coverage or pay a penalty.

Informed consent: A legally recognized patient right, formalized in a document for a patient's signature, to ensure patients' understanding of the risks and benefits of a medical intervention.

Institutional review board (IRB): Professionally constituted, expert groups of individuals who judge the merit of research studies and ensure appropriate and ethical participant safeguards are provided to protect research subjects' safety. A primary function of an IRB is to ensure fully informed consent and research subjects' understanding of risks and benefits of participation.

International medical graduates (IMGs): Physicians trained in medical schools outside the United States who fill the annual shortfall in U.S. medical school graduates required to staff hospitals. Responsibility for evaluating credentials of IMGs entering the United States' residency programs lies with the Educational Commission for Foreign Medical Graduates.

Laboratory technologists and technicians: Clinical laboratory personnel who analyze body fluids, tissues, and cells checking for bacteria and other micro-organisms; analyze chemical content of body fluids, test drug levels in blood to monitor the effectiveness of treatment, and match blood for transfusion. Technologists typically have a bachelor's or higher degree; technicians typically hold associate's degrees or certificates.

Licensure: The most restrictive form of health professional regulation is administered by individual states. It defines a professional's scope of practice and educational and testing requirements to legally engage in the practice of a profession.

Managed behavioral healthcare organization (MBHO): A corporate entity to which a health plan may outsource the management of mental health services for its subscribers. The MBHO assumes the financial risks and benefits of managing treatment budgets and authorization for access to mental health services.

Managed care backlash: Beginning in the late 1990s, organized medicine, other health care providers, and consumers railed against MCO policies on choice of providers, referrals, and other practices that were viewed as unduly restrictive. Public concerns driving sentiments toward more government regulation of the managed care industry included the belief that managed care was hurting the quality of patient care and that the managed care industry was not doing as good a job for patients as other sectors of the health care industry. Since 1998, all 50 state legislatures enacted over 900 laws and regulations addressing both consumer and provider protections relative to managed care policies.

Meaningful use: The criterion defined by the ONC in collaboration with the Centers for Medicare and Medicaid Services that entails meeting a set of time-delineated requirements for eligible professionals and hospitals to qualify for incentive payments under the HITECH Act.

Medicaid: Title XIX amendment to the Social Security Act of 1935 Medicaid, is a joint federal/state program that provides insurance coverage for a prescribed scope of basic health care services to Americans who qualify based on income parameters, established on a state-by-state basis. Unlike Medicare, Medicaid is not an "entitlement" program funded by payroll taxes. Rather, Medicaid is funded by personal income and corporate and excise taxes, with funds transferred from more economically affluent individuals to those in need. Unlike Medicare, which reimburses providers through intermediaries such as Blue Cross, Medicaid directly reimburses service providers. Rate-setting formulas, procedures, and policies vary widely among states and as such, Medicaid has been described as "50 different programs."

Medicare: Title XVIII amendment to the Social Security Act of 1935, Madicare guarantees a minimum level of health insurance benefits to all Americans beginning at age 65 (and other special needs groups without regard to age). Medicare funds derive largely from payroll taxes levied on all American workers.

Mental health parity: Equating annual and aggregate lifetime insurance coverage limits for mental health services with annual and aggregate lifetime insurance coverage for medical care.

Monolithic model of health information exchange: An HIE design in which all member institutions send clinical data to one central repository where all data reside together in one universal and standardized format. In this model, authorized users may access individual, transinstitutional patient records from the central repository.

National alliance on mental illness: A grassroots organization dedicated to advocating for access to services, treatment, supports, and research for the mentally ill.

National Committee on Quality Assurance (NCQA): The most influential managed care quality assurance organization formed in 1979 by the merger of two managed care trade organizations, the American Managed Care and Review Association and the Group Health Association of America, under the title of the American Association of Health Plans. Primary functions of the NCQA are accreditation for MCOs, PPOs, managed behavioral health care organizations, new health plans, and disease management programs; certifying organizations that verify provider credentials and consultation on physician organizations, utilization management organizations, patient-centered medical homes, and disease management organizations and programs.

National Institute for Complementary and Alternative Medicine: A division of the National Institutes of Health devoted to conducting and reporting on research focused on complementary and alternative therapies.

National Health Care Workforce Commission (NHCWC): Established by the ACA, the NHCWC has the mandate to evaluate and make recommendations for numerous dimensions of the nation's health care workforce including education and training support for existing and potential new workers at all levels, efficient workforce deployment, professional compensation, and coordination among different types of providers.

National Prevention, Health Promotion, and Public Health Council: Established by the ACA and chaired by the U.S. Surgeon General, an organization charged with developing and leading a national prevention strategy and making recommendations to the President and Congress for federal policy changes that support public health goals. The Council provides leadership to and coordination of public health activities of 17 federal departments, agencies, and offices and receives input from a 22 nonfederal member, presidentially appointed Prevention Advisory Group.

Natural history of disease: A matrix used by epidemiologists and health services planners that places everything known about a particular disease or condition in the sequence of its origin and progression when untreated; the matrix identifies causes and stages of a particular disease or condition and facilitates matching of causes and stages with appropriate types of interventions intended to prevent the condition's occurrence or to arrest its progress after onset.

Naturally occurring retirement community (NORC): Apartment complexes, neighborhoods, or sections of communities where residents have opted to remain in their homes as they age.

Never events: Egregious medical errors occurring in hospitals, the treatment for which the DHHS will not provide reimbursement.

Nonquantitative treatment limitations (NQTLs): Limitations or restrictions of covered insurance benefits which though not numerically expressed, otherwise limit the scope or duration of benefits for treatment. In assuring parity of mental health with medical/surgical benefits, insurance plans must apply NQTLs in a "comparable and no more stringent manner" to mental health as compared and medical/surgical benefits.

Nurse practitioner: A registered nurse, typically with a master's degree, who may specialize in a particular area of nursing practice such as primary care, geriatrics, psychiatry, emergency medicine, or other medical fields. Nurse practitioners function under the supervision of physicians and provide diagnostic, preventive, and therapeutic health care services and may prescribe medications as allowed by law as delegated by physicians.

Office of the National Coordinator for Health Information Technology (ONC): The federal principal agency created to coordinate nationwide efforts to implement health information technology and exchange of health information.

Oregon Death with Dignity Act of 1994: Also known as the Oregon Physician-Assisted Suicide Act, it legalized allowing "an adult resident of Oregon, who is terminally ill to voluntarily request a prescription for medication to take his or her life." The person must have "an incurable and irreversible disease that will, within reasonable medical judgment, produce death within six months."

Osteopathic medicine: A philosophy of medical education with particular focus on the musculoskeletal system. Graduates receive a DO rather than MD degree and are considered as rigorously trained and qualified as their MD degree counterparts.

Palliative care: Treatment given to relieve the symptoms of a disease rather than attempting to cure the disease.

Patient-centered medical home (PCMH): A team-based model of care led by a personal physician who provides continuous and coordinated care throughout a patient's lifetime to maximize health outcomes, including appropriately arranging patients' care with other qualified professionals for preventive services, treatment of acute and chronic illness, and assistance with end-of-life issues.

Physician assistant (PA): Provides health care services under the supervision of a physician. Most hold master's degrees. PAs are trained to provide diagnostic, preventive, and therapeutic health care services as delegated by physicians. PAs take medical histories, order and interpret laboratory tests and x-rays, make diagnoses, and prescribe medications as allowed by law. Many PAs are employed in specialties such as internal medicine, pediatrics, family medicine, orthopedics, emergency medicine, and surgery.

Physician Compare: The CMS Website, mandated by the ACA, to provide basic contact, practice characteristics, and clinical quality data on Medicare participating physicians and other health care professionals.

Policy development: Generating recommendations from available data to address public health problems, analyzing options for solutions and mobilizing public and community organizations through implementation plans.

Population health focus: A health care system orientation to providing medical care and health-related services that shifts emphasis from individual medical interventions with piecemeal reimbursement to providers' accountability for the outcomes of medical care and overall health status of a defined population group.

Preferred provider organization (PPO): Formed by physicians and hospitals to serve the needs of private, third-party payers and self-insured firms, PPOs guarantee a certain volume of business to hospitals and physicians in return for a negotiated discount in fees. PPOs offer attractive features to both physicians and hospitals. Physicians are not required to share in financial risk as a condition of participation, and PPOs help hospitals to shore up declining occupancy rates and attenuate the competition for admissions with other hospitals. To control costs, PPOs use negotiated discount fees, requirements that members receive care exclusively from contracted providers (or incur financial penalty), requirements for preauthorization of hospital admission, and second opinions for major procedures. Currently, PPOs are the most popular managed care plans, encompassing 56% of employer-covered workers in 2012.

Prevention and Public Health Fund: Established by the ACA, the nation's first mandatory funding stream dedicated to improving public health. The Fund is intended to eliminate the prior shortcomings of unpredictable federal budget appropriations for public health and prevention programs. The ACA mandates the Fund's use to improve health and help restrain the rate of growth in private and public sector health care costs through programs at the local, state, and federal levels to "curb tobacco use, increase access to primary preventive care services, and help state and local governments respond to public health threats and outbreaks."

Primary prevention: Measures designed to promote health and prevent disease or other adverse health occurrences, e.g., health education to encourage good nutrition, exercise, and genetic counseling, and specific protections, e.g., immunization and the use of seat belts.

Readmissions reduction program: Mandated by the ACA, a Medicare program through which payments to hospitals are reduced based on the readmission of patients with specified diagnoses within 30 days of a prior hospitalization. Penalty determinations are based on 3 prior years' hospital discharge data.

Recovery oriented systems of care (ROSC): A holistic, integrated, person-centered and strength-based approach to mental health interventions. ROSC views recovery as a process of pursuing a fulfilling life and seeks to enhance a person's positive self-image and identity through linking their strengths with family and community resources. The ROSC shifts care from the old episodic care model to one that emphasizes continuity and provides choice through the treatment planning process.

Regional health information organization (RHIO): Organizations that create systems agreements, process, and technology to manage and facilitate exchange of health information between institutions and across different vendor platforms within specific geographic areas. RHIOs administer HIEs.

Respite care: Temporary surrogate care given to a patient when that patient's primary caregiver must be absent. It includes any family managed care program that helps to avoid or forestall the placement of a patient in a full-time institutionalized environment by providing planned, intermittent caregiver relief.

Retail clinic: Operated at retail sites such as pharmacies and supermarkets under consumer-friendly names, such as "MinuteClinic" and "TakeCare." Staffed by nurse practitioners or physician assistants; a physician is not required on site; clinics have physician consultation available by phone.

Registration: Begun as a method to facilitate contacts among professionals and potential employers, registration is the least restrictive form of health professional regulation. Most registration programs are voluntary and range from listings of individuals offering a specific service to professional or occupational groups requiring educational qualifications and testing.

Rural health networks: To address challenges of providing a continuum of care with scarce resources, networks join rural health care providers in formal, not-for-profit corporations or through informal linkages to achieve a defined set of mutually beneficial purposes. Networks may advocate at local and state levels on rural health care issues, cooperate in joint community outreach activities, and seek opportunities to negotiate with insurers to cover services for their communities' populations.

Secondary prevention: Early detection and prompt treatment of a disease or condition to achieve an early cure, if possible, or to slow progression, prevent complications, and limit disability. Most preventive health care is currently focused on this level.

Skilled nursing facility (SNF): A facility, or distinct part of one, primarily engaged in providing skilled nursing care and related services for people requiring medical or nursing care, or rehabilitation services. Skilled nursing care is provided by or under the direct supervision of licensed nursing personnel and provides 24-hour nursing care and other types of services.

Self-funded health insurance: A mechanism through which an employer (or other group, such as a union or trade association) collects premiums and pools these into a fund or account that it uses to pay for medical benefit claims instead of using a commercial carrier. Self-funded plans often use the services of an actuarial firm to set premium rates and a third-party administrator to administer benefits, pay claims, and collect data on utilization. Self-funded plans offer advantages to employers, such as avoiding additional administrative and other charges made by commercial carriers, avoiding premium taxes, and enabling interest accrual on cash reserves held in the benefit accounts.

Social Security Act of 1935: The most significant social initiative ever passed by any Congress; it was the legislative basis for a number of major health and welfare programs, including the Medicare and Medicaid programs.

Teaching hospital: A hospital affiliated with a medical school that provides clinical education for medical students, medical and dental residents, and other health professionals.

Tertiary prevention: Rehabilitation and maximizing remaining functional capacity when a disease or condition has occurred and left residual damage.

The Health Insurance Portability and Accountability Act of 1996 (HIPAA): Permitted individuals to continue insurance coverage after a loss or change of employment by mandating the renewal of insurance coverage except for specific reasons; regulated the circumstances in which an insurance plan may limit benefits because of preexisting conditions; established privacy standards for patient health information; established "Administrative Simplification," by calling for computerization of medical records by 2003.

Therapeutic science practitioner: Therapeutic sciences practitioners include physical therapists, occupational therapists, speech language pathology and audiology therapists, radiation therapists, and respiratory therapists, representing some of the allied health disciplines in this category. Depending on their field, therapeutic science practitioners' required credentials range from bachelor's degree to doctoral level educational preparation.

Urgent care center: Facilities that provide walk-in, extended-hour access for acute illness and injury care that is either beyond the scope or the availability of the typical primary care practice or retail clinic. Urgent care centers may also provide other health services such as occupational medicine, travel medicine, sports and school physicals.

Value-based purchasing (VBP): Mandated by the ACA; a Medicare program through which participating hospitals may earn incentive payments based on clinical outcomes and patient satisfaction or incur reductions in Medicare payments based on compliance with Medicare-determined criteria for "clinical processes of care" and "patient experience of care measures."

Vertical integration: A process through which one entity unites related and complementary organizations to create a system that provides a continuum of care. In its most complete form, a vertically integrated system encompasses medical and health-related services required throughout an individual's life span.

Voluntary ambulatory health agency: Community-based, not-for-profit organization governed by a volunteer board of directors that may provide direct medical care, education, advocacy, or a combination of these services. Many voluntary agencies were established by interest groups to address unmet health or health-related needs of specific population groups. Sources of financial support may include government grants, fees for services, third-party reimbursement, and private contributions.

Index

Note: Page numbers followed by *f,* or *t* indicate material in figures, or tables, respectively.